WEIRDO

For every kid who's ever felt weird.
Shine on.
To Mom, Dad, Yesenia, and LENAR.

—TONY

To kids who spend
most of their time
at the library.

—JES

To Mom and Dad,
for confusedly supporting a
superhero-obsessed kid and now adult.

—CIN

WEIRDO

written by

TONY WEAVER, JR.

art by

JES AND CIN WIBOWO

:01
First Second
NEW YORK

CONTENT NOTE:
This story includes mentions
of attempted suicide.

CHAPTER 1

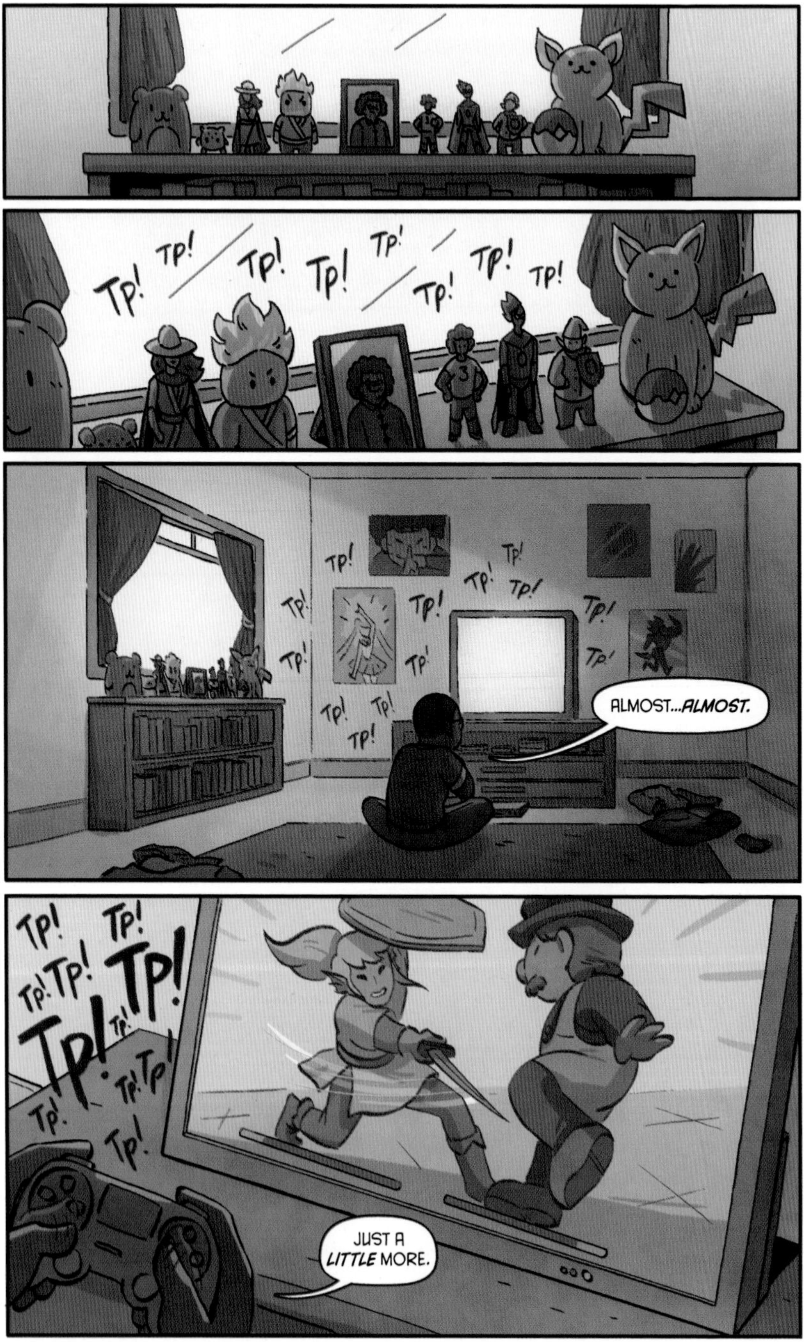
Tp! Tp! Tp! Tp! Tp! Tp! Tp! Tp!
Tp! Tp! Tp! Tp! Tp! Tp! Tp! Tp! Tp! Tp! Tp! Tp!
ALMOST...*ALMOST.*
Tp! Tp! Tp! Tp! Tp! Tp! Tp! Tp! Tp! Tp!
JUST A *LITTLE* MORE.

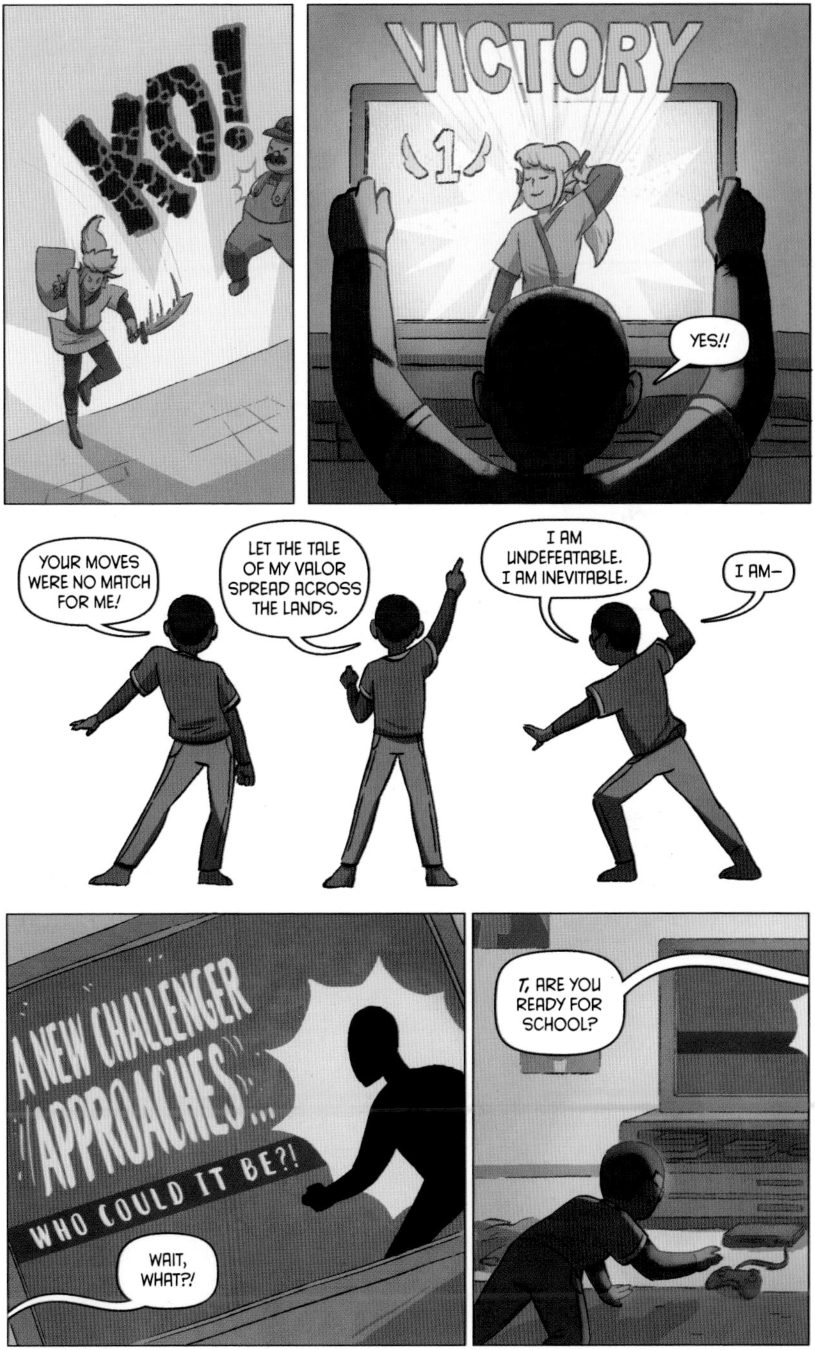
KO!
VICTORY
1
YES!!
YOUR MOVES WERE NO MATCH FOR ME!
LET THE TALE OF MY VALOR SPREAD ACROSS THE LANDS.
I AM UNDEFEATABLE. I AM INEVITABLE.
I AM–
A NEW CHALLENGER APPROACHES...
WHO COULD IT BE?!
WAIT, WHAT?!
T, ARE YOU READY FOR SCHOOL?

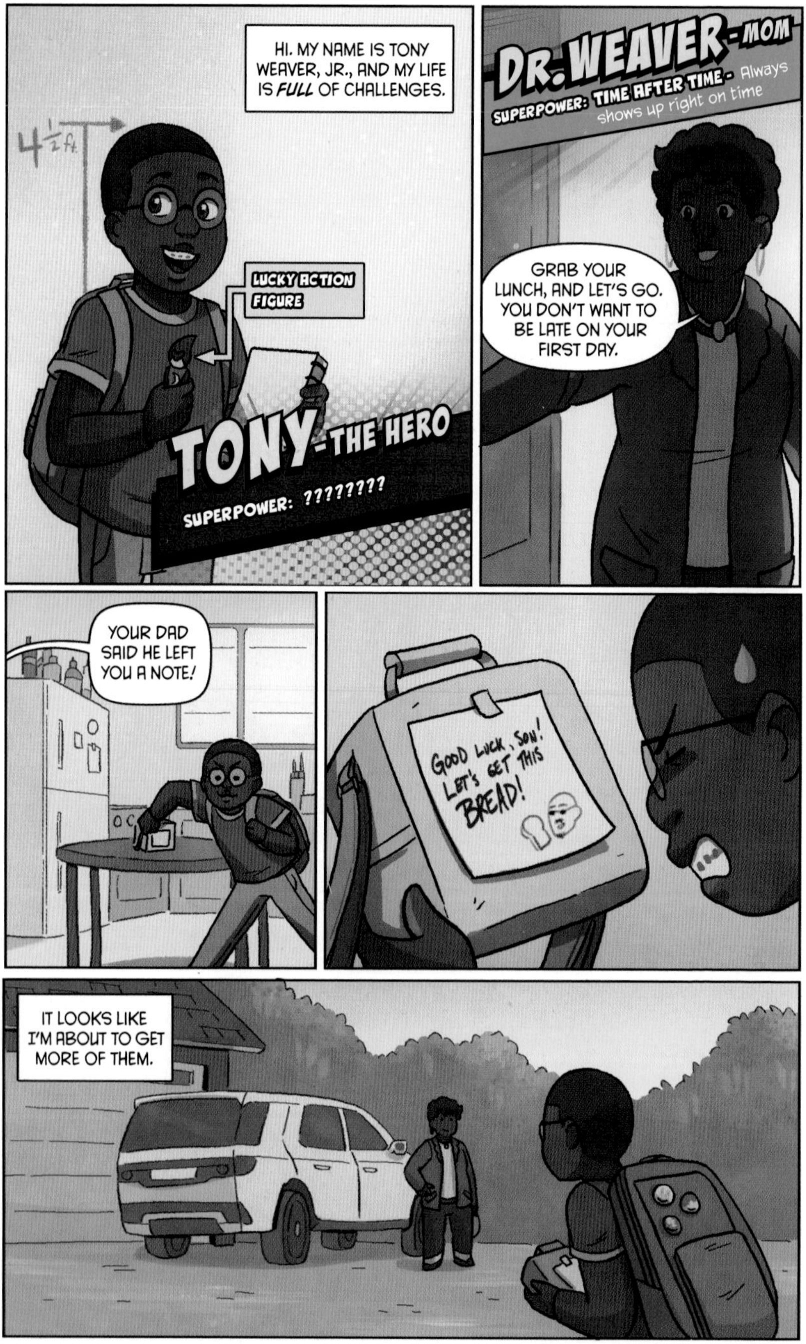

HI. MY NAME IS TONY WEAVER, JR., AND MY LIFE IS FULL OF CHALLENGES.
4 1/2 ft.
LUCKY ACTION FIGURE
TONY - THE HERO
SUPERPOWER: ????????
DR. WEAVER - MOM
SUPERPOWER: TIME AFTER TIME - Always shows up right on time
GRAB YOUR LUNCH, AND LET'S GO. YOU DON'T WANT TO BE LATE ON YOUR FIRST DAY.
YOUR DAD SAID HE LEFT YOU A NOTE!
GOOD LUCK, SON! LET'S GET THIS BREAD!
IT LOOKS LIKE I'M ABOUT TO GET MORE OF THEM.

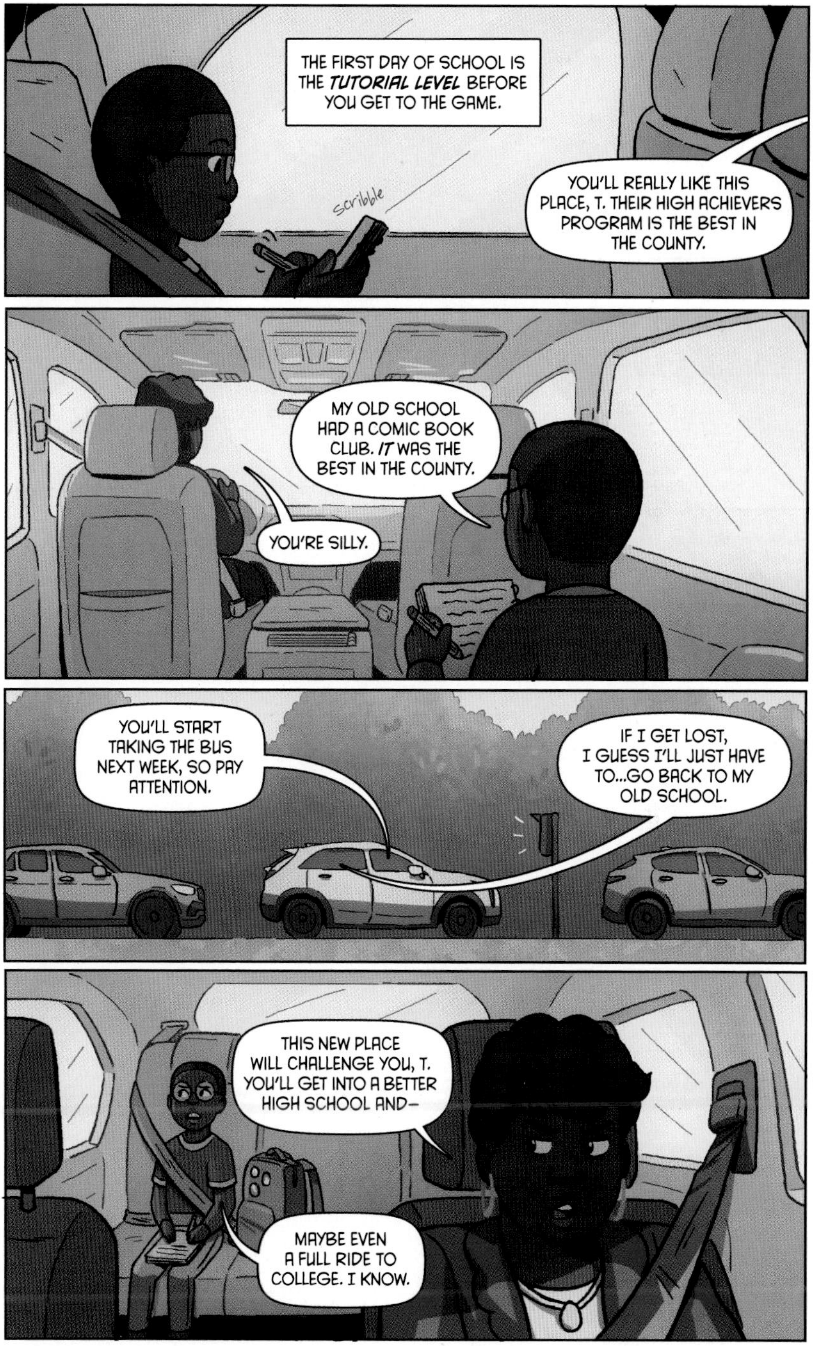
THE FIRST DAY OF SCHOOL IS THE *TUTORIAL LEVEL* BEFORE YOU GET TO THE GAME.
scribble
YOU'LL REALLY LIKE THIS PLACE, T. THEIR HIGH ACHIEVERS PROGRAM IS THE BEST IN THE COUNTY.
MY OLD SCHOOL HAD A COMIC BOOK CLUB. *IT* WAS THE BEST IN THE COUNTY.
YOU'RE SILLY.
YOU'LL START TAKING THE BUS NEXT WEEK, SO PAY ATTENTION.
IF I GET LOST, I GUESS I'LL JUST HAVE TO...GO BACK TO MY OLD SCHOOL.
THIS NEW PLACE WILL CHALLENGE YOU, T. YOU'LL GET INTO A BETTER HIGH SCHOOL AND—
MAYBE EVEN A FULL RIDE TO COLLEGE. I KNOW.

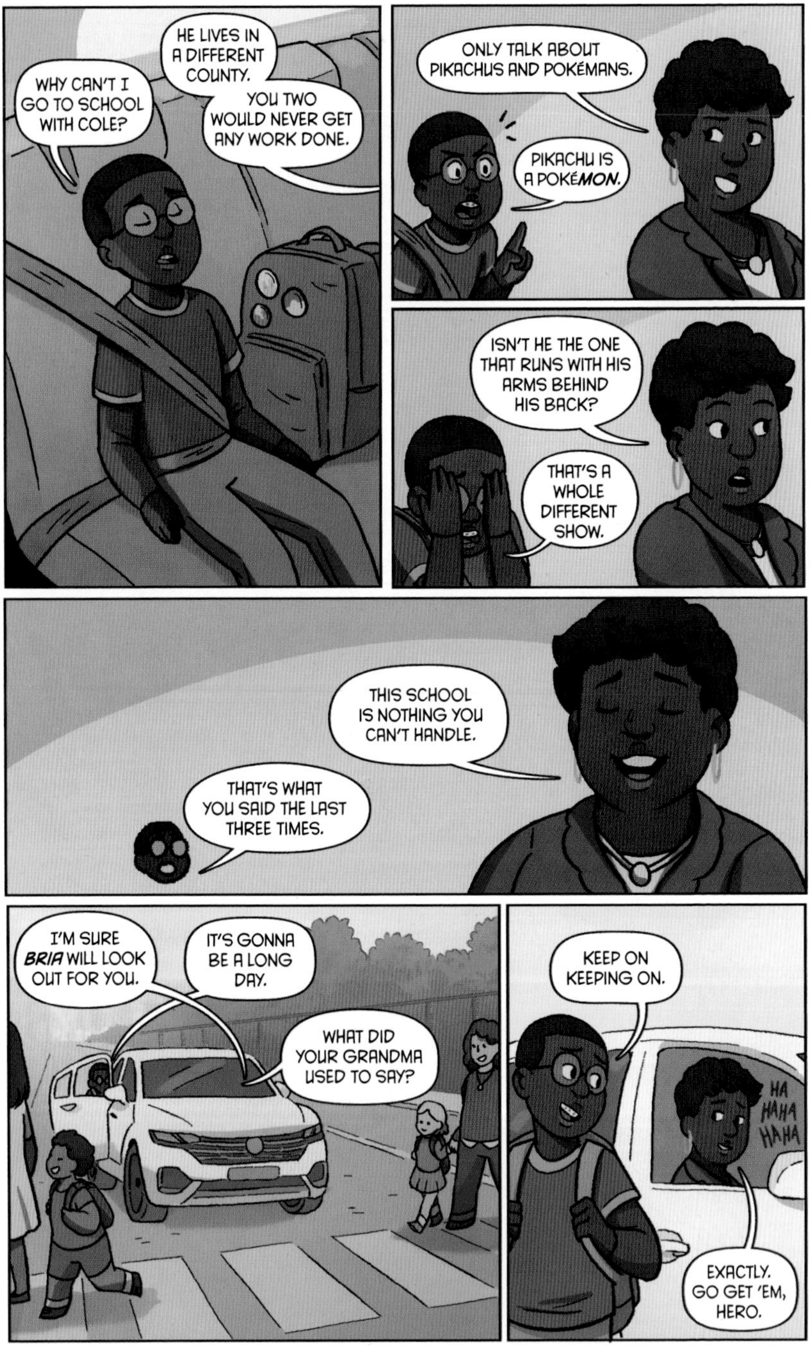
WHY CAN'T I GO TO SCHOOL WITH COLE?
HE LIVES IN A DIFFERENT COUNTY.
YOU TWO WOULD NEVER GET ANY WORK DONE.
ONLY TALK ABOUT PIKACHUS AND POKÉMANS.
PIKACHU IS A POKÉ*MON.*
ISN'T HE THE ONE THAT RUNS WITH HIS ARMS BEHIND HIS BACK?
THAT'S A WHOLE DIFFERENT SHOW.
THIS SCHOOL IS NOTHING YOU CAN'T HANDLE.
THAT'S WHAT YOU SAID THE LAST THREE TIMES.
I'M SURE *BRIA* WILL LOOK OUT FOR YOU.
IT'S GONNA BE A LONG DAY.
WHAT DID YOUR GRANDMA USED TO SAY?
KEEP ON KEEPING ON.
HA HAHA HAHA
EXACTLY. GO GET 'EM, HERO.

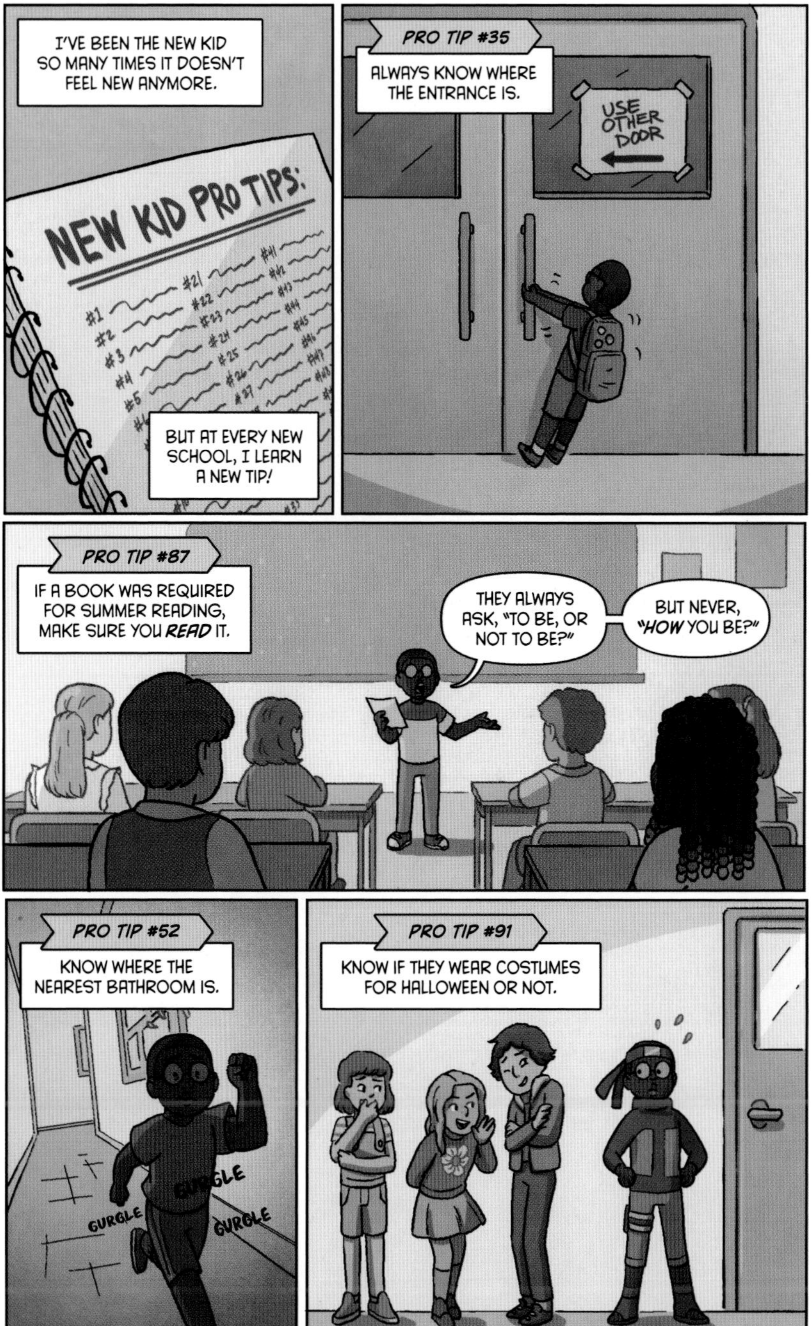
I'VE BEEN THE NEW KID SO MANY TIMES IT DOESN'T FEEL NEW ANYMORE.
NEW KID PRO TIPS:
BUT AT EVERY NEW SCHOOL, I LEARN A NEW TIP!
PRO TIP #35
ALWAYS KNOW WHERE THE ENTRANCE IS.
USE OTHER DOOR
PRO TIP #87
IF A BOOK WAS REQUIRED FOR SUMMER READING, MAKE SURE YOU *READ* IT.
THEY ALWAYS ASK, "TO BE, OR NOT TO BE?"
BUT NEVER, "*HOW* YOU BE?"
PRO TIP #52
KNOW WHERE THE NEAREST BATHROOM IS.
GURGLE
GURGLE
GURGLE
PRO TIP #91
KNOW IF THEY WEAR COSTUMES FOR HALLOWEEN OR NOT.

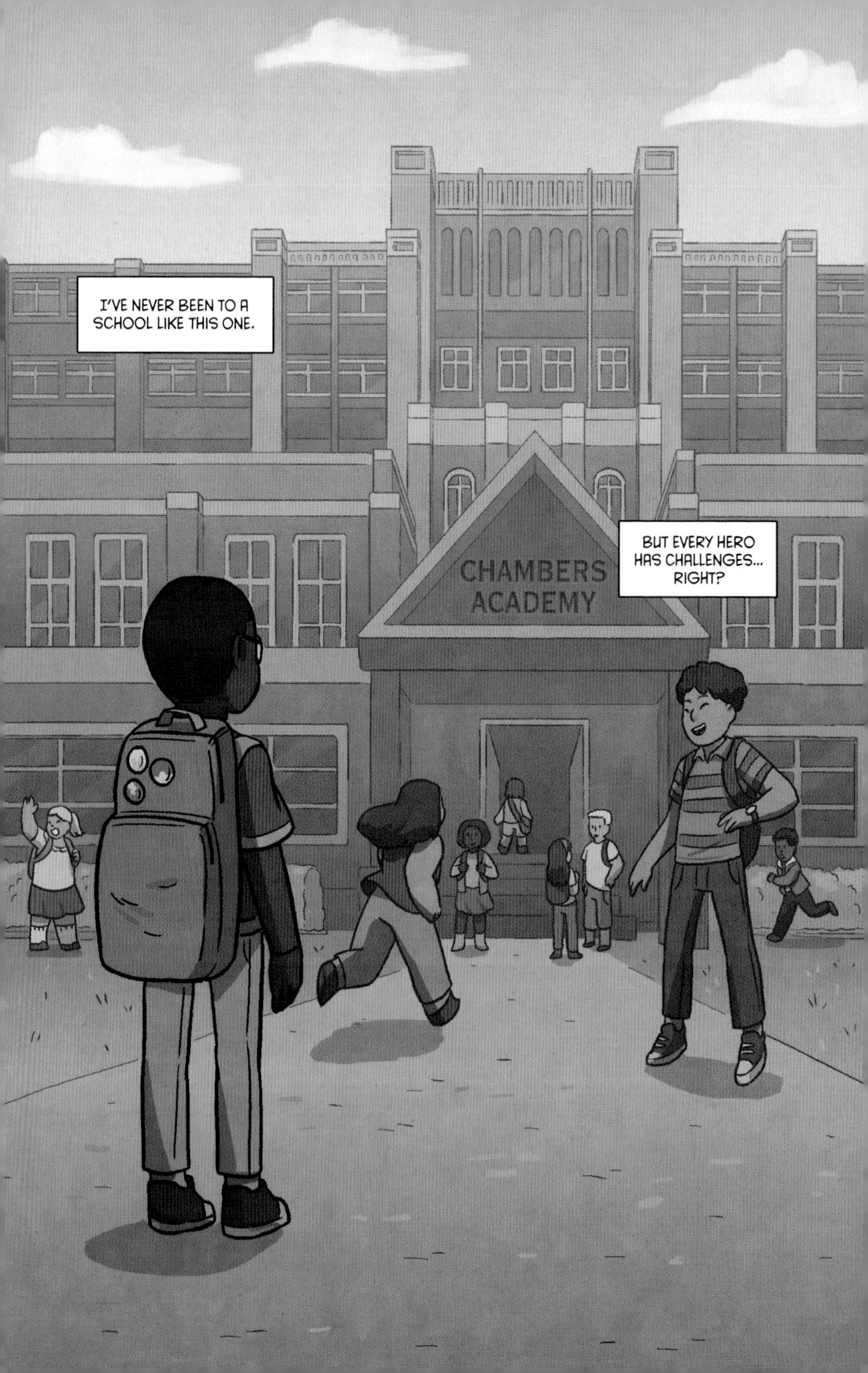
I'VE NEVER BEEN TO A SCHOOL LIKE THIS ONE.
CHAMBERS ACADEMY
BUT EVERY HERO HAS CHALLENGES... RIGHT?

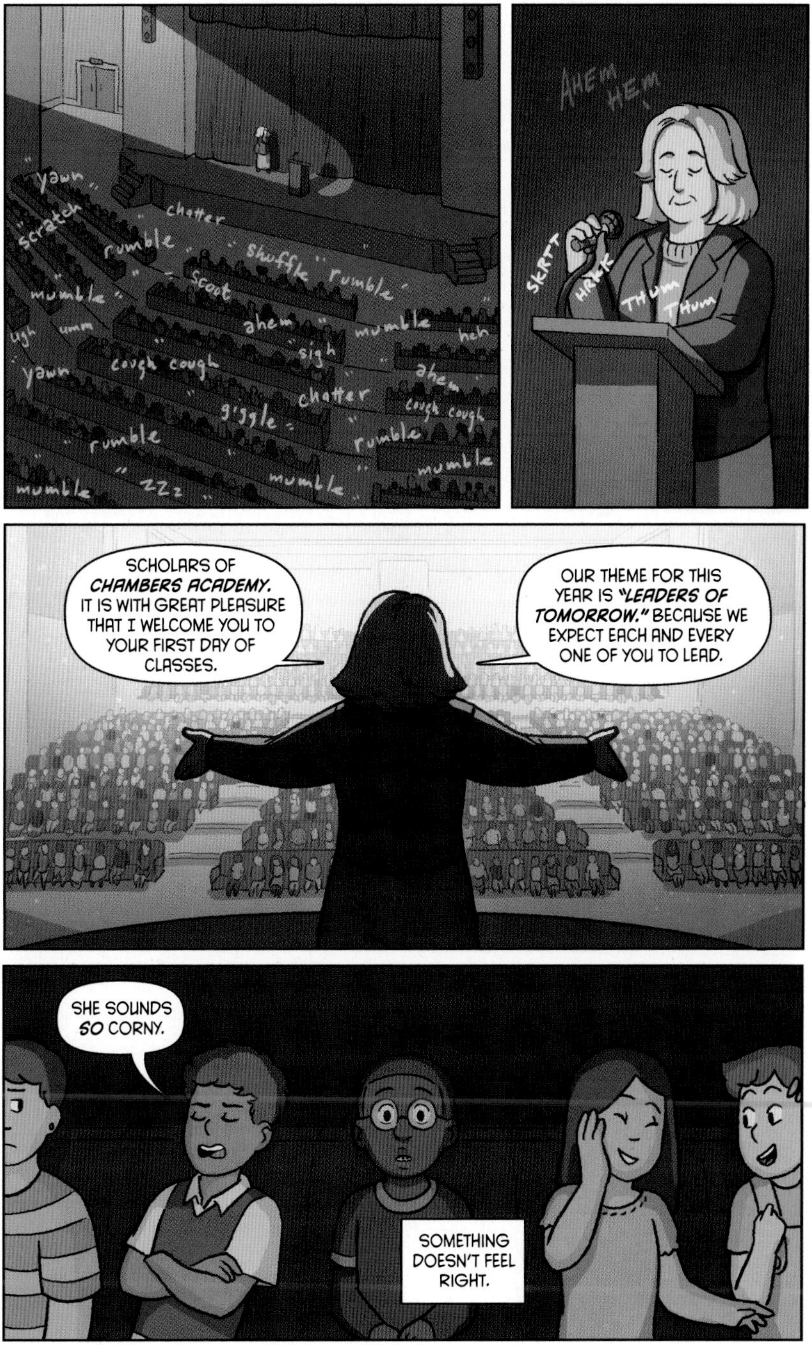
yawn
scratch
chatter
rumble
shuffle
rumble
mumble
scoot
ahem
mumble
heh
ugh
umm
sigh
yawn
cough cough
ahem
chatter
cough cough
giggle
rumble
rumble
mumble
mumble
ZZz
mumble
AHEM
HEM
SKRTT
HRKK
THUM
THUM
SCHOLARS OF CHAMBERS ACADEMY. IT IS WITH GREAT PLEASURE THAT I WELCOME YOU TO YOUR FIRST DAY OF CLASSES.
OUR THEME FOR THIS YEAR IS "LEADERS OF TOMORROW." BECAUSE WE EXPECT EACH AND EVERY ONE OF YOU TO LEAD.
SHE SOUNDS SO CORNY.
SOMETHING DOESN'T FEEL RIGHT.

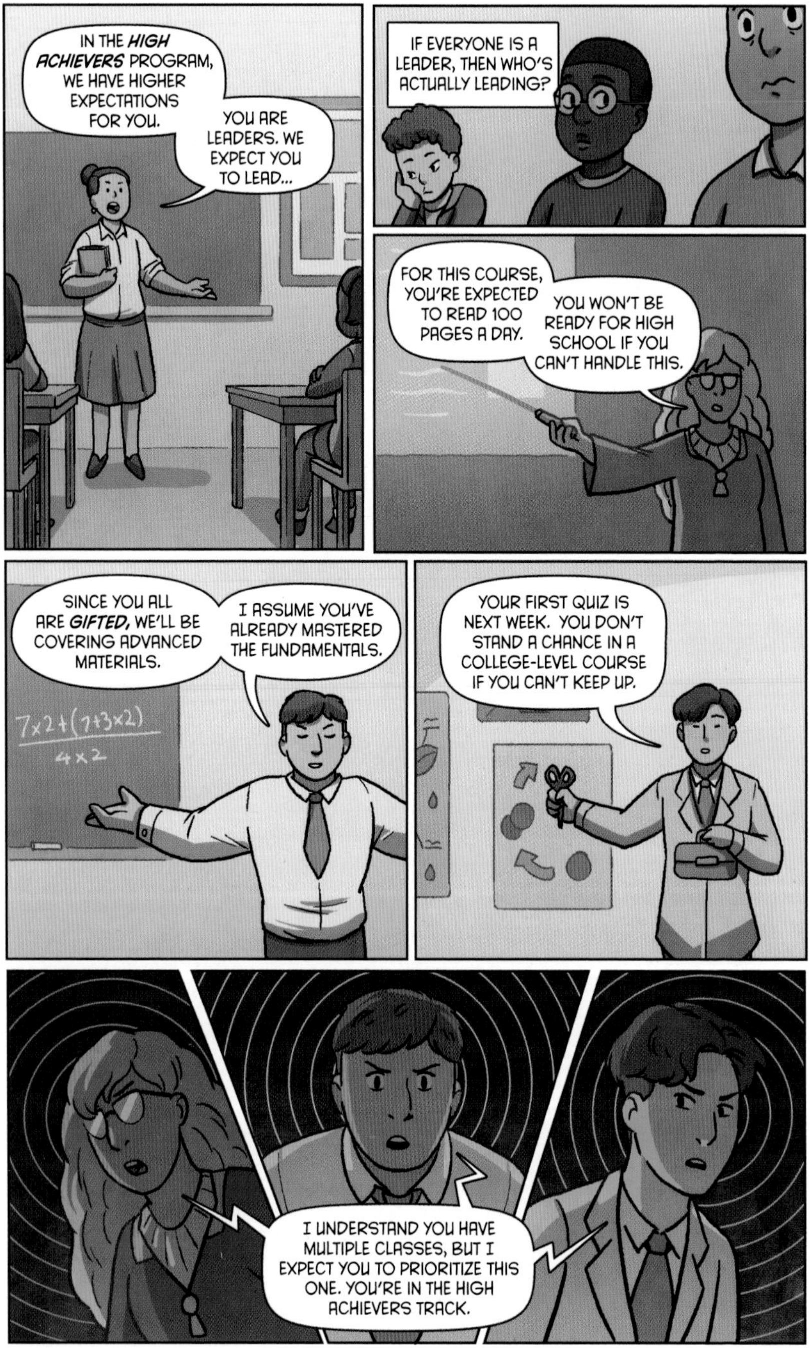
IN THE *HIGH ACHIEVERS* PROGRAM, WE HAVE HIGHER EXPECTATIONS FOR YOU.
YOU ARE LEADERS. WE EXPECT YOU TO LEAD...
IF EVERYONE IS A LEADER, THEN WHO'S ACTUALLY LEADING?
FOR THIS COURSE, YOU'RE EXPECTED TO READ 100 PAGES A DAY.
YOU WON'T BE READY FOR HIGH SCHOOL IF YOU CAN'T HANDLE THIS.
SINCE YOU ALL ARE *GIFTED,* WE'LL BE COVERING ADVANCED MATERIALS.
I ASSUME YOU'VE ALREADY MASTERED THE FUNDAMENTALS.
7x2+(7+3x2)
4x2
YOUR FIRST QUIZ IS NEXT WEEK. YOU DON'T STAND A CHANCE IN A COLLEGE-LEVEL COURSE IF YOU CAN'T KEEP UP.
I UNDERSTAND YOU HAVE MULTIPLE CLASSES, BUT I EXPECT YOU TO PRIORITIZE THIS ONE. YOU'RE IN THE HIGH ACHIEVERS TRACK.

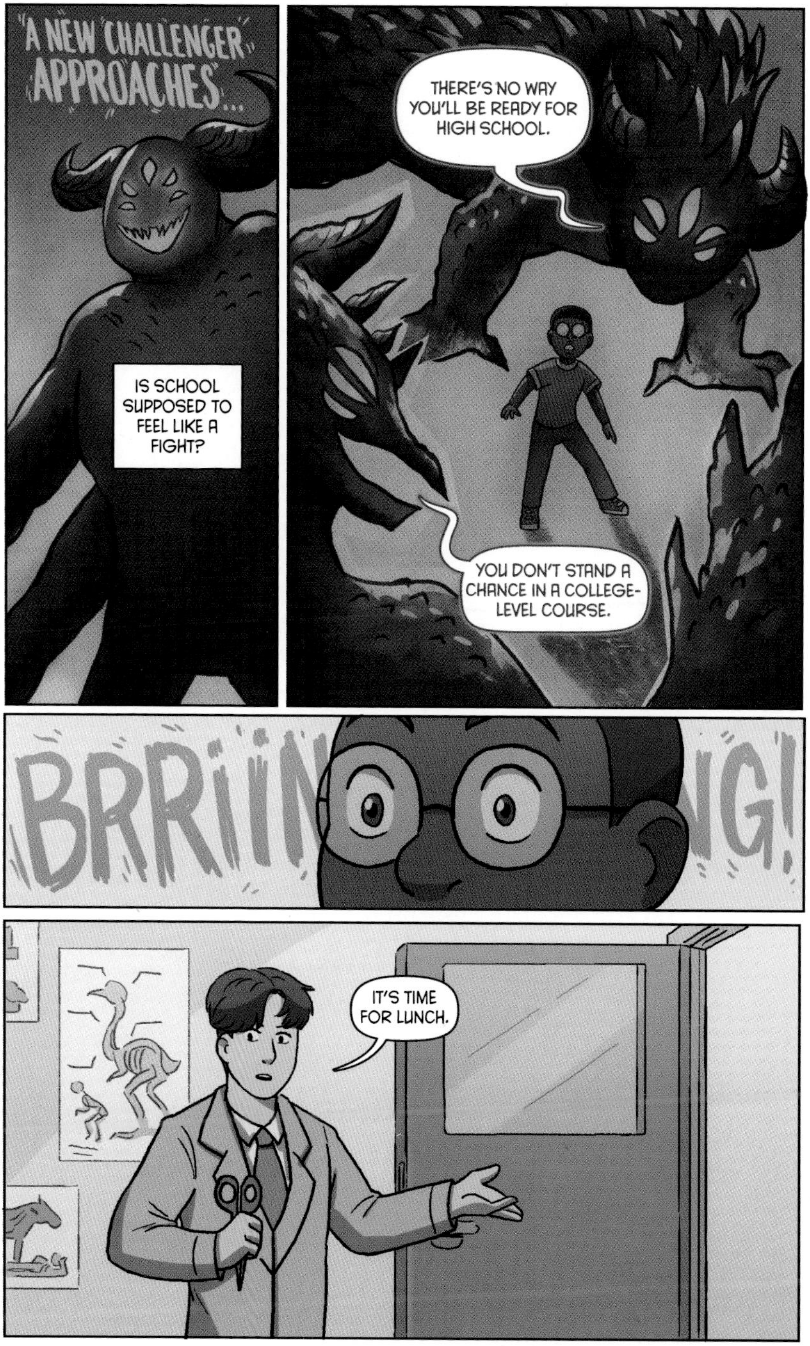
"A NEW CHALLENGER APPROACHES"...
IS SCHOOL SUPPOSED TO FEEL LIKE A FIGHT?
THERE'S NO WAY YOU'LL BE READY FOR HIGH SCHOOL.
YOU DON'T STAND A CHANCE IN A COLLEGE-LEVEL COURSE.
BRRIIN
NG!
IT'S TIME FOR LUNCH.

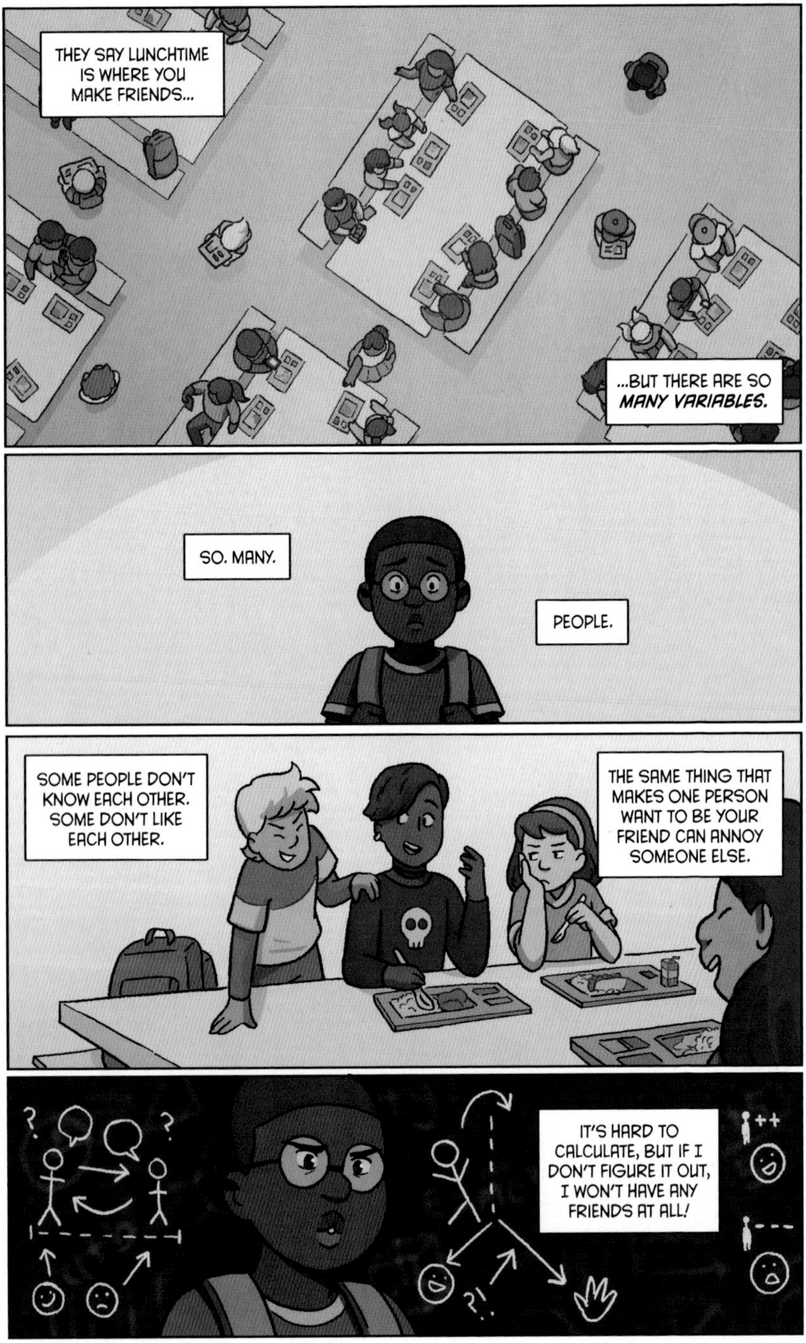
THEY SAY LUNCHTIME IS WHERE YOU MAKE FRIENDS...
...BUT THERE ARE SO *MANY VARIABLES.*
SO. MANY.
PEOPLE.
SOME PEOPLE DON'T KNOW EACH OTHER. SOME DON'T LIKE EACH OTHER.
THE SAME THING THAT MAKES ONE PERSON WANT TO BE YOUR FRIEND CAN ANNOY SOMEONE ELSE.
IT'S HARD TO CALCULATE, BUT IF I DON'T FIGURE IT OUT, I WON'T HAVE ANY FRIENDS AT ALL!

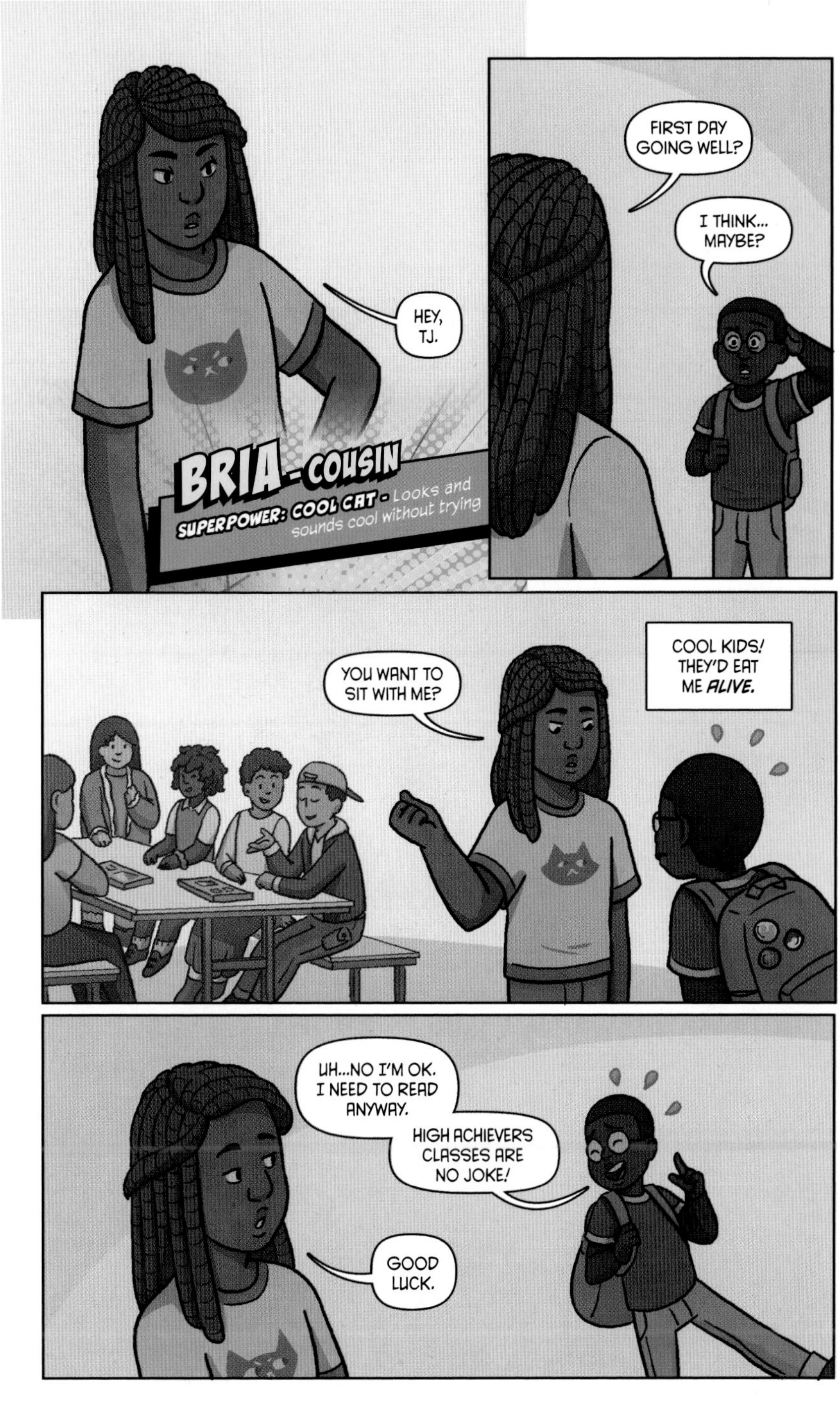
HEY, TJ.
BRIA - COUSIN
SUPERPOWER: COOL CAT - Looks and sounds cool without trying
FIRST DAY GOING WELL?
I THINK... MAYBE?
YOU WANT TO SIT WITH ME?
COOL KIDS! THEY'D EAT ME *ALIVE*.
UH...NO I'M OK. I NEED TO READ ANYWAY.
HIGH ACHIEVERS CLASSES ARE NO JOKE!
GOOD LUCK.

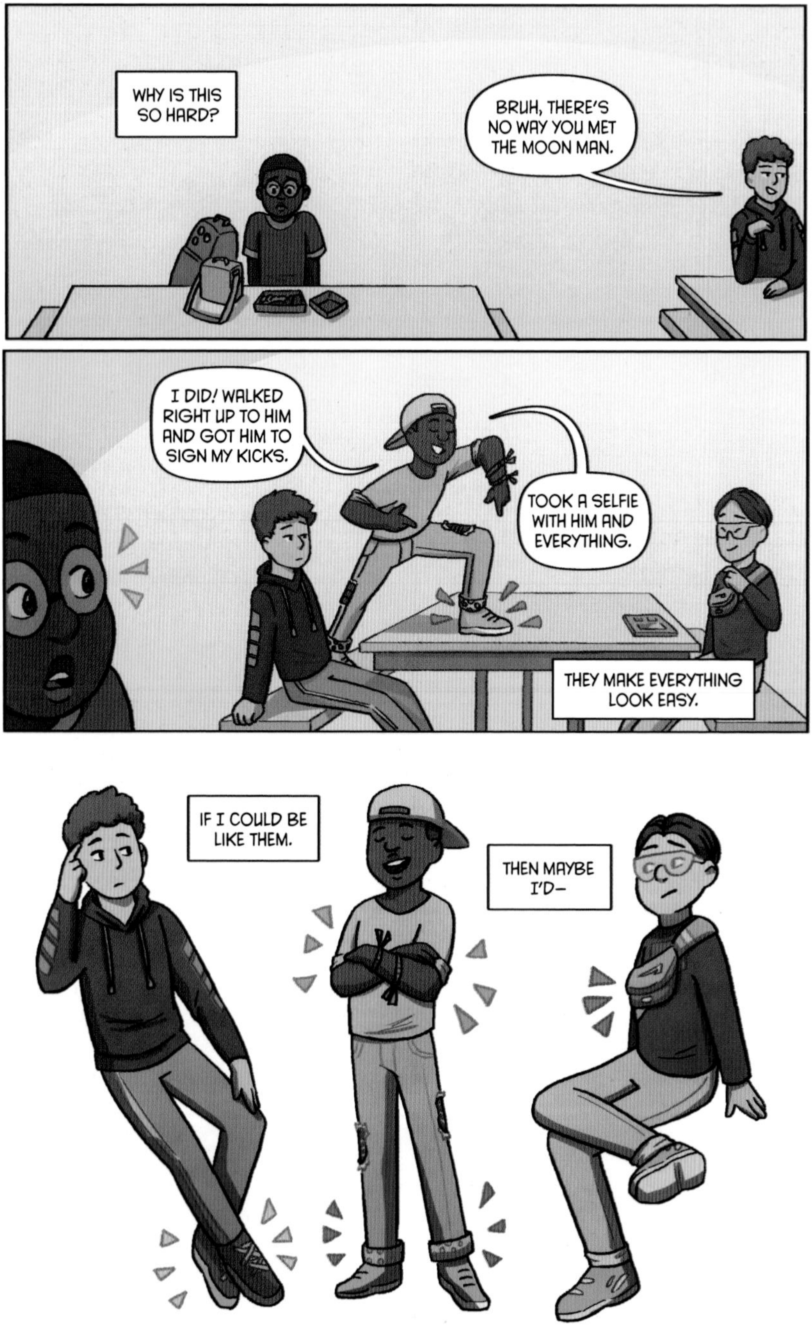

WHY IS THIS SO HARD?
BRUH, THERE'S NO WAY YOU MET THE MOON MAN.
I DID! WALKED RIGHT UP TO HIM AND GOT HIM TO SIGN MY KICKS.
TOOK A SELFIE WITH HIM AND EVERYTHING.
THEY MAKE EVERYTHING LOOK EASY.
IF I COULD BE LIKE THEM.
THEN MAYBE I'D–

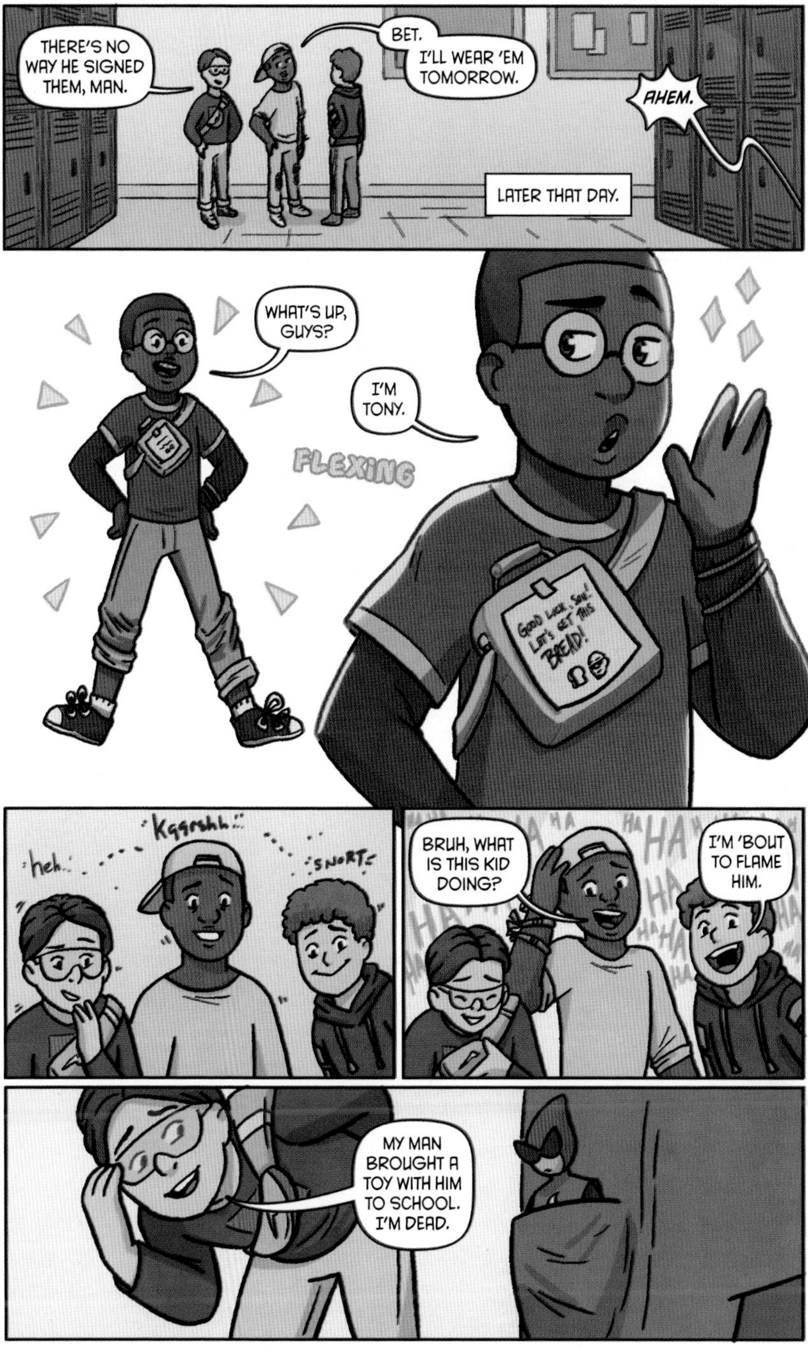
THERE'S NO WAY HE SIGNED THEM, MAN.
BET. I'LL WEAR 'EM TOMORROW.
AHEM.
LATER THAT DAY.
WHAT'S UP, GUYS?
I'M TONY.
FLEXING
GOOD LUCK, SON! LET'S GET THIS BREAD!
heh..
Kggrshh..
SNORT
BRUH, WHAT IS THIS KID DOING?
I'M 'BOUT TO FLAME HIM.
MY MAN BROUGHT A TOY WITH HIM TO SCHOOL. I'M DEAD.

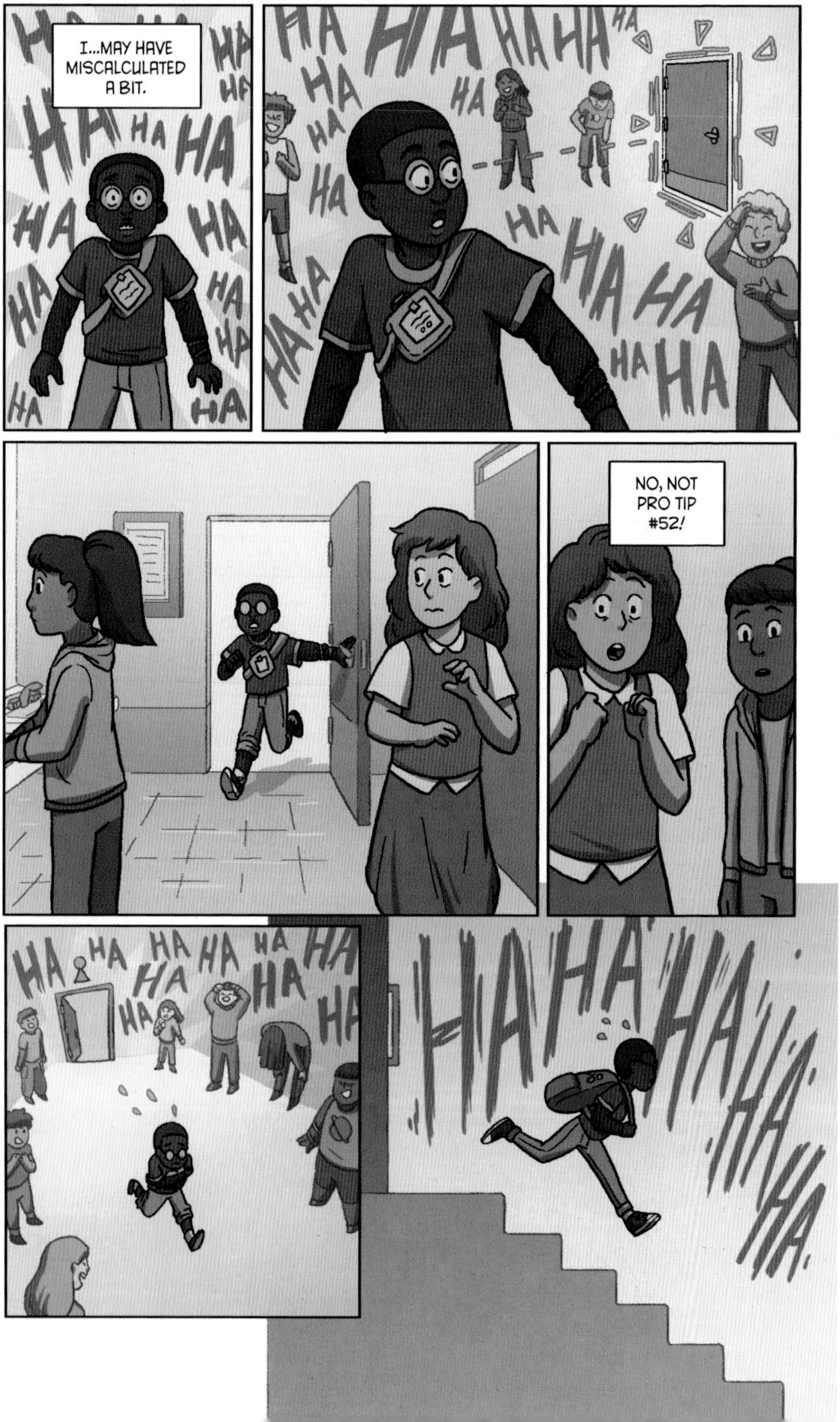
HA HA HA
I...MAY HAVE MISCALCULATED A BIT.
HA HA HA HA HA
HA HA HA HA HA HA HA HA HA HA
HA HA HA HA HA HA HA HA HA HA HA HA HA HA
NO, NOT PRO TIP #52!
HA HA HA HA HA HA HA HA HA HA HA HA
HAHAHAHAHAHAHA.

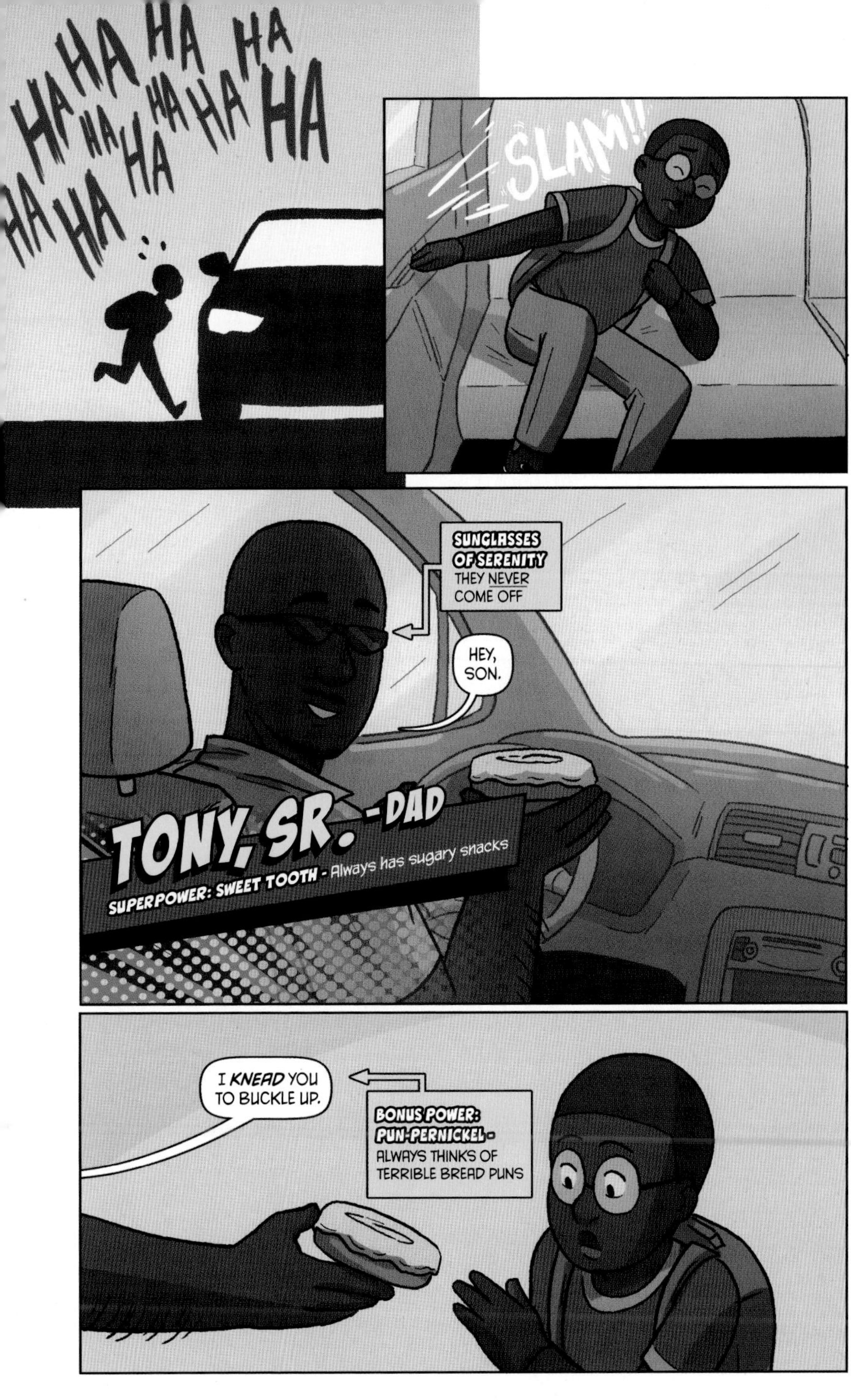
HA HA HA HA HA HA HA HA HA HA HA HA HA HA
SLAM!!
SUNGLASSES OF SERENITY THEY NEVER COME OFF
HEY, SON.
TONY, SR. -DAD
SUPERPOWER: SWEET TOOTH - Always has sugary snacks
I KNEAD YOU TO BUCKLE UP.
BONUS POWER: PUN-PERNICKEL - ALWAYS THINKS OF TERRIBLE BREAD PUNS

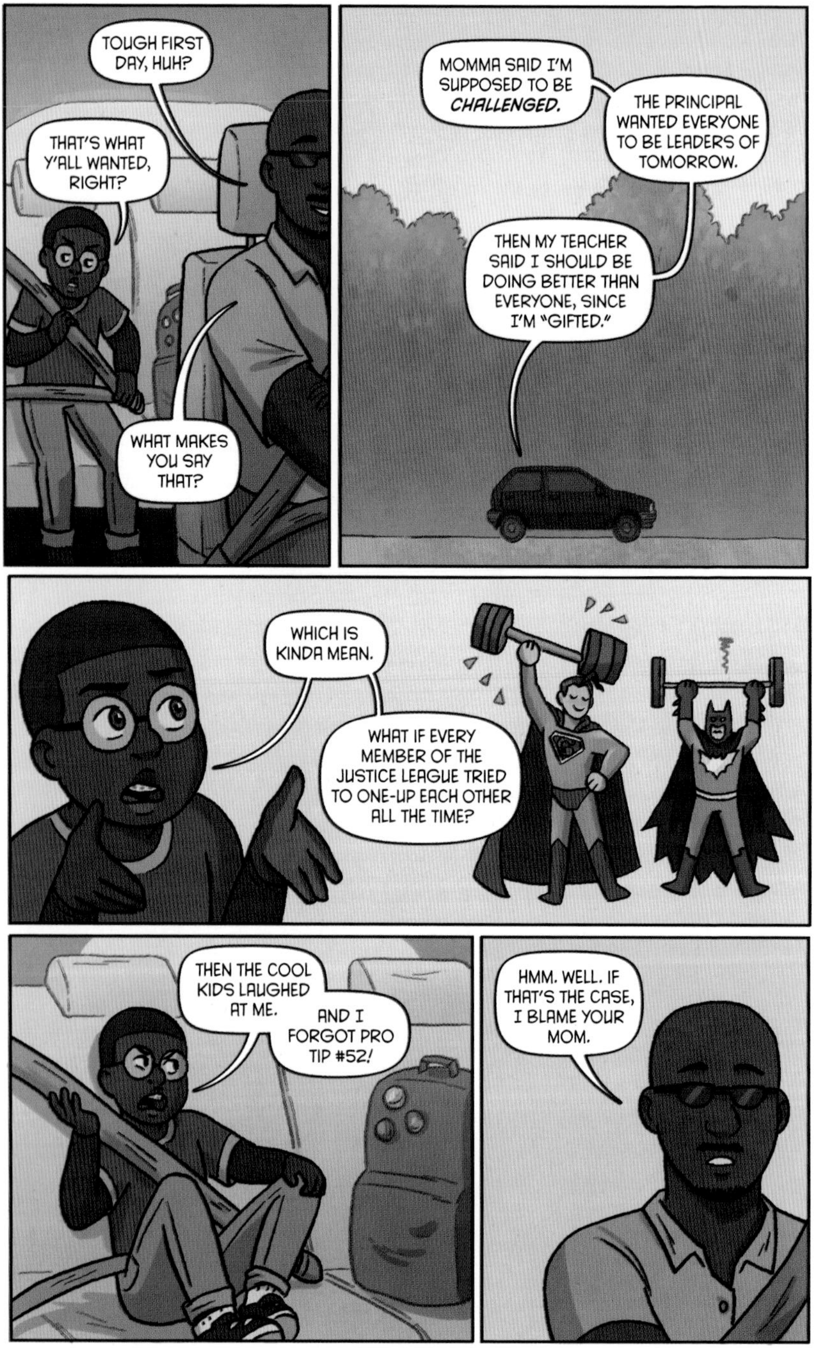
TOUGH FIRST DAY, HUH?
THAT'S WHAT Y'ALL WANTED, RIGHT?
WHAT MAKES YOU SAY THAT?
MOMMA SAID I'M SUPPOSED TO BE ***CHALLENGED.***
THE PRINCIPAL WANTED EVERYONE TO BE LEADERS OF TOMORROW.
THEN MY TEACHER SAID I SHOULD BE DOING BETTER THAN EVERYONE, SINCE I'M "GIFTED."
WHICH IS KINDA MEAN.
WHAT IF EVERY MEMBER OF THE JUSTICE LEAGUE TRIED TO ONE-UP EACH OTHER ALL THE TIME?
THEN THE COOL KIDS LAUGHED AT ME.
AND I FORGOT PRO TIP #52!
HMM. WELL. IF THAT'S THE CASE, I BLAME YOUR MOM.

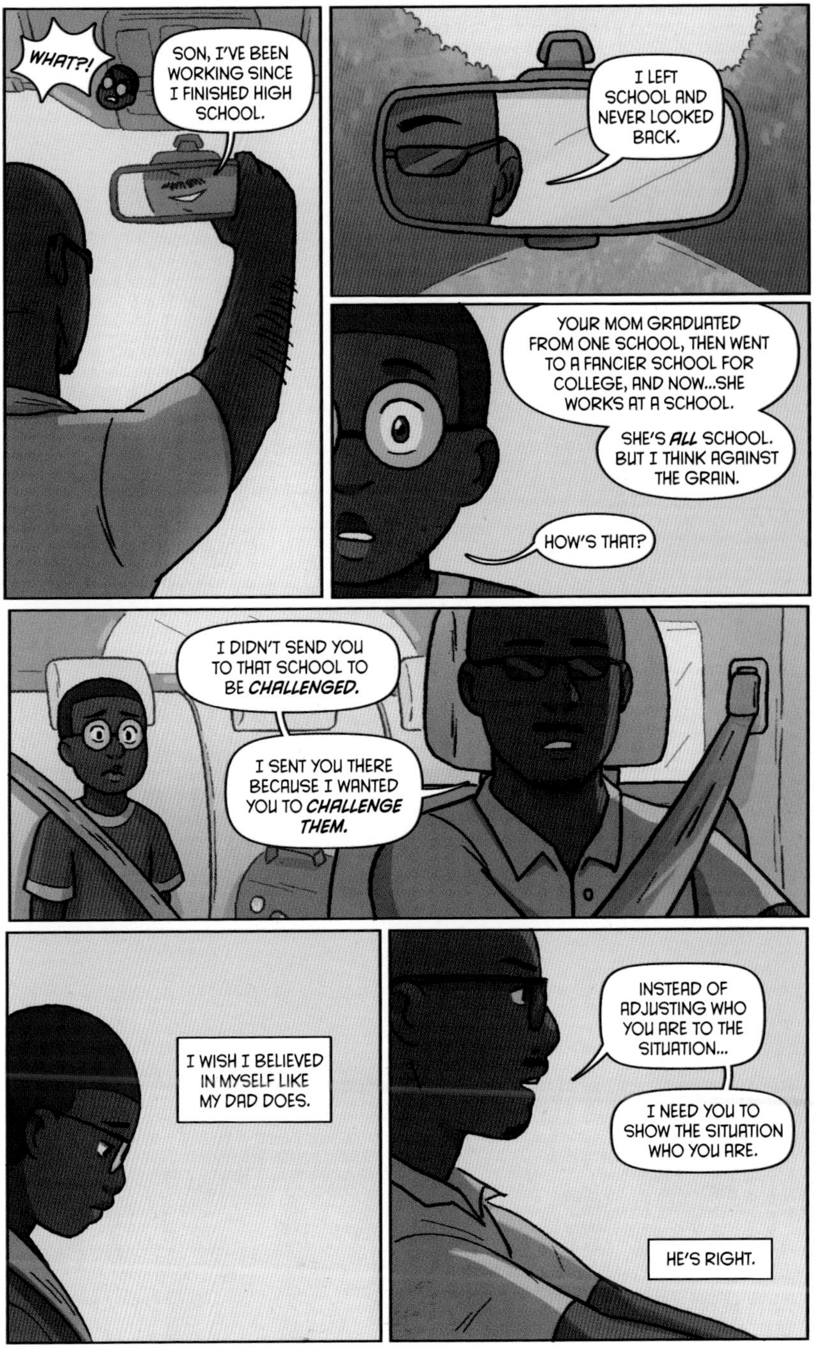
SON, I'VE BEEN WORKING SINCE I FINISHED HIGH SCHOOL.
WHAT?!
I LEFT SCHOOL AND NEVER LOOKED BACK.
YOUR MOM GRADUATED FROM ONE SCHOOL, THEN WENT TO A FANCIER SCHOOL FOR COLLEGE, AND NOW...SHE WORKS AT A SCHOOL.
SHE'S *ALL* SCHOOL. BUT I THINK AGAINST THE GRAIN.
HOW'S THAT?
I DIDN'T SEND YOU TO THAT SCHOOL TO BE ***CHALLENGED.***
I SENT YOU THERE BECAUSE I WANTED YOU TO ***CHALLENGE THEM.***
I WISH I BELIEVED IN MYSELF LIKE MY DAD DOES.
INSTEAD OF ADJUSTING WHO YOU ARE TO THE SITUATION...
I NEED YOU TO SHOW THE SITUATION WHO YOU ARE.
HE'S RIGHT.

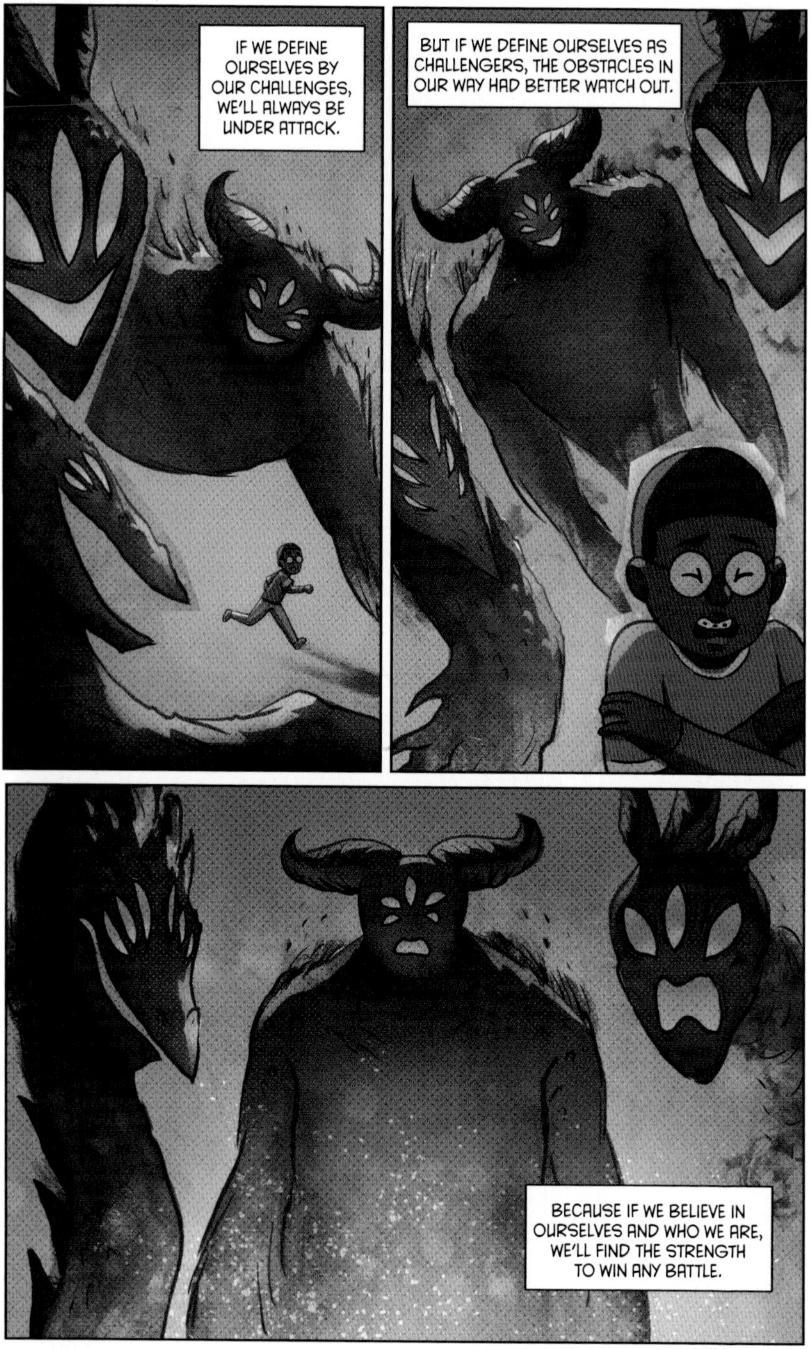
IF WE DEFINE OURSELVES BY OUR CHALLENGES, WE'LL ALWAYS BE UNDER ATTACK.
BUT IF WE DEFINE OURSELVES AS CHALLENGERS, THE OBSTACLES IN OUR WAY HAD BETTER WATCH OUT.
BECAUSE IF WE BELIEVE IN OURSELVES AND WHO WE ARE, WE'LL FIND THE STRENGTH TO WIN ANY BATTLE.

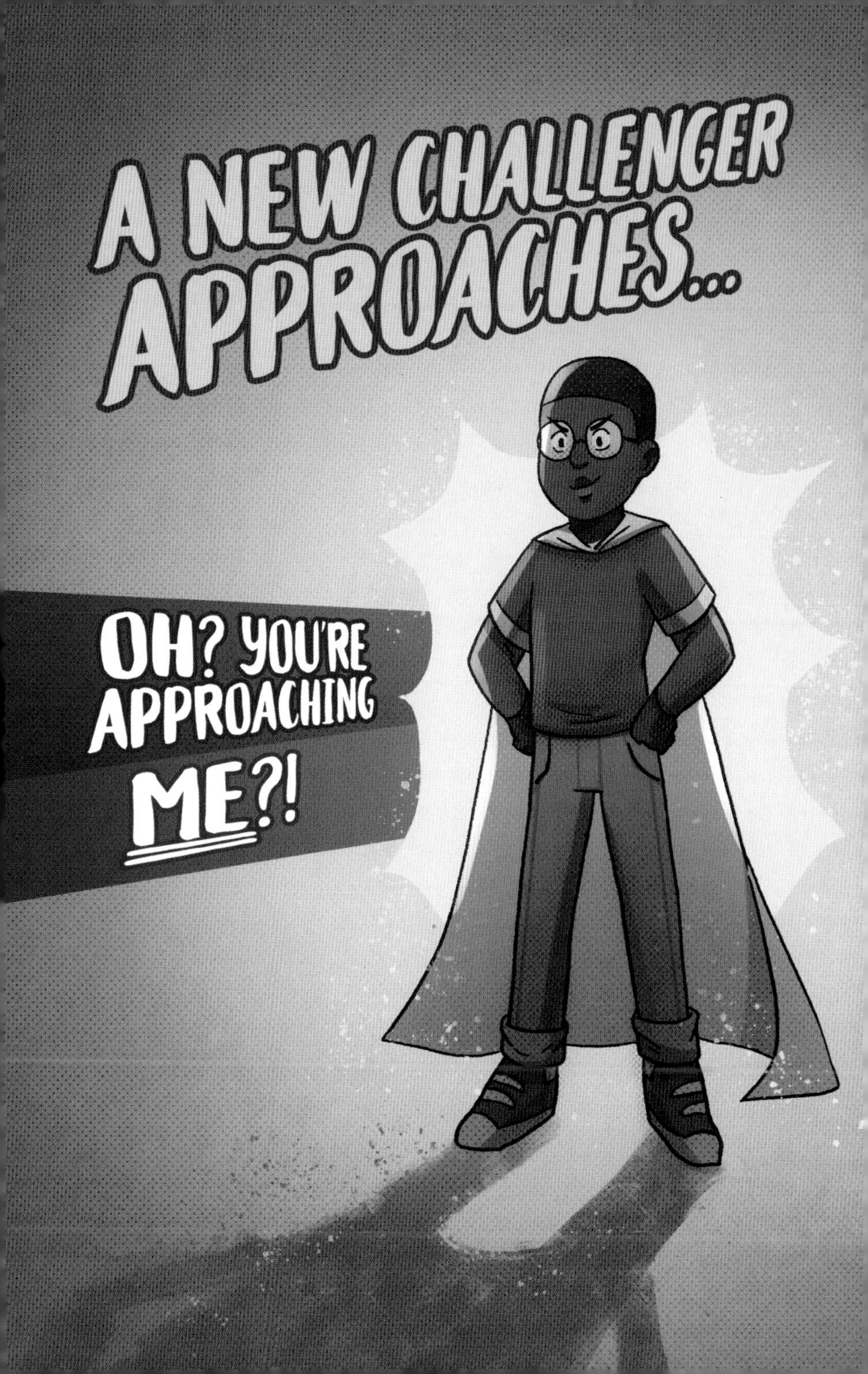
A NEW CHALLENGER APPROACHES...
OH? YOU'RE APPROACHING ME?!

CHAPTER 2

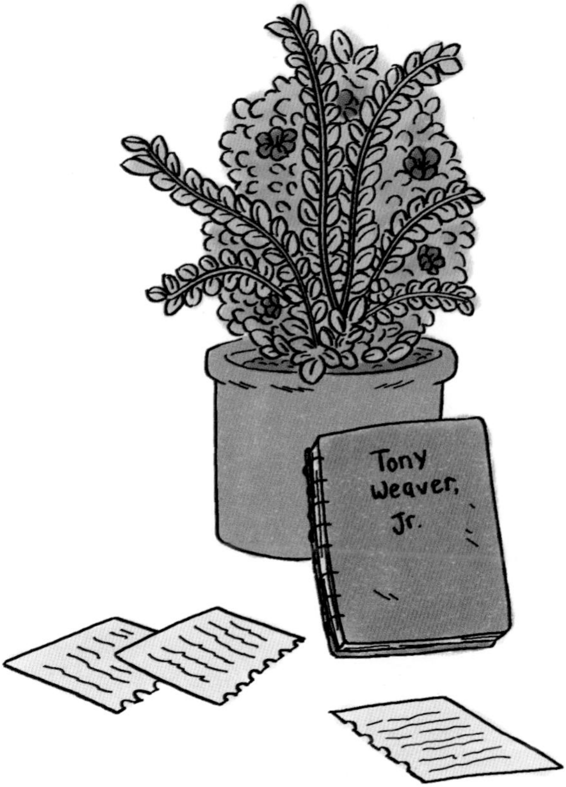
Tony
Weaver,
Jr.

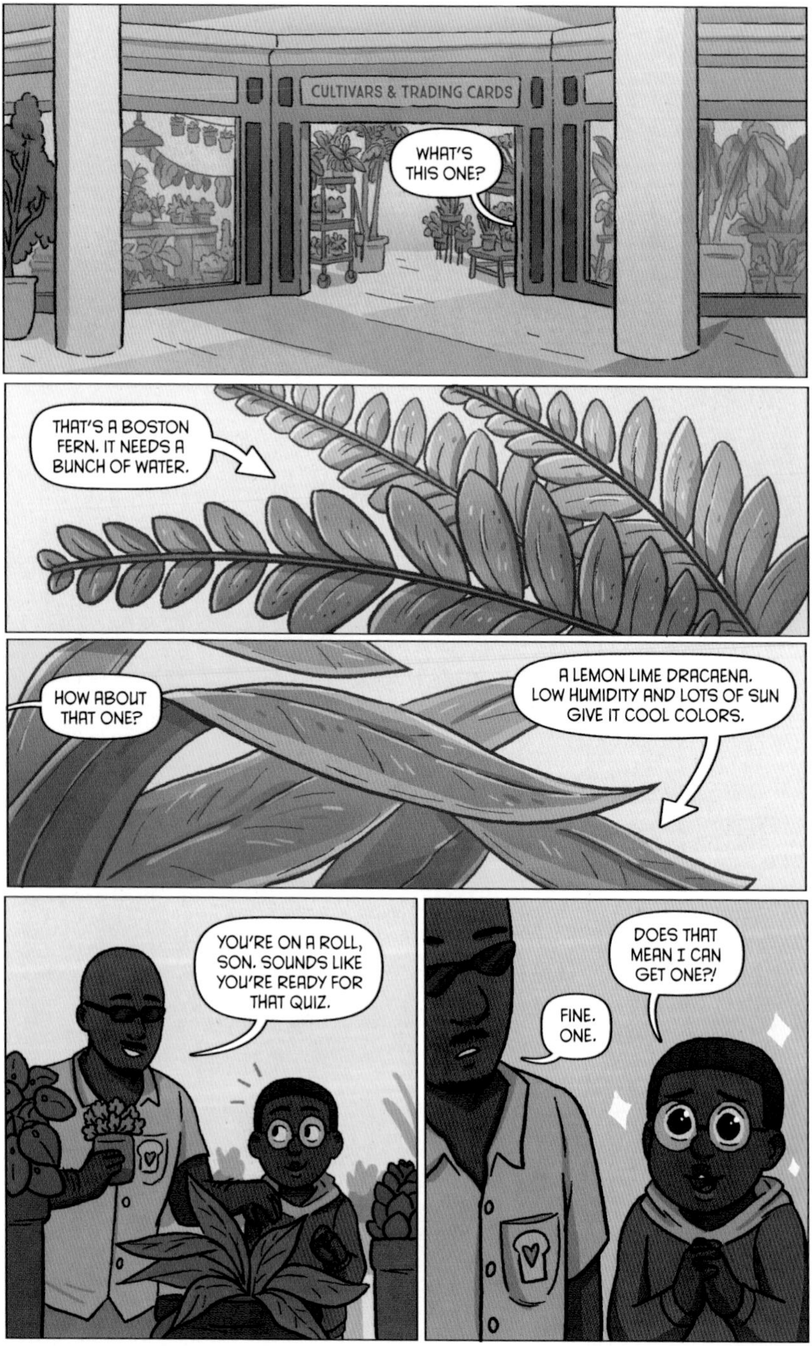
CULTIVARS & TRADING CARDS
WHAT'S THIS ONE?
THAT'S A BOSTON FERN. IT NEEDS A BUNCH OF WATER.
HOW ABOUT THAT ONE?
A LEMON LIME DRACAENA. LOW HUMIDITY AND LOTS OF SUN GIVE IT COOL COLORS.
YOU'RE ON A ROLL, SON. SOUNDS LIKE YOU'RE READY FOR THAT QUIZ.
DOES THAT MEAN I CAN GET ONE?!
FINE. ONE.

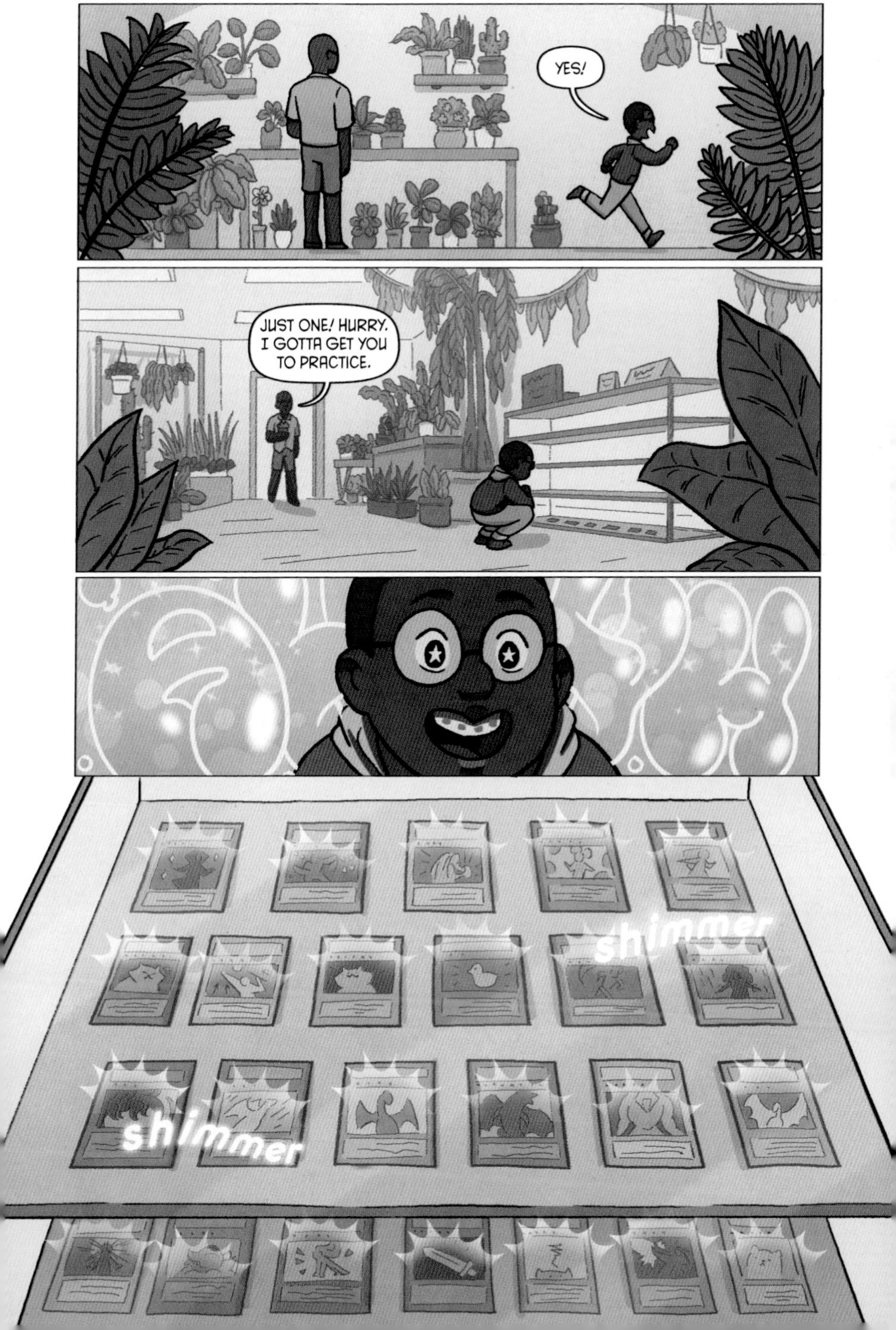
YES!
JUST ONE! HURRY. I GOTTA GET YOU TO PRACTICE.
shimmer
shimmer

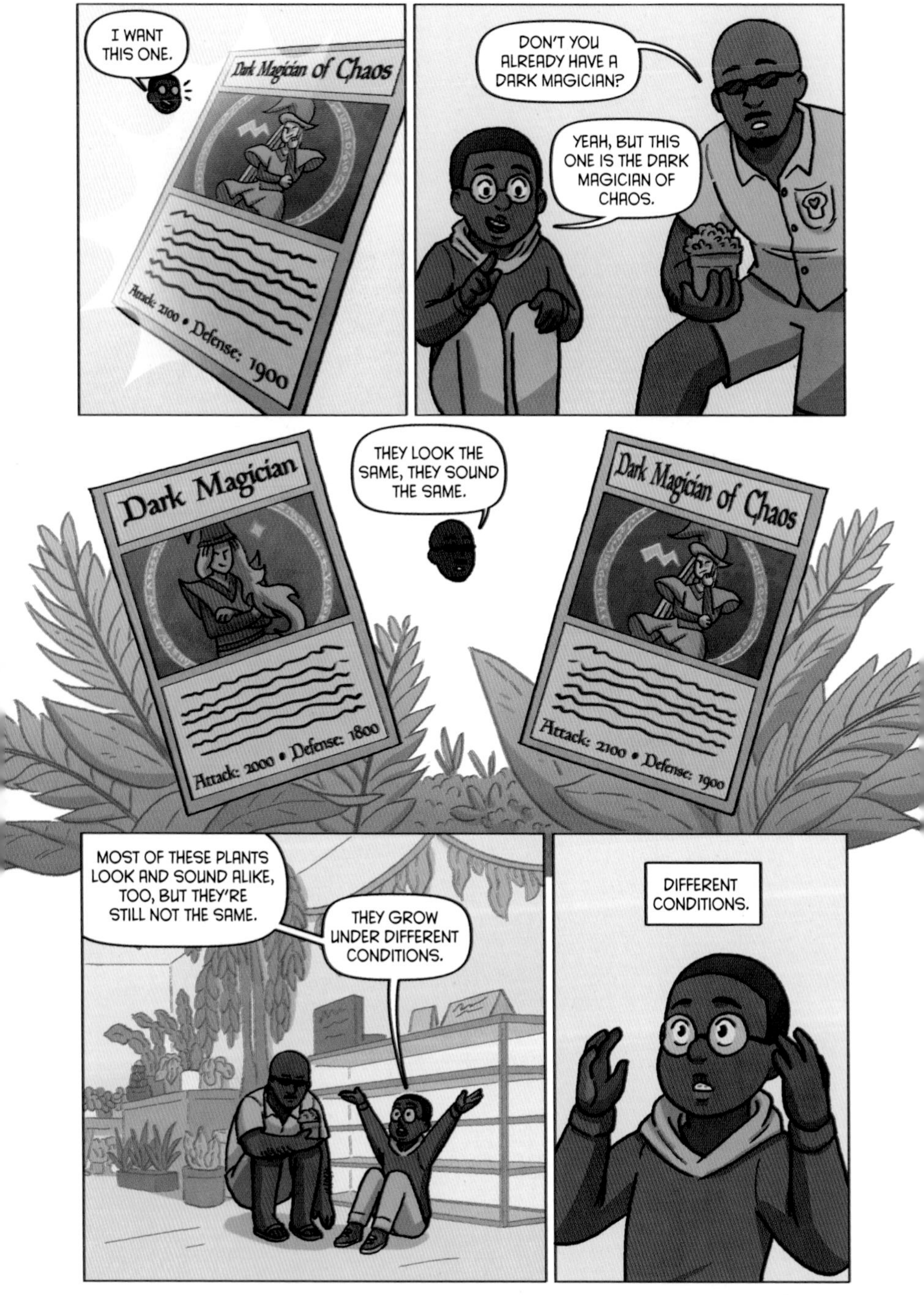
I WANT THIS ONE.
Dark Magician of Chaos
Attack: 2100 • Defense: 1900
DON'T YOU ALREADY HAVE A DARK MAGICIAN?
YEAH, BUT THIS ONE IS THE DARK MAGICIAN OF CHAOS.
Dark Magician
Attack: 2000 • Defense: 1800
THEY LOOK THE SAME, THEY SOUND THE SAME.
Dark Magician of Chaos
Attack: 2100 • Defense: 1900
MOST OF THESE PLANTS LOOK AND SOUND ALIKE, TOO, BUT THEY'RE STILL NOT THE SAME.
THEY GROW UNDER DIFFERENT CONDITIONS.
DIFFERENT CONDITIONS.

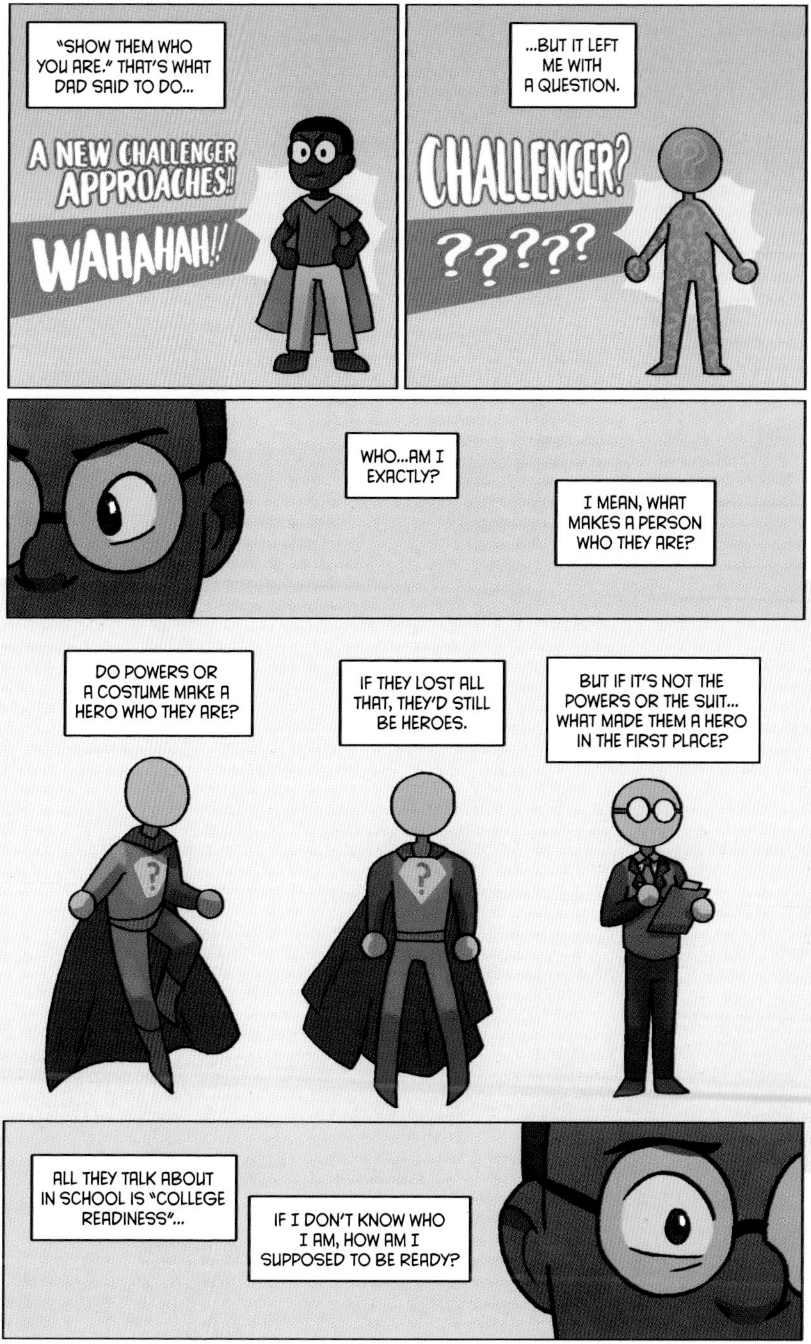
"SHOW THEM WHO YOU ARE." THAT'S WHAT DAD SAID TO DO...
A NEW CHALLENGER APPROACHES!!
WAHAHAH!!
...BUT IT LEFT ME WITH A QUESTION.
CHALLENGER?
????
WHO...AM I EXACTLY?
I MEAN, WHAT MAKES A PERSON WHO THEY ARE?
DO POWERS OR A COSTUME MAKE A HERO WHO THEY ARE?
IF THEY LOST ALL THAT, THEY'D STILL BE HEROES.
BUT IF IT'S NOT THE POWERS OR THE SUIT... WHAT MADE THEM A HERO IN THE FIRST PLACE?
ALL THEY TALK ABOUT IN SCHOOL IS "COLLEGE READINESS"...
IF I DON'T KNOW WHO I AM, HOW AM I SUPPOSED TO BE READY?

IF PLANTS ARE IDENTIFIED BY WHAT ALLOWS THEM TO BLOSSOM AND THRIVE, WHAT IF PEOPLE ARE THE SAME?

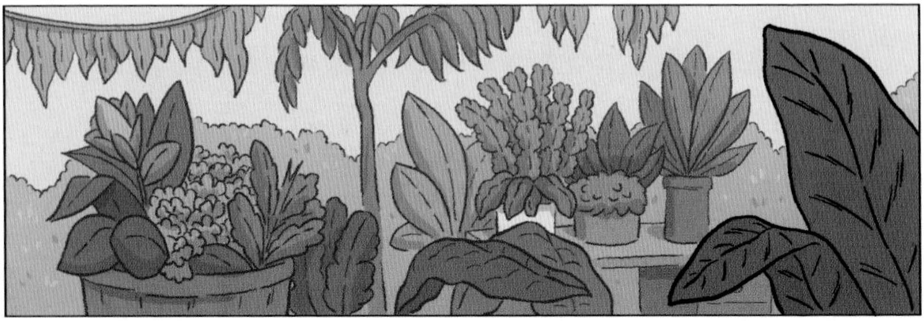

DOES THAT MEAN I HAVE TO FIGURE OUT WHAT THOSE THINGS ARE?

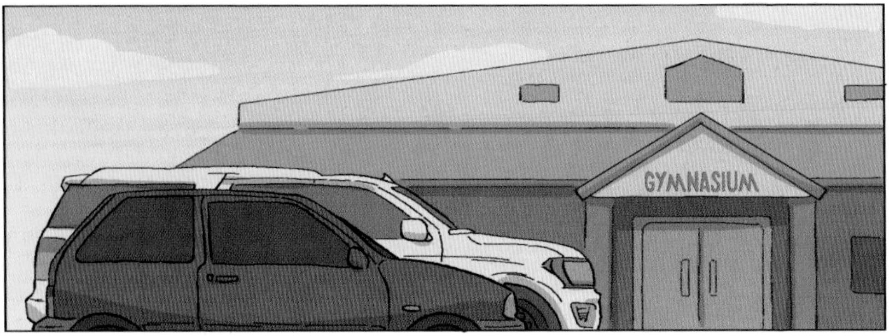
GYMNASIUM

IF IT'LL MAKE ME HAPPY, MAYBE IT'S WORTH GIVING IT A SHOT.

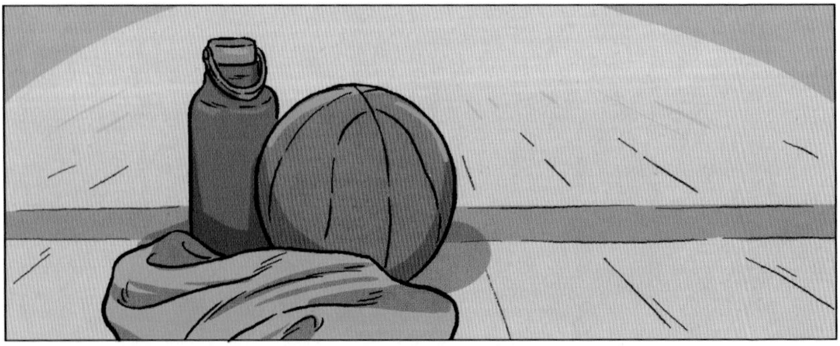

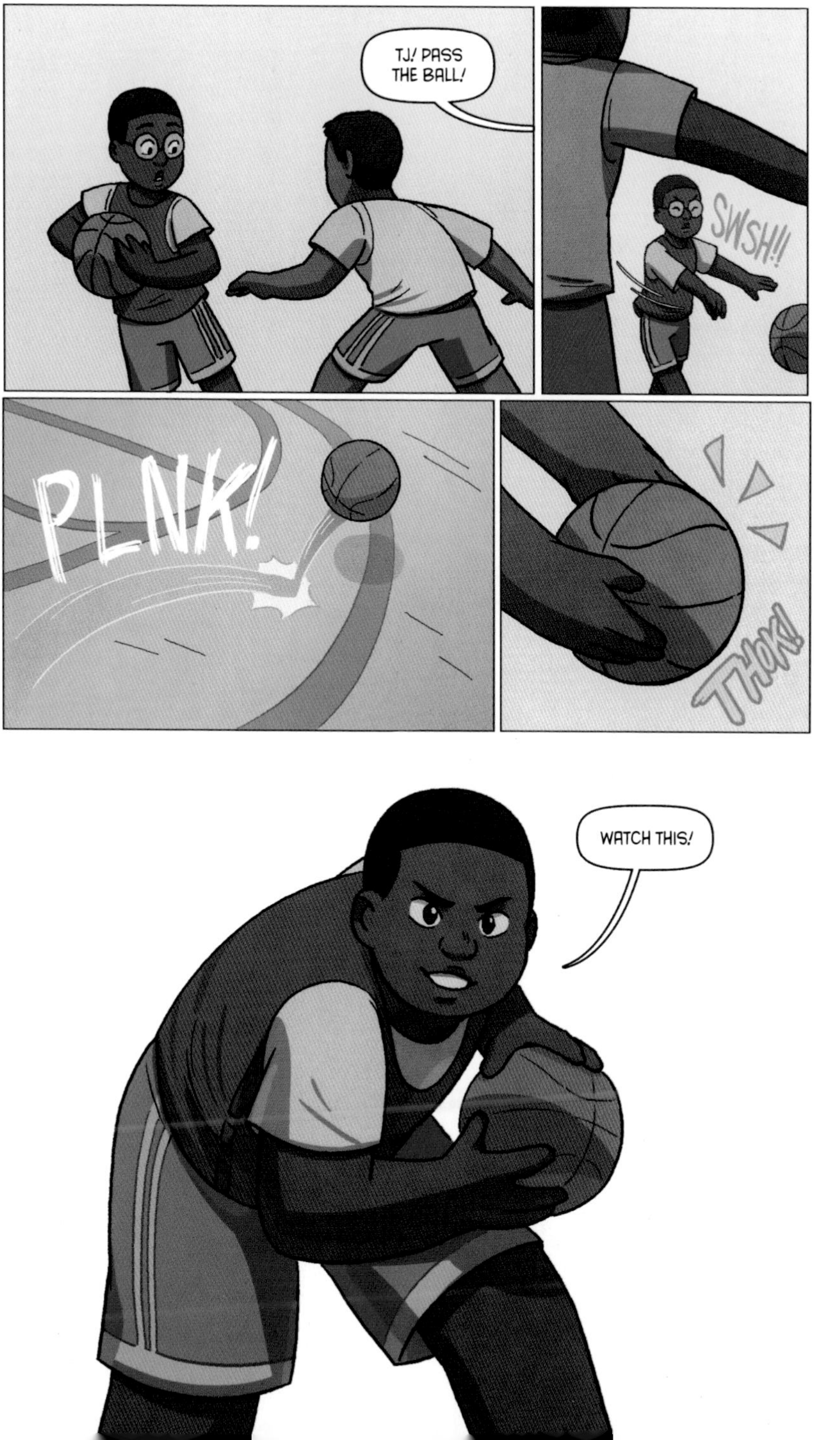
TJ! PASS THE BALL!
SWSH!!
PLNK!
THOK!
WATCH THIS!

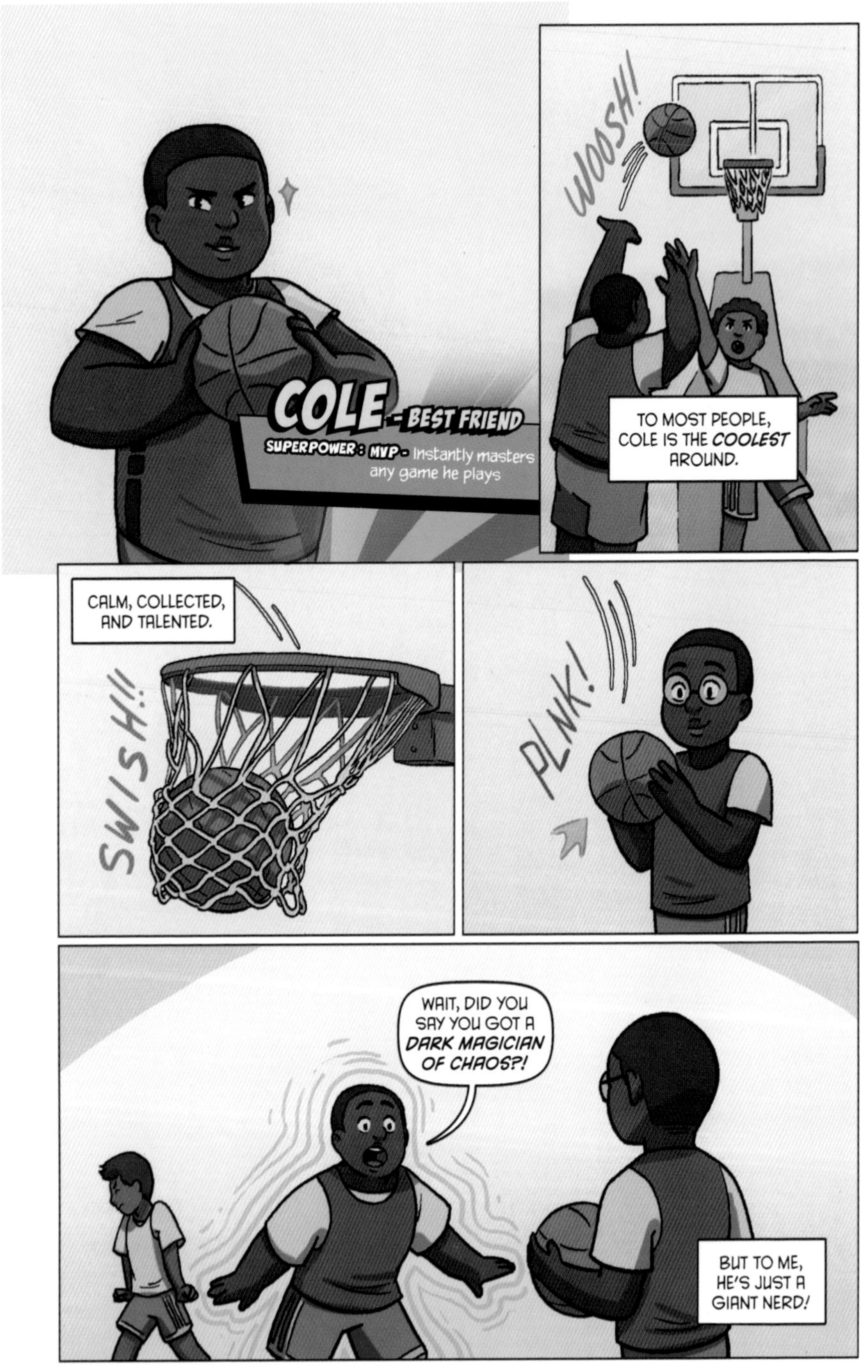
COLE - BEST FRIEND
SUPERPOWER: MVP - Instantly masters any game he plays
WOOSH!
TO MOST PEOPLE, COLE IS THE COOLEST AROUND.
CALM, COLLECTED, AND TALENTED.
SWISH!!
PLNK!
WAIT, DID YOU SAY YOU GOT A DARK MAGICIAN OF CHAOS?!
BUT TO ME, HE'S JUST A GIANT NERD!

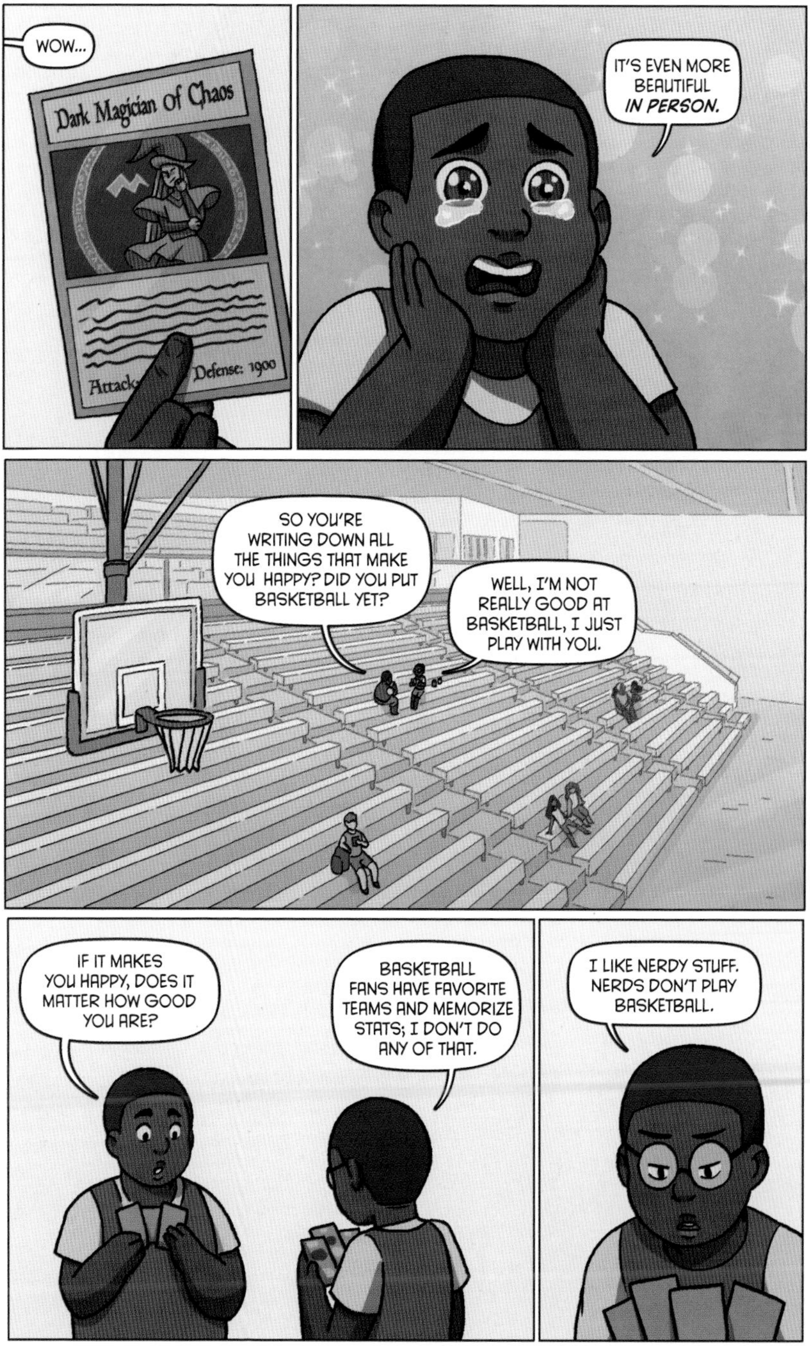
WOW...
Dark Magician of Chaos
Attack Defense: 1900
IT'S EVEN MORE BEAUTIFUL *IN PERSON.*
SO YOU'RE WRITING DOWN ALL THE THINGS THAT MAKE YOU HAPPY? DID YOU PUT BASKETBALL YET?
WELL, I'M NOT REALLY GOOD AT BASKETBALL, I JUST PLAY WITH YOU.
IF IT MAKES YOU HAPPY, DOES IT MATTER HOW GOOD YOU ARE?
BASKETBALL FANS HAVE FAVORITE TEAMS AND MEMORIZE STATS; I DON'T DO ANY OF THAT.
I LIKE NERDY STUFF. NERDS DON'T PLAY BASKETBALL.

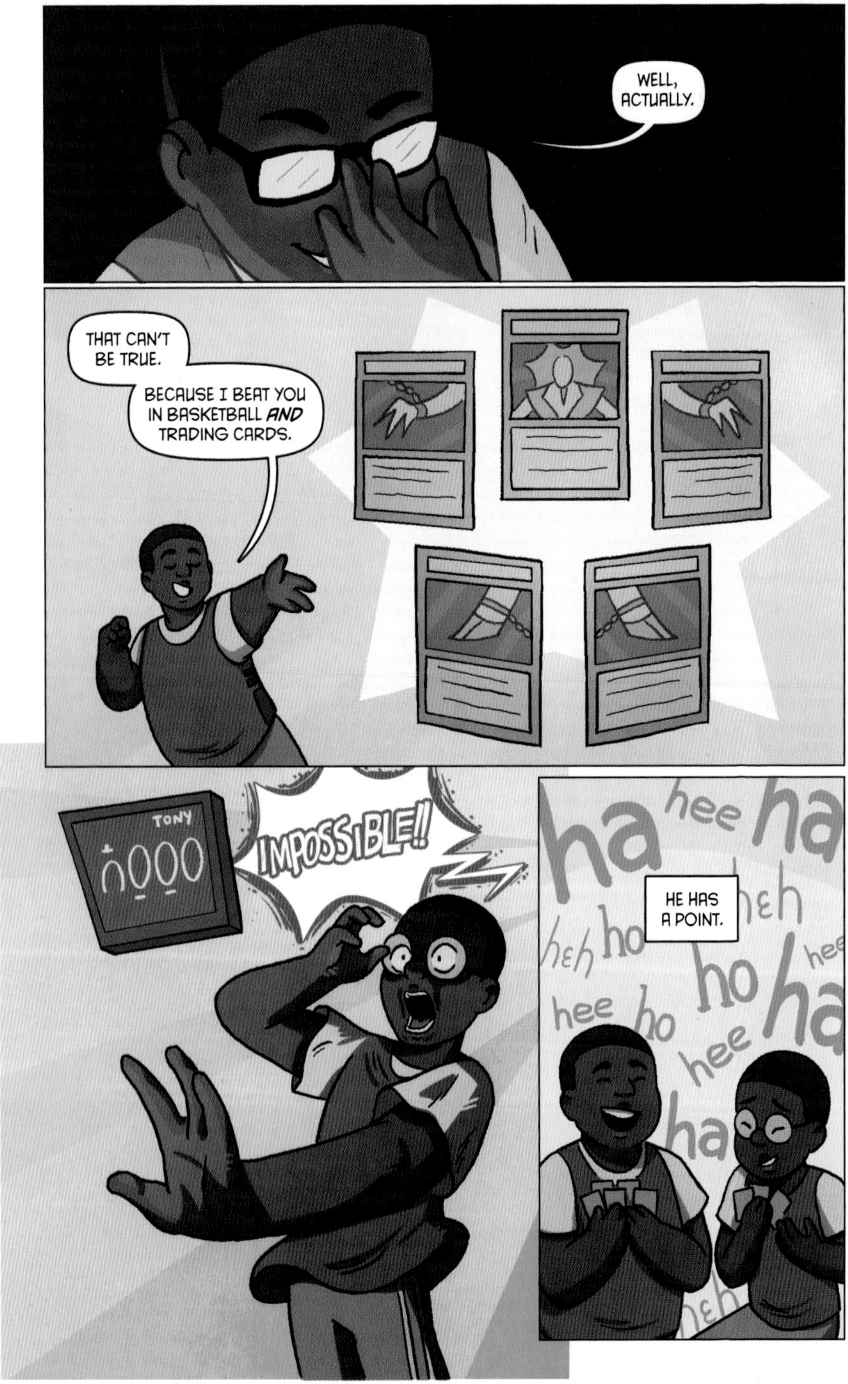
WELL, ACTUALLY.
THAT CAN'T BE TRUE.
BECAUSE I BEAT YOU IN BASKETBALL *AND* TRADING CARDS.
TONY
IMPOSSIBLE!!
HE HAS A POINT.
ha hee ha
heh ho heh
ho hee
hee ho hee ha
ha
heh

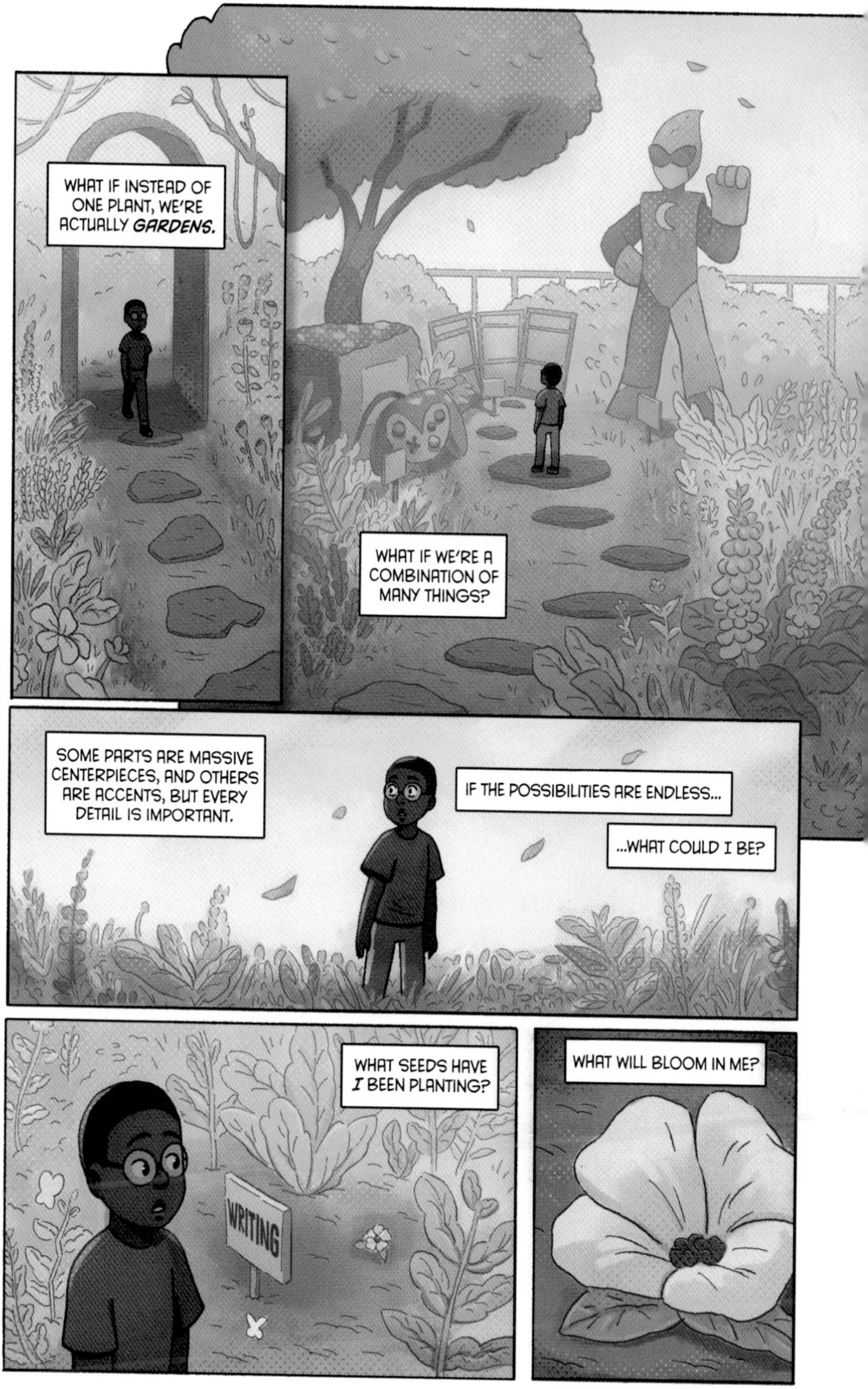
WHAT IF INSTEAD OF ONE PLANT, WE'RE ACTUALLY *GARDENS*.
WHAT IF WE'RE A COMBINATION OF MANY THINGS?
SOME PARTS ARE MASSIVE CENTERPIECES, AND OTHERS ARE ACCENTS, BUT EVERY DETAIL IS IMPORTANT.
IF THE POSSIBILITIES ARE ENDLESS...
...WHAT COULD I BE?
WHAT SEEDS HAVE *I* BEEN PLANTING?
WRITING
WHAT WILL BLOOM IN ME?

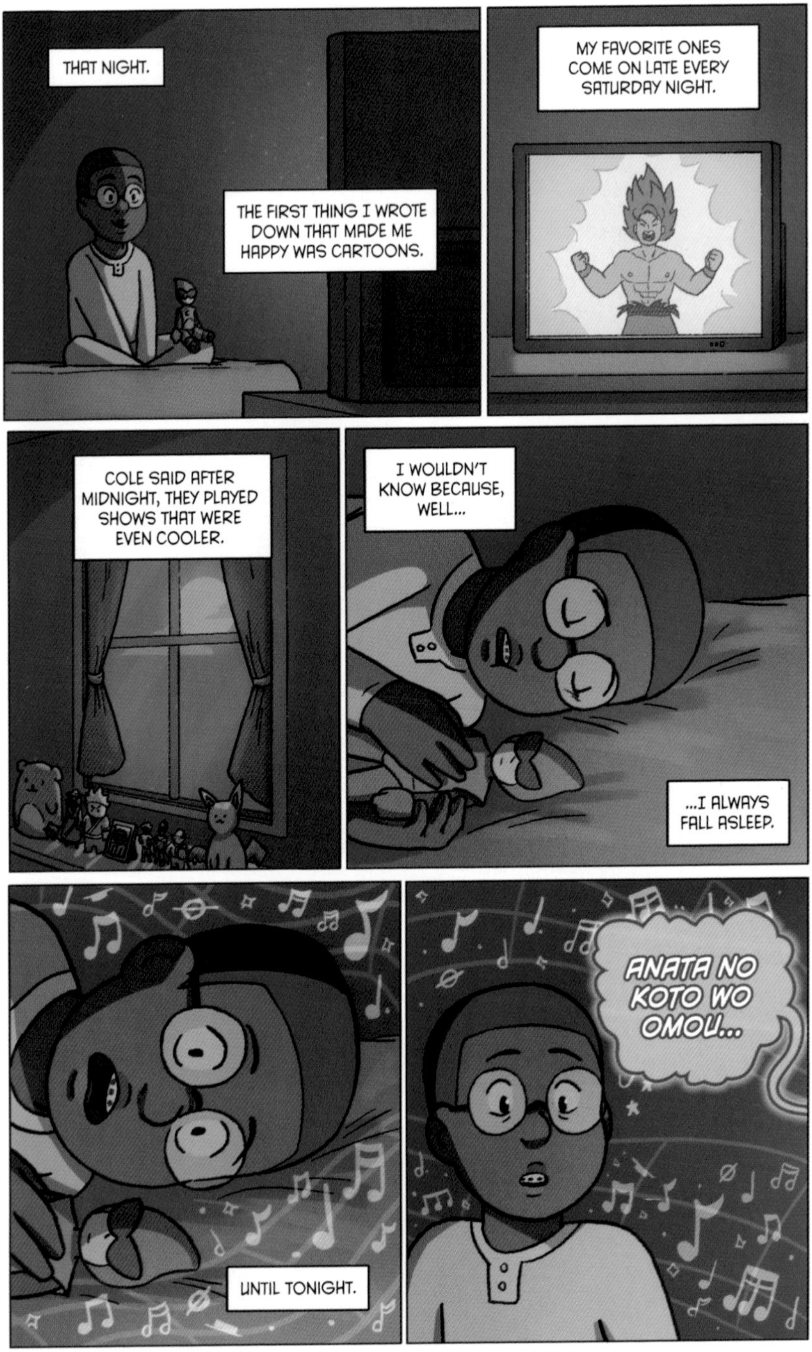
THAT NIGHT.
THE FIRST THING I WROTE DOWN THAT MADE ME HAPPY WAS CARTOONS.
MY FAVORITE ONES COME ON LATE EVERY SATURDAY NIGHT.
COLE SAID AFTER MIDNIGHT, THEY PLAYED SHOWS THAT WERE EVEN COOLER.
I WOULDN'T KNOW BECAUSE, WELL...
...I ALWAYS FALL ASLEEP.
UNTIL TONIGHT.
ANATA NO KOTO WO OMOU...

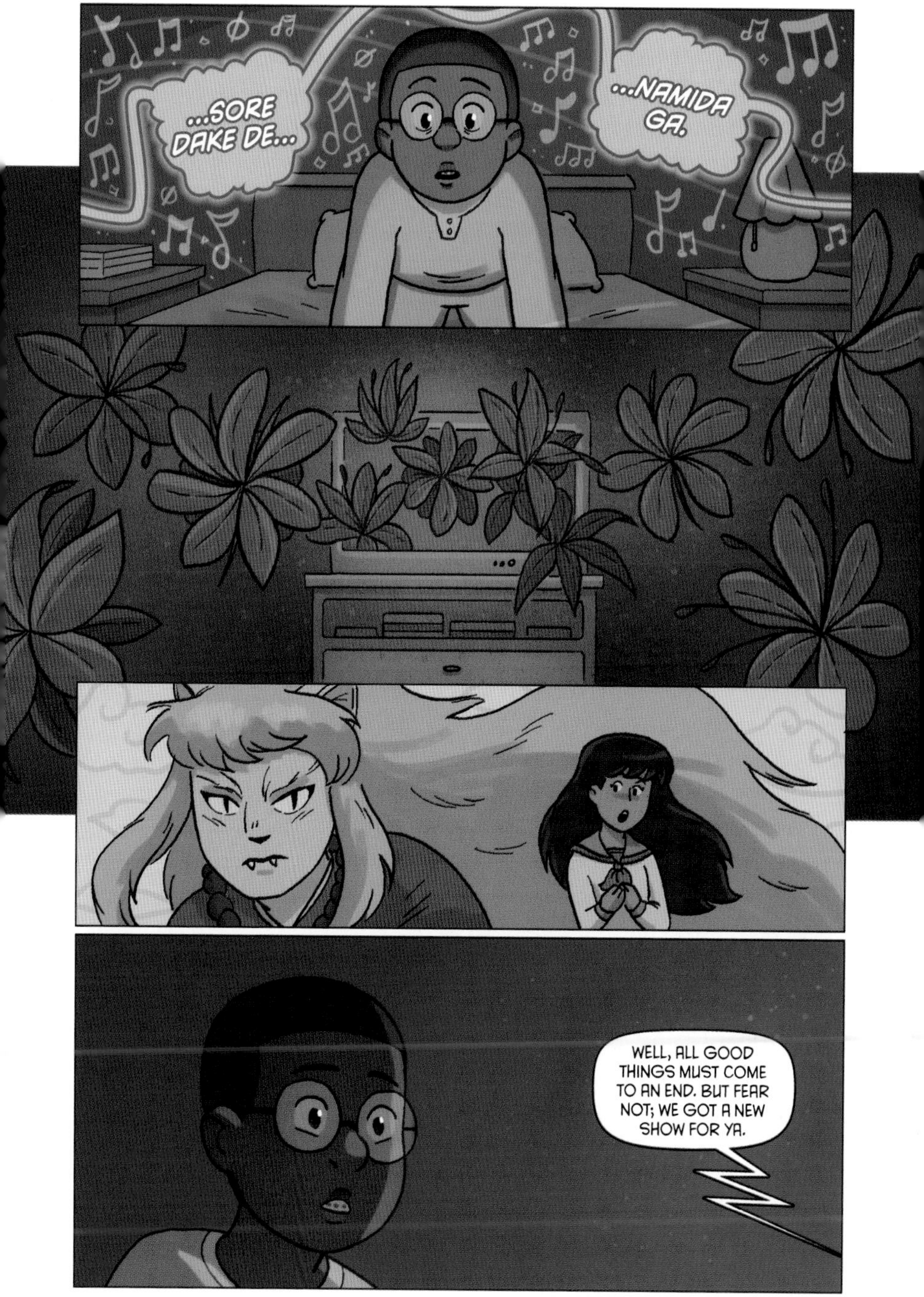
...SORE DAKE DE...
...NAMIDA GA.
WELL, ALL GOOD THINGS MUST COME TO AN END. BUT FEAR NOT; WE GOT A NEW SHOW FOR YA.

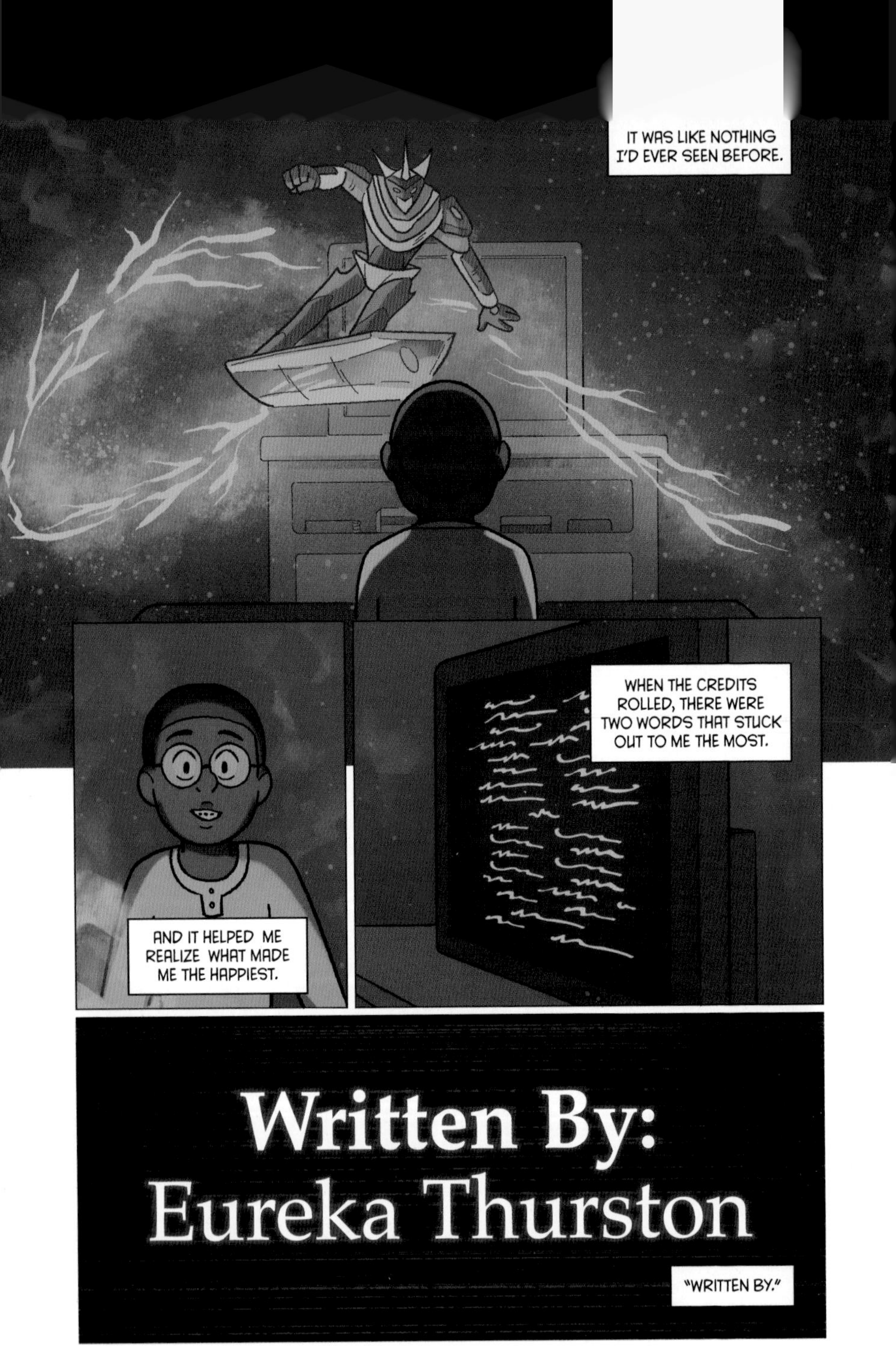
IT WAS LIKE NOTHING I'D EVER SEEN BEFORE.
AND IT HELPED ME REALIZE WHAT MADE ME THE HAPPIEST.
WHEN THE CREDITS ROLLED, THERE WERE TWO WORDS THAT STUCK OUT TO ME THE MOST.
Written By:
Eureka Thurston
"WRITTEN BY."

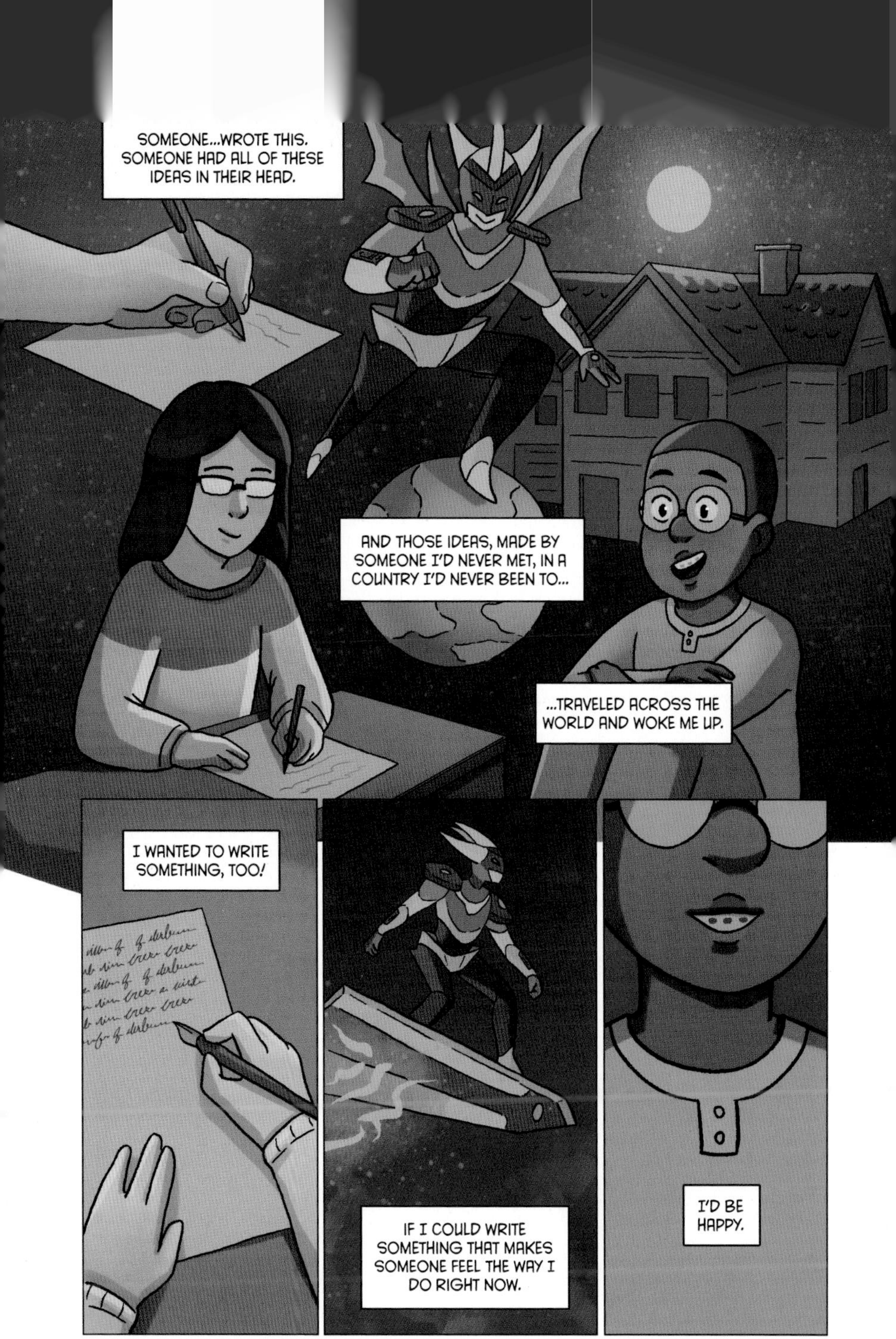
SOMEONE...WROTE THIS. SOMEONE HAD ALL OF THESE IDEAS IN THEIR HEAD.
AND THOSE IDEAS, MADE BY SOMEONE I'D NEVER MET, IN A COUNTRY I'D NEVER BEEN TO...
...TRAVELED ACROSS THE WORLD AND WOKE ME UP.
I WANTED TO WRITE SOMETHING, TOO!
IF I COULD WRITE SOMETHING THAT MAKES SOMEONE FEEL THE WAY I DO RIGHT NOW.
I'D BE HAPPY.

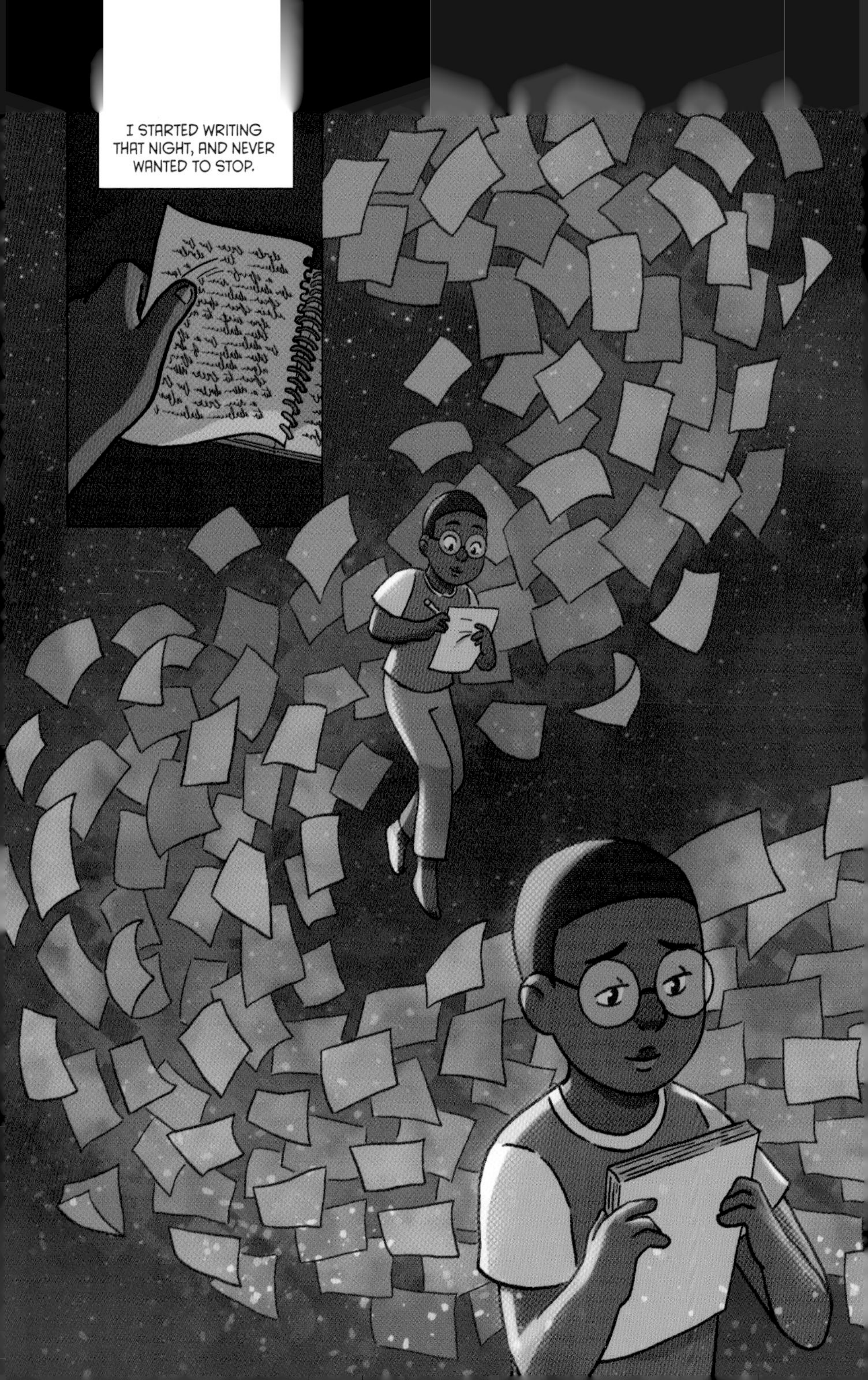
I STARTED WRITING THAT NIGHT, AND NEVER WANTED TO STOP.

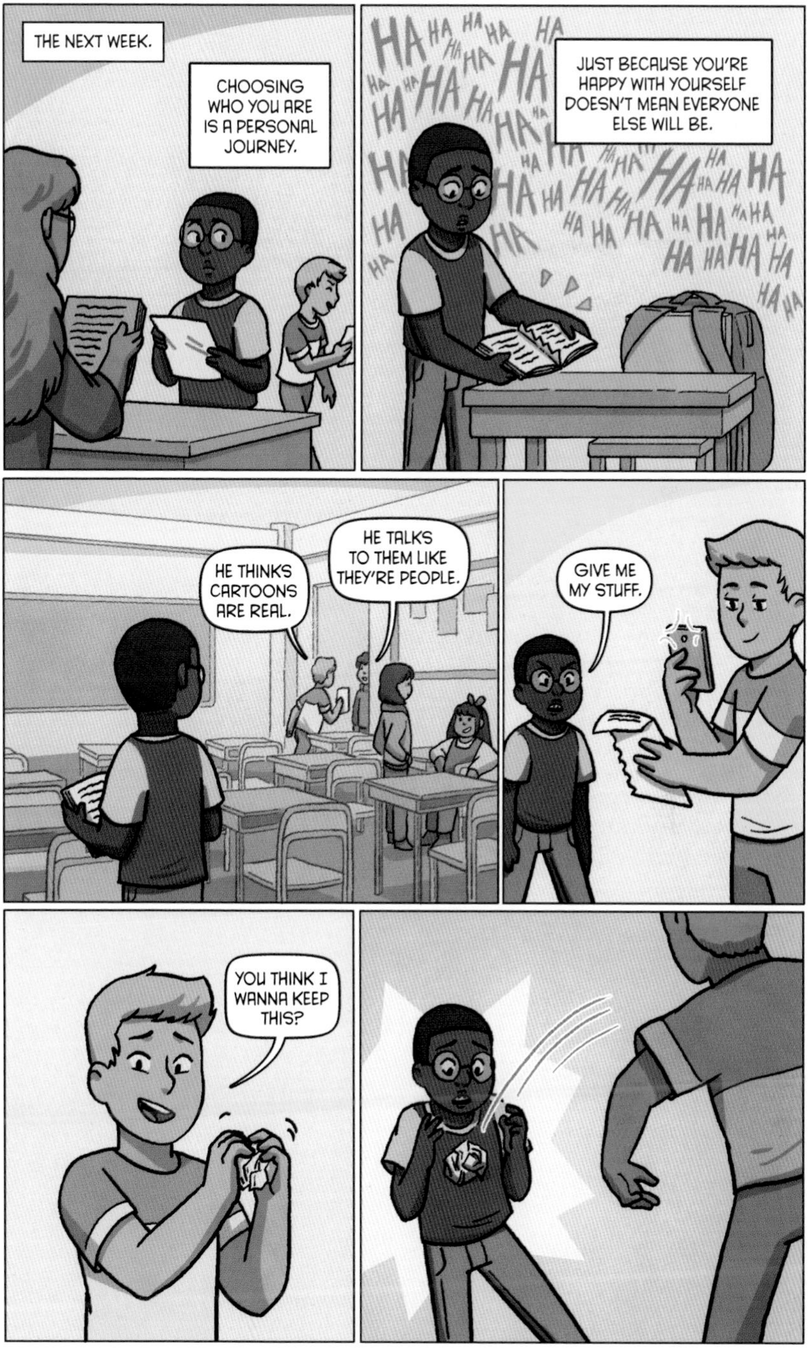
THE NEXT WEEK.
CHOOSING WHO YOU ARE IS A PERSONAL JOURNEY.
JUST BECAUSE YOU'RE HAPPY WITH YOURSELF DOESN'T MEAN EVERYONE ELSE WILL BE.
HA HA HA HA HA HA HA HA HA HA HA HA HA HA HA HA HA HA HA HA HA HA HA HA HA HA HA HA HA HA HA HA HA HA
HE THINKS CARTOONS ARE REAL.
HE TALKS TO THEM LIKE THEY'RE PEOPLE.
GIVE ME MY STUFF.
YOU THINK I WANNA KEEP THIS?

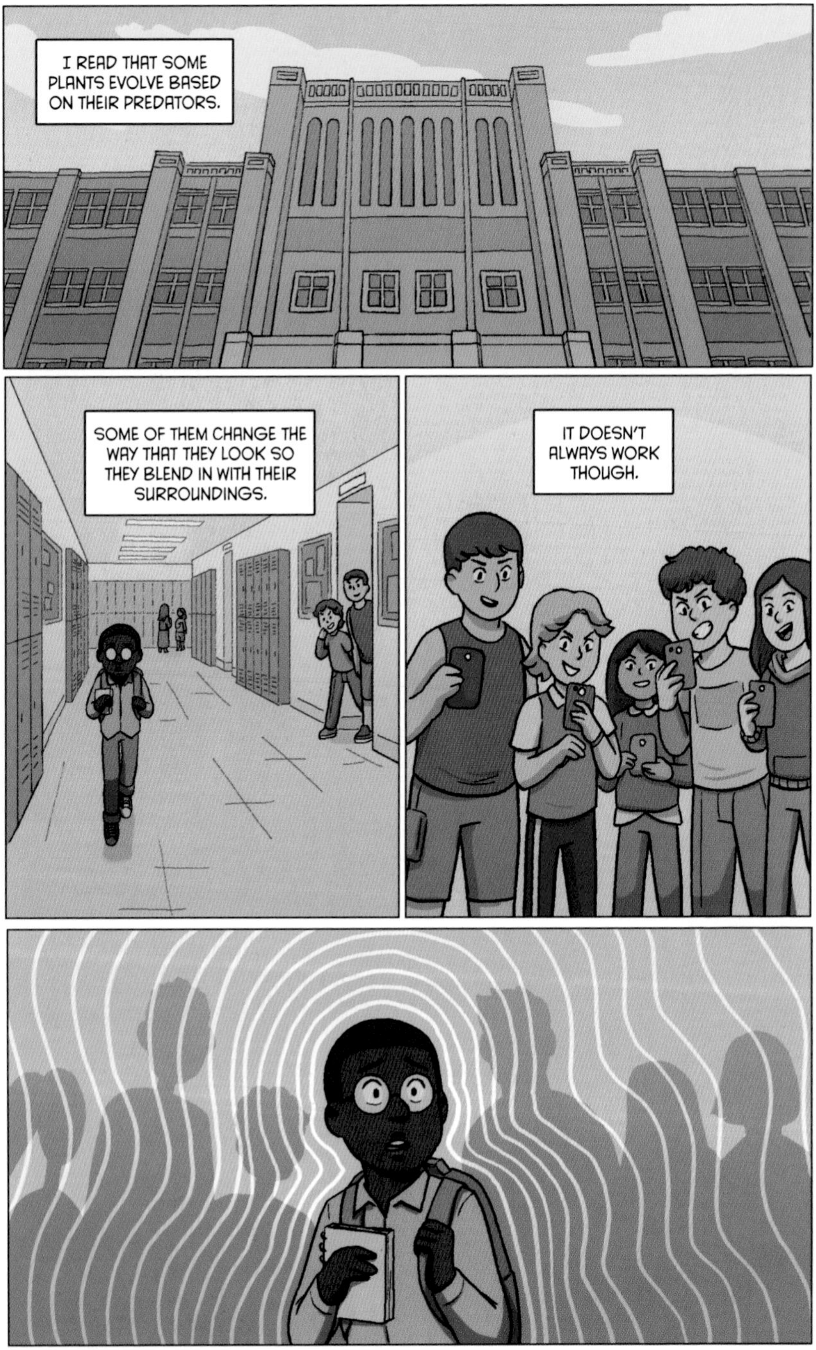
I READ THAT SOME PLANTS EVOLVE BASED ON THEIR PREDATORS.
SOME OF THEM CHANGE THE WAY THAT THEY LOOK SO THEY BLEND IN WITH THEIR SURROUNDINGS.
IT DOESN'T ALWAYS WORK THOUGH.

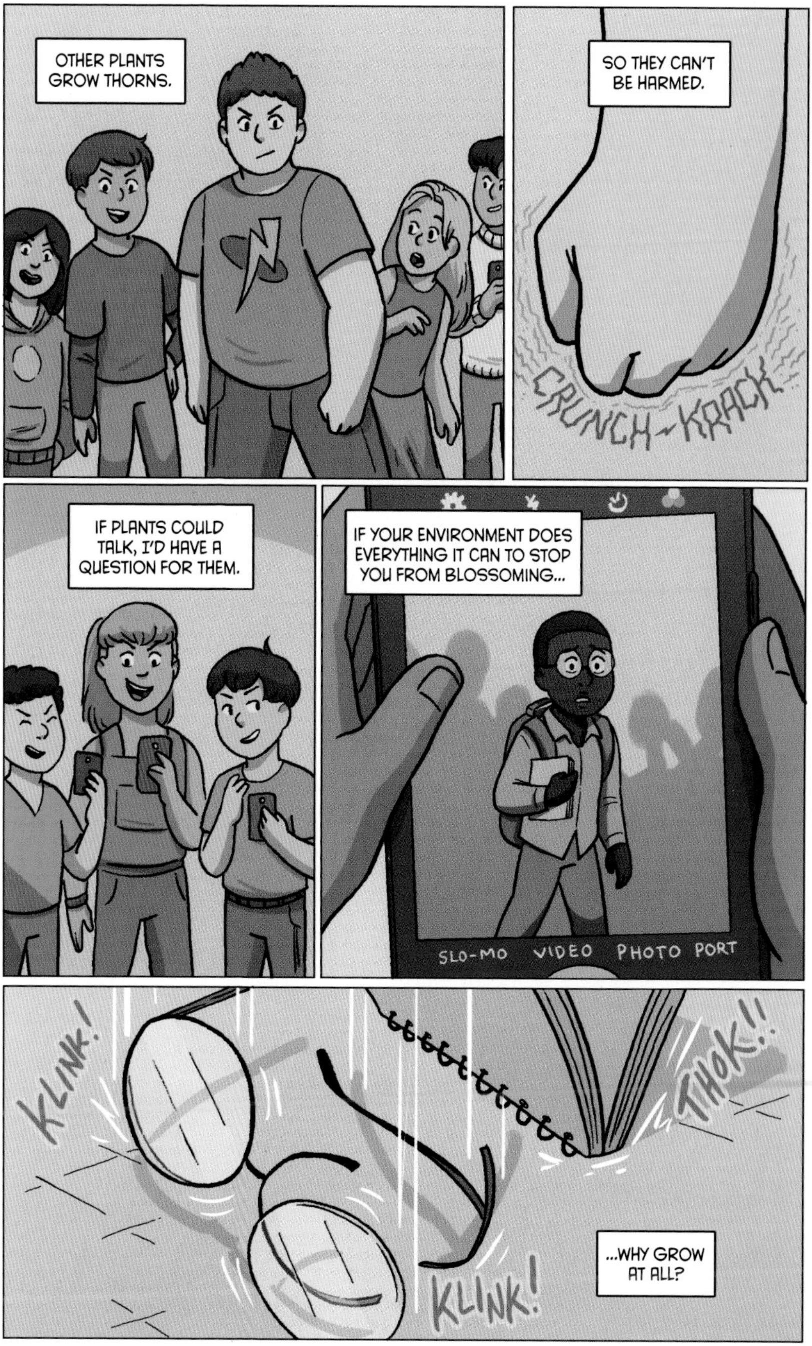
OTHER PLANTS GROW THORNS.
SO THEY CAN'T BE HARMED.
CRUNCH-KRACK
IF PLANTS COULD TALK, I'D HAVE A QUESTION FOR THEM.
IF YOUR ENVIRONMENT DOES EVERYTHING IT CAN TO STOP YOU FROM BLOSSOMING...
SLO-MO VIDEO PHOTO PORT
KLINK!
THOK!!
KLINK!
...WHY GROW AT ALL?

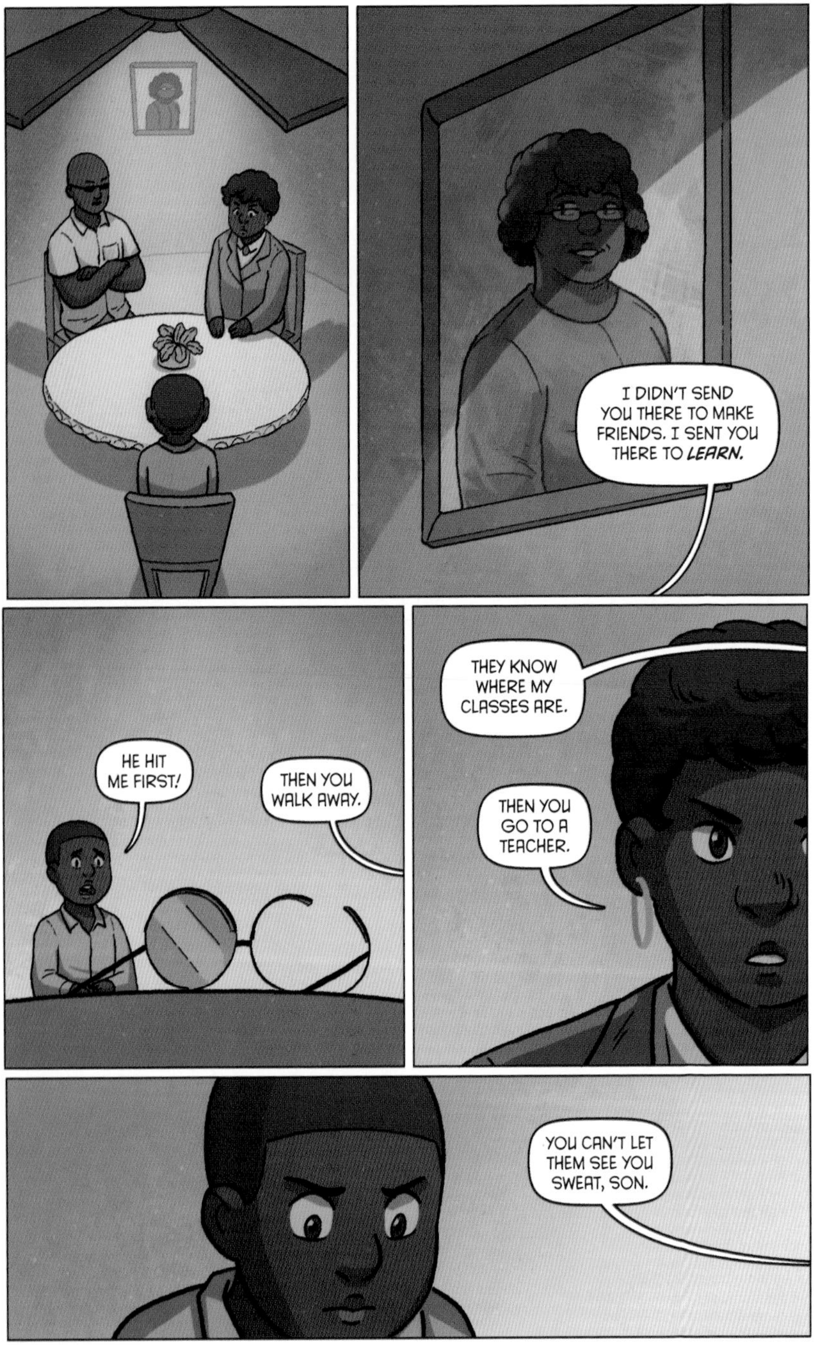
I DIDN'T SEND YOU THERE TO MAKE FRIENDS. I SENT YOU THERE TO *LEARN.*
HE HIT ME FIRST!
THEN YOU WALK AWAY.
THEY KNOW WHERE MY CLASSES ARE.
THEN YOU GO TO A TEACHER.
YOU CAN'T LET THEM SEE YOU SWEAT, SON.

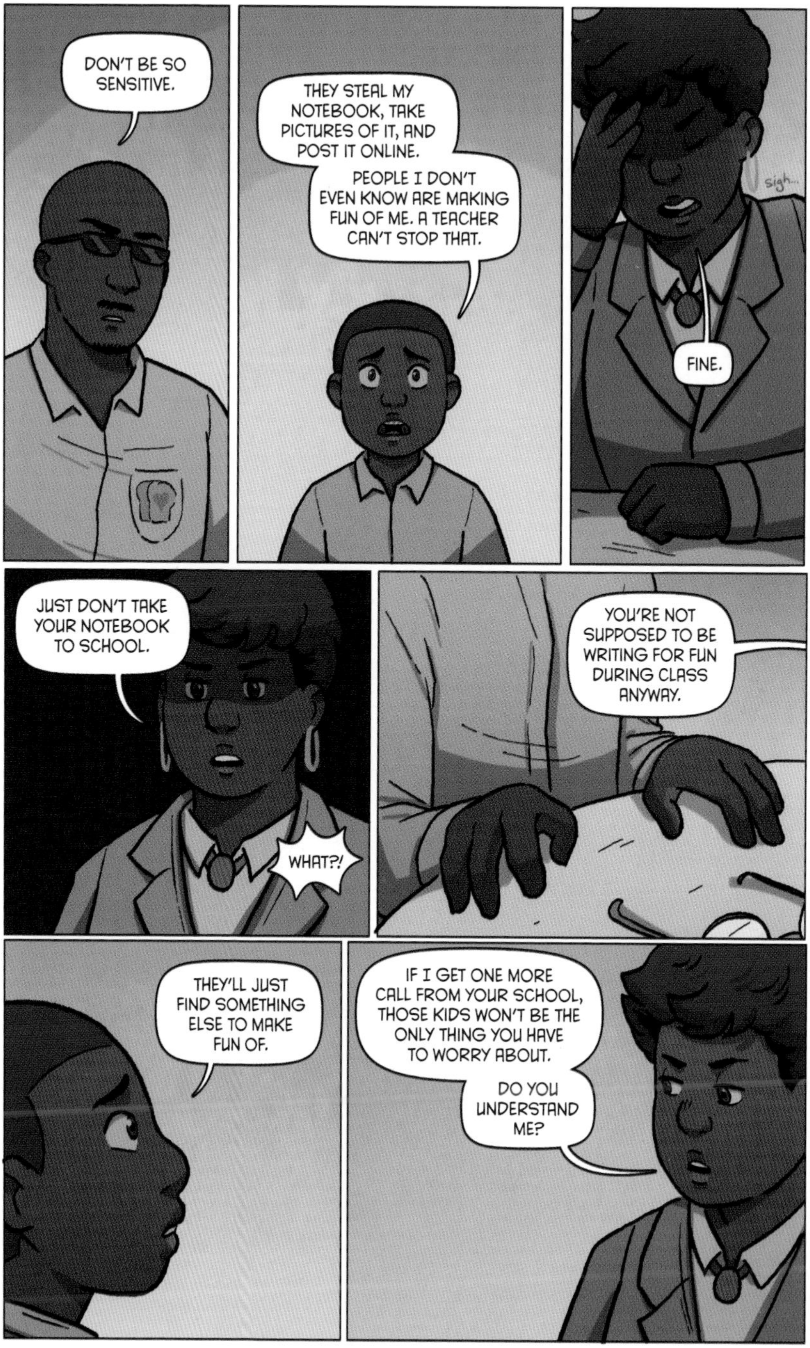
DON'T BE SO SENSITIVE.
THEY STEAL MY NOTEBOOK, TAKE PICTURES OF IT, AND POST IT ONLINE.
PEOPLE I DON'T EVEN KNOW ARE MAKING FUN OF ME. A TEACHER CAN'T STOP THAT.
sigh...
FINE.
JUST DON'T TAKE YOUR NOTEBOOK TO SCHOOL.
WHAT?!
YOU'RE NOT SUPPOSED TO BE WRITING FOR FUN DURING CLASS ANYWAY.
THEY'LL JUST FIND SOMETHING ELSE TO MAKE FUN OF.
IF I GET ONE MORE CALL FROM YOUR SCHOOL, THOSE KIDS WON'T BE THE ONLY THING YOU HAVE TO WORRY ABOUT.
DO YOU UNDERSTAND ME?

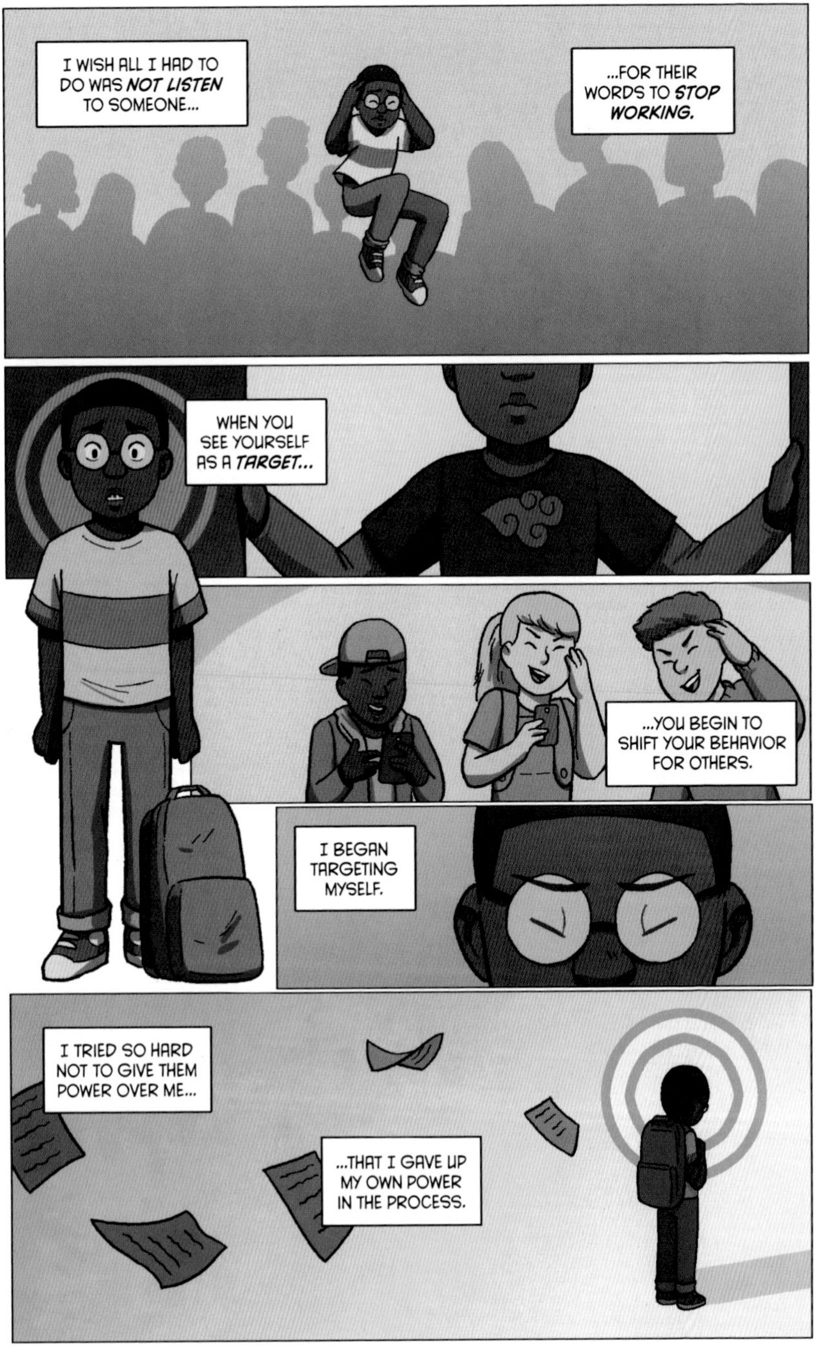
I WISH ALL I HAD TO DO WAS *NOT LISTEN* TO SOMEONE...
...FOR THEIR WORDS TO *STOP WORKING.*
WHEN YOU SEE YOURSELF AS A *TARGET...*
...YOU BEGIN TO SHIFT YOUR BEHAVIOR FOR OTHERS.
I BEGAN TARGETING MYSELF.
I TRIED SO HARD NOT TO GIVE THEM POWER OVER ME...
...THAT I GAVE UP MY OWN POWER IN THE PROCESS.

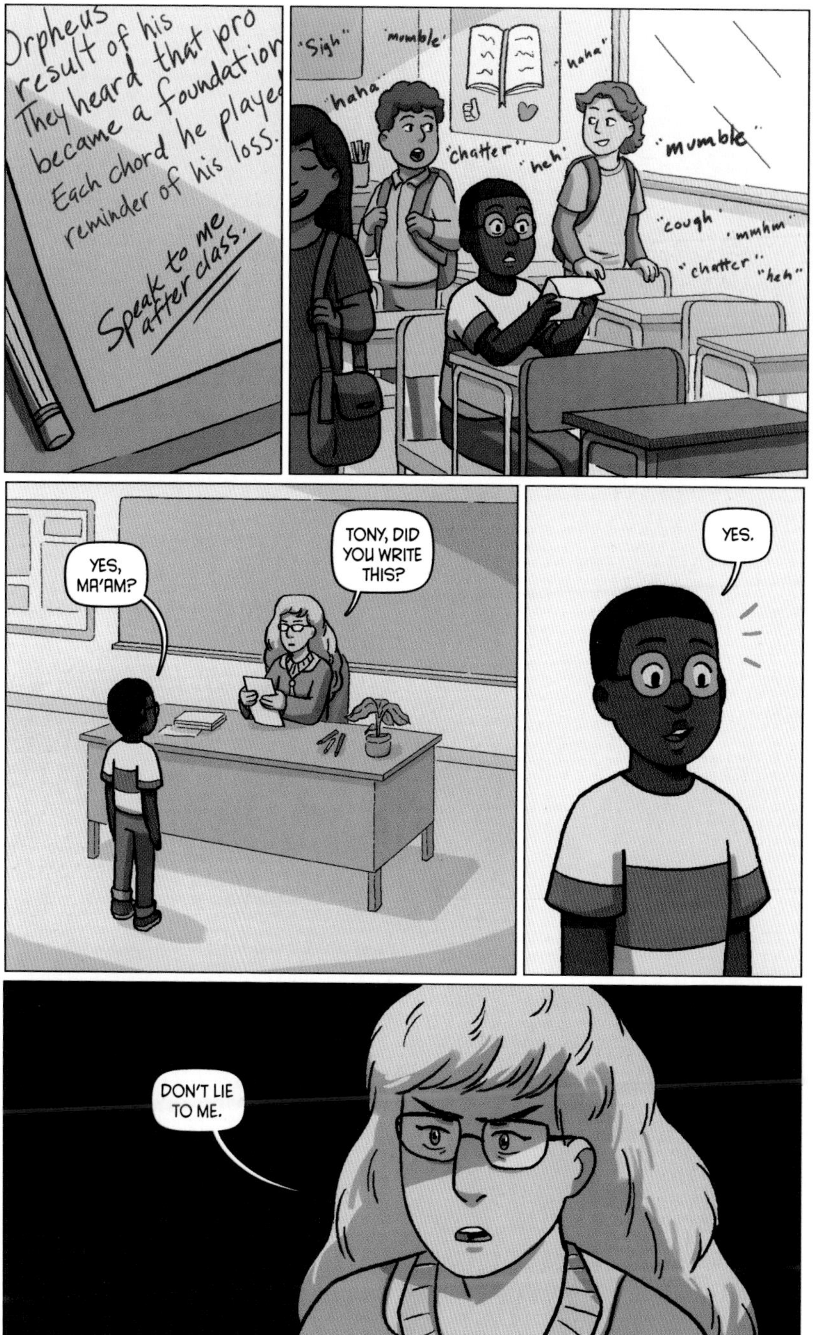

Orpheus
result of his
They heard that pro
became a foundation
Each chord he played
reminder of his loss.
Speak to me after class.
"sigh"
"mumble"
"haha"
"haha"
"chatter"
"heh"
"mumble"
"cough"
"mmhm"
"chatter"
"heh"
YES, MA'AM?
TONY, DID YOU WRITE THIS?
YES.
DON'T LIE TO ME.

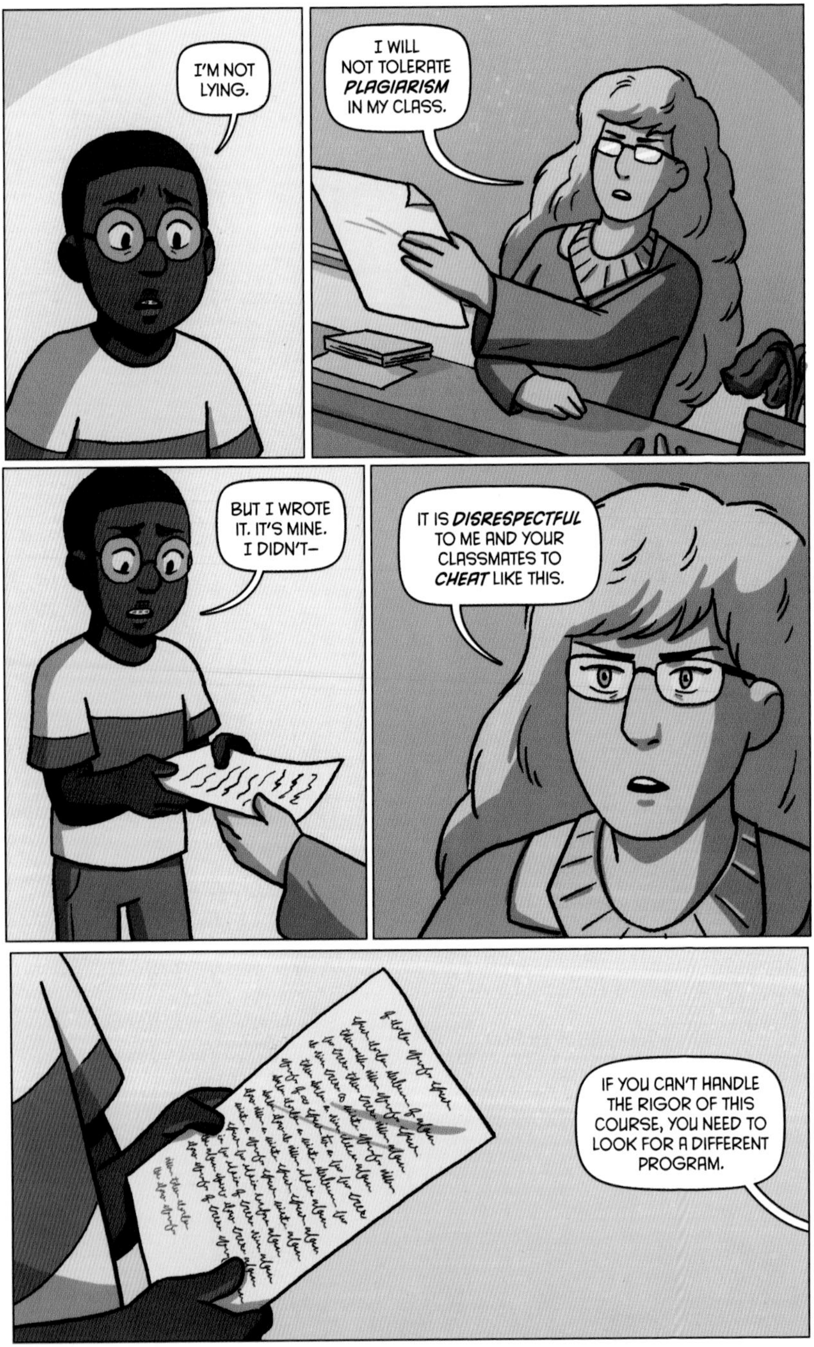
I'M NOT LYING.
I WILL NOT TOLERATE PLAGIARISM IN MY CLASS.
BUT I WROTE IT. IT'S MINE. I DIDN'T—
IT IS DISRESPECTFUL TO ME AND YOUR CLASSMATES TO CHEAT LIKE THIS.
IF YOU CAN'T HANDLE THE RIGOR OF THIS COURSE, YOU NEED TO LOOK FOR A DIFFERENT PROGRAM.

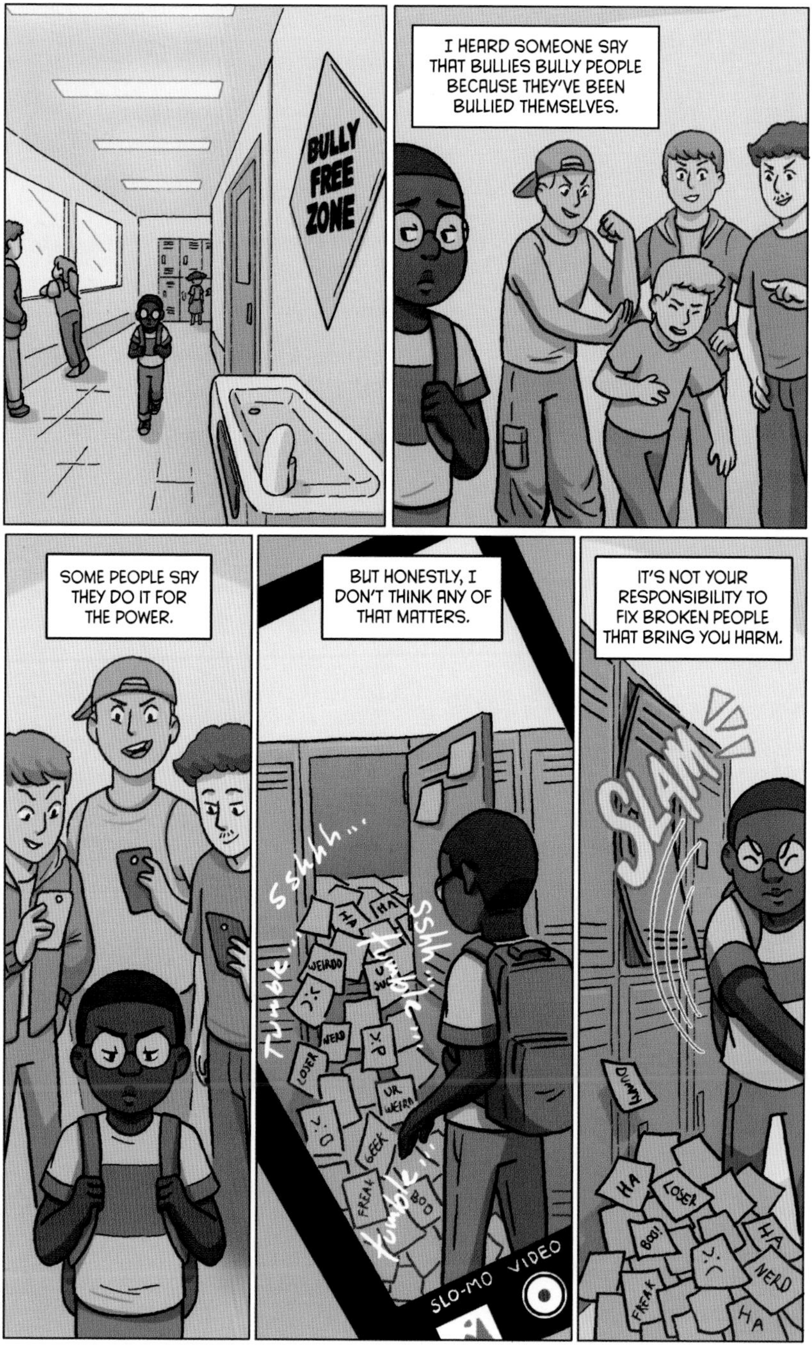
BULLY FREE ZONE
I HEARD SOMEONE SAY THAT BULLIES BULLY PEOPLE BECAUSE THEY'VE BEEN BULLIED THEMSELVES.
SOME PEOPLE SAY THEY DO IT FOR THE POWER.
BUT HONESTLY, I DON'T THINK ANY OF THAT MATTERS.
sshhh...
sshh...
tumble...
tumble...
tumble...
WEIRDO
HA
NERD
LOSER
UR WEIRD
GEEK
FREAK
BOO
SLO-MO VIDEO
IT'S NOT YOUR RESPONSIBILITY TO FIX BROKEN PEOPLE THAT BRING YOU HARM.
SLAM
DUMMY
HA
LOSER
BOO!
HA
NERD
FREAK
HA

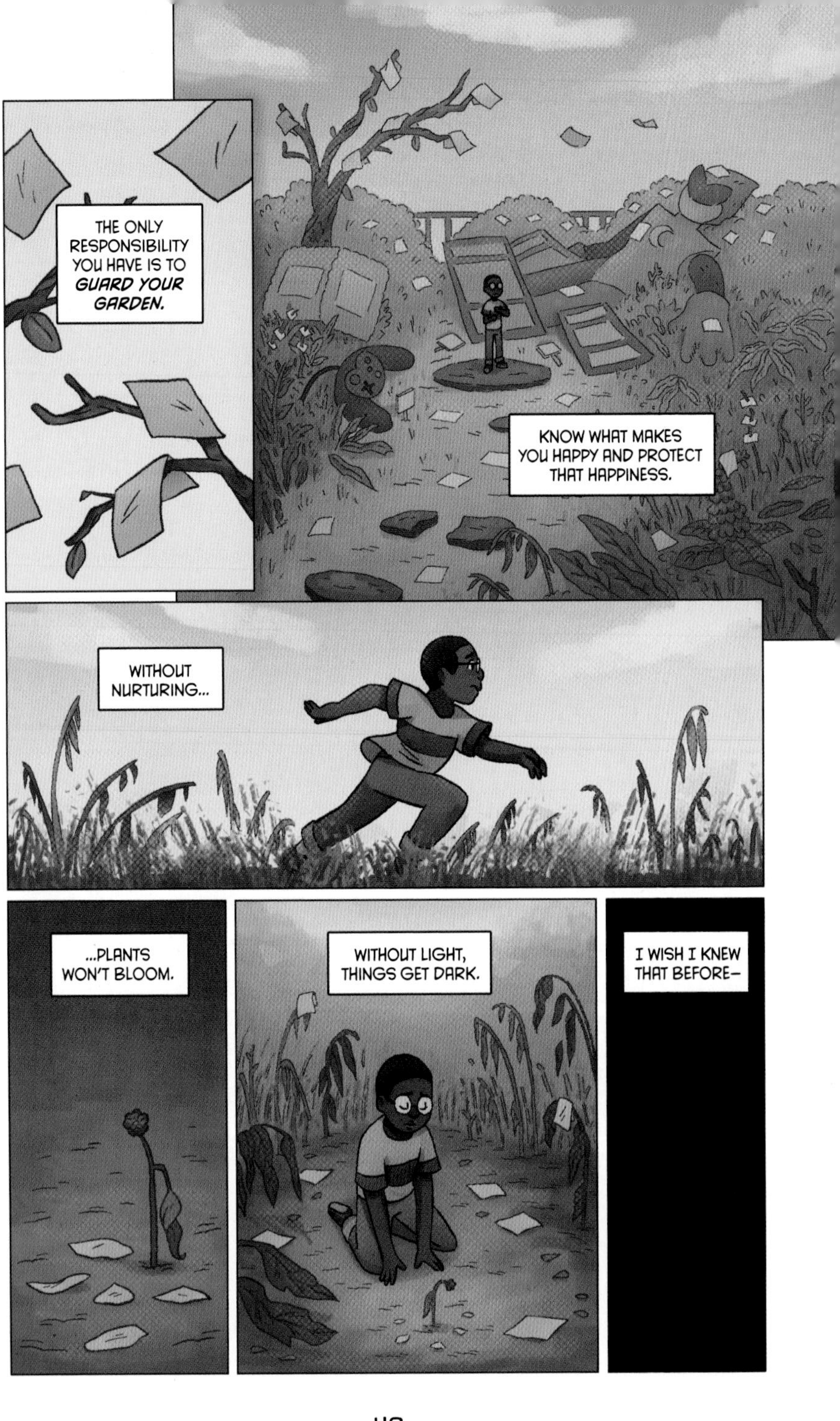
THE ONLY RESPONSIBILITY YOU HAVE IS TO *GUARD YOUR GARDEN.*
KNOW WHAT MAKES YOU HAPPY AND PROTECT THAT HAPPINESS.
WITHOUT NURTURING...
...PLANTS WON'T BLOOM.
WITHOUT LIGHT, THINGS GET DARK.
I WISH I KNEW THAT BEFORE–

CHAPTER 3

NEW KID
PRO TIP #72

Things can get
really dark sometimes.
but there's always

something on the
other side.

ALWAYS.

I PROMISE.

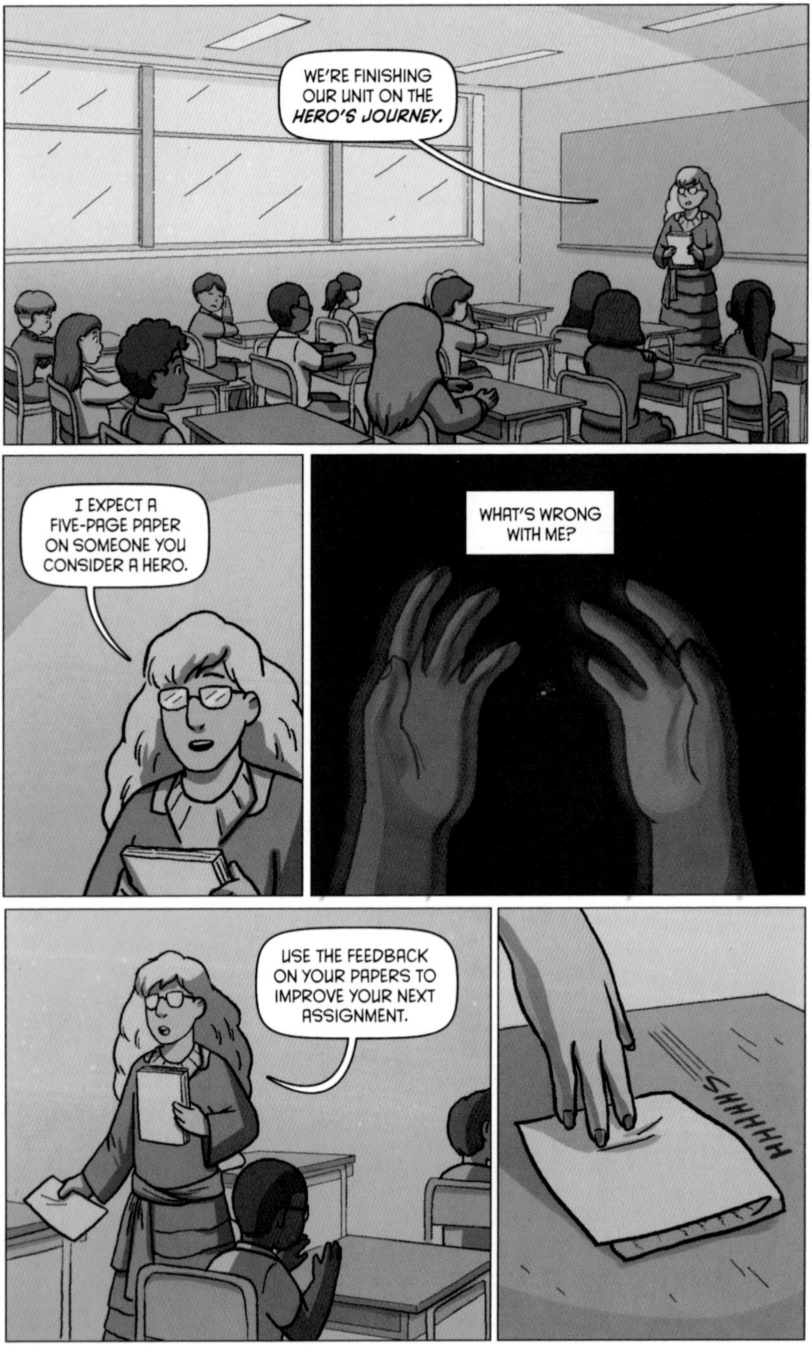
WE'RE FINISHING OUR UNIT ON THE *HERO'S JOURNEY.*
I EXPECT A FIVE-PAGE PAPER ON SOMEONE YOU CONSIDER A HERO.
WHAT'S WRONG WITH ME?
USE THE FEEDBACK ON YOUR PAPERS TO IMPROVE YOUR NEXT ASSIGNMENT.
SHHHHHH

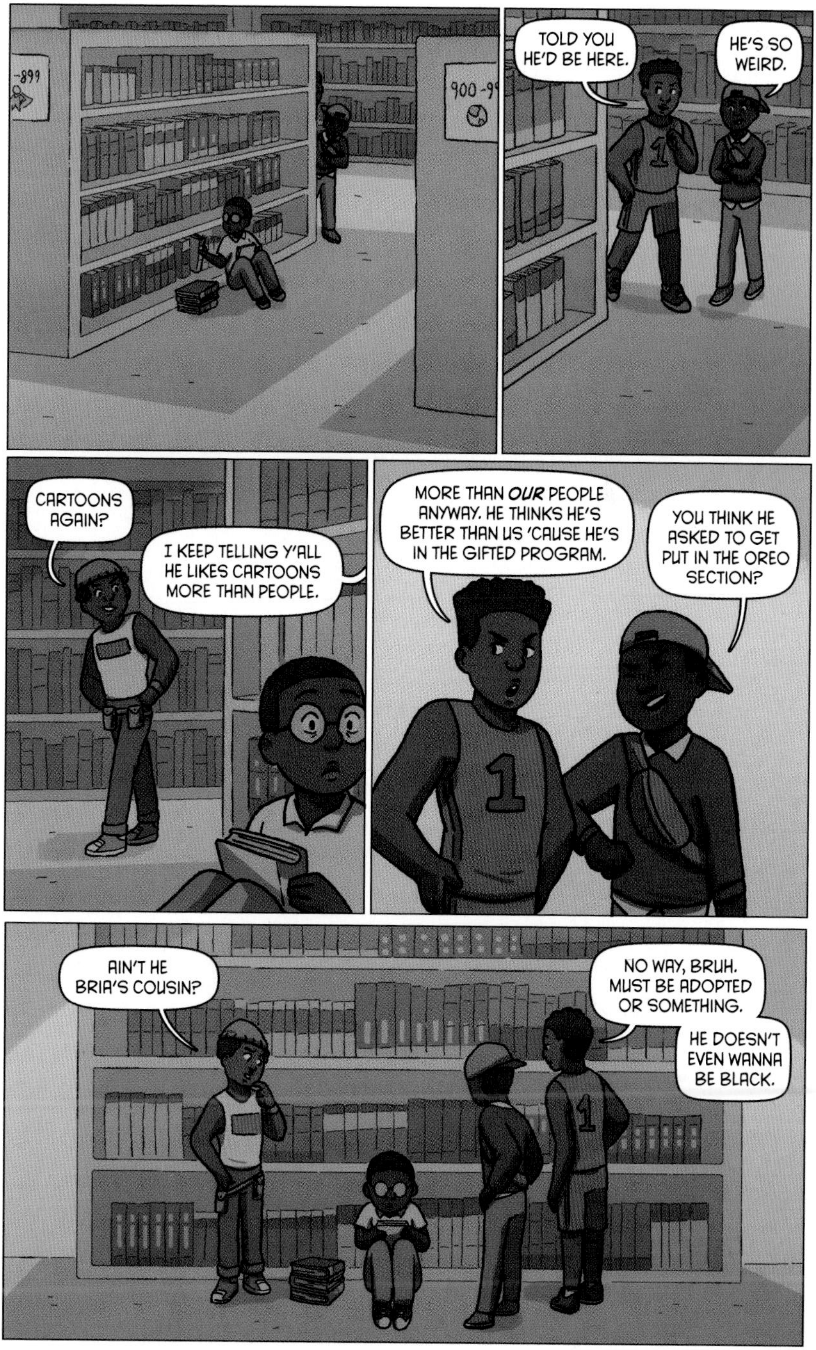
-899
900-9
TOLD YOU HE'D BE HERE.
HE'S SO WEIRD.
CARTOONS AGAIN?
I KEEP TELLING Y'ALL HE LIKES CARTOONS MORE THAN PEOPLE.
MORE THAN *OUR* PEOPLE ANYWAY. HE THINKS HE'S BETTER THAN US 'CAUSE HE'S IN THE GIFTED PROGRAM.
YOU THINK HE ASKED TO GET PUT IN THE OREO SECTION?
AIN'T HE BRIA'S COUSIN?
NO WAY, BRUH. MUST BE ADOPTED OR SOMETHING.
HE DOESN'T EVEN WANNA BE BLACK.

LET'S LEAVE HIM ALONE.

I DON'T WANNA BE THE ONE HE LOOKS FOR WHEN HE SNAPS.

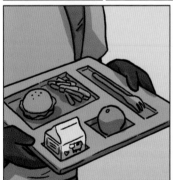

IMAGINE IF NO MATTER WHAT YOU DID...

...THINGS WENT WRONG.

SHUFFLE

CAN ANYONE TELL ME WHAT PLANT CELLS HAVE THAT ANIMAL CELLS DON'T?

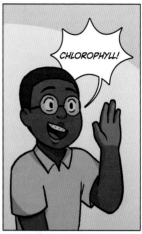

CHLOROPHYLL!

CORRECT!

CHLOROPHYLL IS WHAT ALLOWS PLANTS TO HARNESS ENERGY FROM LIGHT.

LIGHT IS ESSENTIAL FOR—

PLCK!

WHO WOULD YOU THINK THE PROBLEM WAS?

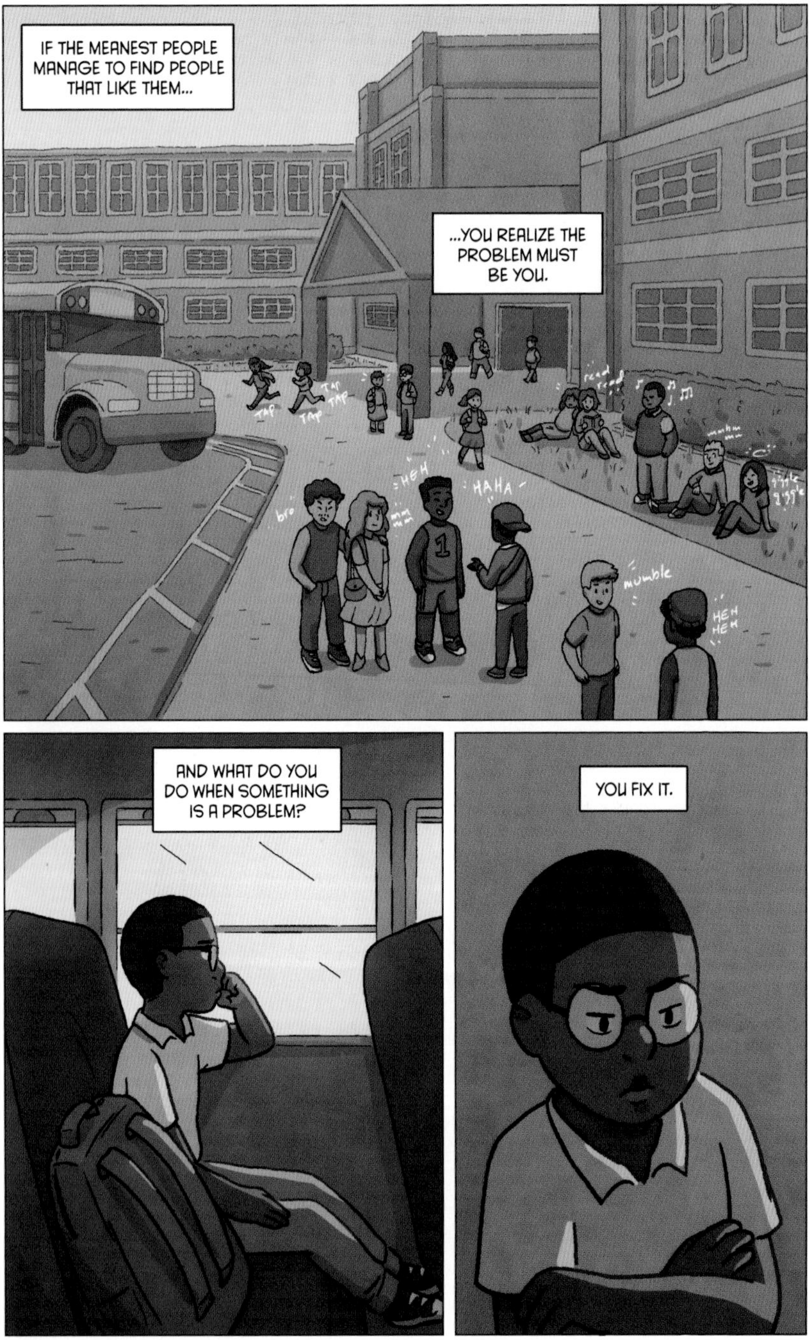
IF THE MEANEST PEOPLE MANAGE TO FIND PEOPLE THAT LIKE THEM...
...YOU REALIZE THE PROBLEM MUST BE YOU.
TAP TAP
TAP TAP
bro
HEH
HAHA
mumble
HEH HEH
AND WHAT DO YOU DO WHEN SOMETHING IS A PROBLEM?
YOU FIX IT.

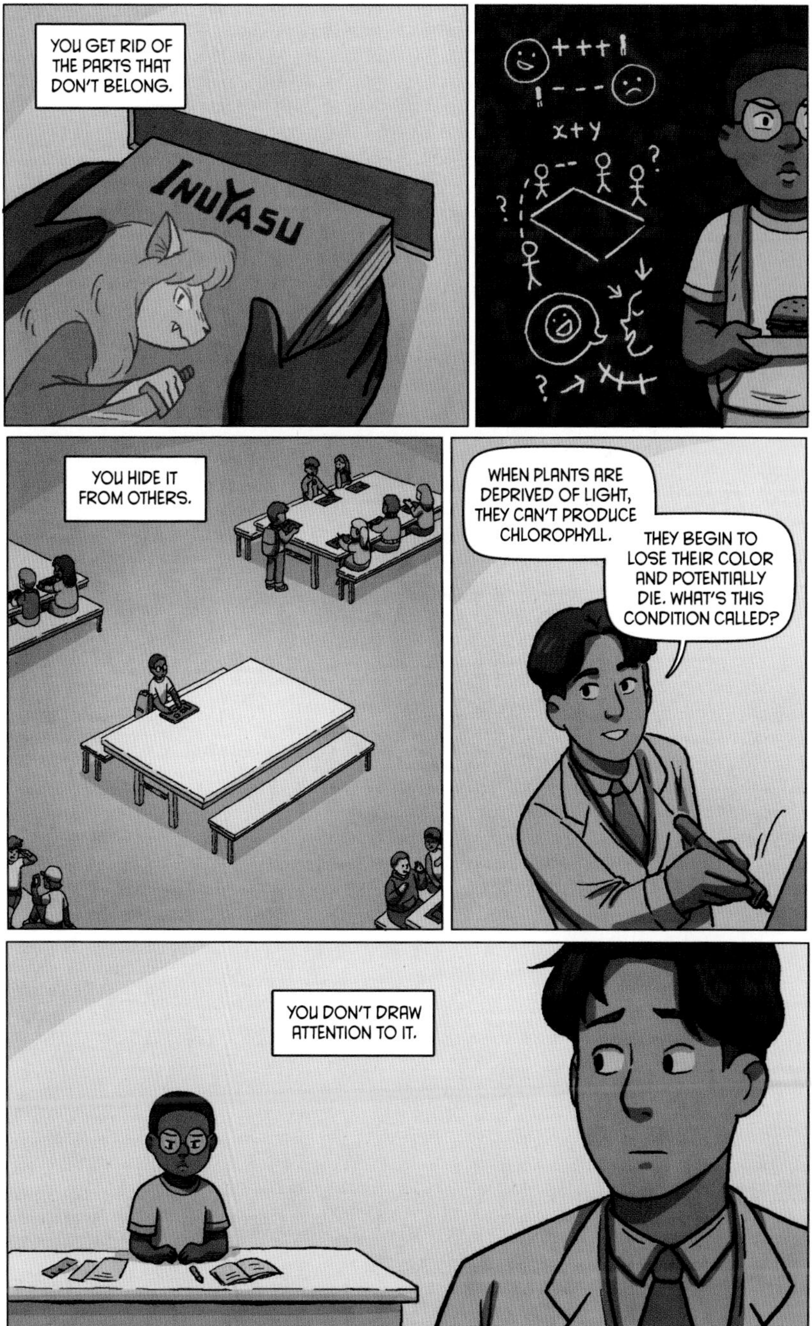
YOU GET RID OF THE PARTS THAT DON'T BELONG.
INUYASU
x+y
YOU HIDE IT FROM OTHERS.
WHEN PLANTS ARE DEPRIVED OF LIGHT, THEY CAN'T PRODUCE CHLOROPHYLL.
THEY BEGIN TO LOSE THEIR COLOR AND POTENTIALLY DIE. WHAT'S THIS CONDITION CALLED?
YOU DON'T DRAW ATTENTION TO IT.

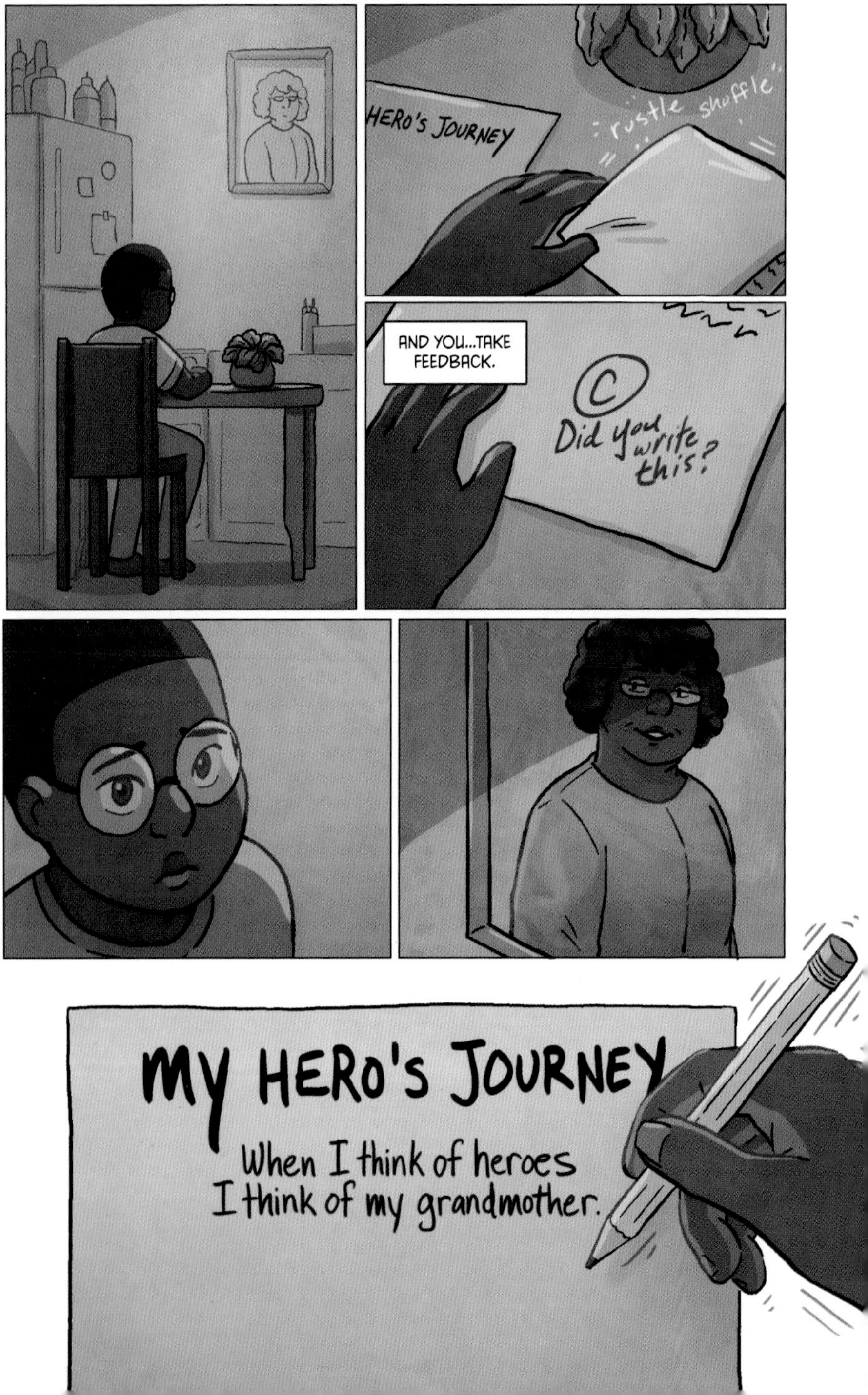
HERO's JOURNEY
rustle shuffle
AND YOU...TAKE FEEDBACK.
C
Did you write this?
MY HERO's JOURNEY
When I think of heroes
I think of my grandmother.

HEROES ARE PEOPLE THAT MAKE THE WORLD AROUND THEM BETTER.

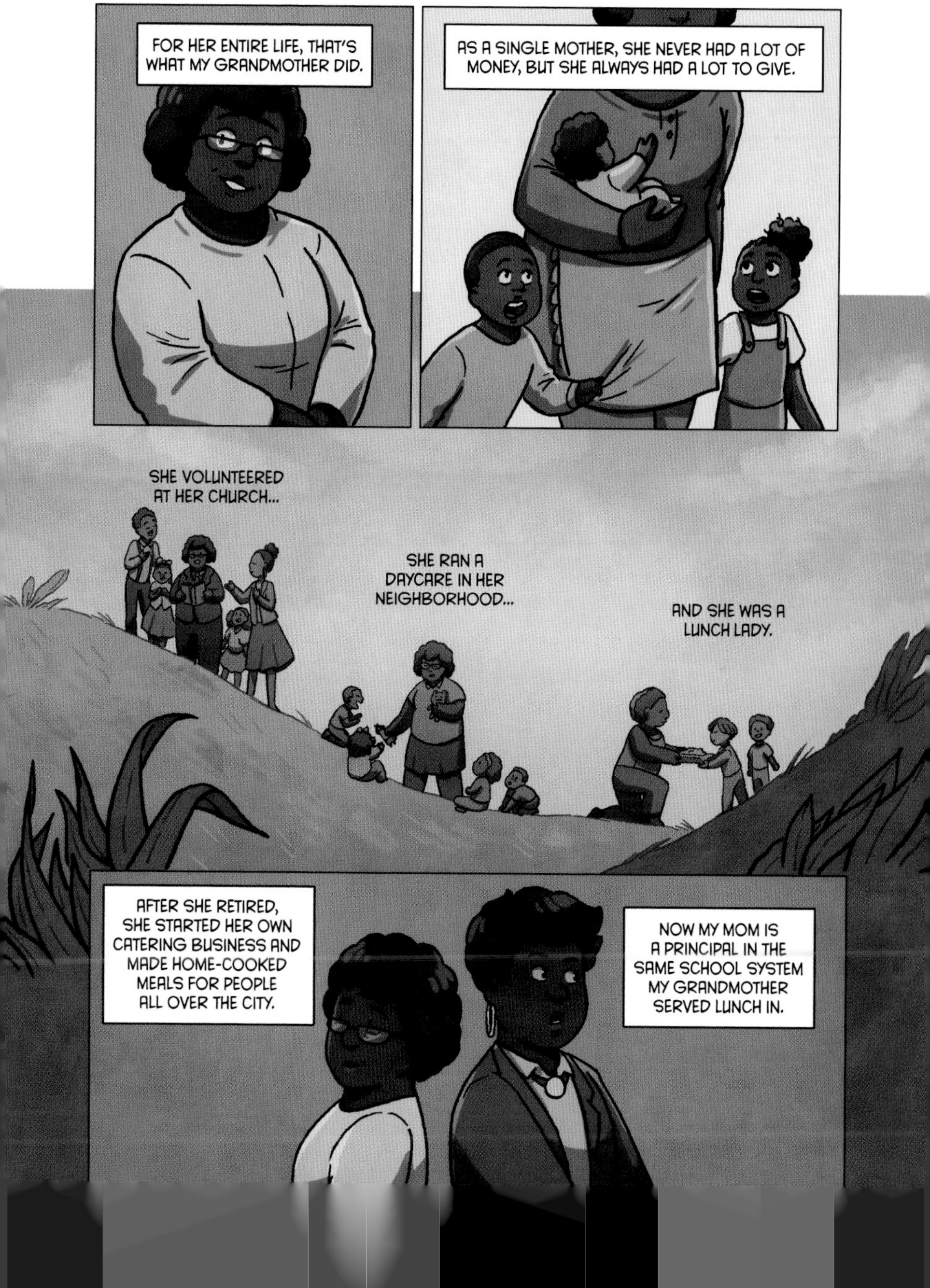

FOR HER ENTIRE LIFE, THAT'S WHAT MY GRANDMOTHER DID.
AS A SINGLE MOTHER, SHE NEVER HAD A LOT OF MONEY, BUT SHE ALWAYS HAD A LOT TO GIVE.
SHE VOLUNTEERED AT HER CHURCH...
SHE RAN A DAYCARE IN HER NEIGHBORHOOD...
AND SHE WAS A LUNCH LADY.
AFTER SHE RETIRED, SHE STARTED HER OWN CATERING BUSINESS AND MADE HOME-COOKED MEALS FOR PEOPLE ALL OVER THE CITY.
NOW MY MOM IS A PRINCIPAL IN THE SAME SCHOOL SYSTEM MY GRANDMOTHER SERVED LUNCH IN.

MY GRANDMA TAUGHT ME THE THING YOU CAN ALWAYS GIVE A PERSON IS YOUR TIME.

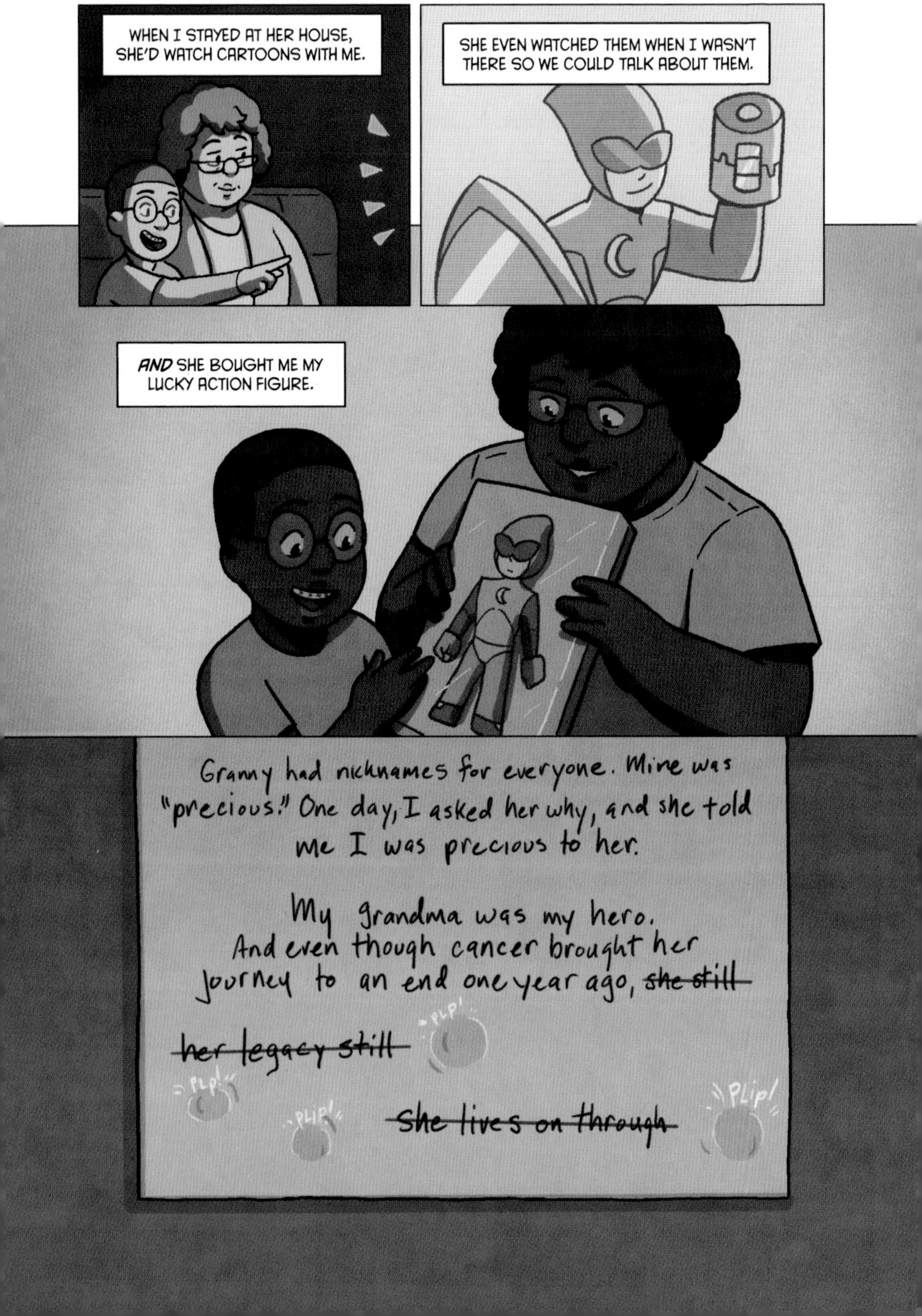

WHEN I STAYED AT HER HOUSE, SHE'D WATCH CARTOONS WITH ME.
SHE EVEN WATCHED THEM WHEN I WASN'T THERE SO WE COULD TALK ABOUT THEM.
AND SHE BOUGHT ME MY LUCKY ACTION FIGURE.
Granny had nicknames for everyone. Mine was "precious." One day, I asked her why, and she told me I was precious to her.
My grandma was my hero. And even though cancer brought her journey to an end one year ago, ~~she still~~
~~her legacy still~~
PLIP!
PLIP!
PLIP!
~~She lives on through~~
PLIP!

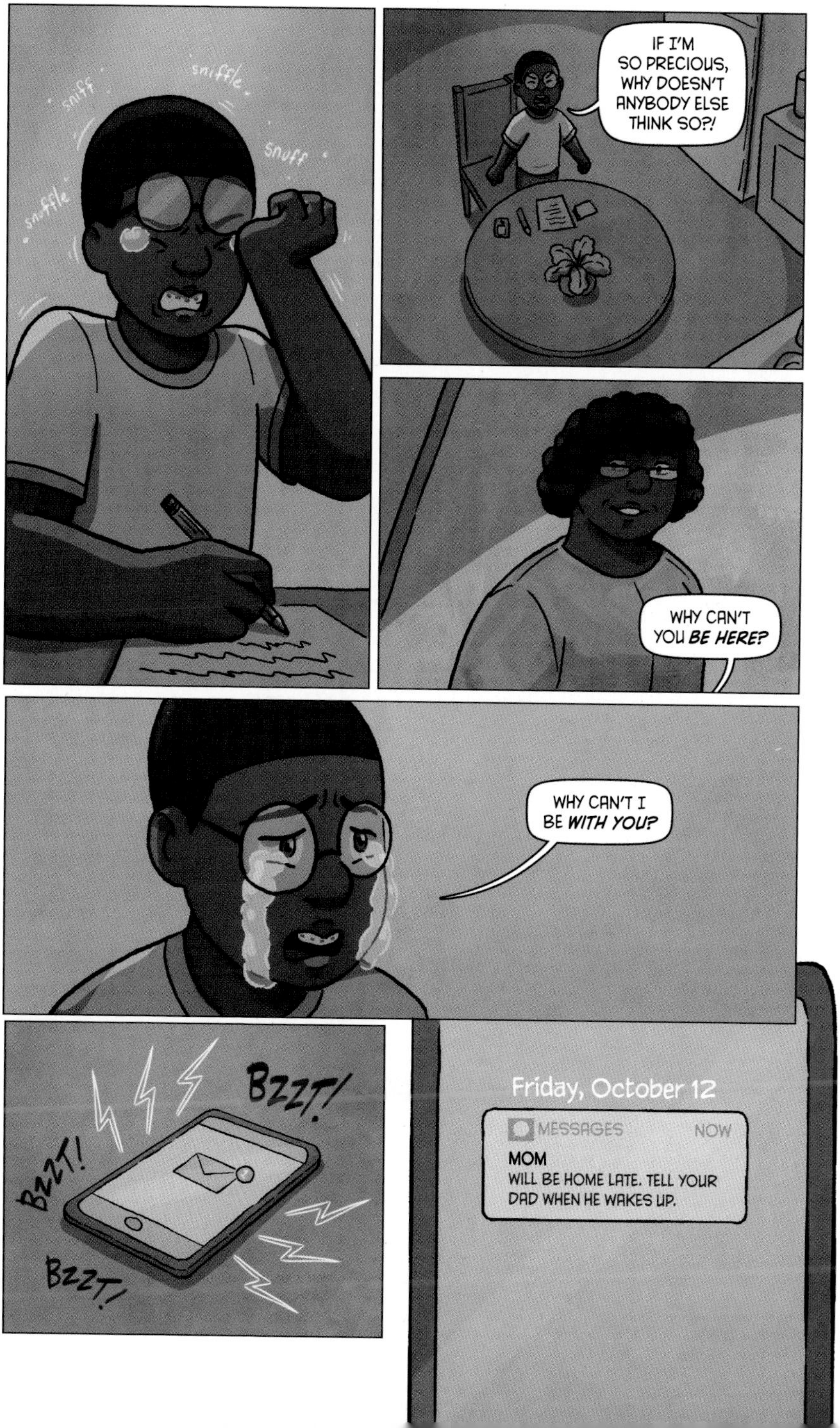
sniff
sniffle
snuff
snuffle
IF I'M SO PRECIOUS, WHY DOESN'T ANYBODY ELSE THINK SO?!
WHY CAN'T YOU *BE HERE?*
WHY CAN'T I BE *WITH YOU?*
BZZT!
BZZT!
BZZT!
Friday, October 12
MESSAGES
NOW
MOM
WILL BE HOME LATE. TELL YOUR DAD WHEN HE WAKES UP.

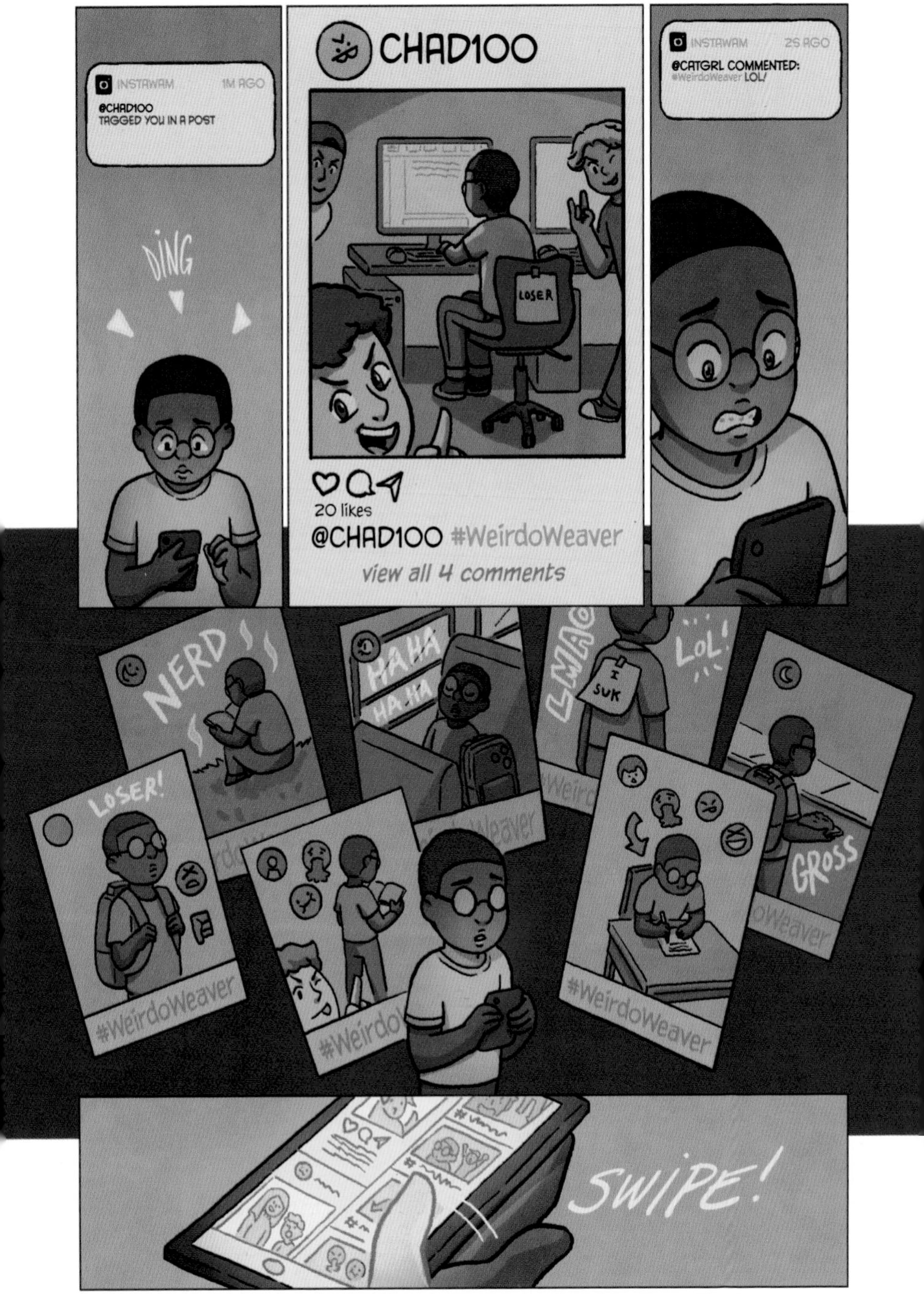
INSTAWAM 1M AGO
@CHAD100
TAGGED YOU IN A POST
DING
CHAD100
LOSER
20 likes
@CHAD100 #WeirdoWeaver
view all 4 comments
INSTAWAM 2S AGO
@CATGRL COMMENTED:
#WeirdoWeaver LOL!
NERD
HAHA
HAHA
LMAO
I SUK
LOL!
LOSER!
#WeirdoWeaver
#WeirdoW
#WeirdoWeaver
GROSS
SWIPE!

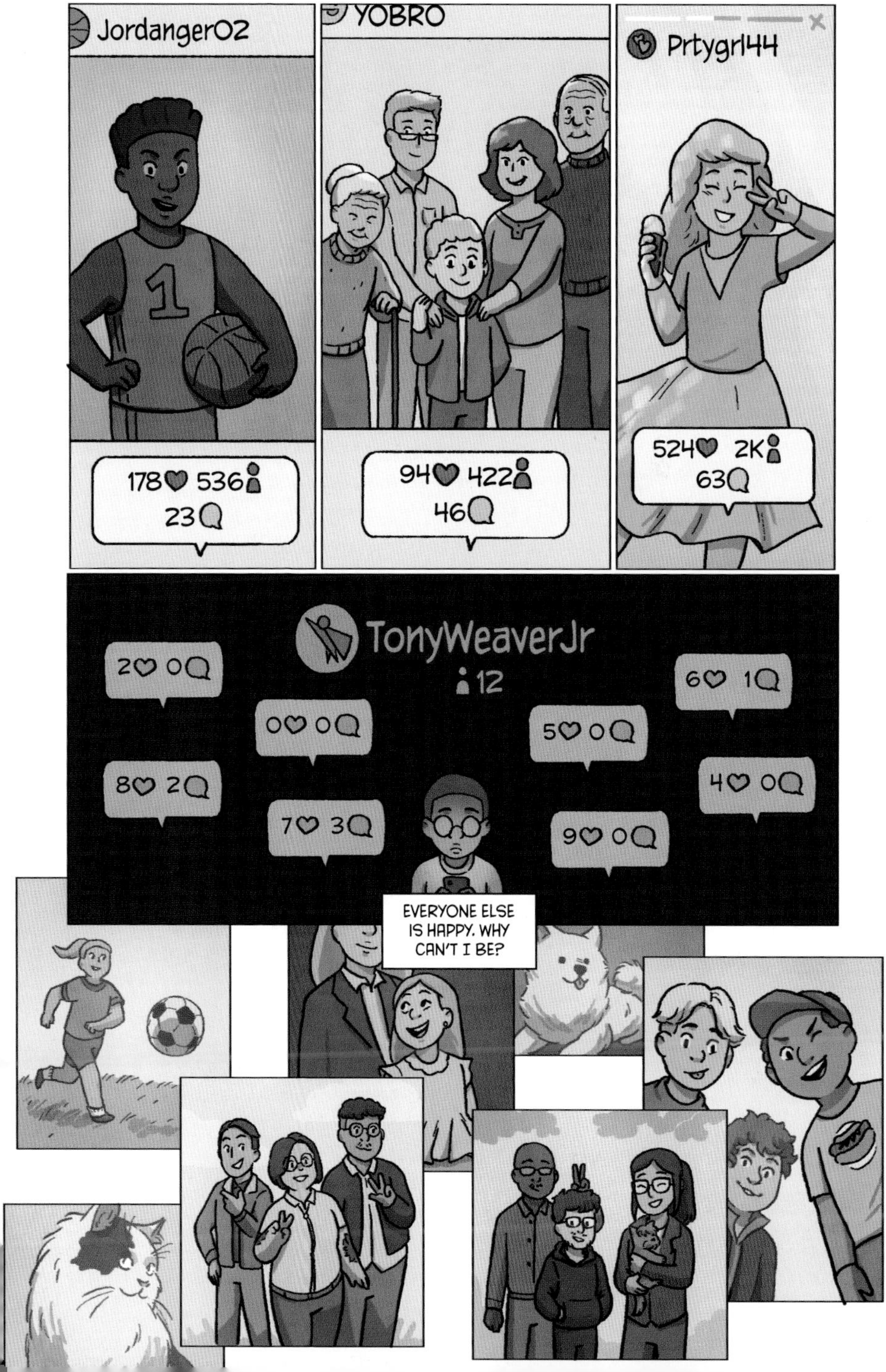

Jordanger02
178 536
23
YOBRO
94 422
46
Prtygrl44
524 2K
63
TonyWeaverJr
12
2 0
0 0
8 2
7 3
5 0
6 1
4 0
9 0
EVERYONE ELSE IS HAPPY. WHY CAN'T I BE?

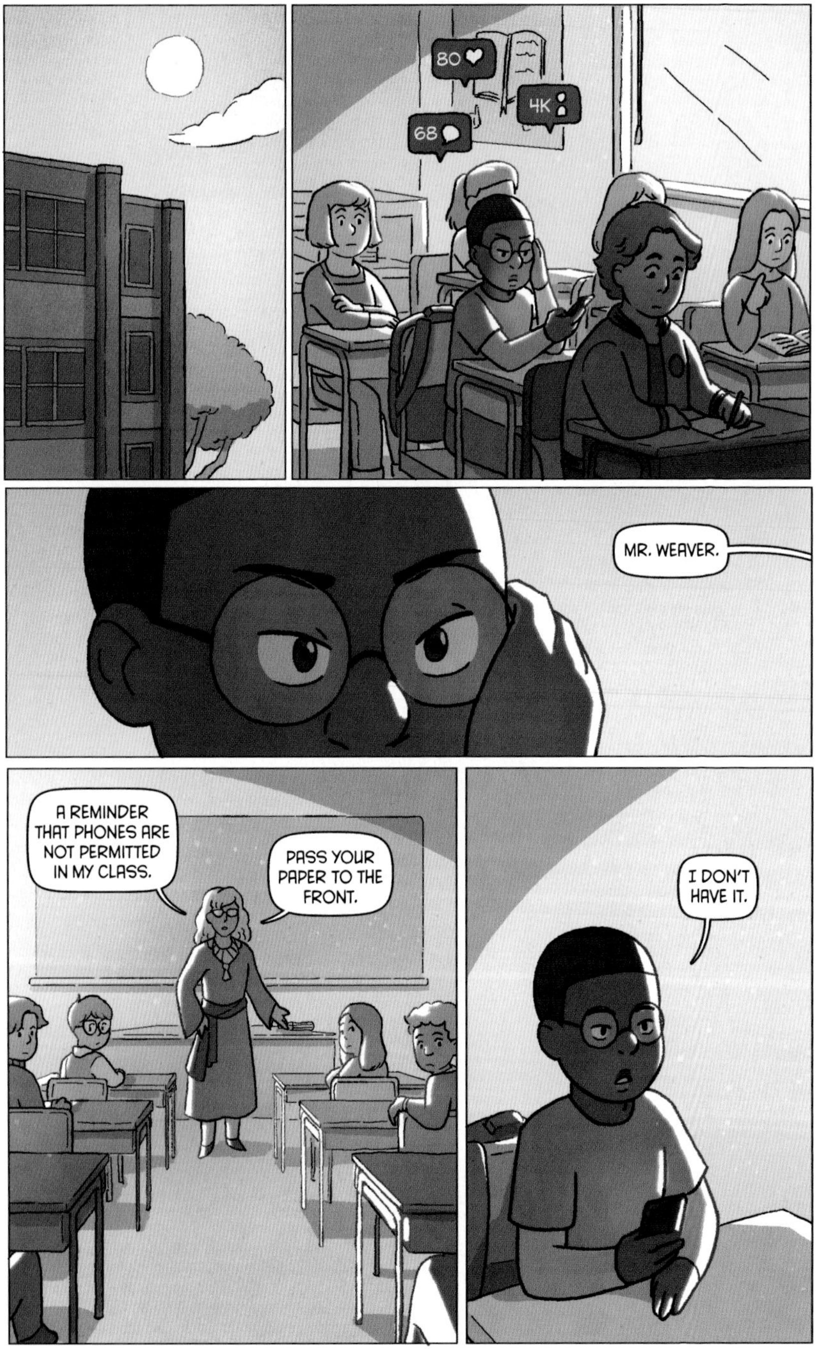
80
4K
68
MR. WEAVER.
A REMINDER THAT PHONES ARE NOT PERMITTED IN MY CLASS.
PASS YOUR PAPER TO THE FRONT.
I DON'T HAVE IT.

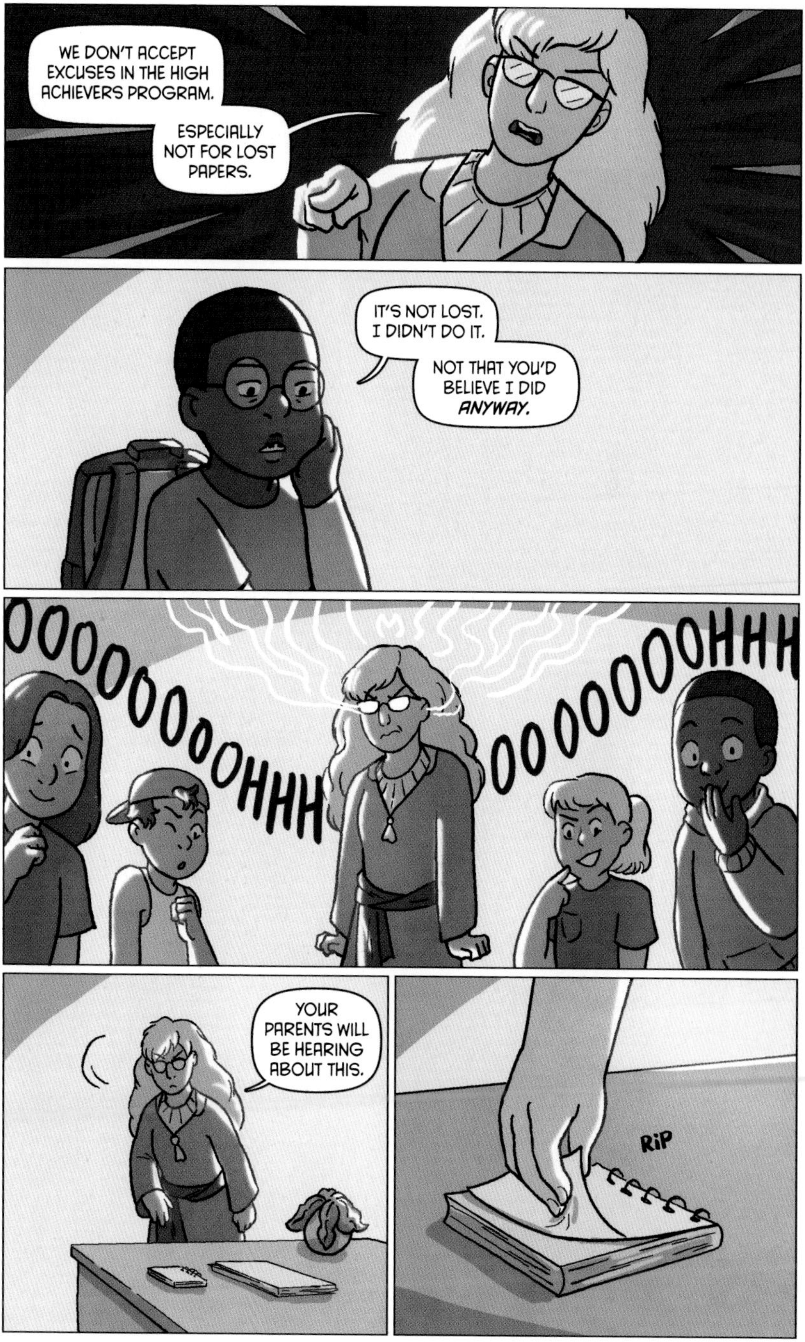
WE DON'T ACCEPT EXCUSES IN THE HIGH ACHIEVERS PROGRAM.
ESPECIALLY NOT FOR LOST PAPERS.
IT'S NOT LOST. I DIDN'T DO IT.
NOT THAT YOU'D BELIEVE I DID *ANYWAY.*
OOOOOOOOOOHHH
OOOOOOOOOOHHH
YOUR PARENTS WILL BE HEARING ABOUT THIS.
RIP

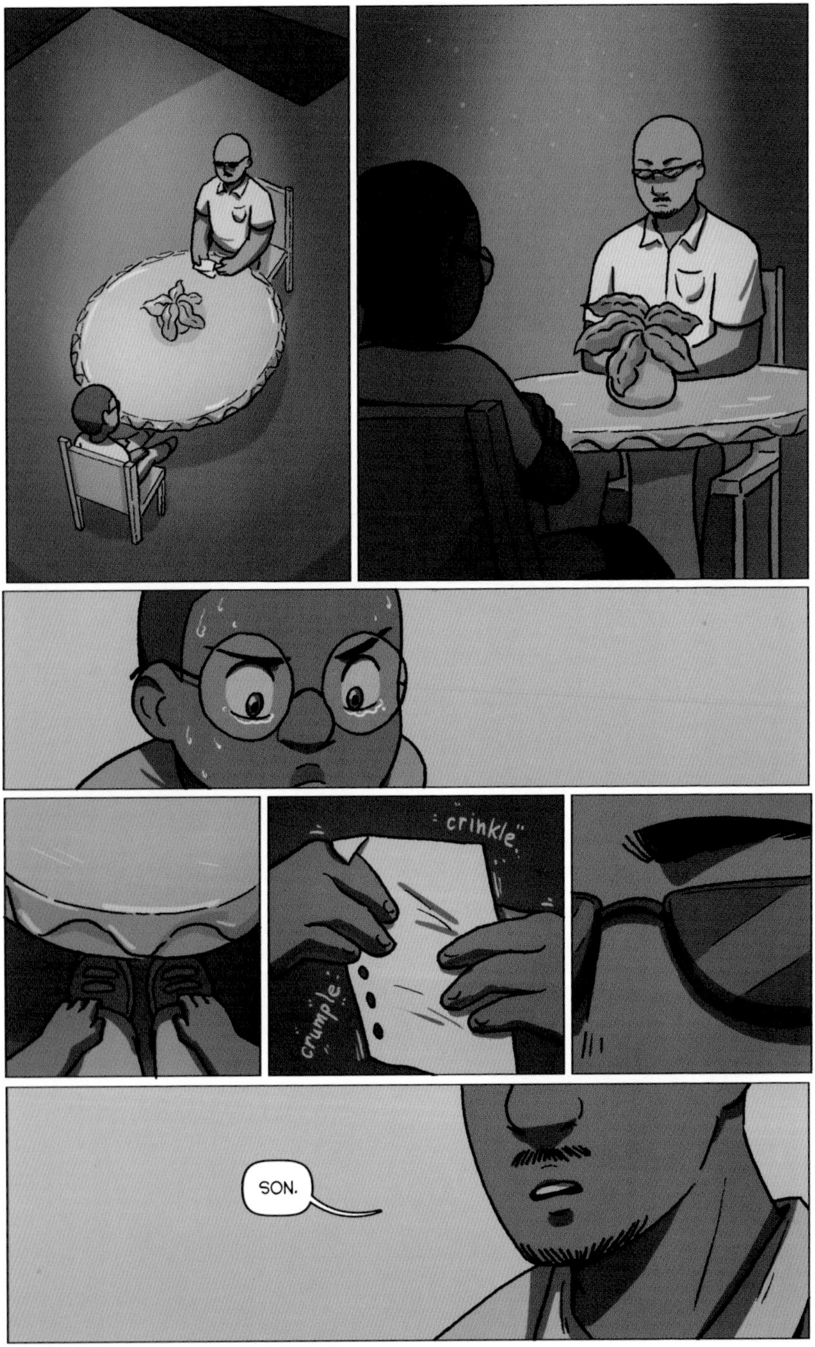
crinkle
crumple
SON.

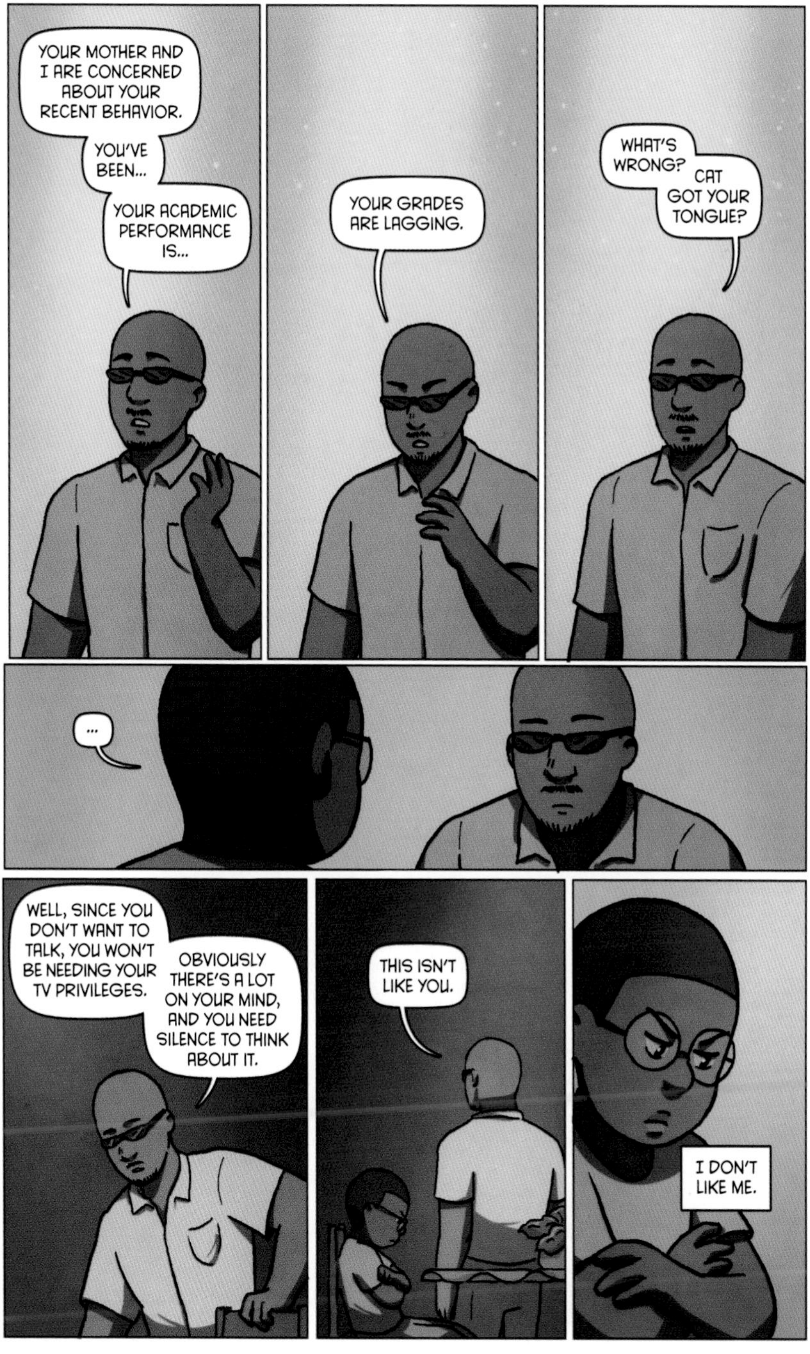
YOUR MOTHER AND I ARE CONCERNED ABOUT YOUR RECENT BEHAVIOR.
YOU'VE BEEN...
YOUR ACADEMIC PERFORMANCE IS...
YOUR GRADES ARE LAGGING.
WHAT'S WRONG?
CAT GOT YOUR TONGUE?
...
WELL, SINCE YOU DON'T WANT TO TALK, YOU WON'T BE NEEDING YOUR TV PRIVILEGES.
OBVIOUSLY THERE'S A LOT ON YOUR MIND, AND YOU NEED SILENCE TO THINK ABOUT IT.
THIS ISN'T LIKE YOU.
I DON'T LIKE ME.

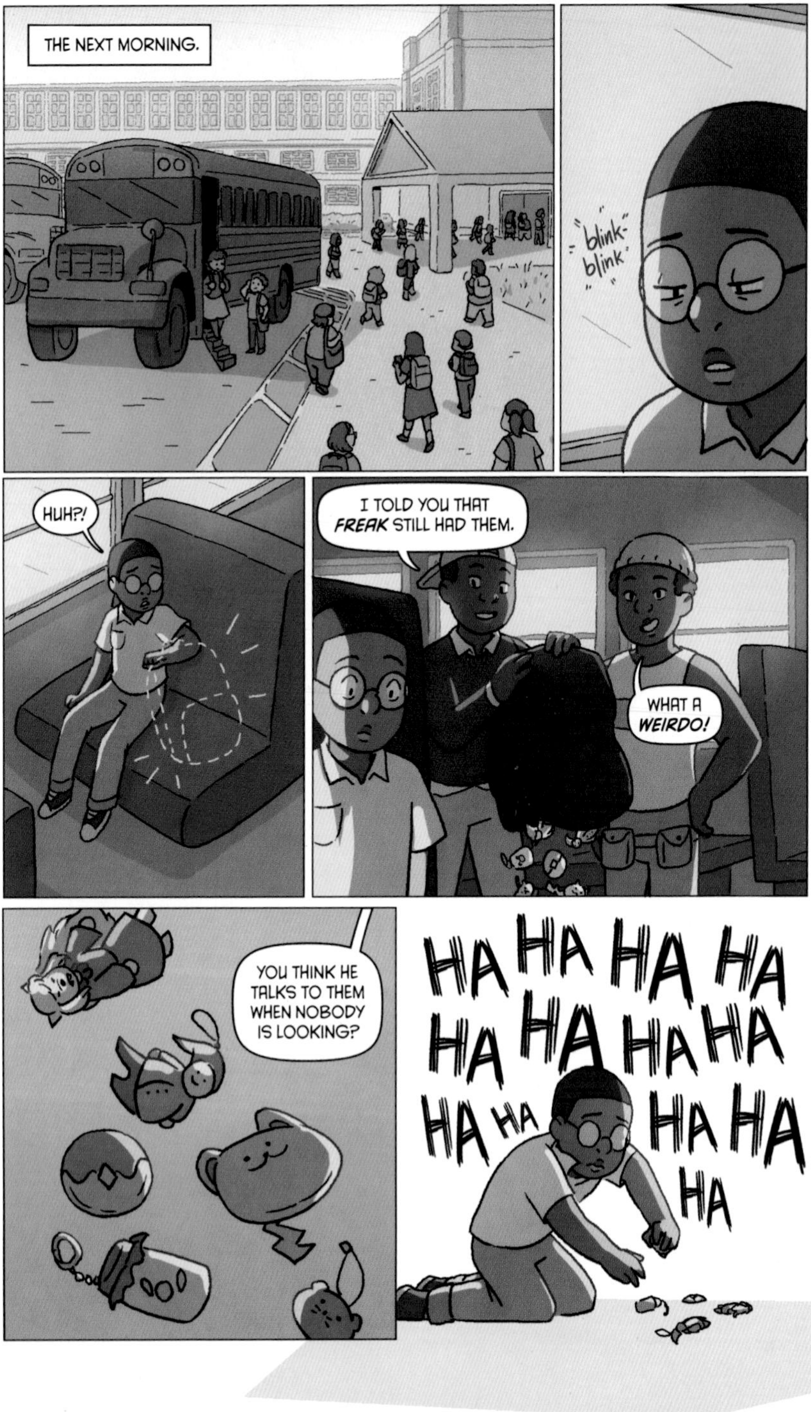
THE NEXT MORNING.
blink-blink
HUH?!
I TOLD YOU THAT FREAK STILL HAD THEM.
WHAT A WEIRDO!
YOU THINK HE TALKS TO THEM WHEN NOBODY IS LOOKING?
HA HA HA HA HA HA HA HA HA HA HA HA HA HA HA

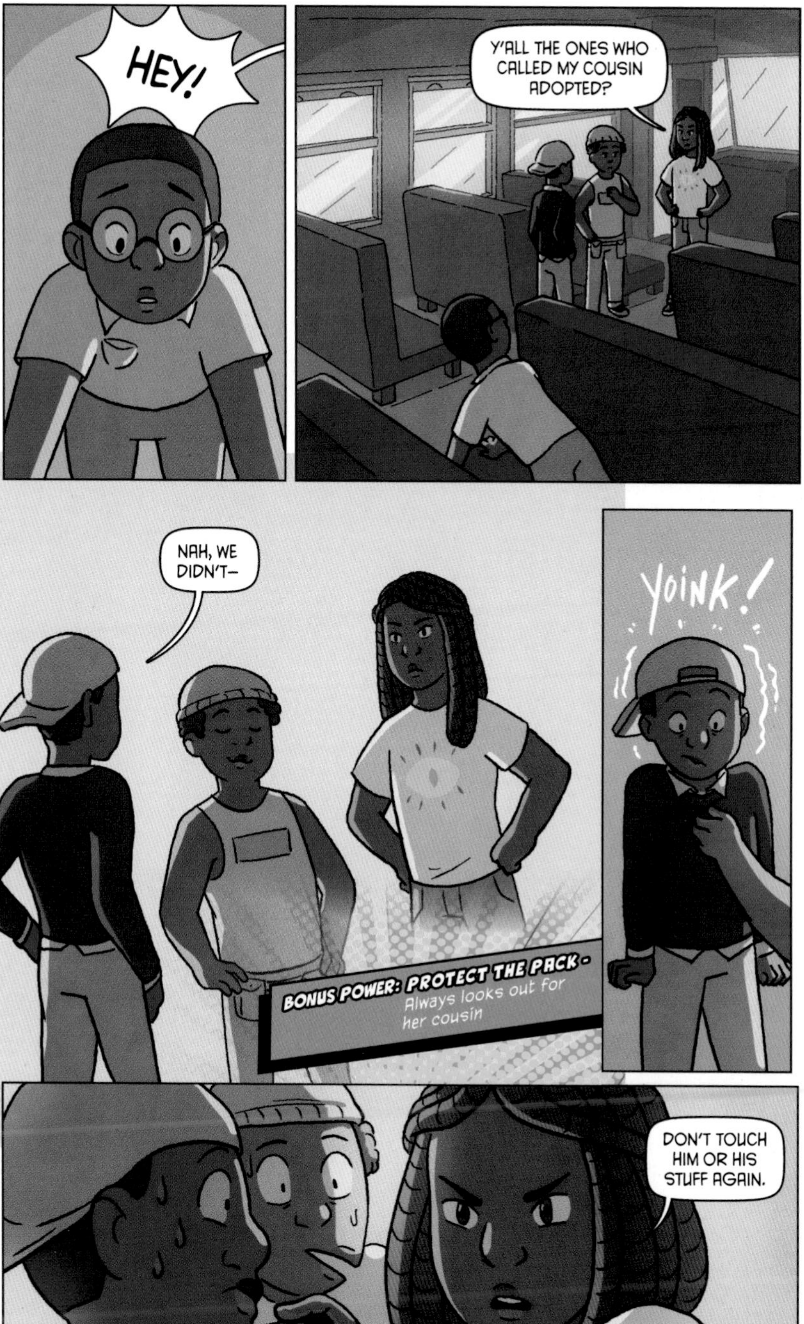
HEY!
Y'ALL THE ONES WHO CALLED MY COUSIN ADOPTED?
NAH, WE DIDN'T—
BONUS POWER: PROTECT THE PACK - Always looks out for her cousin
YOINK!
DON'T TOUCH HIM OR HIS STUFF AGAIN.

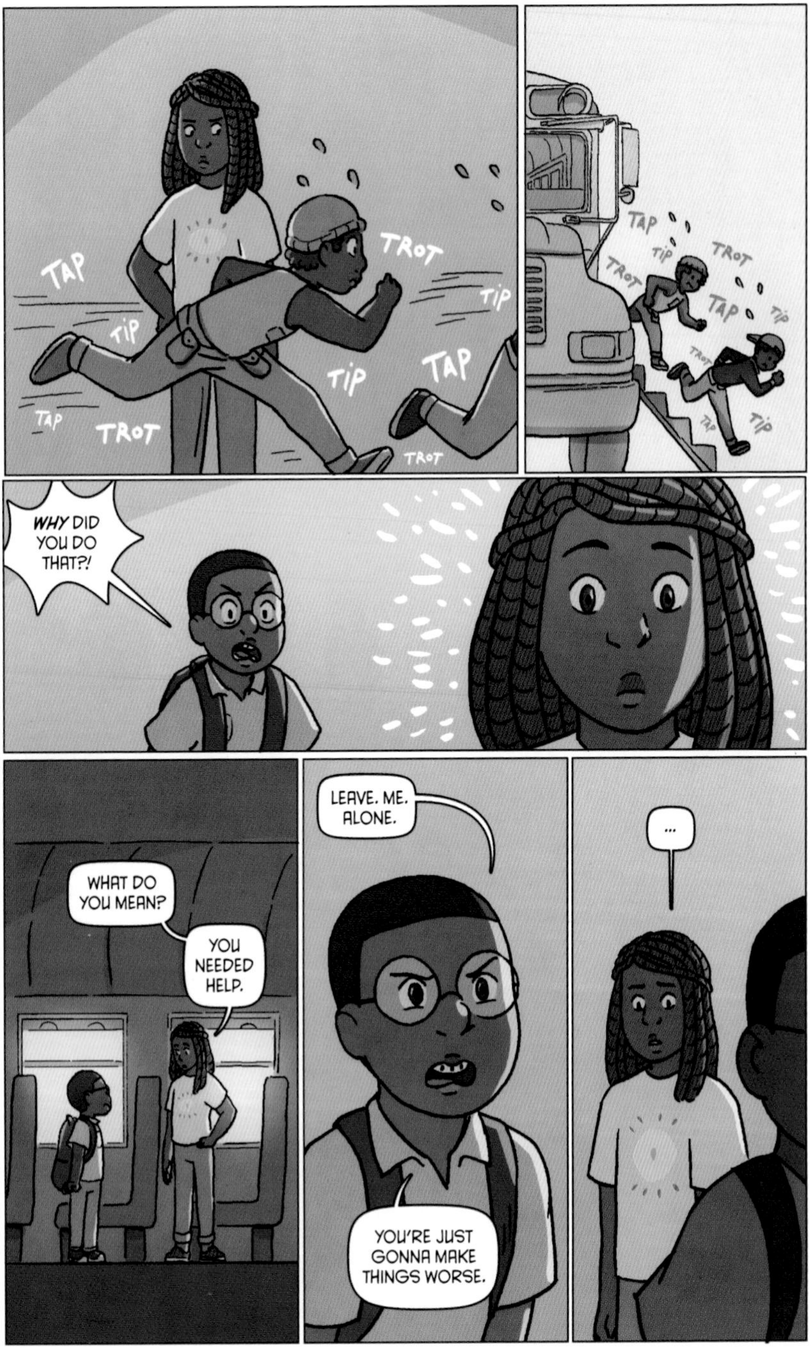
TAP
TIP
TROT
TIP
TAP
TROT
TIP
TAP
TRIP
TROT
TAP
TIP
TROT
TROT
TAP
TIP
TIP
WHY DID YOU DO THAT?!
WHAT DO YOU MEAN?
YOU NEEDED HELP.
LEAVE. ME. ALONE.
YOU'RE JUST GONNA MAKE THINGS WORSE.
...

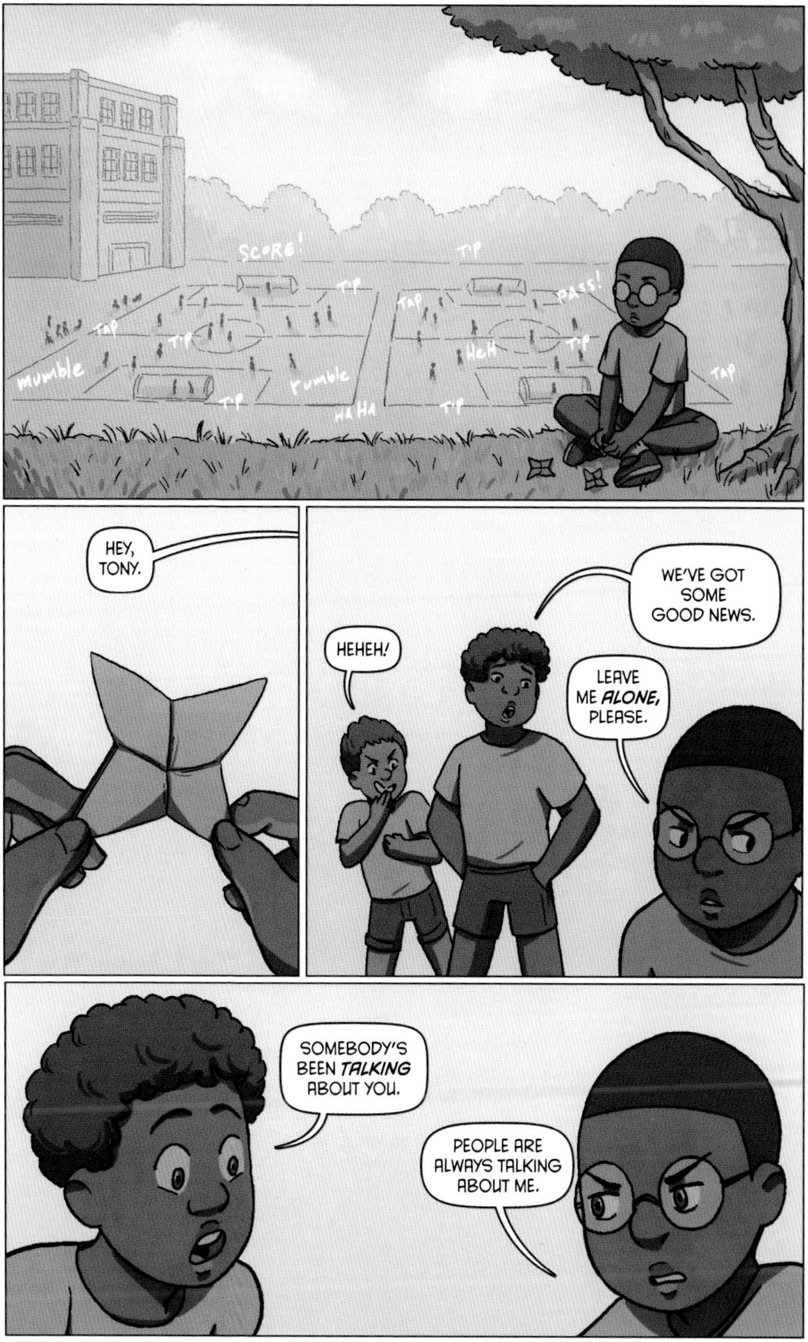
SCORE!
TIP
TIP
TAP
PASS!
TAP
TIP
HEH
TIP
MUMBLE
RUMBLE
TAP
TIP
HAHA
TIP
HEY, TONY.
WE'VE GOT SOME GOOD NEWS.
HEHEH!
LEAVE ME *ALONE,* PLEASE.
SOMEBODY'S BEEN *TALKING* ABOUT YOU.
PEOPLE ARE ALWAYS TALKING ABOUT ME.

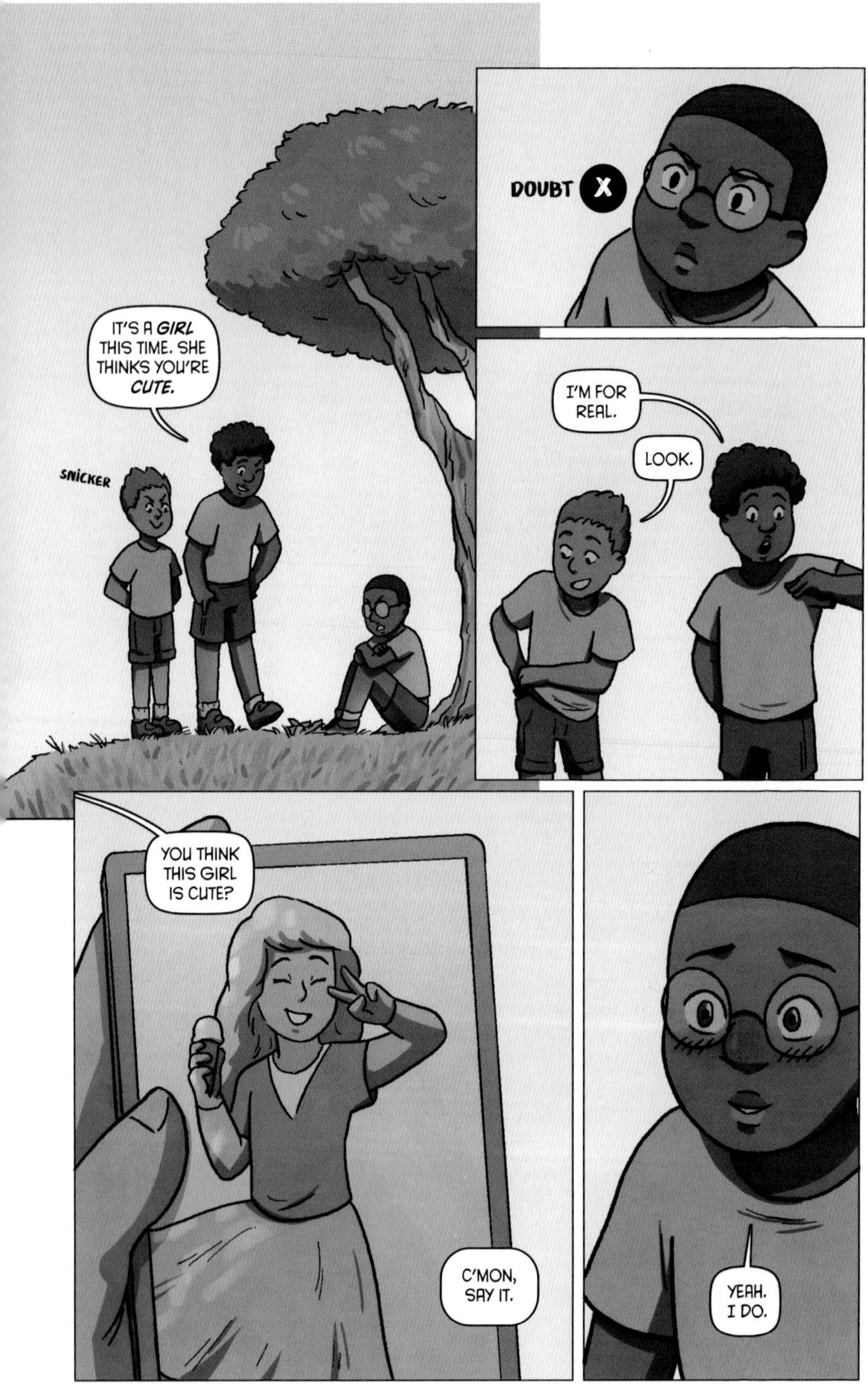

DOUBT X
IT'S A *GIRL* THIS TIME. SHE THINKS YOU'RE *CUTE.*
SNICKER
I'M FOR REAL.
LOOK.
YOU THINK THIS GIRL IS CUTE?
C'MON, SAY IT.
YEAH. I DO.

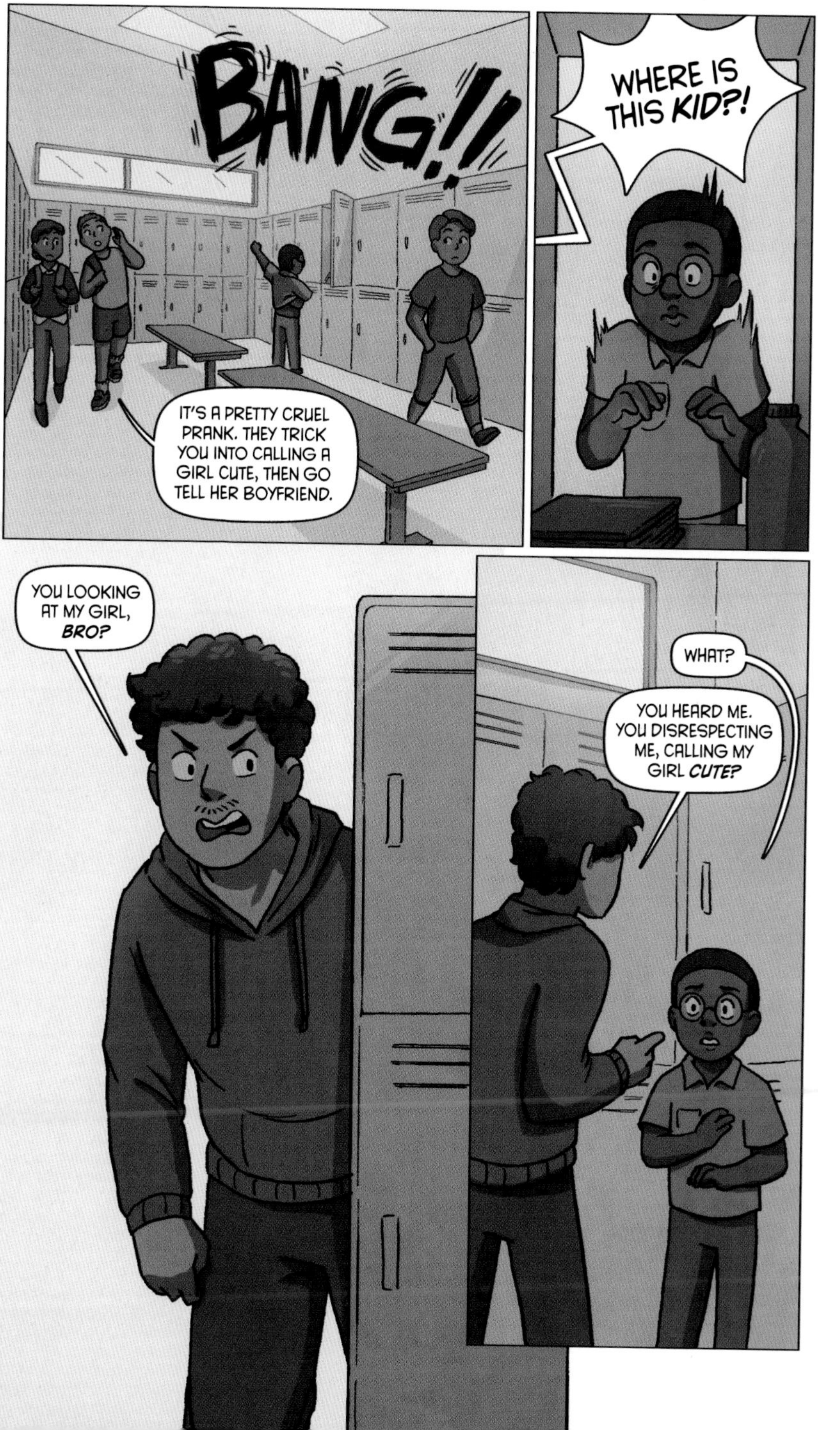
BANG!!
IT'S A PRETTY CRUEL PRANK. THEY TRICK YOU INTO CALLING A GIRL CUTE, THEN GO TELL HER BOYFRIEND.
WHERE IS THIS KID?!
YOU LOOKING AT MY GIRL, BRO?
WHAT?
YOU HEARD ME. YOU DISRESPECTING ME, CALLING MY GIRL CUTE?

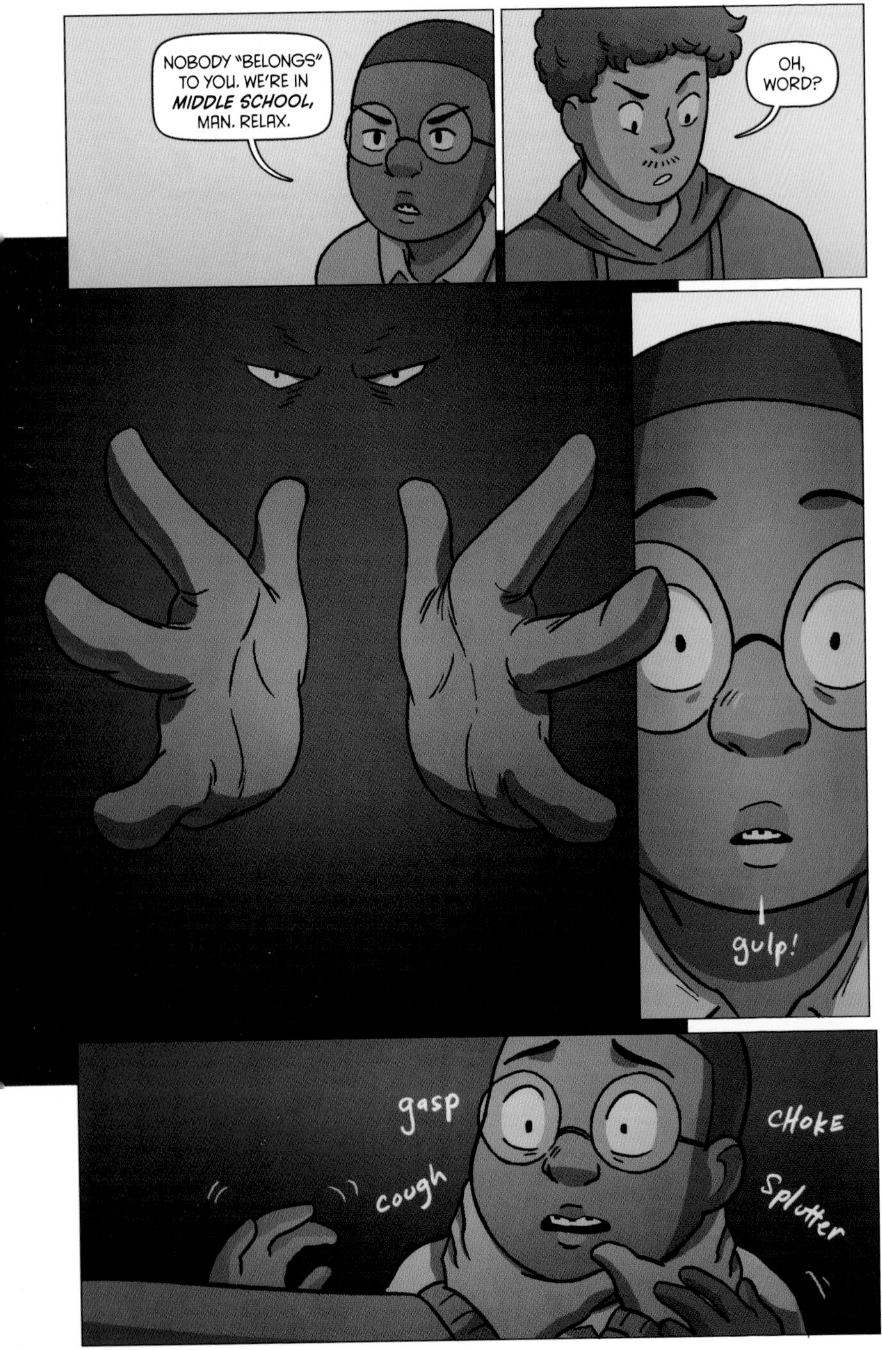
NOBODY "BELONGS" TO YOU. WE'RE IN *MIDDLE SCHOOL,* MAN. RELAX.
OH, WORD?
gulp!
gasp
cough
CHOKE
Splutter

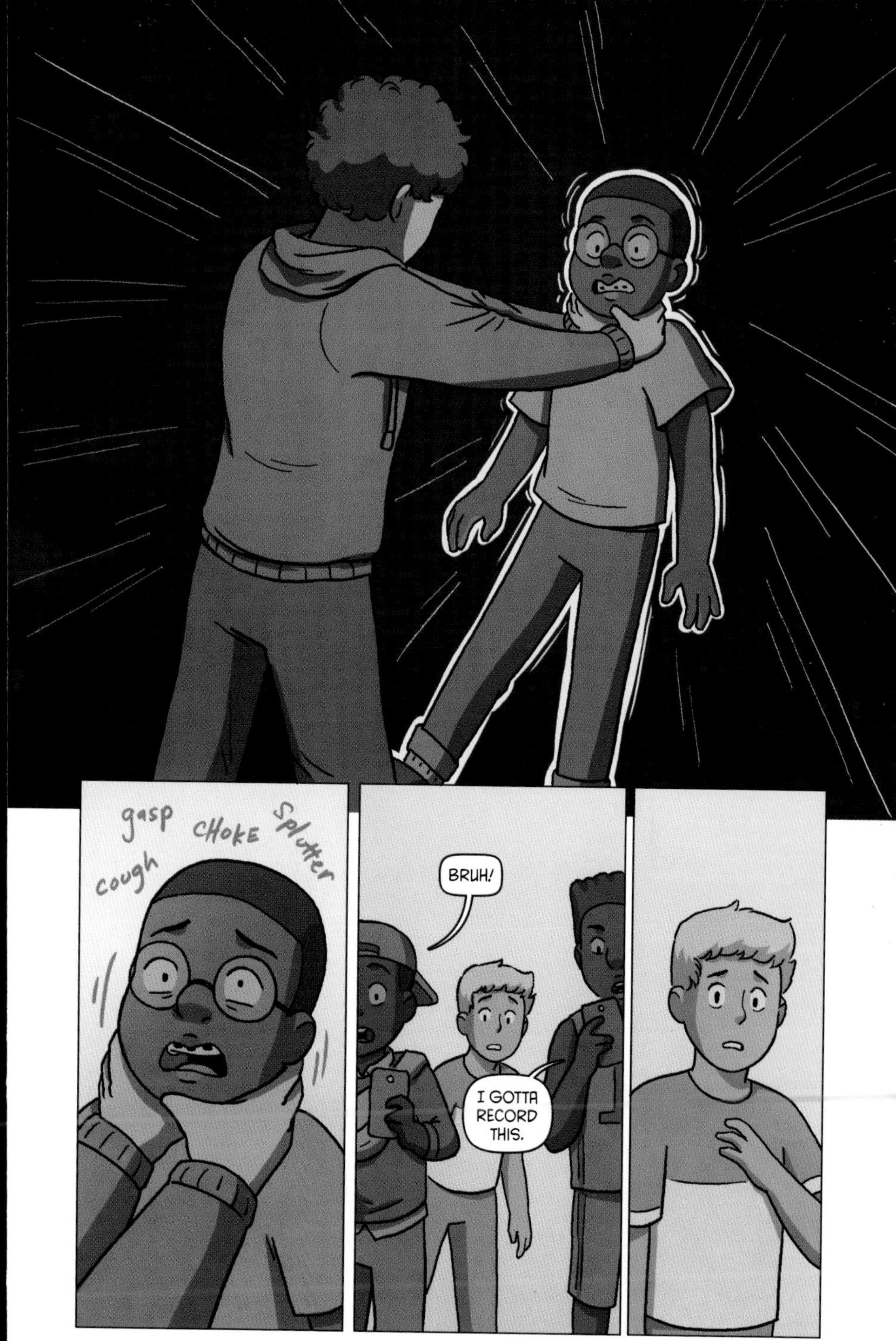
gasp
CHOKE
splutter
cough
BRUH!
I GOTTA RECORD THIS.

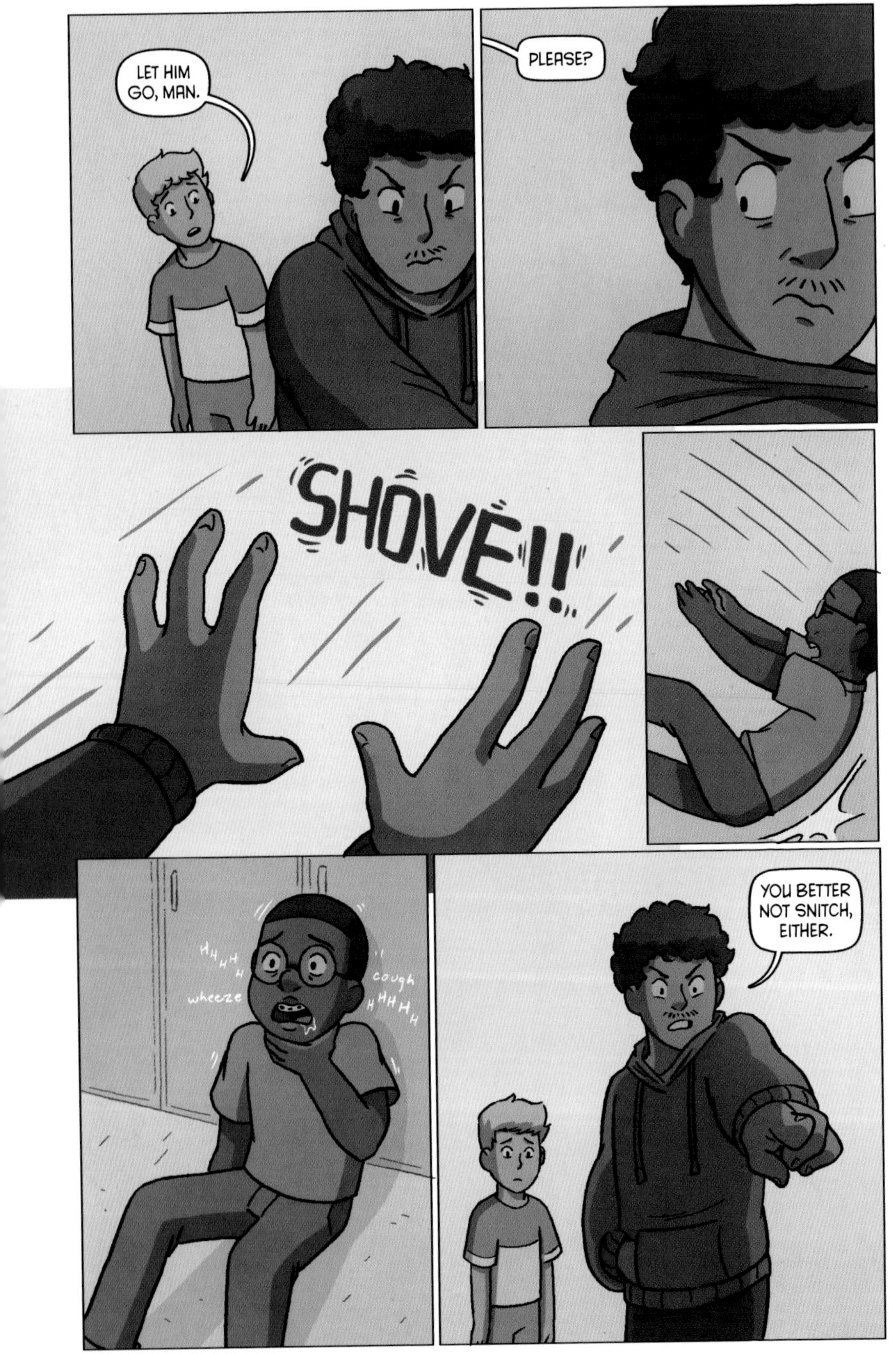
LET HIM GO, MAN.
PLEASE?
SHOVE!!
HHHHH
wheeze
cough
HHHHH
YOU BETTER NOT SNITCH, EITHER.

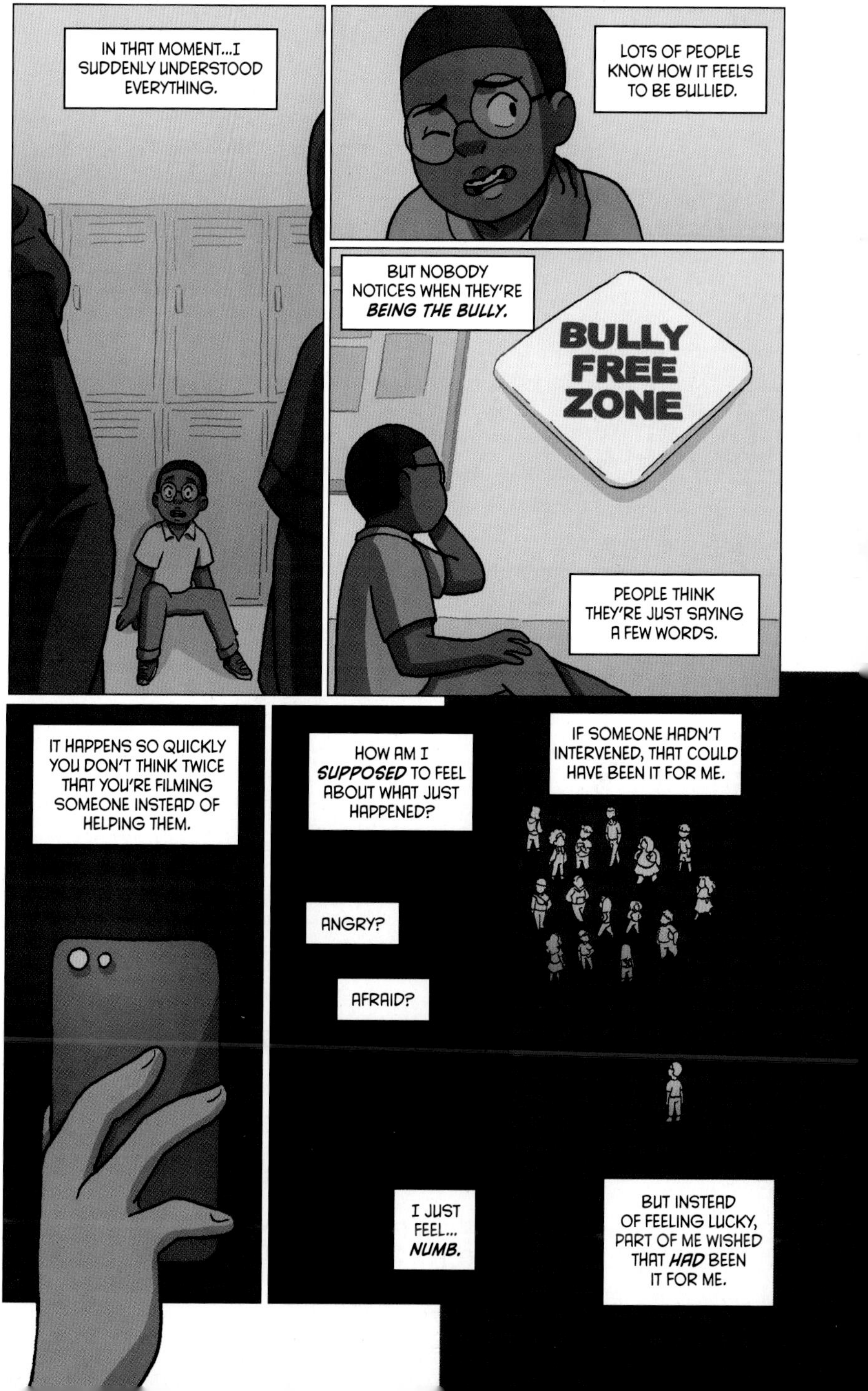
IN THAT MOMENT...I SUDDENLY UNDERSTOOD EVERYTHING.
LOTS OF PEOPLE KNOW HOW IT FEELS TO BE BULLIED.
BUT NOBODY NOTICES WHEN THEY'RE *BEING THE BULLY.*
BULLY FREE ZONE
PEOPLE THINK THEY'RE JUST SAYING A FEW WORDS.
IT HAPPENS SO QUICKLY YOU DON'T THINK TWICE THAT YOU'RE FILMING SOMEONE INSTEAD OF HELPING THEM.
HOW AM I *SUPPOSED* TO FEEL ABOUT WHAT JUST HAPPENED?
ANGRY?
AFRAID?
I JUST FEEL... *NUMB.*
IF SOMEONE HADN'T INTERVENED, THAT COULD HAVE BEEN IT FOR ME.
BUT INSTEAD OF FEELING LUCKY, PART OF ME WISHED THAT *HAD* BEEN IT FOR ME.

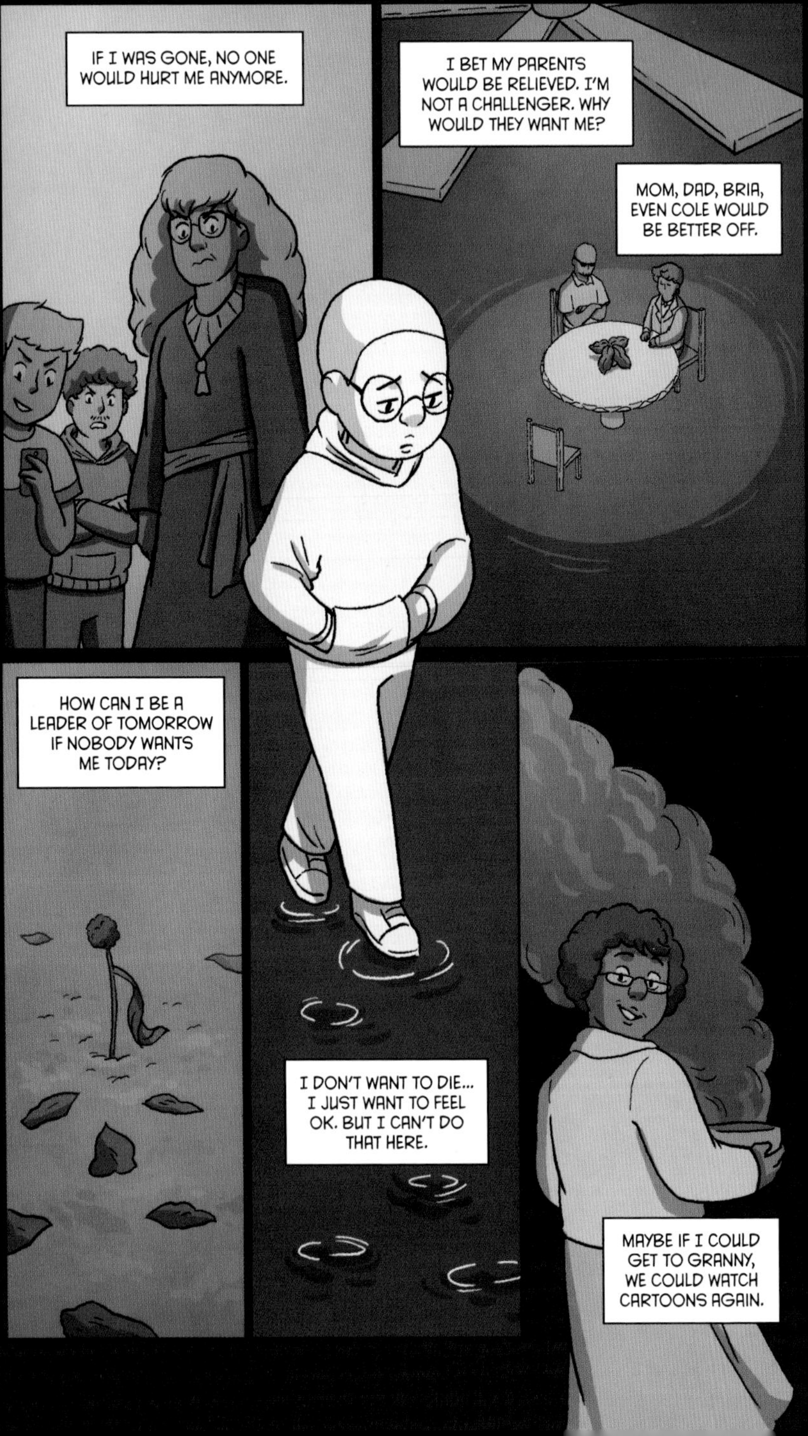
IF I WAS GONE, NO ONE WOULD HURT ME ANYMORE.
I BET MY PARENTS WOULD BE RELIEVED. I'M NOT A CHALLENGER. WHY WOULD THEY WANT ME?
MOM, DAD, BRIA, EVEN COLE WOULD BE BETTER OFF.
HOW CAN I BE A LEADER OF TOMORROW IF NOBODY WANTS ME TODAY?
I DON'T WANT TO DIE... I JUST WANT TO FEEL OK. BUT I CAN'T DO THAT HERE.
MAYBE IF I COULD GET TO GRANNY, WE COULD WATCH CARTOONS AGAIN.

I DECIDED THAT I WAS RIGHT.

THAT ME DISAPPEARING WOULD BE BEST FOR EVERYONE.

AN END TO MY PAIN AND THEIRS.

I WON'T TELL YOU HOW I DID IT,
AND I'M BEGGING YOU, DON'T TRY TO GUESS.

THINGS GOT SO DARK I FORGOT THERE WAS ANYTHING ELSE.

INSTEAD OF TRYING TO GET AWAY FROM IT, I RAN INTO IT.

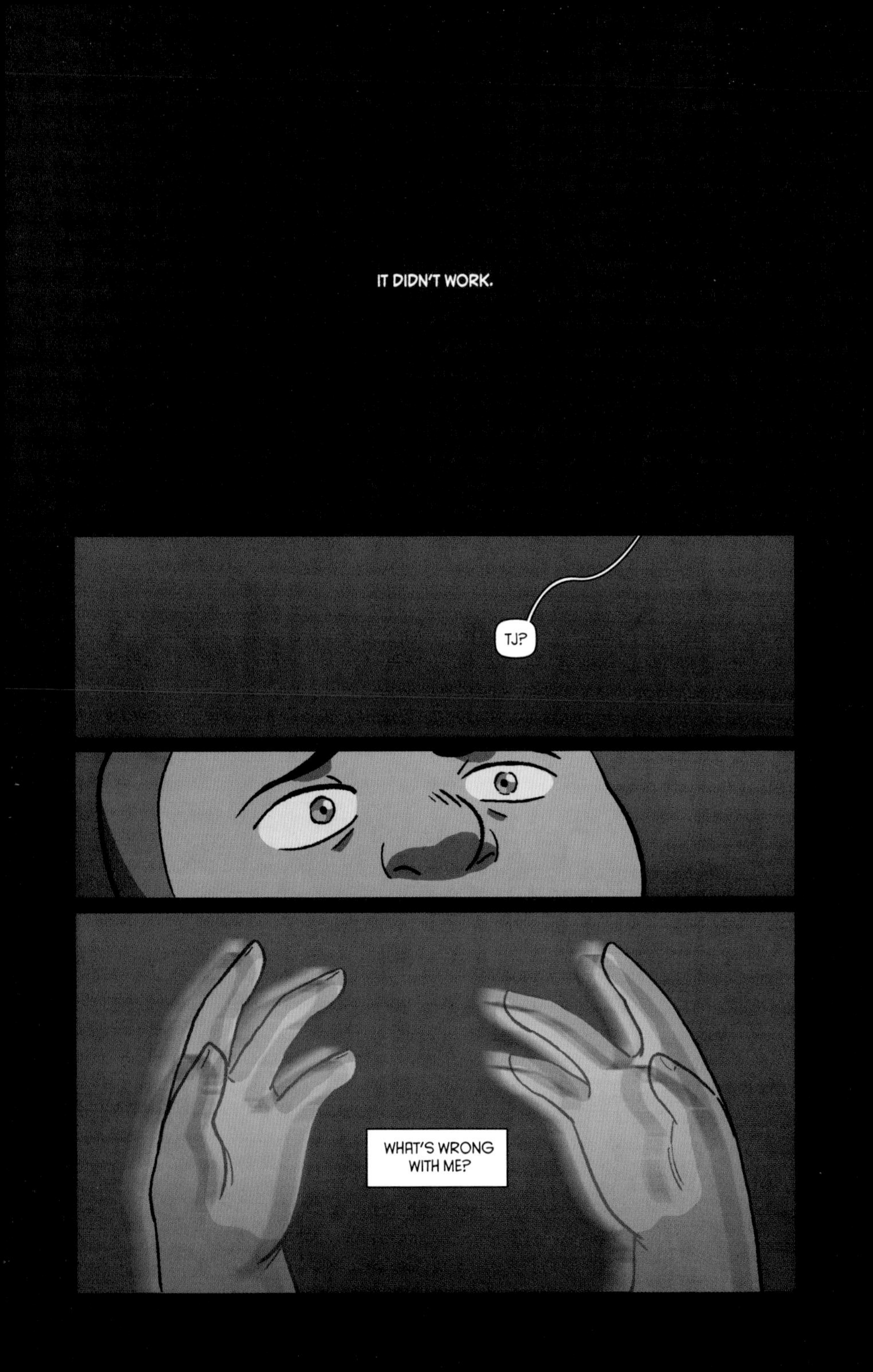
IT DIDN'T WORK.
TJ?
WHAT'S WRONG WITH ME?

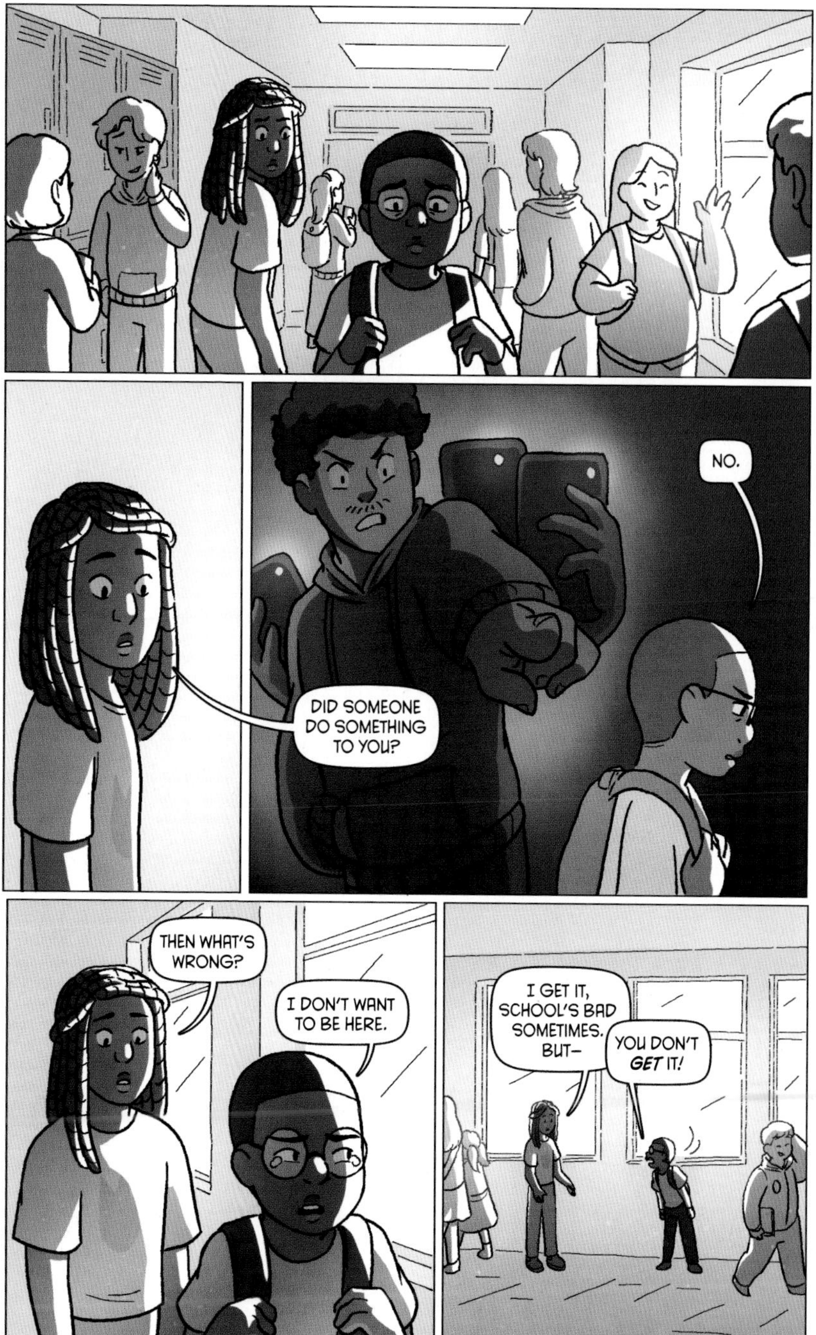
NO.
DID SOMEONE DO SOMETHING TO YOU?
THEN WHAT'S WRONG?
I DON'T WANT TO BE HERE.
I GET IT, SCHOOL'S BAD SOMETIMES. BUT—
YOU DON'T *GET* IT!

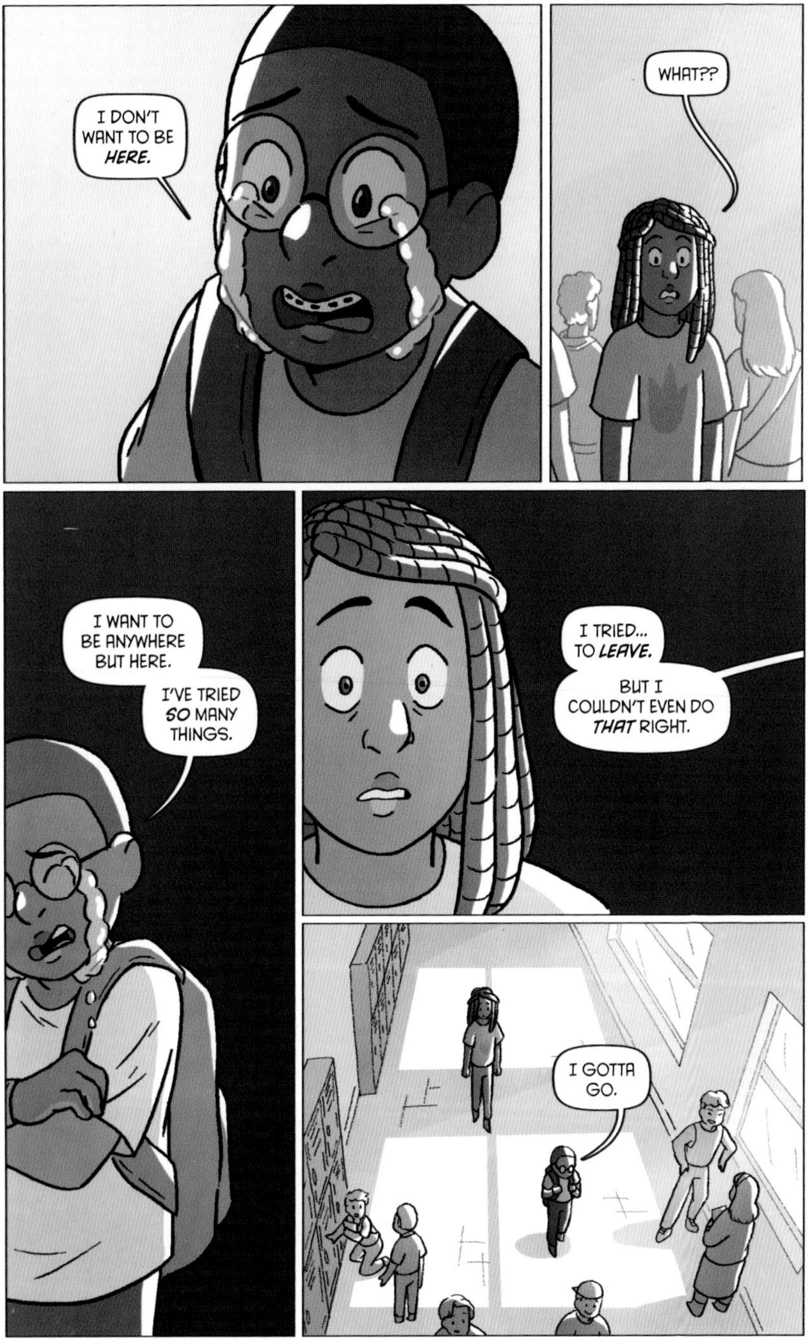
I DON'T WANT TO BE *HERE.*
WHAT??
I WANT TO BE ANYWHERE BUT HERE.
I'VE TRIED *SO* MANY THINGS.
I TRIED... TO *LEAVE.*
BUT I COULDN'T EVEN DO *THAT* RIGHT.
I GOTTA GO.

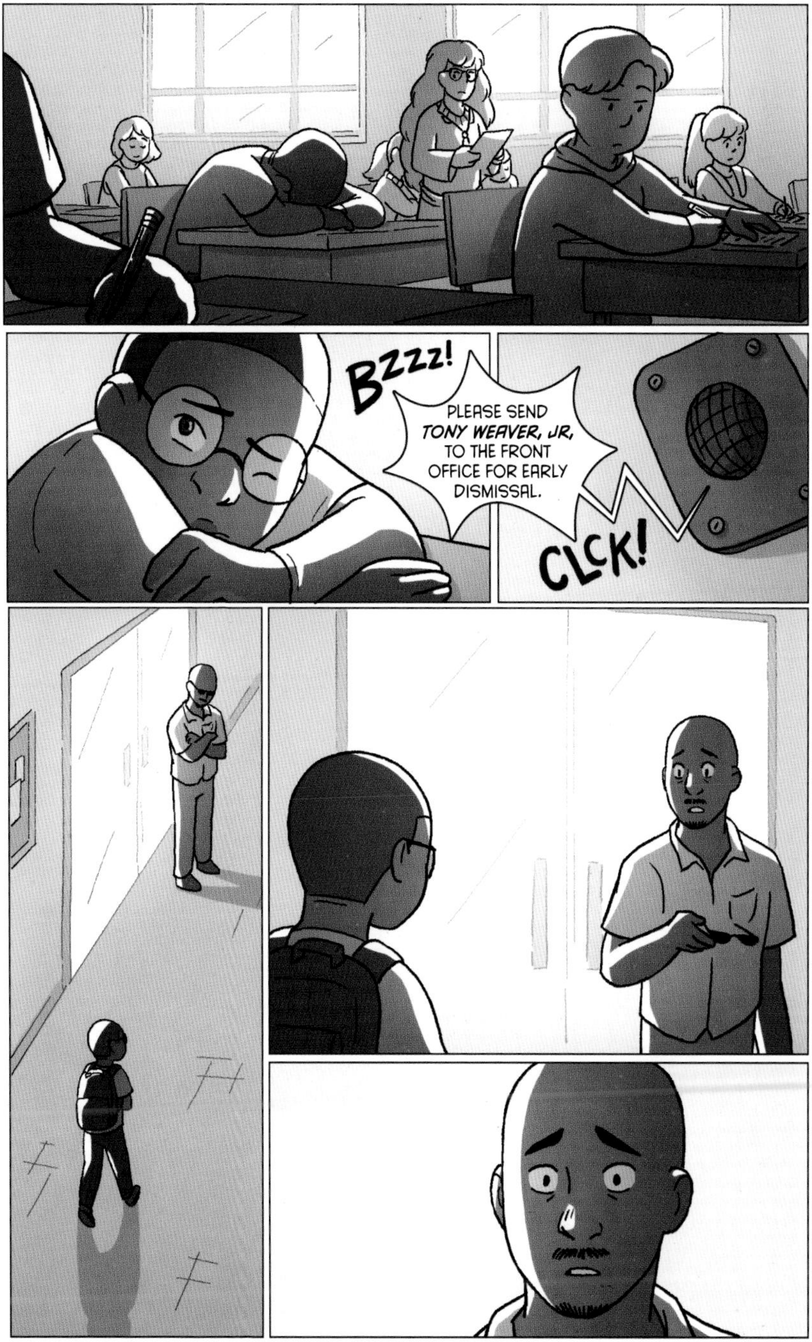
BZZZ!
PLEASE SEND *TONY WEAVER, JR,* TO THE FRONT OFFICE FOR EARLY DISMISSAL.
CLCK!

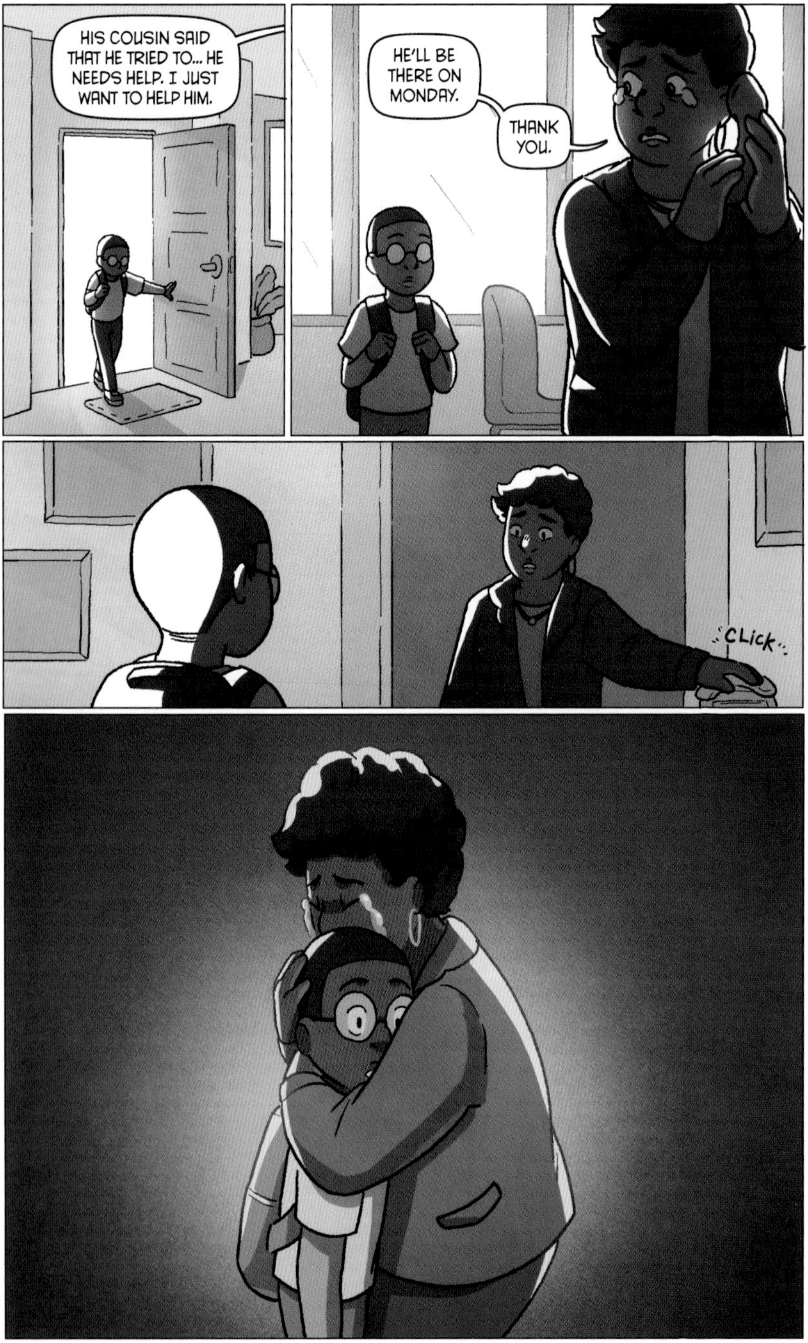
HIS COUSIN SAID THAT HE TRIED TO... HE NEEDS HELP. I JUST WANT TO HELP HIM.
HE'LL BE THERE ON MONDAY.
THANK YOU.
CLICK

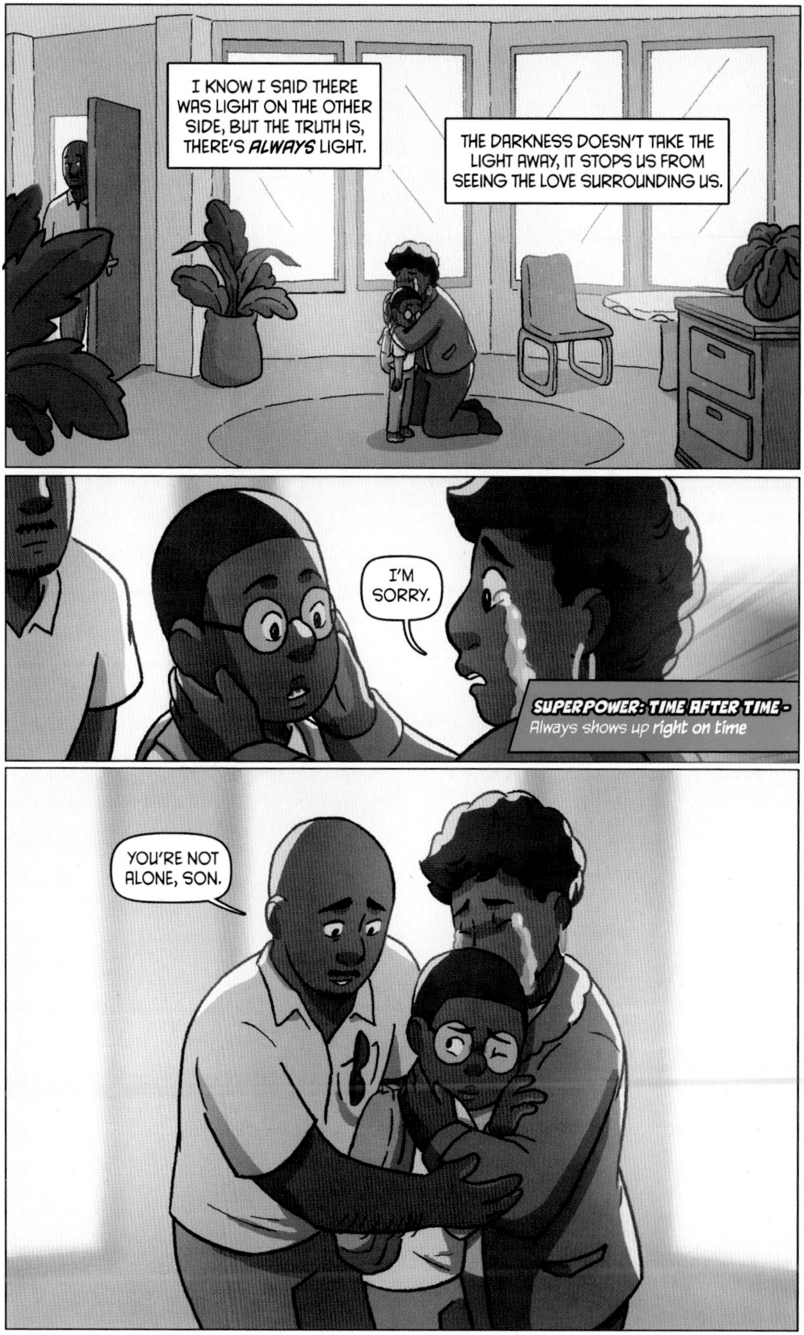
I KNOW I SAID THERE WAS LIGHT ON THE OTHER SIDE, BUT THE TRUTH IS, THERE'S *ALWAYS* LIGHT.
THE DARKNESS DOESN'T TAKE THE LIGHT AWAY, IT STOPS US FROM SEEING THE LOVE SURROUNDING US.
I'M SORRY.
SUPERPOWER: TIME AFTER TIME - Always shows up right on time
YOU'RE NOT ALONE, SON.

NEVER LOSE SIGHT OF THE LIGHT.

EVEN IF I'M NOT LIKE EVERYONE ELSE, I CAN STILL BE A SPLENDID LEADER. I WILL PROVE IT TO THE WORLD!

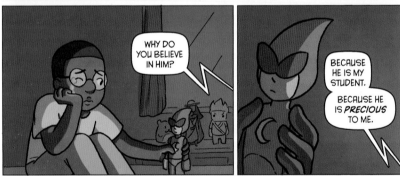

WHY DO YOU BELIEVE IN HIM?

BECAUSE HE IS MY STUDENT.

BECAUSE HE IS *PRECIOUS* TO ME.

SOMETIMES IT COMES FROM THE MOST UNEXPECTED PLACES.

CHAPTER 4

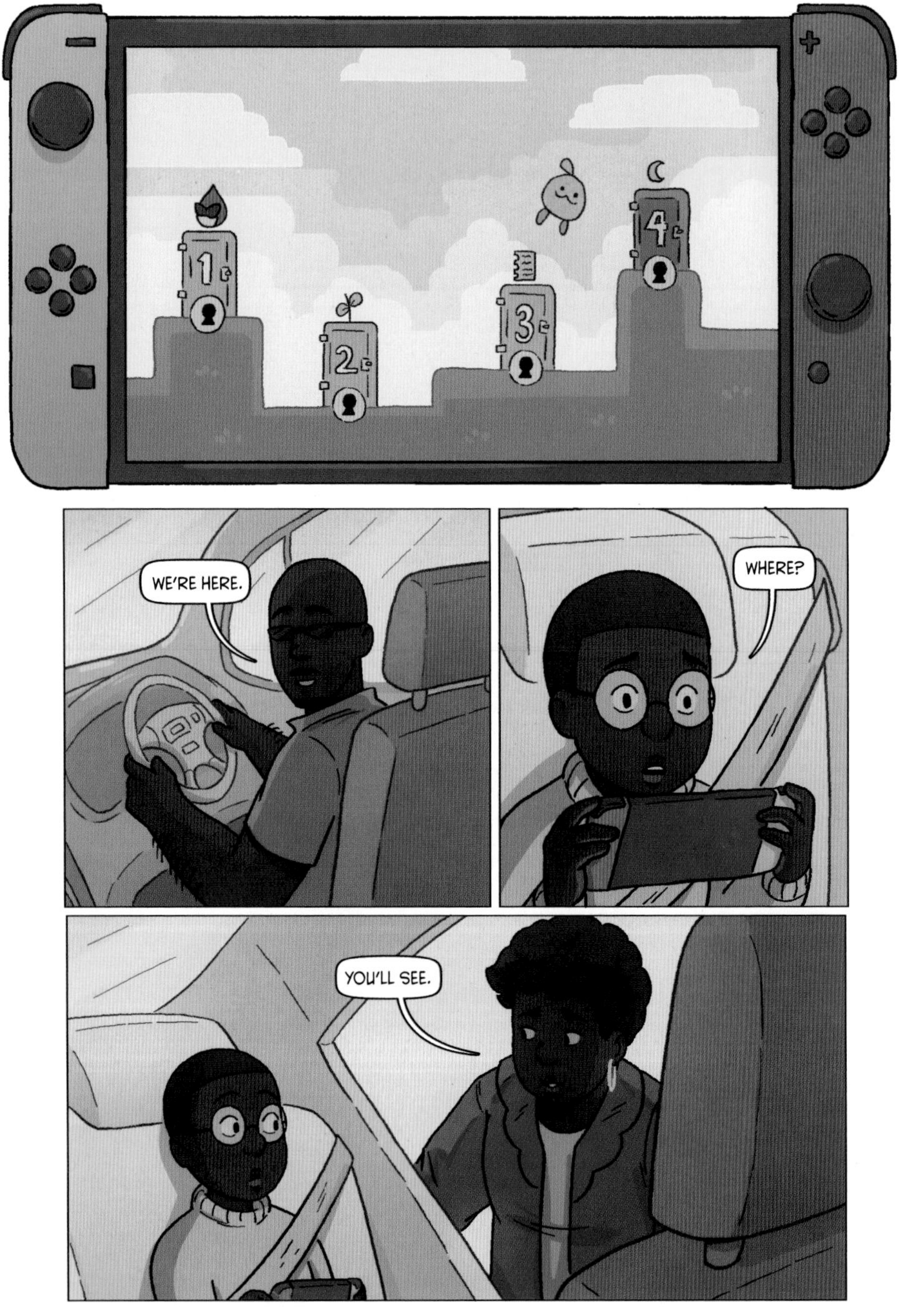
1
2
3
4
WE'RE HERE.
WHERE?
YOU'LL SEE.

CREAK

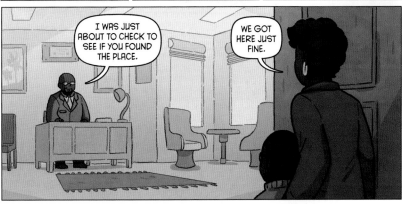

I WAS JUST ABOUT TO CHECK TO SEE IF YOU FOUND THE PLACE.

WE GOT HERE JUST FINE.

WE APPRECIATE YOU BEING AVAILABLE ON SUCH SHORT NOTICE.

IT'S NOT A PROBLEM AT ALL.

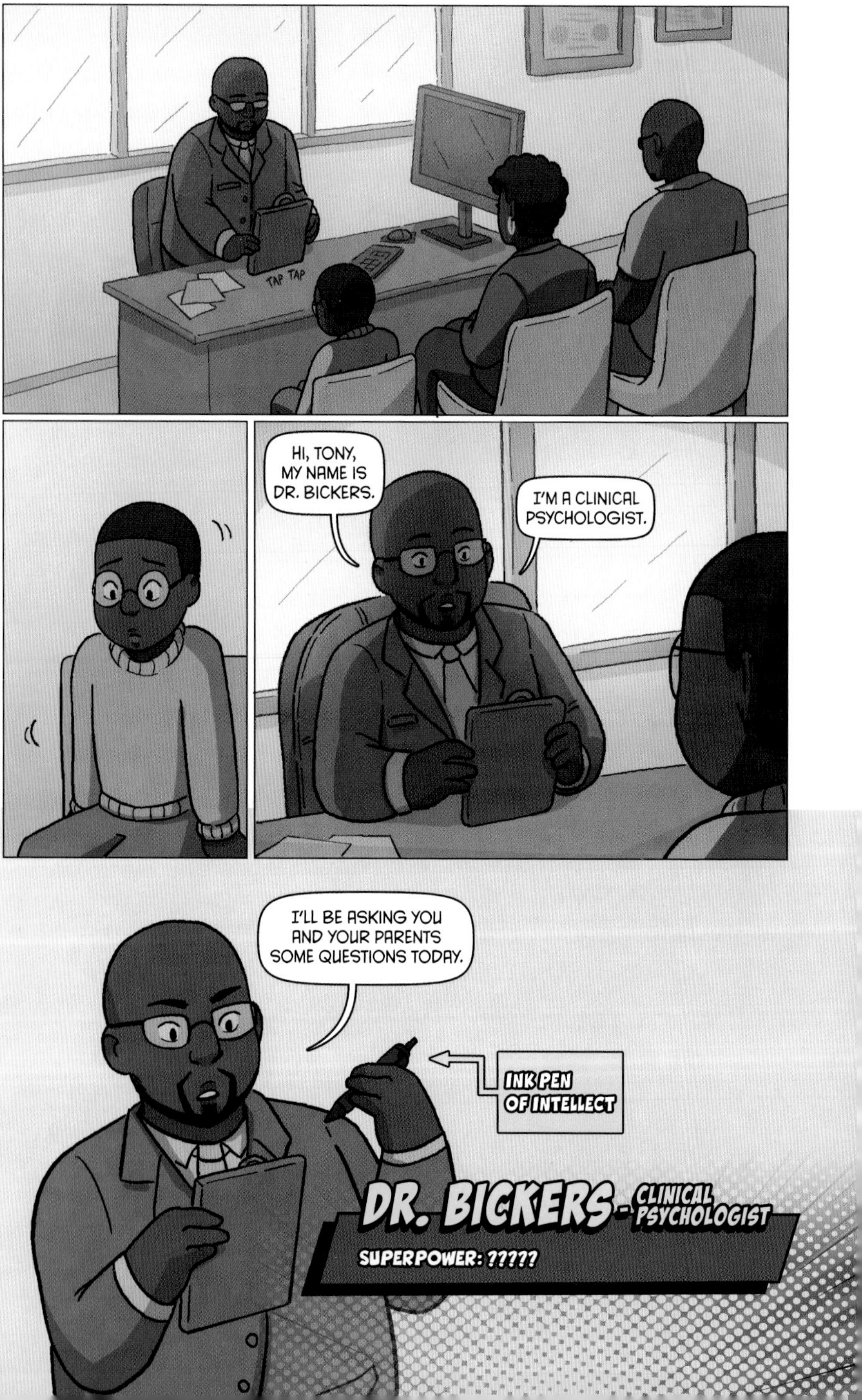
TAP TAP
HI, TONY, MY NAME IS DR. BICKERS.
I'M A CLINICAL PSYCHOLOGIST.
I'LL BE ASKING YOU AND YOUR PARENTS SOME QUESTIONS TODAY.
INK PEN OF INTELLECT
DR. BICKERS - CLINICAL PSYCHOLOGIST
SUPERPOWER: ?????

YOU ALL ARE HIS BIOLOGICAL PARENTS CORRECT?
YES.
WHAT GRADE IS TONY IN RIGHT NOW?
7TH.
DOES HE HAVE ANY HOBBIES?
HE WRITES.
DOES HE *SMOKE* OR *DRINK?* ANY *DRUG USE?*
NO.
NO.
HOW ABOUT ELECTRONICS, TV, VIDEO GAMES, *INTERNET?*
A *LOT* OF THAT.
HAVE THERE BEEN ANY RECENT *DEATHS* IN THE FAMILY?
YES...HIS GRANDMOTHER.
IS THERE A *GUN* IN THE HOME THAT HE HAS ACCESS TO?
NO. NONE AT ALL.

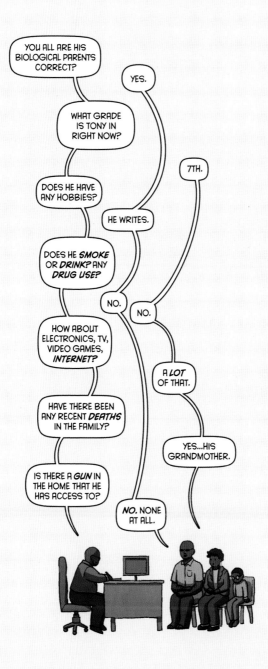

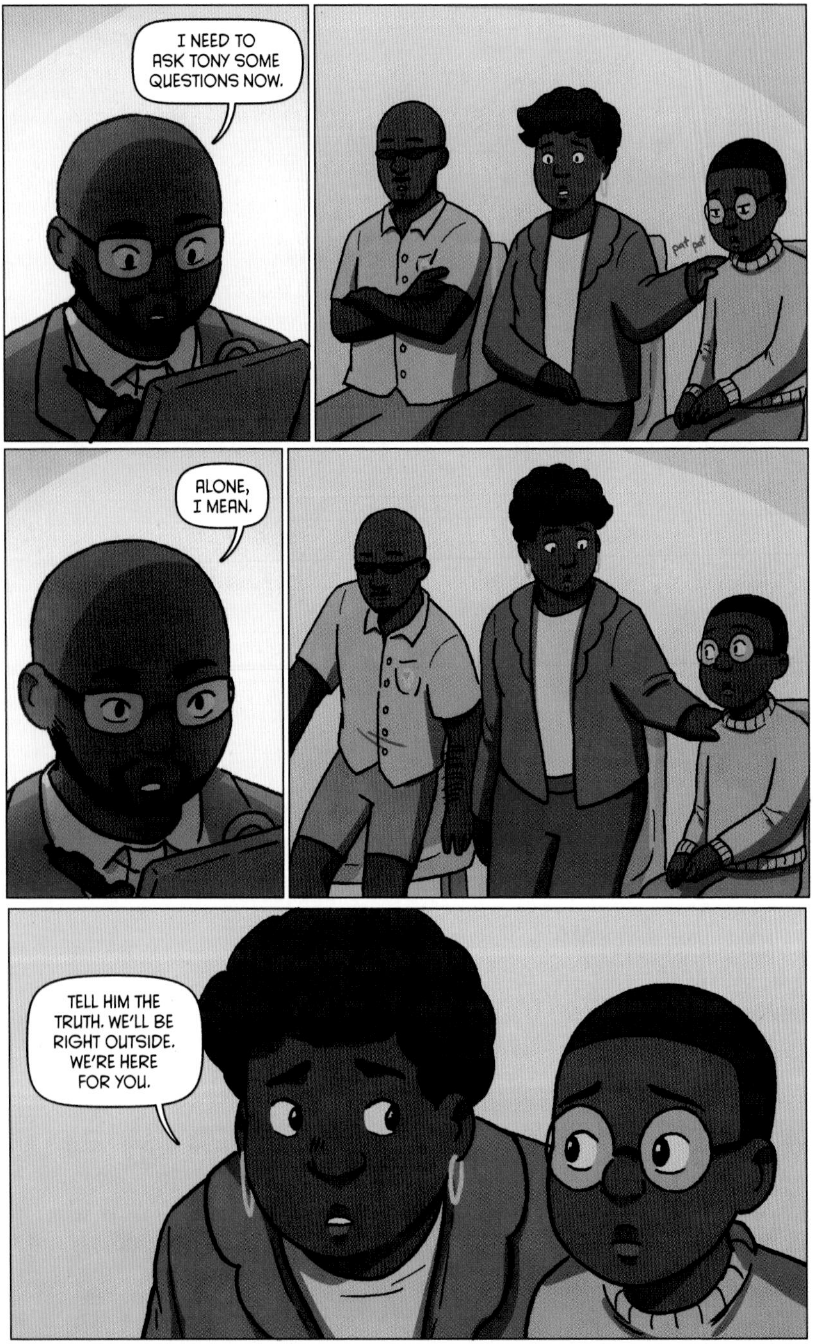
I NEED TO ASK TONY SOME QUESTIONS NOW.
pat pat
ALONE, I MEAN.
TELL HIM THE TRUTH. WE'LL BE RIGHT OUTSIDE. WE'RE HERE FOR YOU.

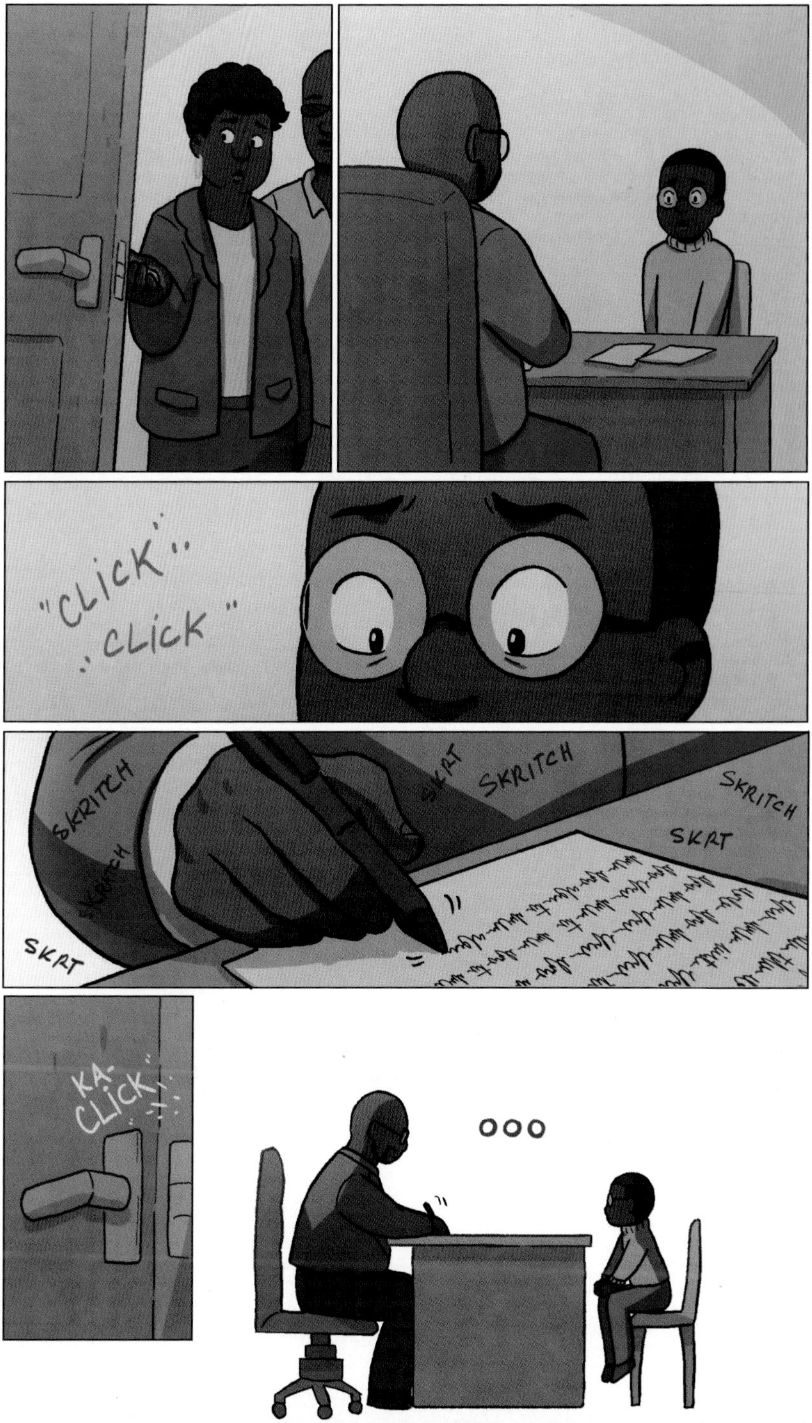
"CLICK"
"CLICK"
SKRITCH
SKRITCH
SKRT
SKRITCH
SKRITCH
SKRT
SKRT
KA-CLICK
OOO

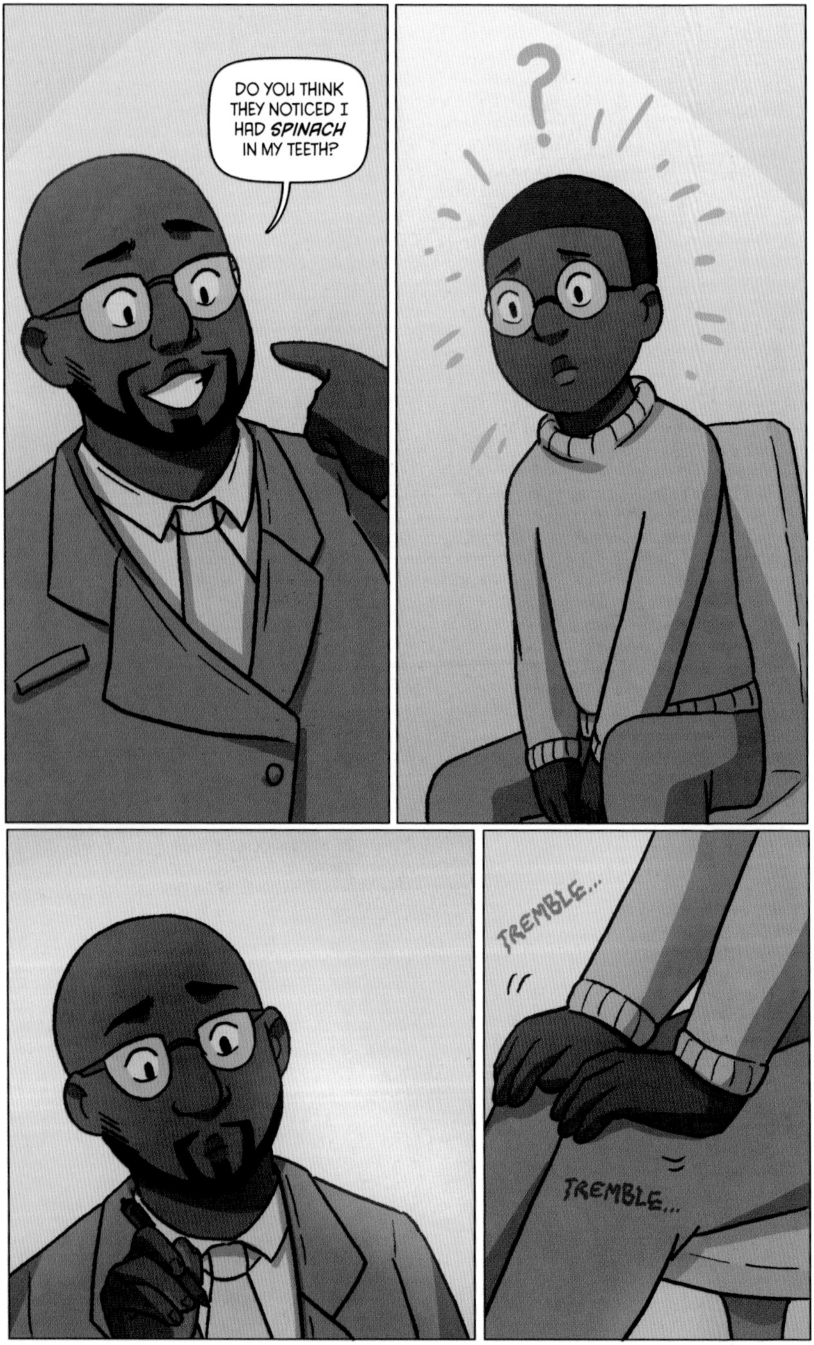
DO YOU THINK THEY NOTICED I HAD *SPINACH* IN MY TEETH?
?
TREMBLE...
TREMBLE...

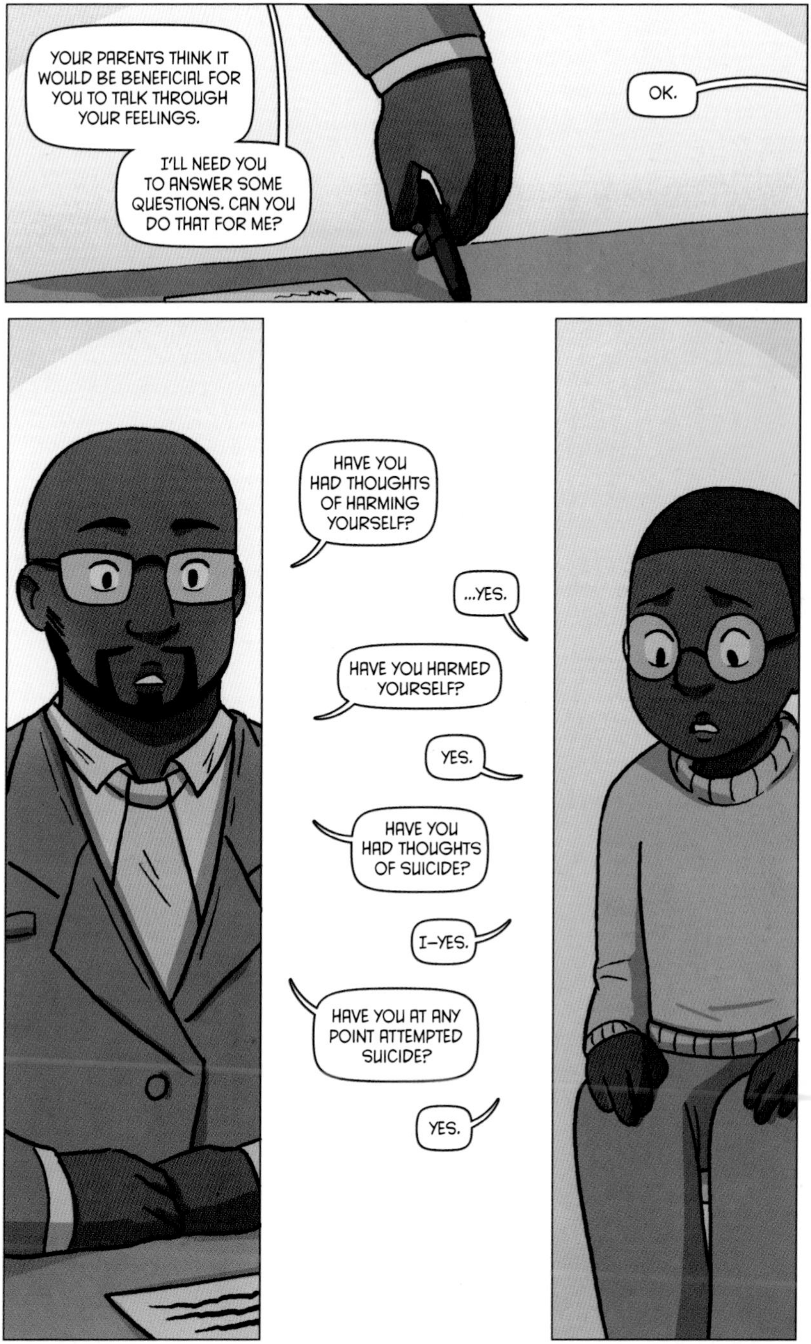
YOUR PARENTS THINK IT WOULD BE BENEFICIAL FOR YOU TO TALK THROUGH YOUR FEELINGS.
I'LL NEED YOU TO ANSWER SOME QUESTIONS. CAN YOU DO THAT FOR ME?
OK.
HAVE YOU HAD THOUGHTS OF HARMING YOURSELF?
...YES.
HAVE YOU HARMED YOURSELF?
YES.
HAVE YOU HAD THOUGHTS OF SUICIDE?
I—YES.
HAVE YOU AT ANY POINT ATTEMPTED SUICIDE?
YES.

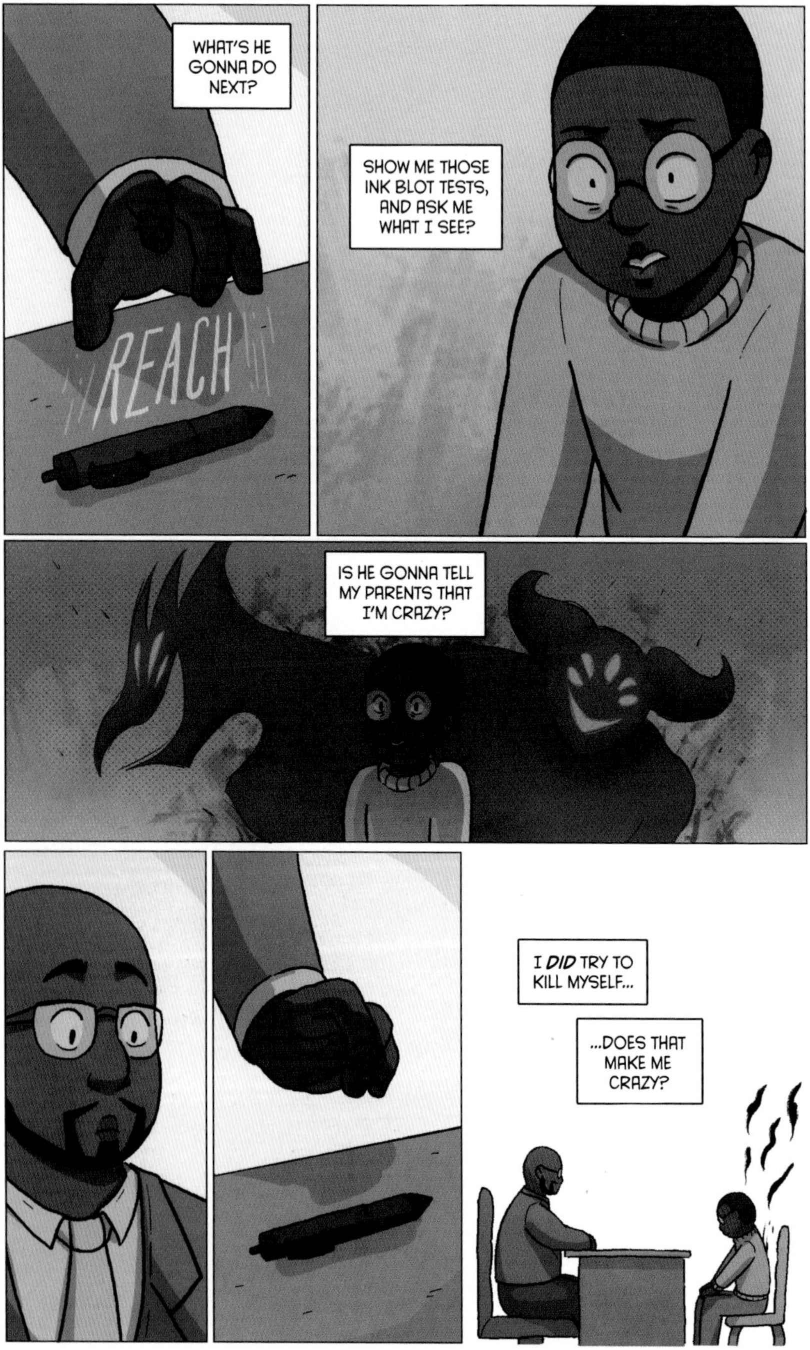
WHAT'S HE GONNA DO NEXT?
REACH
SHOW ME THOSE INK BLOT TESTS, AND ASK ME WHAT I SEE?
IS HE GONNA TELL MY PARENTS THAT I'M CRAZY?
I *DID* TRY TO KILL MYSELF...
...DOES THAT MAKE ME CRAZY?

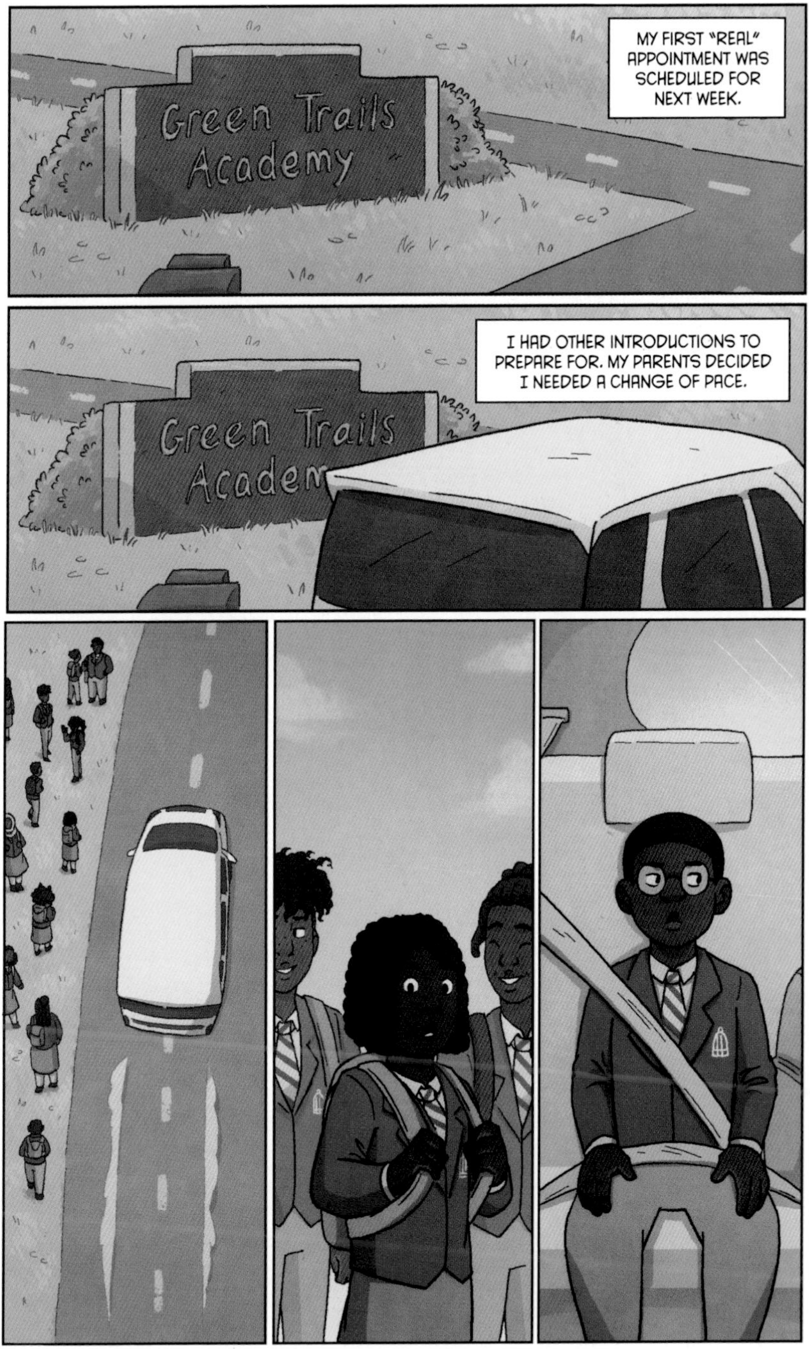
Green Trails Academy
MY FIRST "REAL" APPOINTMENT WAS SCHEDULED FOR NEXT WEEK.
I HAD OTHER INTRODUCTIONS TO PREPARE FOR. MY PARENTS DECIDED I NEEDED A CHANGE OF PACE.

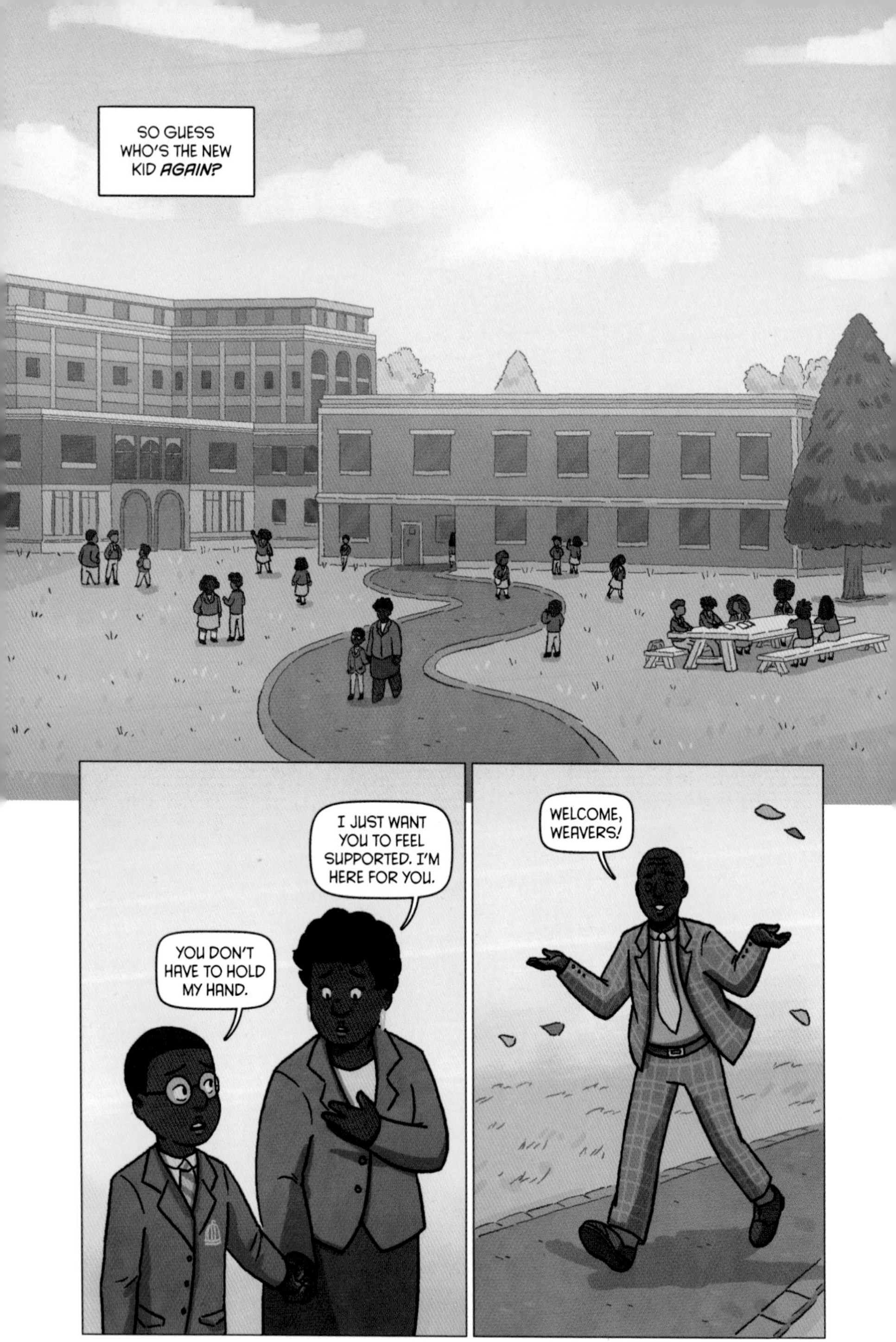
SO GUESS WHO'S THE NEW KID *AGAIN?*
I JUST WANT YOU TO FEEL SUPPORTED. I'M HERE FOR YOU.
YOU DON'T HAVE TO HOLD MY HAND.
WELCOME, WEAVERS!

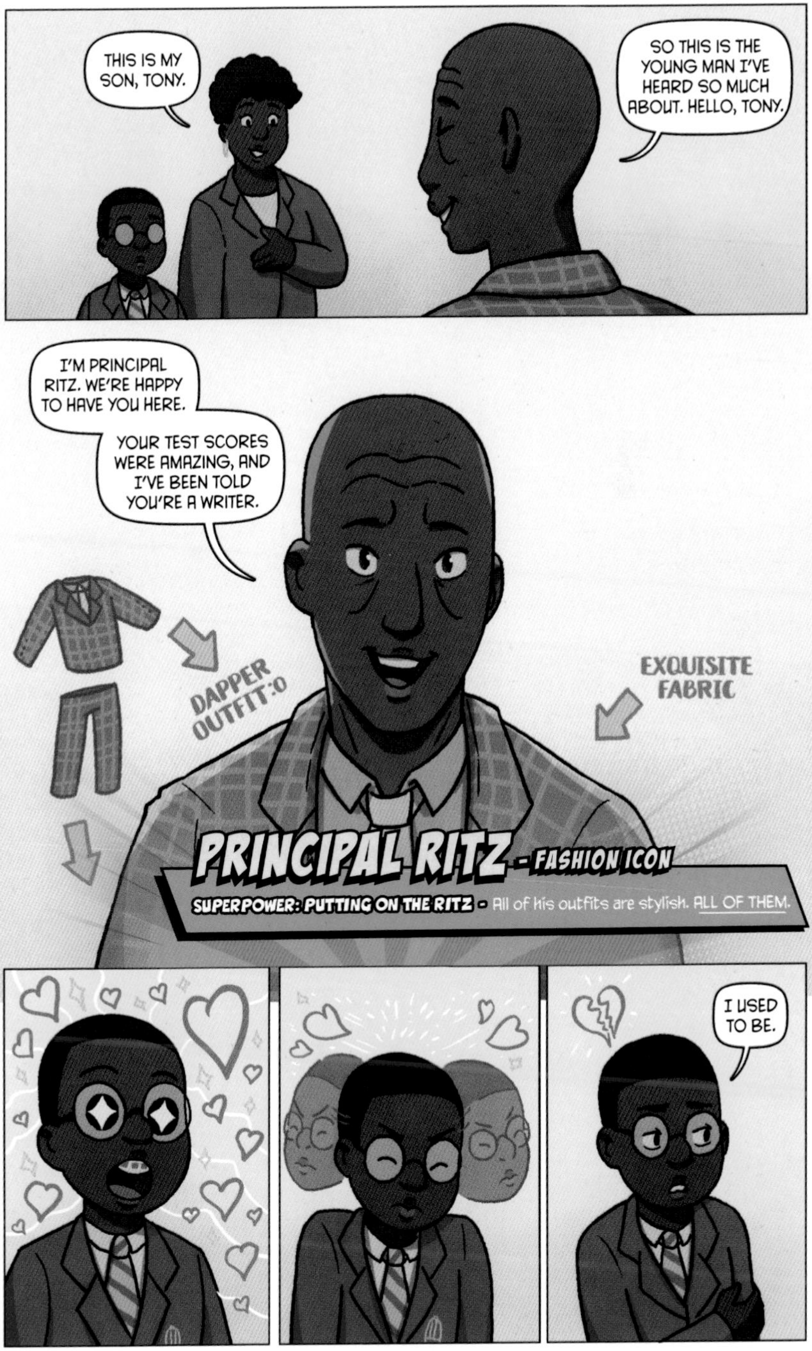
THIS IS MY SON, TONY.
SO THIS IS THE YOUNG MAN I'VE HEARD SO MUCH ABOUT. HELLO, TONY.
I'M PRINCIPAL RITZ. WE'RE HAPPY TO HAVE YOU HERE.
YOUR TEST SCORES WERE AMAZING, AND I'VE BEEN TOLD YOU'RE A WRITER.
DAPPER OUTFIT :O
EXQUISITE FABRIC
PRINCIPAL RITZ - FASHION ICON
SUPERPOWER: PUTTING ON THE RITZ - All of his outfits are stylish. ALL OF THEM.
I USED TO BE.

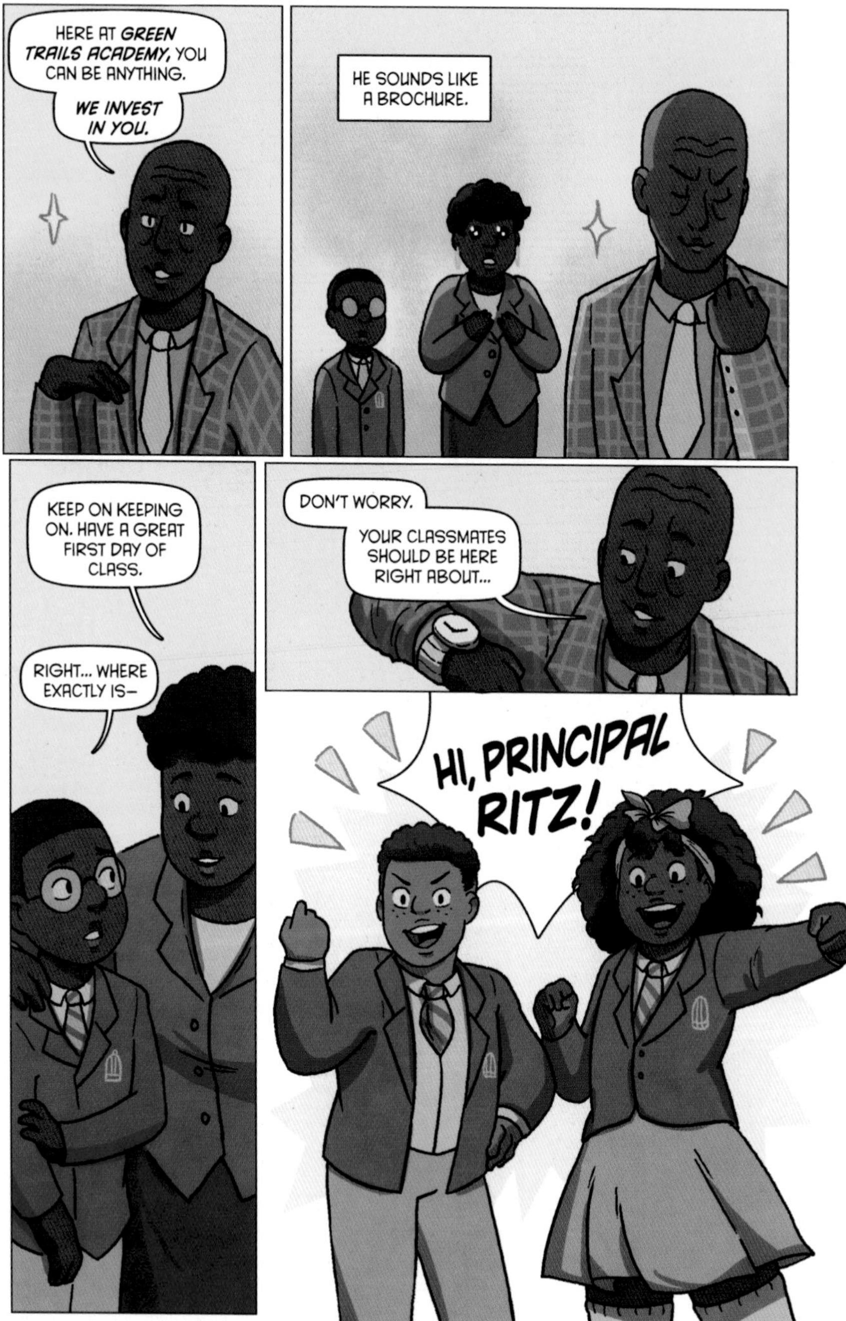

HERE AT GREEN TRAILS ACADEMY, YOU CAN BE ANYTHING.
WE INVEST IN YOU.
HE SOUNDS LIKE A BROCHURE.
KEEP ON KEEPING ON. HAVE A GREAT FIRST DAY OF CLASS.
RIGHT... WHERE EXACTLY IS—
DON'T WORRY.
YOUR CLASSMATES SHOULD BE HERE RIGHT ABOUT...
HI, PRINCIPAL RITZ!

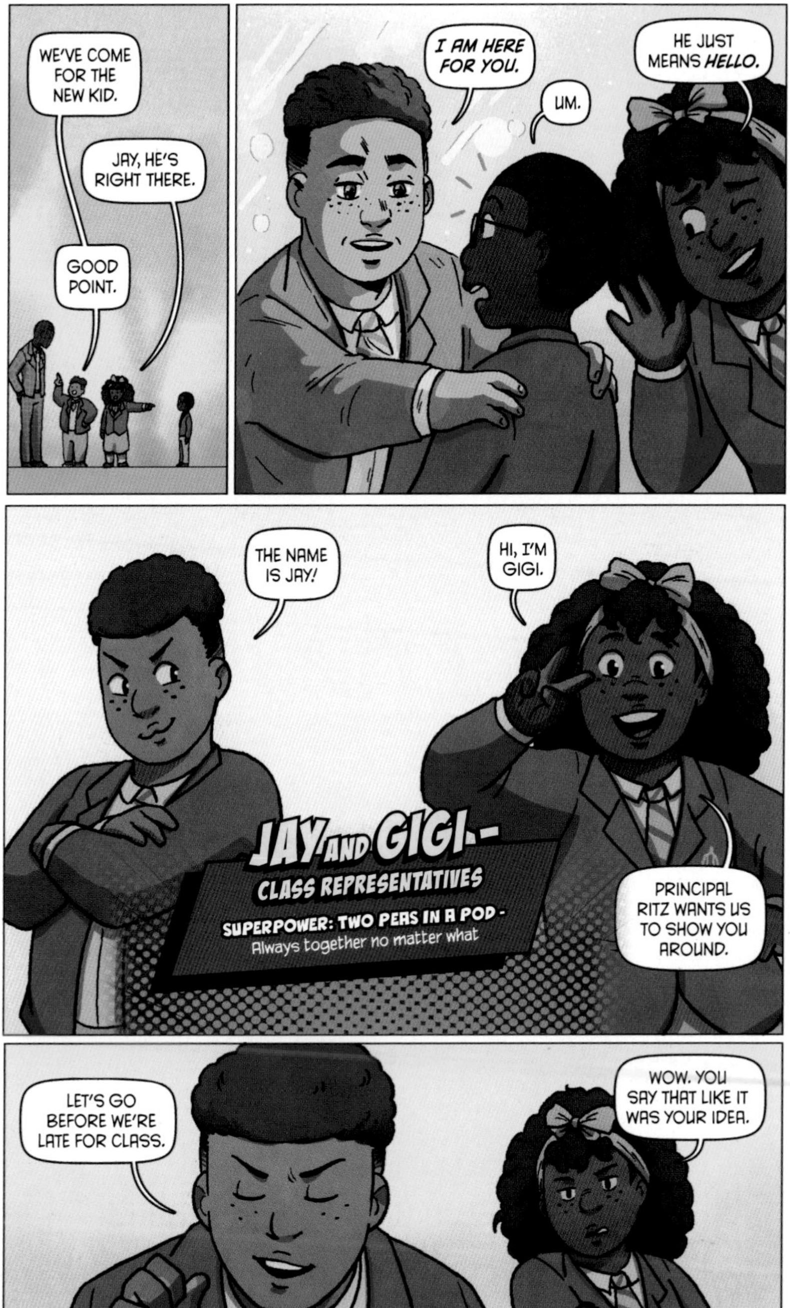
WE'VE COME FOR THE NEW KID.
JAY, HE'S RIGHT THERE.
GOOD POINT.
I AM HERE FOR YOU.
UM.
HE JUST MEANS HELLO.
THE NAME IS JAY!
HI, I'M GIGI.
JAY AND GIGI -
CLASS REPRESENTATIVES
SUPERPOWER: TWO PEAS IN A POD -
Always together no matter what
PRINCIPAL RITZ WANTS US TO SHOW YOU AROUND.
LET'S GO BEFORE WE'RE LATE FOR CLASS.
WOW. YOU SAY THAT LIKE IT WAS YOUR IDEA.

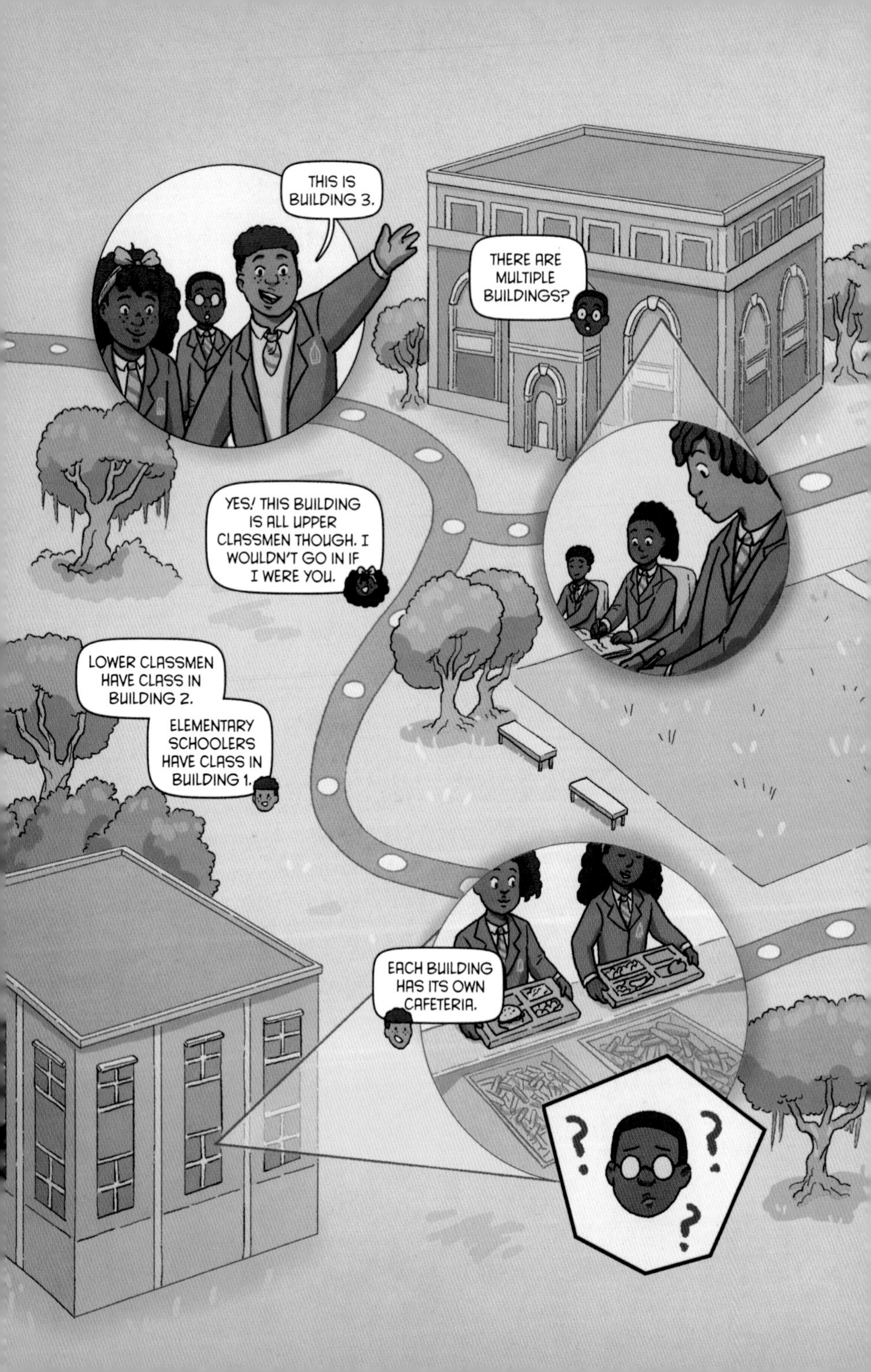
THIS IS BUILDING 3.
THERE ARE MULTIPLE BUILDINGS?
YES! THIS BUILDING IS ALL UPPER CLASSMEN THOUGH. I WOULDN'T GO IN IF I WERE YOU.
LOWER CLASSMEN HAVE CLASS IN BUILDING 2.
ELEMENTARY SCHOOLERS HAVE CLASS IN BUILDING 1.
EACH BUILDING HAS ITS OWN CAFETERIA.
?
?
?

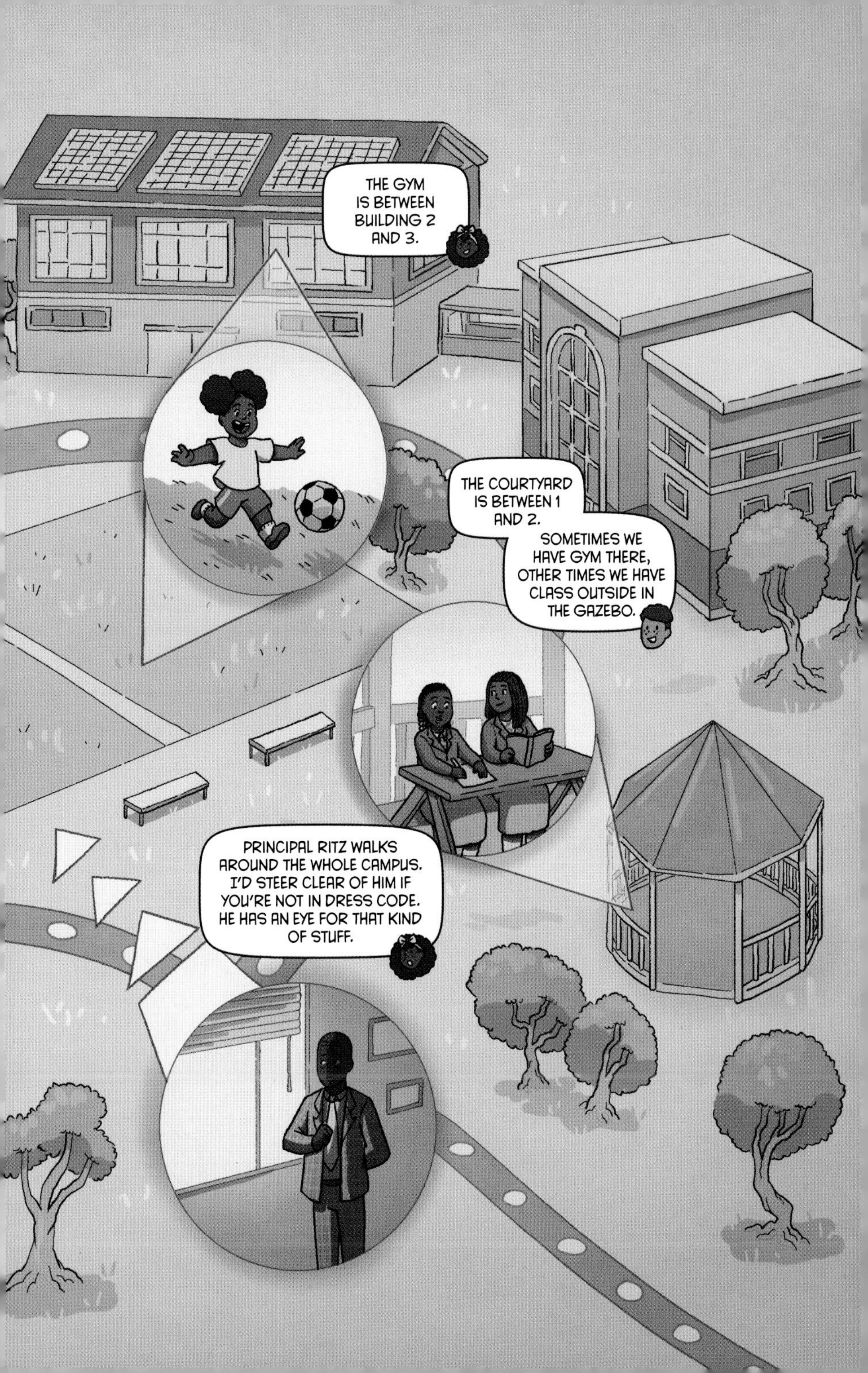
THE GYM IS BETWEEN BUILDING 2 AND 3.
THE COURTYARD IS BETWEEN 1 AND 2.
SOMETIMES WE HAVE GYM THERE, OTHER TIMES WE HAVE CLASS OUTSIDE IN THE GAZEBO.
PRINCIPAL RITZ WALKS AROUND THE WHOLE CAMPUS. I'D STEER CLEAR OF HIM IF YOU'RE NOT IN DRESS CODE. HE HAS AN EYE FOR THAT KIND OF STUFF.

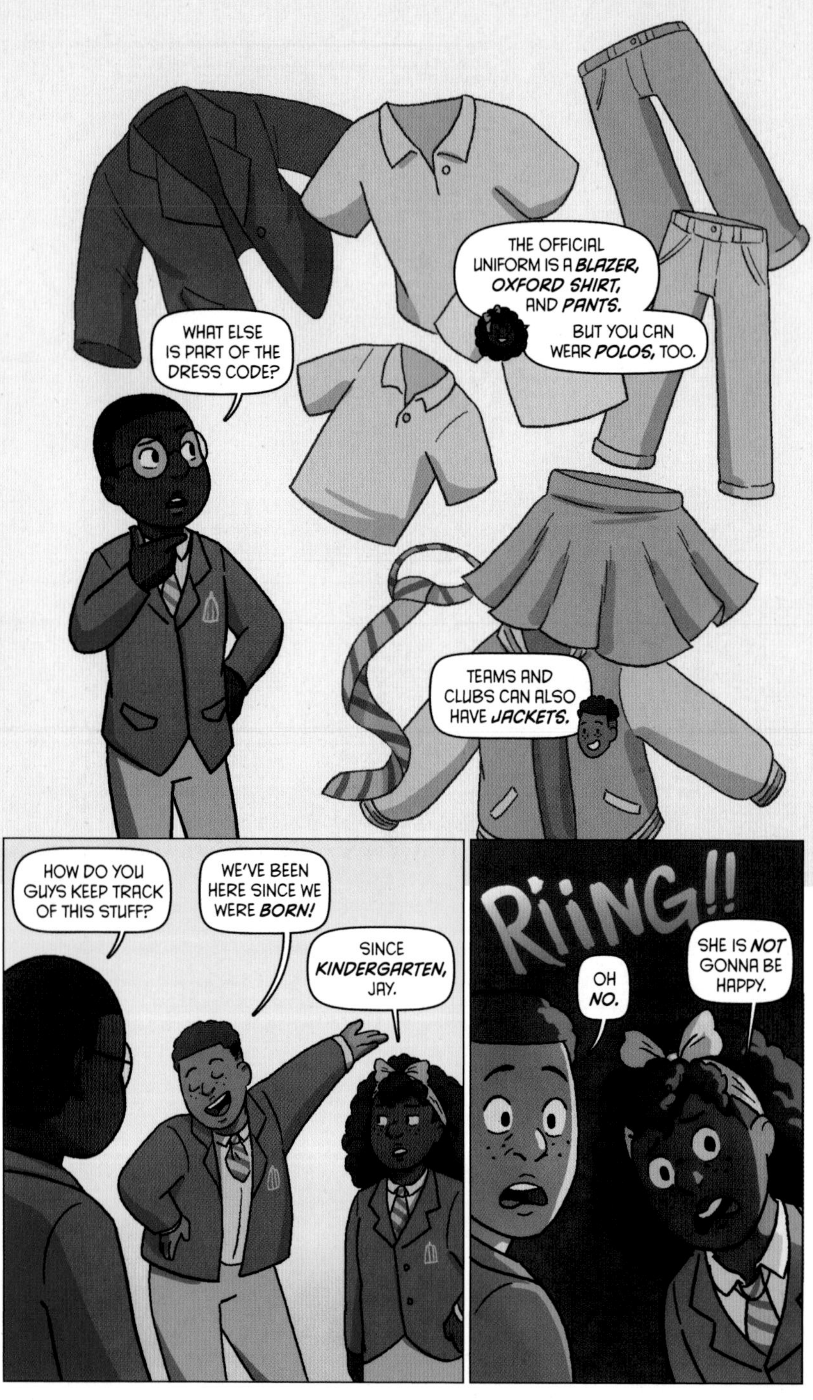
WHAT ELSE IS PART OF THE DRESS CODE?
THE OFFICIAL UNIFORM IS A BLAZER, OXFORD SHIRT, AND PANTS.
BUT YOU CAN WEAR POLOS, TOO.
TEAMS AND CLUBS CAN ALSO HAVE JACKETS.
HOW DO YOU GUYS KEEP TRACK OF THIS STUFF?
WE'VE BEEN HERE SINCE WE WERE BORN!
SINCE KINDERGARTEN, JAY.
RIING!!
OH NO.
SHE IS NOT GONNA BE HAPPY.

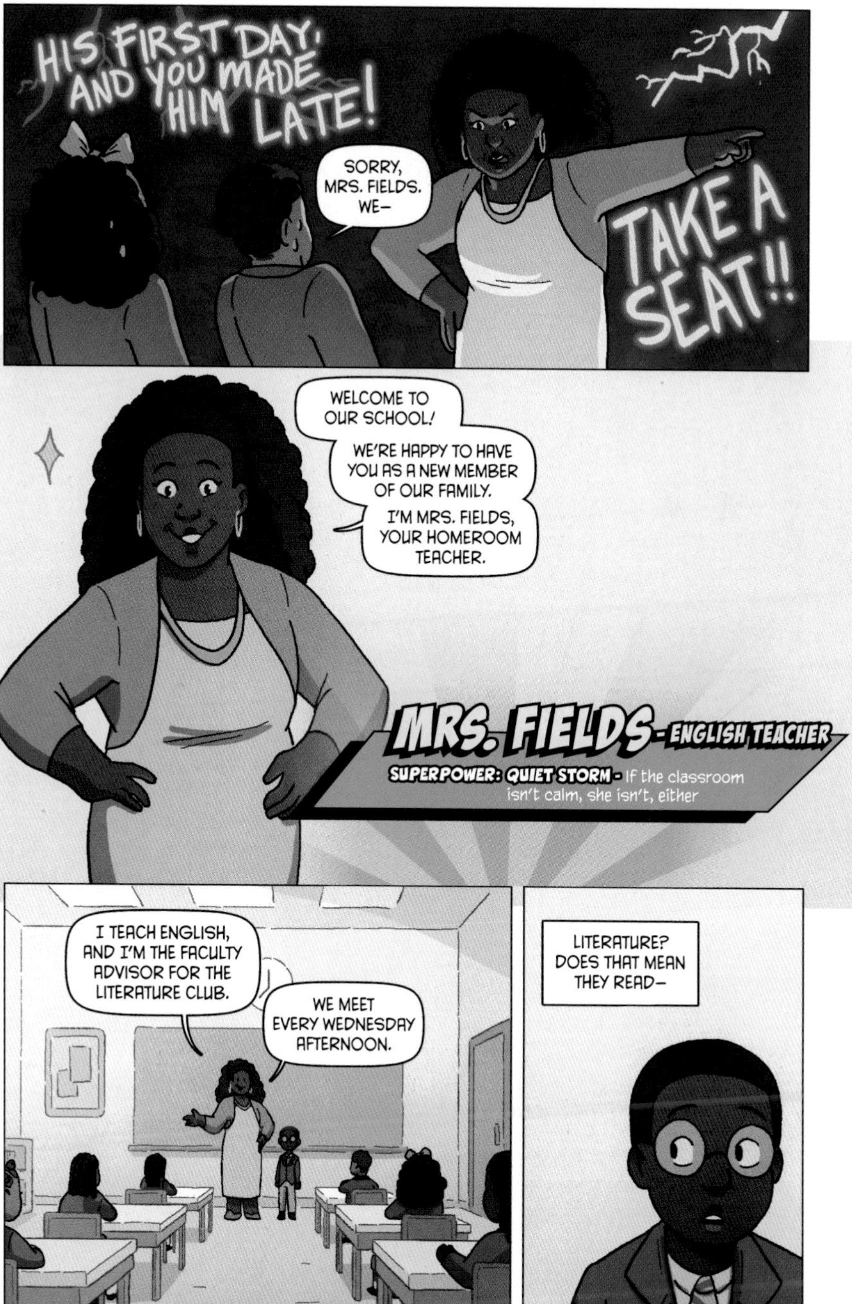
HIS FIRST DAY, AND YOU MADE HIM LATE!
SORRY, MRS. FIELDS. WE—
TAKE A SEAT!!
WELCOME TO OUR SCHOOL!
WE'RE HAPPY TO HAVE YOU AS A NEW MEMBER OF OUR FAMILY.
I'M MRS. FIELDS, YOUR HOMEROOM TEACHER.
MRS. FIELDS - ENGLISH TEACHER
SUPERPOWER: QUIET STORM - If the classroom isn't calm, she isn't, either
I TEACH ENGLISH, AND I'M THE FACULTY ADVISOR FOR THE LITERATURE CLUB.
WE MEET EVERY WEDNESDAY AFTERNOON.
LITERATURE? DOES THAT MEAN THEY READ—

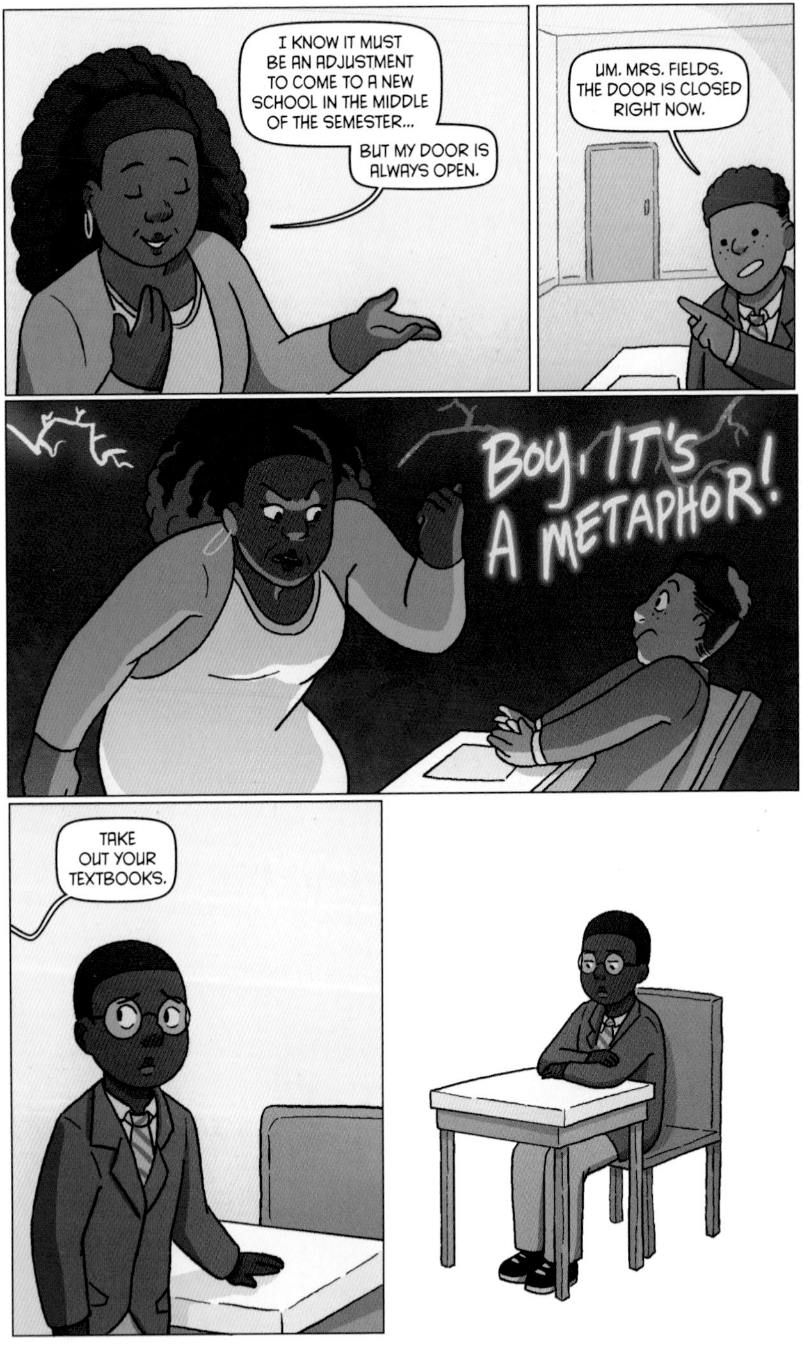
I KNOW IT MUST BE AN ADJUSTMENT TO COME TO A NEW SCHOOL IN THE MIDDLE OF THE SEMESTER...
BUT MY DOOR IS ALWAYS OPEN.
UM. MRS. FIELDS. THE DOOR IS CLOSED RIGHT NOW.
BOY, IT'S A METAPHOR!
TAKE OUT YOUR TEXTBOOKS.

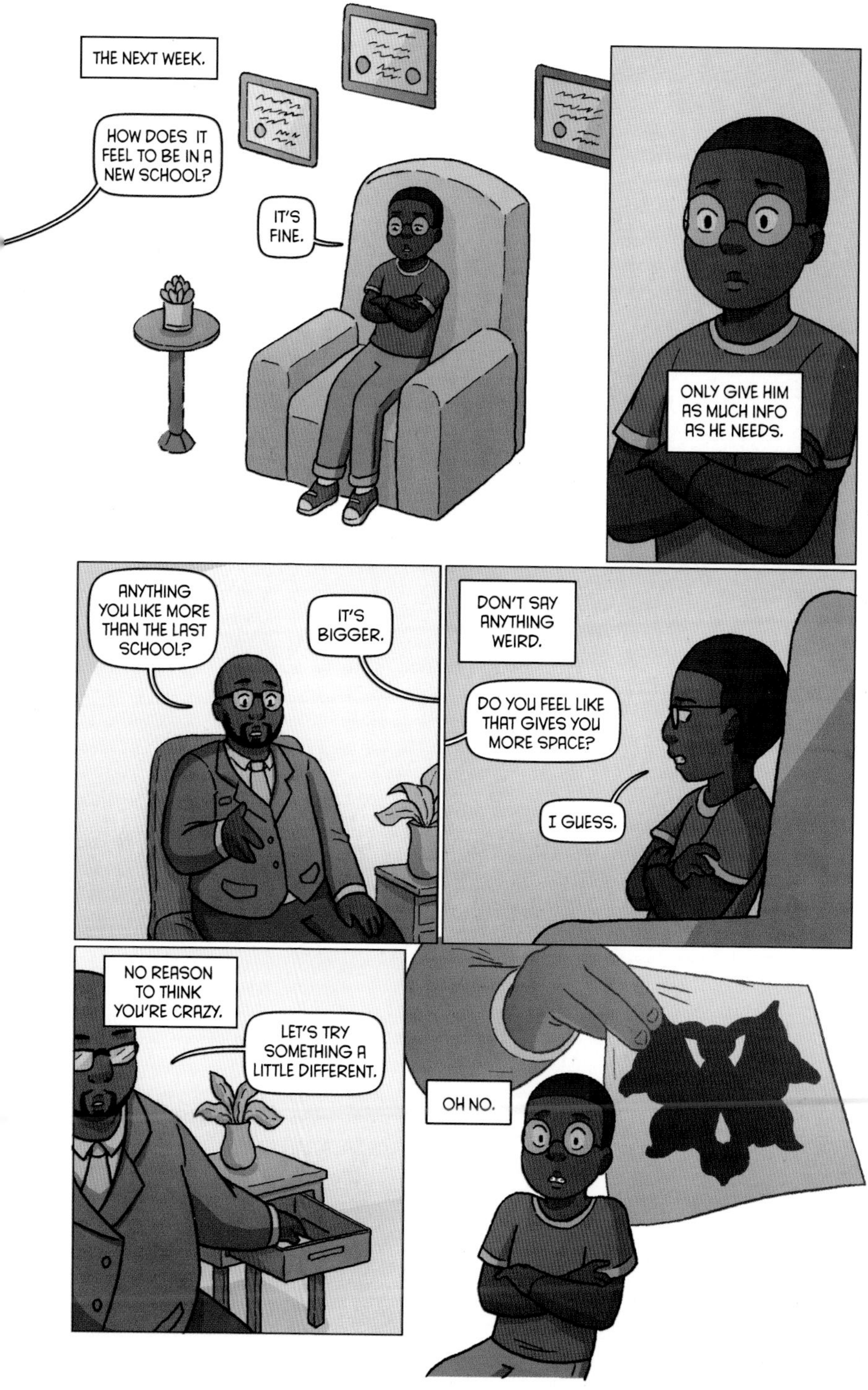
THE NEXT WEEK.
HOW DOES IT FEEL TO BE IN A NEW SCHOOL?
IT'S FINE.
ONLY GIVE HIM AS MUCH INFO AS HE NEEDS.
ANYTHING YOU LIKE MORE THAN THE LAST SCHOOL?
IT'S BIGGER.
DON'T SAY ANYTHING WEIRD.
DO YOU FEEL LIKE THAT GIVES YOU MORE SPACE?
I GUESS.
NO REASON TO THINK YOU'RE CRAZY.
LET'S TRY SOMETHING A LITTLE DIFFERENT.
OH NO.

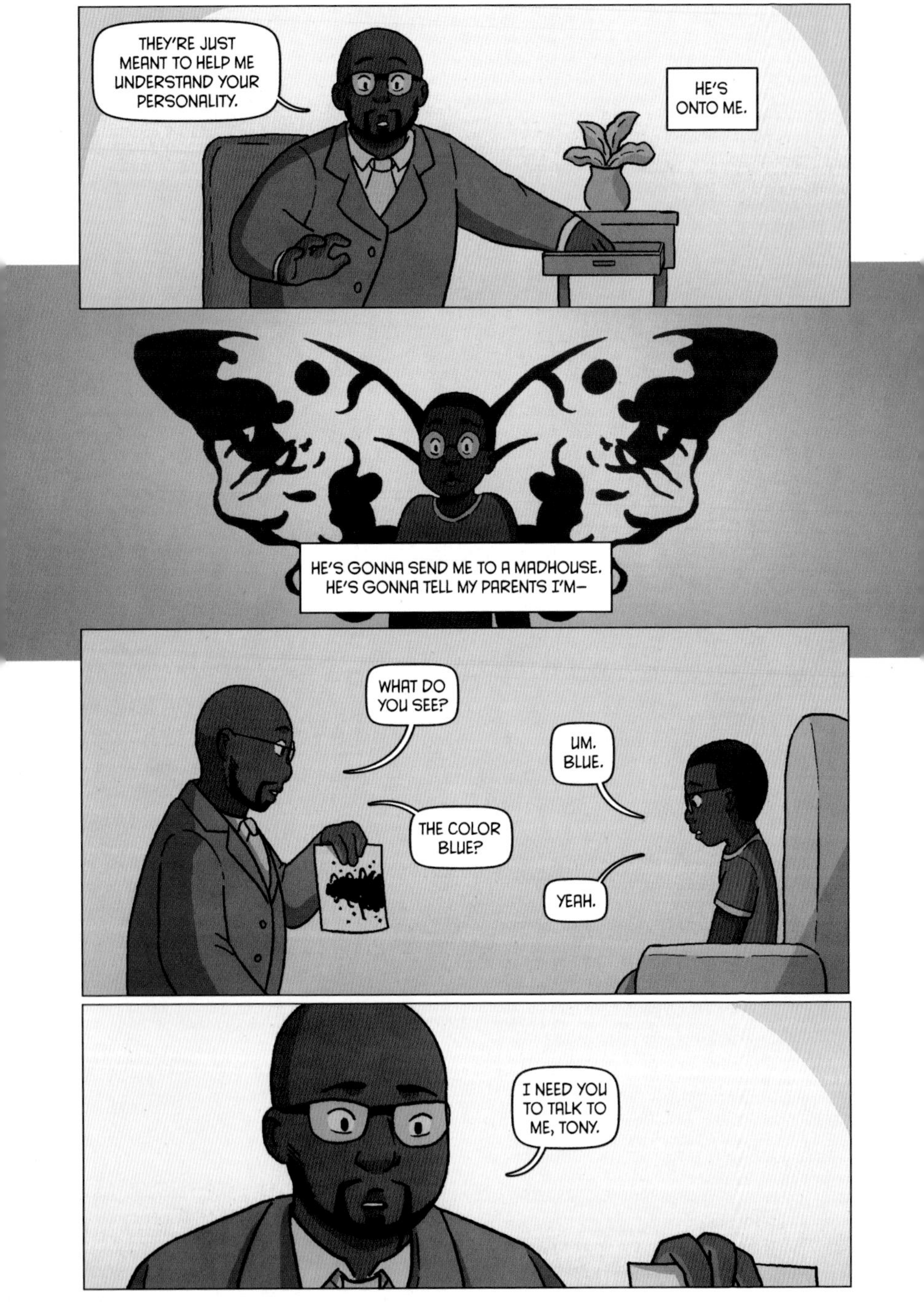
THEY'RE JUST MEANT TO HELP ME UNDERSTAND YOUR PERSONALITY.
HE'S ONTO ME.
HE'S GONNA SEND ME TO A MADHOUSE. HE'S GONNA TELL MY PARENTS I'M–
WHAT DO YOU SEE?
UM. BLUE.
THE COLOR BLUE?
YEAH.
I NEED YOU TO TALK TO ME, TONY.

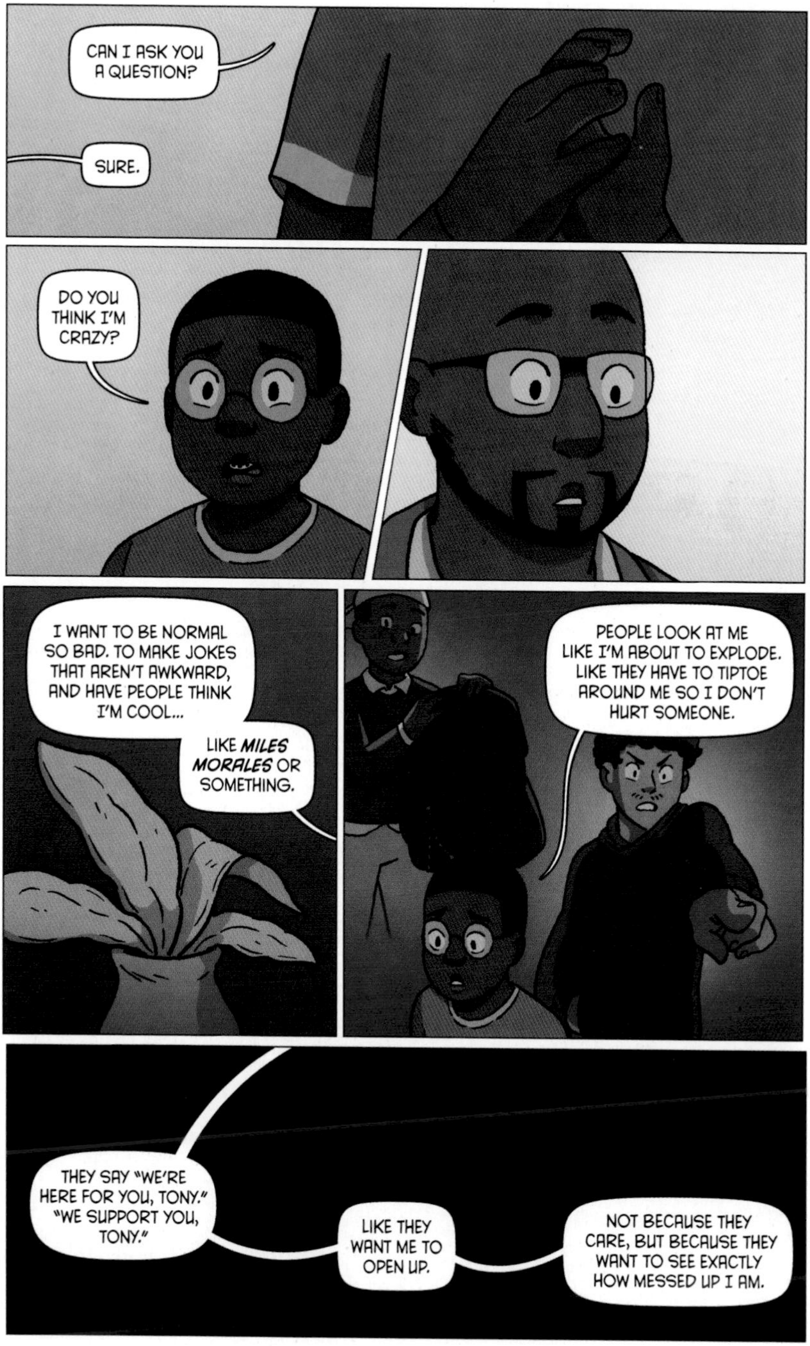
CAN I ASK YOU A QUESTION?
SURE.
DO YOU THINK I'M CRAZY?
I WANT TO BE NORMAL SO BAD. TO MAKE JOKES THAT AREN'T AWKWARD, AND HAVE PEOPLE THINK I'M COOL...
LIKE *MILES MORALES* OR SOMETHING.
PEOPLE LOOK AT ME LIKE I'M ABOUT TO EXPLODE. LIKE THEY HAVE TO TIPTOE AROUND ME SO I DON'T HURT SOMEONE.
THEY SAY "WE'RE HERE FOR YOU, TONY." "WE SUPPORT YOU, TONY."
LIKE THEY WANT ME TO OPEN UP.
NOT BECAUSE THEY CARE, BUT BECAUSE THEY WANT TO SEE EXACTLY HOW MESSED UP I AM.

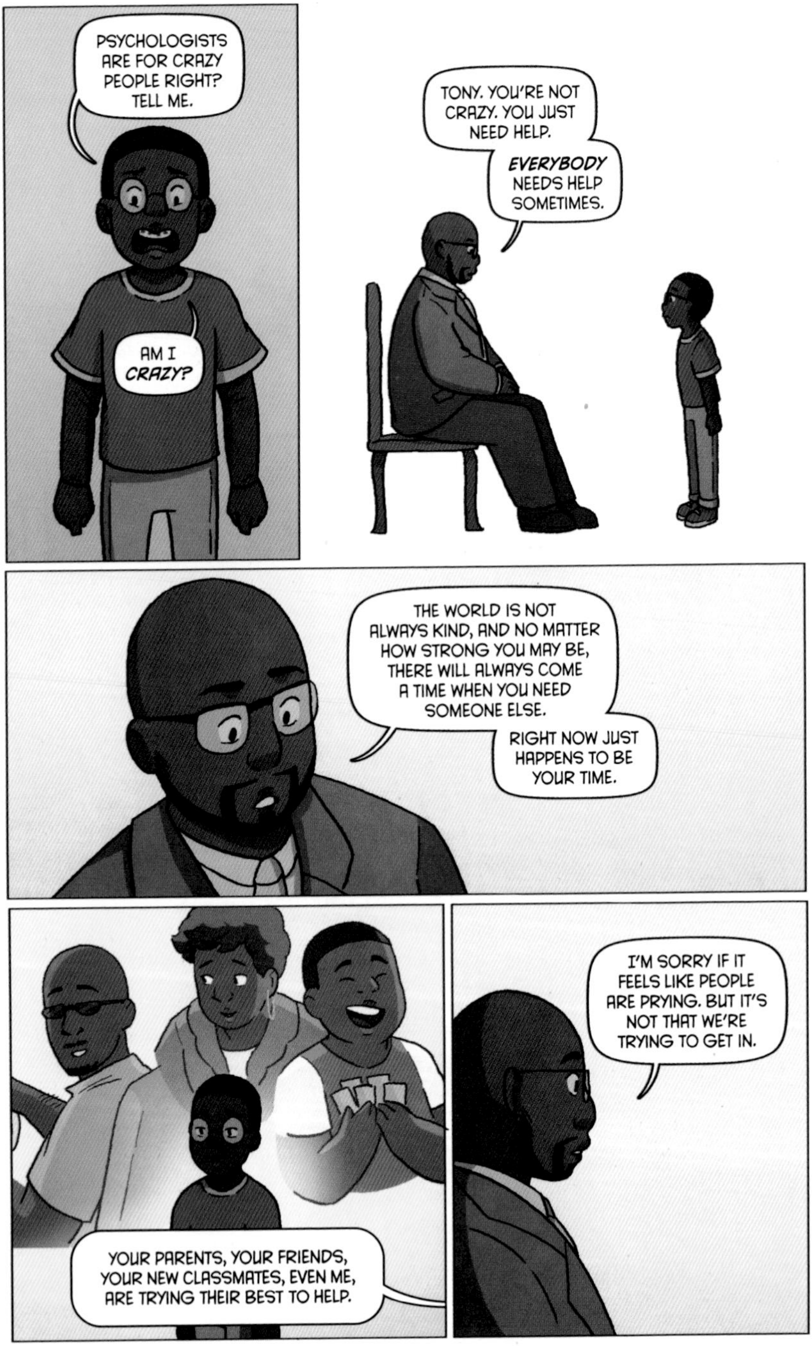
PSYCHOLOGISTS ARE FOR CRAZY PEOPLE RIGHT? TELL ME.
AM I *CRAZY?*
TONY. YOU'RE NOT CRAZY. YOU JUST NEED HELP.
EVERYBODY NEEDS HELP SOMETIMES.
THE WORLD IS NOT ALWAYS KIND, AND NO MATTER HOW STRONG YOU MAY BE, THERE WILL ALWAYS COME A TIME WHEN YOU NEED SOMEONE ELSE.
RIGHT NOW JUST HAPPENS TO BE YOUR TIME.
YOUR PARENTS, YOUR FRIENDS, YOUR NEW CLASSMATES, EVEN ME, ARE TRYING THEIR BEST TO HELP.
I'M SORRY IF IT FEELS LIKE PEOPLE ARE PRYING. BUT IT'S NOT THAT WE'RE TRYING TO GET IN.

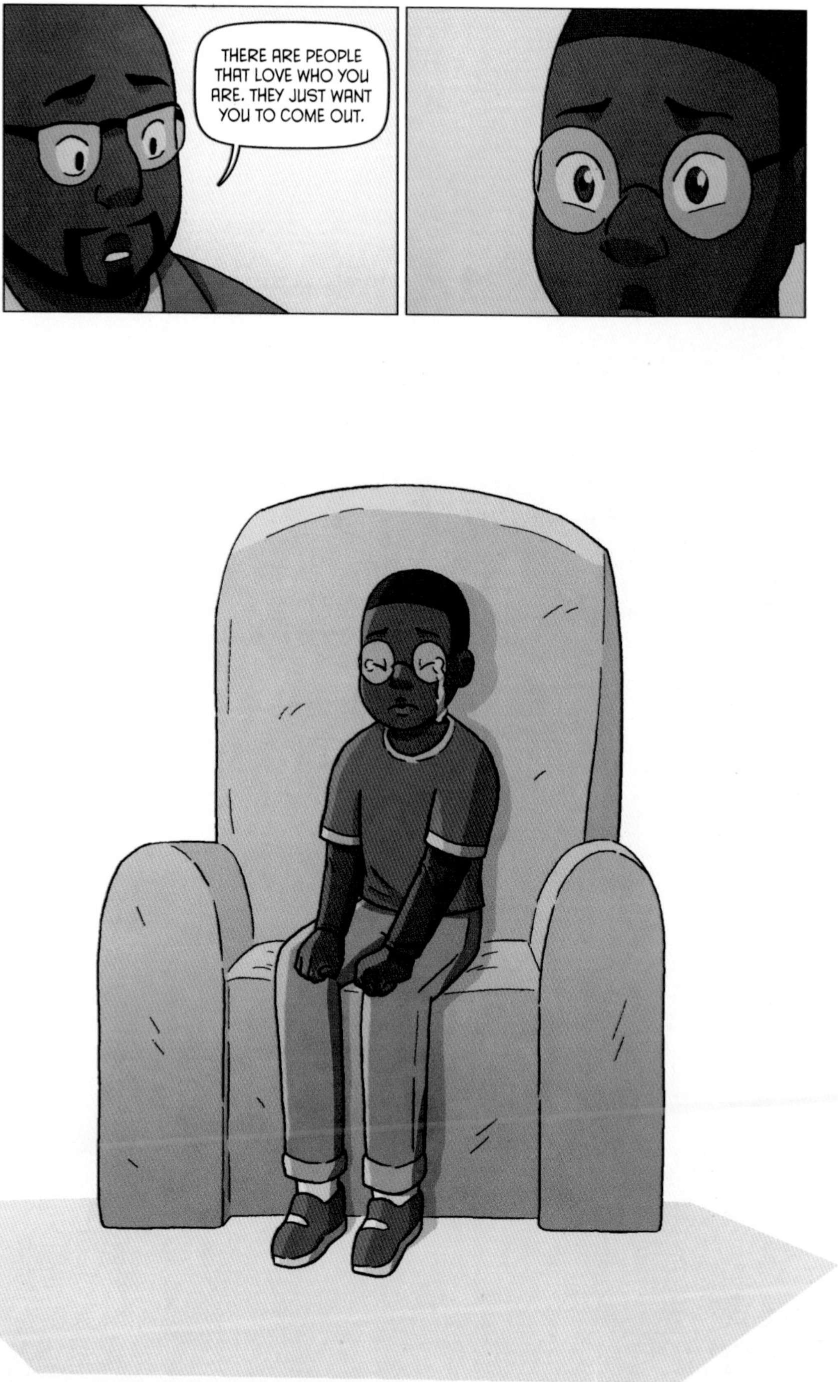
THERE ARE PEOPLE THAT LOVE WHO YOU ARE. THEY JUST WANT YOU TO COME OUT.

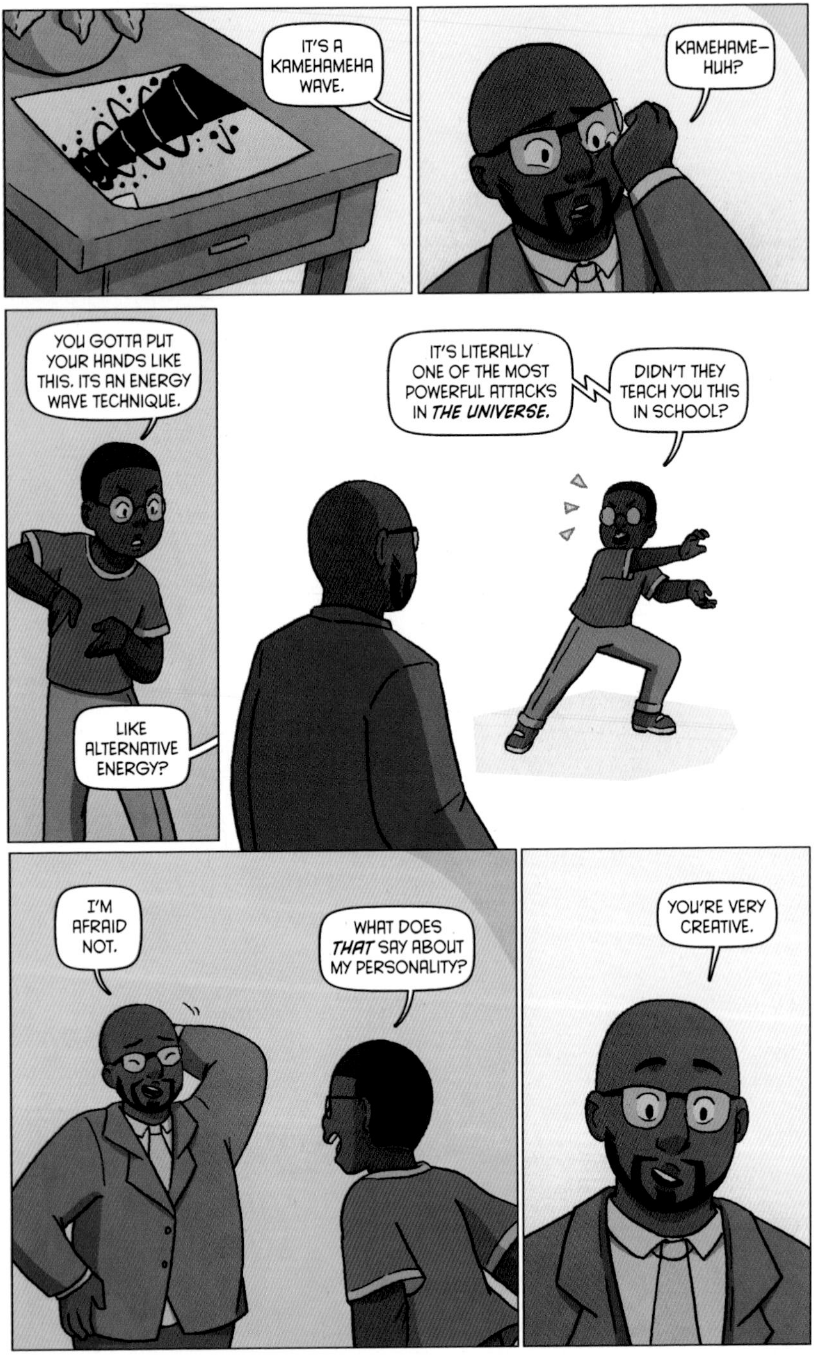
IT'S A KAMEHAMEHA WAVE.
KAMEHAME—HUH?
YOU GOTTA PUT YOUR HANDS LIKE THIS. ITS AN ENERGY WAVE TECHNIQUE.
LIKE ALTERNATIVE ENERGY?
IT'S LITERALLY ONE OF THE MOST POWERFUL ATTACKS IN *THE UNIVERSE.*
DIDN'T THEY TEACH YOU THIS IN SCHOOL?
I'M AFRAID NOT.
WHAT DOES *THAT* SAY ABOUT MY PERSONALITY?
YOU'RE VERY CREATIVE.

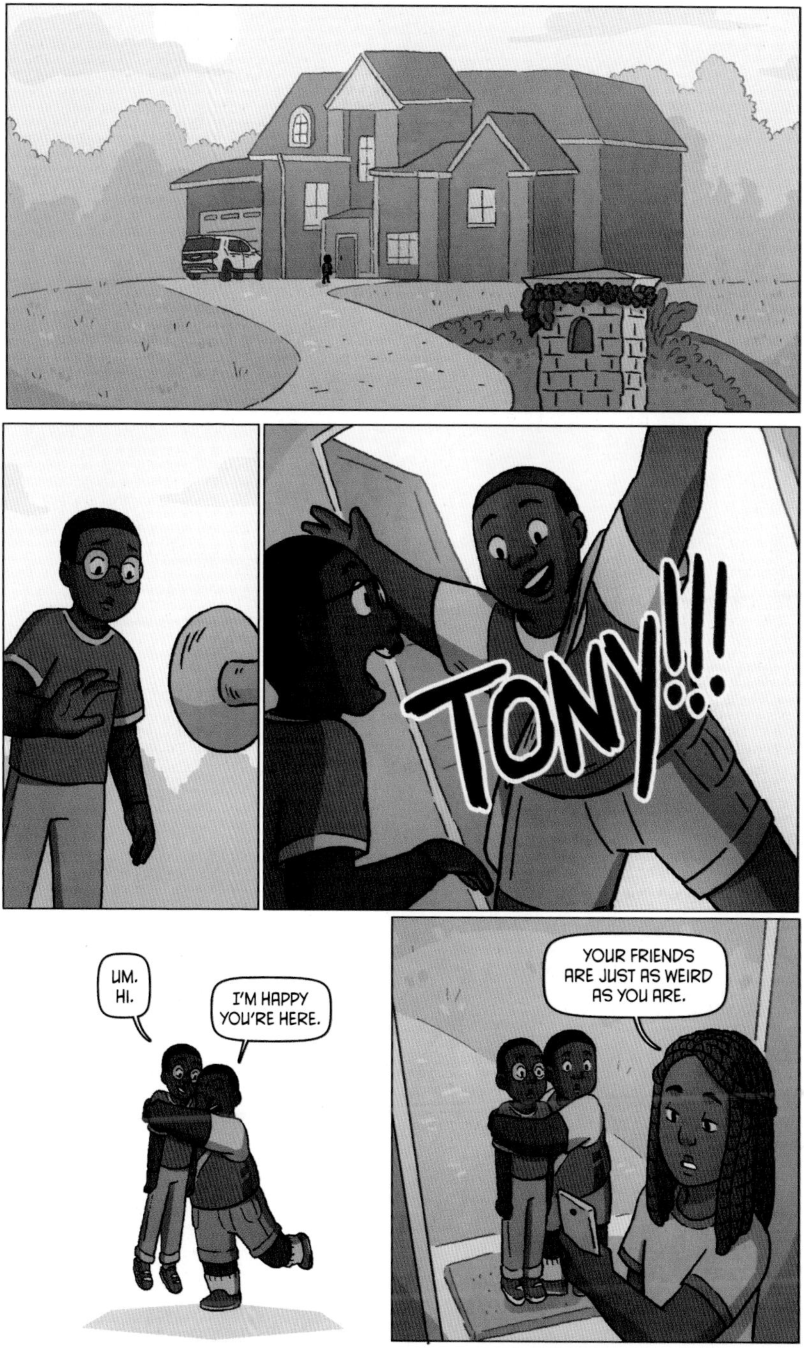
TONY!!!
UM. HI.
I'M HAPPY YOU'RE HERE.
YOUR FRIENDS ARE JUST AS WEIRD AS YOU ARE.

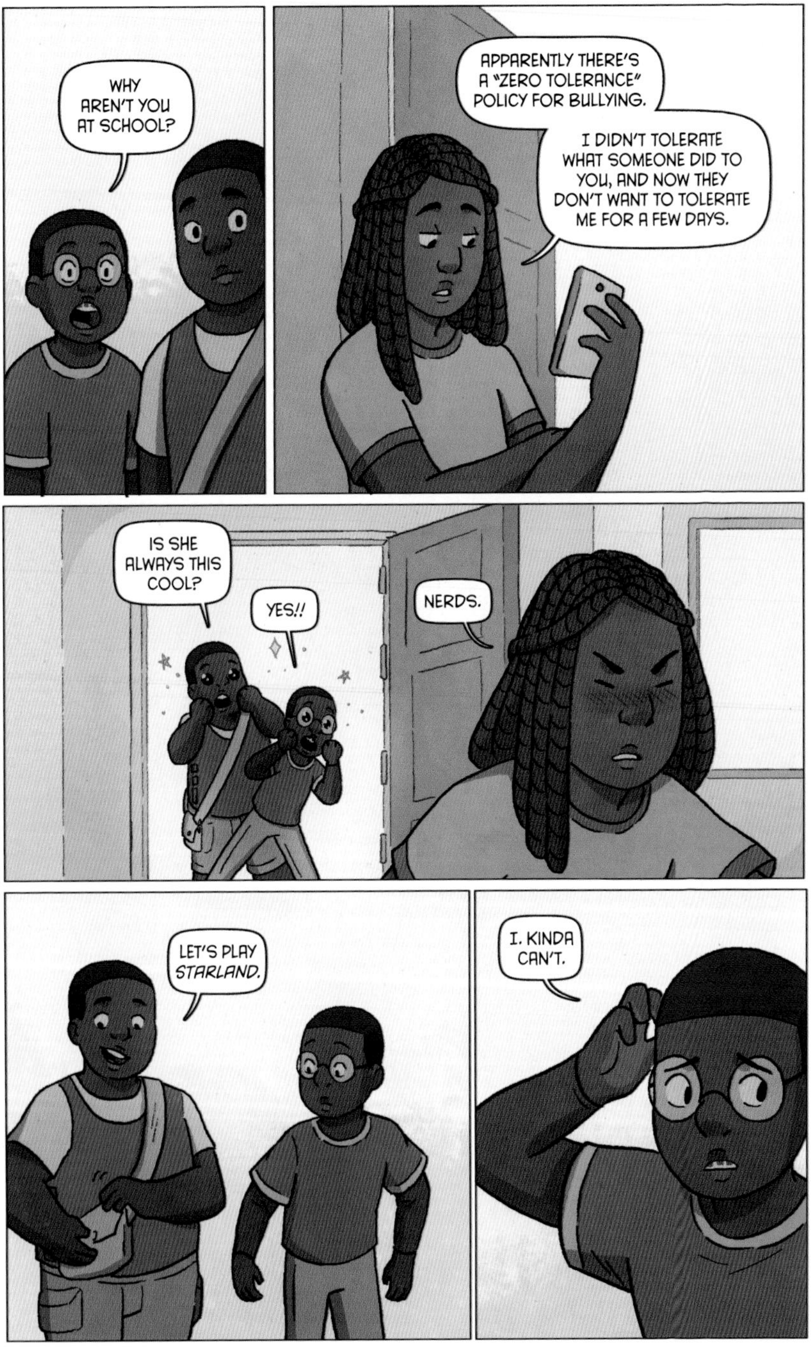
WHY AREN'T YOU AT SCHOOL?
APPARENTLY THERE'S A "ZERO TOLERANCE" POLICY FOR BULLYING.
I DIDN'T TOLERATE WHAT SOMEONE DID TO YOU, AND NOW THEY DON'T WANT TO TOLERATE ME FOR A FEW DAYS.
IS SHE ALWAYS THIS COOL?
YES!!
NERDS.
LET'S PLAY *STARLAND.*
I. KINDA CAN'T.

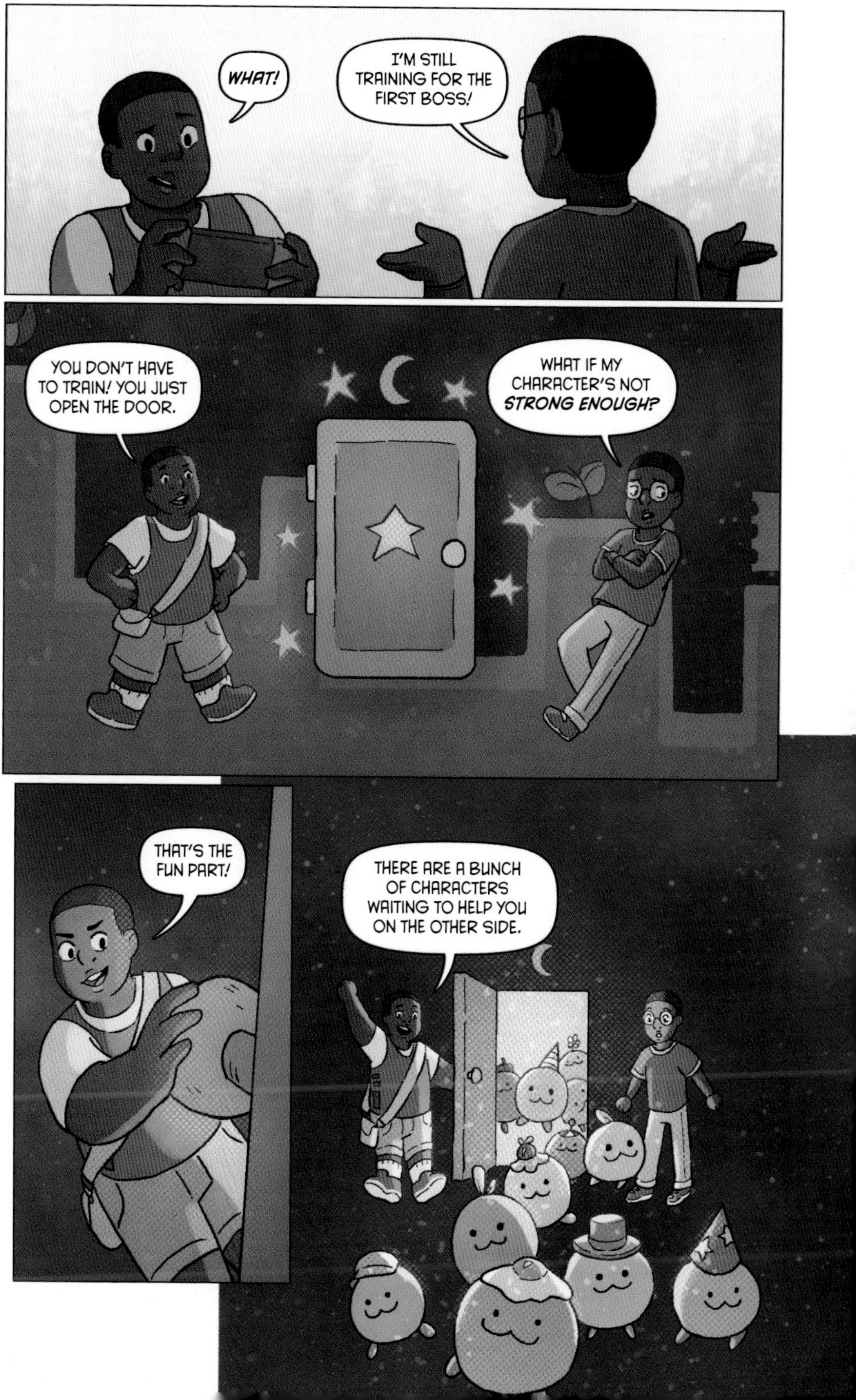
WHAT!
I'M STILL TRAINING FOR THE FIRST BOSS!
YOU DON'T HAVE TO TRAIN! YOU JUST OPEN THE DOOR.
WHAT IF MY CHARACTER'S NOT STRONG ENOUGH?
THAT'S THE FUN PART!
THERE ARE A BUNCH OF CHARACTERS WAITING TO HELP YOU ON THE OTHER SIDE.

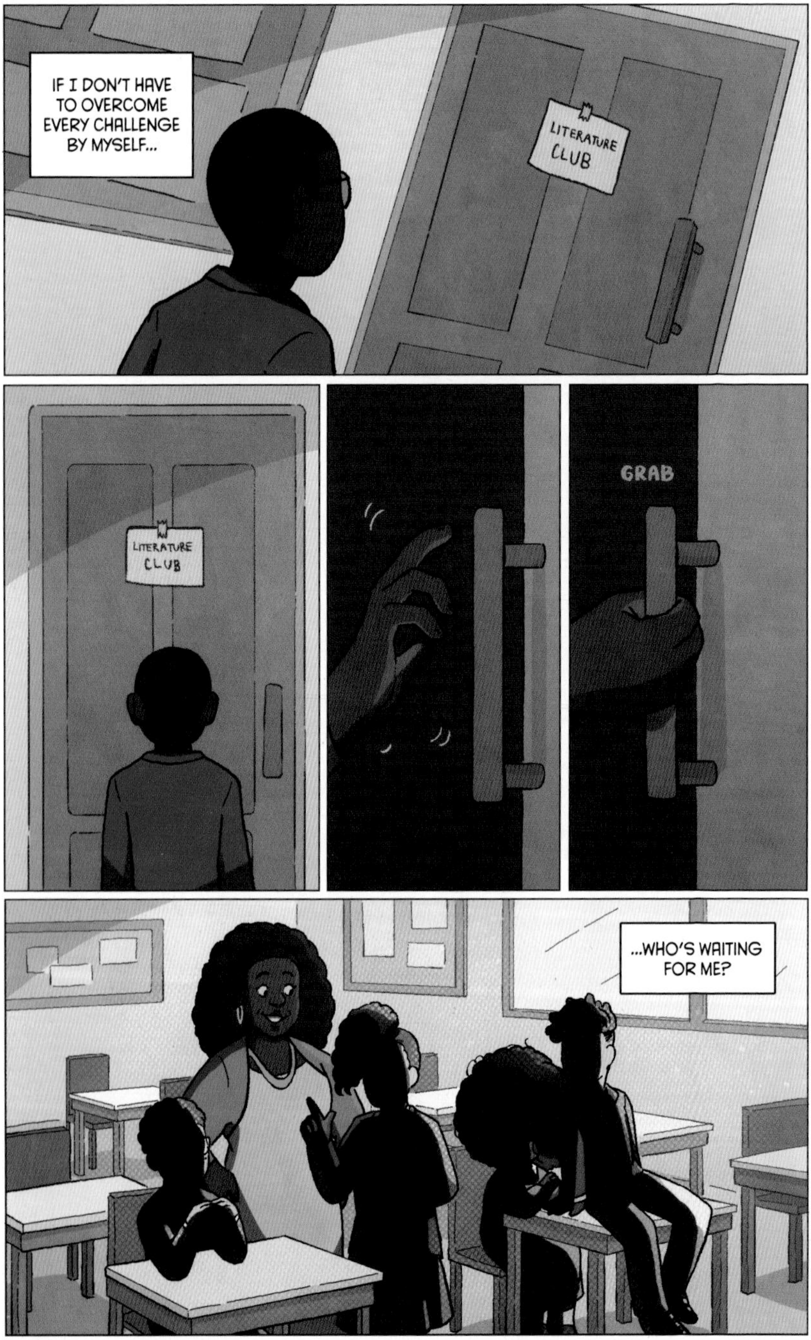
IF I DON'T HAVE TO OVERCOME EVERY CHALLENGE BY MYSELF...
LITERATURE CLUB
LITERATURE CLUB
GRAB
...WHO'S WAITING FOR ME?

CHAPTER 5

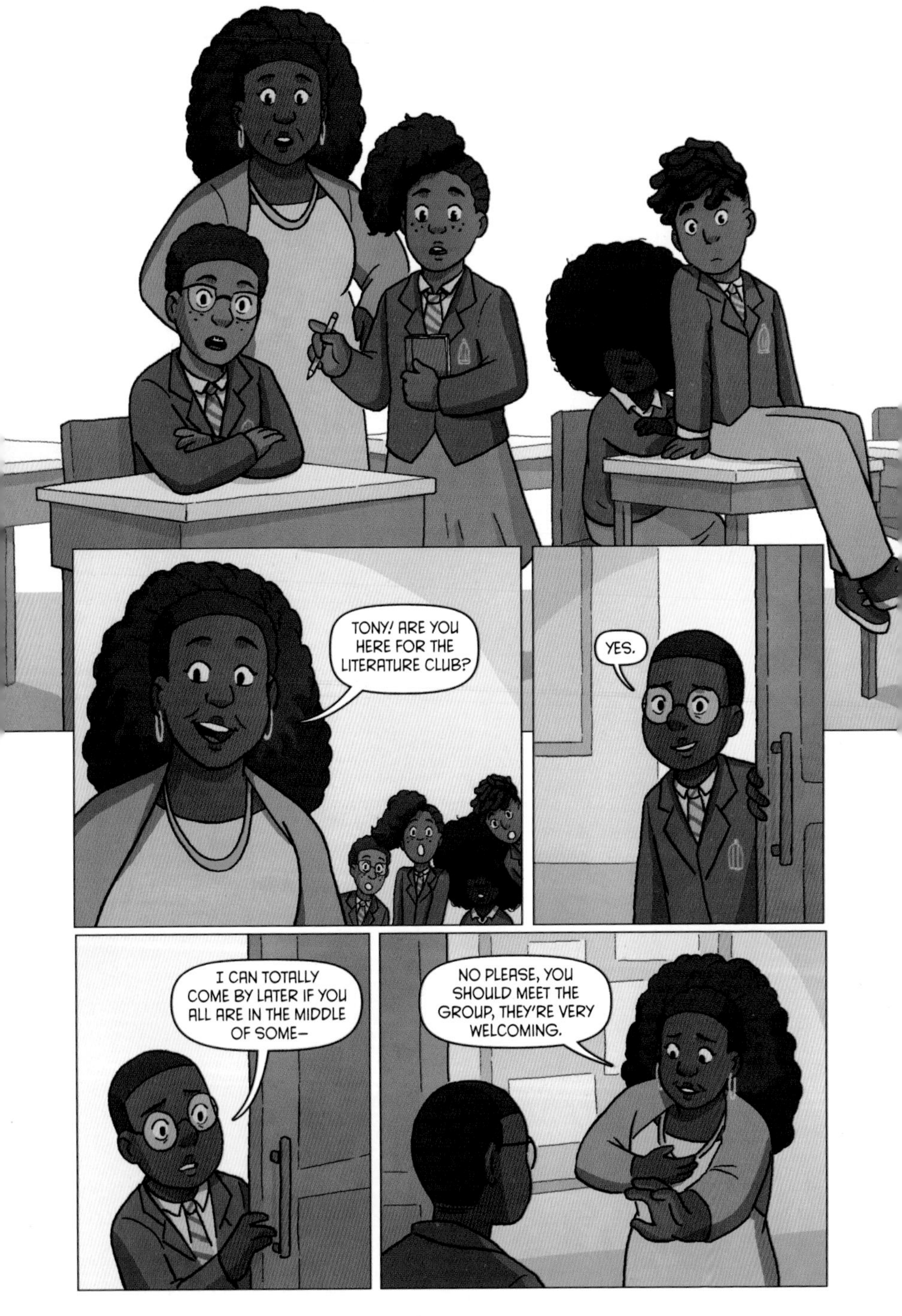
TONY! ARE YOU HERE FOR THE LITERATURE CLUB?
YES.
I CAN TOTALLY COME BY LATER IF YOU ALL ARE IN THE MIDDLE OF SOME—
NO PLEASE, YOU SHOULD MEET THE GROUP, THEY'RE VERY WELCOMING.

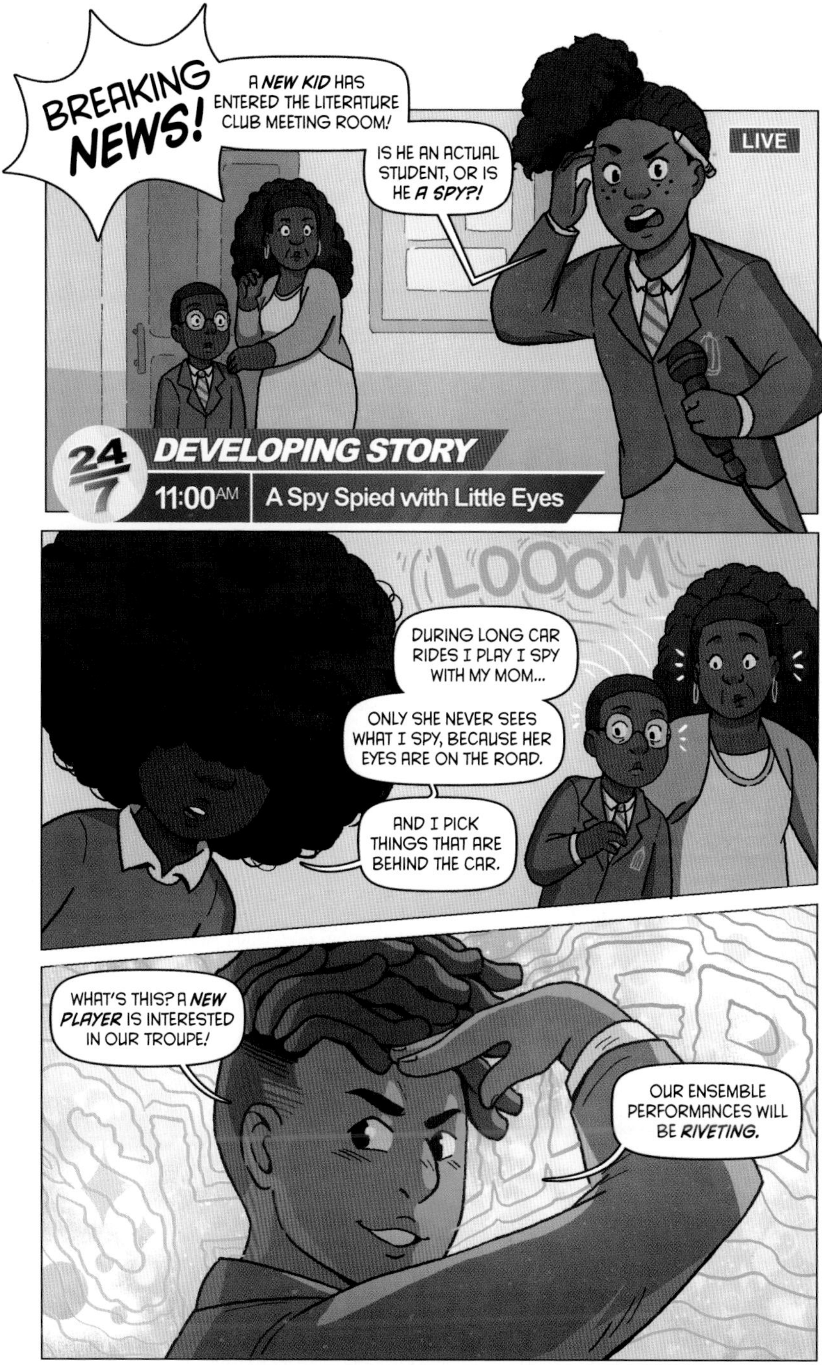
BREAKING NEWS!
A NEW KID HAS ENTERED THE LITERATURE CLUB MEETING ROOM!
IS HE AN ACTUAL STUDENT, OR IS HE A SPY?!
LIVE
24/7
DEVELOPING STORY
11:00AM
A Spy Spied with Little Eyes
LOOOM
DURING LONG CAR RIDES I PLAY I SPY WITH MY MOM...
ONLY SHE NEVER SEES WHAT I SPY, BECAUSE HER EYES ARE ON THE ROAD.
AND I PICK THINGS THAT ARE BEHIND THE CAR.
WHAT'S THIS? A NEW PLAYER IS INTERESTED IN OUR TROUPE!
OUR ENSEMBLE PERFORMANCES WILL BE RIVETING.

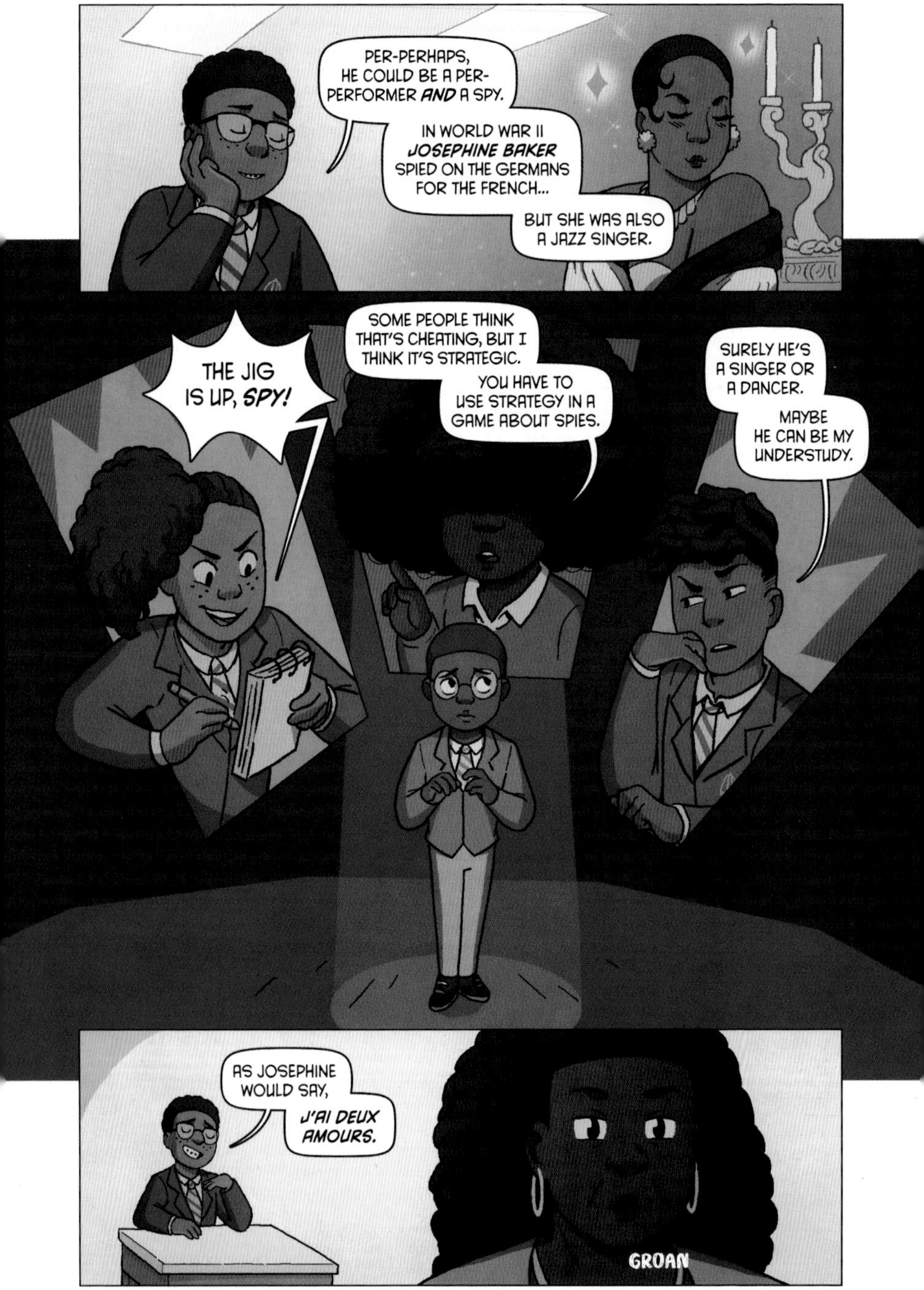
PER-PERHAPS, HE COULD BE A PER-PERFORMER AND A SPY.
IN WORLD WAR II JOSEPHINE BAKER SPIED ON THE GERMANS FOR THE FRENCH...
BUT SHE WAS ALSO A JAZZ SINGER.
THE JIG IS UP, SPY!
SOME PEOPLE THINK THAT'S CHEATING, BUT I THINK IT'S STRATEGIC.
YOU HAVE TO USE STRATEGY IN A GAME ABOUT SPIES.
SURELY HE'S A SINGER OR A DANCER.
MAYBE HE CAN BE MY UNDERSTUDY.
AS JOSEPHINE WOULD SAY,
J'AI DEUX AMOURS.
GROAN

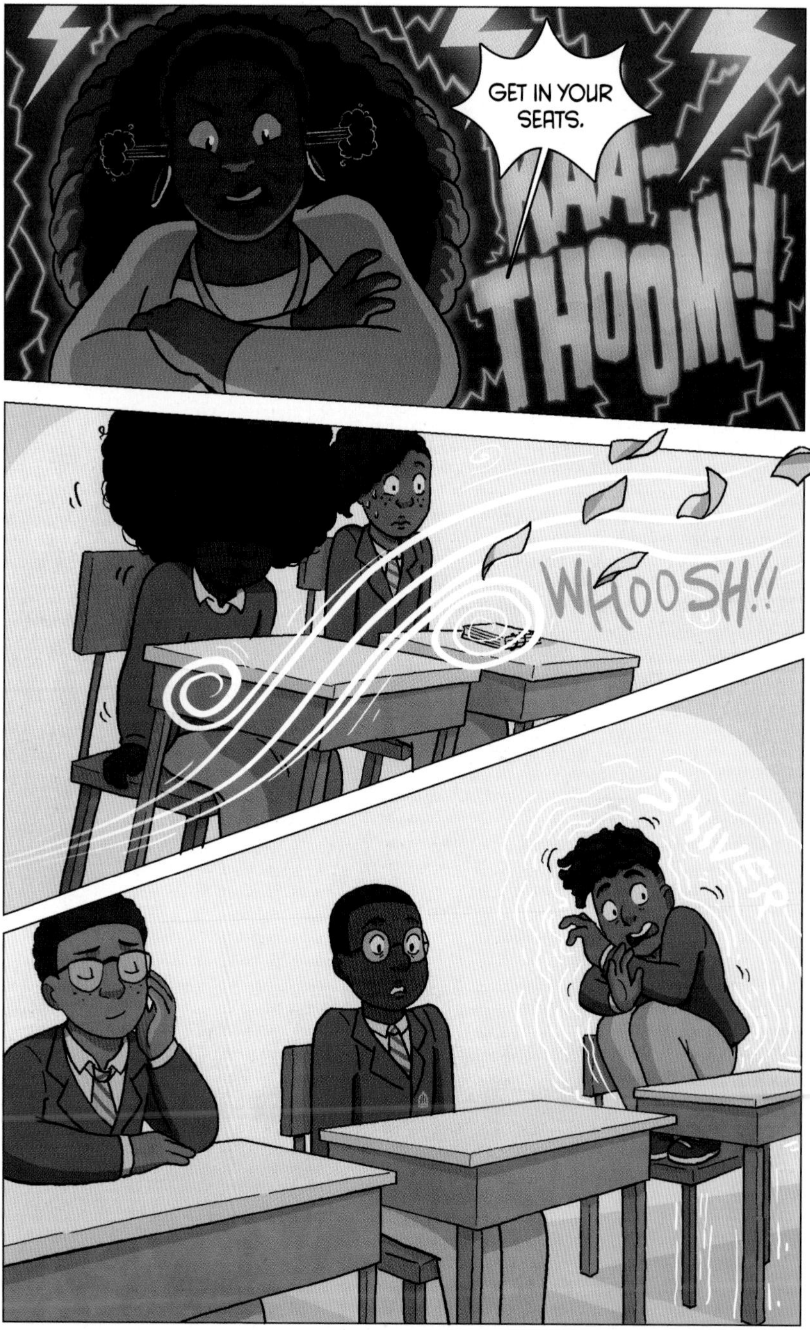
GET IN YOUR SEATS.
THOOM!!
WHOOSH!!
SHIVER

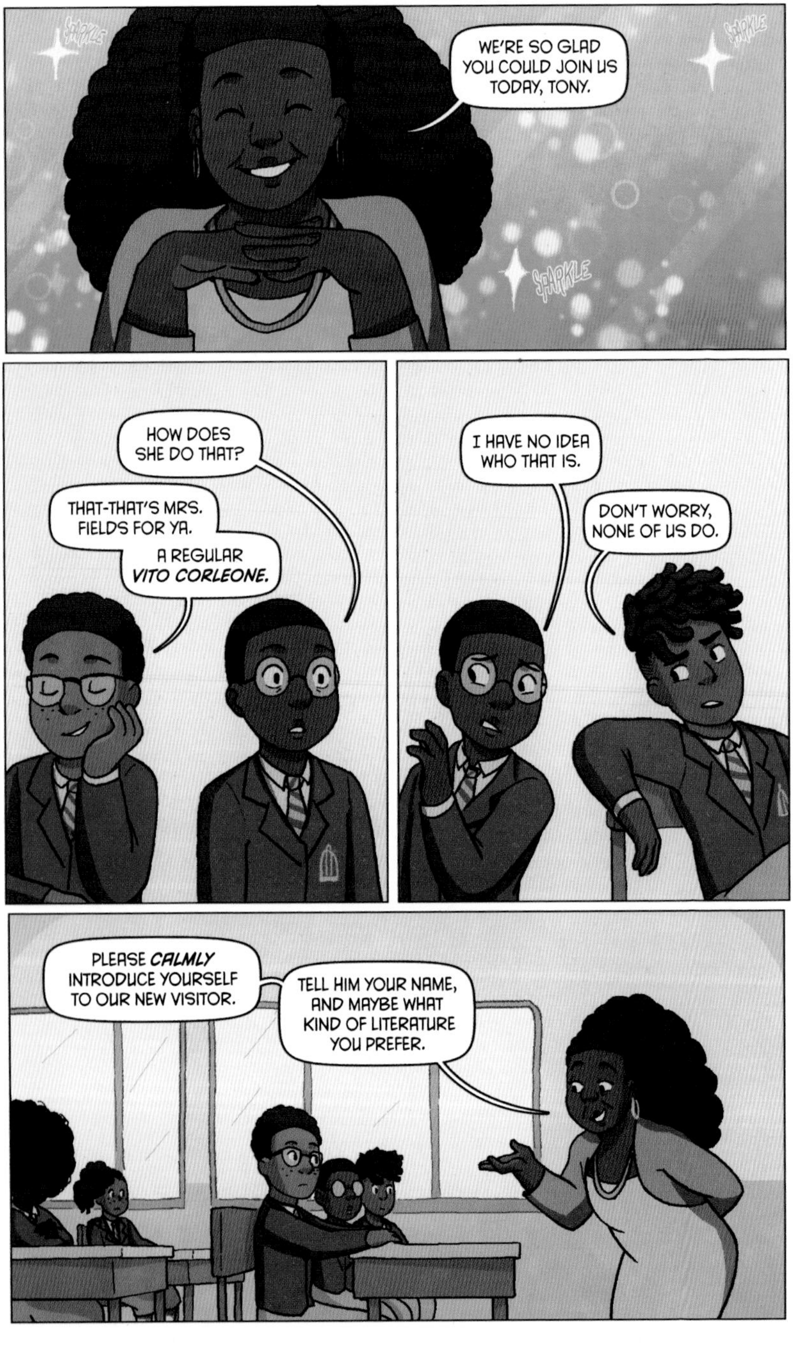
SPARKLE
SPARKLE
WE'RE SO GLAD YOU COULD JOIN US TODAY, TONY.
SPARKLE
HOW DOES SHE DO THAT?
THAT-THAT'S MRS. FIELDS FOR YA.
A REGULAR *VITO CORLEONE.*
I HAVE NO IDEA WHO THAT IS.
DON'T WORRY, NONE OF US DO.
PLEASE *CALMLY* INTRODUCE YOURSELF TO OUR NEW VISITOR.
TELL HIM YOUR NAME, AND MAYBE WHAT KIND OF LITERATURE YOU PREFER.

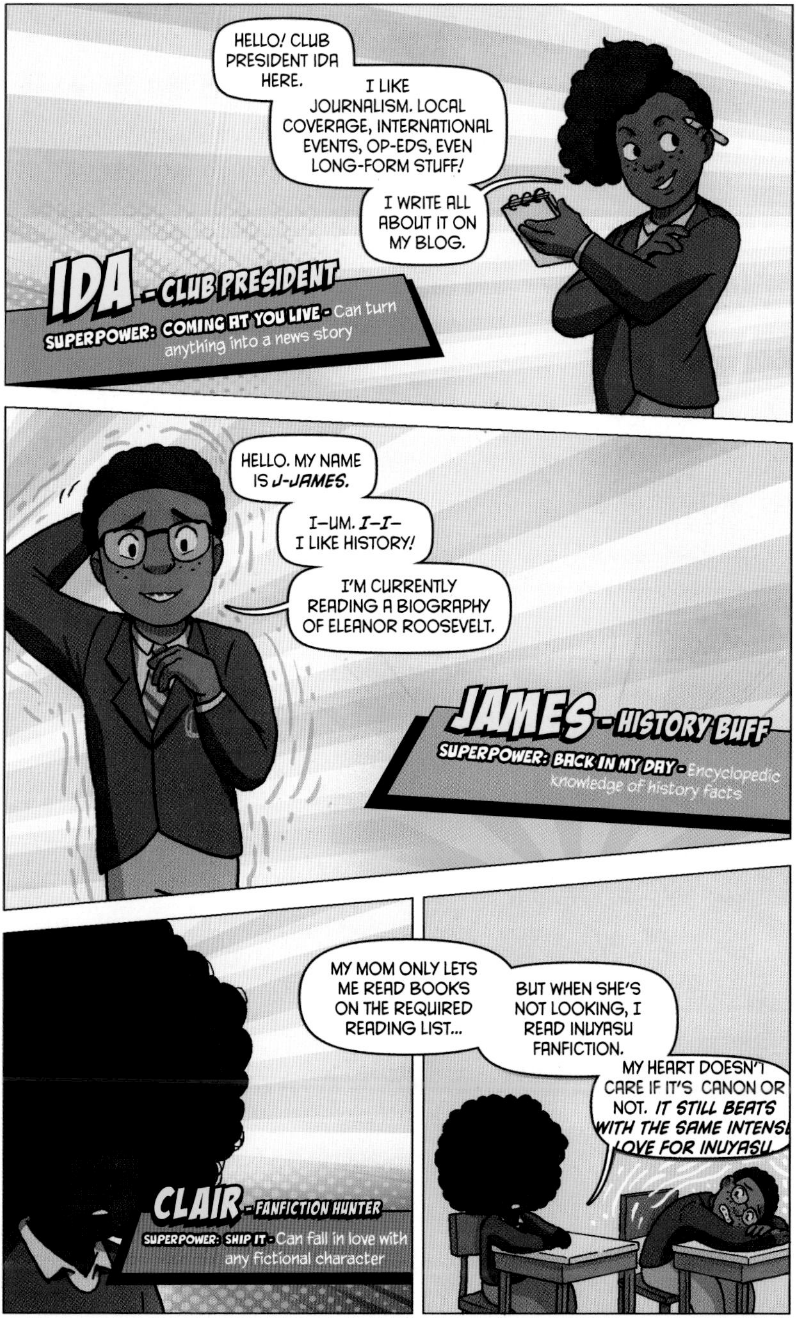
HELLO! CLUB PRESIDENT IDA HERE.
I LIKE JOURNALISM. LOCAL COVERAGE, INTERNATIONAL EVENTS, OP-EDS, EVEN LONG-FORM STUFF!
I WRITE ALL ABOUT IT ON MY BLOG.
IDA - CLUB PRESIDENT
SUPERPOWER: COMING AT YOU LIVE - Can turn anything into a news story
HELLO. MY NAME IS J-JAMES.
I-UM. I-I- I LIKE HISTORY!
I'M CURRENTLY READING A BIOGRAPHY OF ELEANOR ROOSEVELT.
JAMES - HISTORY BUFF
SUPERPOWER: BACK IN MY DAY - Encyclopedic knowledge of history facts
CLAIR - FANFICTION HUNTER
SUPERPOWER: SHIP IT - Can fall in love with any fictional character
MY MOM ONLY LETS ME READ BOOKS ON THE REQUIRED READING LIST...
BUT WHEN SHE'S NOT LOOKING, I READ INUYASU FANFICTION.
MY HEART DOESN'T CARE IF IT'S CANON OR NOT. IT STILL BEATS WITH THE SAME INTENSE LOVE FOR INUYASU.

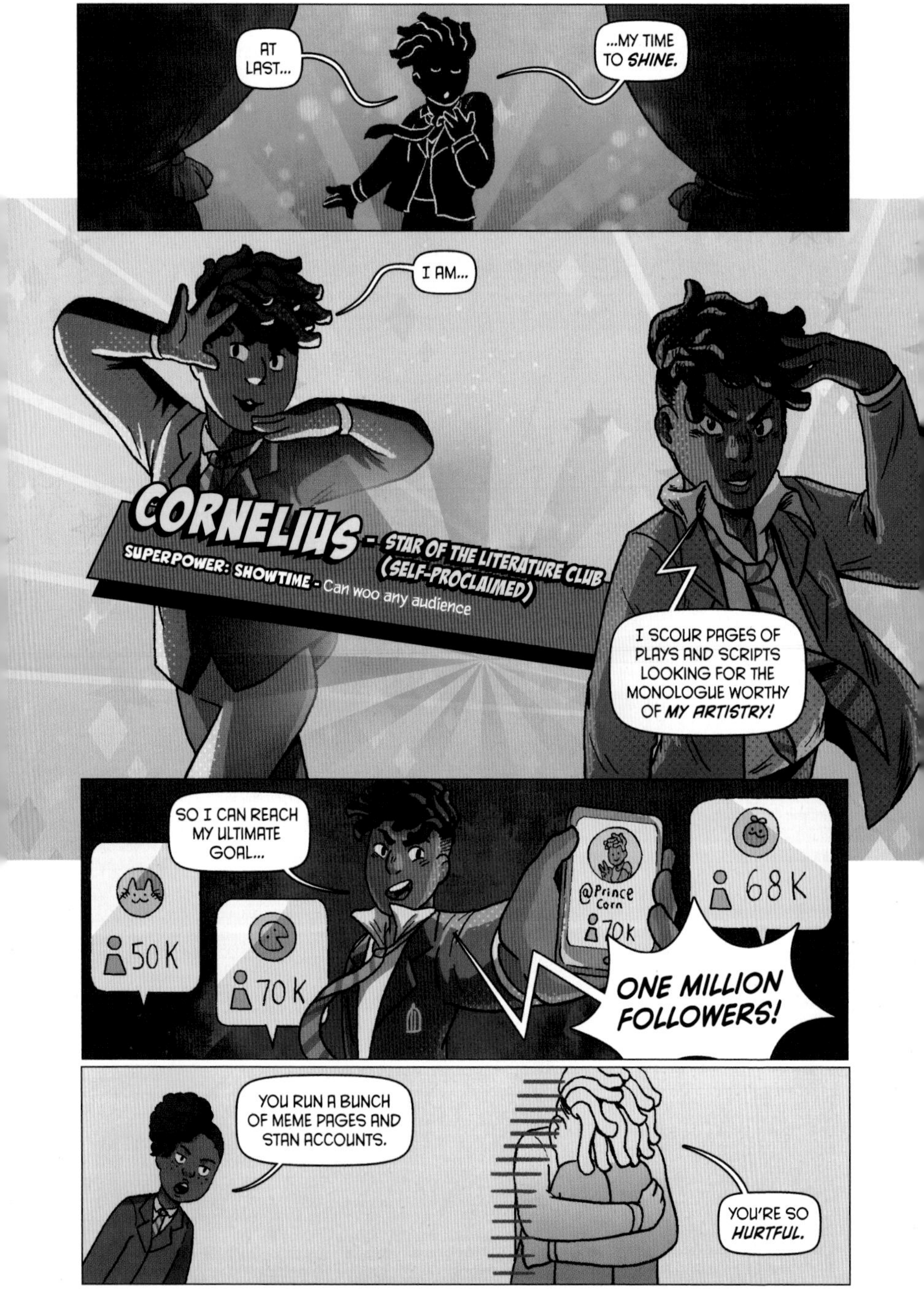
AT LAST...
...MY TIME TO SHINE.
I AM...
CORNELIUS - STAR OF THE LITERATURE CLUB (SELF-PROCLAIMED)
SUPERPOWER: SHOWTIME - Can woo any audience
I SCOUR PAGES OF PLAYS AND SCRIPTS LOOKING FOR THE MONOLOGUE WORTHY OF MY ARTISTRY!
SO I CAN REACH MY ULTIMATE GOAL...
50K
70K
@Prince Corn
70K
68K
ONE MILLION FOLLOWERS!
YOU RUN A BUNCH OF MEME PAGES AND STAN ACCOUNTS.
YOU'RE SO HURTFUL.

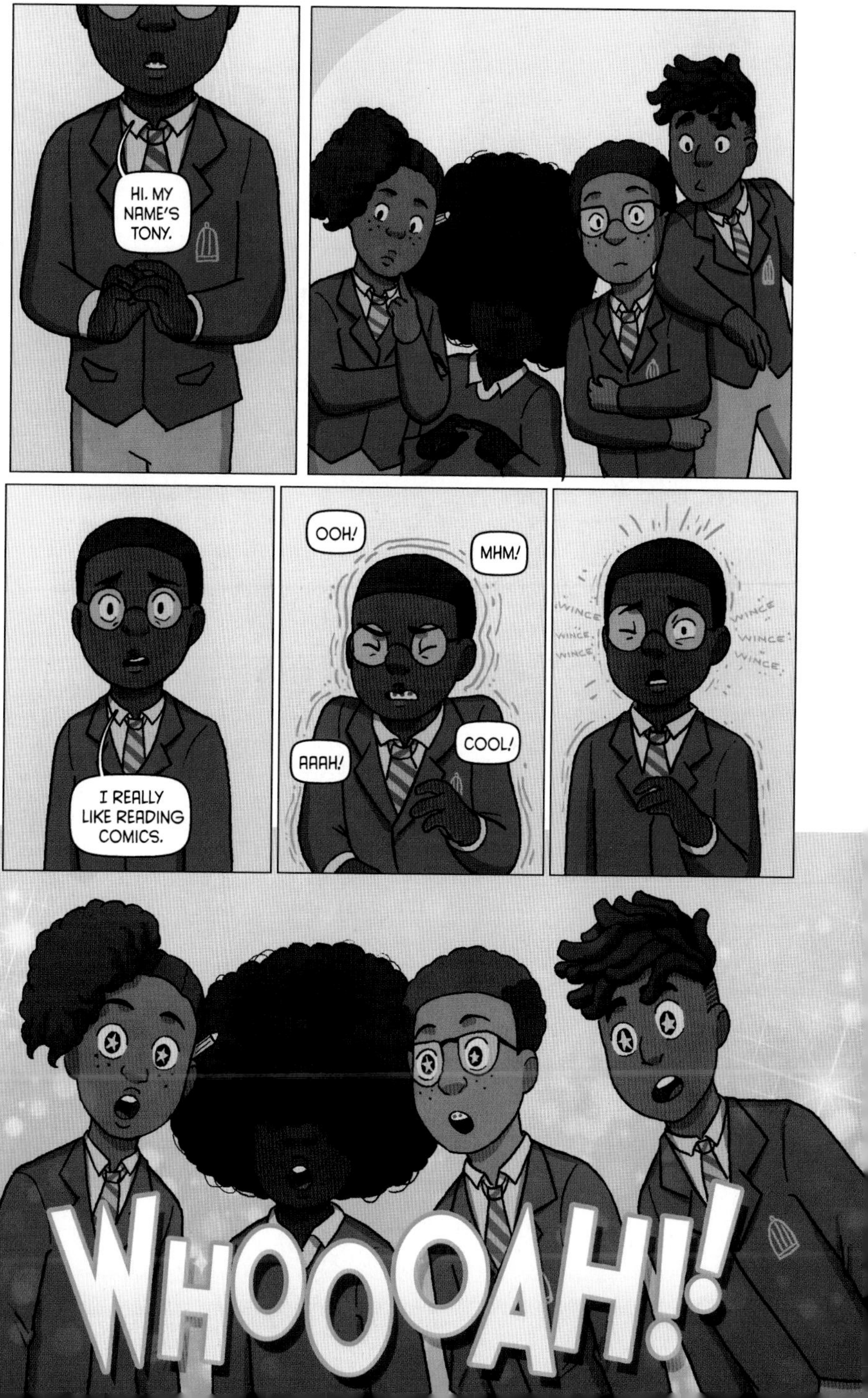
HI. MY NAME'S TONY.
I REALLY LIKE READING COMICS.
OOH!
MHM!
AAAH!
COOL!
WINCE
WINCE
WINCE
WINCE
WINCE
WINCE
WHOOOAH!!

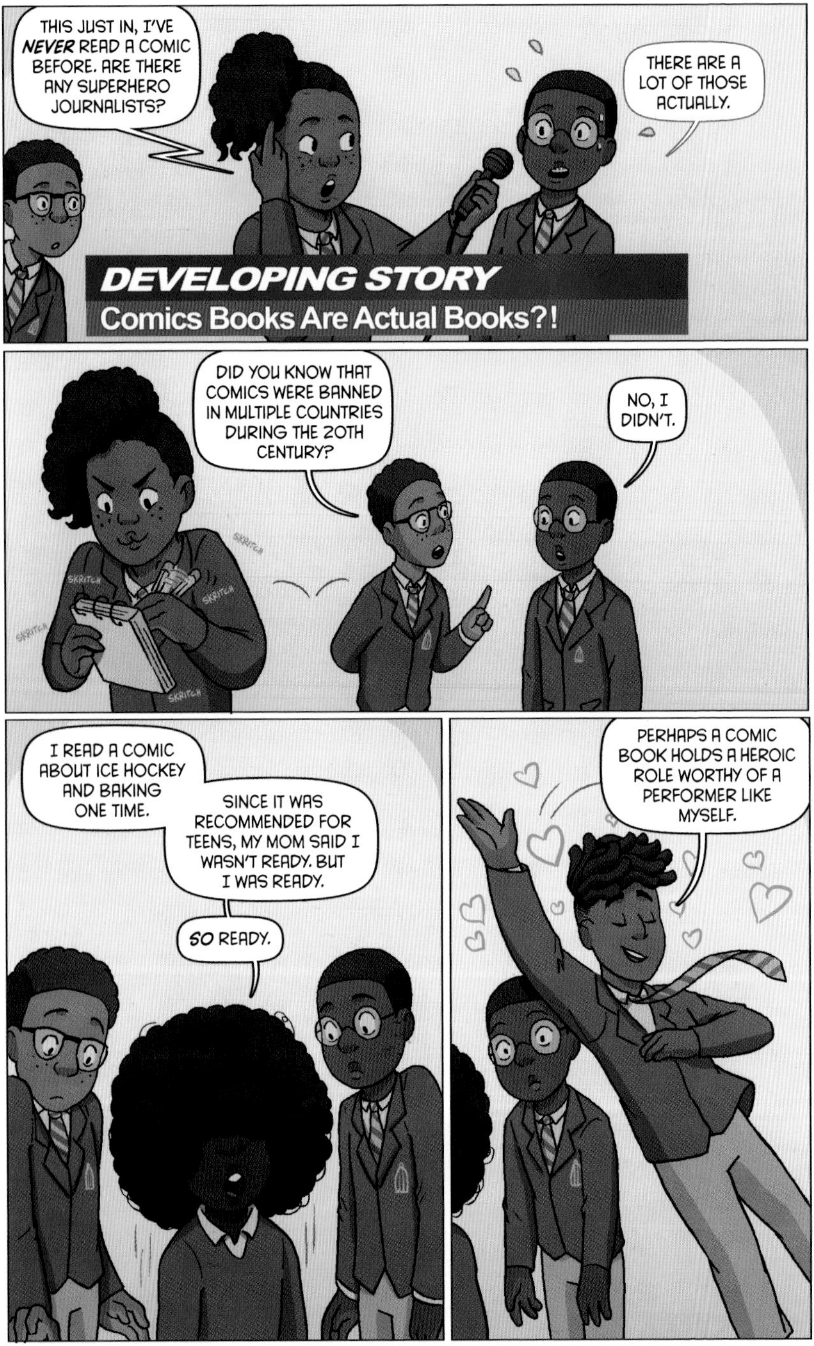
THIS JUST IN, I'VE NEVER READ A COMIC BEFORE. ARE THERE ANY SUPERHERO JOURNALISTS?
THERE ARE A LOT OF THOSE ACTUALLY.
DEVELOPING STORY
Comics Books Are Actual Books?!
DID YOU KNOW THAT COMICS WERE BANNED IN MULTIPLE COUNTRIES DURING THE 20TH CENTURY?
NO, I DIDN'T.
SKRITCH
SKRITCH
SKRITCH
SKRITCH
SKRITCH
I READ A COMIC ABOUT ICE HOCKEY AND BAKING ONE TIME.
SINCE IT WAS RECOMMENDED FOR TEENS, MY MOM SAID I WASN'T READY. BUT I WAS READY.
SO READY.
PERHAPS A COMIC BOOK HOLDS A HEROIC ROLE WORTHY OF A PERFORMER LIKE MYSELF.

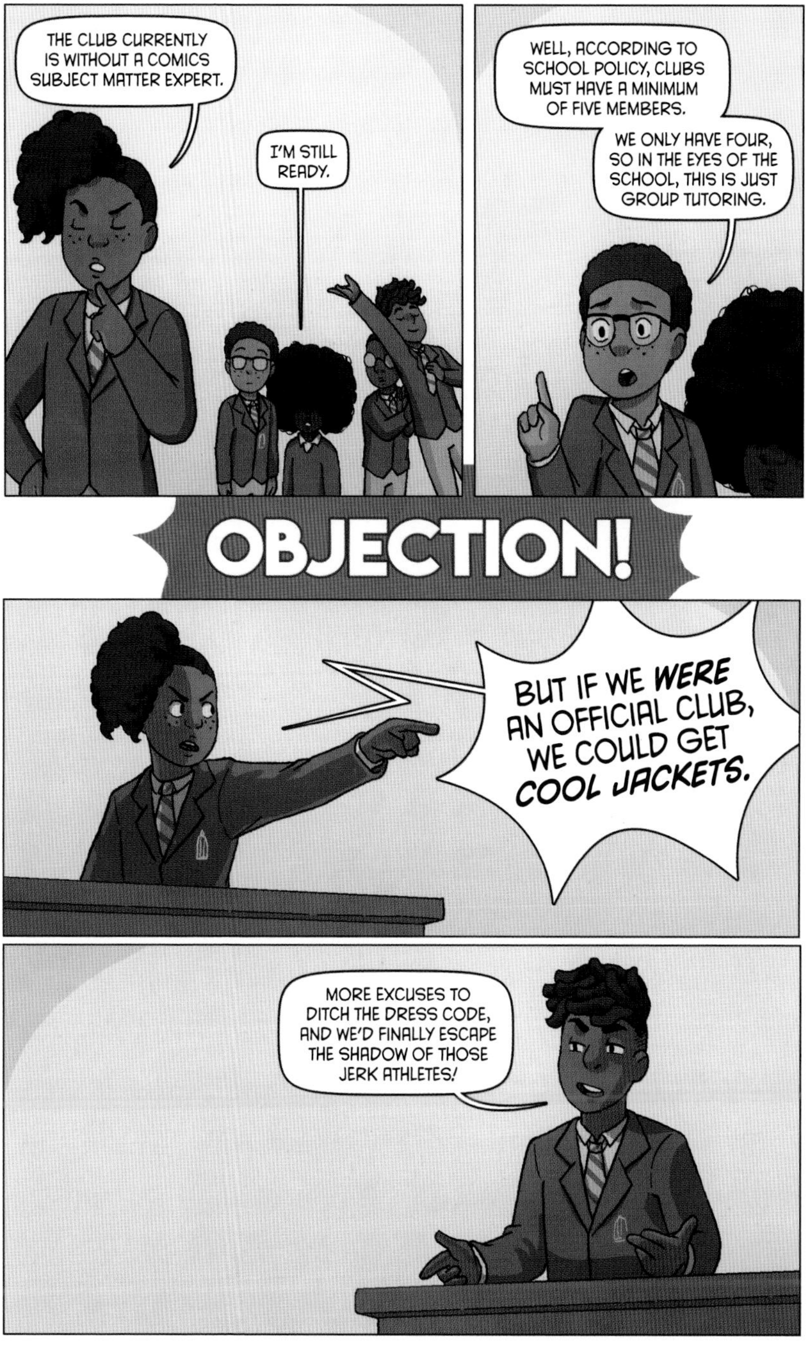
THE CLUB CURRENTLY IS WITHOUT A COMICS SUBJECT MATTER EXPERT.
I'M STILL READY.
WELL, ACCORDING TO SCHOOL POLICY, CLUBS MUST HAVE A MINIMUM OF FIVE MEMBERS.
WE ONLY HAVE FOUR, SO IN THE EYES OF THE SCHOOL, THIS IS JUST GROUP TUTORING.
OBJECTION!
BUT IF WE *WERE* AN OFFICIAL CLUB, WE COULD GET *COOL JACKETS.*
MORE EXCUSES TO DITCH THE DRESS CODE, AND WE'D FINALLY ESCAPE THE SHADOW OF THOSE JERK ATHLETES!

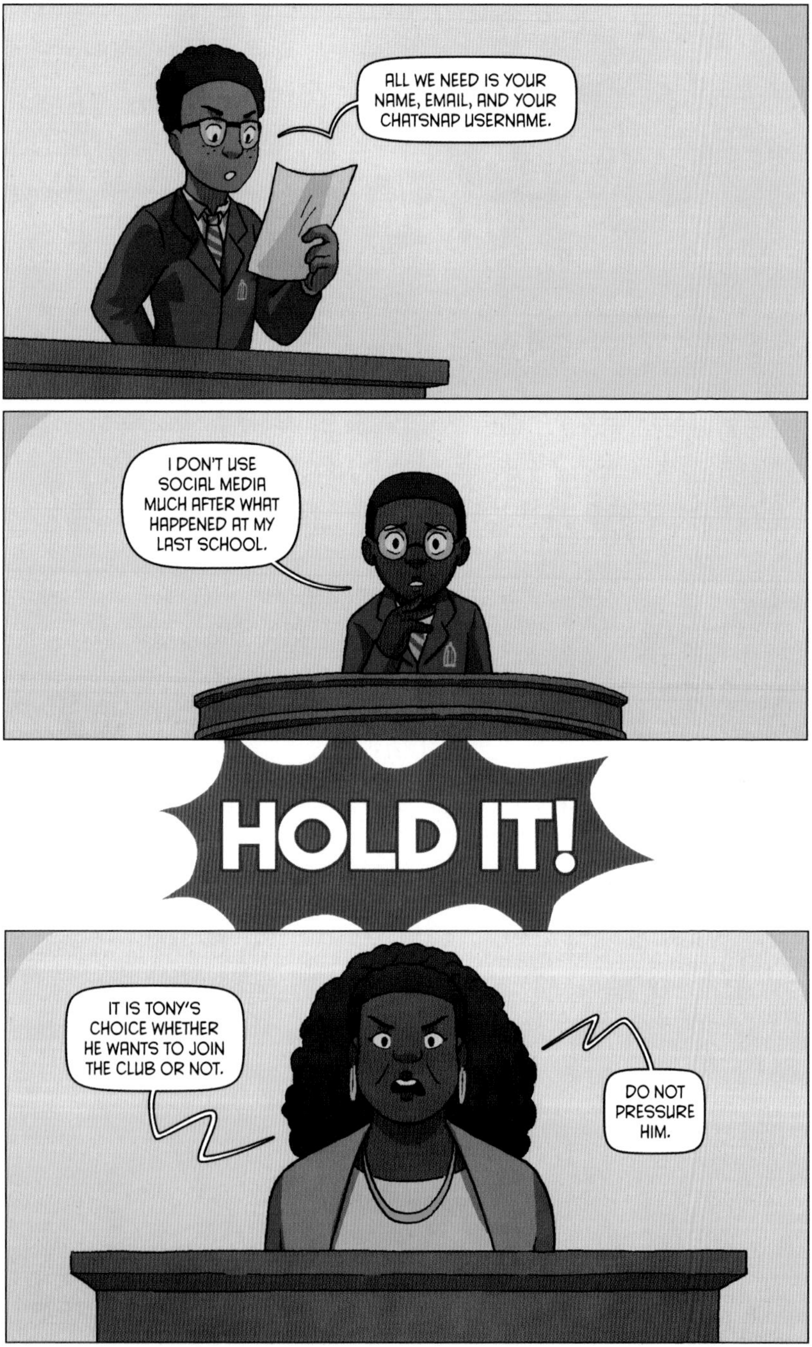
ALL WE NEED IS YOUR NAME, EMAIL, AND YOUR CHATSNAP USERNAME.
I DON'T USE SOCIAL MEDIA MUCH AFTER WHAT HAPPENED AT MY LAST SCHOOL.
HOLD IT!
IT IS TONY'S CHOICE WHETHER HE WANTS TO JOIN THE CLUB OR NOT.
DO NOT PRESSURE HIM.

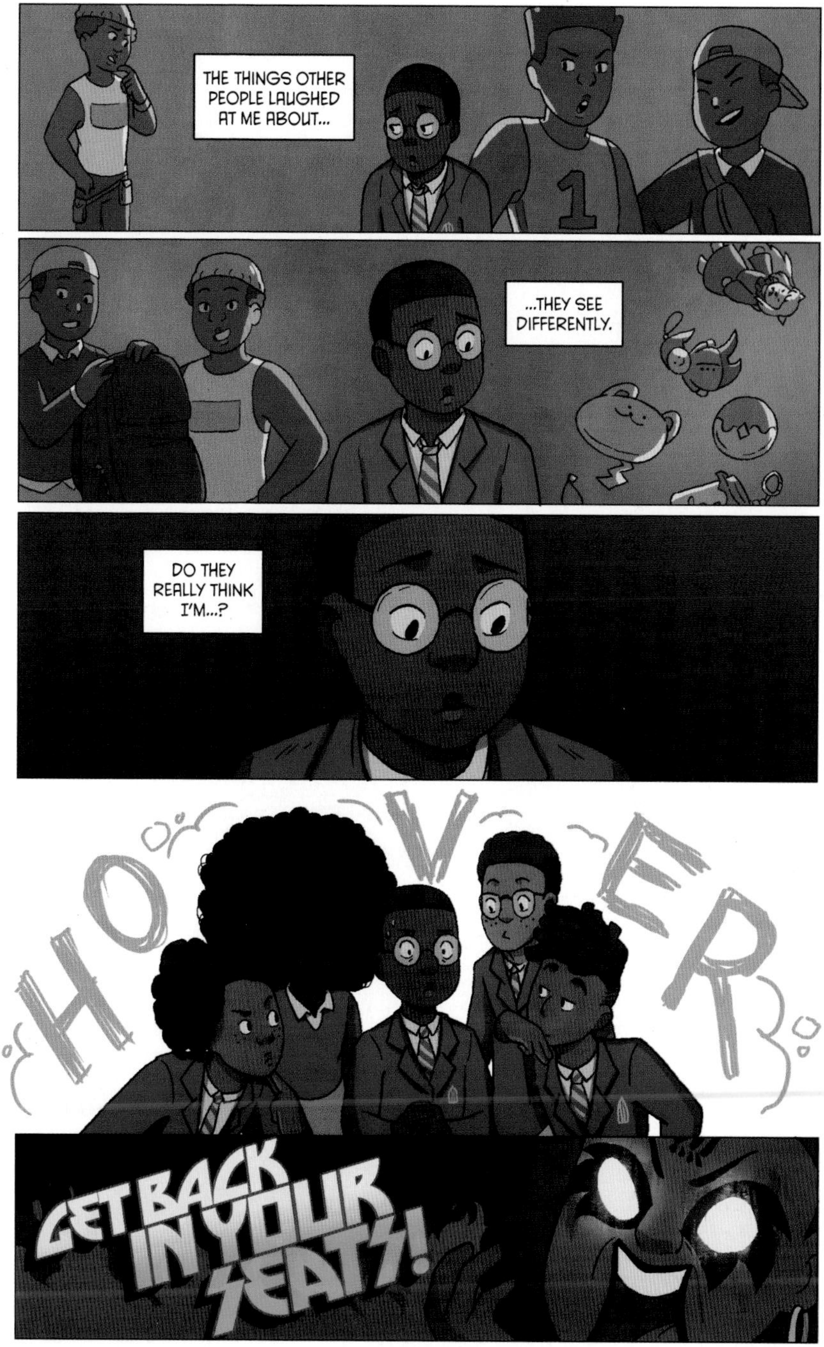
THE THINGS OTHER PEOPLE LAUGHED AT ME ABOUT...
...THEY SEE DIFFERENTLY.
DO THEY REALLY THINK I'M...?
HOVER
GET BACK IN YOUR SEATS!

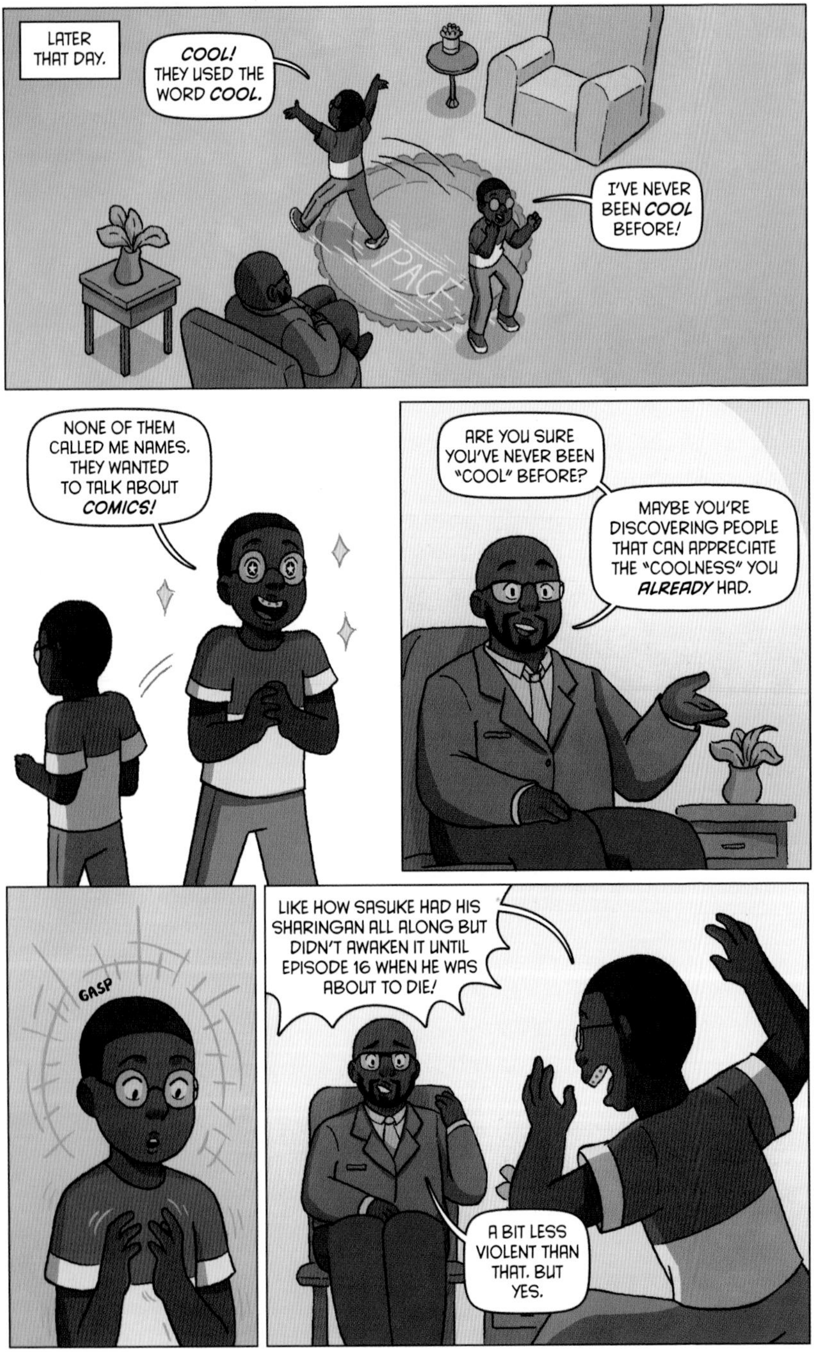
LATER THAT DAY.
COOL! THEY USED THE WORD COOL.
I'VE NEVER BEEN COOL BEFORE!
PACE
NONE OF THEM CALLED ME NAMES. THEY WANTED TO TALK ABOUT COMICS!
ARE YOU SURE YOU'VE NEVER BEEN "COOL" BEFORE?
MAYBE YOU'RE DISCOVERING PEOPLE THAT CAN APPRECIATE THE "COOLNESS" YOU ALREADY HAD.
GASP
LIKE HOW SASUKE HAD HIS SHARINGAN ALL ALONG BUT DIDN'T AWAKEN IT UNTIL EPISODE 16 WHEN HE WAS ABOUT TO DIE!
A BIT LESS VIOLENT THAN THAT. BUT YES.

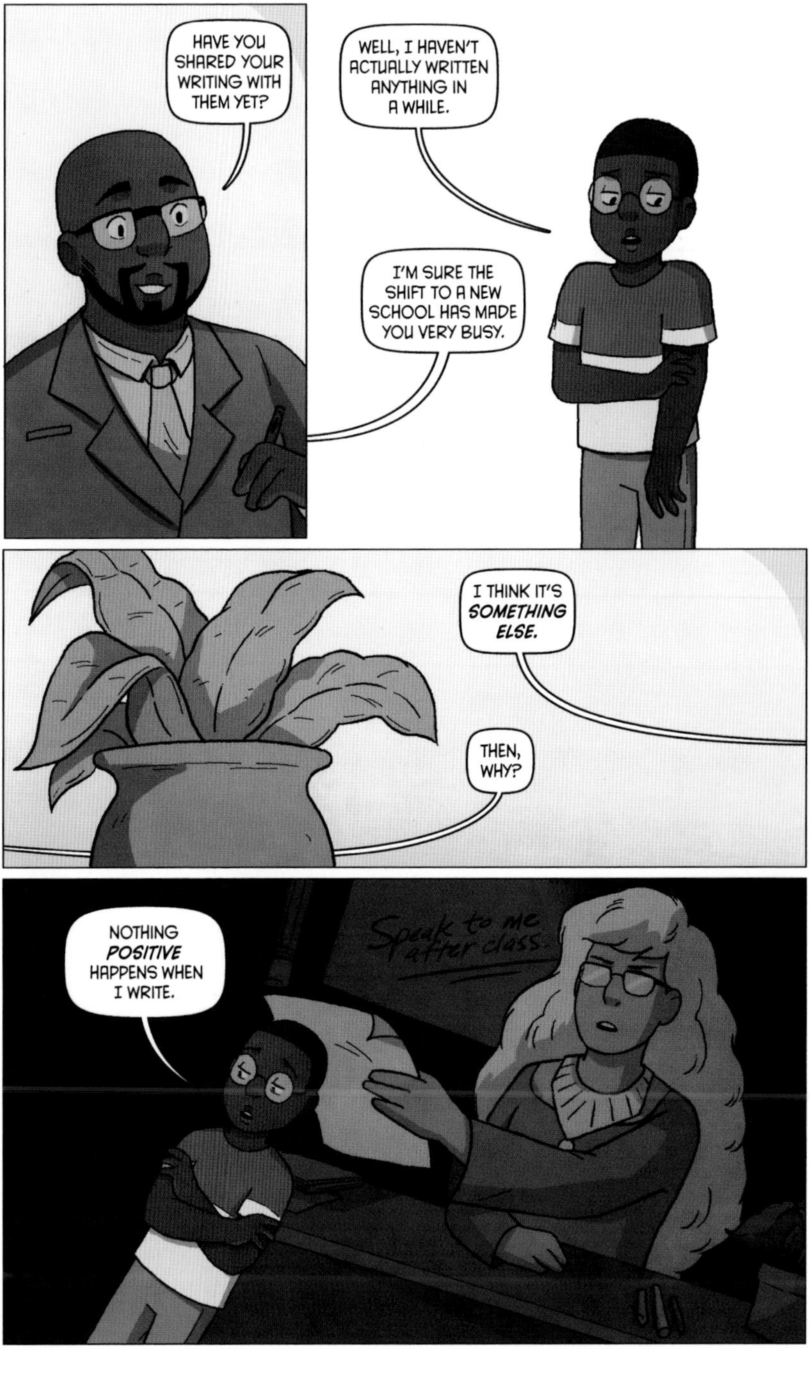
HAVE YOU SHARED YOUR WRITING WITH THEM YET?
WELL, I HAVEN'T ACTUALLY WRITTEN ANYTHING IN A WHILE.
I'M SURE THE SHIFT TO A NEW SCHOOL HAS MADE YOU VERY BUSY.
I THINK IT'S *SOMETHING ELSE.*
THEN, WHY?
NOTHING *POSITIVE* HAPPENS WHEN I WRITE.
Speak to me after class.

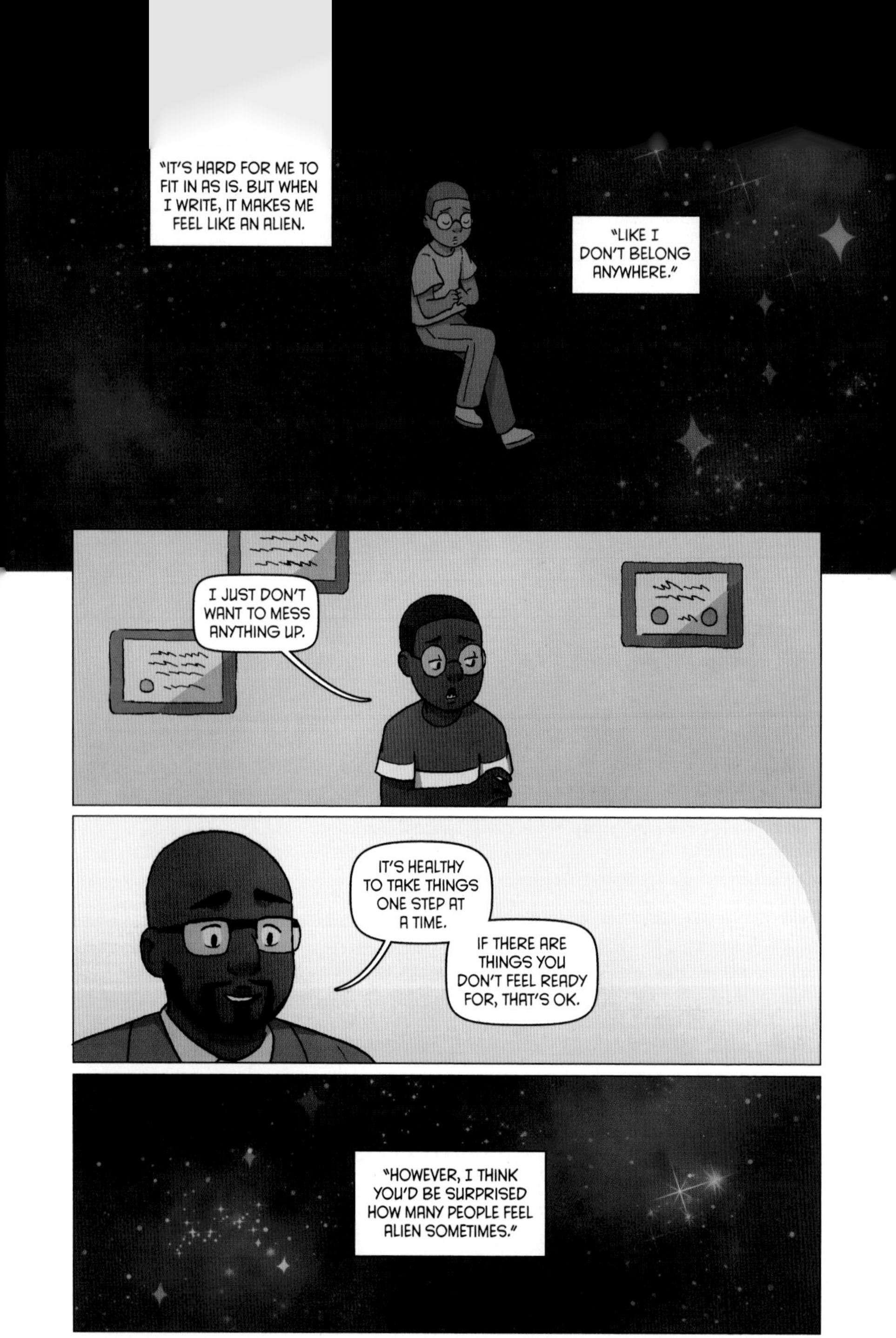
"IT'S HARD FOR ME TO FIT IN AS IS. BUT WHEN I WRITE, IT MAKES ME FEEL LIKE AN ALIEN.
"LIKE I DON'T BELONG ANYWHERE."
I JUST DON'T WANT TO MESS ANYTHING UP.
IT'S HEALTHY TO TAKE THINGS ONE STEP AT A TIME.
IF THERE ARE THINGS YOU DON'T FEEL READY FOR, THAT'S OK.
"HOWEVER, I THINK YOU'D BE SURPRISED HOW MANY PEOPLE FEEL ALIEN SOMETIMES."

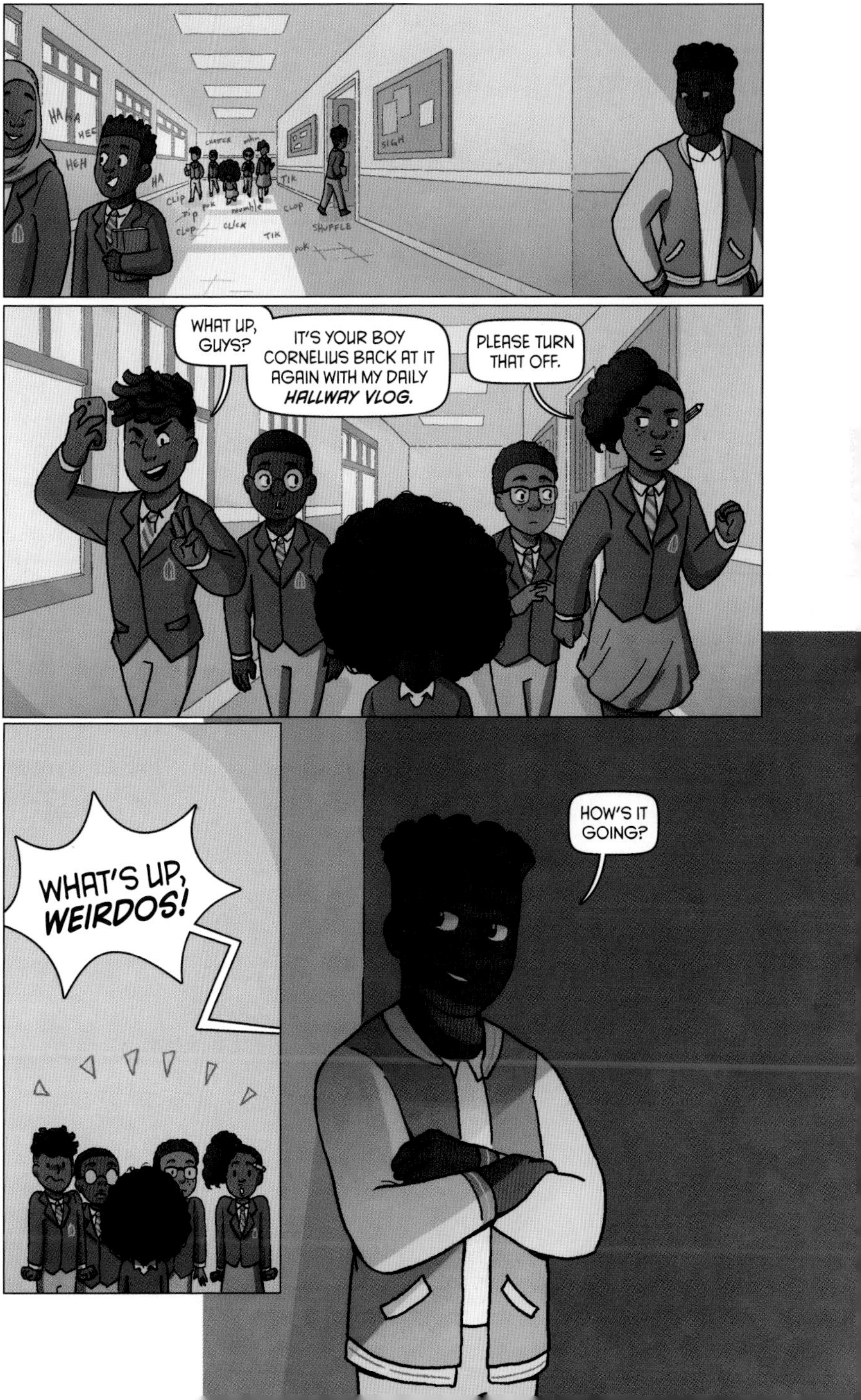
HA HA
HEH
HEH
HA
CHATTER
CLIP
pip
pok
mumble
CLICK
CLOP
TIK
TIK
CLOP
SHUFFLE
pok
SIGH
WHAT UP, GUYS?
IT'S YOUR BOY CORNELIUS BACK AT IT AGAIN WITH MY DAILY *HALLWAY VLOG.*
PLEASE TURN THAT OFF.
WHAT'S UP, *WEIRDOS!*
HOW'S IT GOING?

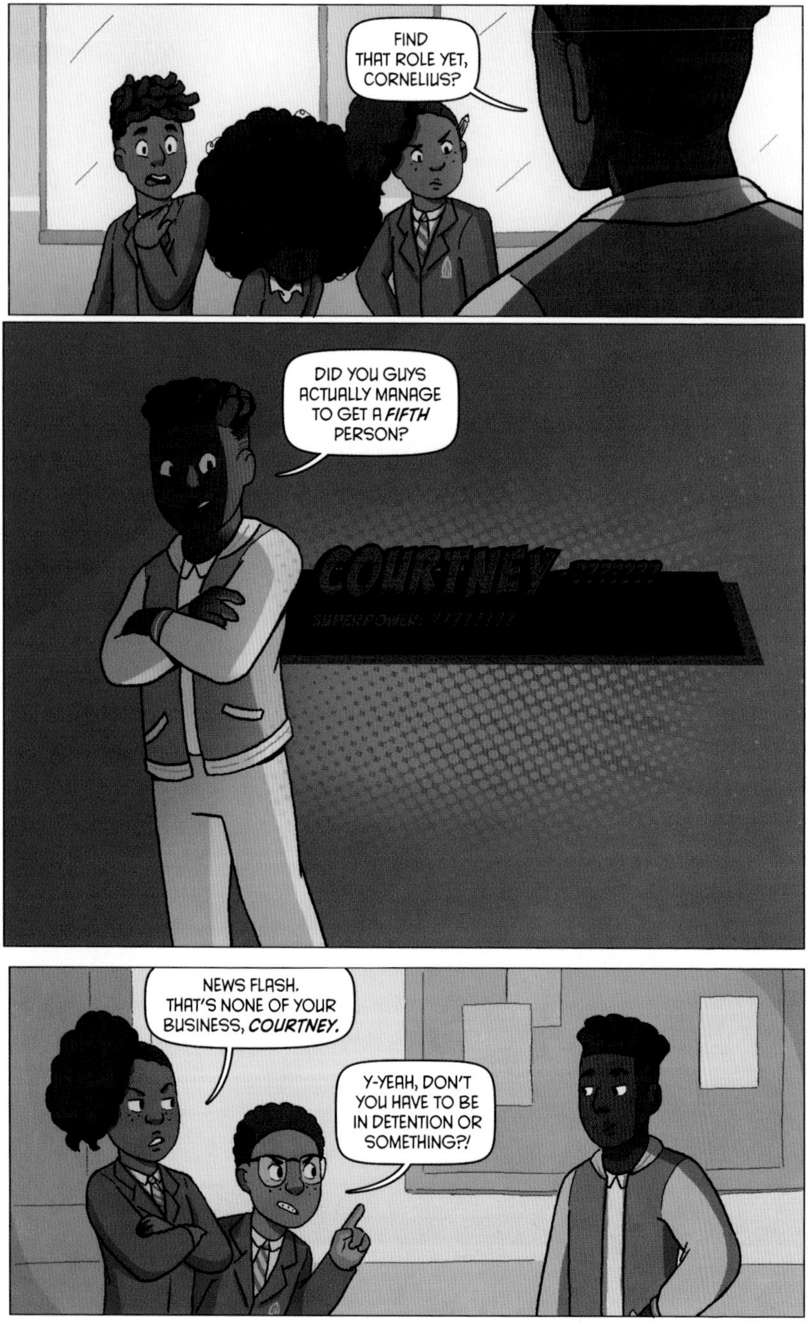
FIND THAT ROLE YET, CORNELIUS?
DID YOU GUYS ACTUALLY MANAGE TO GET A *FIFTH* PERSON?
COURTNEY - ????????
SUPERPOWER: ????????
NEWS FLASH. THAT'S NONE OF YOUR BUSINESS, ***COURTNEY.***
Y-YEAH, DON'T YOU HAVE TO BE IN DETENTION OR SOMETHING?!

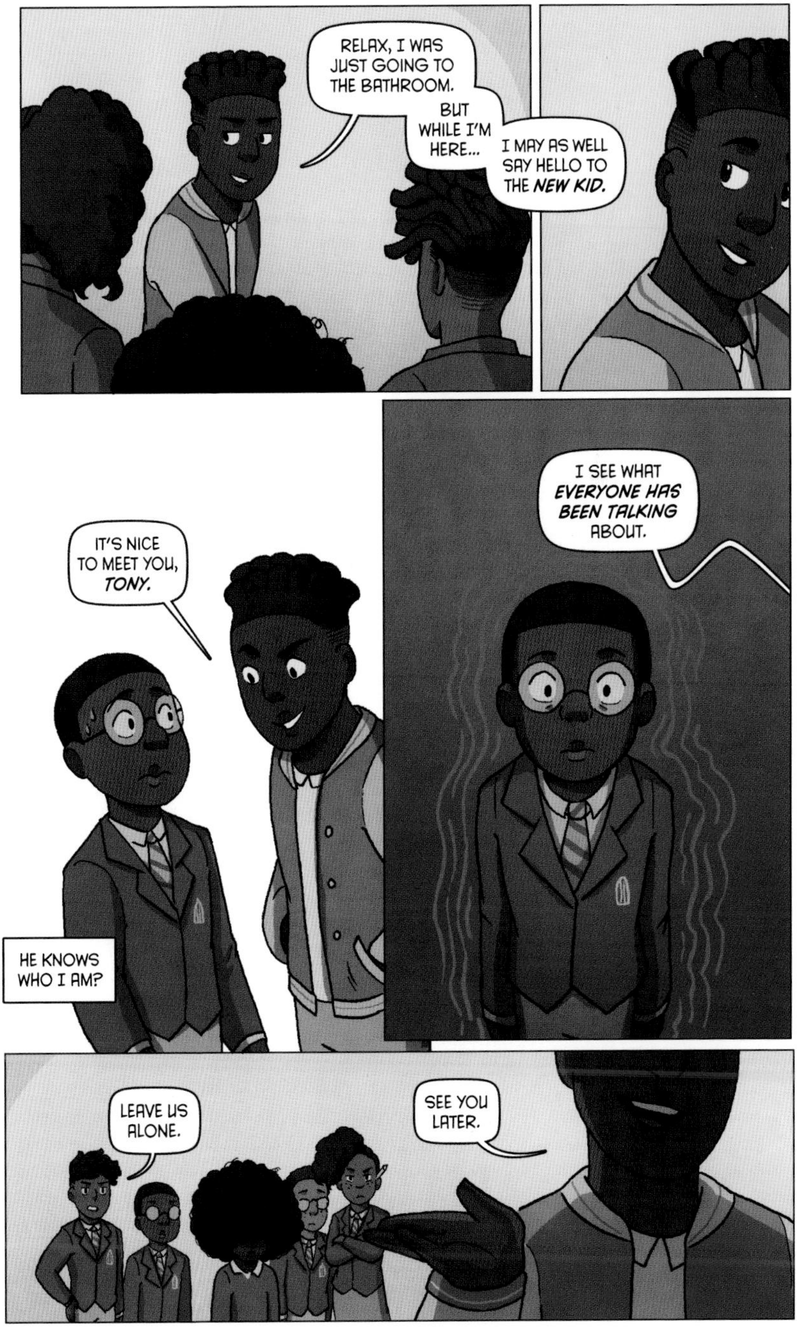
RELAX, I WAS JUST GOING TO THE BATHROOM.
BUT WHILE I'M HERE...
I MAY AS WELL SAY HELLO TO THE *NEW KID.*
IT'S NICE TO MEET YOU, *TONY.*
HE KNOWS WHO I AM?
I SEE WHAT *EVERYONE HAS BEEN TALKING* ABOUT.
LEAVE US ALONE.
SEE YOU LATER.

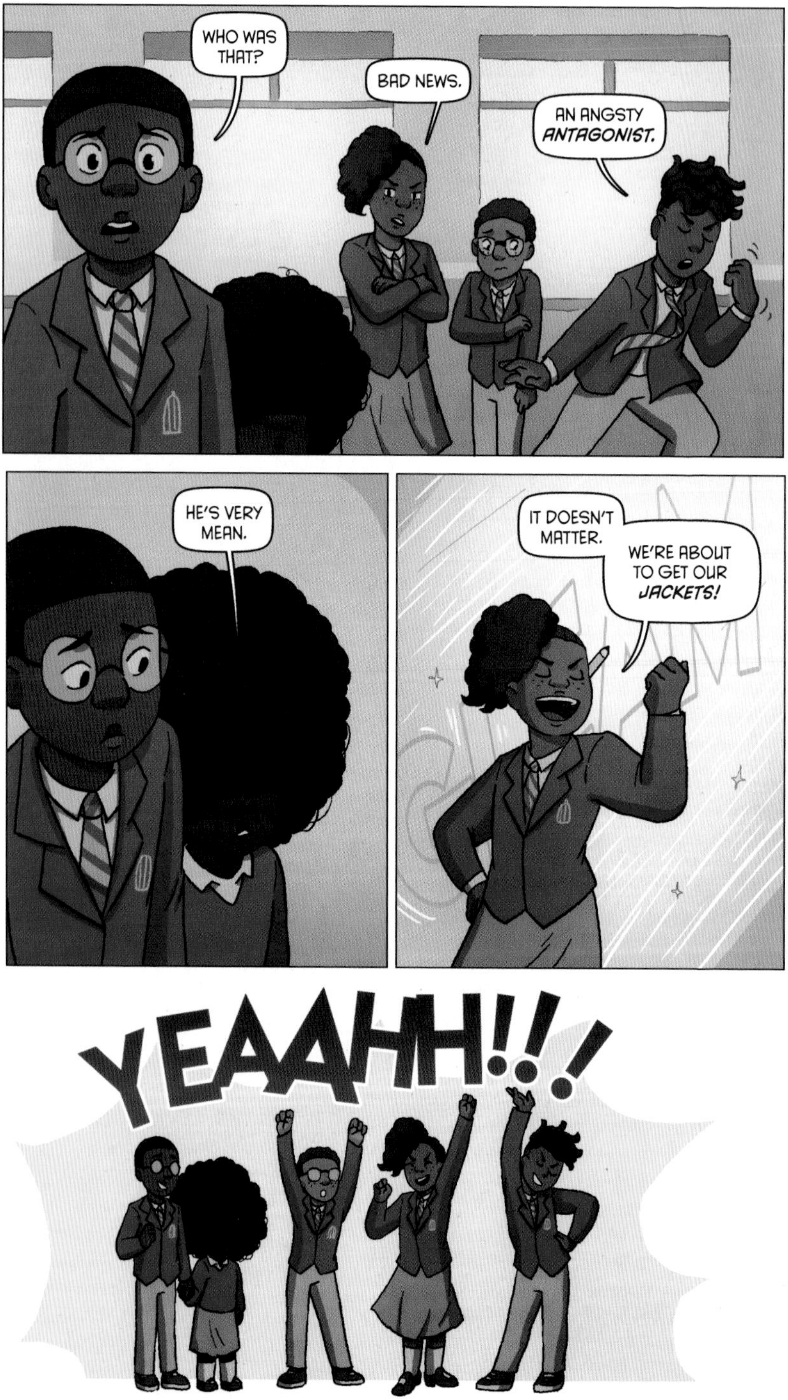
WHO WAS THAT?
BAD NEWS.
AN ANGSTY *ANTAGONIST.*
HE'S VERY MEAN.
IT DOESN'T MATTER.
WE'RE ABOUT TO GET OUR *JACKETS!*
YEAAHH!!!

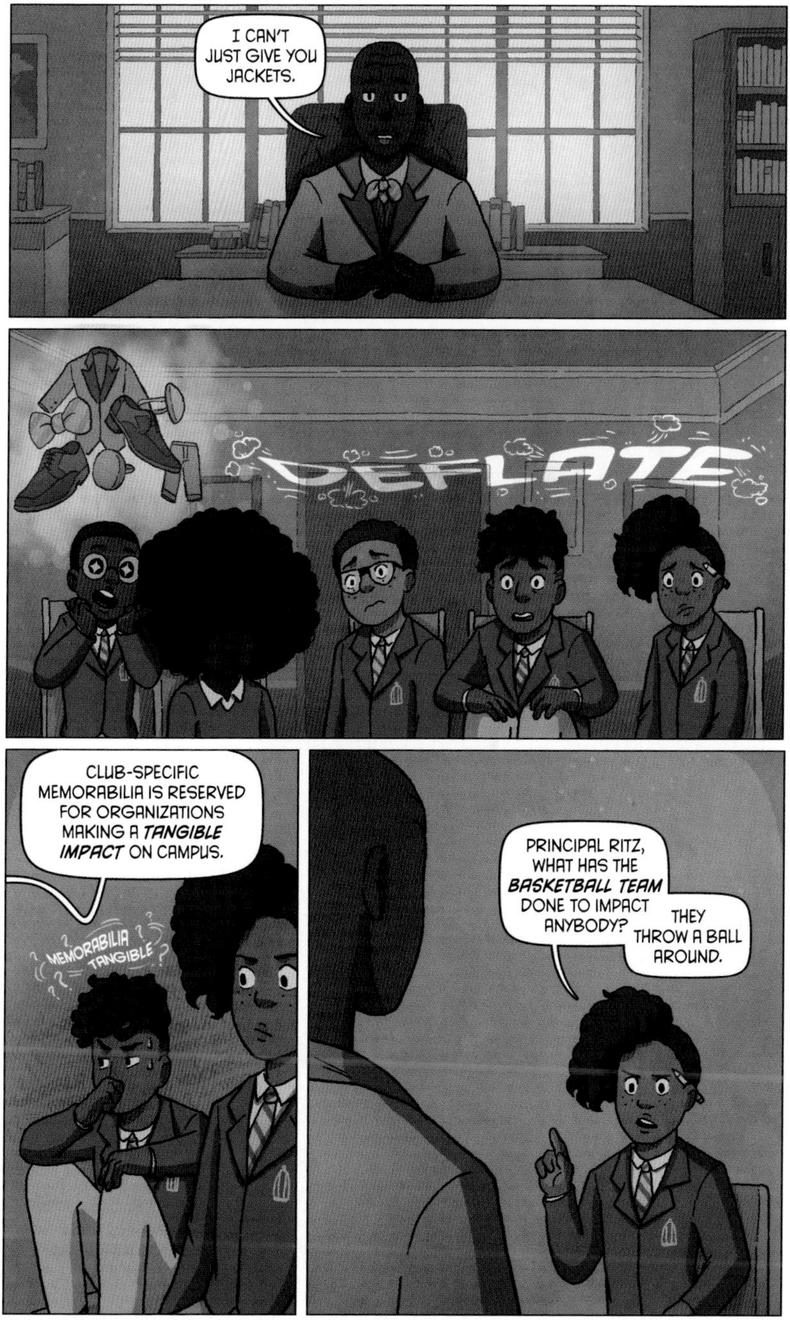
I CAN'T JUST GIVE YOU JACKETS.
DEFLATE
CLUB-SPECIFIC MEMORABILIA IS RESERVED FOR ORGANIZATIONS MAKING A *TANGIBLE IMPACT* ON CAMPUS.
MEMORABILIA TANGIBLE
PRINCIPAL RITZ, WHAT HAS THE *BASKETBALL TEAM* DONE TO IMPACT ANYBODY?
THEY THROW A BALL AROUND.

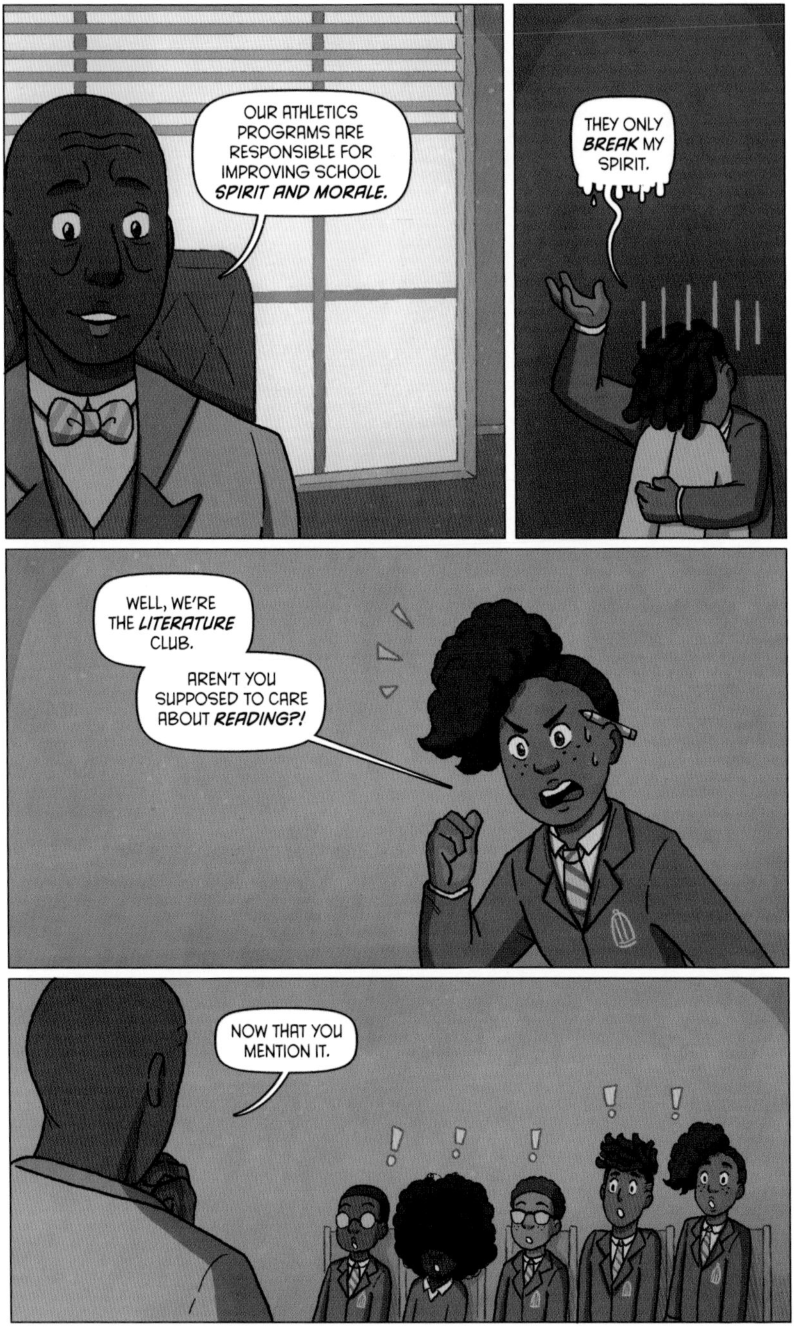
OUR ATHLETICS PROGRAMS ARE RESPONSIBLE FOR IMPROVING SCHOOL SPIRIT AND MORALE.
THEY ONLY BREAK MY SPIRIT.
WELL, WE'RE THE LITERATURE CLUB.
AREN'T YOU SUPPOSED TO CARE ABOUT READING?!
NOW THAT YOU MENTION IT.

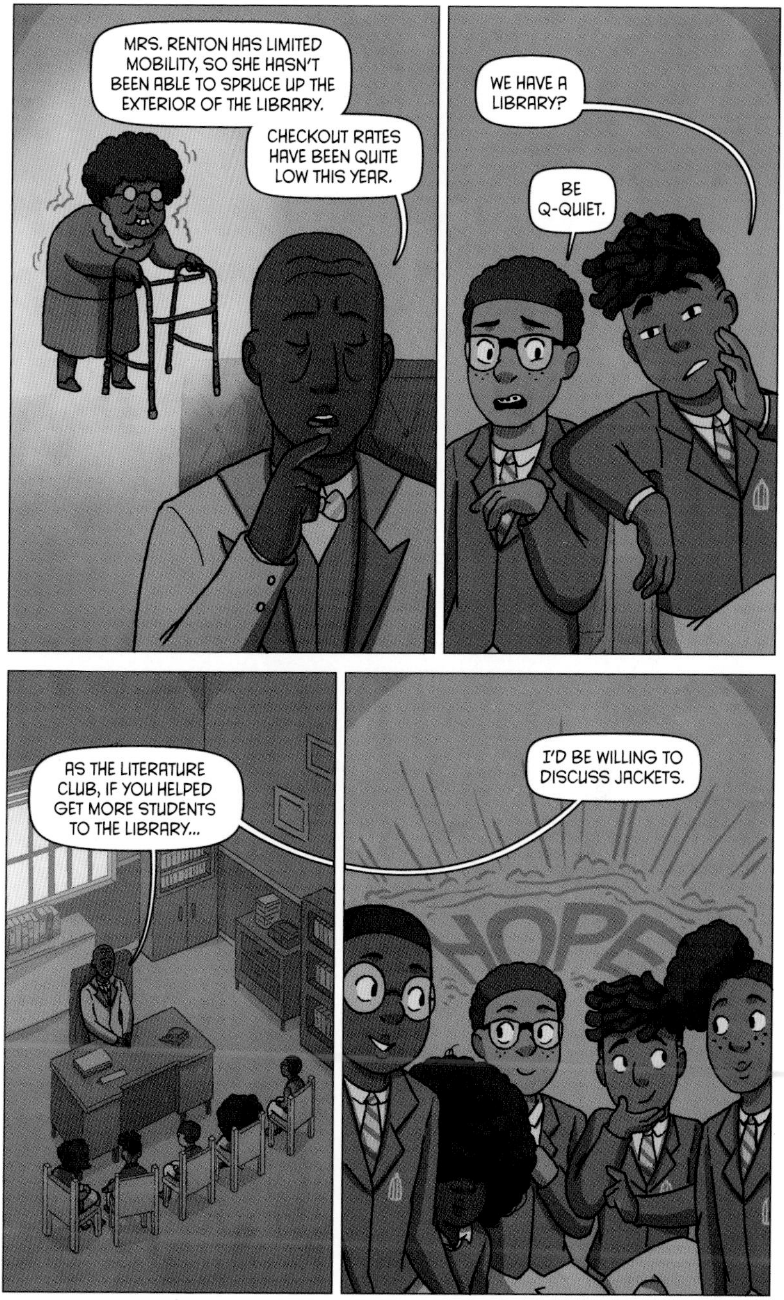
MRS. RENTON HAS LIMITED MOBILITY, SO SHE HASN'T BEEN ABLE TO SPRUCE UP THE EXTERIOR OF THE LIBRARY.
CHECKOUT RATES HAVE BEEN QUITE LOW THIS YEAR.
WE HAVE A LIBRARY?
BE Q-QUIET.
AS THE LITERATURE CLUB, IF YOU HELPED GET MORE STUDENTS TO THE LIBRARY...
I'D BE WILLING TO DISCUSS JACKETS.
HOPE

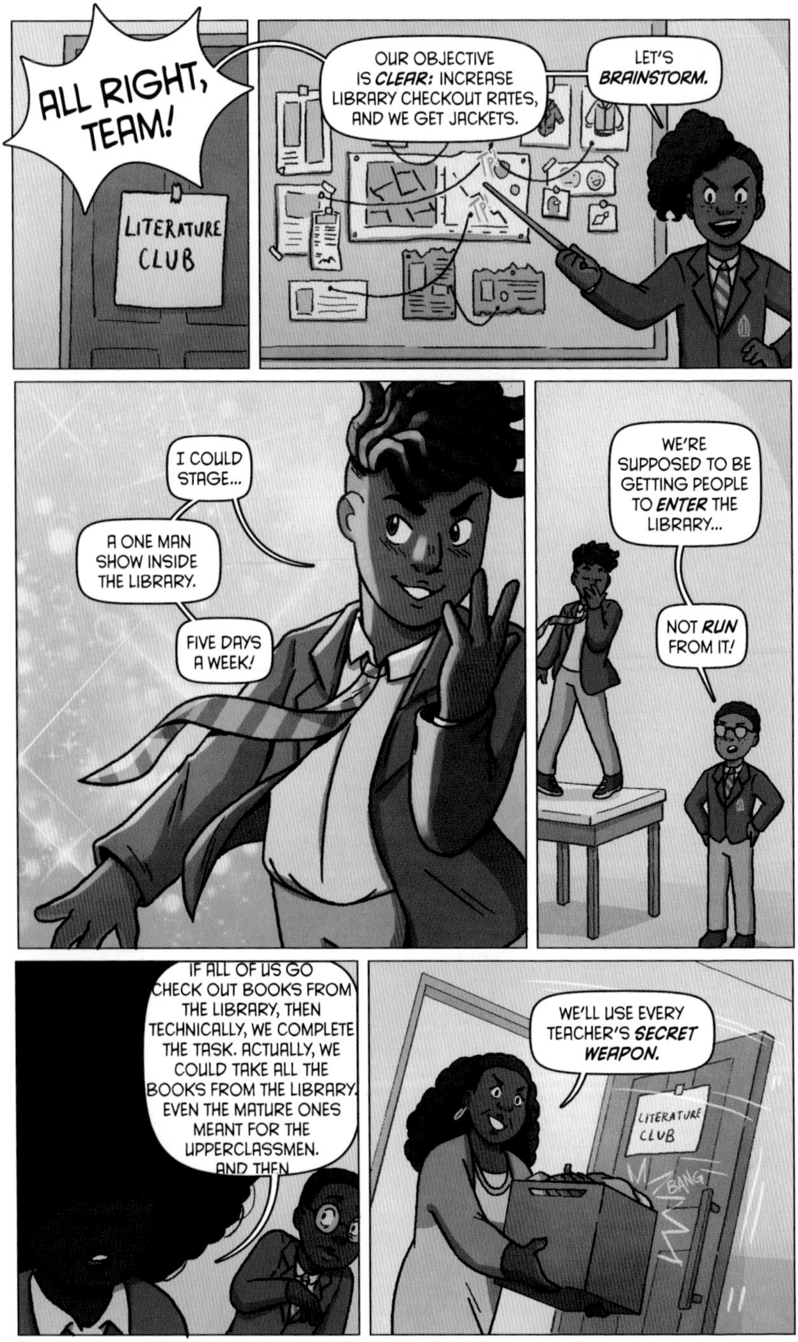

ALL RIGHT, TEAM!
OUR OBJECTIVE IS CLEAR: INCREASE LIBRARY CHECKOUT RATES, AND WE GET JACKETS.
LET'S BRAINSTORM.
LITERATURE CLUB
I COULD STAGE...
A ONE MAN SHOW INSIDE THE LIBRARY.
FIVE DAYS A WEEK!
WE'RE SUPPOSED TO BE GETTING PEOPLE TO ENTER THE LIBRARY...
NOT RUN FROM IT!
IF ALL OF US GO CHECK OUT BOOKS FROM THE LIBRARY, THEN TECHNICALLY, WE COMPLETE THE TASK. ACTUALLY, WE COULD TAKE ALL THE BOOKS FROM THE LIBRARY. EVEN THE MATURE ONES MEANT FOR THE UPPERCLASSMEN. AND THEN
WE'LL USE EVERY TEACHER'S SECRET WEAPON.
LITERATURE CLUB
BANG

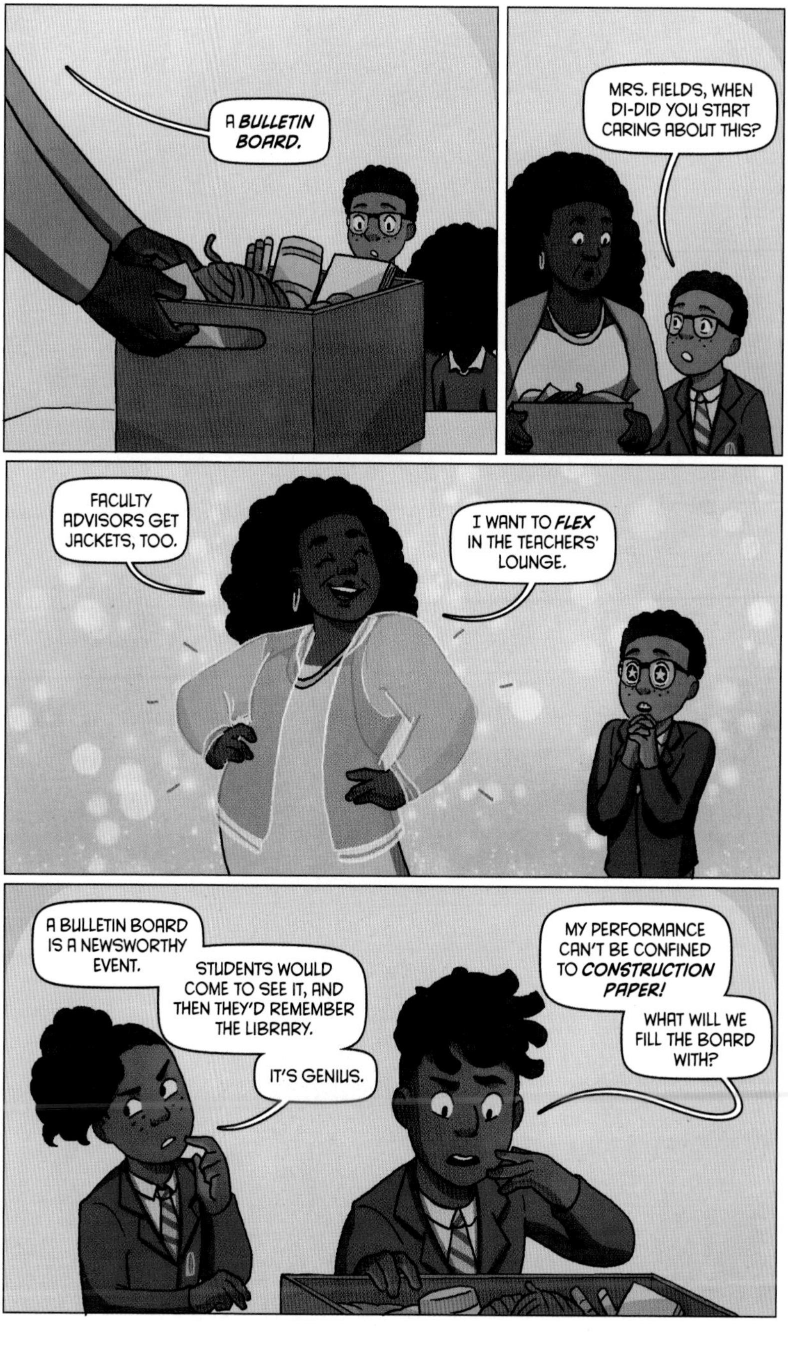
A BULLETIN BOARD.
MRS. FIELDS, WHEN DI-DID YOU START CARING ABOUT THIS?
FACULTY ADVISORS GET JACKETS, TOO.
I WANT TO FLEX IN THE TEACHERS' LOUNGE.
A BULLETIN BOARD IS A NEWSWORTHY EVENT.
STUDENTS WOULD COME TO SEE IT, AND THEN THEY'D REMEMBER THE LIBRARY.
IT'S GENIUS.
MY PERFORMANCE CAN'T BE CONFINED TO CONSTRUCTION PAPER!
WHAT WILL WE FILL THE BOARD WITH?

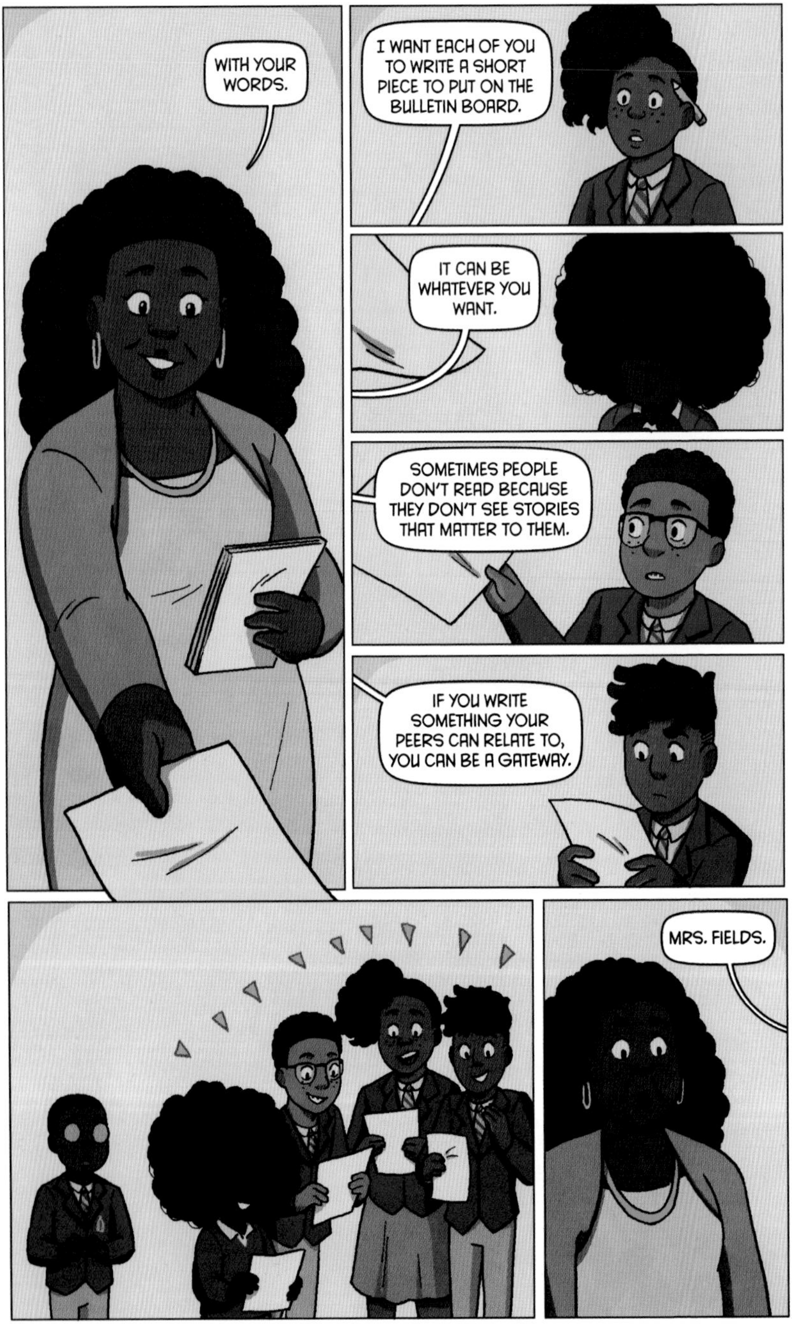
WITH YOUR WORDS.
I WANT EACH OF YOU TO WRITE A SHORT PIECE TO PUT ON THE BULLETIN BOARD.
IT CAN BE WHATEVER YOU WANT.
SOMETIMES PEOPLE DON'T READ BECAUSE THEY DON'T SEE STORIES THAT MATTER TO THEM.
IF YOU WRITE SOMETHING YOUR PEERS CAN RELATE TO, YOU CAN BE A GATEWAY.
MRS. FIELDS.

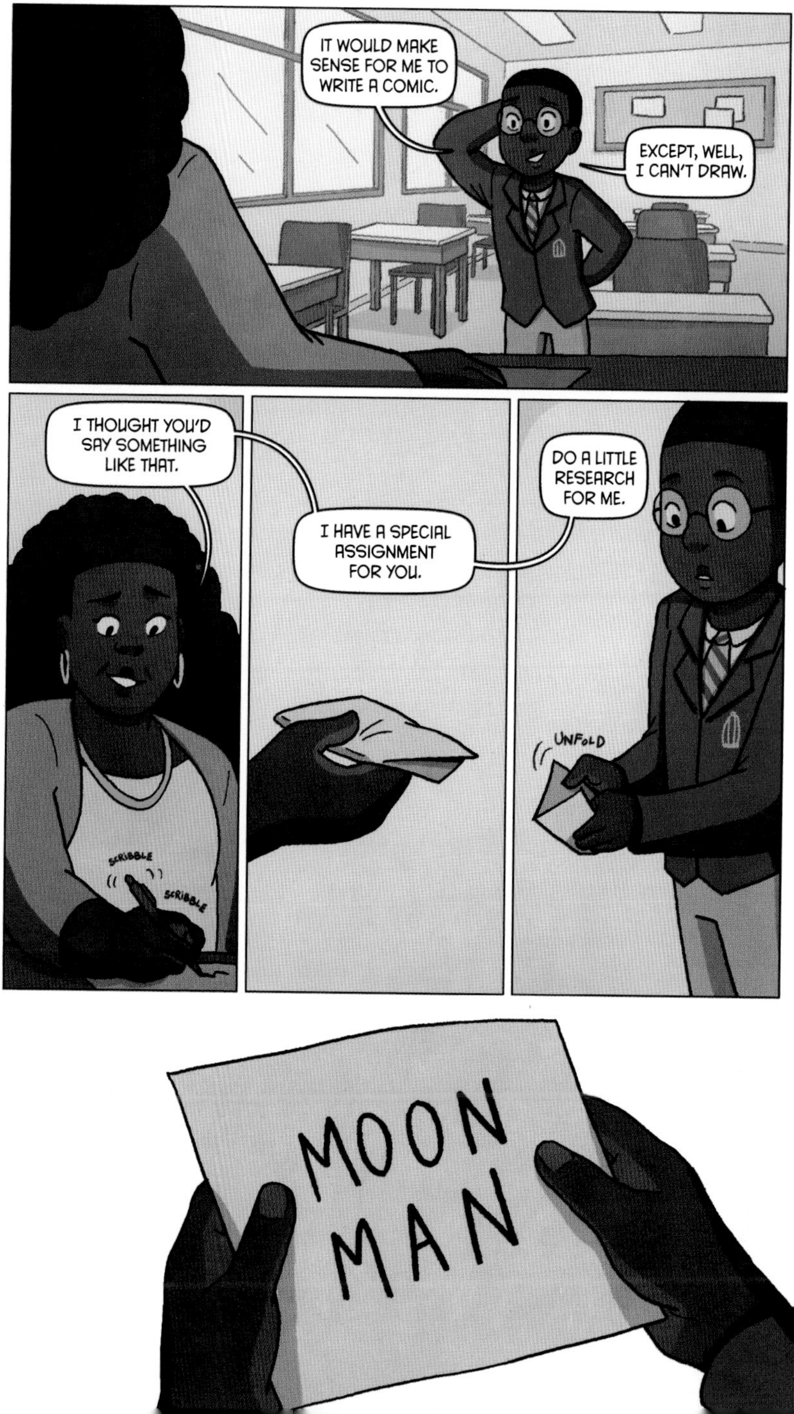
IT WOULD MAKE SENSE FOR ME TO WRITE A COMIC.
EXCEPT, WELL, I CAN'T DRAW.
I THOUGHT YOU'D SAY SOMETHING LIKE THAT.
I HAVE A SPECIAL ASSIGNMENT FOR YOU.
DO A LITTLE RESEARCH FOR ME.
SCRIBBLE
SCRIBBLE
UNFOLD
MOON MAN

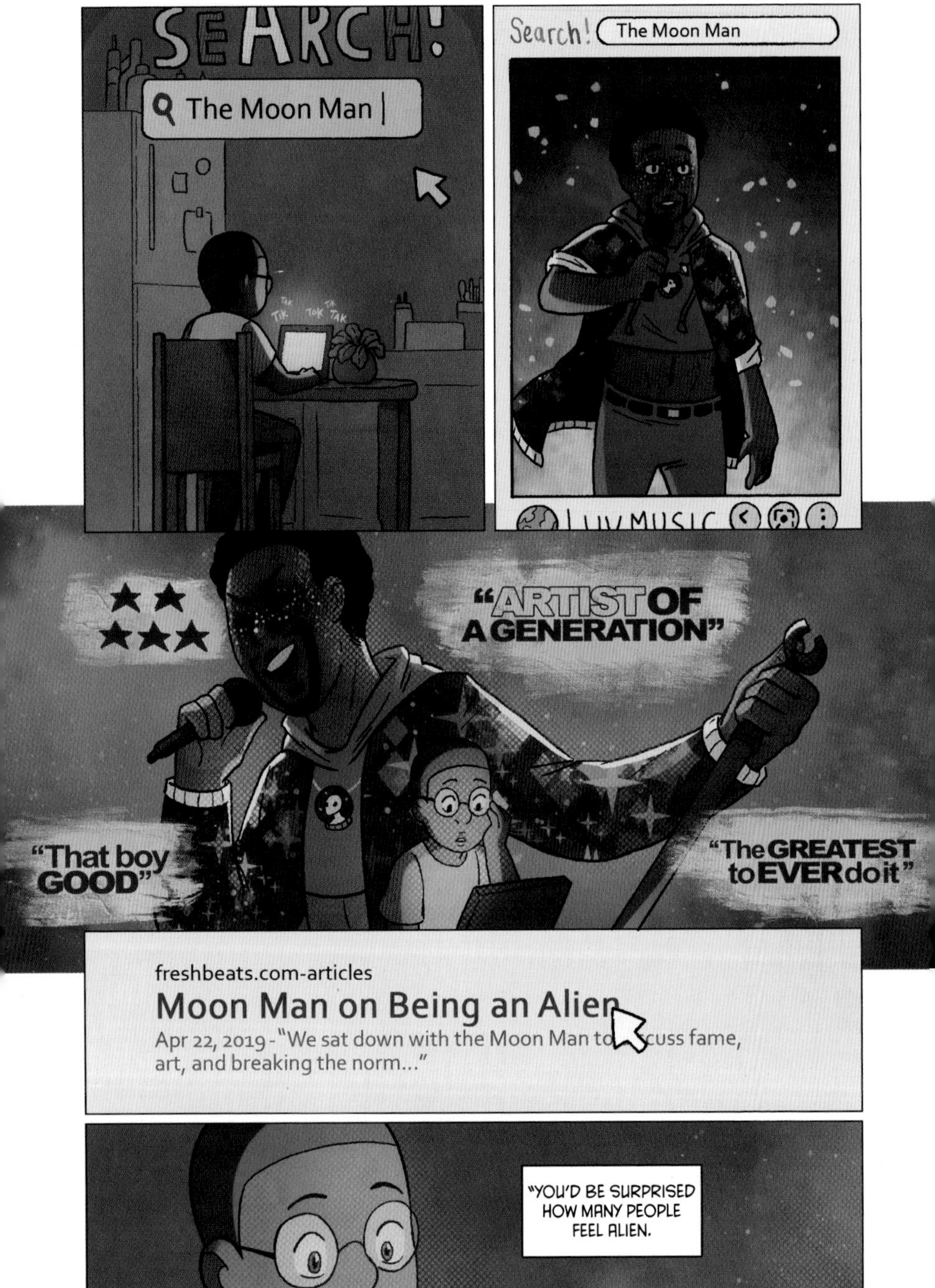
SEARCH!
The Moon Man
Search!
The Moon Man
"ARTIST OF A GENERATION"
"That boy GOOD"
"The GREATEST to EVER do it"
freshbeats.com-articles
Moon Man on Being an Alien
Apr 22, 2019 - "We sat down with the Moon Man to … cuss fame, art, and breaking the norm…"
"YOU'D BE SURPRISED HOW MANY PEOPLE FEEL ALIEN.

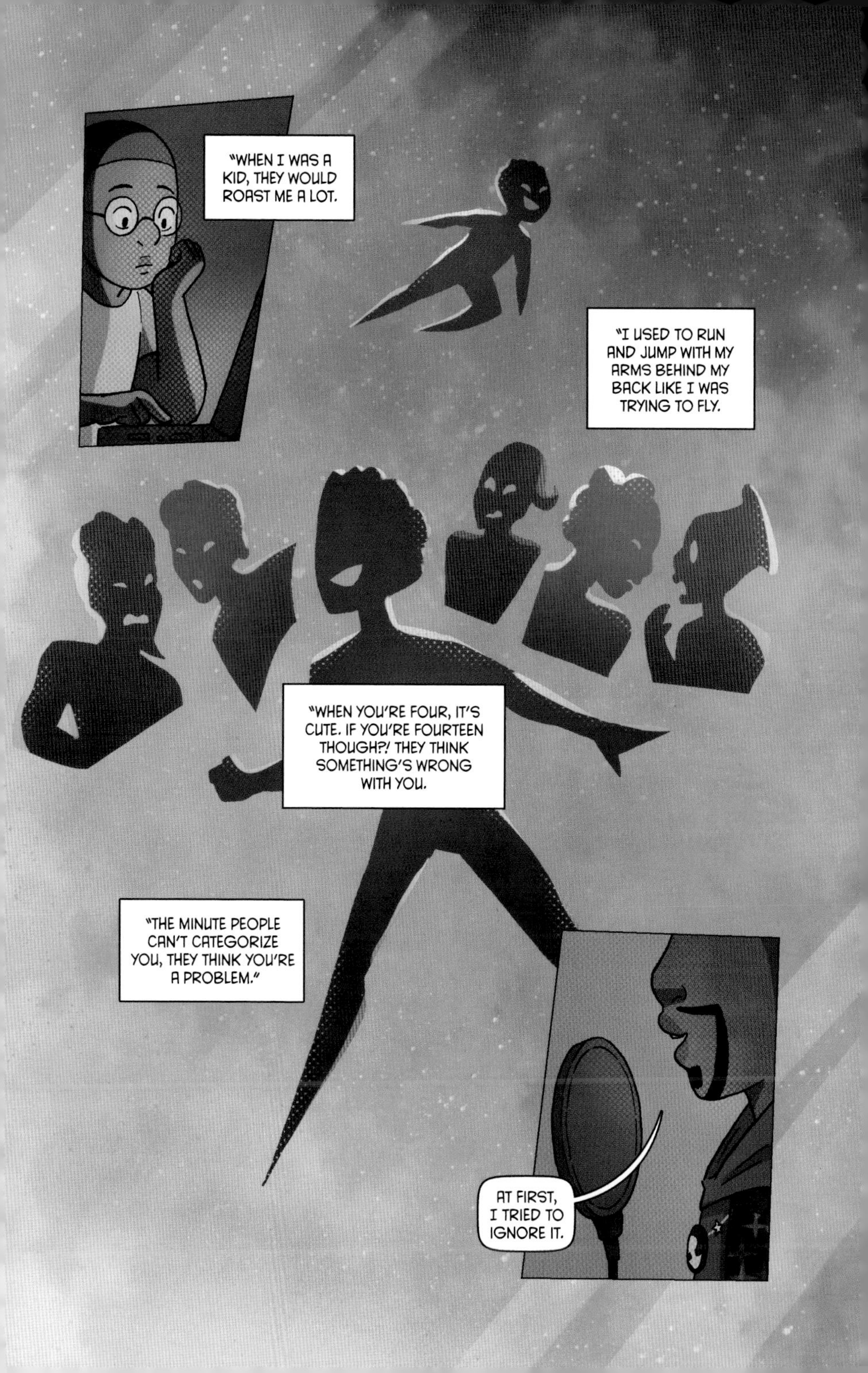
"WHEN I WAS A KID, THEY WOULD ROAST ME A LOT.
"I USED TO RUN AND JUMP WITH MY ARMS BEHIND MY BACK LIKE I WAS TRYING TO FLY.
"WHEN YOU'RE FOUR, IT'S CUTE. IF YOU'RE FOURTEEN THOUGH?! THEY THINK SOMETHING'S WRONG WITH YOU.
"THE MINUTE PEOPLE CAN'T CATEGORIZE YOU, THEY THINK YOU'RE A PROBLEM."
AT FIRST, I TRIED TO IGNORE IT.

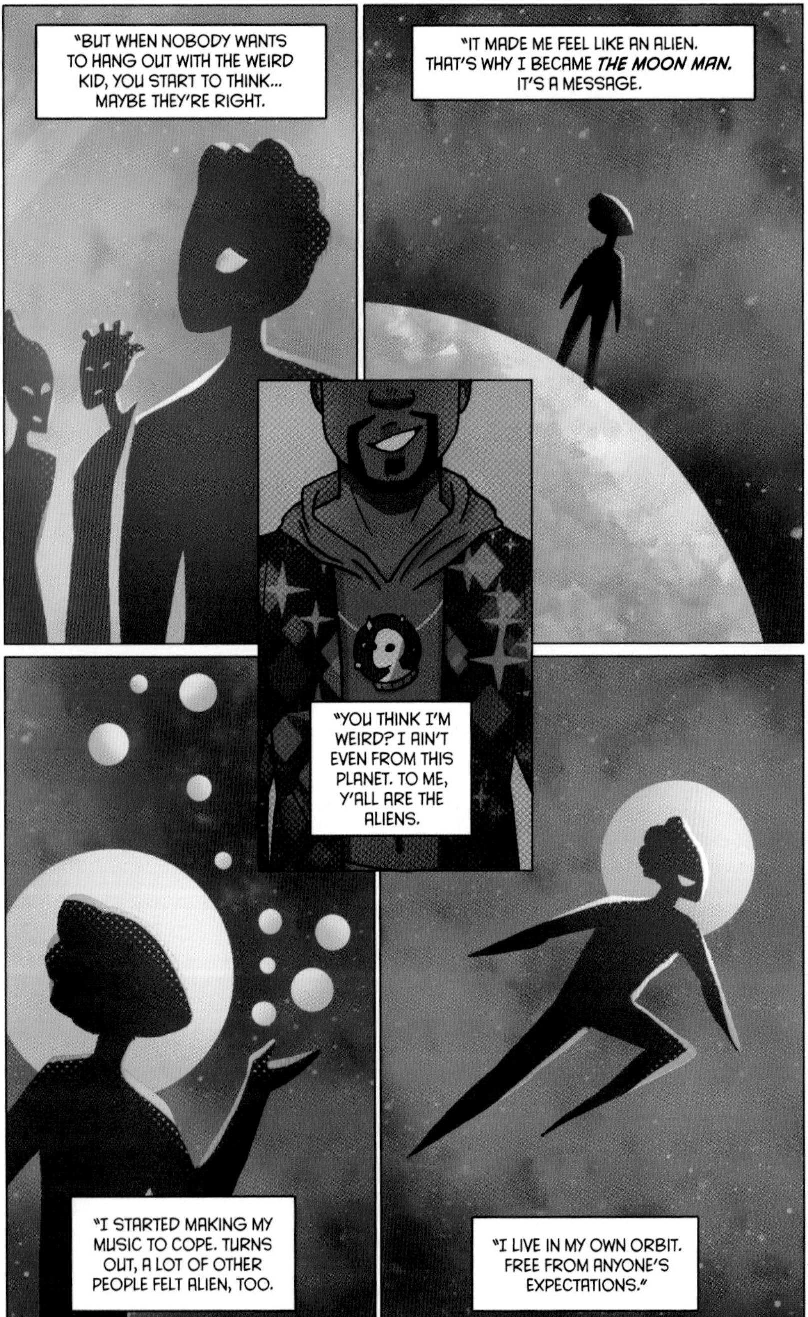
"BUT WHEN NOBODY WANTS TO HANG OUT WITH THE WEIRD KID, YOU START TO THINK... MAYBE THEY'RE RIGHT.
"IT MADE ME FEEL LIKE AN ALIEN. THAT'S WHY I BECAME *THE MOON MAN.* IT'S A MESSAGE.
"YOU THINK I'M WEIRD? I AIN'T EVEN FROM THIS PLANET. TO ME, Y'ALL ARE THE ALIENS.
"I STARTED MAKING MY MUSIC TO COPE. TURNS OUT, A LOT OF OTHER PEOPLE FELT ALIEN, TOO.
"I LIVE IN MY OWN ORBIT. FREE FROM ANYONE'S EXPECTATIONS."

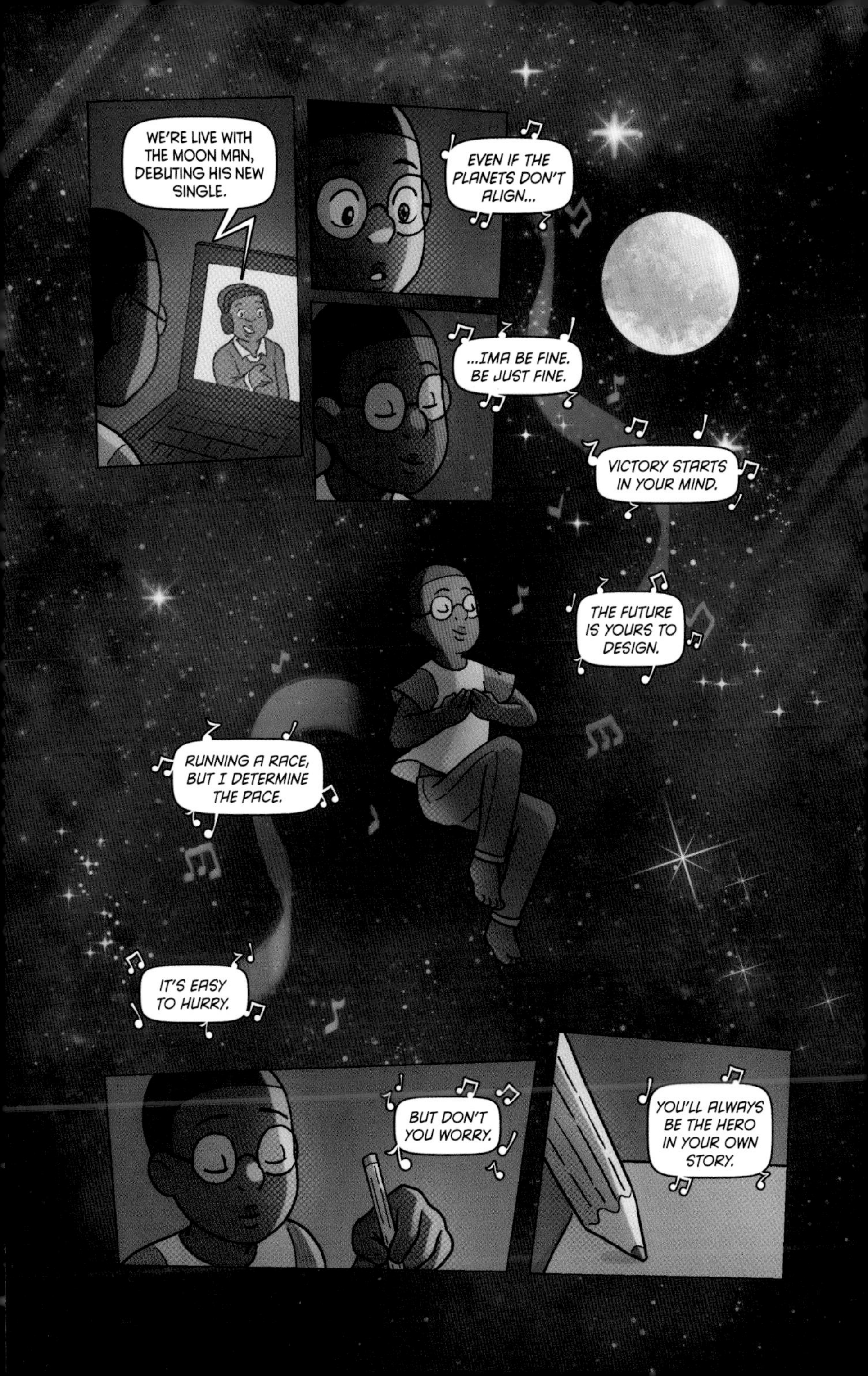
WE'RE LIVE WITH THE MOON MAN, DEBUTING HIS NEW SINGLE.
EVEN IF THE PLANETS DON'T ALIGN...
...IMA BE FINE. BE JUST FINE.
VICTORY STARTS IN YOUR MIND.
THE FUTURE IS YOURS TO DESIGN.
RUNNING A RACE, BUT I DETERMINE THE PACE.
IT'S EASY TO HURRY.
BUT DON'T YOU WORRY.
YOU'LL ALWAYS BE THE HERO IN YOUR OWN STORY.

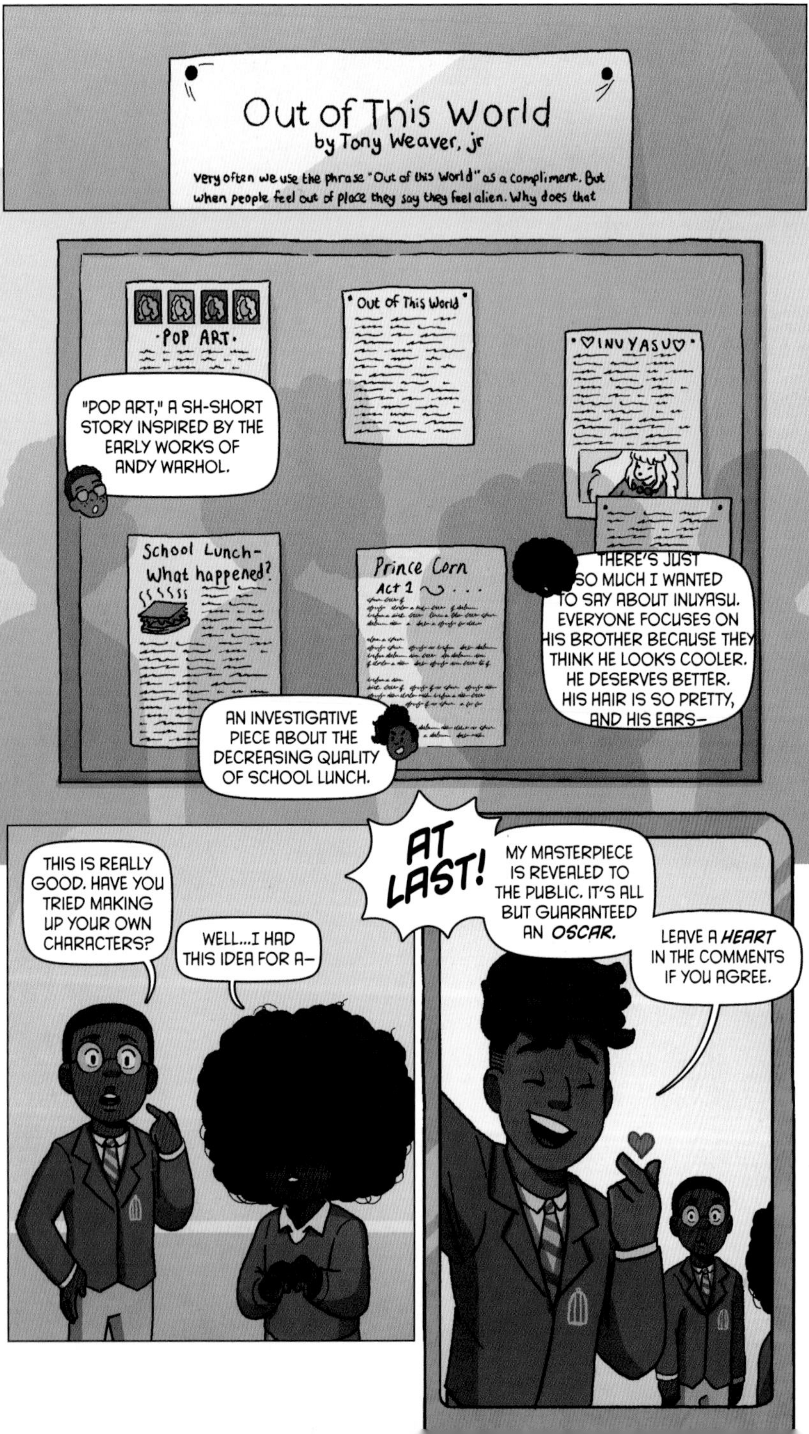

Out of This World
by Tony Weaver, jr
Very often we use the phrase "Out of this World" as a compliment. But when people feel out of place they say they feel alien. Why does that
POP ART
Out of This World
♡INUYASU♡
"POP ART," A SH-SHORT STORY INSPIRED BY THE EARLY WORKS OF ANDY WARHOL.
School Lunch- What happened?
Prince Corn
Act 1
THERE'S JUST SO MUCH I WANTED TO SAY ABOUT INUYASU. EVERYONE FOCUSES ON HIS BROTHER BECAUSE THEY THINK HE LOOKS COOLER. HE DESERVES BETTER. HIS HAIR IS SO PRETTY, AND HIS EARS–
AN INVESTIGATIVE PIECE ABOUT THE DECREASING QUALITY OF SCHOOL LUNCH.
THIS IS REALLY GOOD. HAVE YOU TRIED MAKING UP YOUR OWN CHARACTERS?
WELL...I HAD THIS IDEA FOR A–
AT LAST!
MY MASTERPIECE IS REVEALED TO THE PUBLIC. IT'S ALL BUT GUARANTEED AN OSCAR.
LEAVE A HEART IN THE COMMENTS IF YOU AGREE.

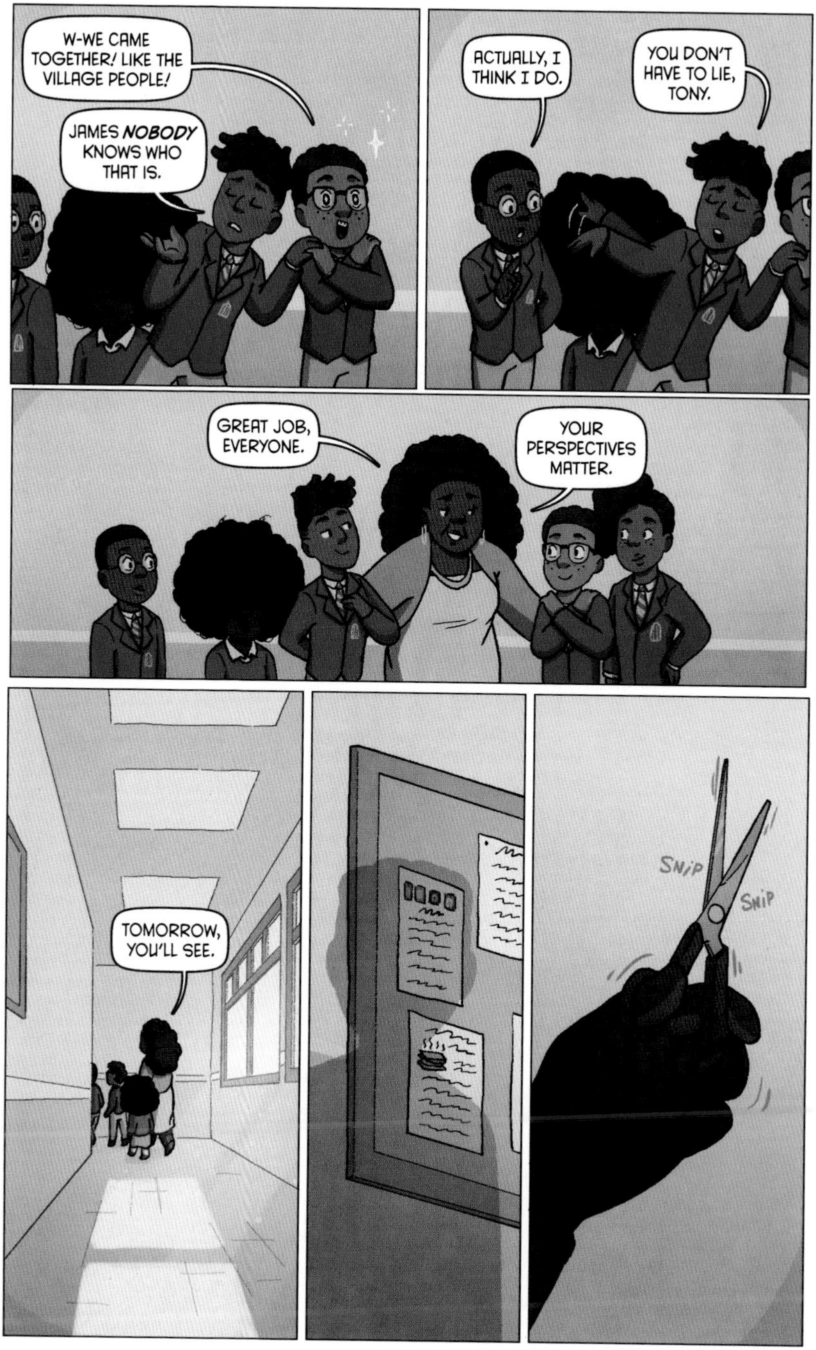
W-WE CAME TOGETHER! LIKE THE VILLAGE PEOPLE!
JAMES *NOBODY* KNOWS WHO THAT IS.
ACTUALLY, I THINK I DO.
YOU DON'T HAVE TO LIE, TONY.
GREAT JOB, EVERYONE.
YOUR PERSPECTIVES MATTER.
TOMORROW, YOU'LL SEE.
SNIP
SNIP

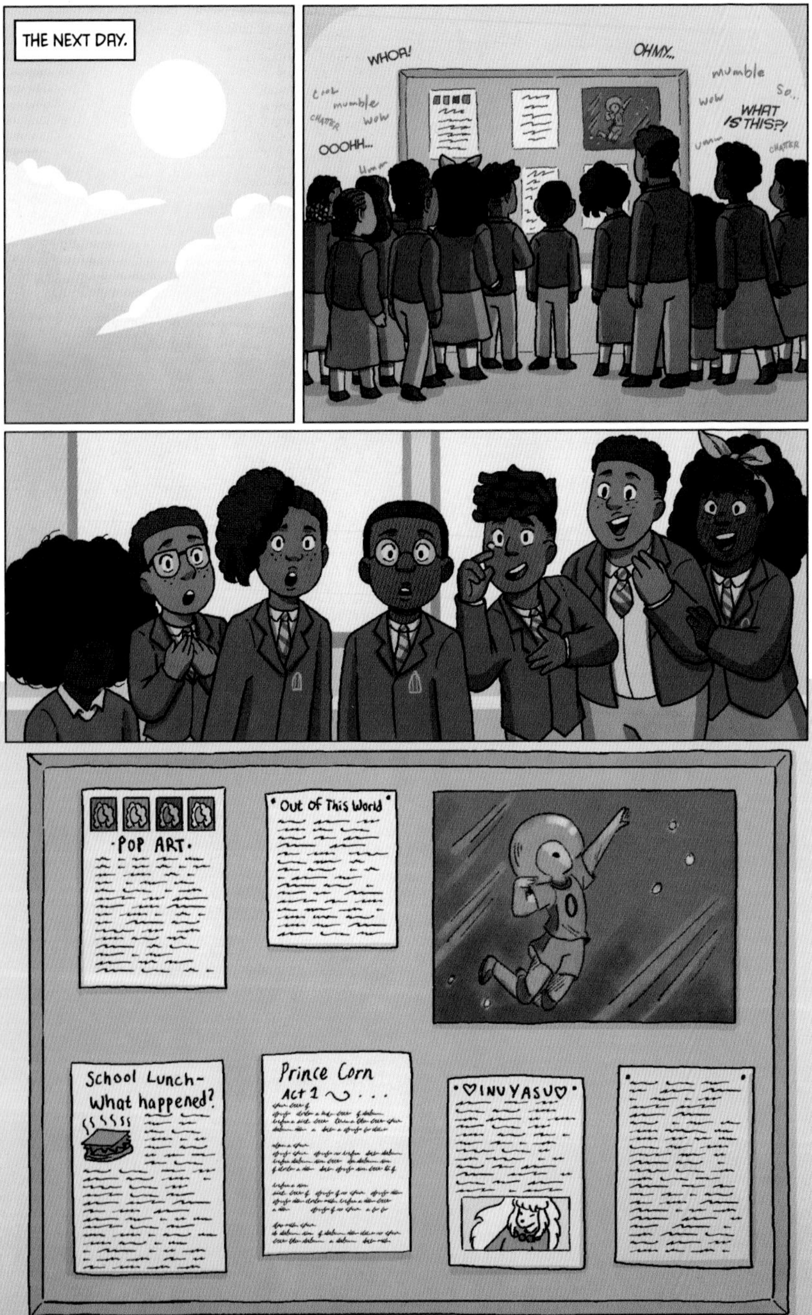
THE NEXT DAY.
WHOA!
cool
mumble
CHATTER
wow
OOOHH...
OHMY...
mumble
So..
wow
WHAT IS THIS?!
CHATTER
POP ART
Out Of This World
School Lunch-
What happened?
Prince Corn
Act 1
♡INUYASU♡

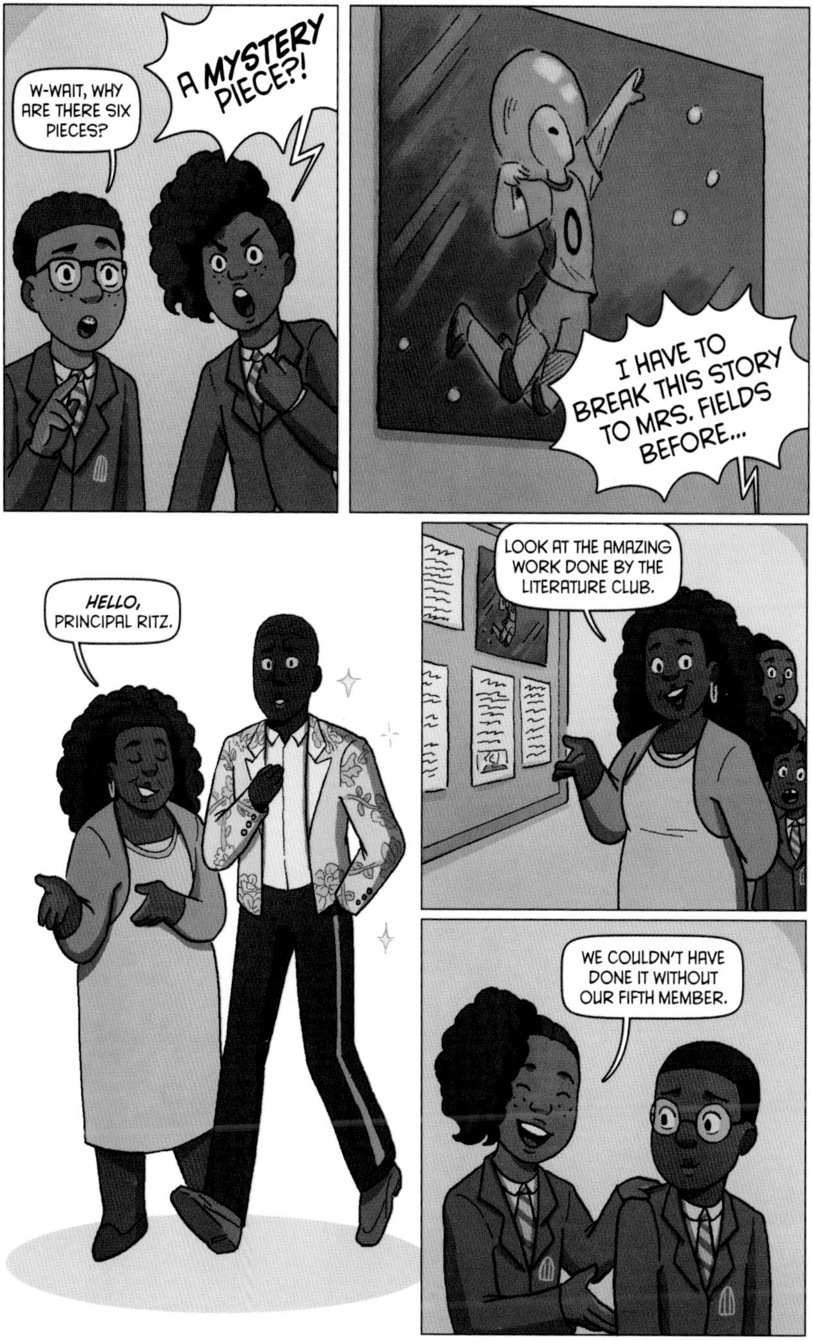
W-WAIT, WHY ARE THERE SIX PIECES?
A *MYSTERY* PIECE?!
I HAVE TO BREAK THIS STORY TO MRS. FIELDS BEFORE...
HELLO, PRINCIPAL RITZ.
LOOK AT THE AMAZING WORK DONE BY THE LITERATURE CLUB.
WE COULDN'T HAVE DONE IT WITHOUT OUR FIFTH MEMBER.

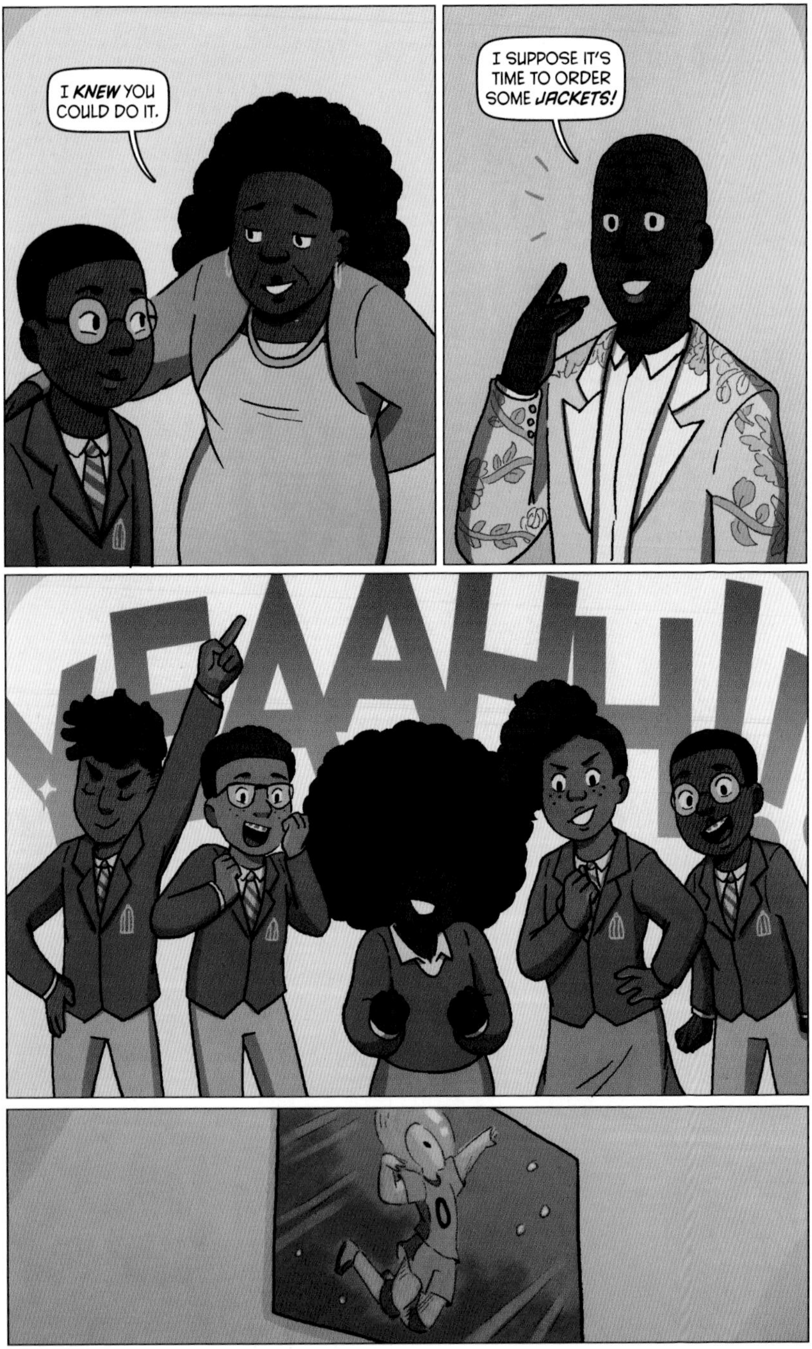
I KNEW YOU COULD DO IT.
I SUPPOSE IT'S TIME TO ORDER SOME JACKETS!

CHAPTER 6

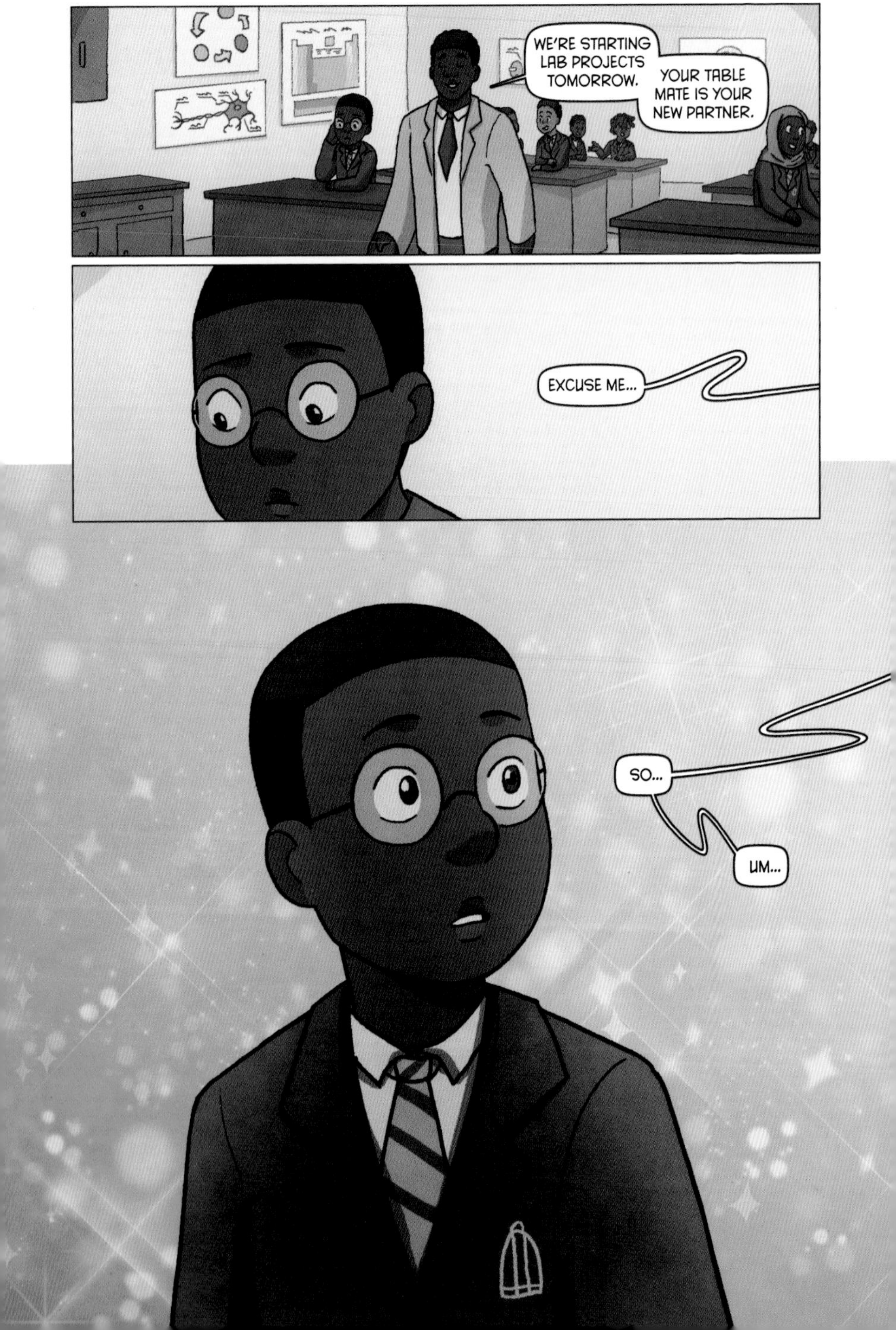
WE'RE STARTING LAB PROJECTS TOMORROW.
YOUR TABLE MATE IS YOUR NEW PARTNER.
EXCUSE ME...
SO...
UM...

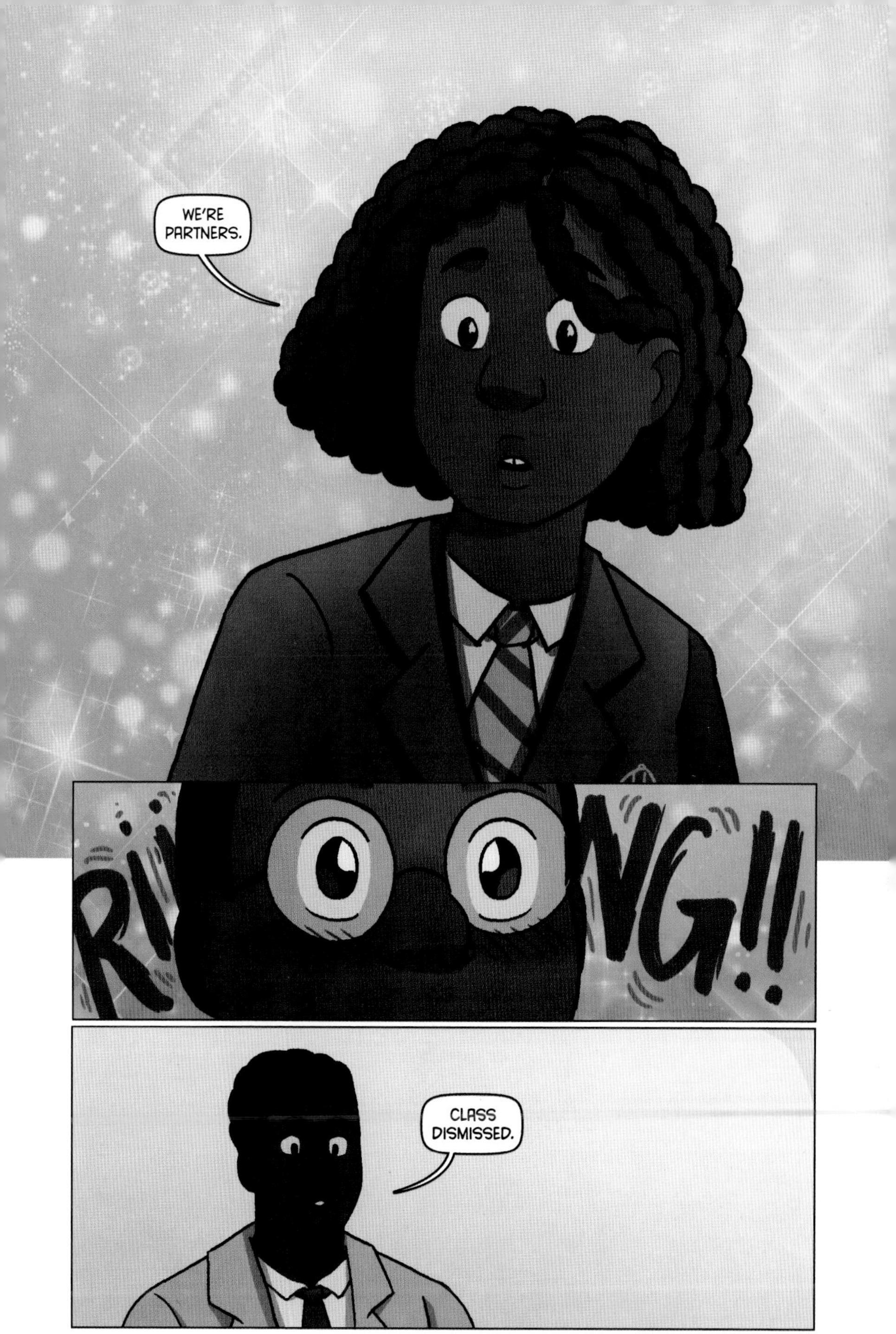
WE'RE PARTNERS.
CLASS DISMISSED.

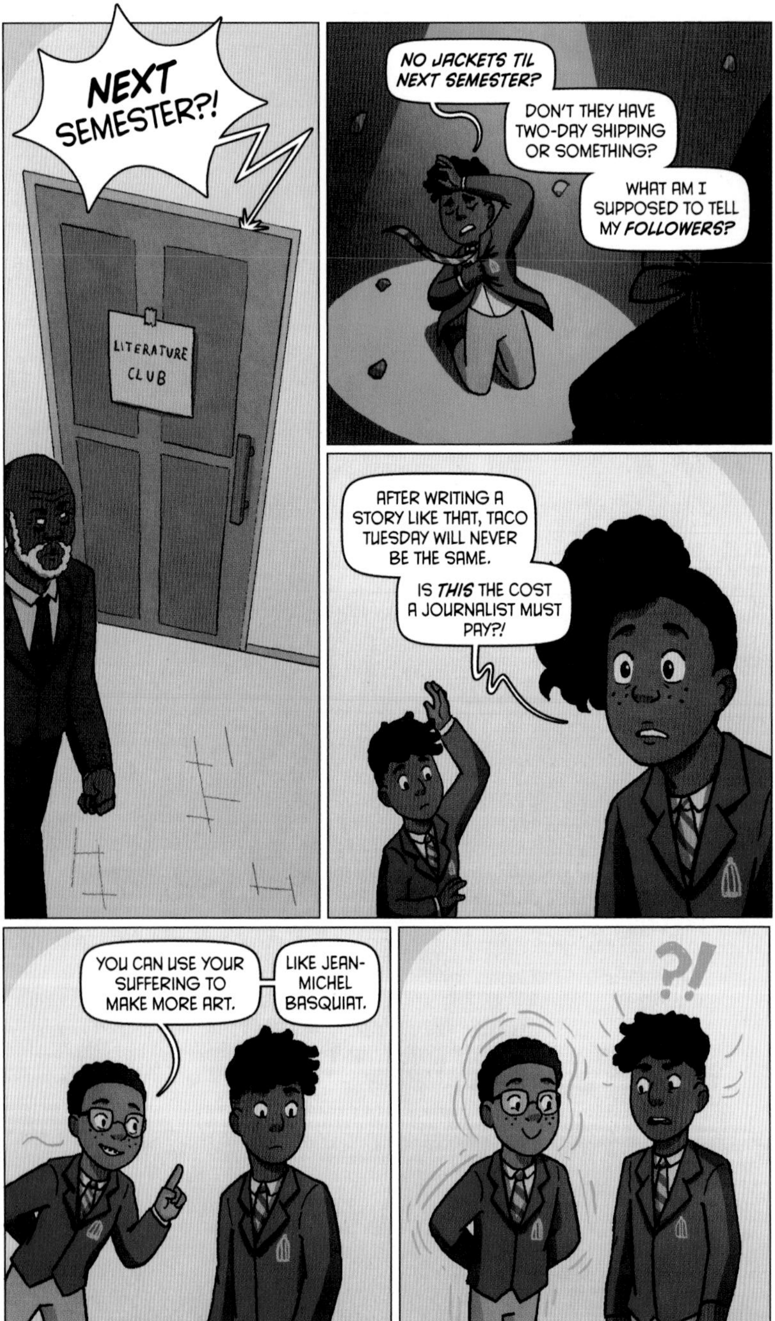
NEXT SEMESTER?!
LITERATURE CLUB
NO JACKETS TIL NEXT SEMESTER?
DON'T THEY HAVE TWO-DAY SHIPPING OR SOMETHING?
WHAT AM I SUPPOSED TO TELL MY FOLLOWERS?
AFTER WRITING A STORY LIKE THAT, TACO TUESDAY WILL NEVER BE THE SAME.
IS THIS THE COST A JOURNALIST MUST PAY?!
YOU CAN USE YOUR SUFFERING TO MAKE MORE ART.
LIKE JEAN-MICHEL BASQUIAT.
?!

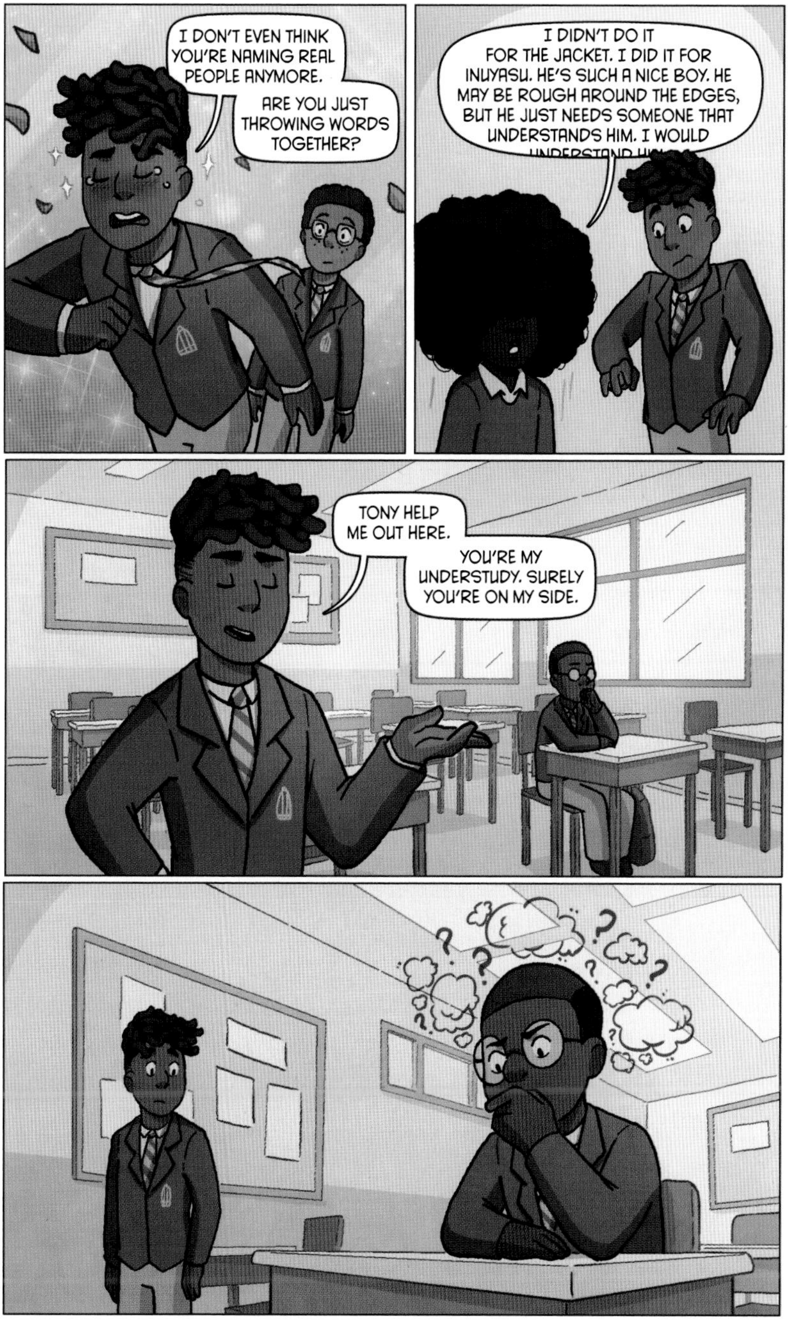
I DON'T EVEN THINK YOU'RE NAMING REAL PEOPLE ANYMORE.
ARE YOU JUST THROWING WORDS TOGETHER?
I DIDN'T DO IT FOR THE JACKET. I DID IT FOR INUYASU. HE'S SUCH A NICE BOY. HE MAY BE ROUGH AROUND THE EDGES, BUT HE JUST NEEDS SOMEONE THAT UNDERSTANDS HIM. I WOULD
TONY HELP ME OUT HERE.
YOU'RE MY UNDERSTUDY. SURELY YOU'RE ON MY SIDE.

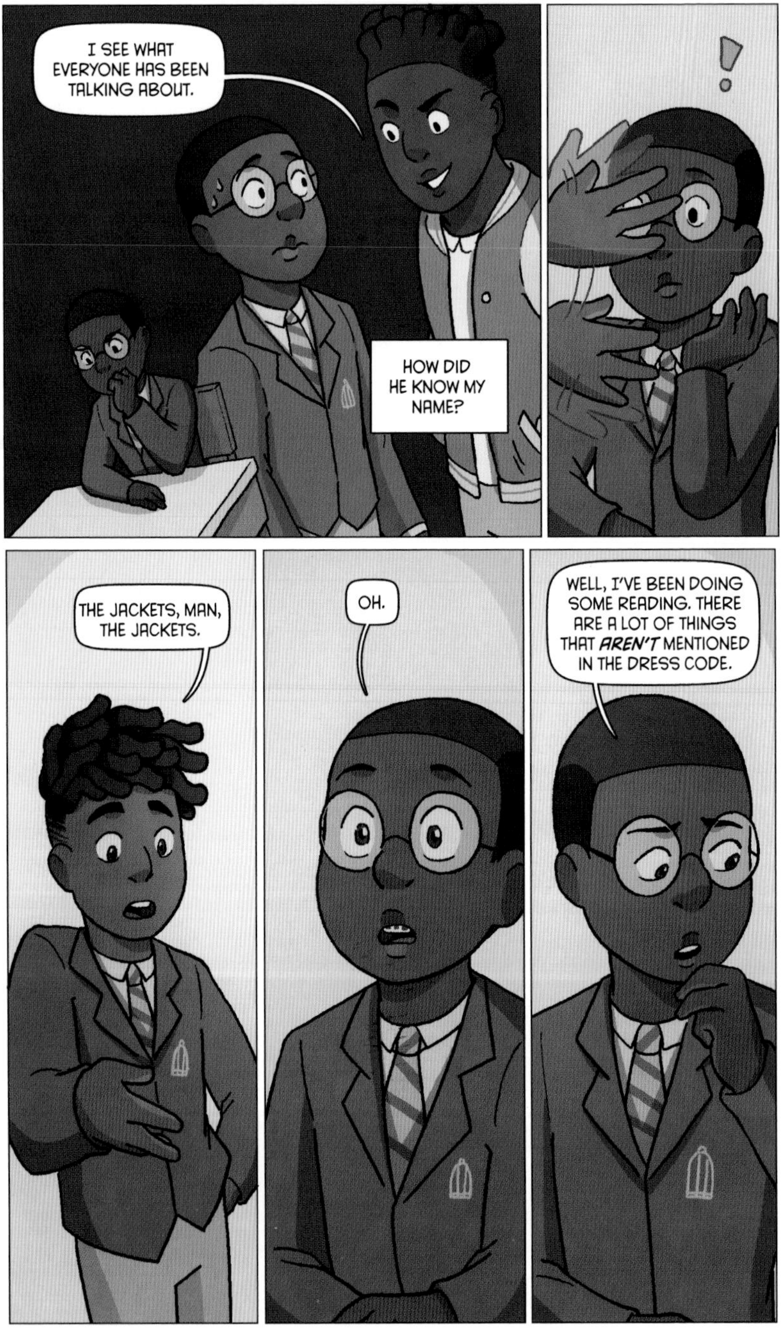
I SEE WHAT EVERYONE HAS BEEN TALKING ABOUT.
HOW DID HE KNOW MY NAME?
!
THE JACKETS, MAN, THE JACKETS.
OH.
WELL, I'VE BEEN DOING SOME READING. THERE ARE A LOT OF THINGS THAT *AREN'T* MENTIONED IN THE DRESS CODE.

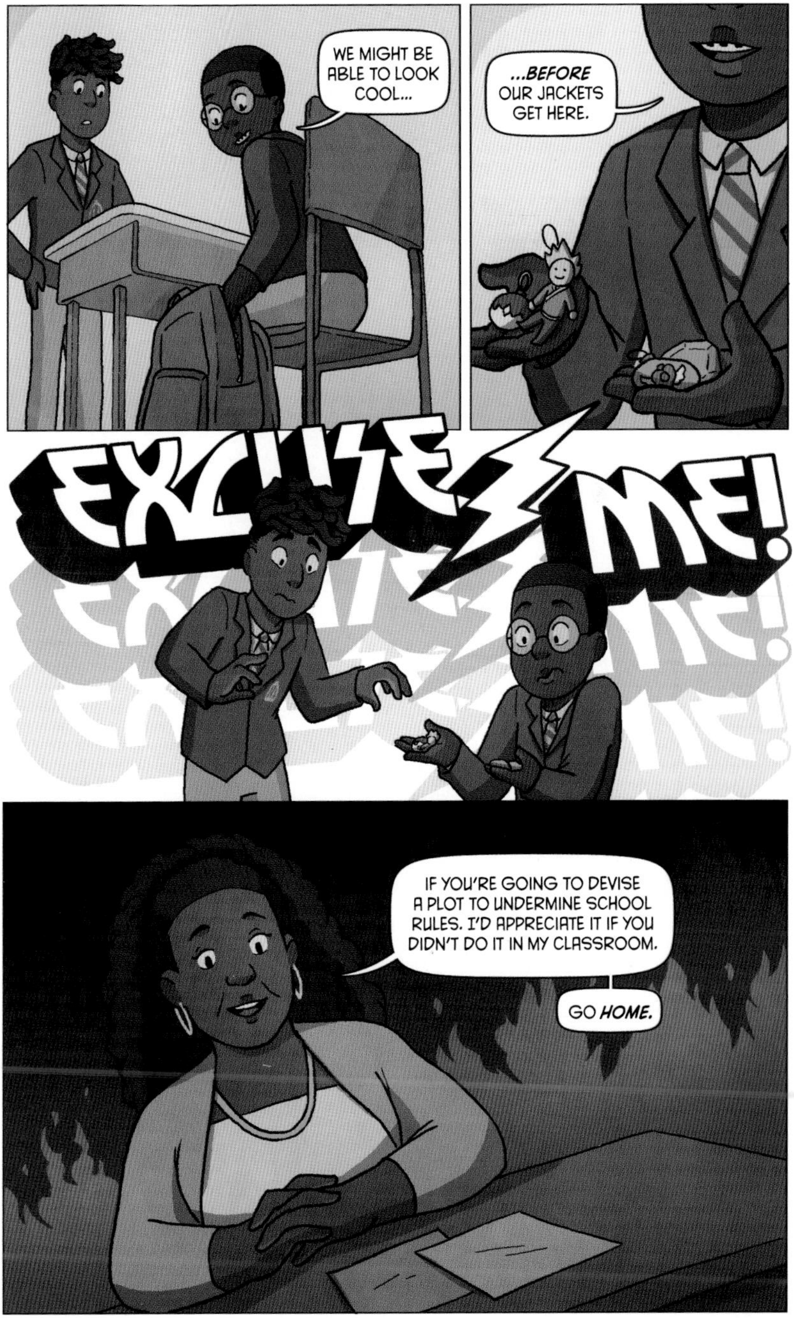
WE MIGHT BE ABLE TO LOOK COOL...
...BEFORE OUR JACKETS GET HERE.
EXCUSE ME!
IF YOU'RE GOING TO DEVISE A PLOT TO UNDERMINE SCHOOL RULES. I'D APPRECIATE IT IF YOU DIDN'T DO IT IN MY CLASSROOM.
GO HOME.

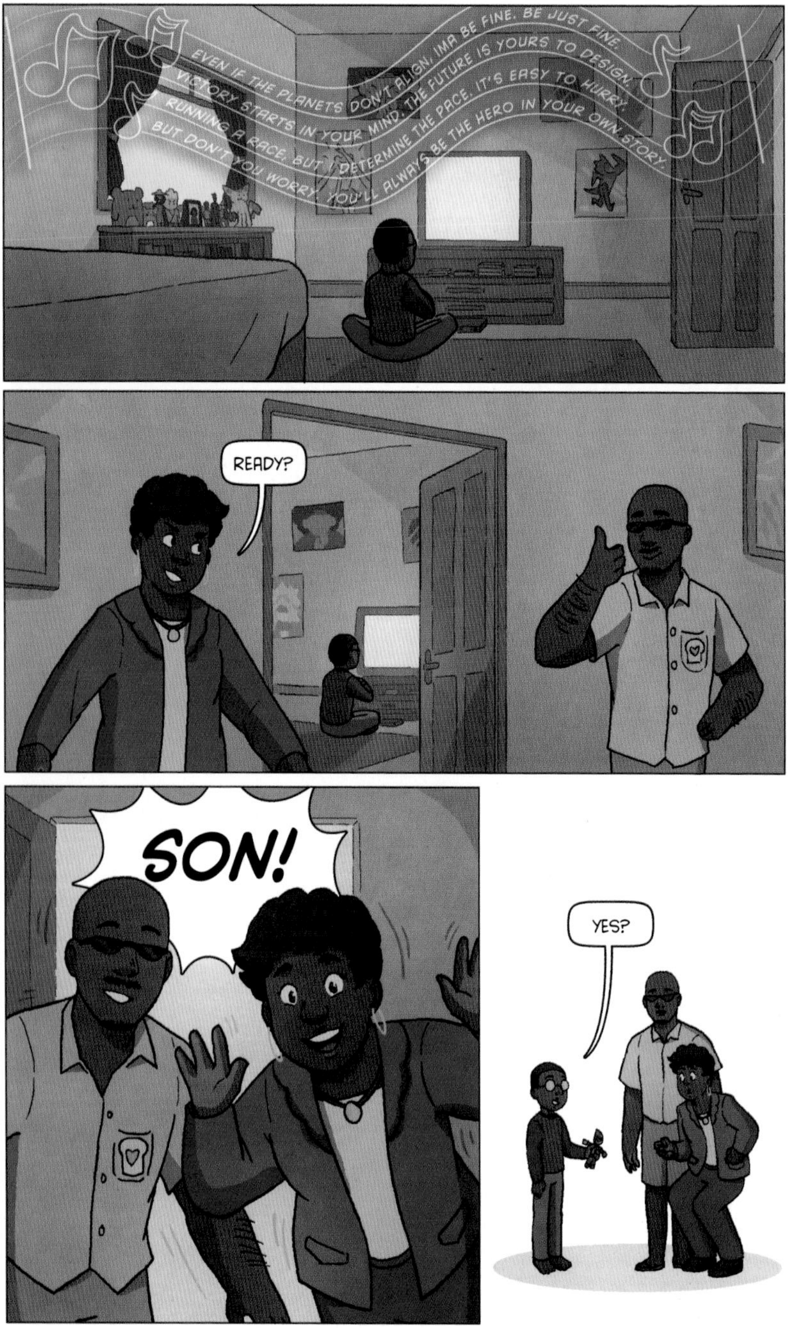
EVEN IF THE PLANETS DON'T ALIGN, IMA BE FINE. BE JUST FINE.
VICTORY STARTS IN YOUR MIND. THE FUTURE IS YOURS TO DESIGN.
RUNNING A RACE, BUT I DETERMINE THE PACE. IT'S EASY TO HURRY.
BUT DON'T YOU WORRY. YOU'LL ALWAYS BE THE HERO IN YOUR OWN STORY.
READY?
SON!
YES?

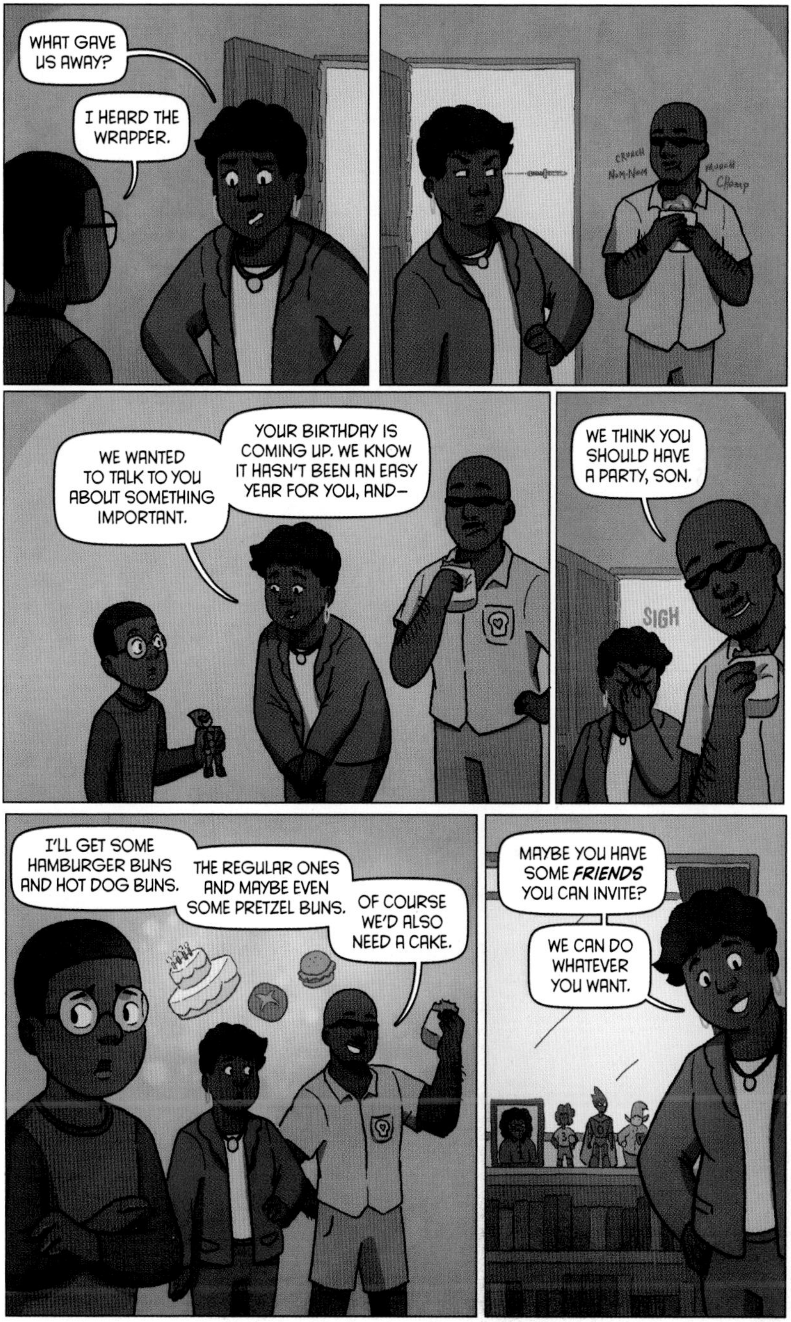
WHAT GAVE US AWAY?
I HEARD THE WRAPPER.
CRUNCH
NOM-NOM
MUNCH
CHOMP
WE WANTED TO TALK TO YOU ABOUT SOMETHING IMPORTANT.
YOUR BIRTHDAY IS COMING UP. WE KNOW IT HASN'T BEEN AN EASY YEAR FOR YOU, AND—
WE THINK YOU SHOULD HAVE A PARTY, SON.
SIGH
I'LL GET SOME HAMBURGER BUNS AND HOT DOG BUNS.
THE REGULAR ONES AND MAYBE EVEN SOME PRETZEL BUNS.
OF COURSE WE'D ALSO NEED A CAKE.
MAYBE YOU HAVE SOME *FRIENDS* YOU CAN INVITE?
WE CAN DO WHATEVER YOU WANT.

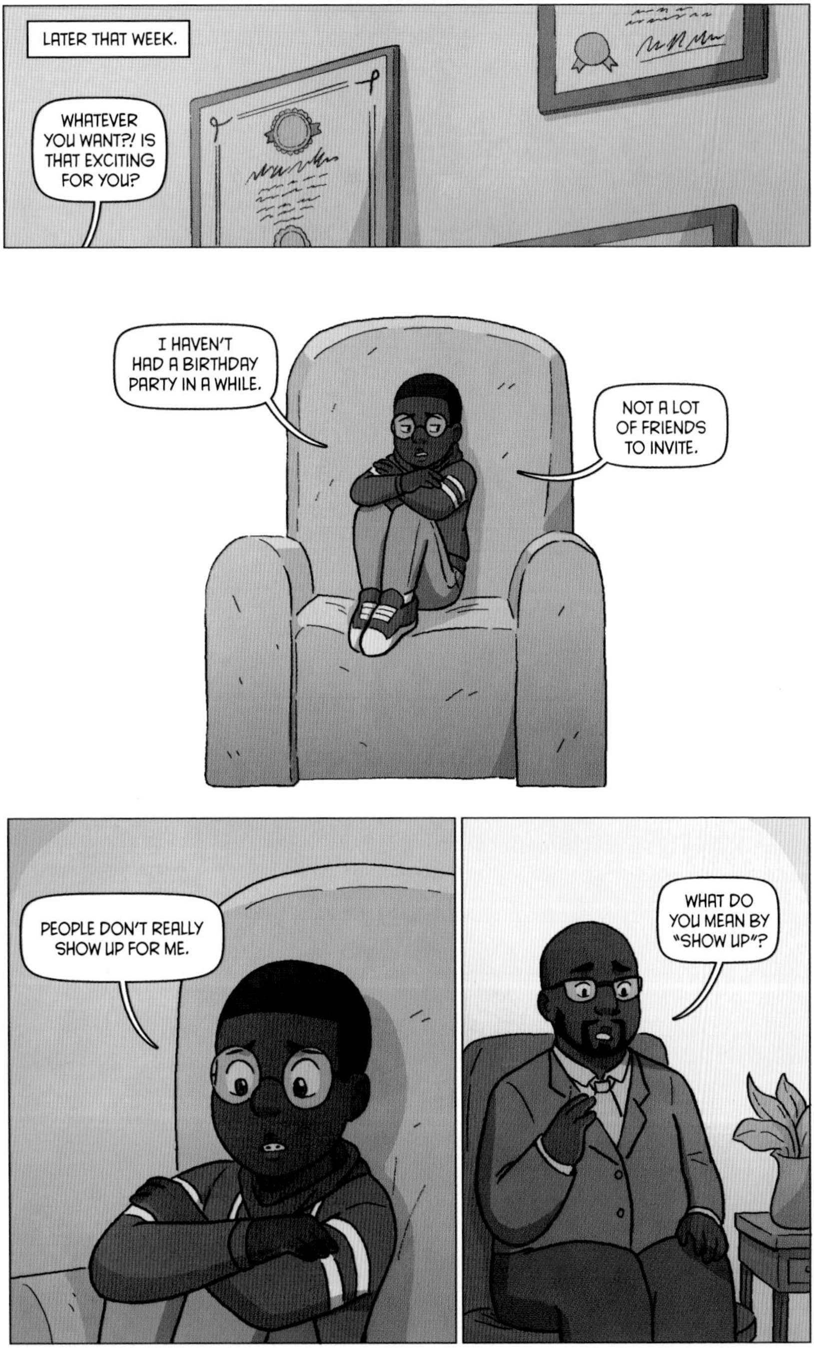
LATER THAT WEEK.
WHATEVER YOU WANT?! IS THAT EXCITING FOR YOU?
I HAVEN'T HAD A BIRTHDAY PARTY IN A WHILE.
NOT A LOT OF FRIENDS TO INVITE.
PEOPLE DON'T REALLY SHOW UP FOR ME.
WHAT DO YOU MEAN BY "SHOW UP"?

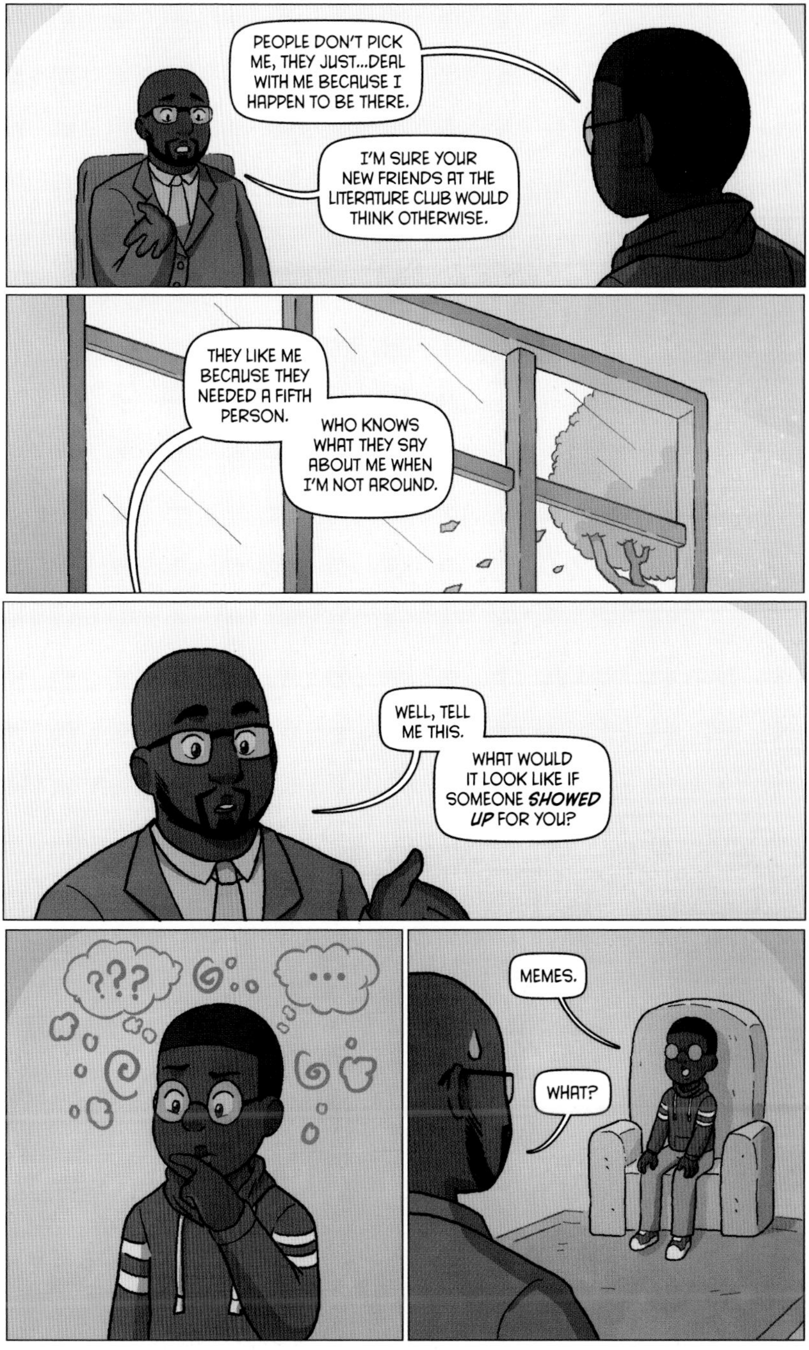
PEOPLE DON'T PICK ME, THEY JUST...DEAL WITH ME BECAUSE I HAPPEN TO BE THERE.
I'M SURE YOUR NEW FRIENDS AT THE LITERATURE CLUB WOULD THINK OTHERWISE.
THEY LIKE ME BECAUSE THEY NEEDED A FIFTH PERSON.
WHO KNOWS WHAT THEY SAY ABOUT ME WHEN I'M NOT AROUND.
WELL, TELL ME THIS.
WHAT WOULD IT LOOK LIKE IF SOMEONE ***SHOWED UP*** FOR YOU?
???
...
MEMES.
WHAT?

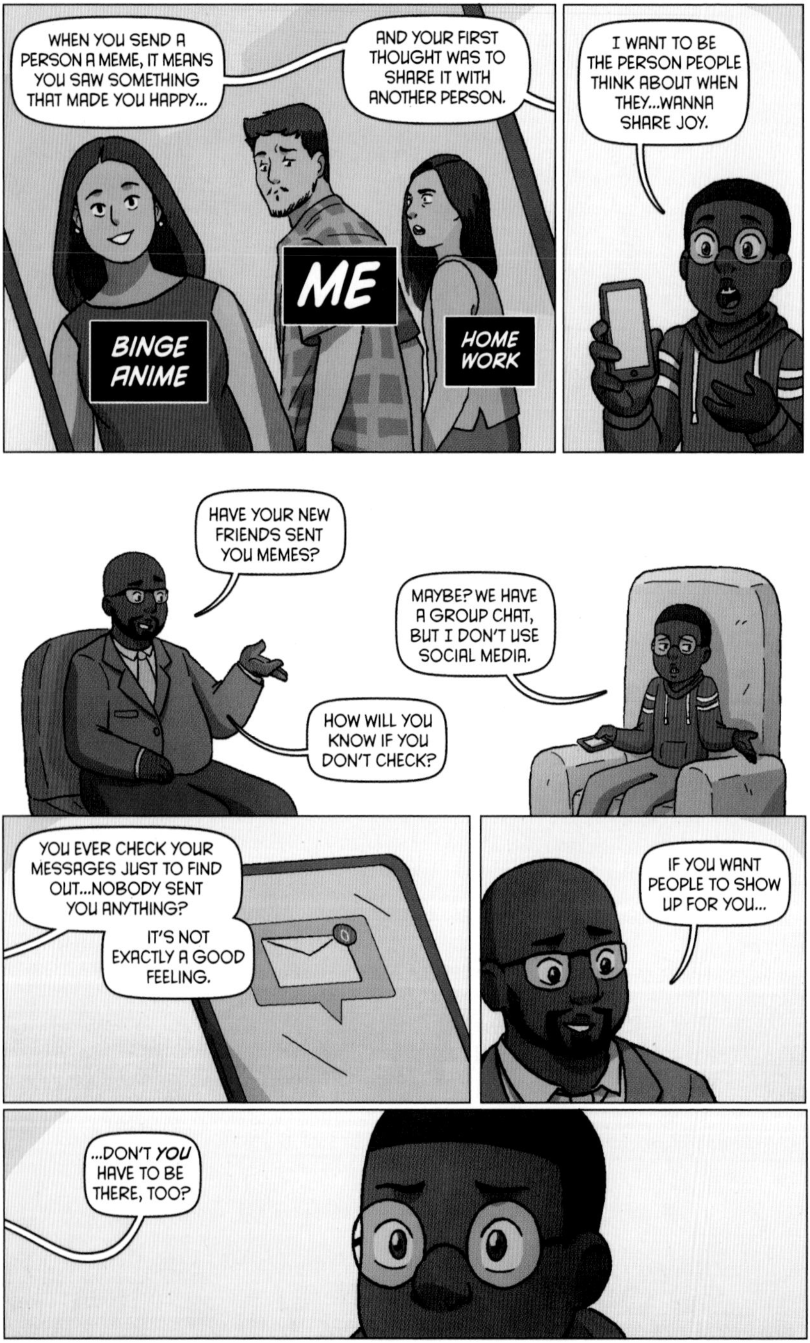
WHEN YOU SEND A PERSON A MEME, IT MEANS YOU SAW SOMETHING THAT MADE YOU HAPPY...
AND YOUR FIRST THOUGHT WAS TO SHARE IT WITH ANOTHER PERSON.
BINGE ANIME
ME
HOME WORK
I WANT TO BE THE PERSON PEOPLE THINK ABOUT WHEN THEY...WANNA SHARE JOY.
HAVE YOUR NEW FRIENDS SENT YOU MEMES?
MAYBE? WE HAVE A GROUP CHAT, BUT I DON'T USE SOCIAL MEDIA.
HOW WILL YOU KNOW IF YOU DON'T CHECK?
YOU EVER CHECK YOUR MESSAGES JUST TO FIND OUT...NOBODY SENT YOU ANYTHING?
IT'S NOT EXACTLY A GOOD FEELING.
0
IF YOU WANT PEOPLE TO SHOW UP FOR YOU...
...DON'T *YOU* HAVE TO BE THERE, TOO?

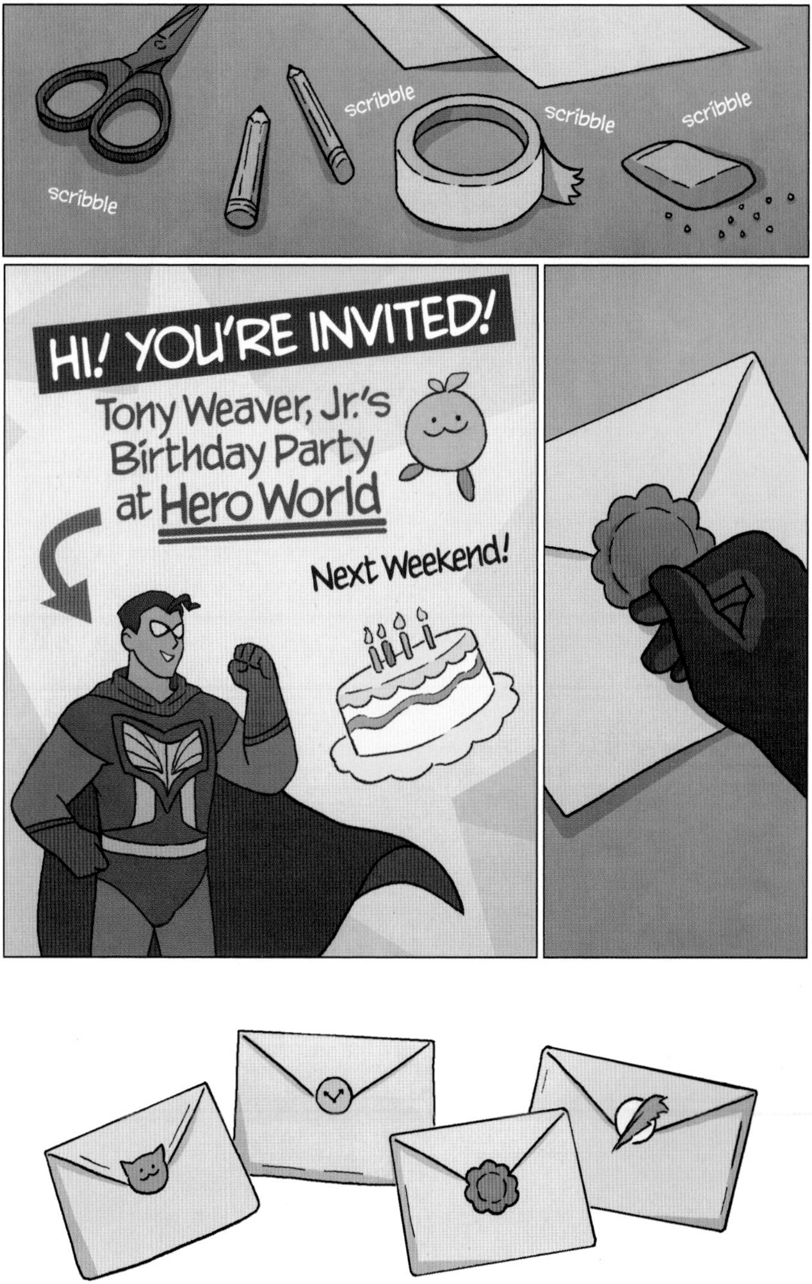
scribble
scribble
scribble
scribble
HI! YOU'RE INVITED!
Tony Weaver, Jr.'s Birthday Party at Hero World
Next Weekend!

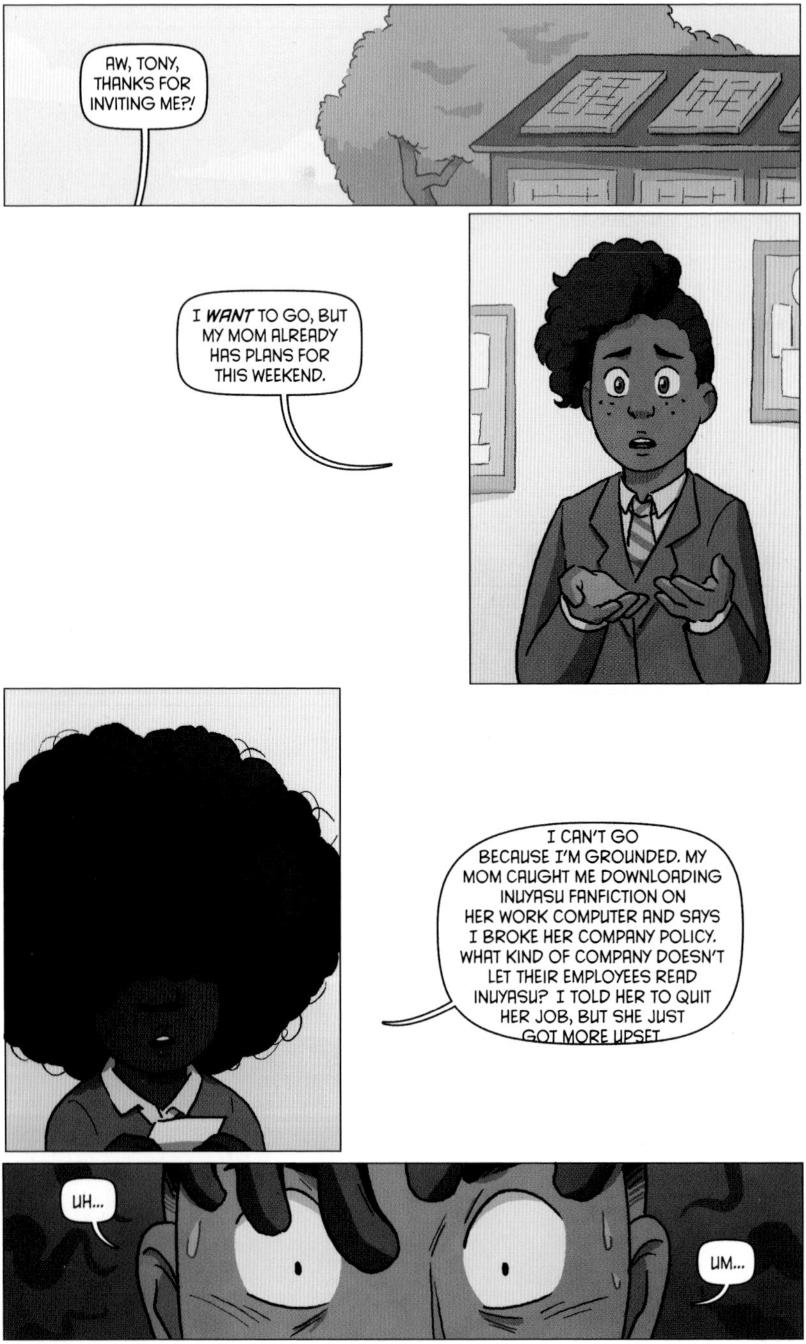
AW, TONY, THANKS FOR INVITING ME?!
I WANT TO GO, BUT MY MOM ALREADY HAS PLANS FOR THIS WEEKEND.
I CAN'T GO BECAUSE I'M GROUNDED. MY MOM CAUGHT ME DOWNLOADING INUYASU FANFICTION ON HER WORK COMPUTER AND SAYS I BROKE HER COMPANY POLICY. WHAT KIND OF COMPANY DOESN'T LET THEIR EMPLOYEES READ INUYASU? I TOLD HER TO QUIT HER JOB, BUT SHE JUST GOT MORE UPSET.
UH...
UM...

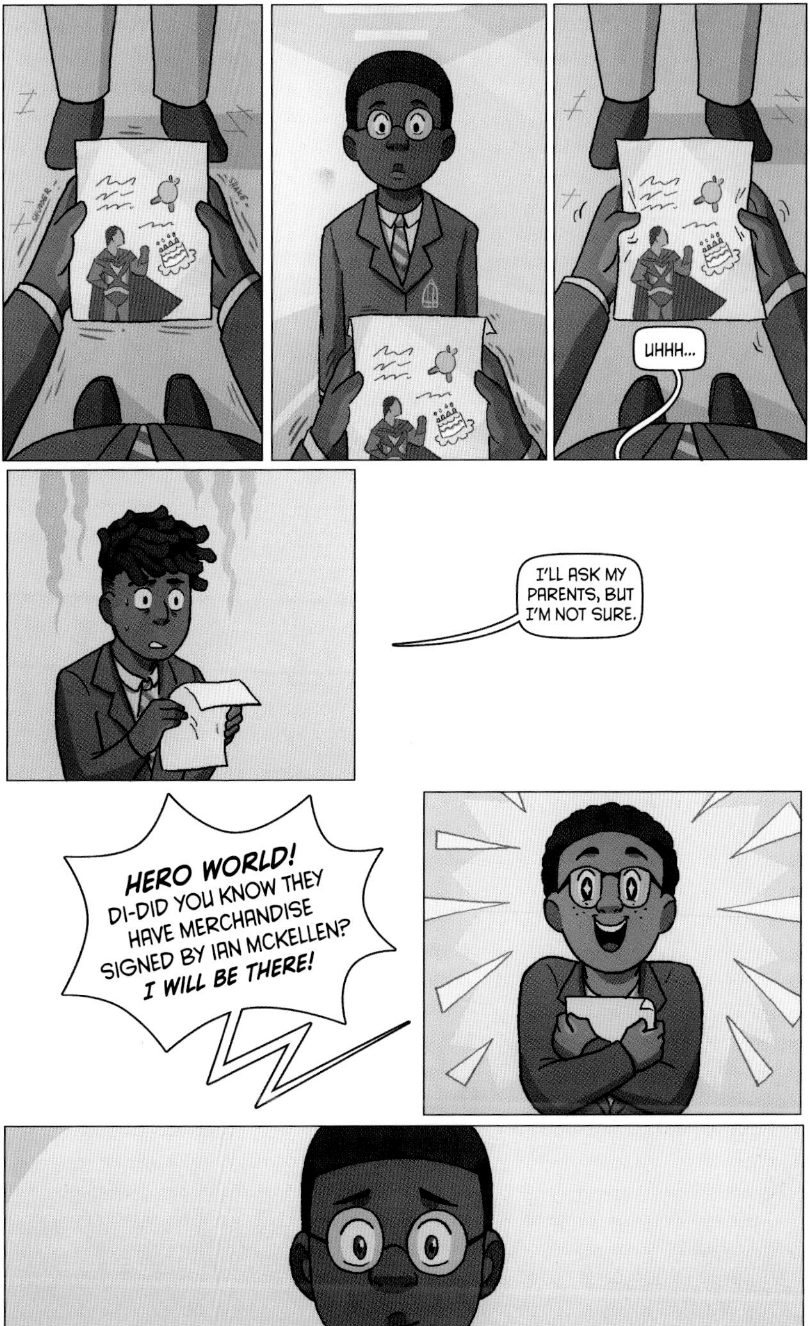
SHUDDER
SHAKE
UHHH...
I'LL ASK MY PARENTS, BUT I'M NOT SURE.
HERO WORLD! DI-DID YOU KNOW THEY HAVE MERCHANDISE SIGNED BY IAN MCKELLEN? I WILL BE THERE!

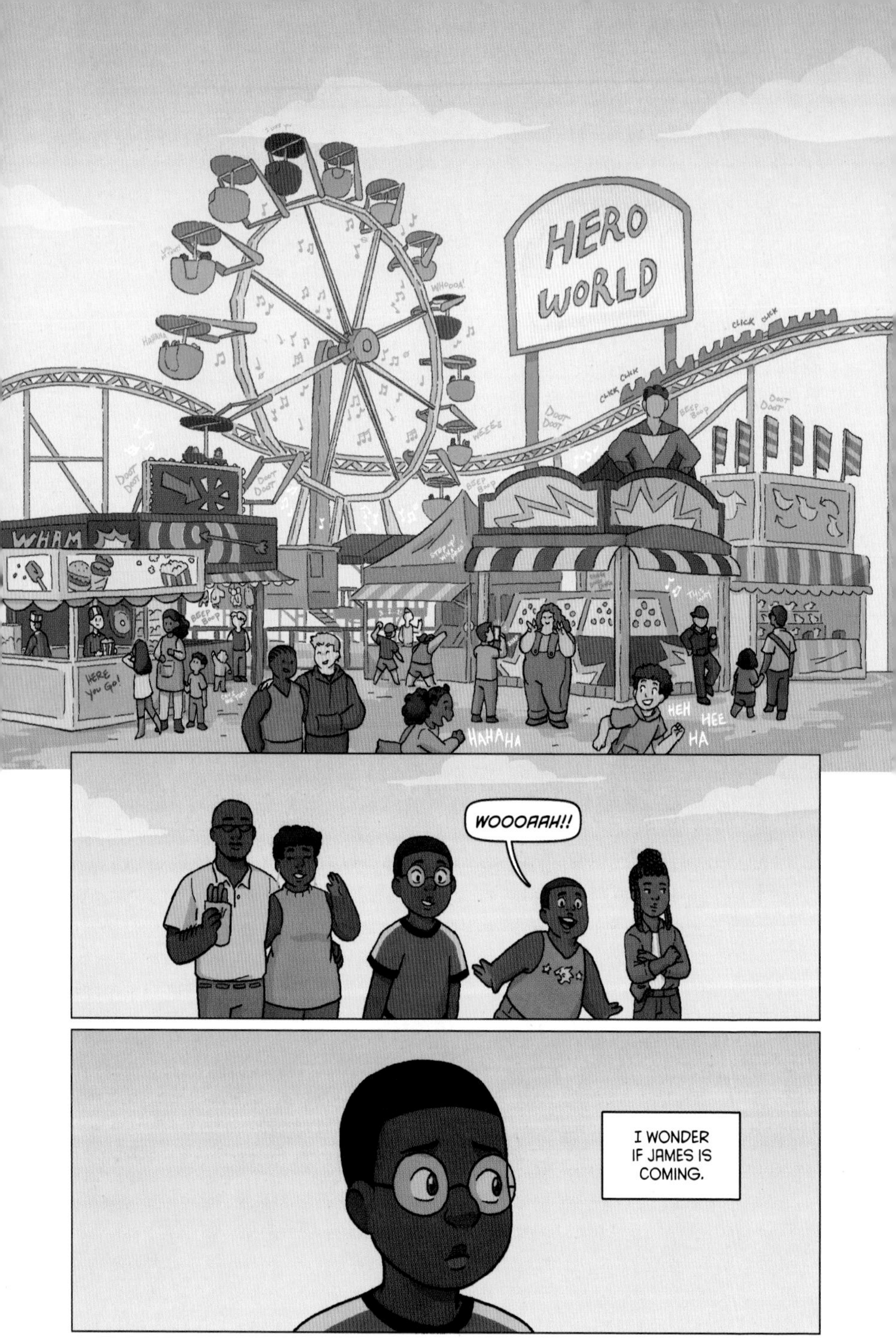
HERO WORLD
WHAM
CLICK CLICK
CLICK CLICK
DOOT DOOT
BEEP BOOP
HERE YOU GO!
HAHAHA
HEH HEE HA
WOOOAAH!!
I WONDER IF JAMES IS COMING.

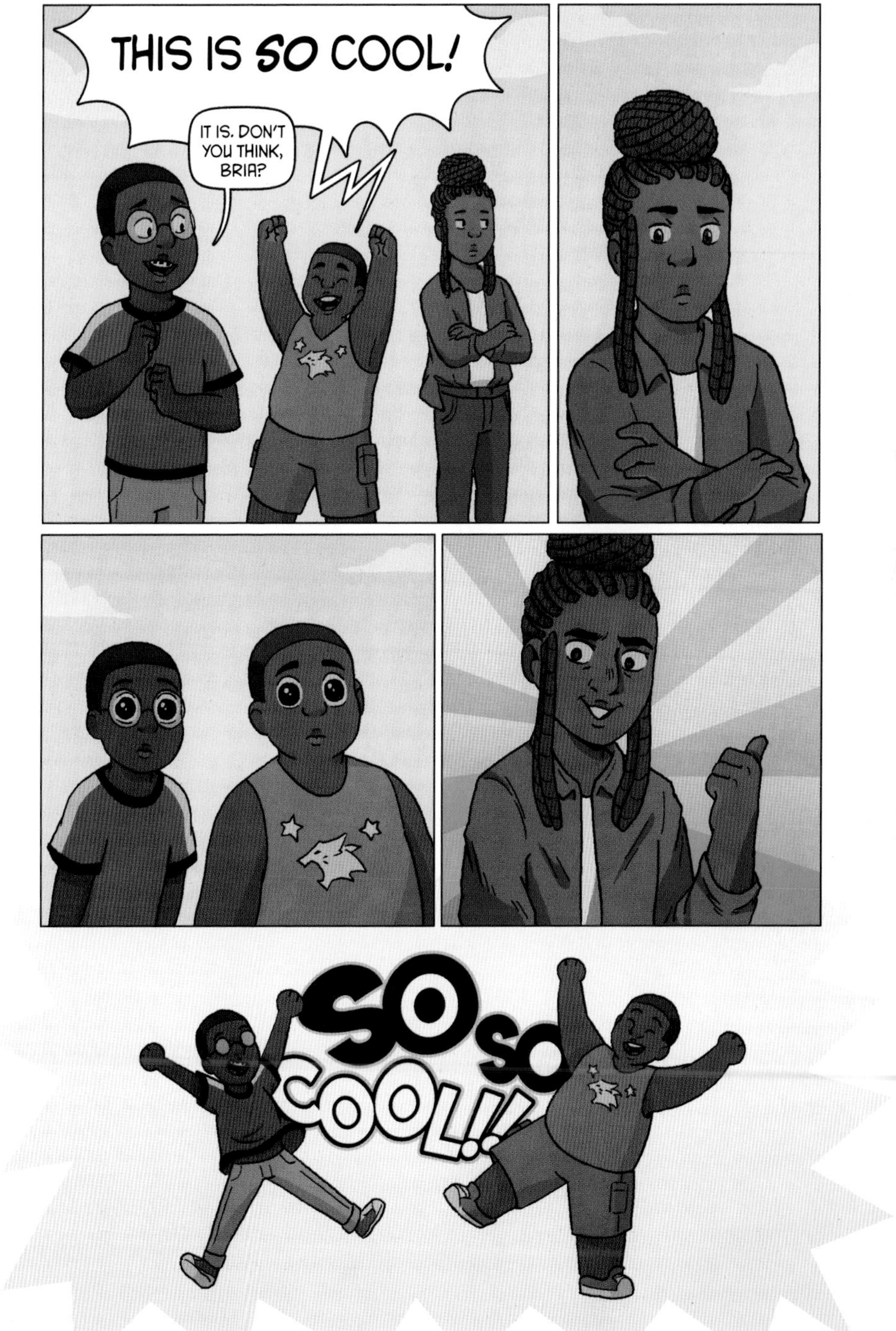
THIS IS SO COOL!
IT IS. DON'T YOU THINK, BRIA?
SO SO COOL!!

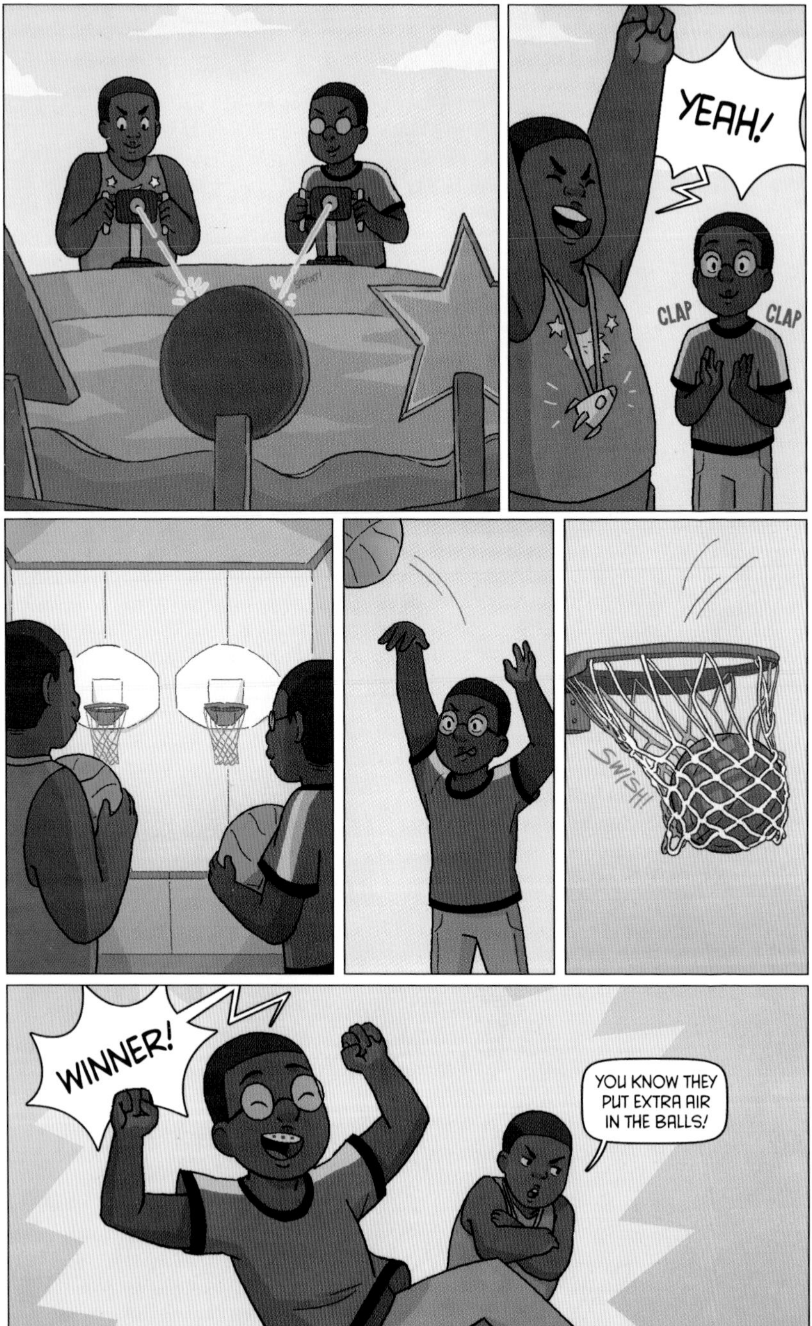
YEAH!
CLAP
CLAP
SWISH!
WINNER!
YOU KNOW THEY PUT EXTRA AIR IN THE BALLS!

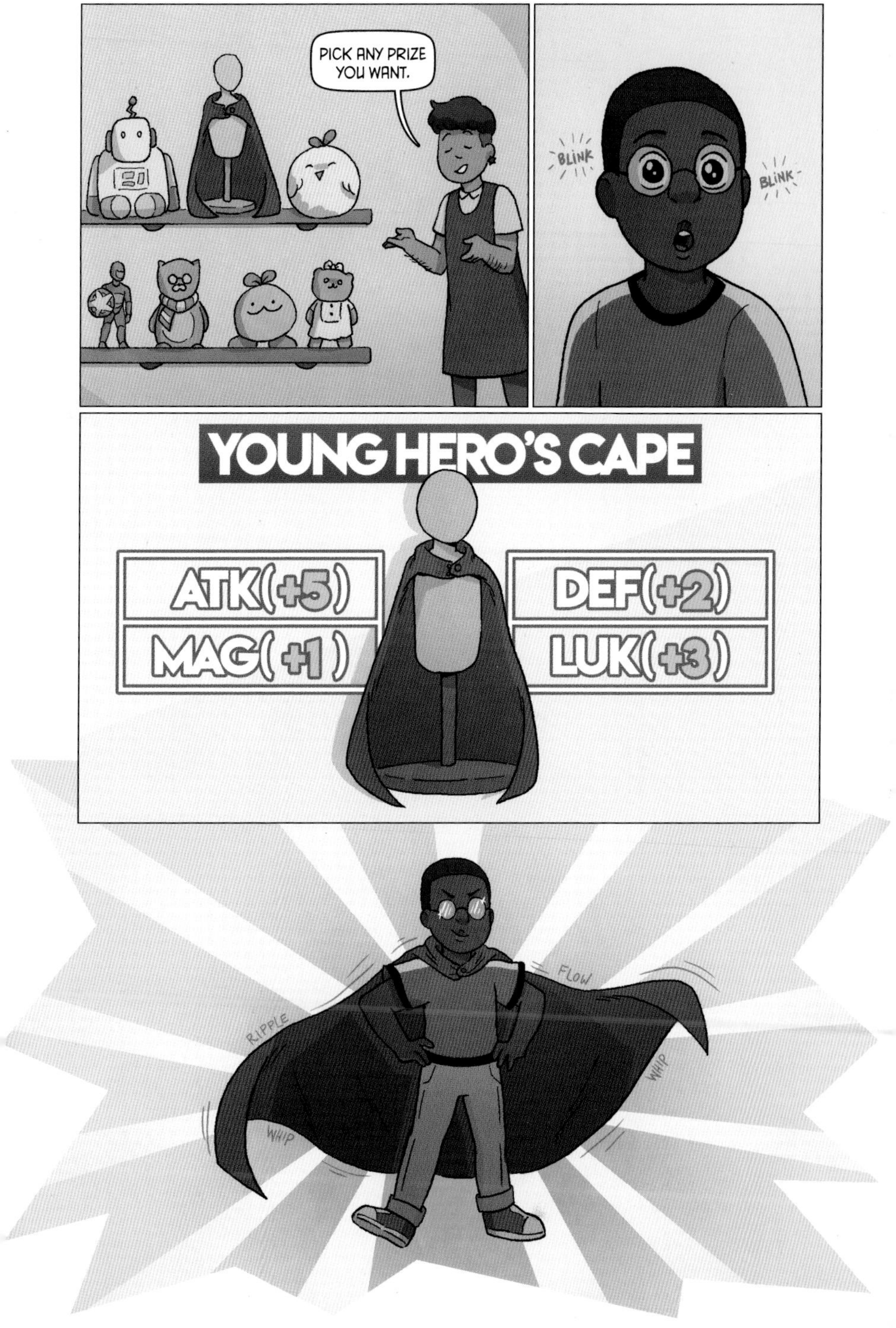
PICK ANY PRIZE YOU WANT.
BLINK
BLINK
YOUNG HERO'S CAPE
ATK(+5)
DEF(+2)
MAG(+1)
LUK(+3)
FLOW
RIPPLE
WHIP
WHIP

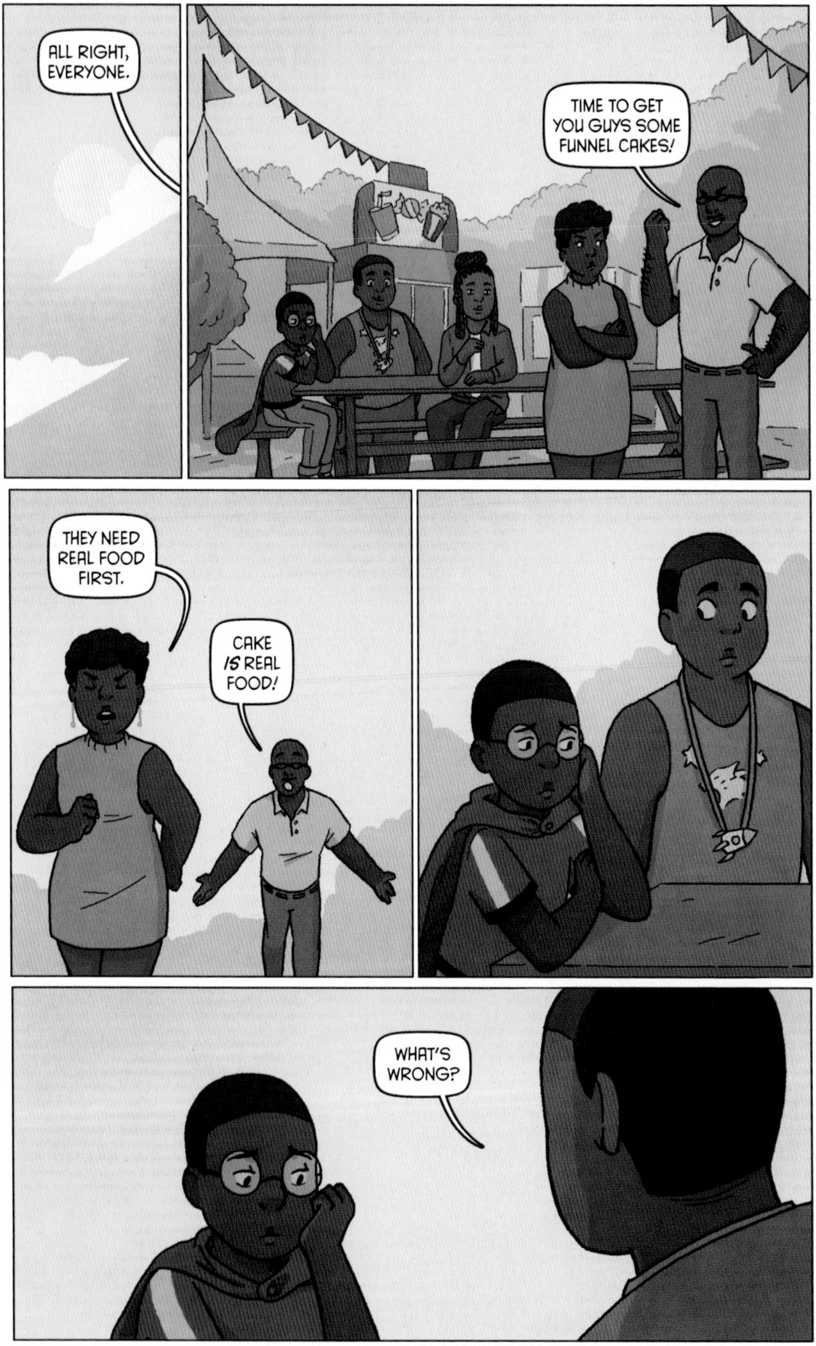
ALL RIGHT, EVERYONE.
TIME TO GET YOU GUYS SOME FUNNEL CAKES!
THEY NEED REAL FOOD FIRST.
CAKE *IS* REAL FOOD!
WHAT'S WRONG?

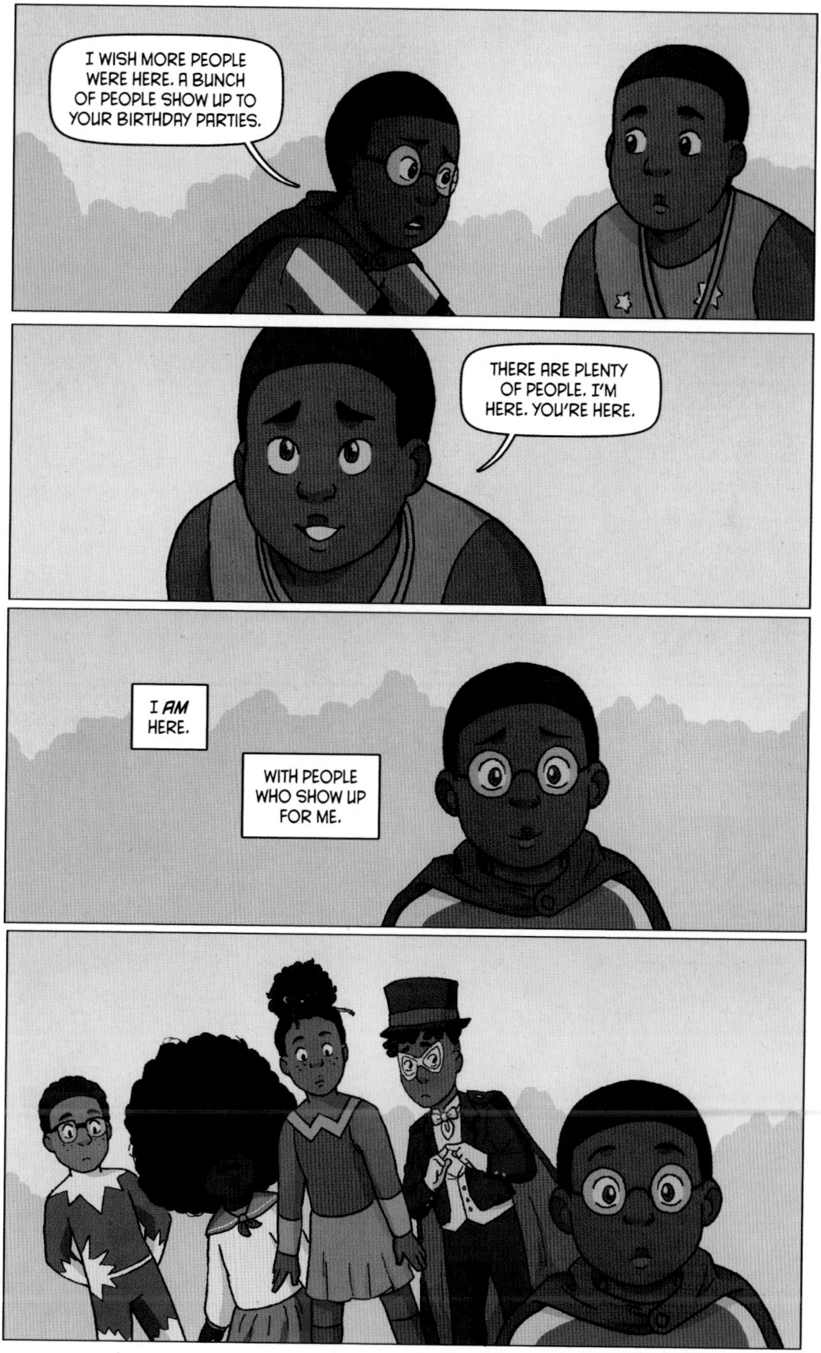
I WISH MORE PEOPLE WERE HERE. A BUNCH OF PEOPLE SHOW UP TO YOUR BIRTHDAY PARTIES.
THERE ARE PLENTY OF PEOPLE. I'M HERE. YOU'RE HERE.
I *AM* HERE.
WITH PEOPLE WHO SHOW UP FOR ME.

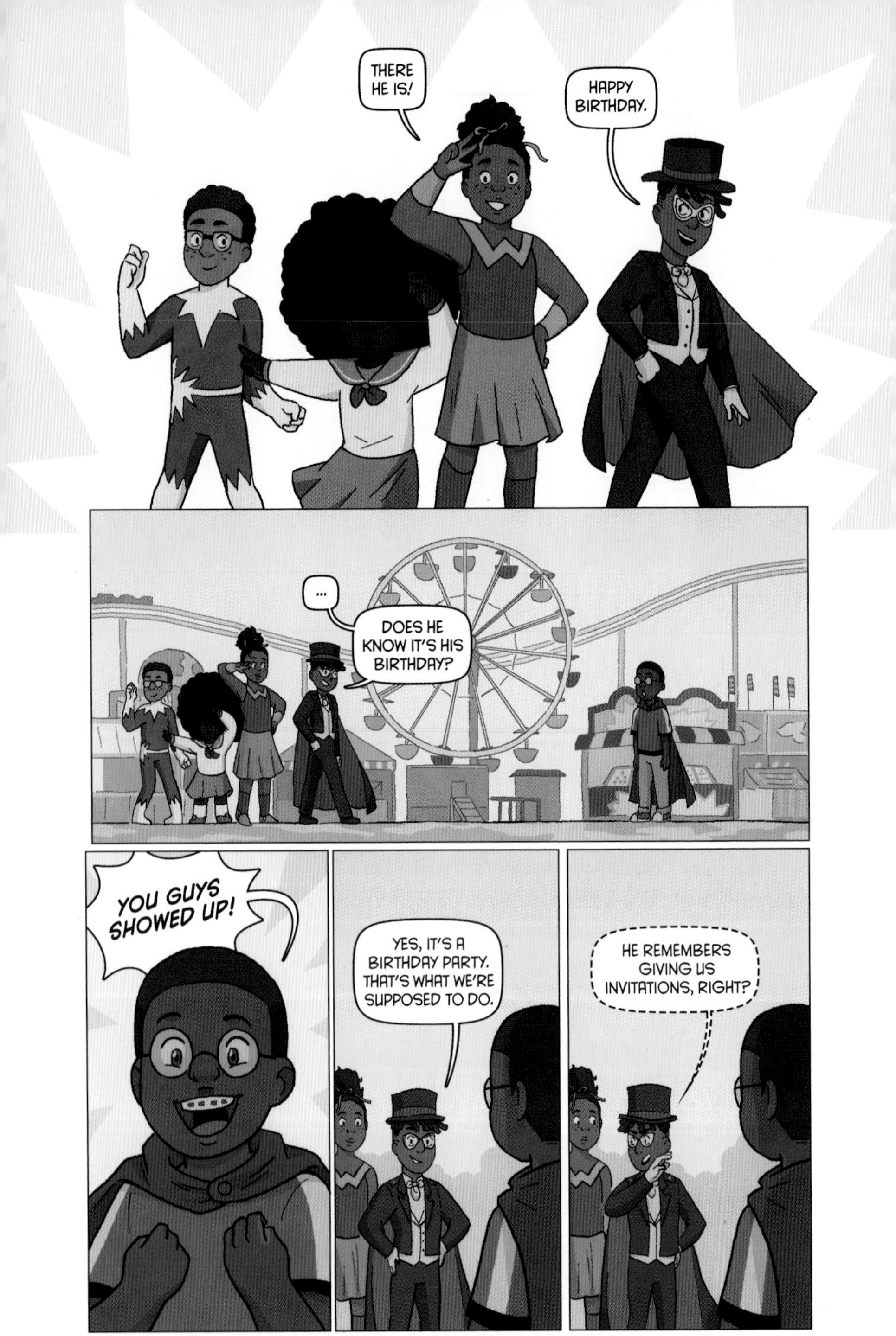
THERE HE IS!
HAPPY BIRTHDAY.
...
DOES HE KNOW IT'S HIS BIRTHDAY?
YOU GUYS SHOWED UP!
YES, IT'S A BIRTHDAY PARTY. THAT'S WHAT WE'RE SUPPOSED TO DO.
HE REMEMBERS GIVING US INVITATIONS, RIGHT?

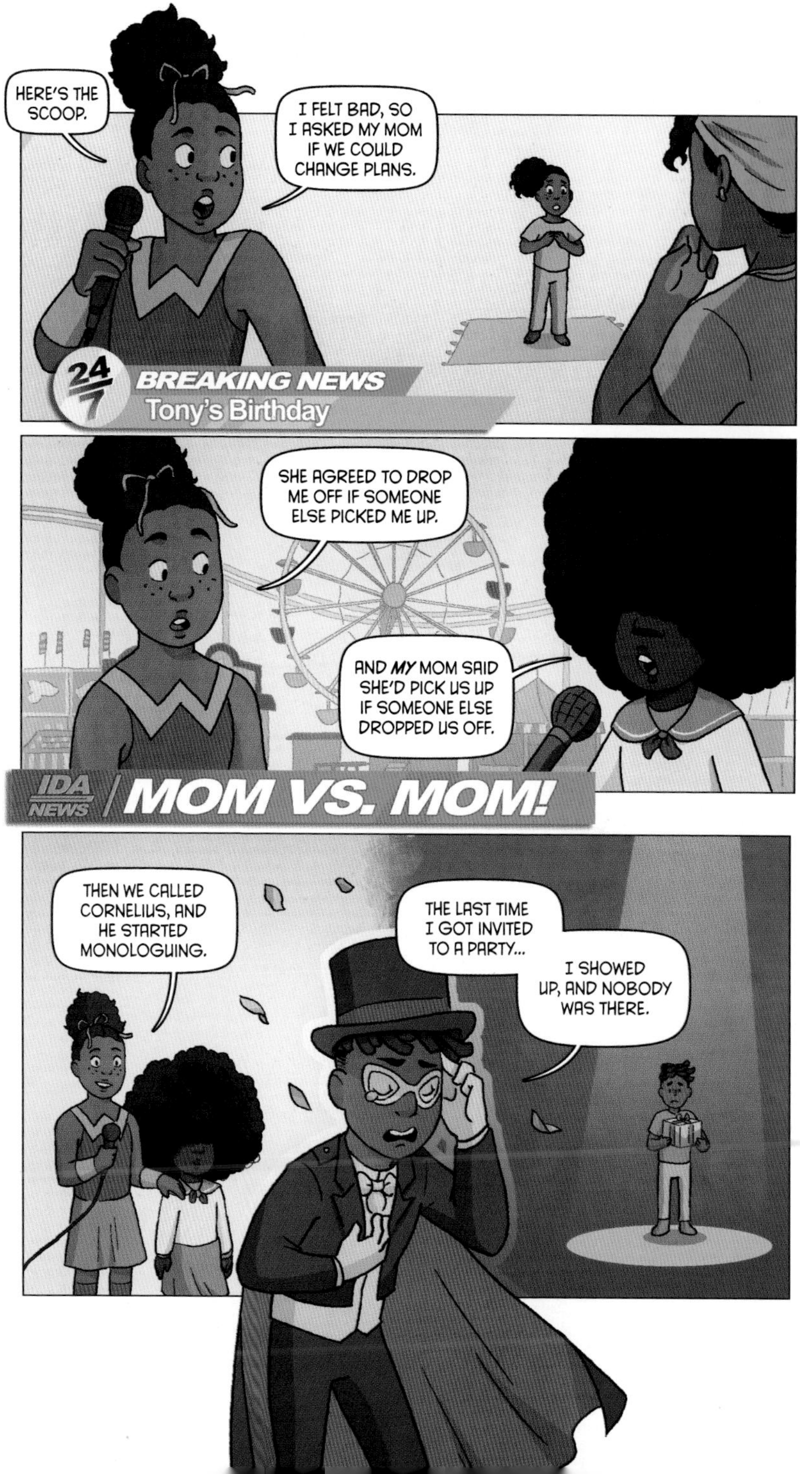
HERE'S THE SCOOP.
I FELT BAD, SO I ASKED MY MOM IF WE COULD CHANGE PLANS.
24 7
BREAKING NEWS
Tony's Birthday
SHE AGREED TO DROP ME OFF IF SOMEONE ELSE PICKED ME UP.
AND *MY* MOM SAID SHE'D PICK US UP IF SOMEONE ELSE DROPPED US OFF.
IDA NEWS
MOM VS. MOM!
THEN WE CALLED CORNELIUS, AND HE STARTED MONOLOGUING.
THE LAST TIME I GOT INVITED TO A PARTY...
I SHOWED UP, AND NOBODY WAS THERE.

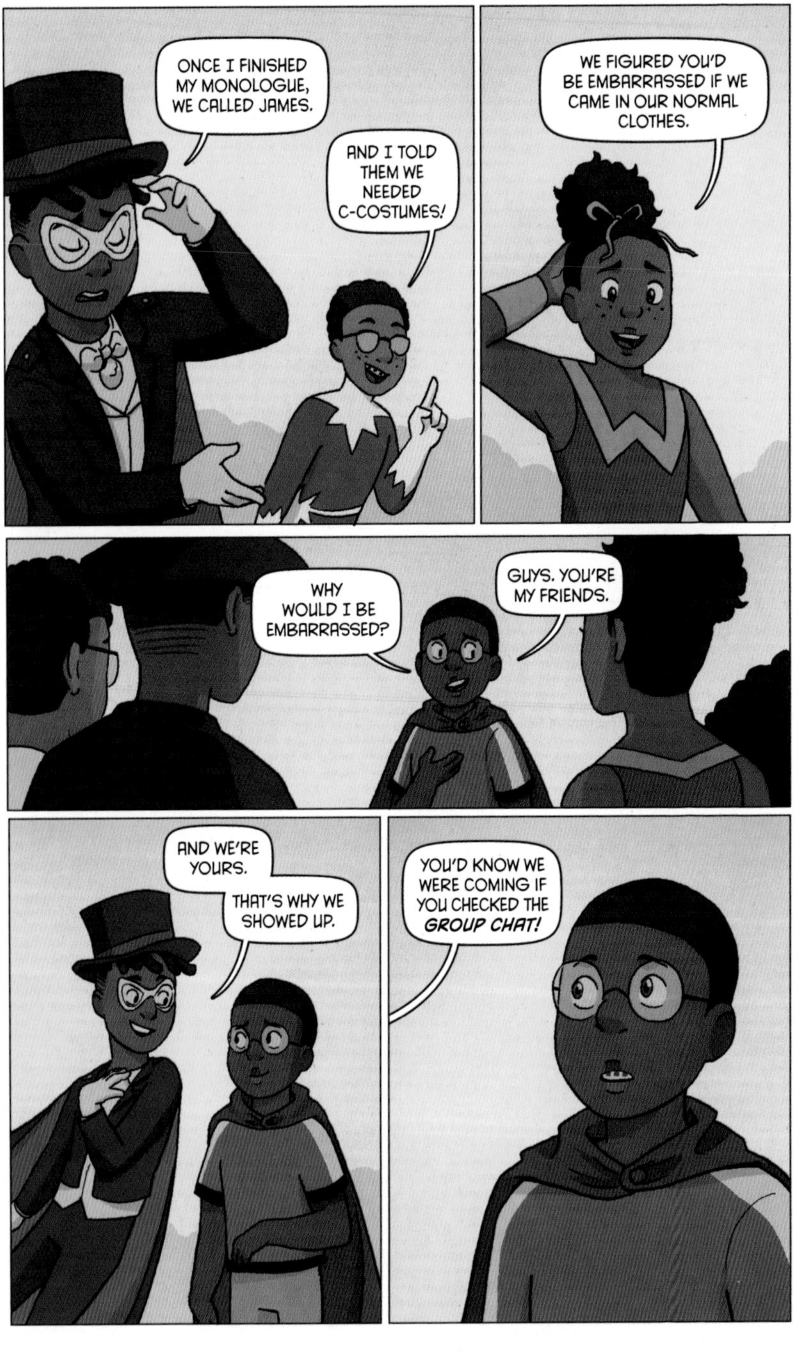
ONCE I FINISHED MY MONOLOGUE, WE CALLED JAMES.
AND I TOLD THEM WE NEEDED C-COSTUMES!
WE FIGURED YOU'D BE EMBARRASSED IF WE CAME IN OUR NORMAL CLOTHES.
WHY WOULD I BE EMBARRASSED?
GUYS. YOU'RE MY FRIENDS.
AND WE'RE YOURS.
THAT'S WHY WE SHOWED UP.
YOU'D KNOW WE WERE COMING IF YOU CHECKED THE GROUP CHAT!

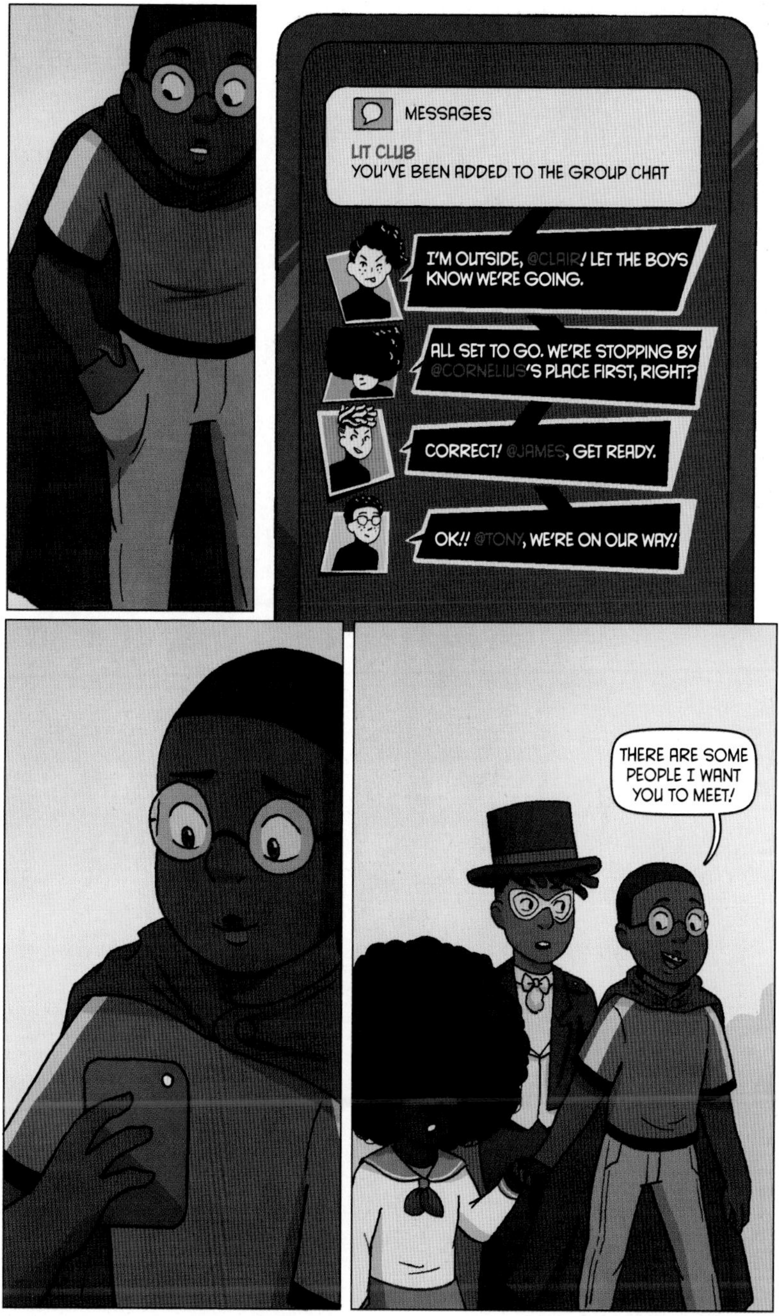
MESSAGES
LIT CLUB
YOU'VE BEEN ADDED TO THE GROUP CHAT
I'M OUTSIDE, @CLAIR! LET THE BOYS KNOW WE'RE GOING.
ALL SET TO GO. WE'RE STOPPING BY @CORNELIUS'S PLACE FIRST, RIGHT?
CORRECT! @JAMES, GET READY.
OK!! @TONY, WE'RE ON OUR WAY!
THERE ARE SOME PEOPLE I WANT YOU TO MEET!

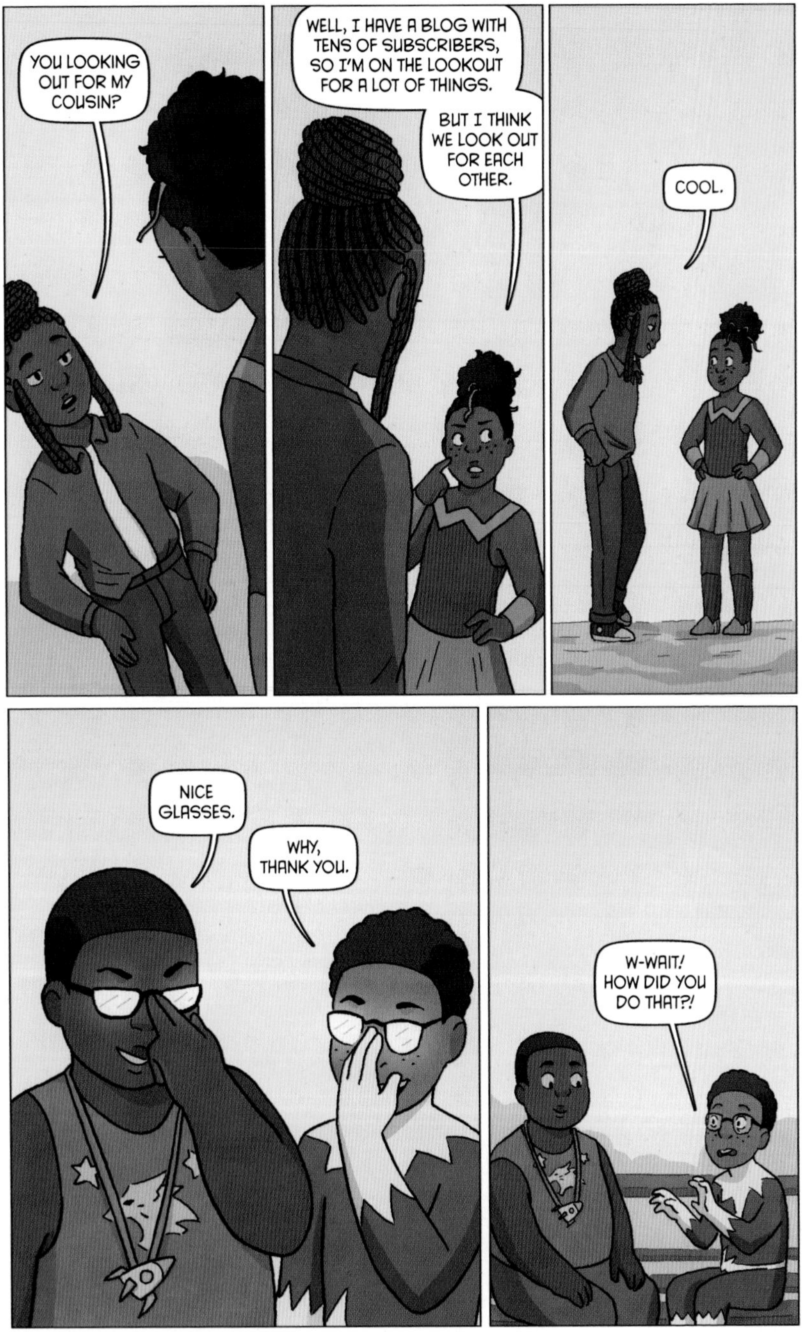
YOU LOOKING OUT FOR MY COUSIN?
WELL, I HAVE A BLOG WITH TENS OF SUBSCRIBERS, SO I'M ON THE LOOKOUT FOR A LOT OF THINGS.
BUT I THINK WE LOOK OUT FOR EACH OTHER.
COOL.
NICE GLASSES.
WHY, THANK YOU.
W-WAIT! HOW DID YOU DO THAT?!

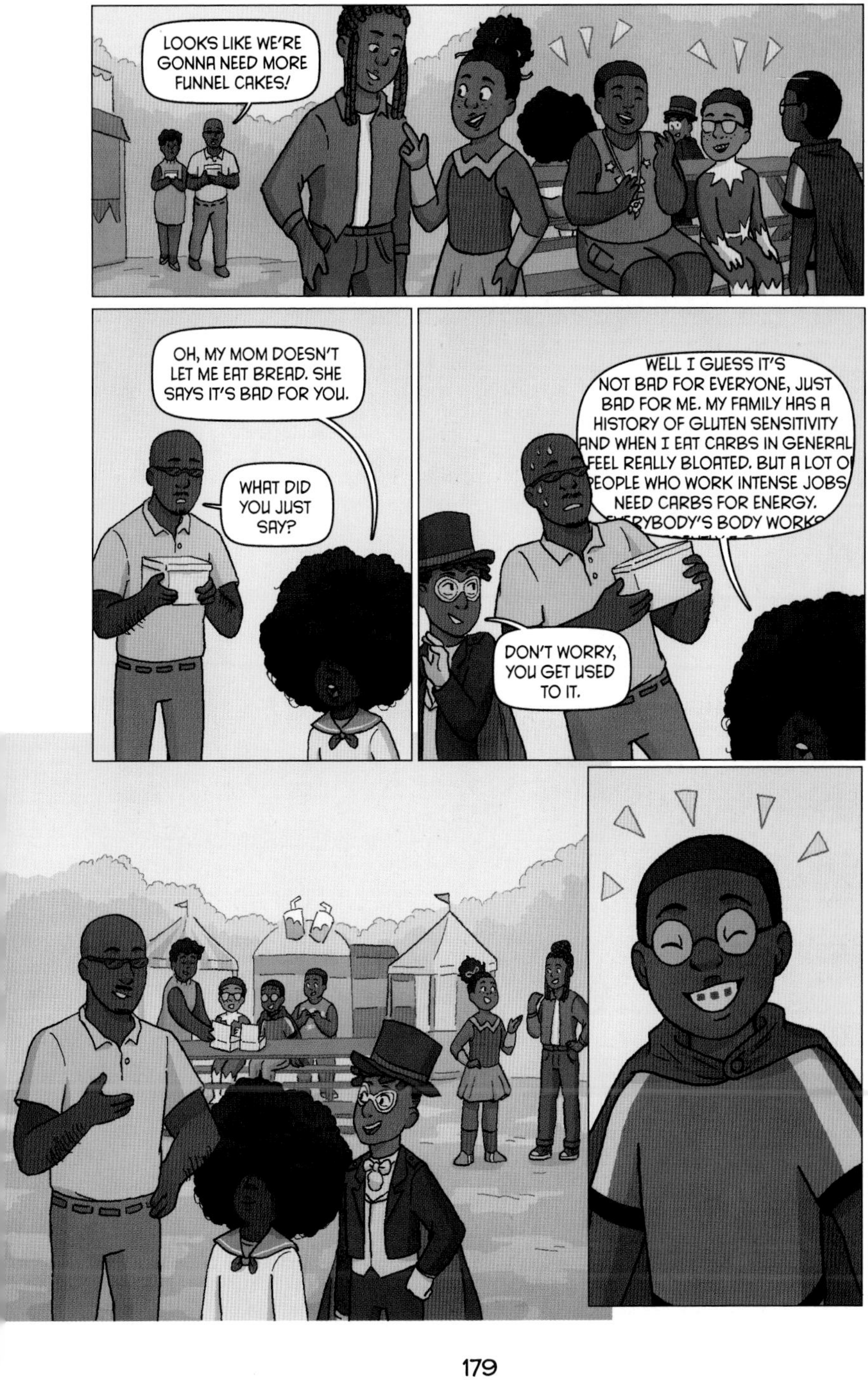
LOOKS LIKE WE'RE GONNA NEED MORE FUNNEL CAKES!
OH, MY MOM DOESN'T LET ME EAT BREAD. SHE SAYS IT'S BAD FOR YOU.
WHAT DID YOU JUST SAY?
WELL I GUESS IT'S NOT BAD FOR EVERYONE, JUST BAD FOR ME. MY FAMILY HAS A HISTORY OF GLUTEN SENSITIVITY AND WHEN I EAT CARBS IN GENERAL FEEL REALLY BLOATED. BUT A LOT O EOPLE WHO WORK INTENSE JOBS NEED CARBS FOR ENERGY. RYBODY'S BODY WORK
DON'T WORRY, YOU GET USED TO IT.

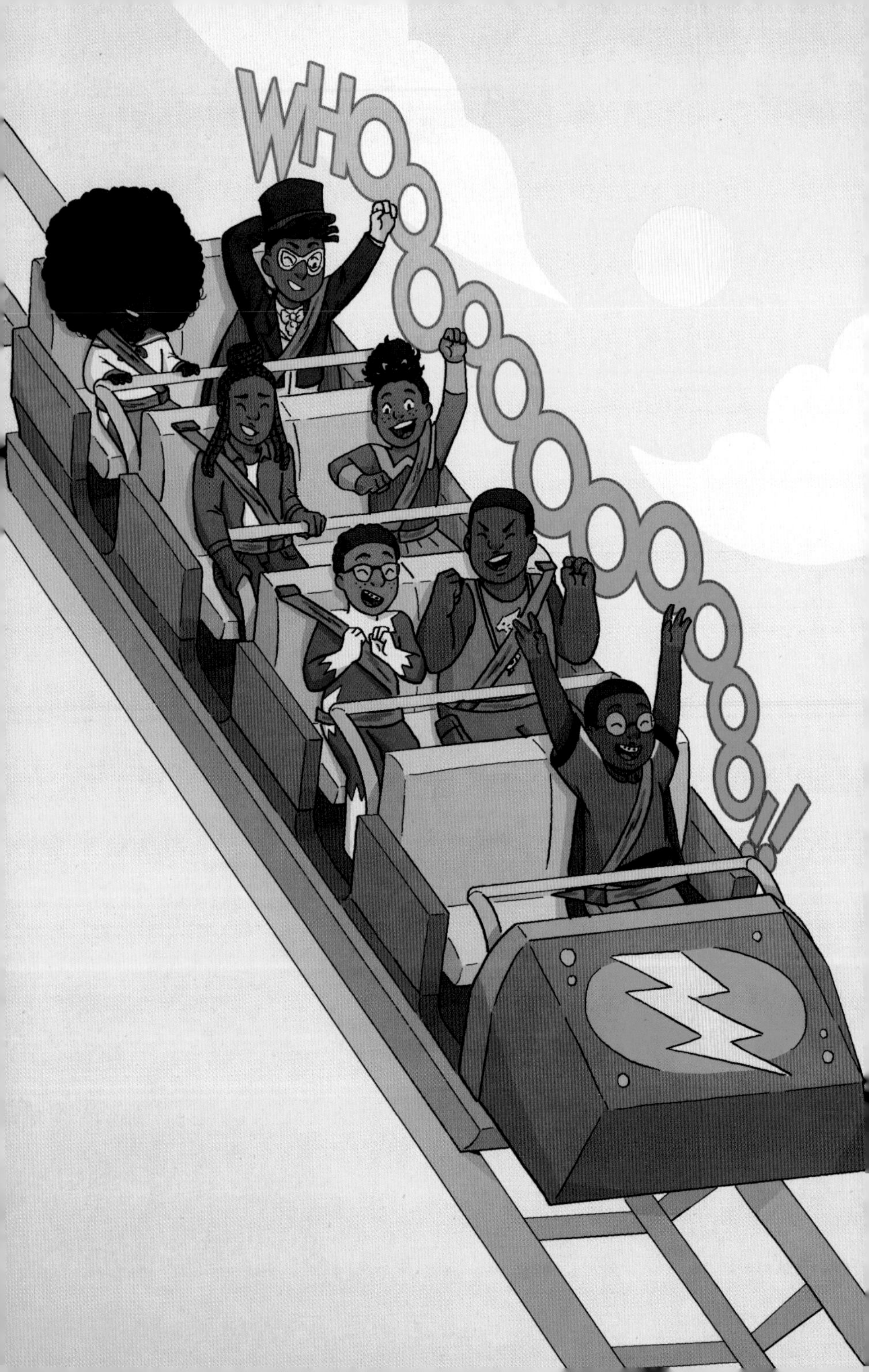
WHOOOOOOOOOO!!

CHAPTER 7

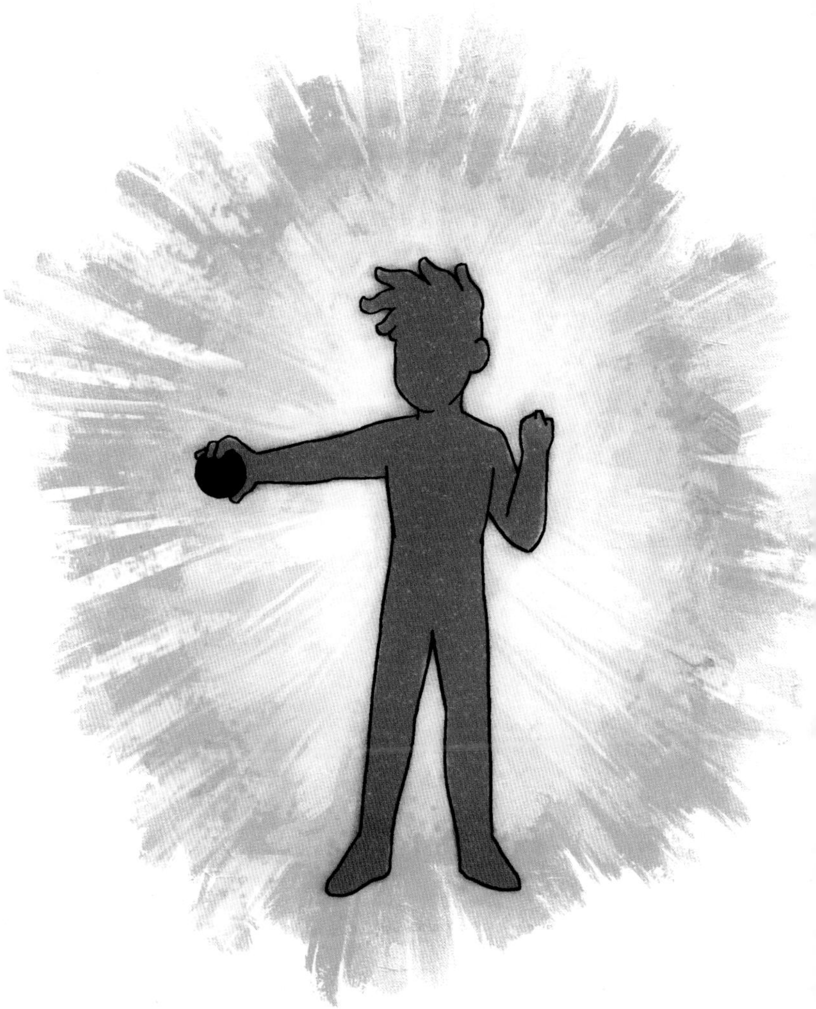

A FEW WEEKS LATER.

SO YOU'RE STARTING YOUR SECOND SEMESTER AT YOUR NEW SCHOOL. HOW DO YOU FEEL?

...

OH DON'T GET SILENT ON ME NOW! IT'S OUR LAST APPOINTMENT.

"LAST" MAKES IT SOUND *SO SAD*.

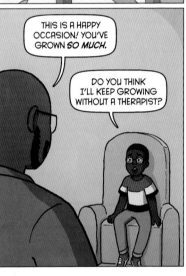

THIS IS A HAPPY OCCASION! YOU'VE GROWN *SO MUCH*.

DO YOU THINK I'LL KEEP GROWING WITHOUT A THERAPIST?

YOU DID ALL THE WORK. I JUST HELPED!

I HAVE NO DOUBT YOU'LL CONTINUE TO.

DR. BICKERS - CLINICAL PSYCHOLOGIST

SUPERPOWER: ONCE MORE, WITH HEALING -
Helps others grow from their pasts

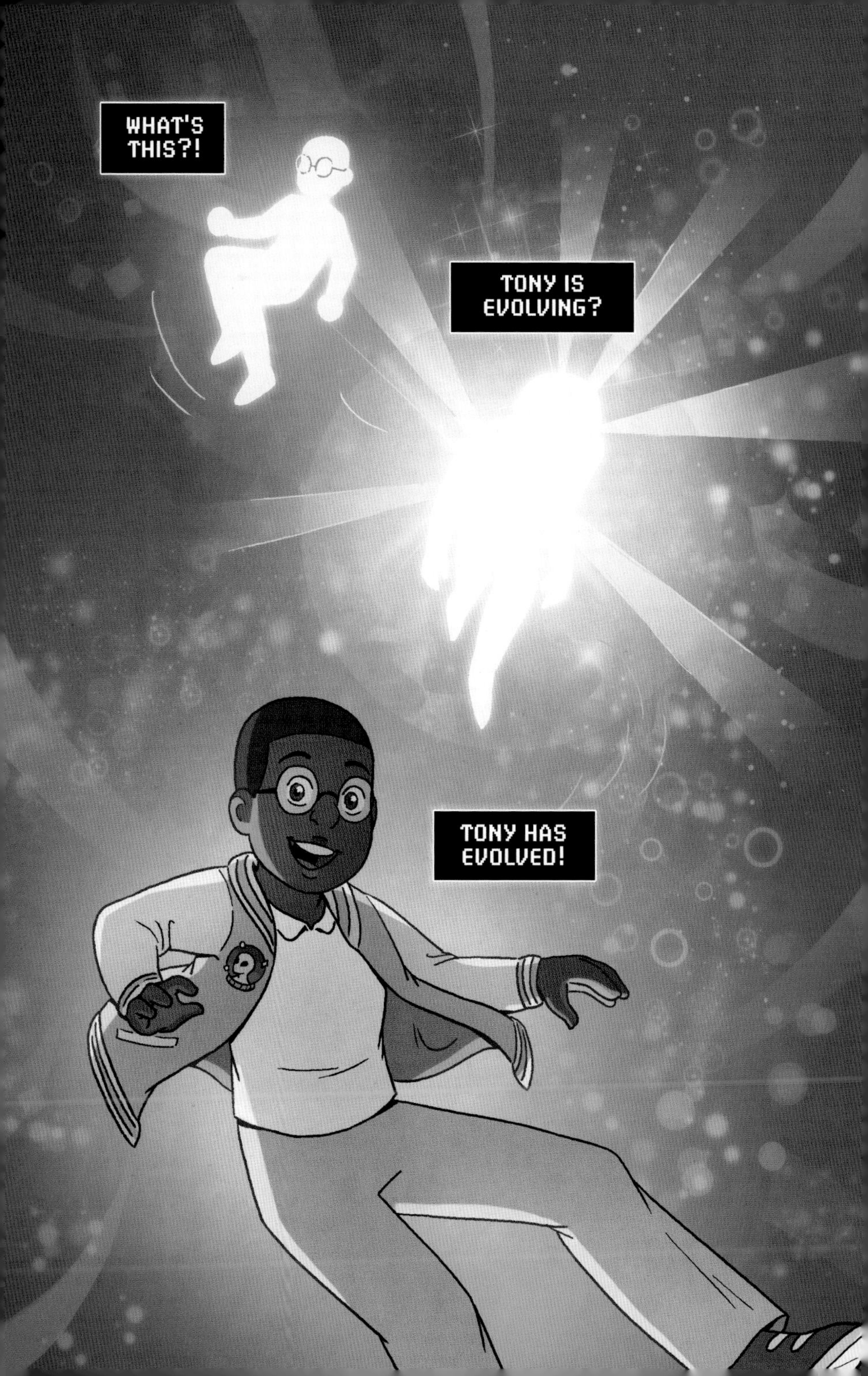
WHAT'S THIS?!
TONY IS EVOLVING?
TONY HAS EVOLVED!

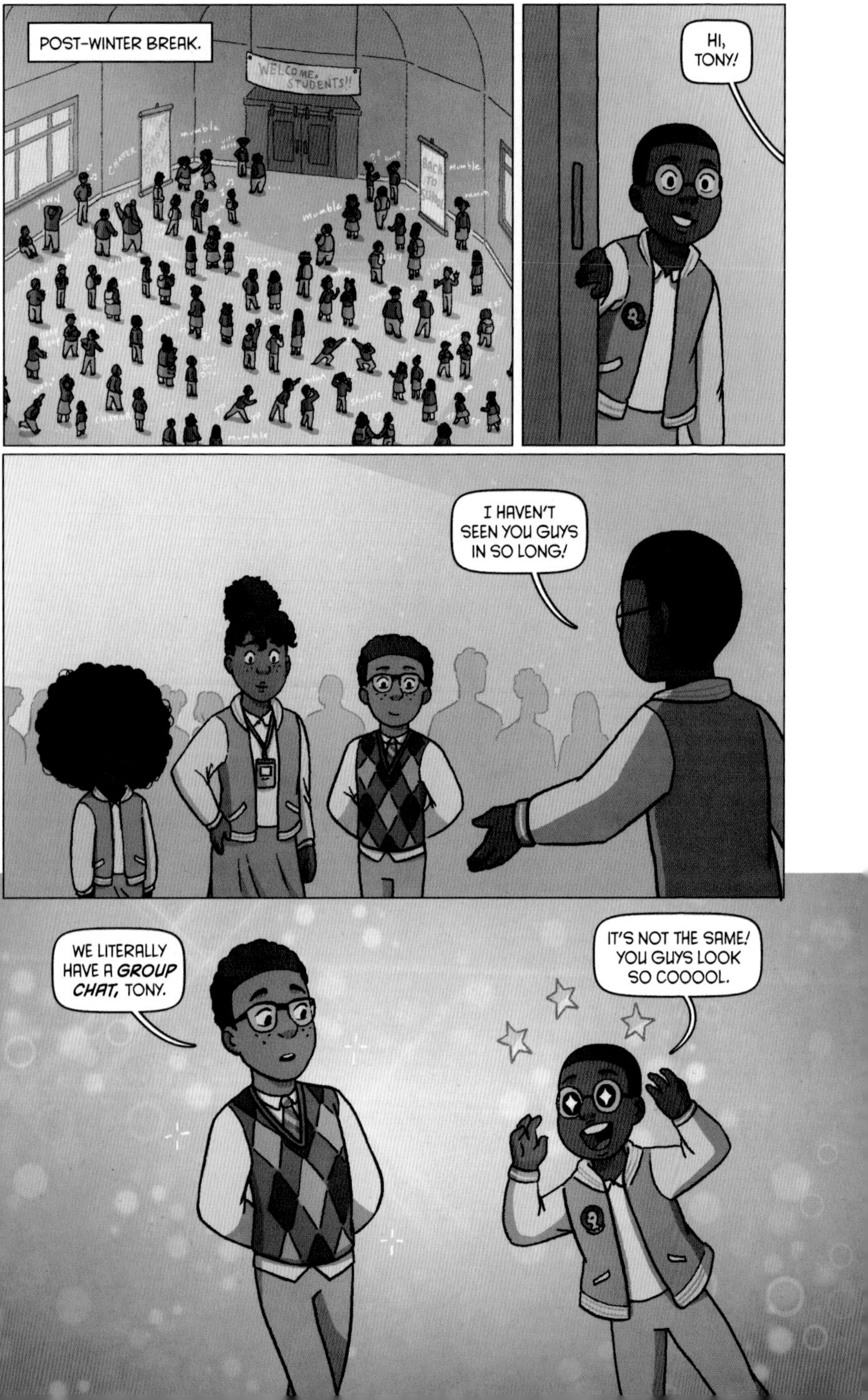
POST-WINTER BREAK.
WELCOME, STUDENTS!!
BACK TO SCHOOL
HI, TONY!
I HAVEN'T SEEN YOU GUYS IN SO LONG!
WE LITERALLY HAVE A *GROUP CHAT,* TONY.
IT'S NOT THE SAME! YOU GUYS LOOK SO COOOOL.

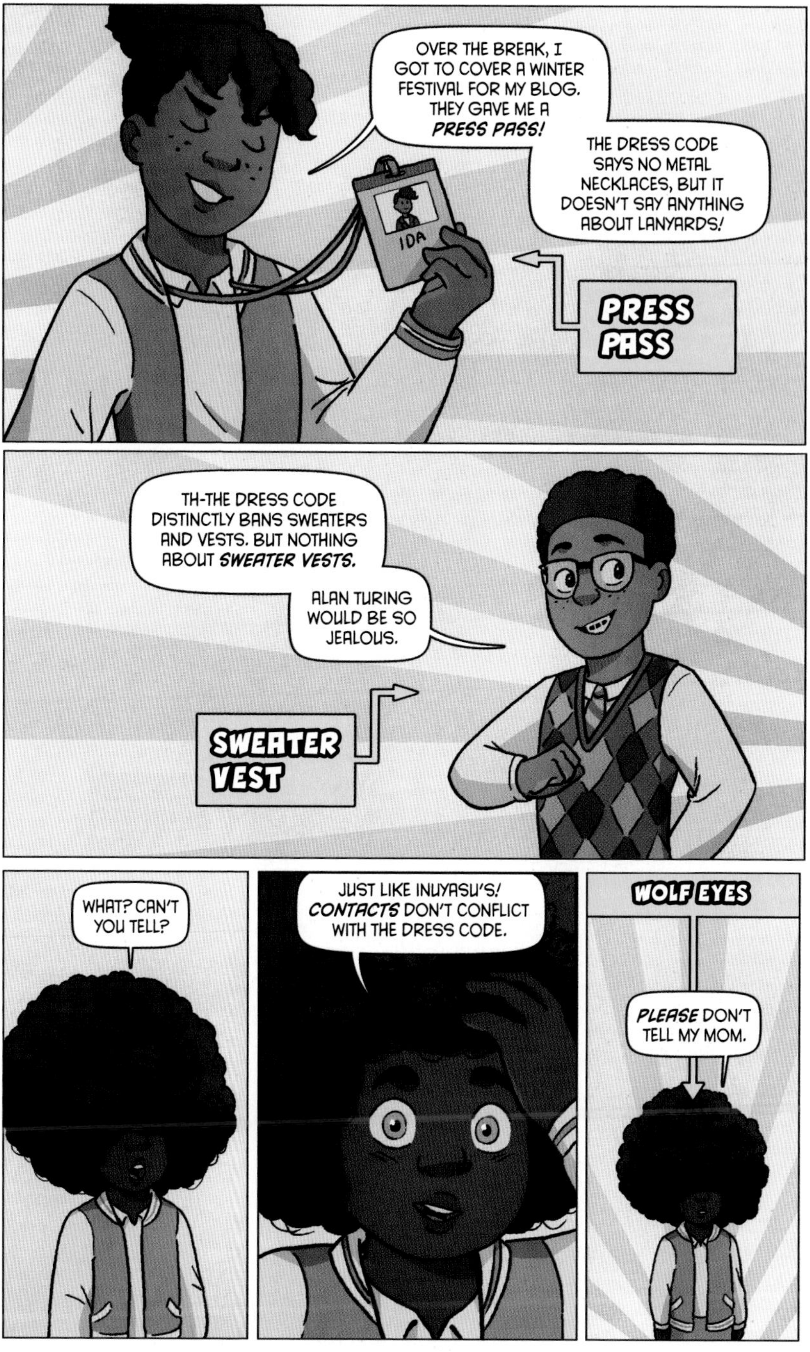
OVER THE BREAK, I GOT TO COVER A WINTER FESTIVAL FOR MY BLOG. THEY GAVE ME A *PRESS PASS!*
THE DRESS CODE SAYS NO METAL NECKLACES, BUT IT DOESN'T SAY ANYTHING ABOUT LANYARDS!
IDA
PRESS PASS
TH-THE DRESS CODE DISTINCTLY BANS SWEATERS AND VESTS. BUT NOTHING ABOUT *SWEATER VESTS.*
ALAN TURING WOULD BE SO JEALOUS.
SWEATER VEST
WHAT? CAN'T YOU TELL?
JUST LIKE INUYASU'S! *CONTACTS* DON'T CONFLICT WITH THE DRESS CODE.
WOLF EYES
PLEASE DON'T TELL MY MOM.

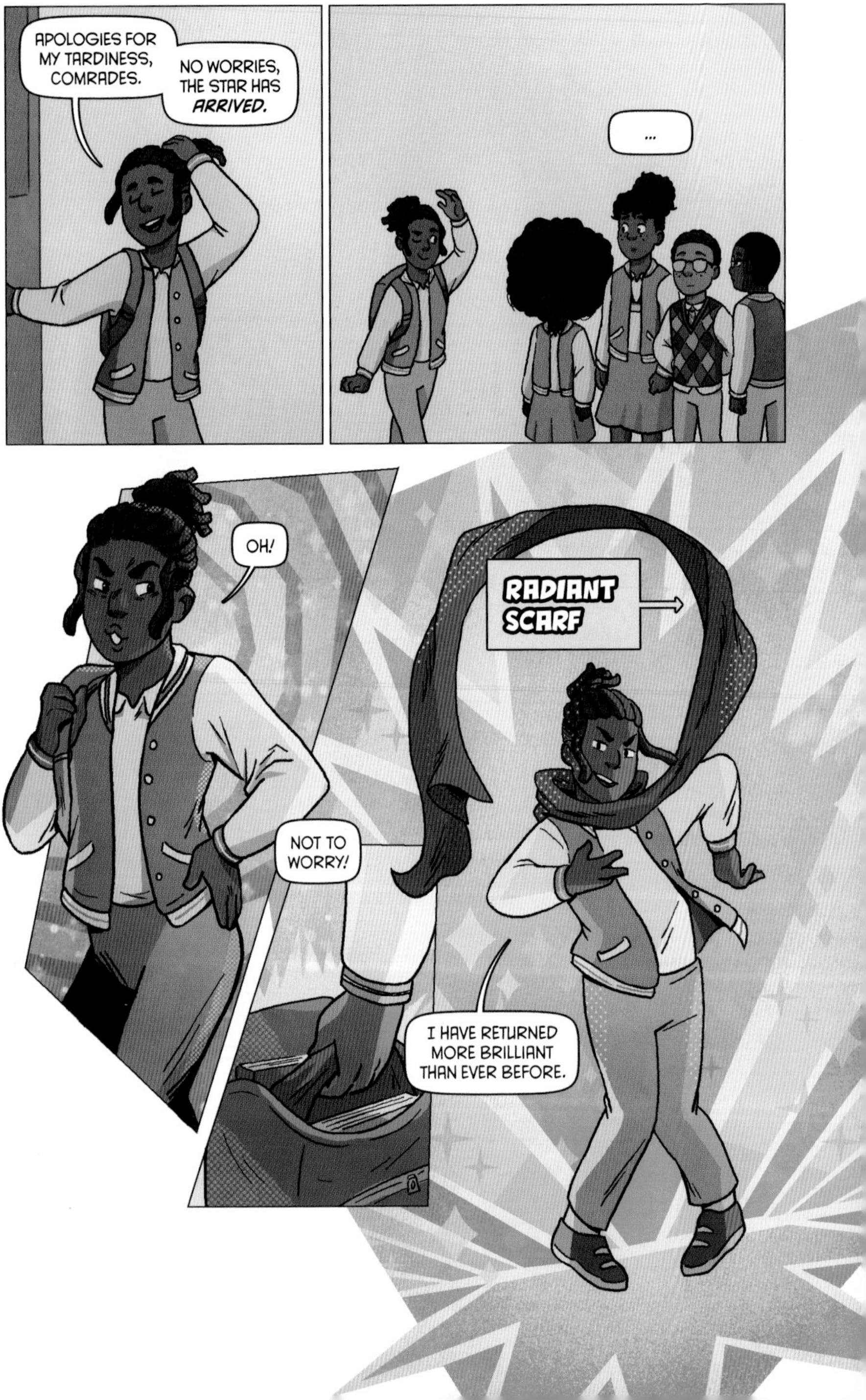
APOLOGIES FOR MY TARDINESS, COMRADES.
NO WORRIES, THE STAR HAS ARRIVED.
...
OH!
RADIANT SCARF
NOT TO WORRY!
I HAVE RETURNED MORE BRILLIANT THAN EVER BEFORE.

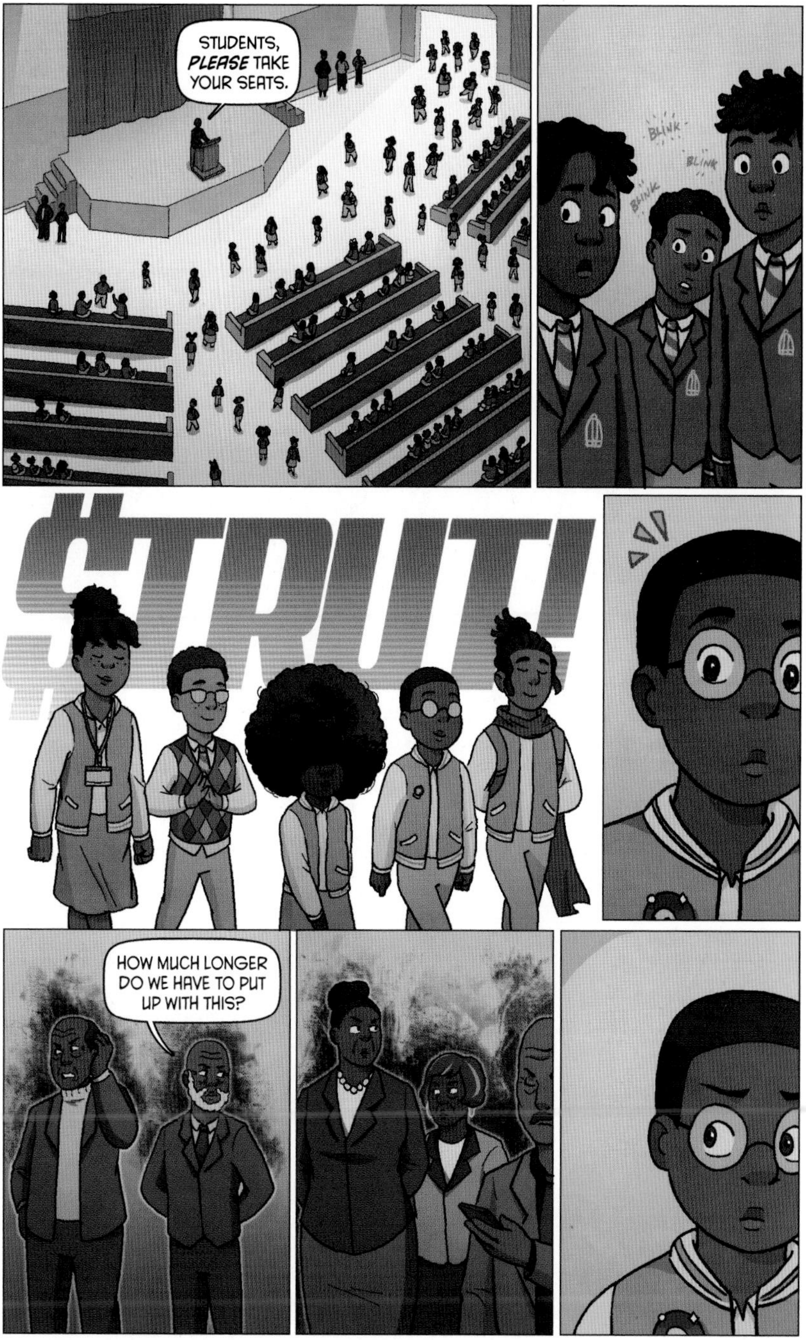
STUDENTS, *PLEASE* TAKE YOUR SEATS.
BLINK
BLINK
BLINK
$TRUT!
HOW MUCH LONGER DO WE HAVE TO PUT UP WITH THIS?

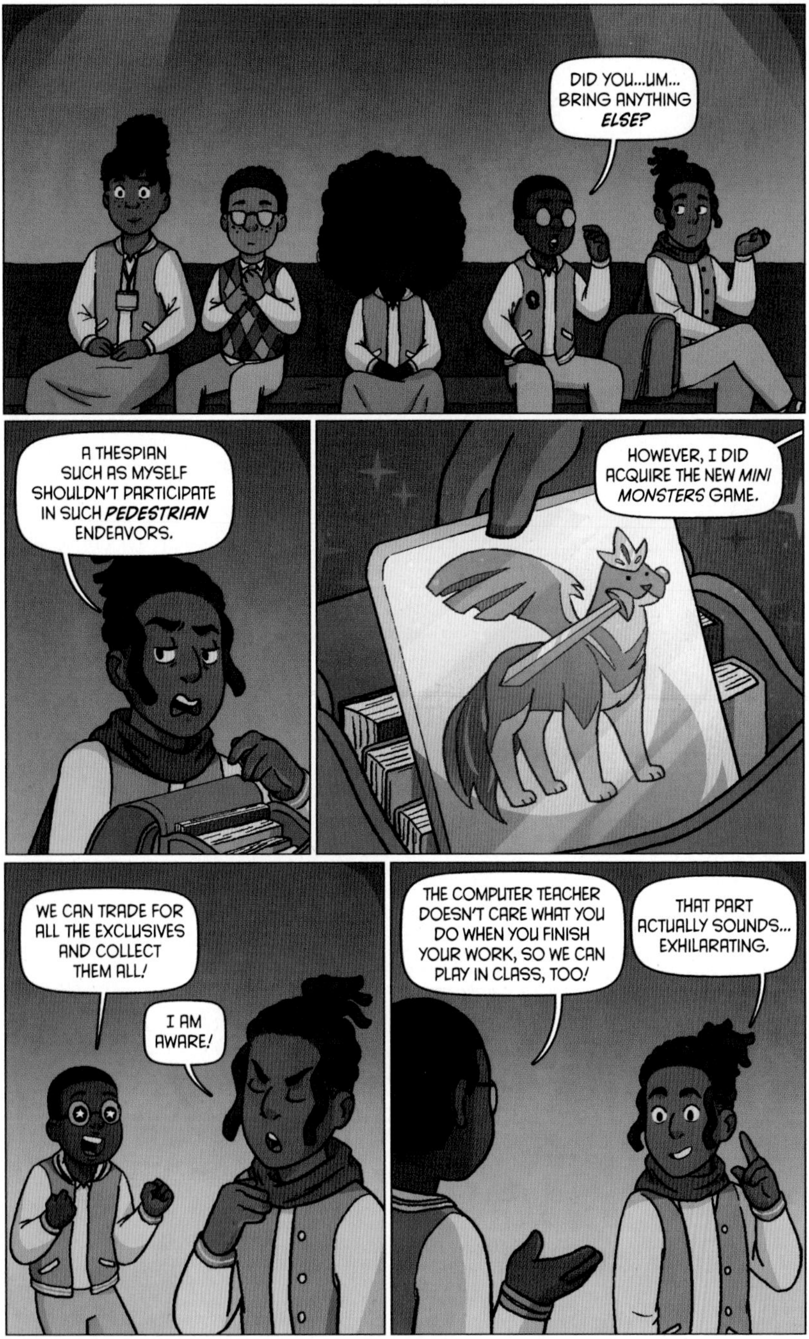
DID YOU...UM... BRING ANYTHING *ELSE?*
A THESPIAN SUCH AS MYSELF SHOULDN'T PARTICIPATE IN SUCH *PEDESTRIAN* ENDEAVORS.
HOWEVER, I DID ACQUIRE THE NEW *MINI MONSTERS* GAME.
WE CAN TRADE FOR ALL THE EXCLUSIVES AND COLLECT THEM ALL!
I AM AWARE!
THE COMPUTER TEACHER DOESN'T CARE WHAT YOU DO WHEN YOU FINISH YOUR WORK, SO WE CAN PLAY IN CLASS, TOO!
THAT PART ACTUALLY SOUNDS... EXHILARATING.

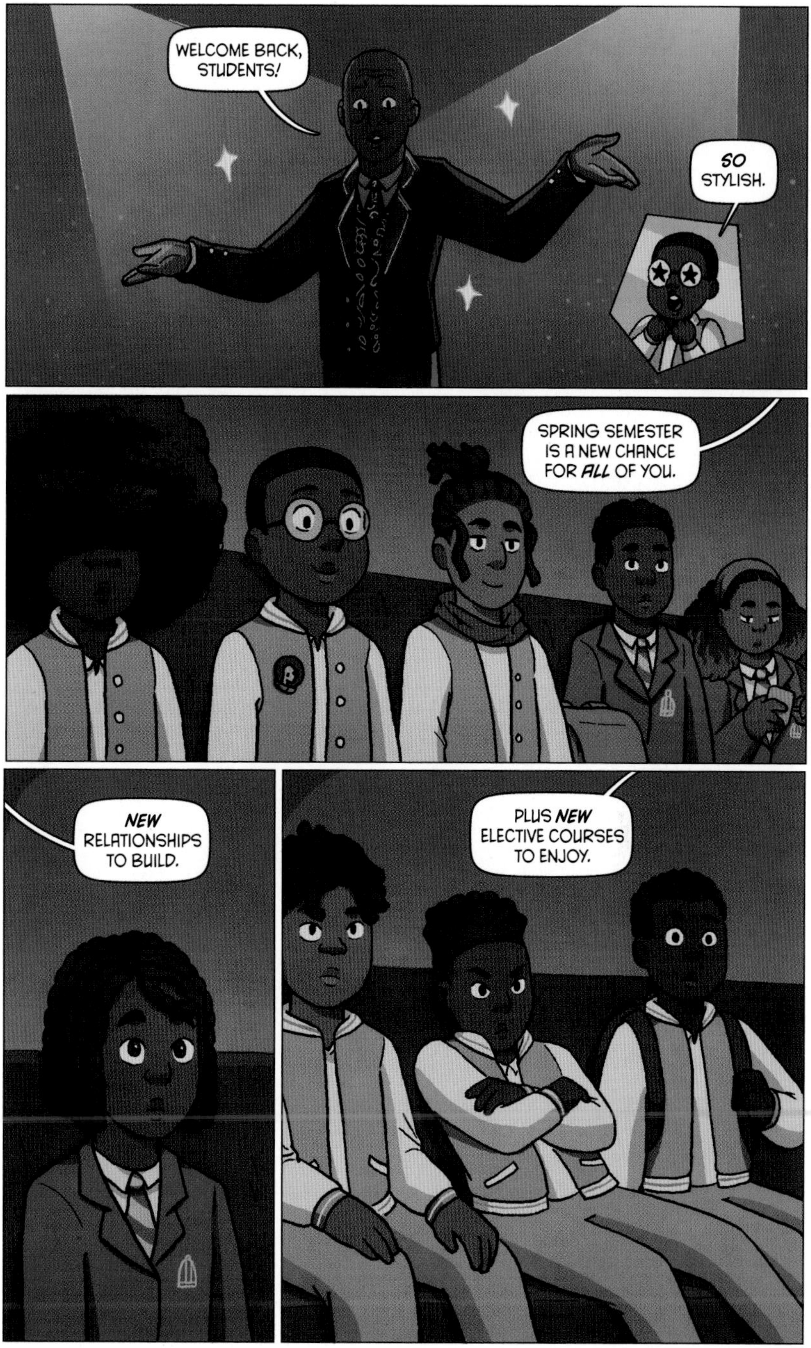
WELCOME BACK, STUDENTS!
SO STYLISH.
SPRING SEMESTER IS A NEW CHANCE FOR ALL OF YOU.
NEW RELATIONSHIPS TO BUILD.
PLUS NEW ELECTIVE COURSES TO ENJOY.

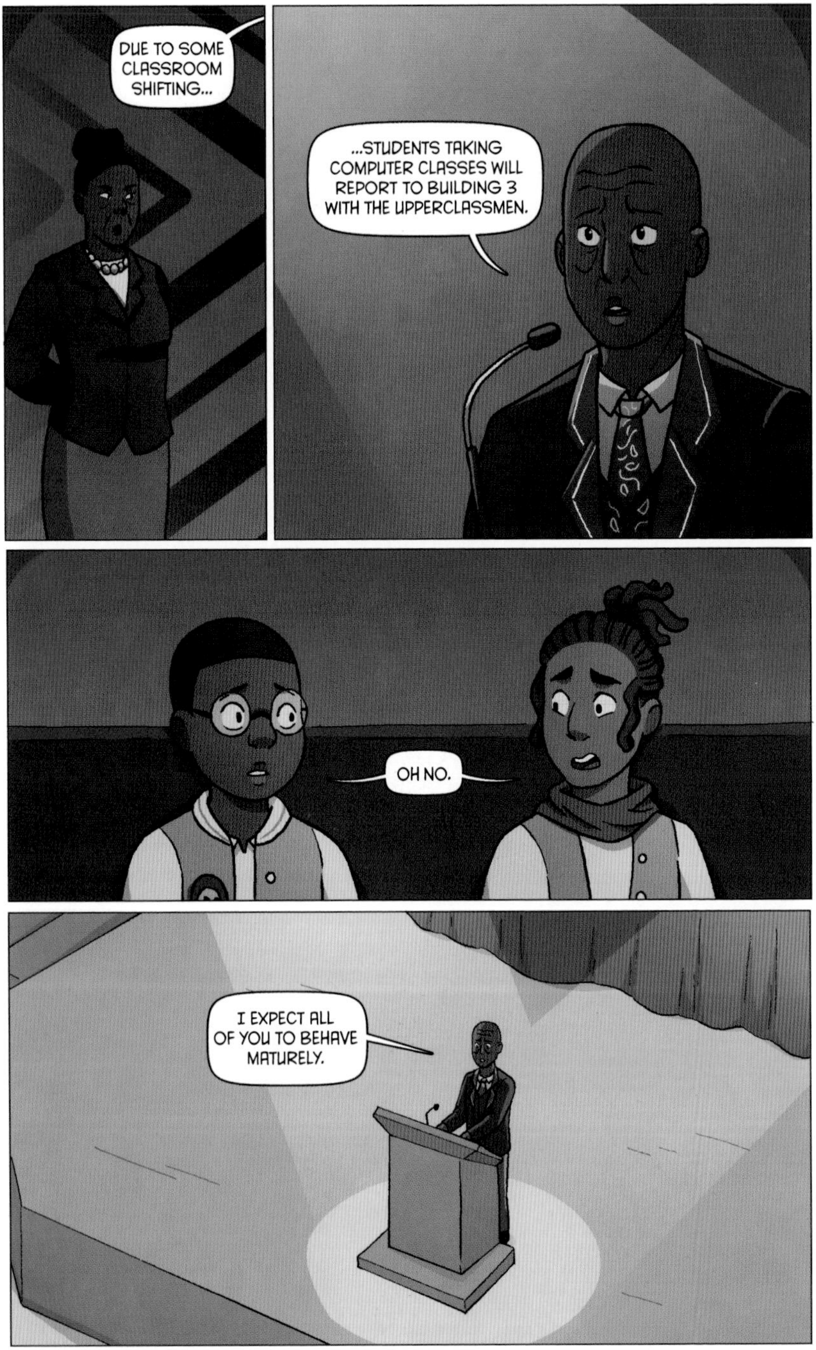
DUE TO SOME CLASSROOM SHIFTING...
...STUDENTS TAKING COMPUTER CLASSES WILL REPORT TO BUILDING 3 WITH THE UPPERCLASSMEN.
OH NO.
I EXPECT ALL OF YOU TO BEHAVE MATURELY.

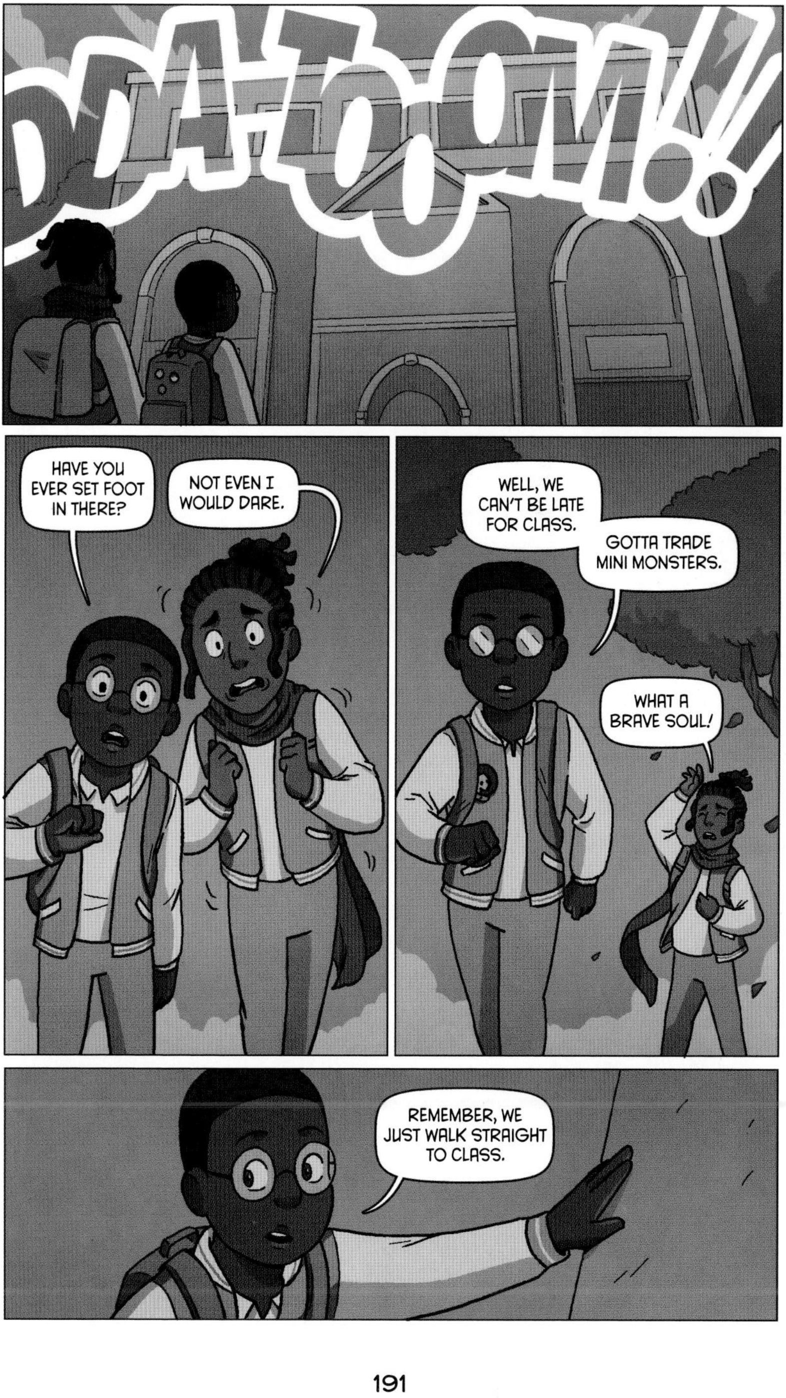
DDATOOOM!!
HAVE YOU EVER SET FOOT IN THERE?
NOT EVEN I WOULD DARE.
WELL, WE CAN'T BE LATE FOR CLASS.
GOTTA TRADE MINI MONSTERS.
WHAT A BRAVE SOUL!
REMEMBER, WE JUST WALK STRAIGHT TO CLASS.

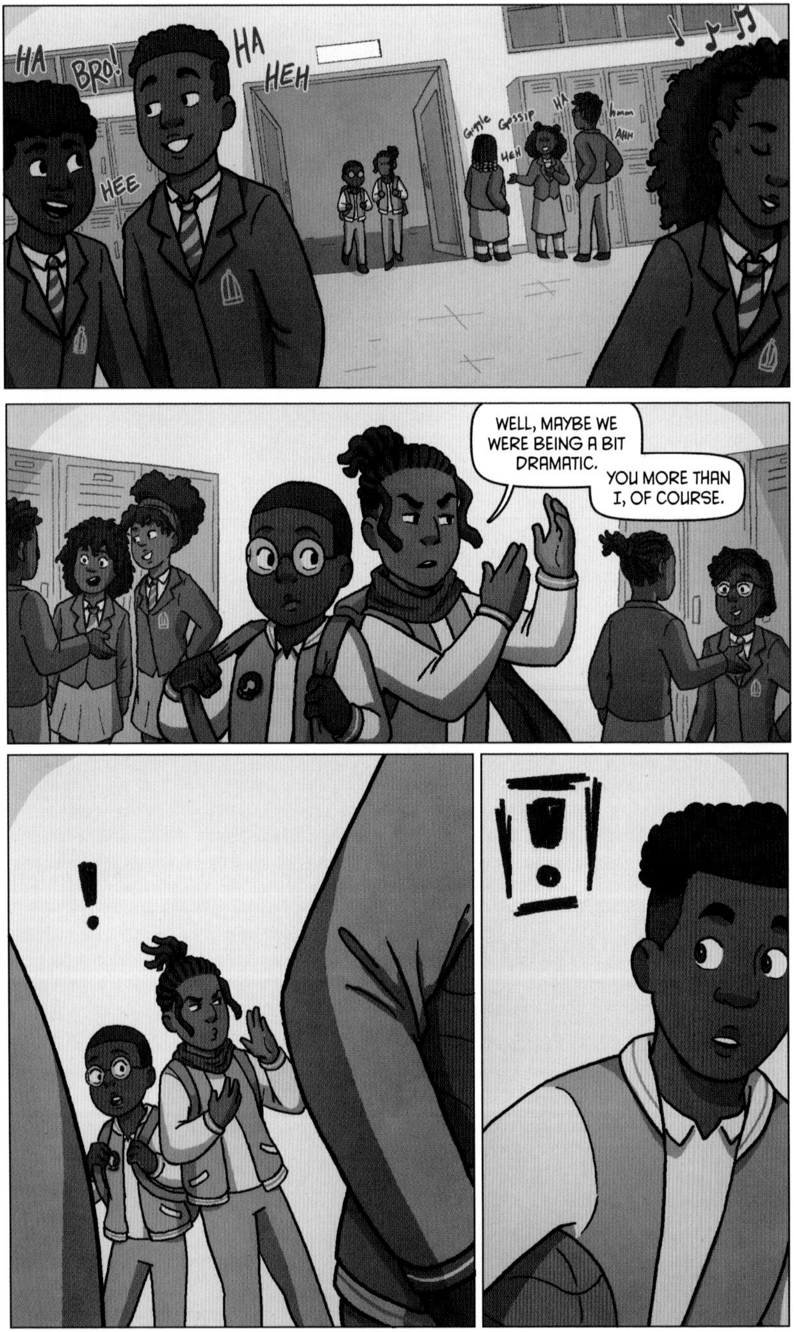
HA
BRO!
HA
HEH
HEE
Giggle
Gossip
HEH
HA
AHH
WELL, MAYBE WE WERE BEING A BIT DRAMATIC.
YOU MORE THAN I, OF COURSE.
!
!

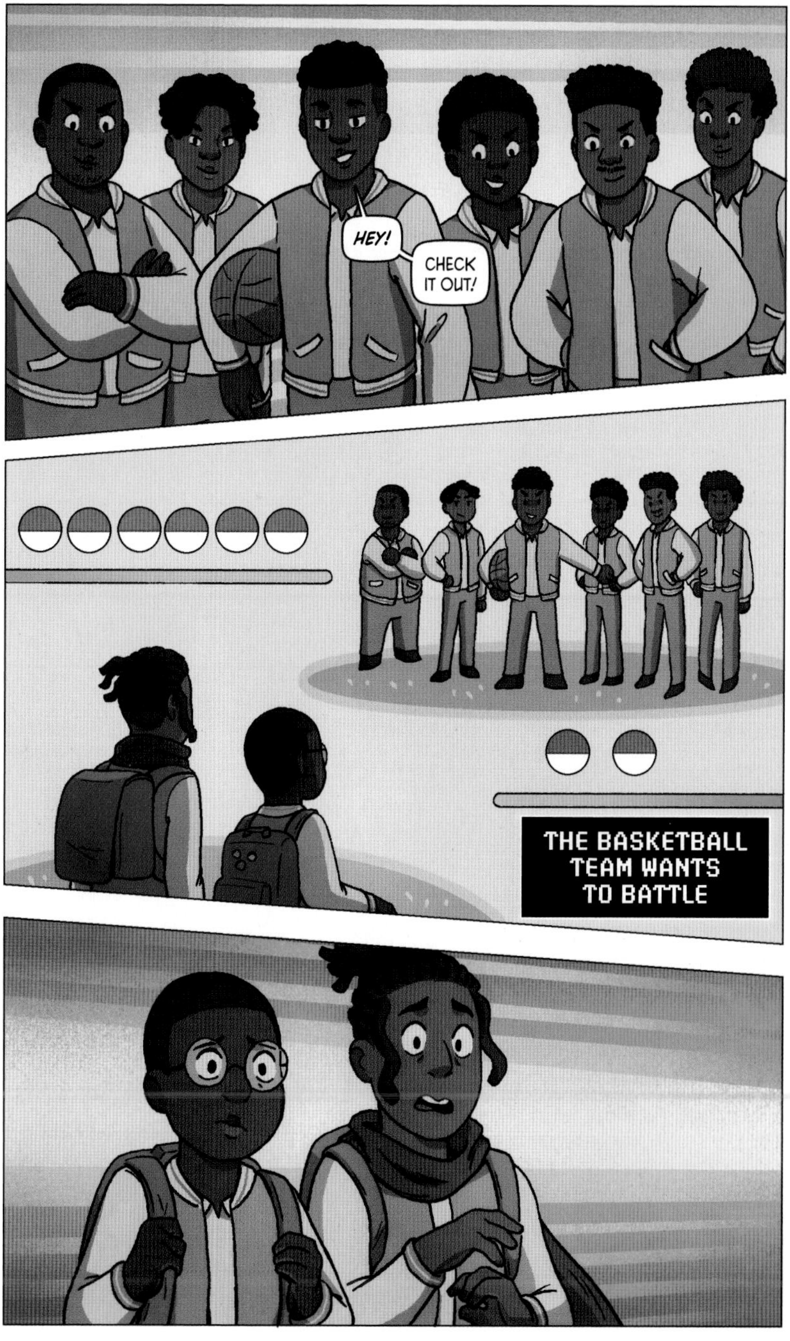
HEY!
CHECK IT OUT!
THE BASKETBALL TEAM WANTS TO BATTLE

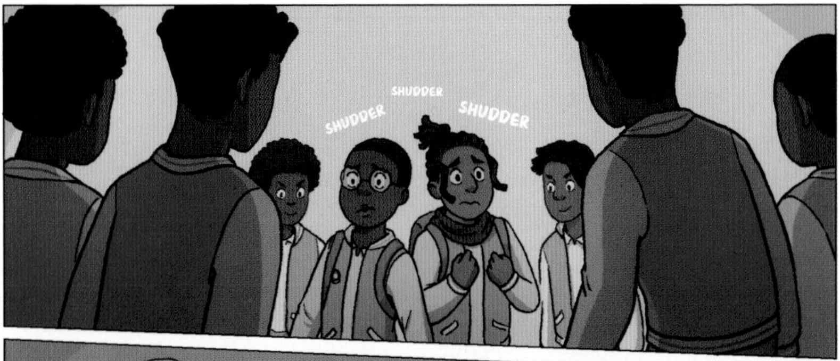
SHUDDER
SHUDDER
SHUDDER

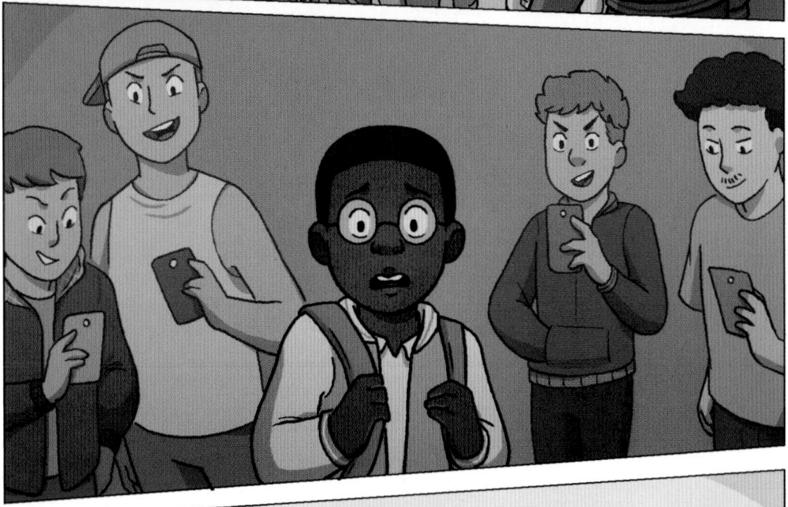

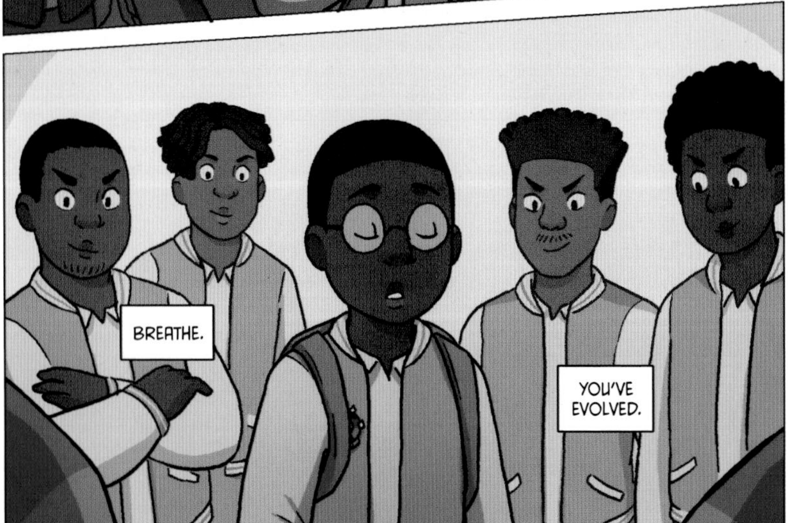
BREATHE.
YOU'VE EVOLVED.

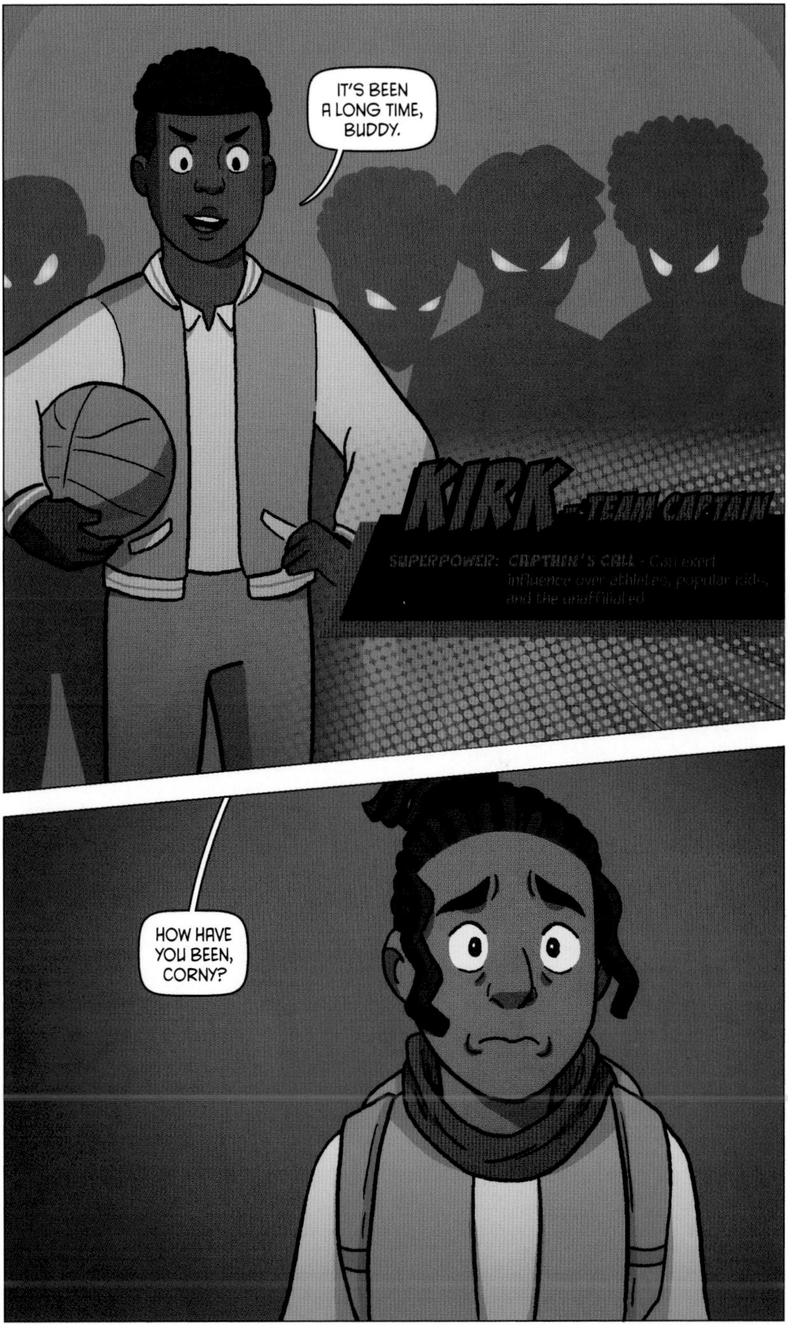
IT'S BEEN A LONG TIME, BUDDY.
KIRK - TEAM CAPTAIN
SUPERPOWER: CAPTAIN'S CALL - Can exert influence over athletes, popular kids, and the unaffiliated
HOW HAVE YOU BEEN, CORNY?

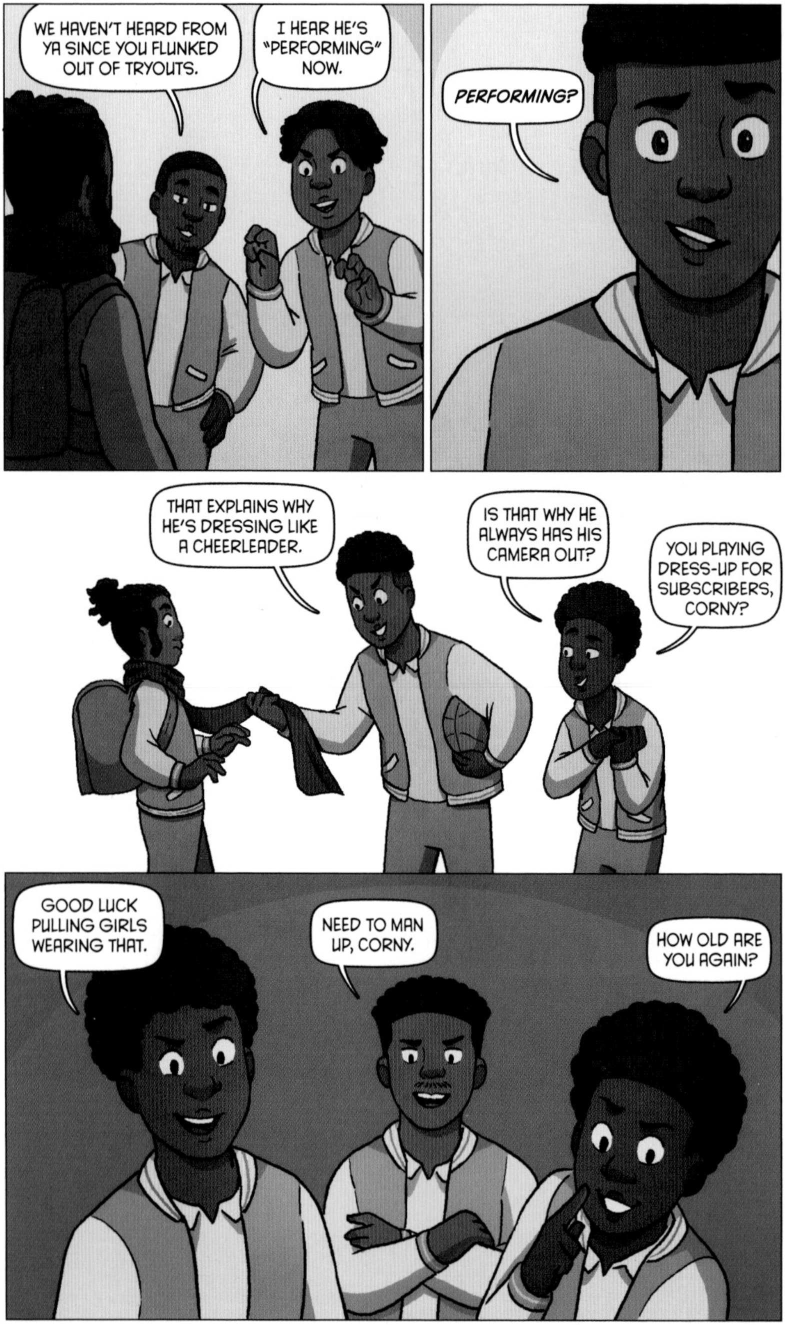
WE HAVEN'T HEARD FROM YA SINCE YOU FLUNKED OUT OF TRYOUTS.
I HEAR HE'S "PERFORMING" NOW.
PERFORMING?
THAT EXPLAINS WHY HE'S DRESSING LIKE A CHEERLEADER.
IS THAT WHY HE ALWAYS HAS HIS CAMERA OUT?
YOU PLAYING DRESS-UP FOR SUBSCRIBERS, CORNY?
GOOD LUCK PULLING GIRLS WEARING THAT.
NEED TO MAN UP, CORNY.
HOW OLD ARE YOU AGAIN?

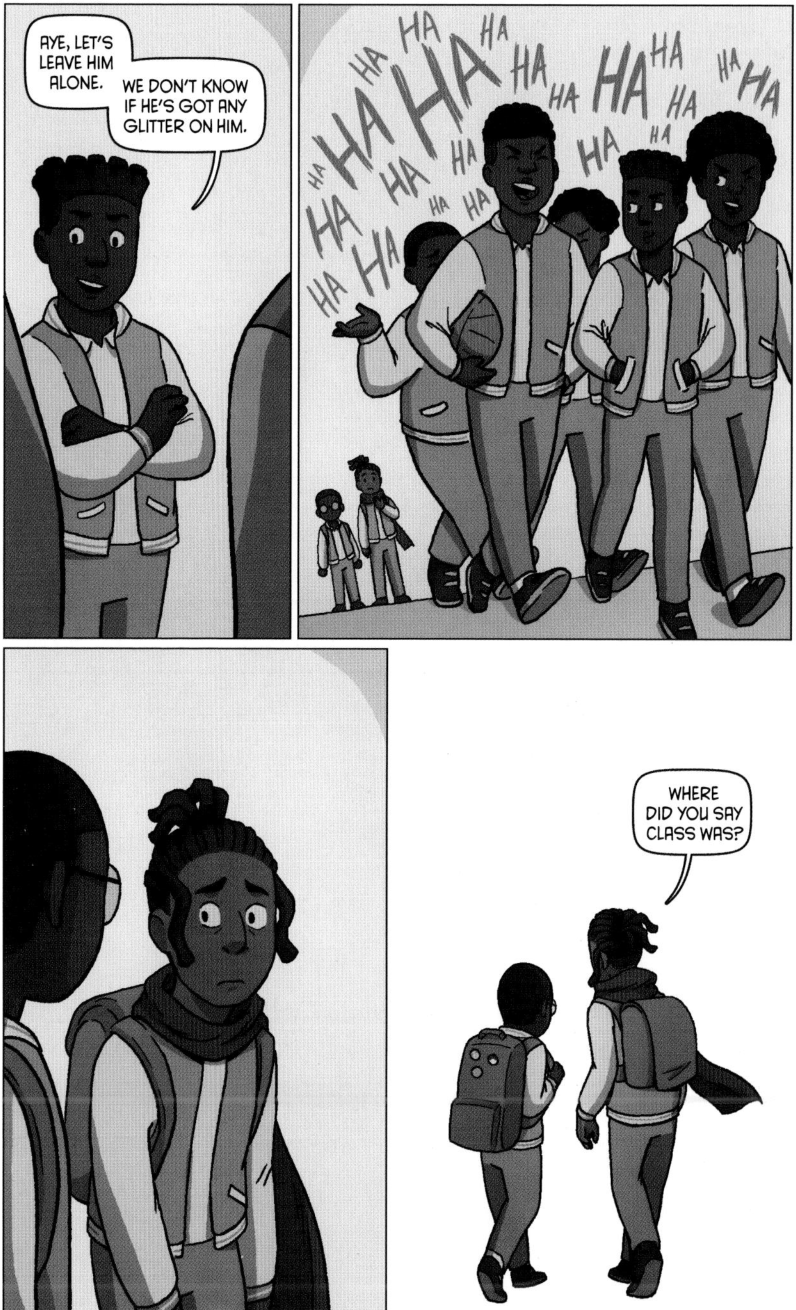
AYE, LET'S LEAVE HIM ALONE.
WE DON'T KNOW IF HE'S GOT ANY GLITTER ON HIM.
HA HA HA HA HA HA HA HA HA HA HA HA HA HA HA HA HA HA HA HA HA HA HA
WHERE DID YOU SAY CLASS WAS?

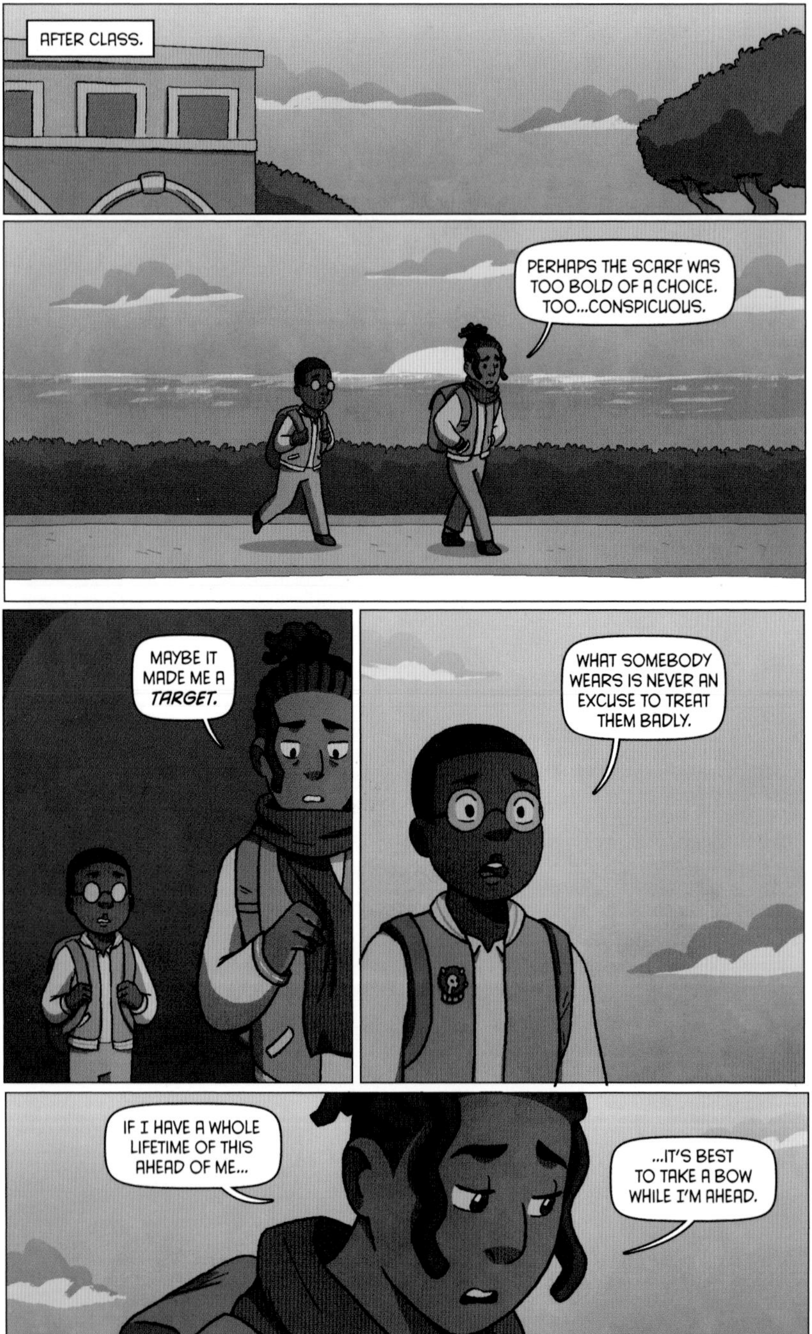
AFTER CLASS.
PERHAPS THE SCARF WAS TOO BOLD OF A CHOICE. TOO...CONSPICUOUS.
MAYBE IT MADE ME A *TARGET.*
WHAT SOMEBODY WEARS IS NEVER AN EXCUSE TO TREAT THEM BADLY.
IF I HAVE A WHOLE LIFETIME OF THIS AHEAD OF ME...
...IT'S BEST TO TAKE A BOW WHILE I'M AHEAD.

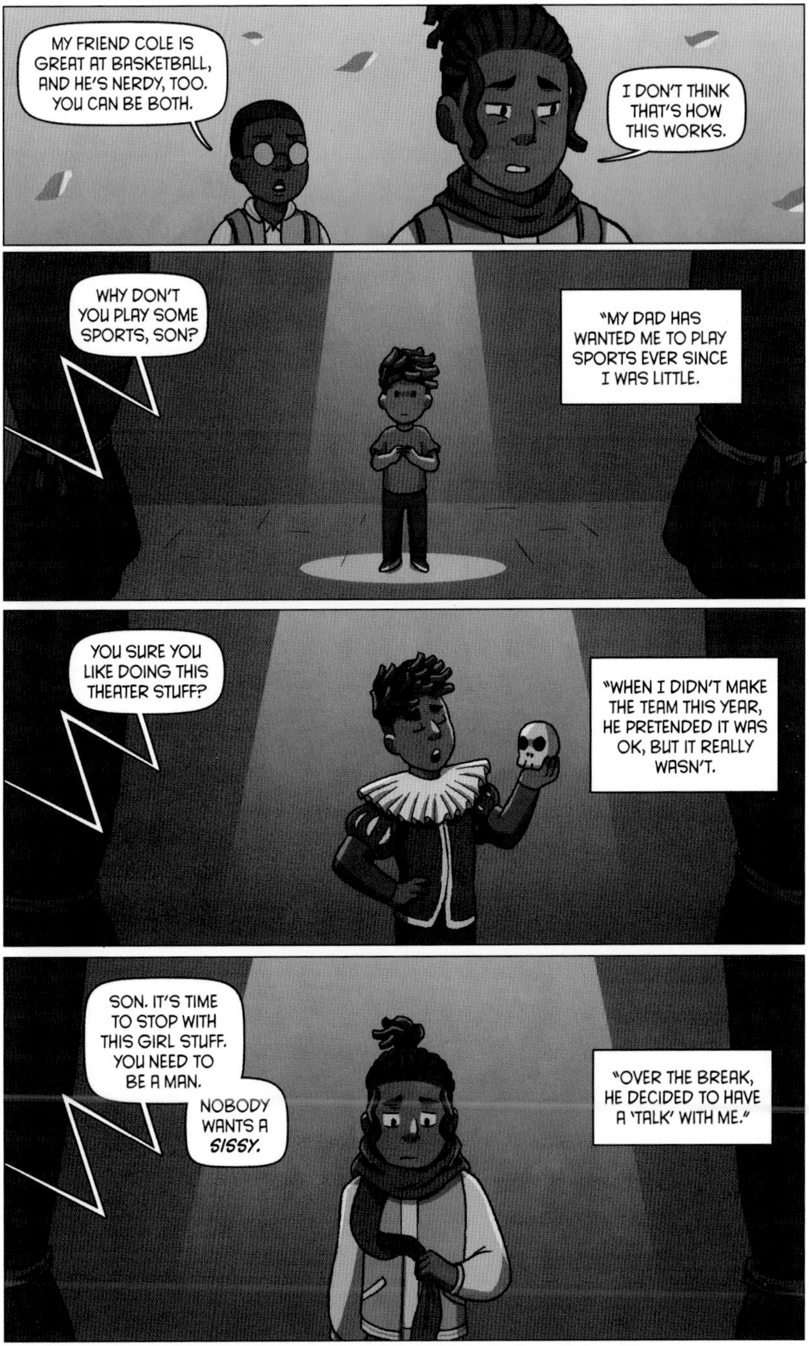

MY FRIEND COLE IS GREAT AT BASKETBALL, AND HE'S NERDY, TOO. YOU CAN BE BOTH.
I DON'T THINK THAT'S HOW THIS WORKS.
WHY DON'T YOU PLAY SOME SPORTS, SON?
"MY DAD HAS WANTED ME TO PLAY SPORTS EVER SINCE I WAS LITTLE.
YOU SURE YOU LIKE DOING THIS THEATER STUFF?
"WHEN I DIDN'T MAKE THE TEAM THIS YEAR, HE PRETENDED IT WAS OK, BUT IT REALLY WASN'T.
SON. IT'S TIME TO STOP WITH THIS GIRL STUFF. YOU NEED TO BE A MAN.
NOBODY WANTS A *SISSY.*
"OVER THE BREAK, HE DECIDED TO HAVE A 'TALK' WITH ME."

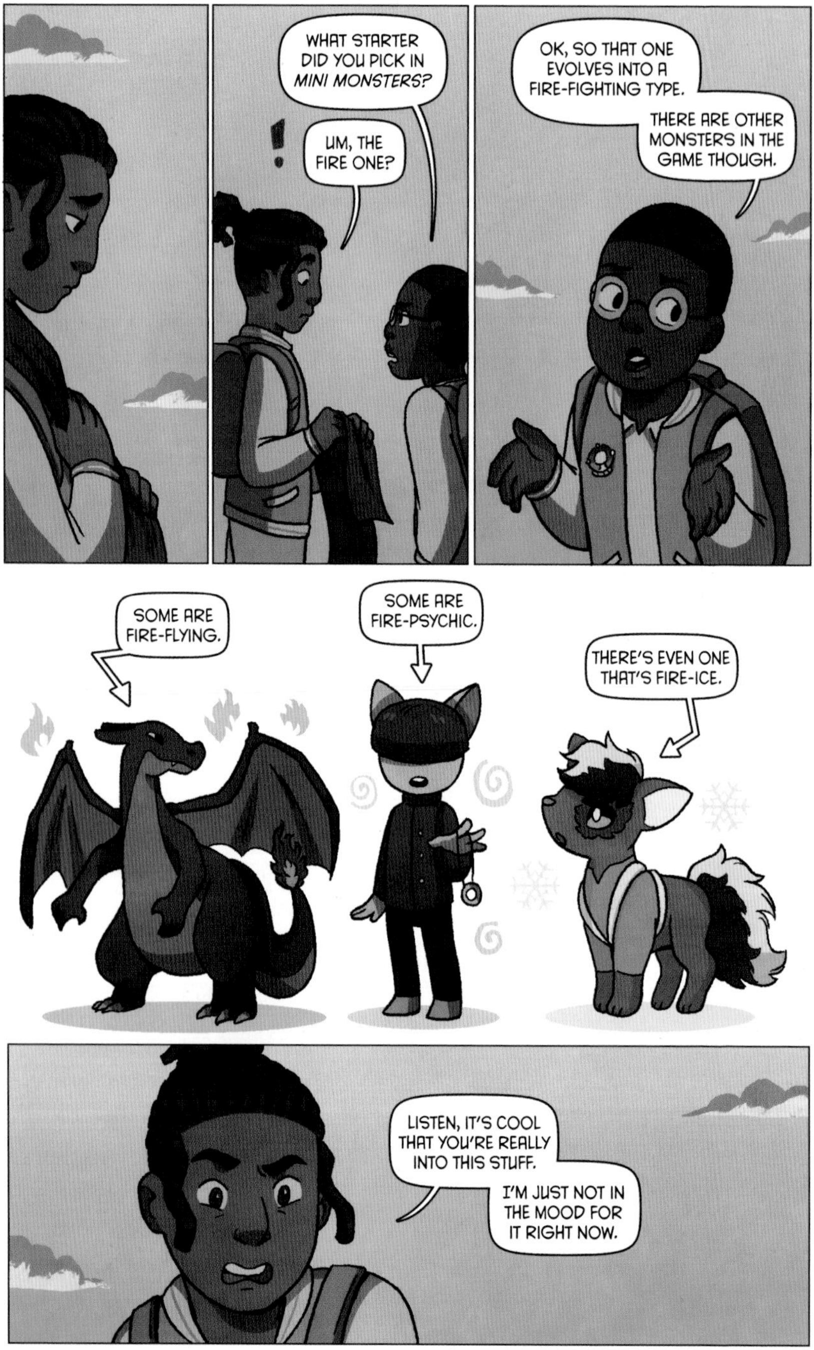
WHAT STARTER DID YOU PICK IN *MINI MONSTERS?*
!
UM, THE FIRE ONE?
OK, SO THAT ONE EVOLVES INTO A FIRE-FIGHTING TYPE.
THERE ARE OTHER MONSTERS IN THE GAME THOUGH.
SOME ARE FIRE-FLYING.
SOME ARE FIRE-PSYCHIC.
THERE'S EVEN ONE THAT'S FIRE-ICE.
LISTEN, IT'S COOL THAT YOU'RE REALLY INTO THIS STUFF.
I'M JUST NOT IN THE MOOD FOR IT RIGHT NOW.

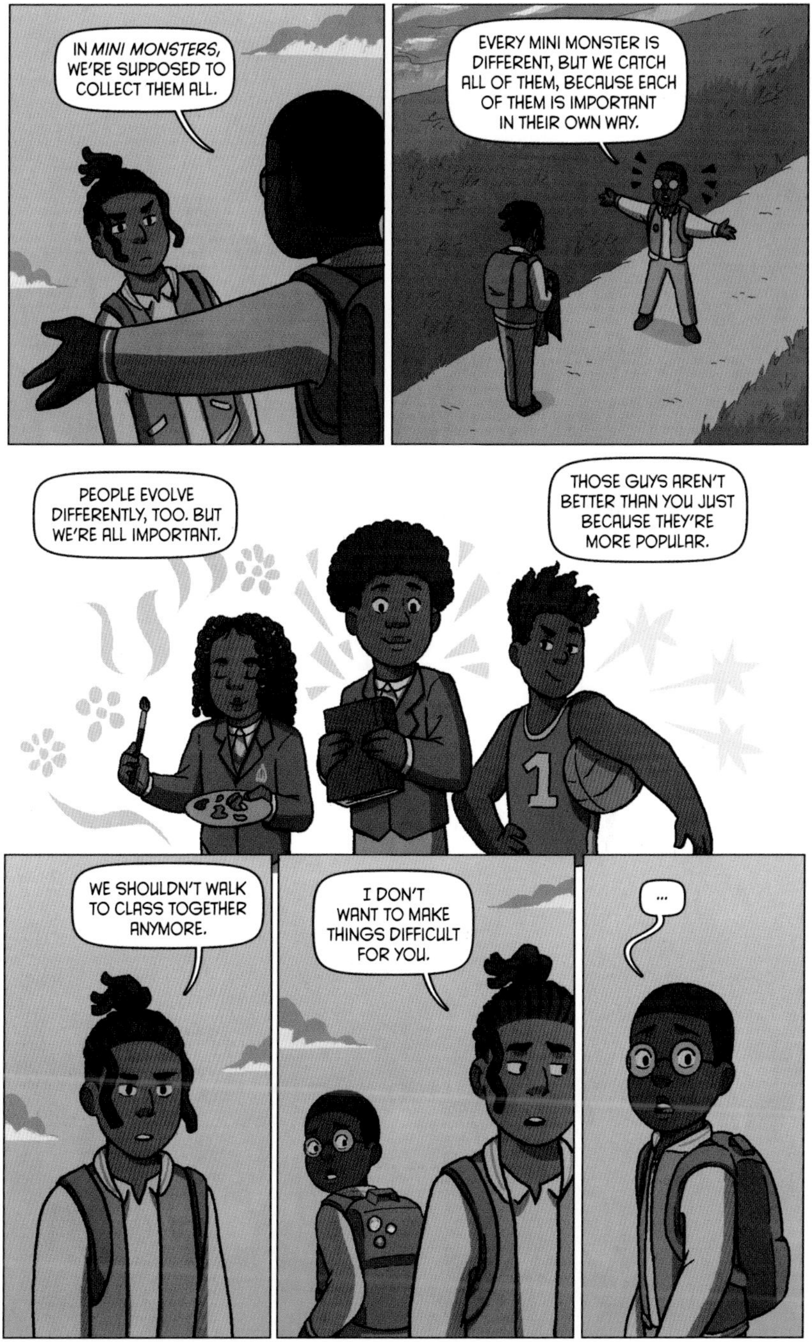
IN *MINI MONSTERS*, WE'RE SUPPOSED TO COLLECT THEM ALL.
EVERY MINI MONSTER IS DIFFERENT, BUT WE CATCH ALL OF THEM, BECAUSE EACH OF THEM IS IMPORTANT IN THEIR OWN WAY.
PEOPLE EVOLVE DIFFERENTLY, TOO. BUT WE'RE ALL IMPORTANT.
THOSE GUYS AREN'T BETTER THAN YOU JUST BECAUSE THEY'RE MORE POPULAR.
1
WE SHOULDN'T WALK TO CLASS TOGETHER ANYMORE.
I DON'T WANT TO MAKE THINGS DIFFICULT FOR YOU.
...

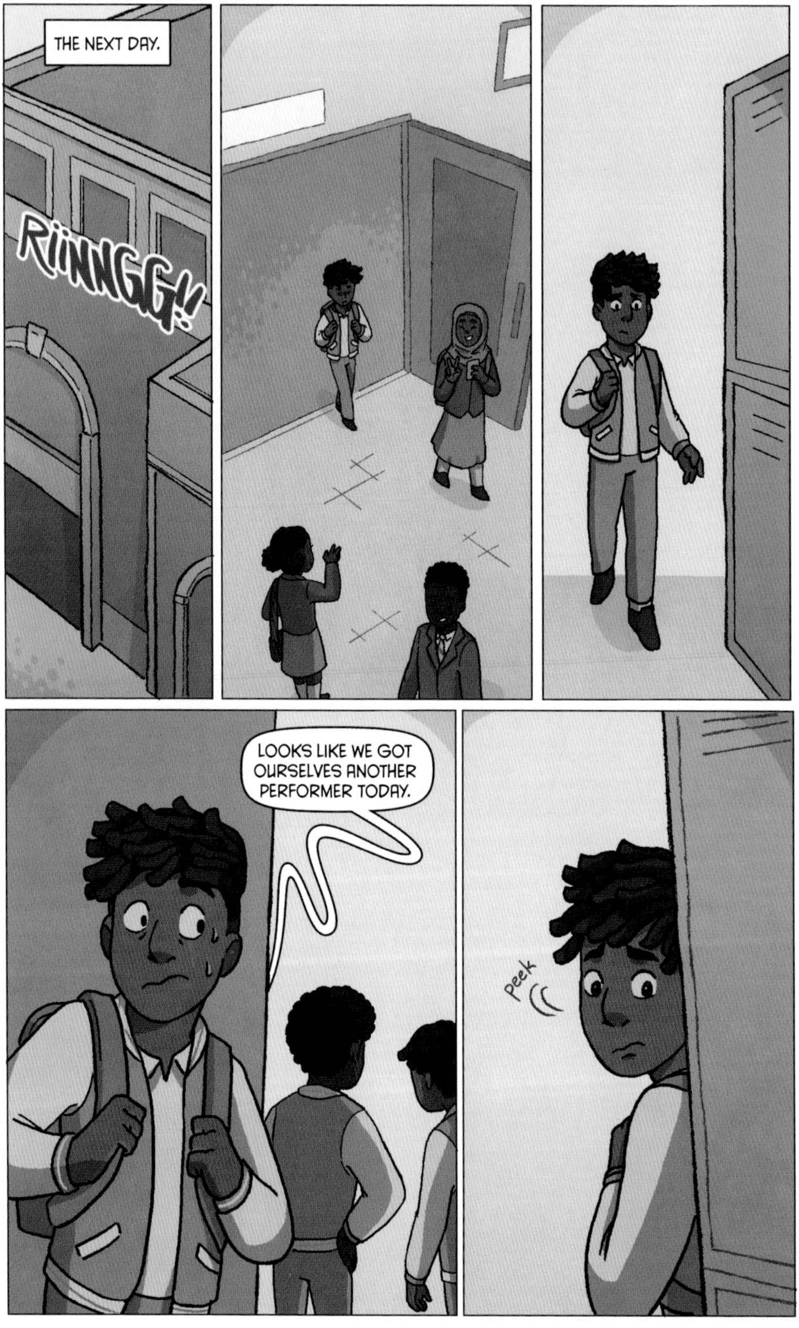
THE NEXT DAY.
RIINNGG!!
LOOKS LIKE WE GOT OURSELVES ANOTHER PERFORMER TODAY.
peek

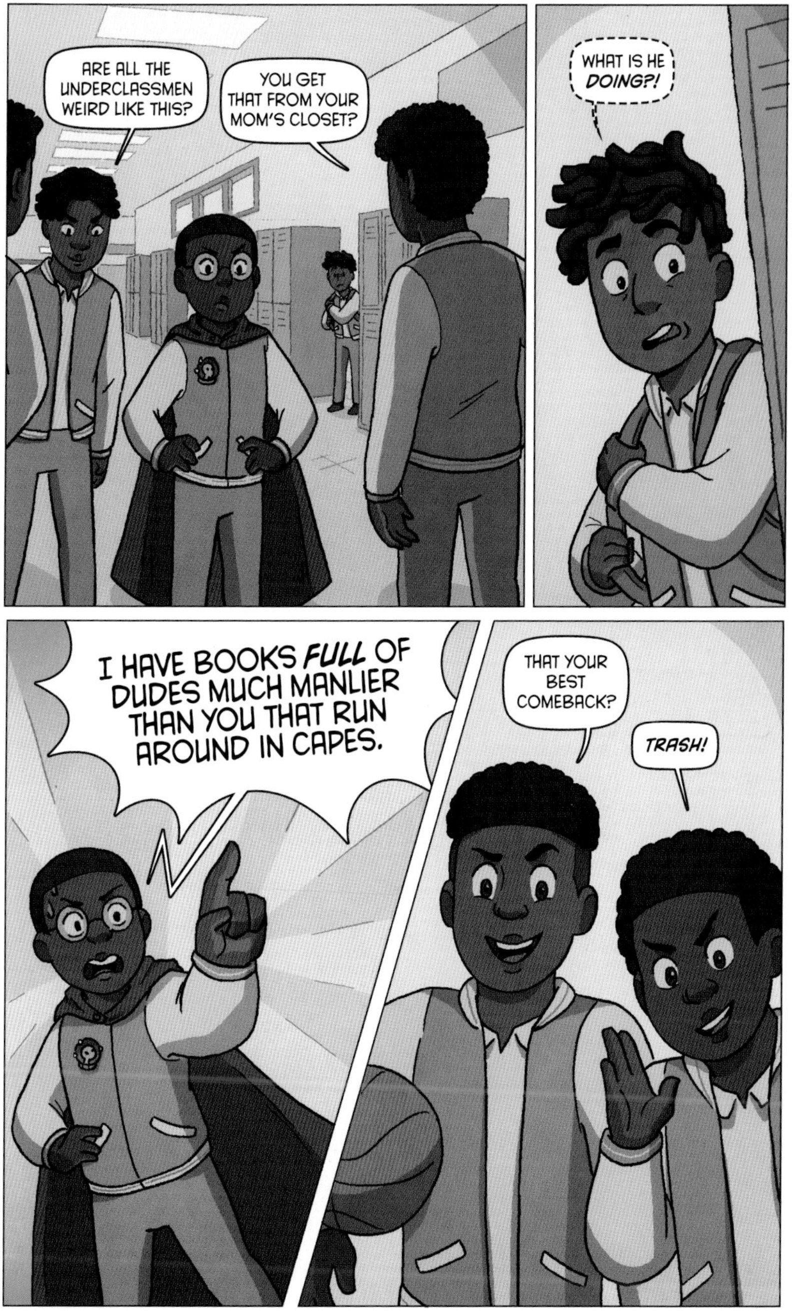
ARE ALL THE UNDERCLASSMEN WEIRD LIKE THIS?
YOU GET THAT FROM YOUR MOM'S CLOSET?
WHAT IS HE *DOING?!*
I HAVE BOOKS *FULL* OF DUDES MUCH MANLIER THAN YOU THAT RUN AROUND IN CAPES.
THAT YOUR BEST COMEBACK?
TRASH!

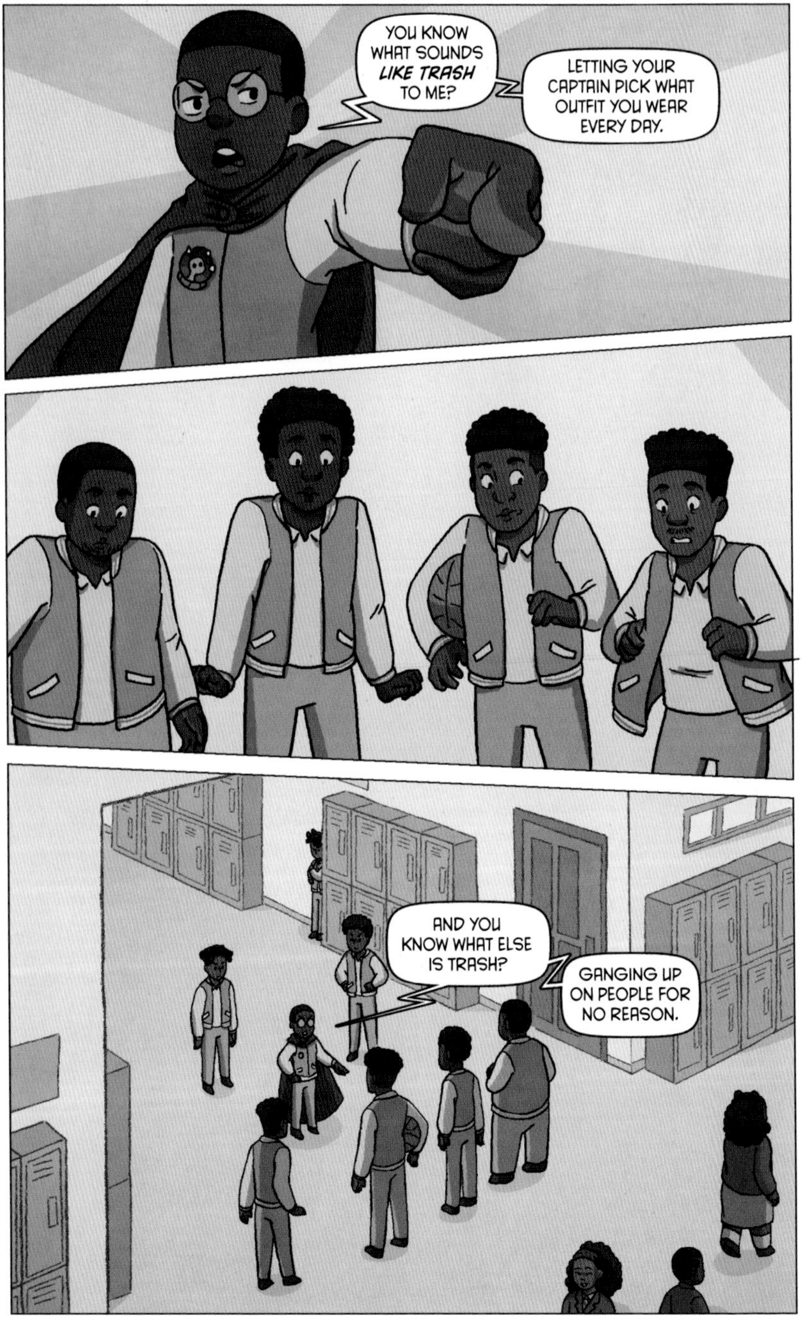
YOU KNOW WHAT SOUNDS *LIKE TRASH* TO ME?
LETTING YOUR CAPTAIN PICK WHAT OUTFIT YOU WEAR EVERY DAY.
AND YOU KNOW WHAT ELSE IS TRASH?
GANGING UP ON PEOPLE FOR NO REASON.

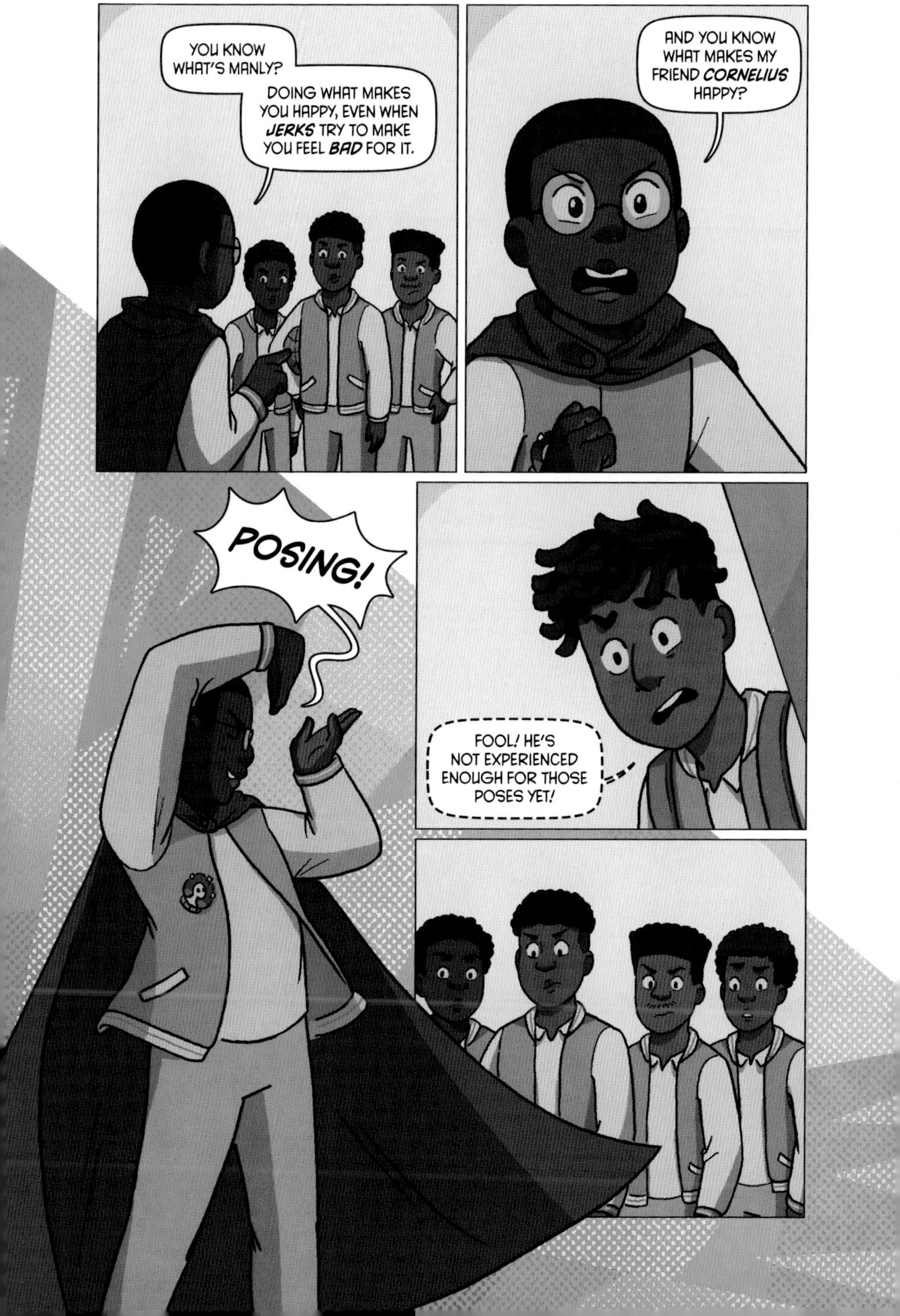
YOU KNOW WHAT'S MANLY?
DOING WHAT MAKES YOU HAPPY, EVEN WHEN JERKS TRY TO MAKE YOU FEEL BAD FOR IT.
AND YOU KNOW WHAT MAKES MY FRIEND CORNELIUS HAPPY?
POSING!
FOOL! HE'S NOT EXPERIENCED ENOUGH FOR THOSE POSES YET!

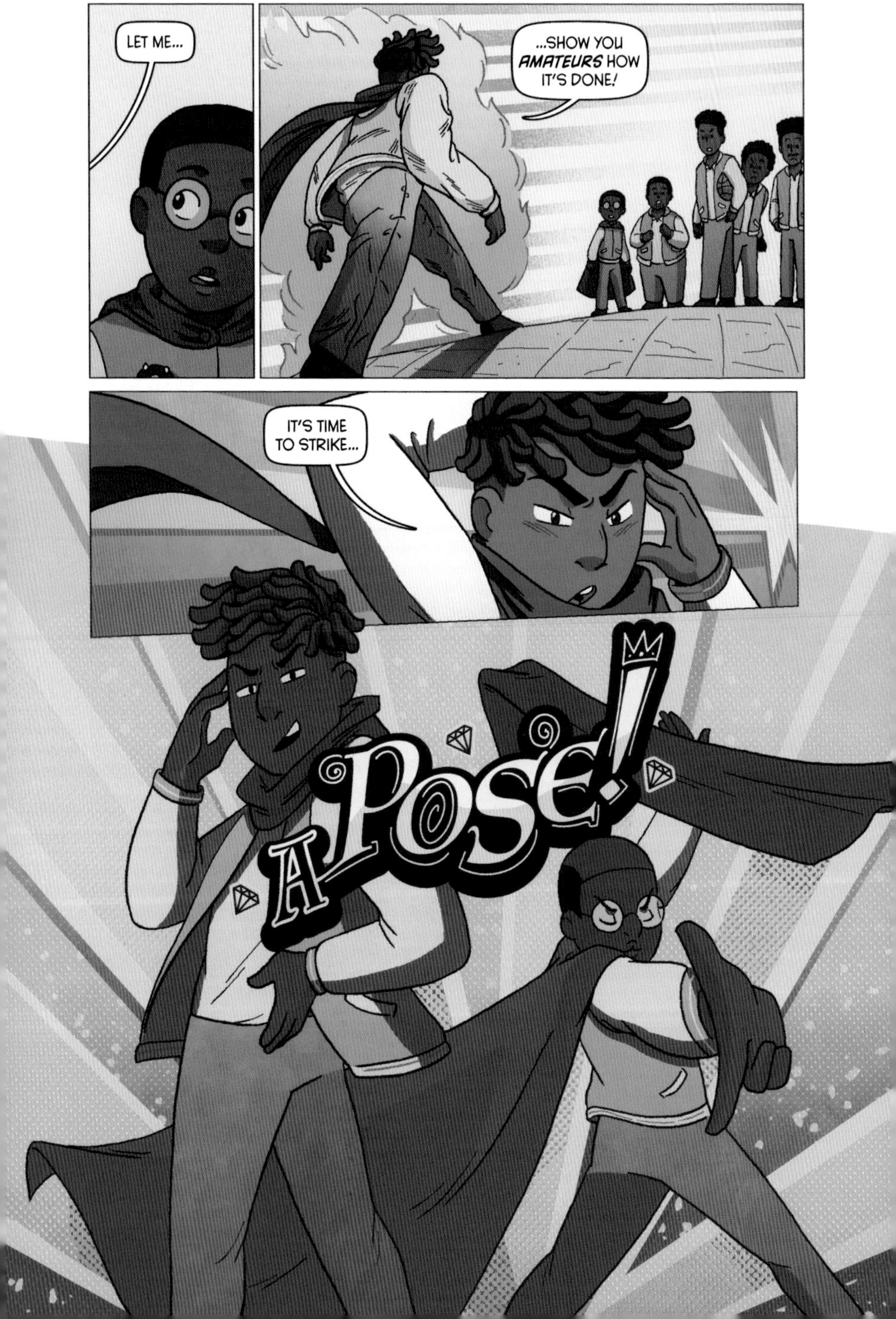
LET ME...
...SHOW YOU AMATEURS HOW IT'S DONE!
IT'S TIME TO STRIKE...
A POSE!

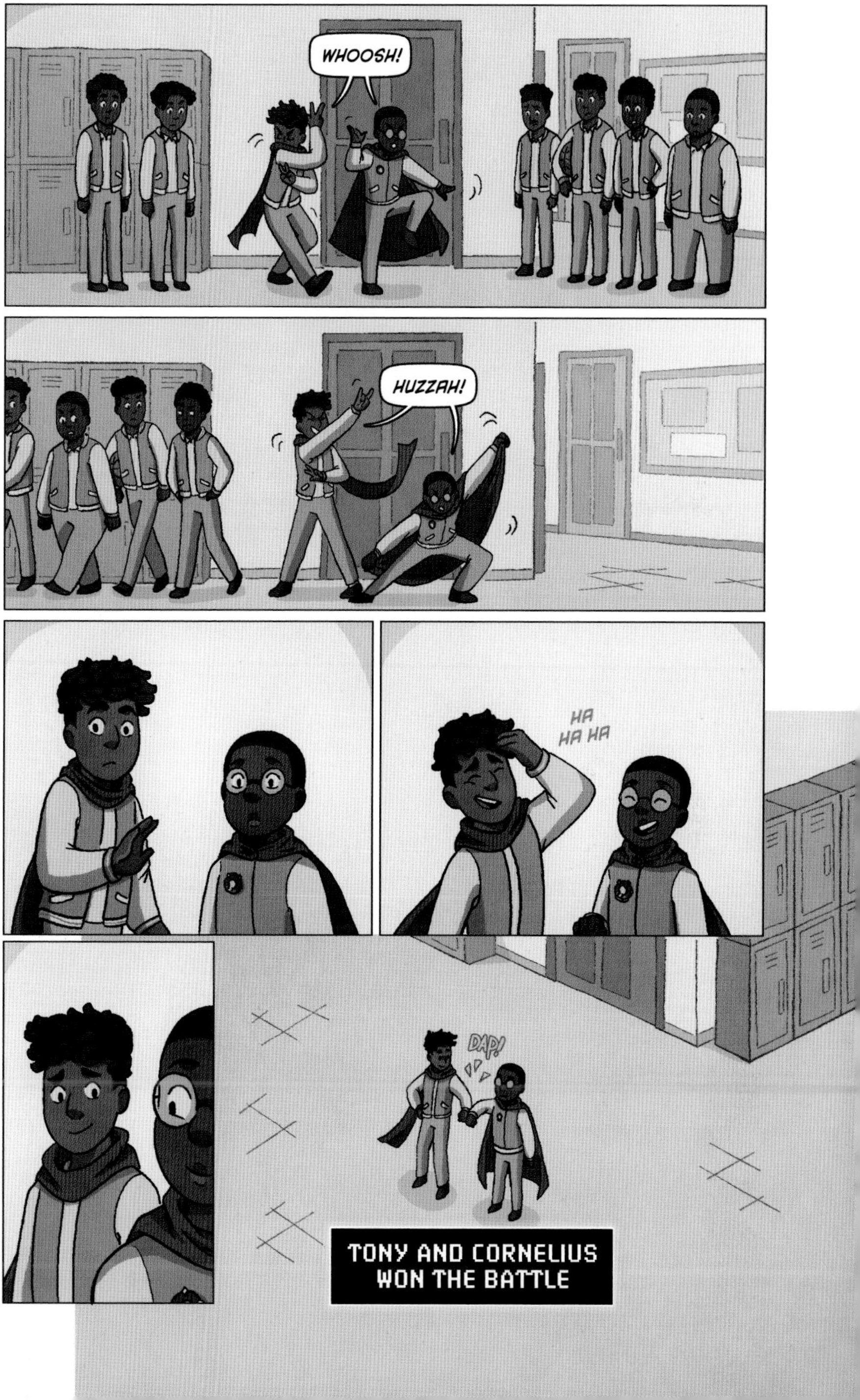
WHOOSH!
HUZZAH!
HA HA HA
DAP!
TONY AND CORNELIUS WON THE BATTLE

CHAPTER 8

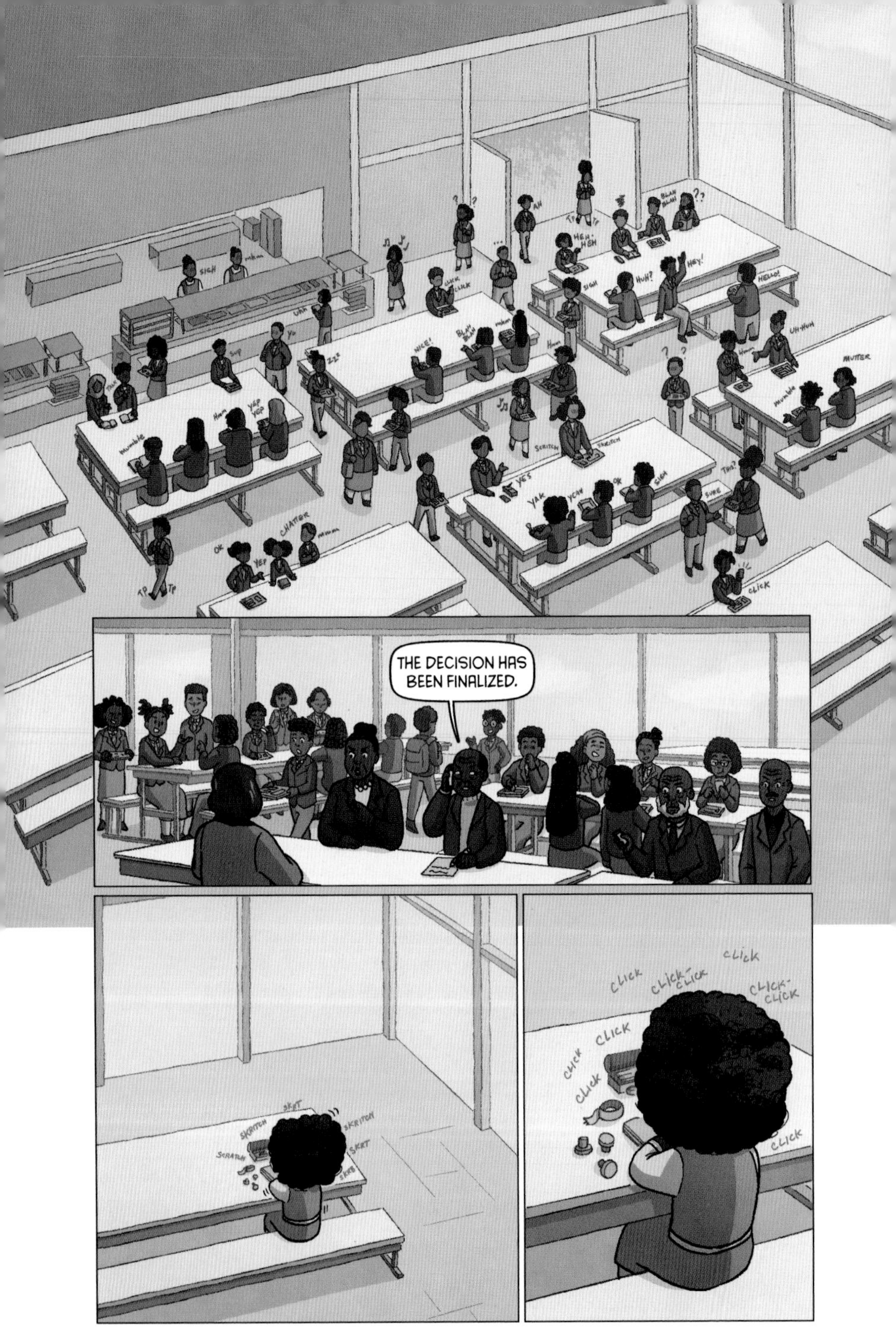
THE DECISION HAS BEEN FINALIZED.

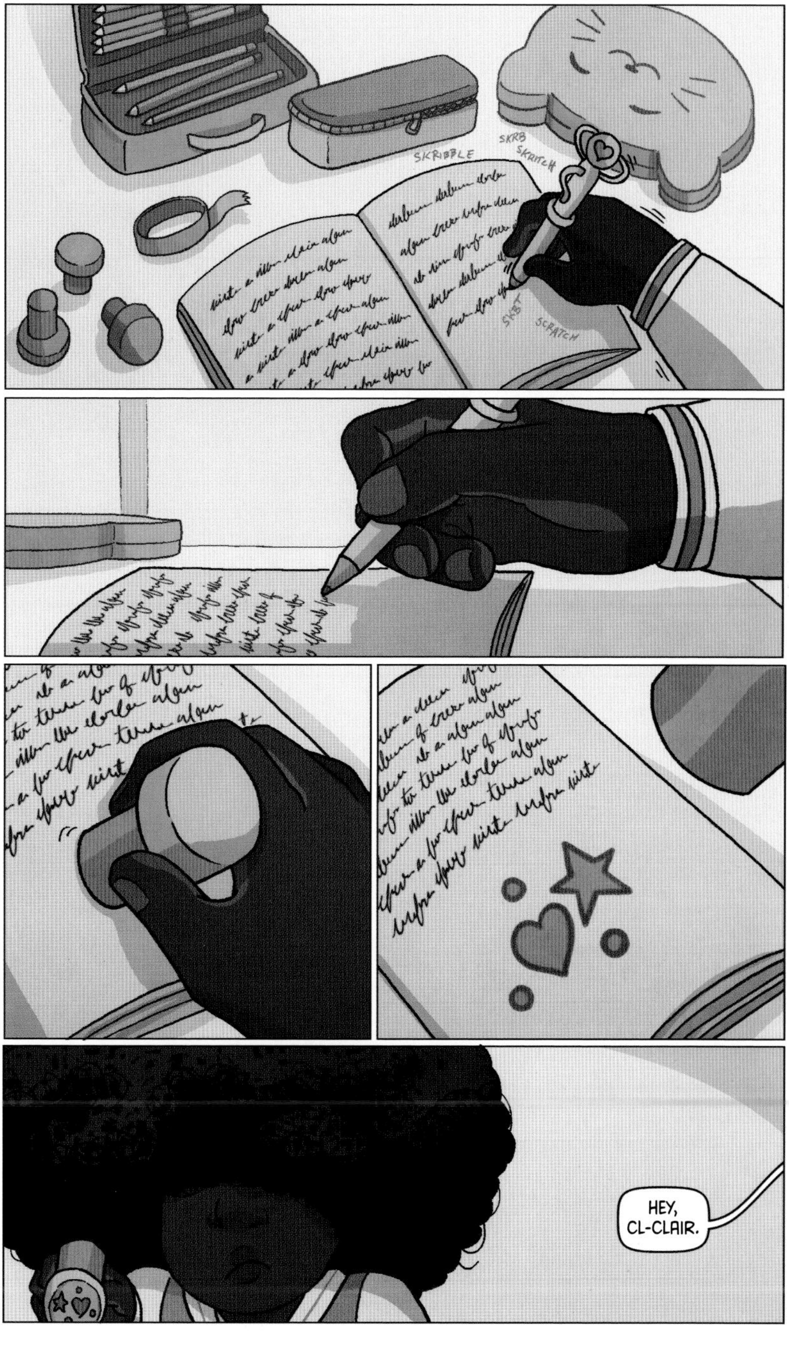
SKRIBBLE
SKRB
SKRITCH
SKBT
SCRATCH
HEY, CL-CLAIR.

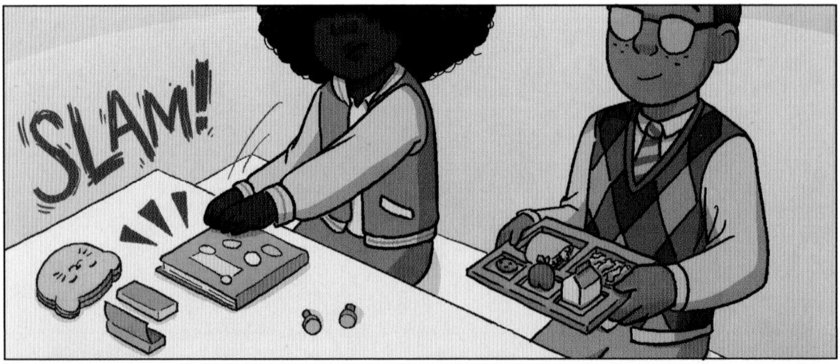
SLAM!

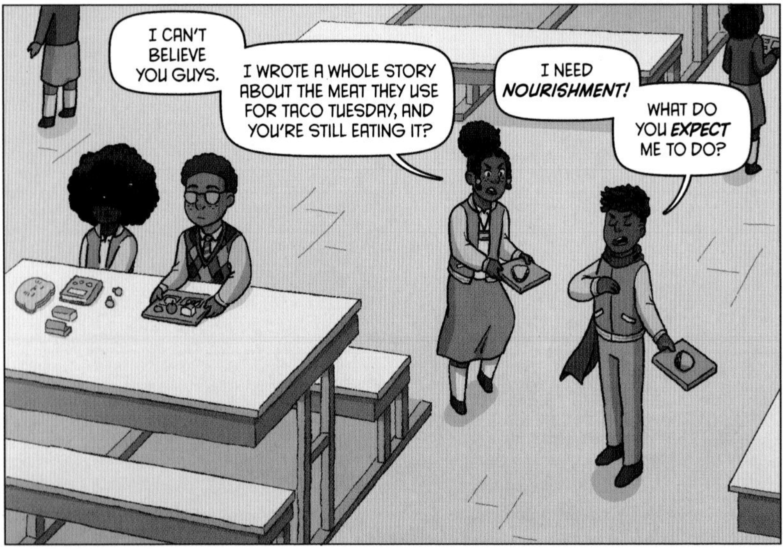
I CAN'T BELIEVE YOU GUYS.
I WROTE A WHOLE STORY ABOUT THE MEAT THEY USE FOR TACO TUESDAY, AND YOU'RE STILL EATING IT?
I NEED ***NOURISHMENT!***
WHAT DO YOU ***EXPECT*** ME TO DO?

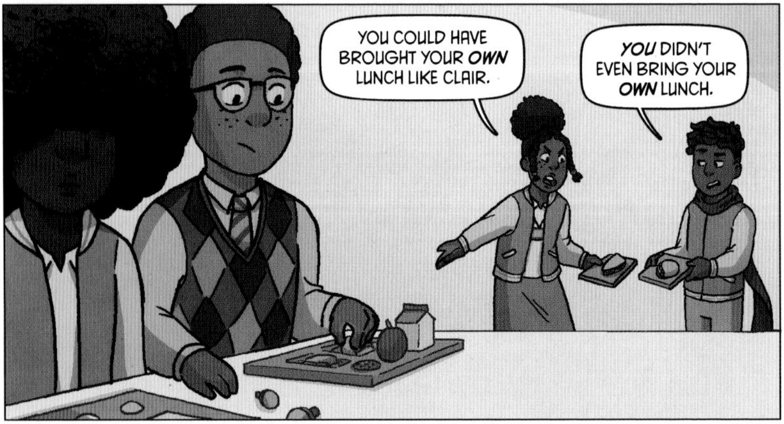
YOU COULD HAVE BROUGHT YOUR ***OWN*** LUNCH LIKE CLAIR.
YOU DIDN'T EVEN BRING YOUR ***OWN*** LUNCH.

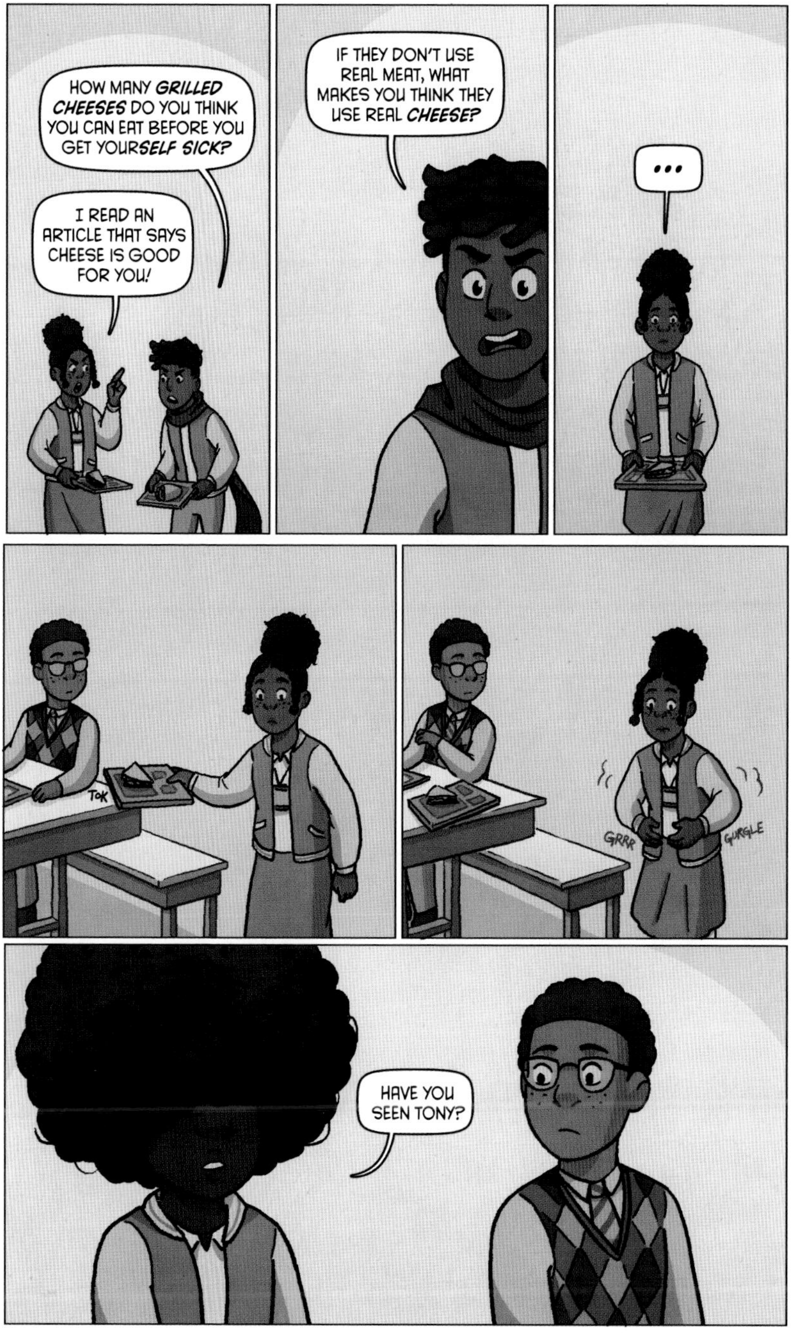
HOW MANY GRILLED CHEESES DO YOU THINK YOU CAN EAT BEFORE YOU GET YOURSELF SICK?
I READ AN ARTICLE THAT SAYS CHEESE IS GOOD FOR YOU!
IF THEY DON'T USE REAL MEAT, WHAT MAKES YOU THINK THEY USE REAL CHEESE?
...
TOK
GRRR
GURGLE
HAVE YOU SEEN TONY?

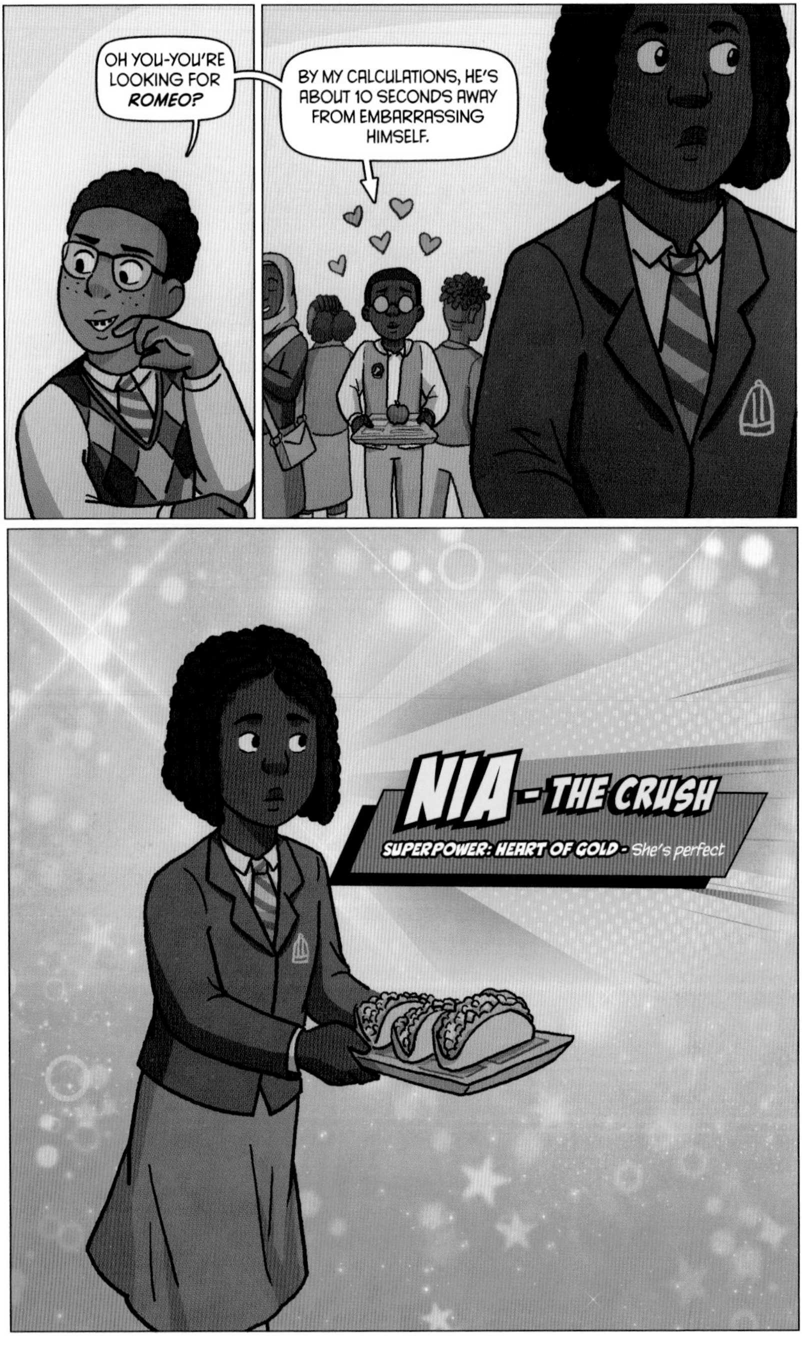
OH YOU-YOU'RE LOOKING FOR *ROMEO?*
BY MY CALCULATIONS, HE'S ABOUT 10 SECONDS AWAY FROM EMBARRASSING HIMSELF.
NIA - THE CRUSH
SUPERPOWER: HEART OF GOLD - She's perfect

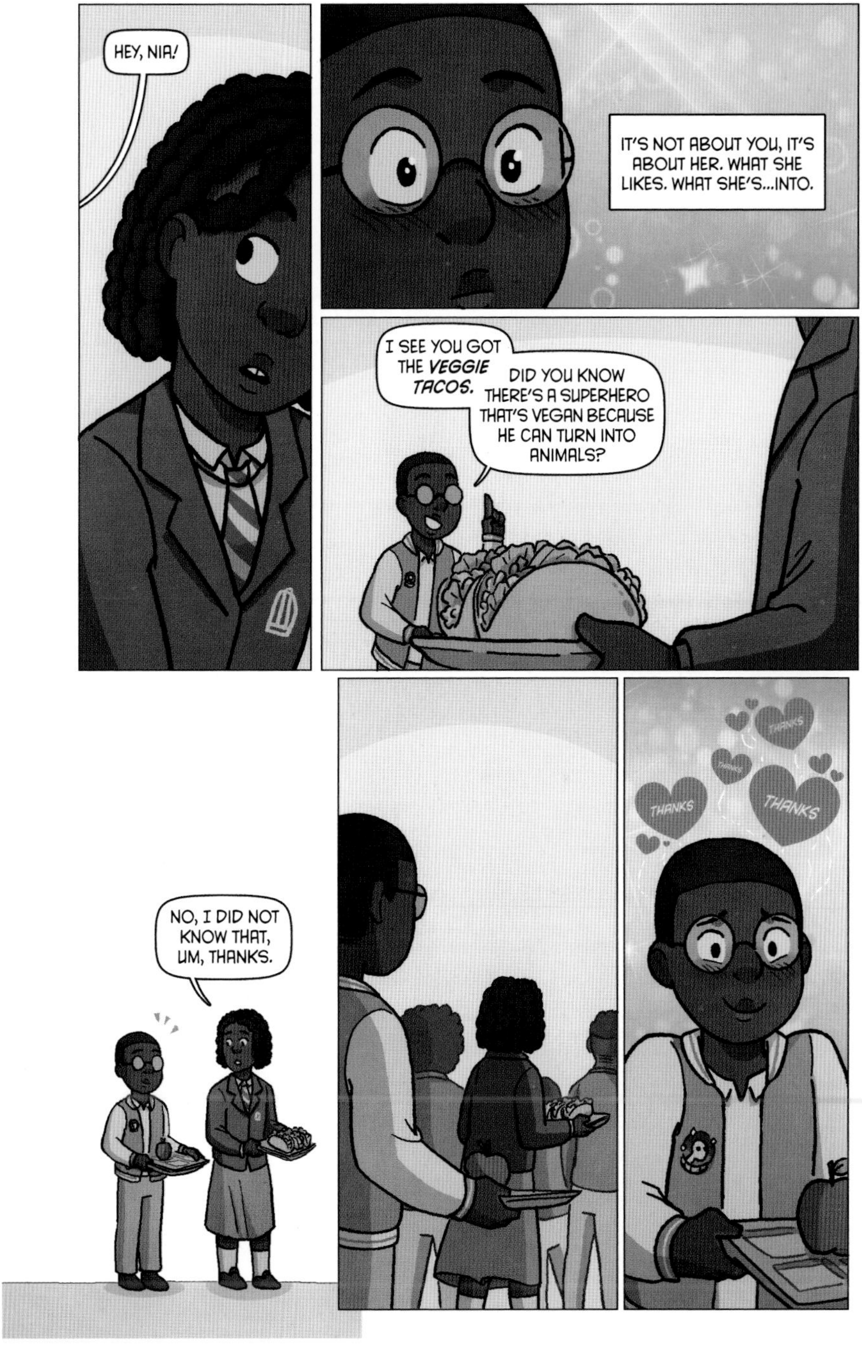
HEY, NIA!
IT'S NOT ABOUT YOU, IT'S ABOUT HER. WHAT SHE LIKES. WHAT SHE'S...INTO.
I SEE YOU GOT THE *VEGGIE TACOS.*
DID YOU KNOW THERE'S A SUPERHERO THAT'S VEGAN BECAUSE HE CAN TURN INTO ANIMALS?
NO, I DID NOT KNOW THAT, UM, THANKS.
THANKS
THANKS
THANKS
THANKS

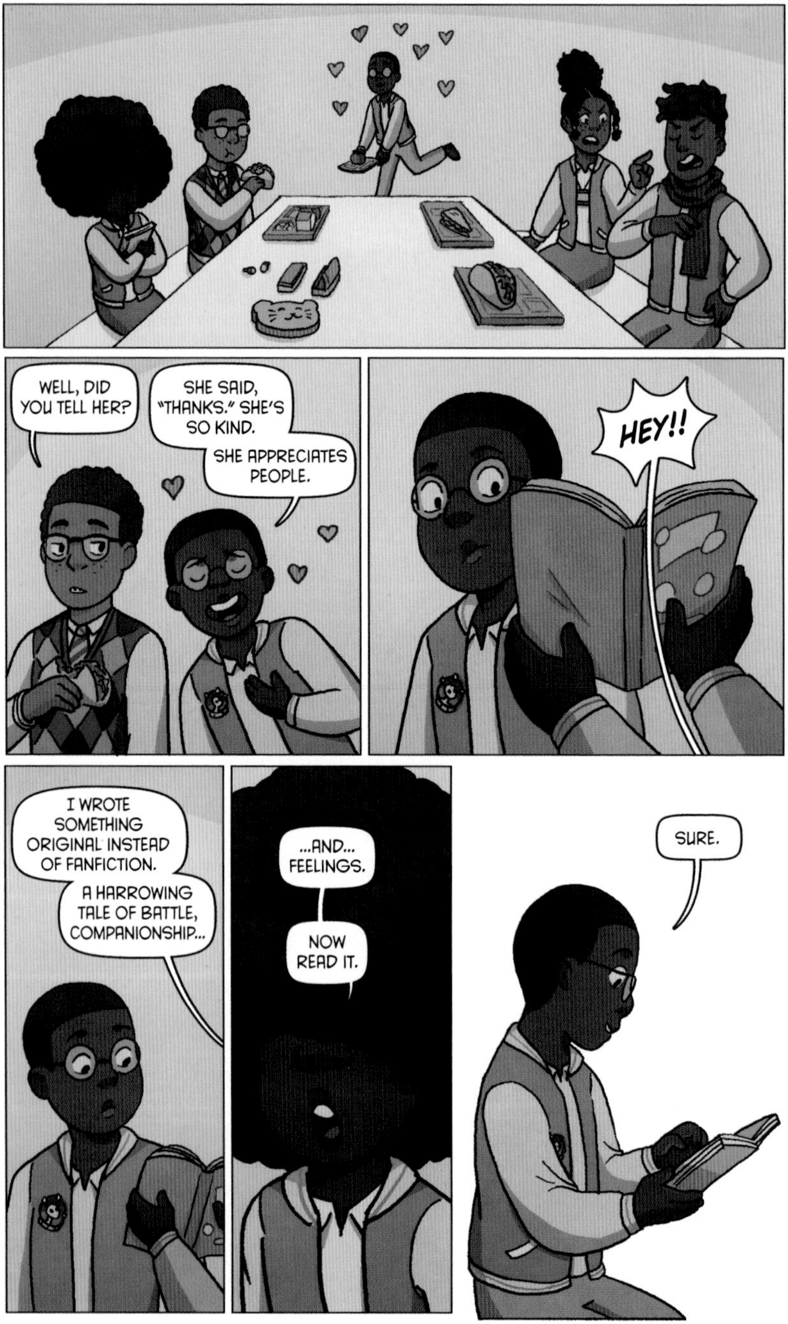
WELL, DID YOU TELL HER?
SHE SAID, "THANKS." SHE'S SO KIND.
SHE APPRECIATES PEOPLE.
HEY!!
I WROTE SOMETHING ORIGINAL INSTEAD OF FANFICTION.
A HARROWING TALE OF BATTLE, COMPANIONSHIP...
...AND... FEELINGS.
NOW READ IT.
SURE.

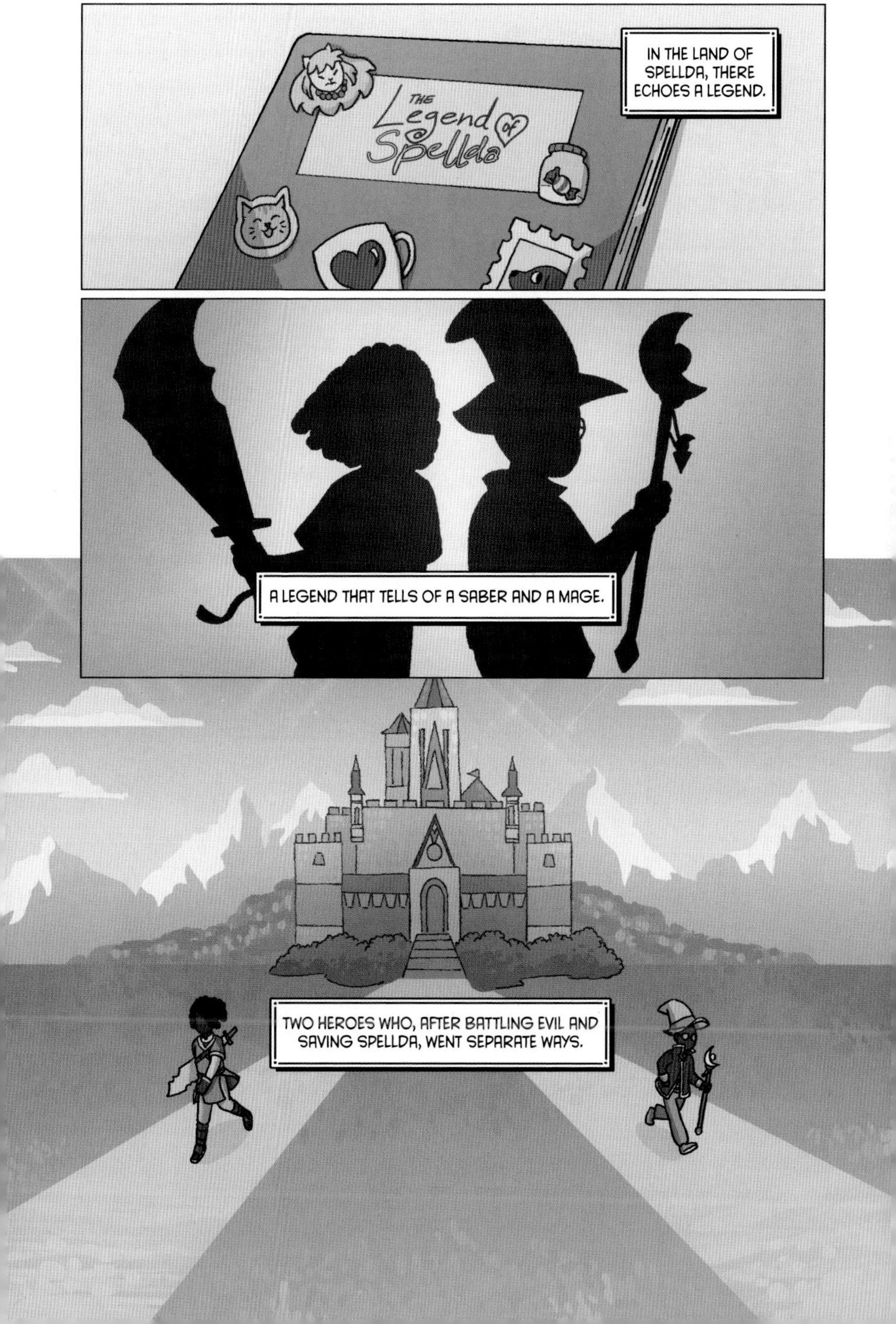
THE Legend of Spellda
IN THE LAND OF SPELLDA, THERE ECHOES A LEGEND.
A LEGEND THAT TELLS OF A SABER AND A MAGE.
TWO HEROES WHO, AFTER BATTLING EVIL AND SAVING SPELLDA, WENT SEPARATE WAYS.

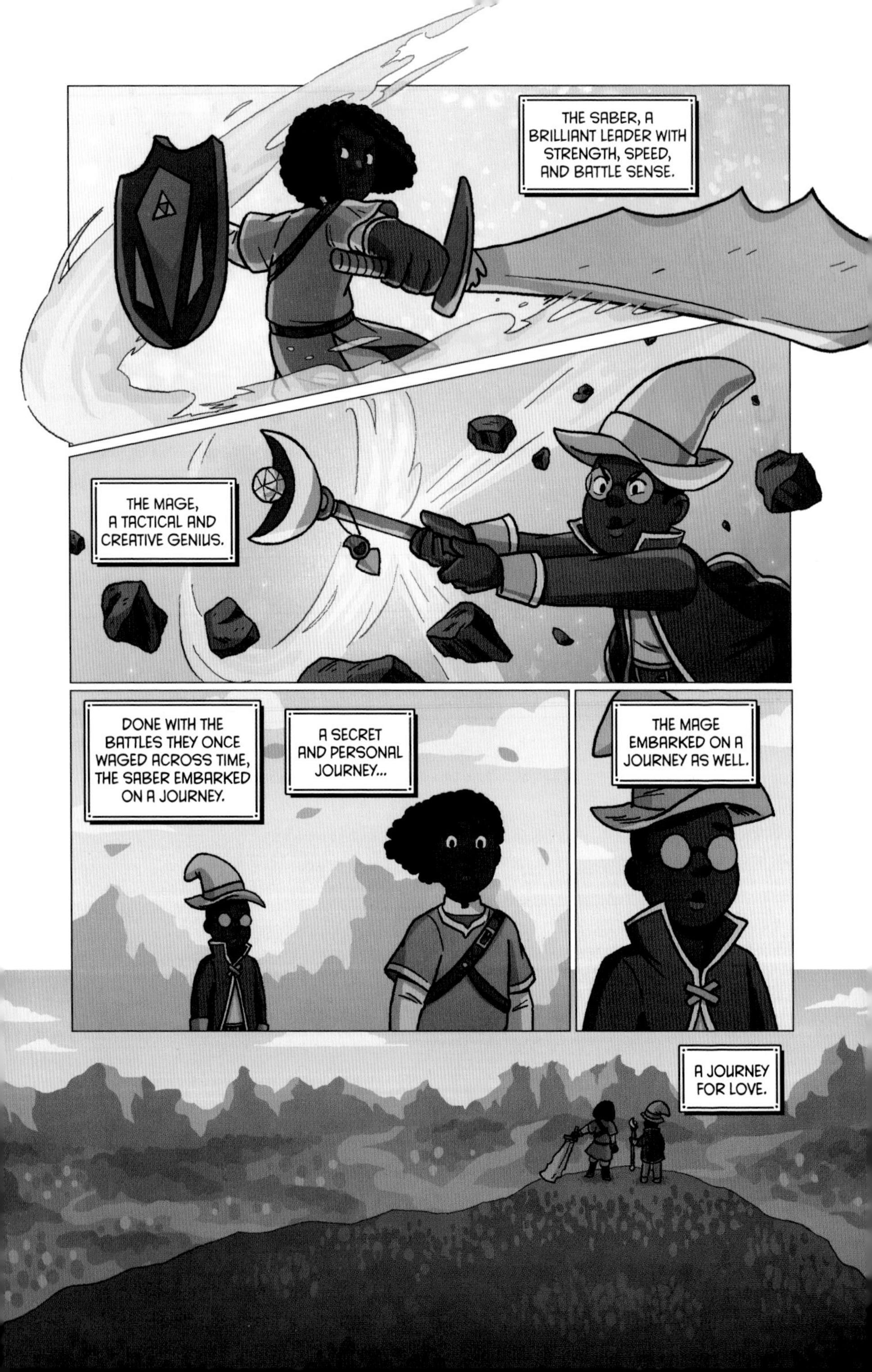
THE SABER, A BRILLIANT LEADER WITH STRENGTH, SPEED, AND BATTLE SENSE.
THE MAGE, A TACTICAL AND CREATIVE GENIUS.
DONE WITH THE BATTLES THEY ONCE WAGED ACROSS TIME, THE SABER EMBARKED ON A JOURNEY.
A SECRET AND PERSONAL JOURNEY...
THE MAGE EMBARKED ON A JOURNEY AS WELL.
A JOURNEY FOR LOVE.

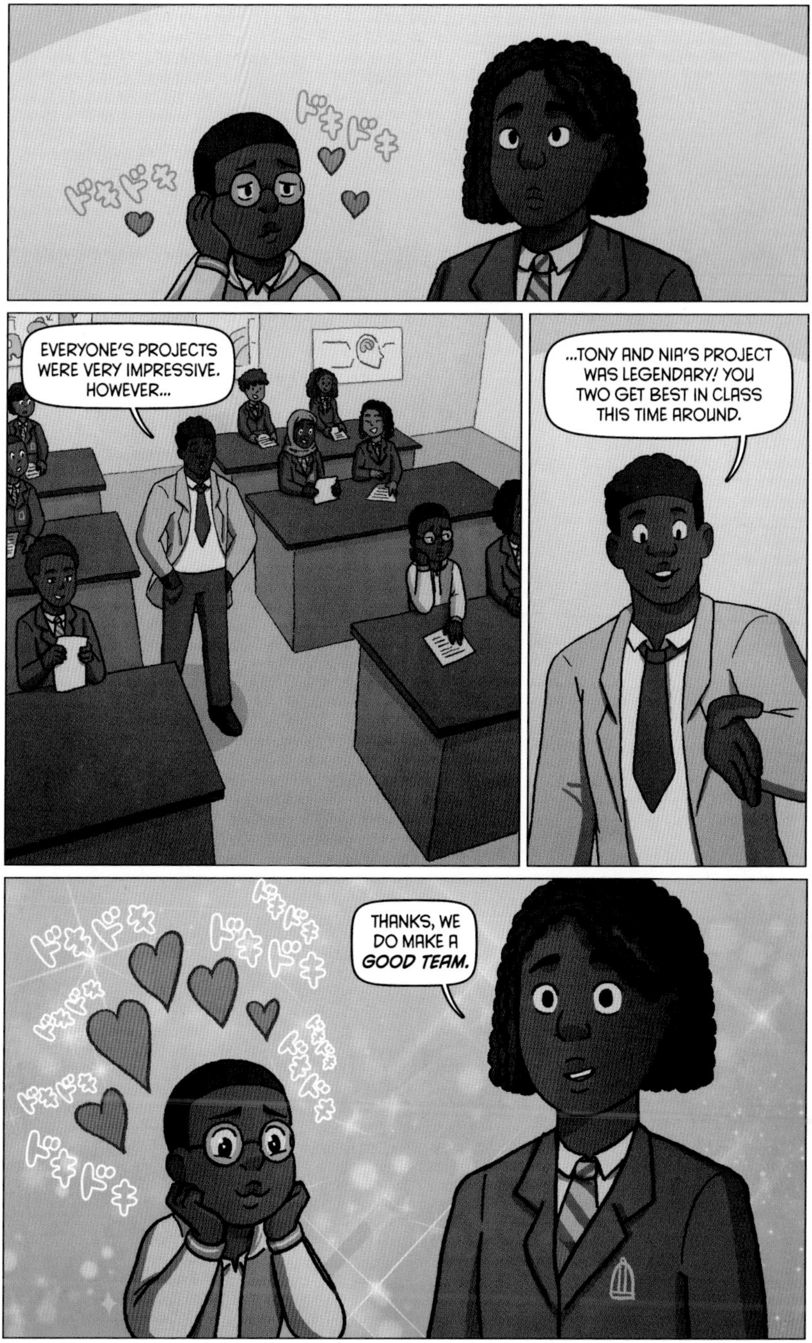
ドキドキ
ドキドキ
EVERYONE'S PROJECTS WERE VERY IMPRESSIVE. HOWEVER...
...TONY AND NIA'S PROJECT WAS LEGENDARY! YOU TWO GET BEST IN CLASS THIS TIME AROUND.
ドキドキ
ドキドキ
ドキドキ
THANKS, WE DO MAKE A *GOOD TEAM.*
ドキドキ
ドキドキ
ドキドキ
ドキドキ

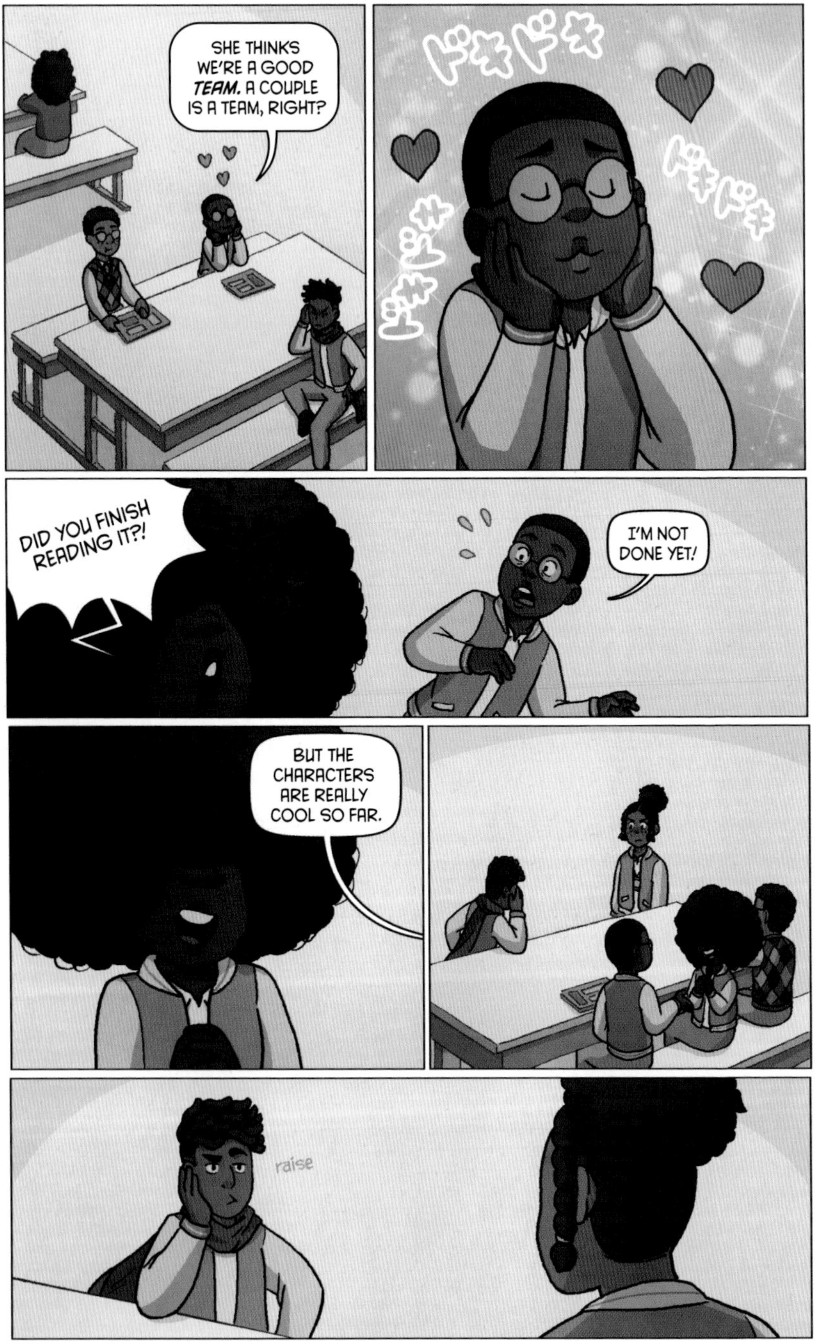
SHE THINKS WE'RE A GOOD *TEAM.* A COUPLE IS A TEAM, RIGHT?
ドキドキ
ドキドキ
ドキドキ
DID YOU FINISH READING IT?!
I'M NOT DONE YET!
BUT THE CHARACTERS ARE REALLY COOL SO FAR.
raise

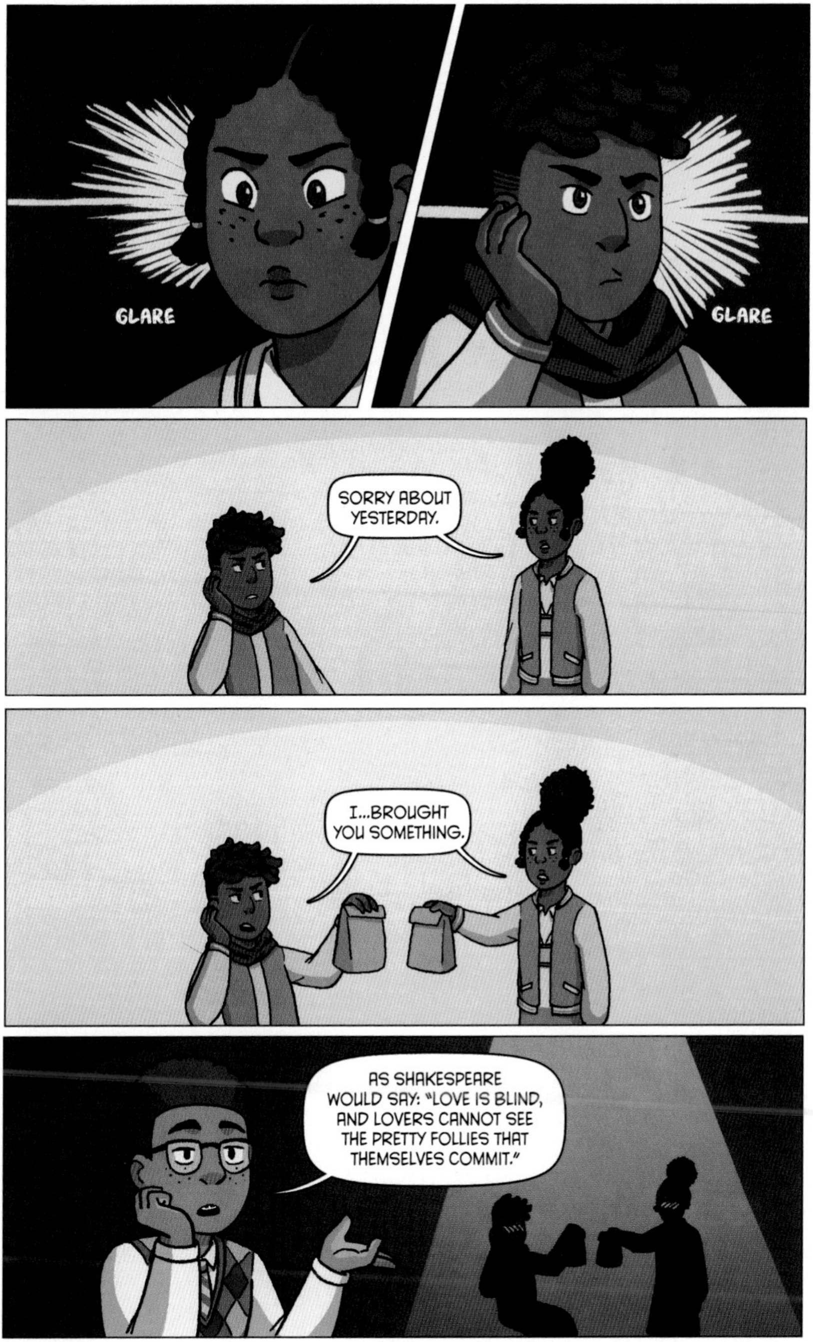
GLARE
GLARE
SORRY ABOUT YESTERDAY.
I...BROUGHT YOU SOMETHING.
AS SHAKESPEARE WOULD SAY: "LOVE IS BLIND, AND LOVERS CANNOT SEE THE PRETTY FOLLIES THAT THEMSELVES COMMIT."

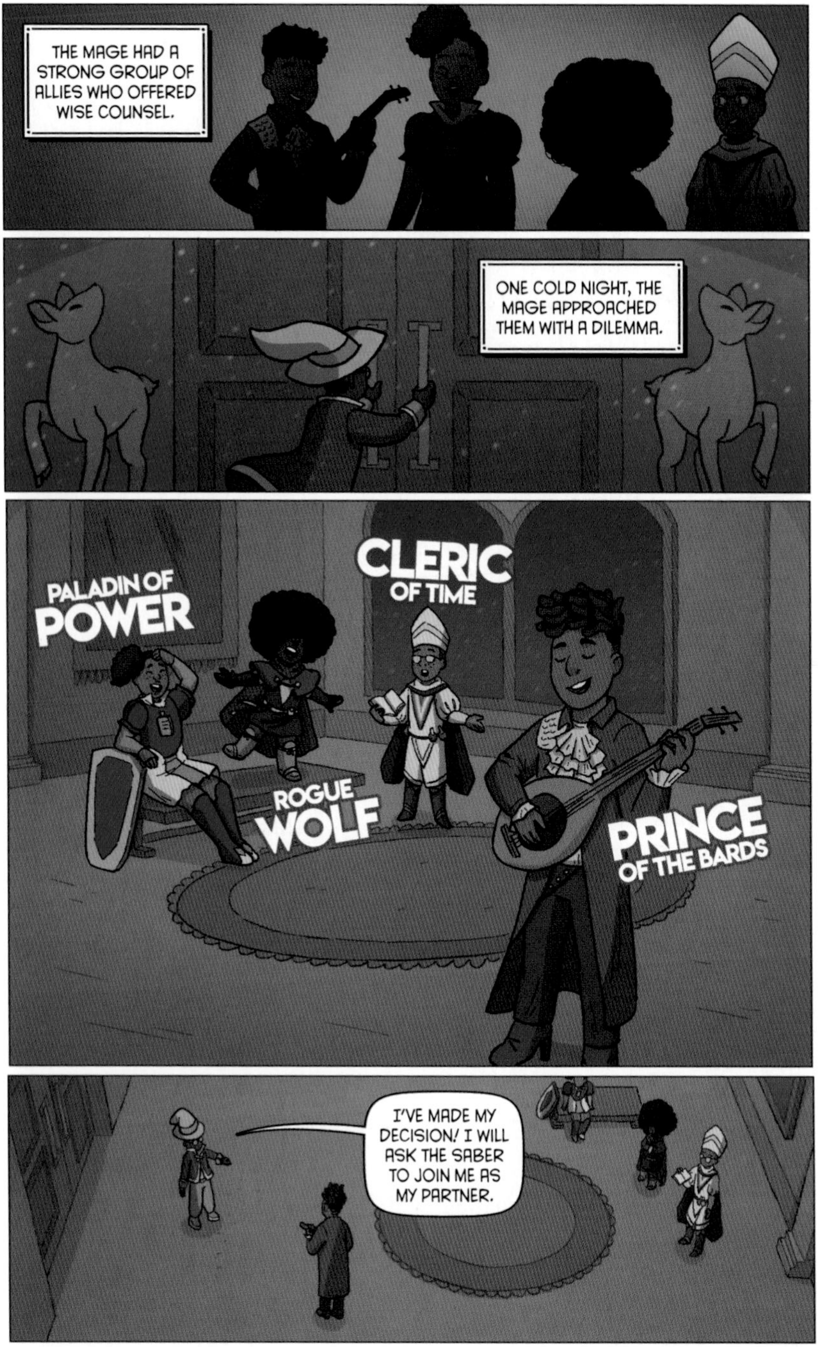
THE MAGE HAD A STRONG GROUP OF ALLIES WHO OFFERED WISE COUNSEL.
ONE COLD NIGHT, THE MAGE APPROACHED THEM WITH A DILEMMA.
PALADIN OF POWER
CLERIC OF TIME
ROGUE WOLF
PRINCE OF THE BARDS
I'VE MADE MY DECISION! I WILL ASK THE SABER TO JOIN ME AS MY PARTNER.

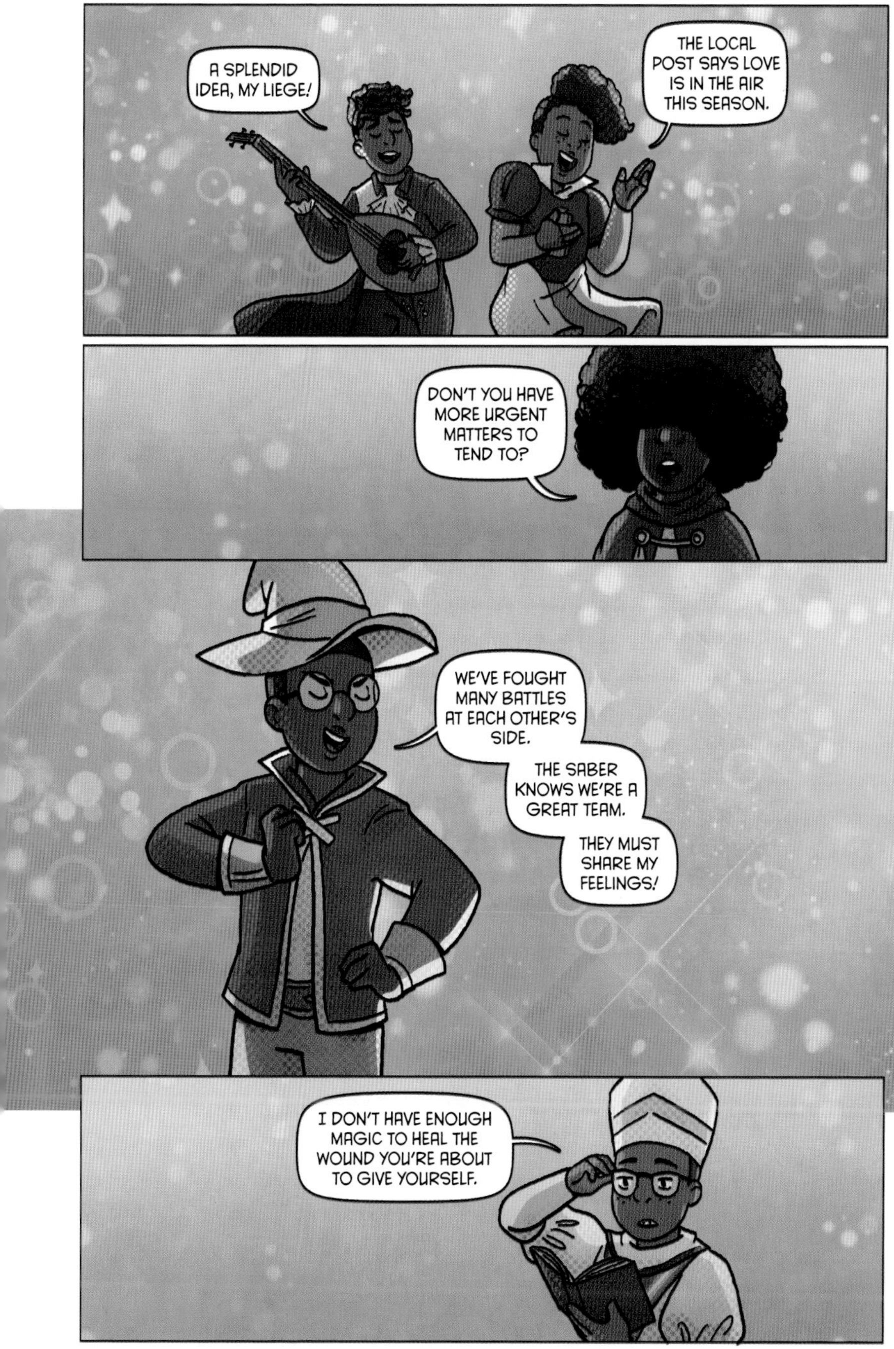
A SPLENDID IDEA, MY LIEGE!
THE LOCAL POST SAYS LOVE IS IN THE AIR THIS SEASON.
DON'T YOU HAVE MORE URGENT MATTERS TO TEND TO?
WE'VE FOUGHT MANY BATTLES AT EACH OTHER'S SIDE.
THE SABER KNOWS WE'RE A GREAT TEAM.
THEY MUST SHARE MY FEELINGS!
I DON'T HAVE ENOUGH MAGIC TO HEAL THE WOUND YOU'RE ABOUT TO GIVE YOURSELF.

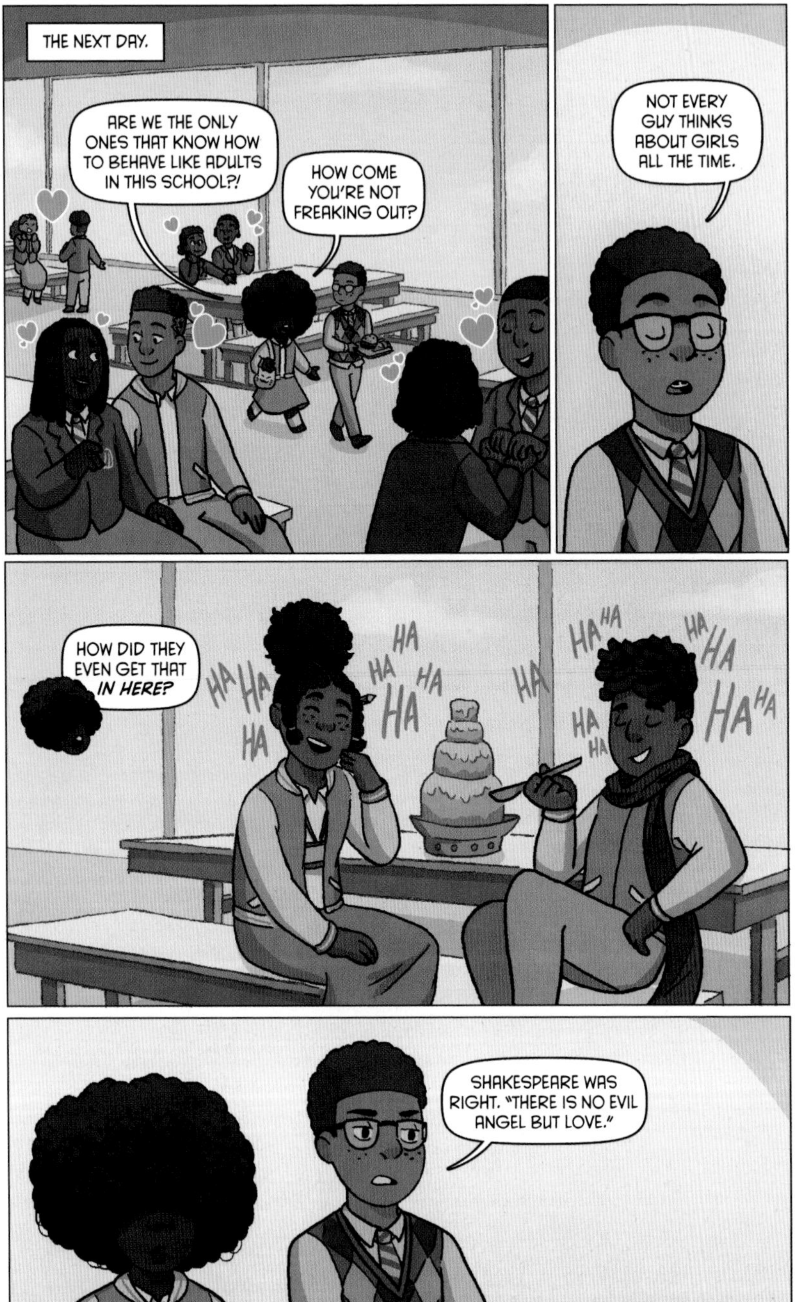
THE NEXT DAY.
ARE WE THE ONLY ONES THAT KNOW HOW TO BEHAVE LIKE ADULTS IN THIS SCHOOL?!
HOW COME YOU'RE NOT FREAKING OUT?
NOT EVERY GUY THINKS ABOUT GIRLS ALL THE TIME.
HOW DID THEY EVEN GET THAT *IN HERE?*
HA HA HA HA HA HA HA HA HA HA HA HA HA HA HA HA HA
SHAKESPEARE WAS RIGHT. "THERE IS NO EVIL ANGEL BUT LOVE."

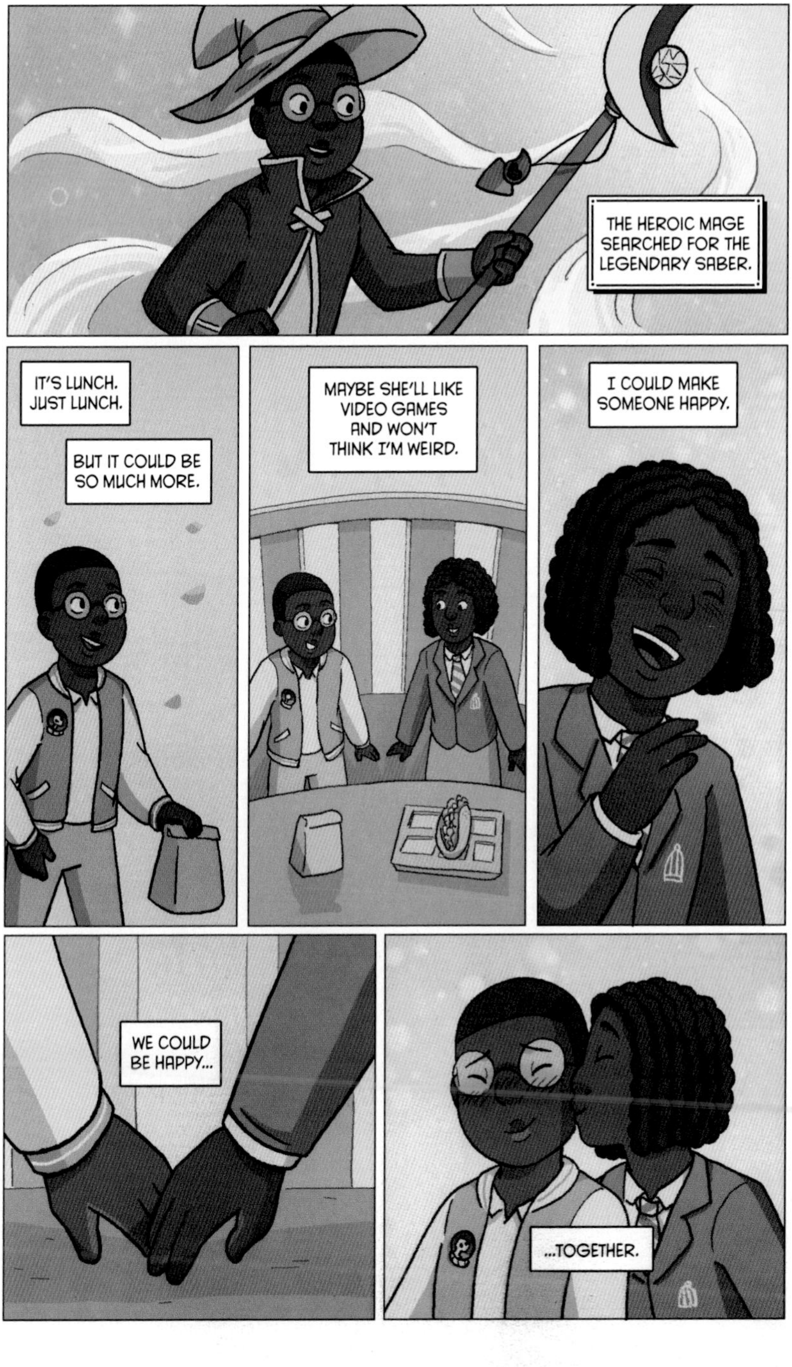
THE HEROIC MAGE SEARCHED FOR THE LEGENDARY SABER.
IT'S LUNCH. JUST LUNCH.
BUT IT COULD BE SO MUCH MORE.
MAYBE SHE'LL LIKE VIDEO GAMES AND WON'T THINK I'M WEIRD.
I COULD MAKE SOMEONE HAPPY.
WE COULD BE HAPPY...
...TOGETHER.

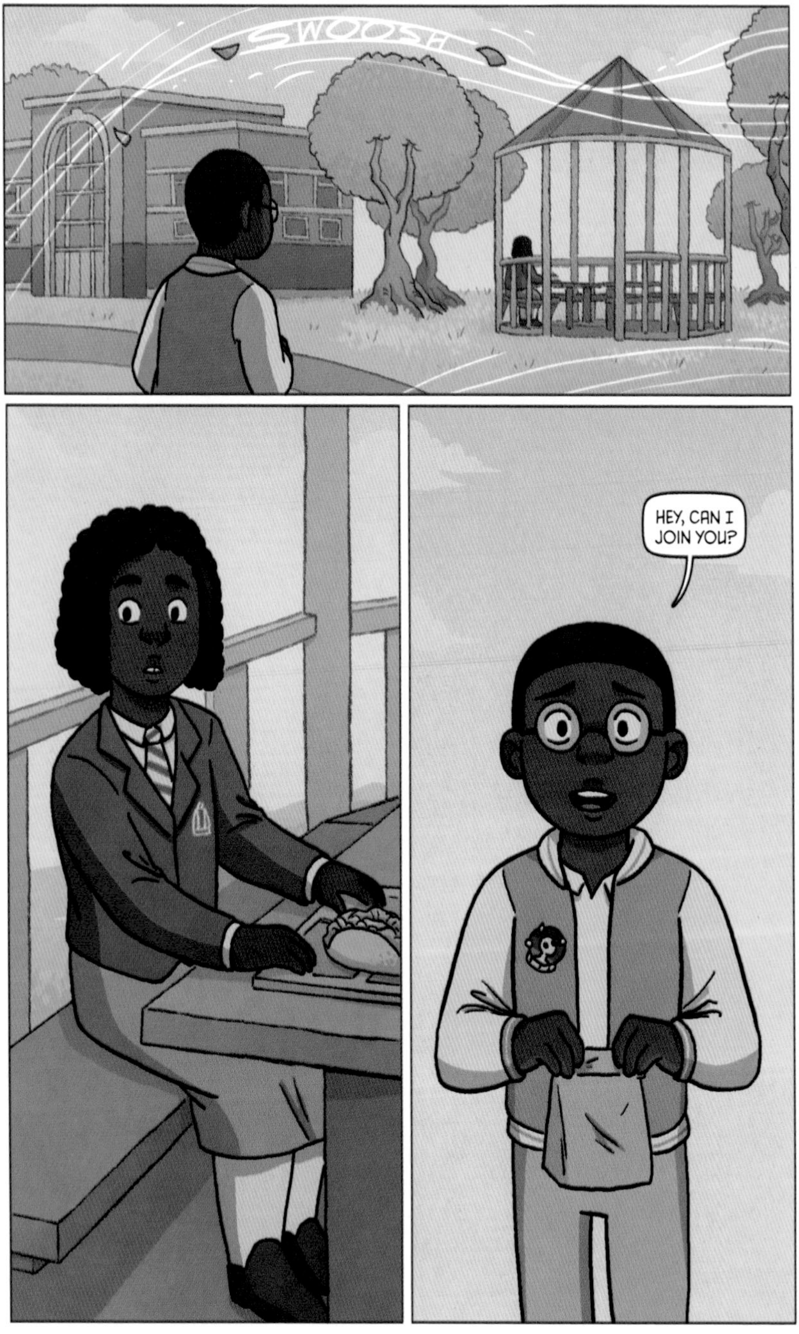
SWOOSH
HEY, CAN I JOIN YOU?

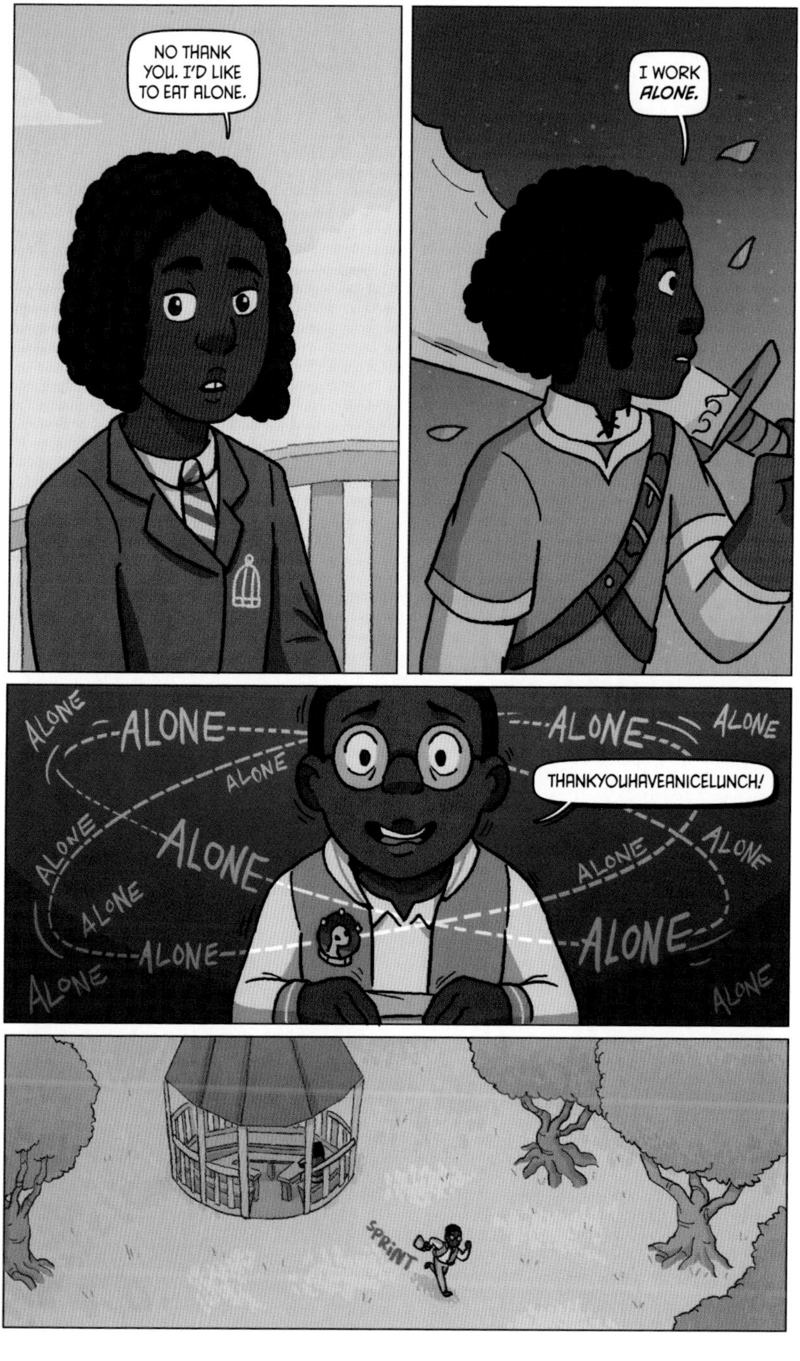
NO THANK YOU. I'D LIKE TO EAT ALONE.
I WORK ALONE.
ALONE
ALONE
ALONE
ALONE
ALONE
ALONE
ALONE
ALONE
ALONE
ALONE
ALONE
ALONE
ALONE
ALONE
ALONE
THANKYOUHAVEANICELUNCH!
SPRINT

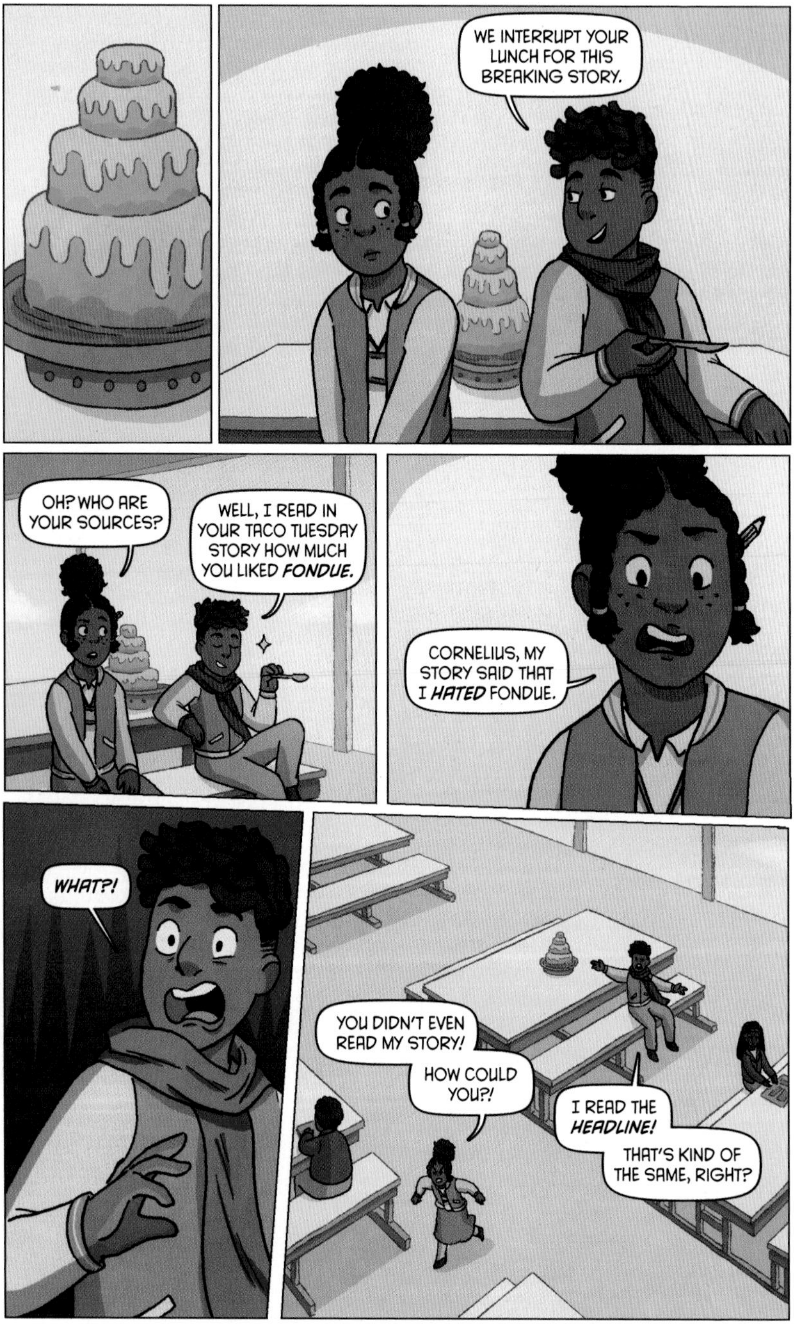
WE INTERRUPT YOUR LUNCH FOR THIS BREAKING STORY.
OH? WHO ARE YOUR SOURCES?
WELL, I READ IN YOUR TACO TUESDAY STORY HOW MUCH YOU LIKED *FONDUE.*
CORNELIUS, MY STORY SAID THAT I *HATED* FONDUE.
WHAT?!
YOU DIDN'T EVEN READ MY STORY!
HOW COULD YOU?!
I READ THE *HEADLINE!*
THAT'S KIND OF THE SAME, RIGHT?

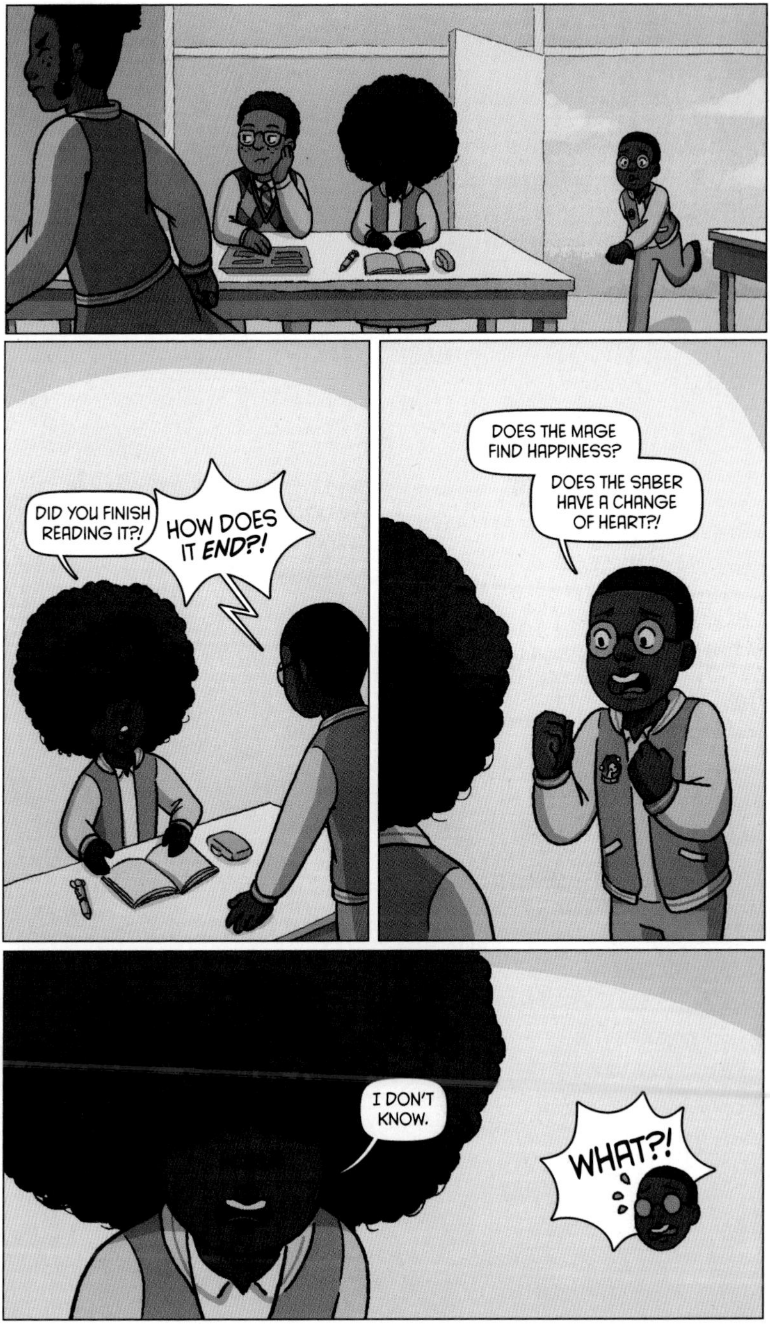
DID YOU FINISH READING IT?!
HOW DOES IT *END?!*
DOES THE MAGE FIND HAPPINESS?
DOES THE SABER HAVE A CHANGE OF HEART?!
I DON'T KNOW.
WHAT?!

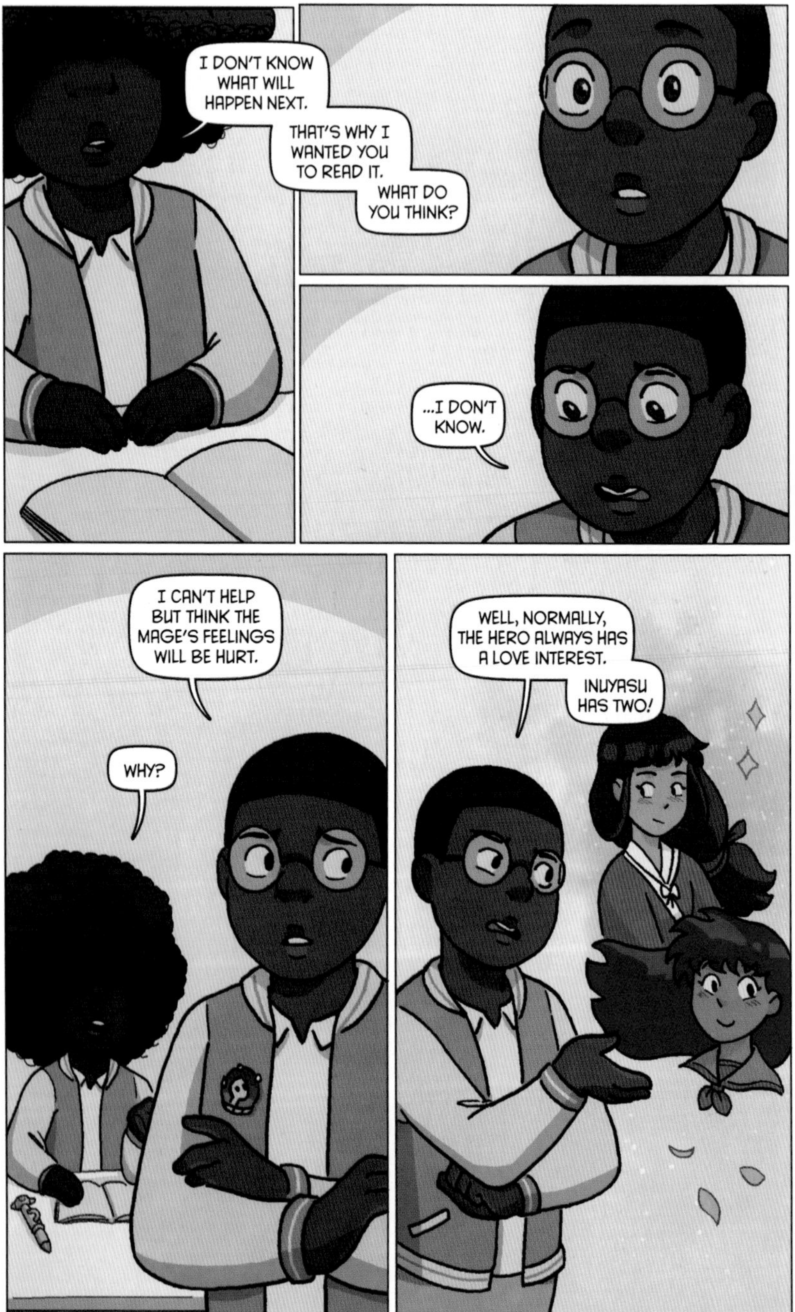
I DON'T KNOW WHAT WILL HAPPEN NEXT.
THAT'S WHY I WANTED YOU TO READ IT.
WHAT DO YOU THINK?
...I DON'T KNOW.
I CAN'T HELP BUT THINK THE MAGE'S FEELINGS WILL BE HURT.
WHY?
WELL, NORMALLY, THE HERO ALWAYS HAS A LOVE INTEREST.
INUYASU HAS TWO!

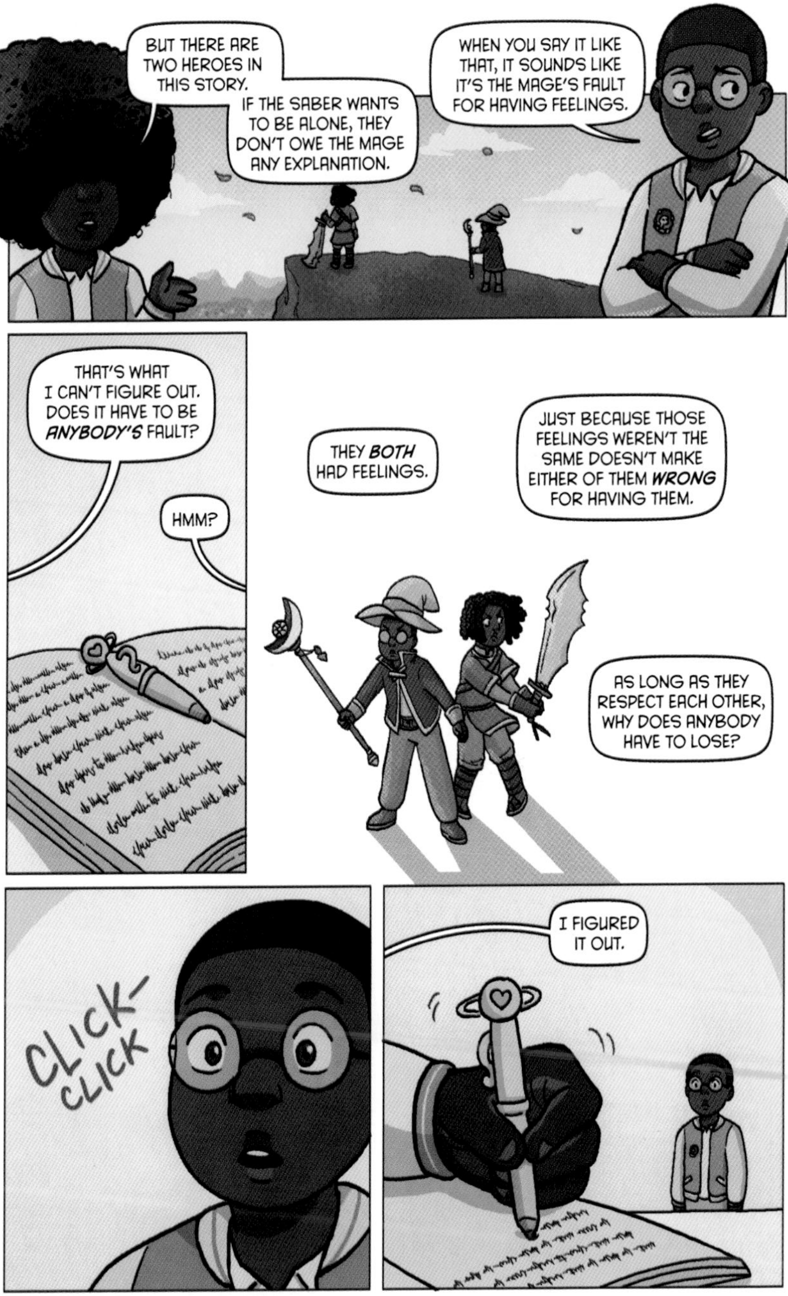

BUT THERE ARE TWO HEROES IN THIS STORY.
IF THE SABER WANTS TO BE ALONE, THEY DON'T OWE THE MAGE ANY EXPLANATION.
WHEN YOU SAY IT LIKE THAT, IT SOUNDS LIKE IT'S THE MAGE'S FAULT FOR HAVING FEELINGS.
THAT'S WHAT I CAN'T FIGURE OUT. DOES IT HAVE TO BE ***ANYBODY'S*** FAULT?
HMM?
THEY ***BOTH*** HAD FEELINGS.
JUST BECAUSE THOSE FEELINGS WEREN'T THE SAME DOESN'T MAKE EITHER OF THEM ***WRONG*** FOR HAVING THEM.
AS LONG AS THEY RESPECT EACH OTHER, WHY DOES ANYBODY HAVE TO LOSE?
CLICK-CLICK
I FIGURED IT OUT.

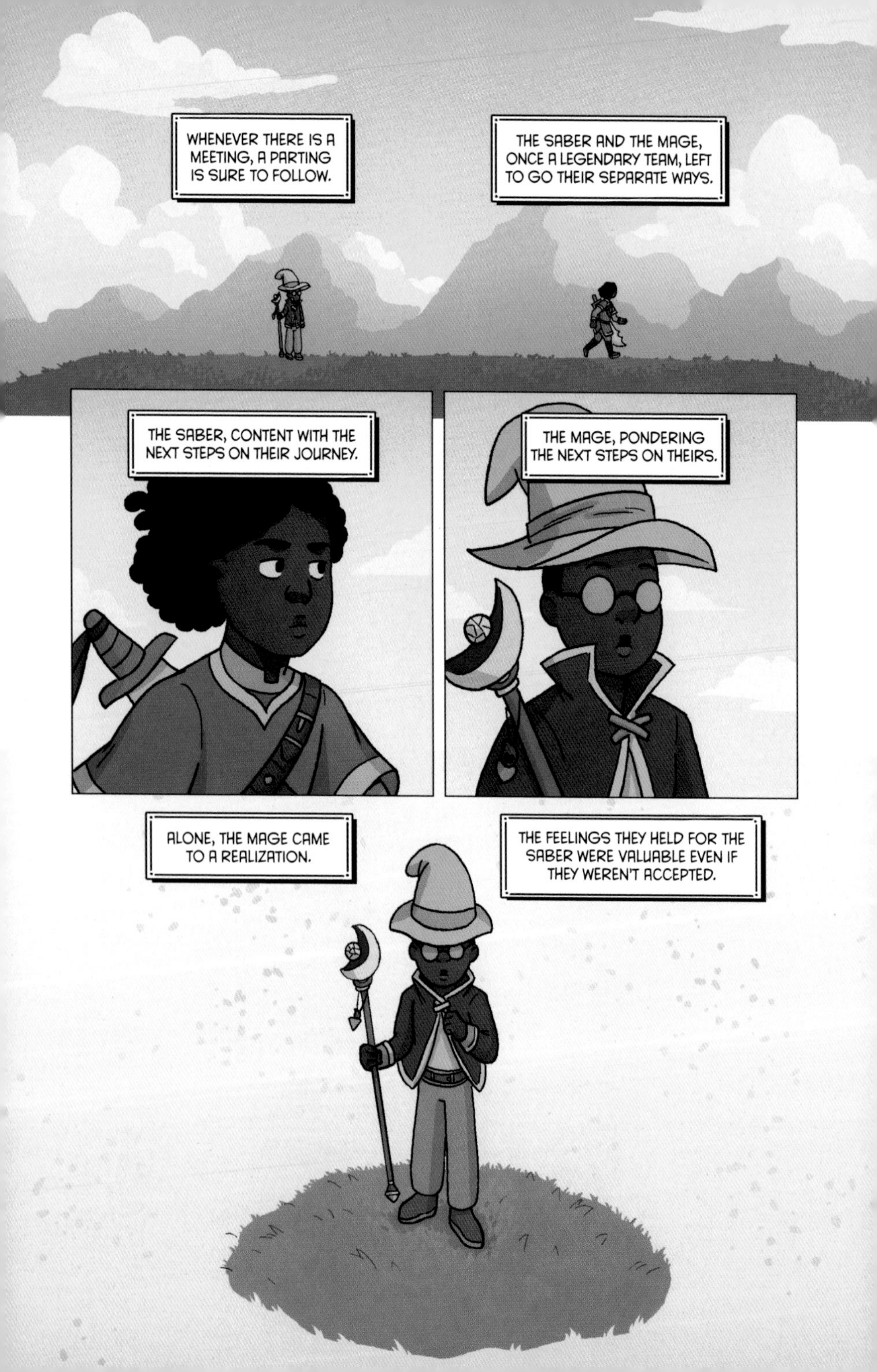
WHENEVER THERE IS A MEETING, A PARTING IS SURE TO FOLLOW.
THE SABER AND THE MAGE, ONCE A LEGENDARY TEAM, LEFT TO GO THEIR SEPARATE WAYS.
THE SABER, CONTENT WITH THE NEXT STEPS ON THEIR JOURNEY.
THE MAGE, PONDERING THE NEXT STEPS ON THEIRS.
ALONE, THE MAGE CAME TO A REALIZATION.
THE FEELINGS THEY HELD FOR THE SABER WERE VALUABLE EVEN IF THEY WEREN'T ACCEPTED.

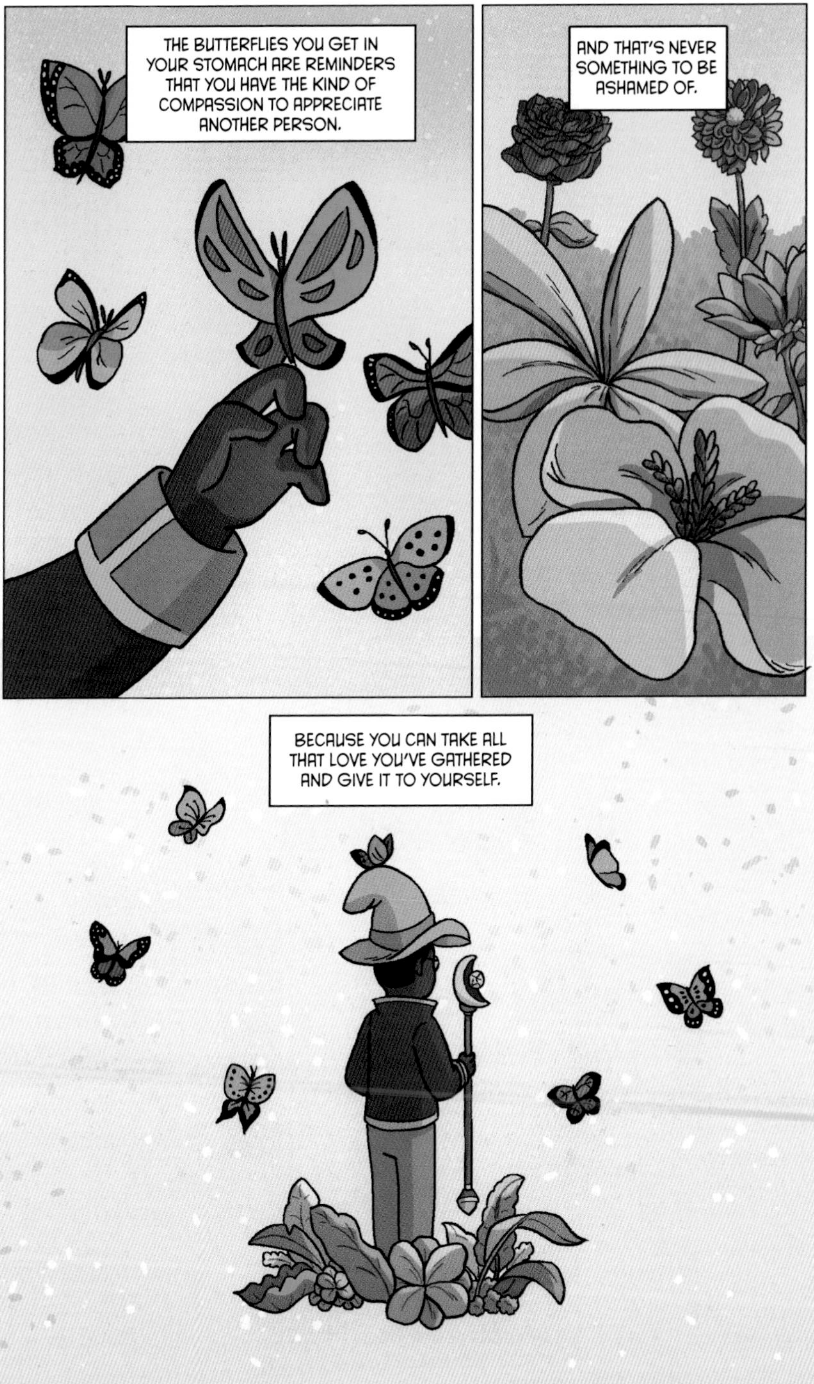
THE BUTTERFLIES YOU GET IN YOUR STOMACH ARE REMINDERS THAT YOU HAVE THE KIND OF COMPASSION TO APPRECIATE ANOTHER PERSON.
AND THAT'S NEVER SOMETHING TO BE ASHAMED OF.
BECAUSE YOU CAN TAKE ALL THAT LOVE YOU'VE GATHERED AND GIVE IT TO YOURSELF.

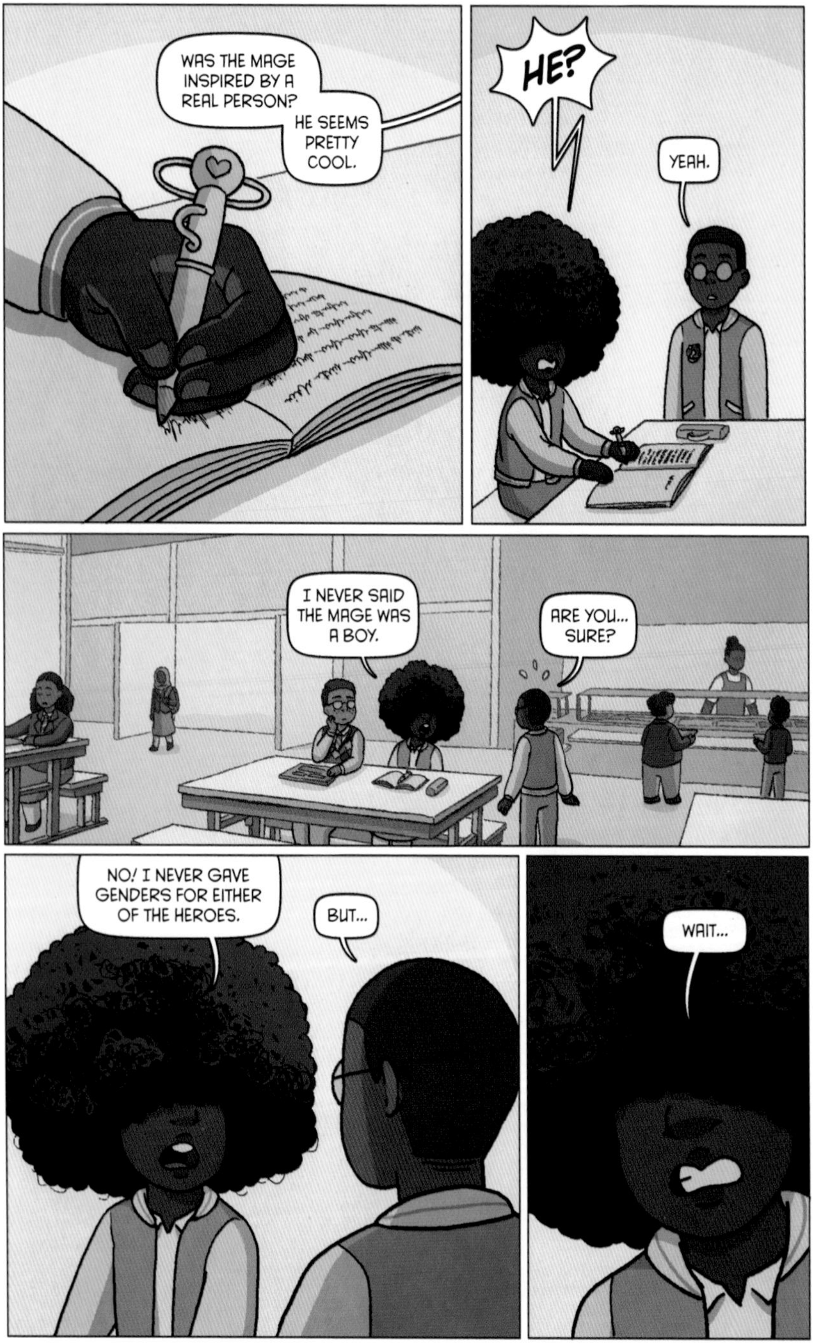
WAS THE MAGE INSPIRED BY A REAL PERSON?
HE SEEMS PRETTY COOL.
HE?
YEAH.
I NEVER SAID THE MAGE WAS A BOY.
ARE YOU... SURE?
NO! I NEVER GAVE GENDERS FOR EITHER OF THE HEROES.
BUT...
WAIT...

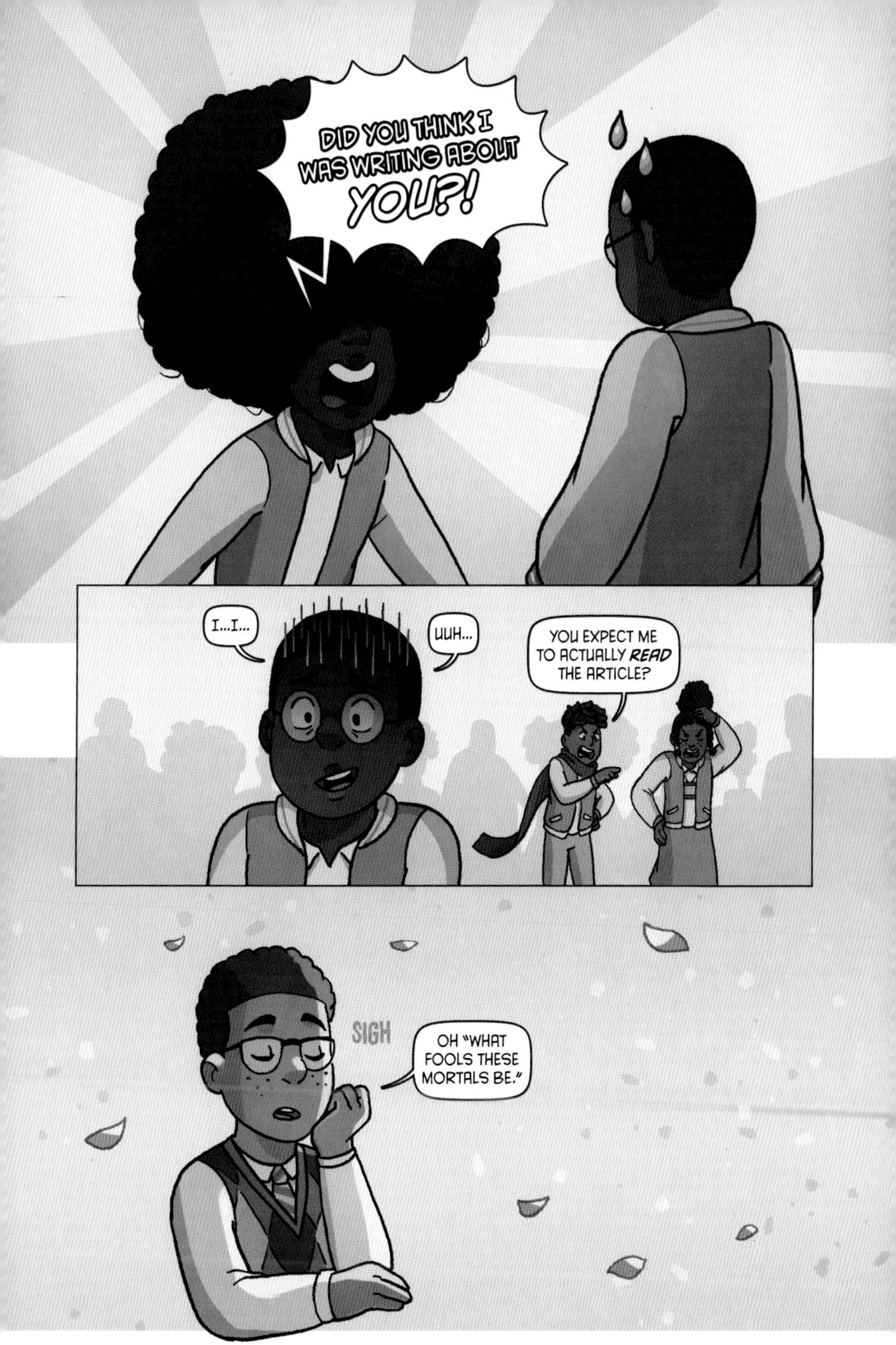
DID YOU THINK I WAS WRITING ABOUT YOU?!
I...I...
UUH...
YOU EXPECT ME TO ACTUALLY READ THE ARTICLE?
SIGH
OH "WHAT FOOLS THESE MORTALS BE."

CHAPTER 9

I KNOW WHAT YOU'RE WONDERING.

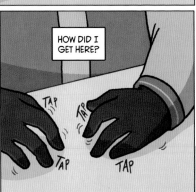

HOW DID I GET HERE?

TAP TAP TAP TAP TAP

IT'S KIND OF A LONG STORY.

CREEEAAAK

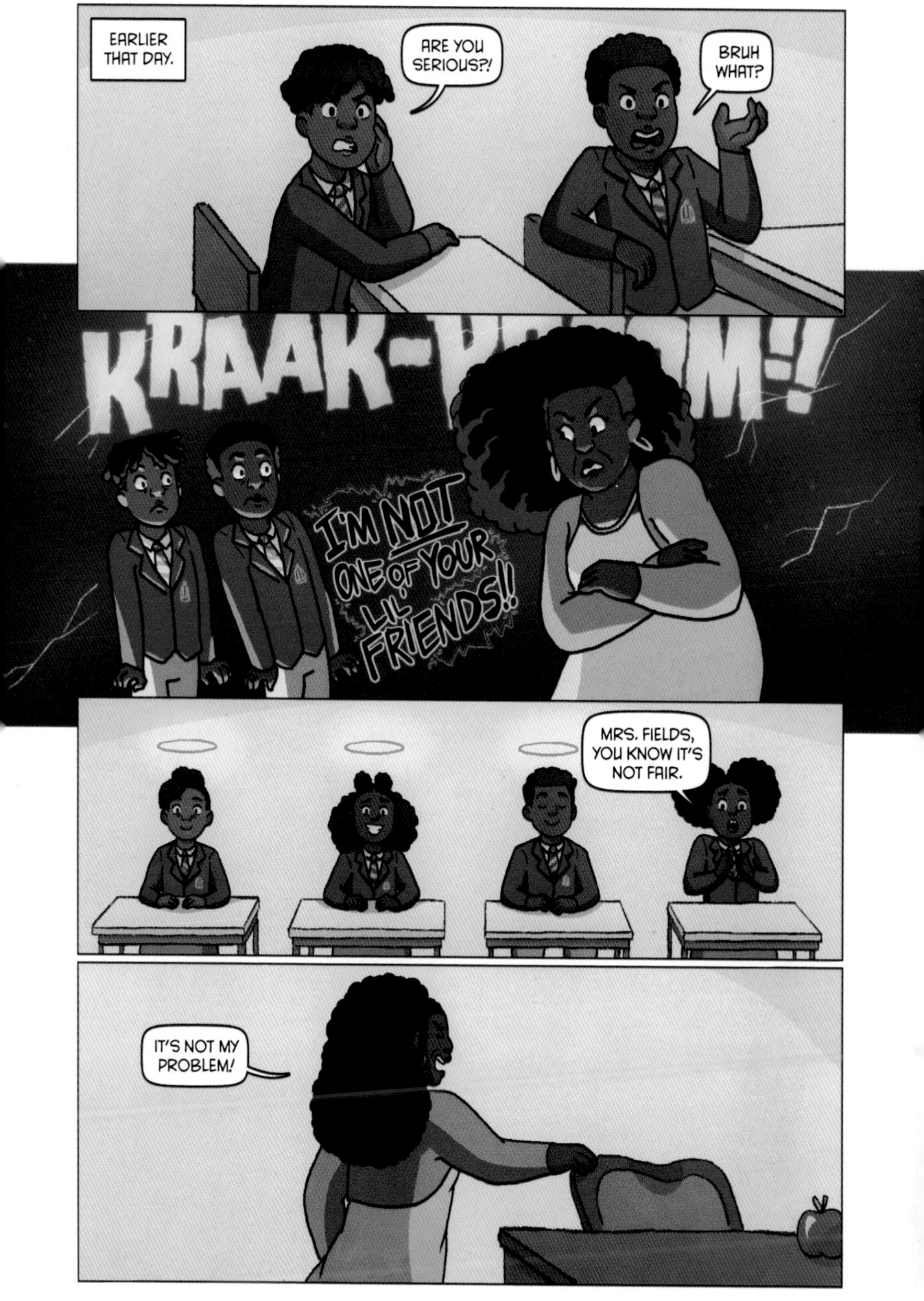
EARLIER THAT DAY.
ARE YOU SERIOUS?!
BRUH WHAT?
KRAAK-
I'M NOT ONE OF YOUR LIL FRIENDS!!
MRS. FIELDS, YOU KNOW IT'S NOT FAIR.
IT'S NOT MY PROBLEM!

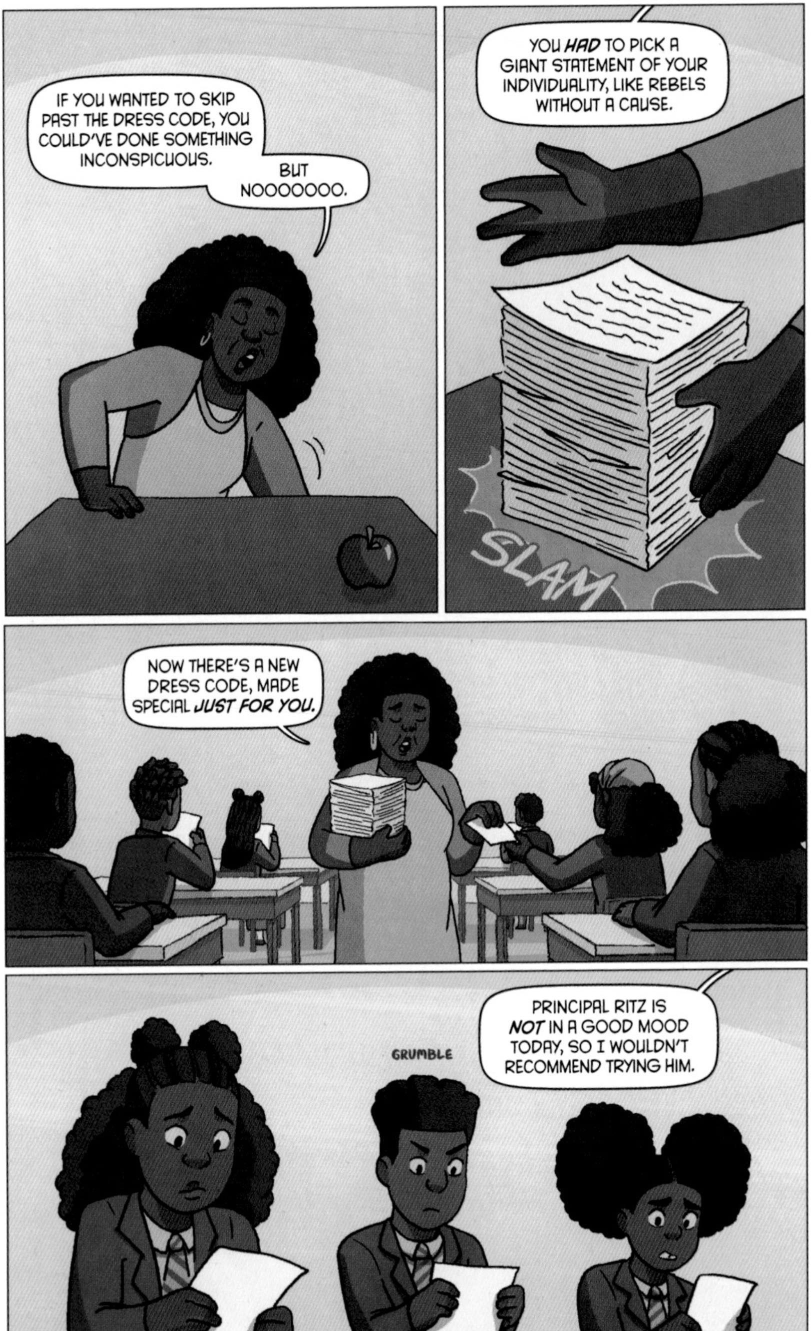
IF YOU WANTED TO SKIP PAST THE DRESS CODE, YOU COULD'VE DONE SOMETHING INCONSPICUOUS.
BUT NOOOOOOO.
YOU HAD TO PICK A GIANT STATEMENT OF YOUR INDIVIDUALITY, LIKE REBELS WITHOUT A CAUSE.
SLAM
NOW THERE'S A NEW DRESS CODE, MADE SPECIAL JUST FOR YOU.
GRUMBLE
PRINCIPAL RITZ IS NOT IN A GOOD MOOD TODAY, SO I WOULDN'T RECOMMEND TRYING HIM.

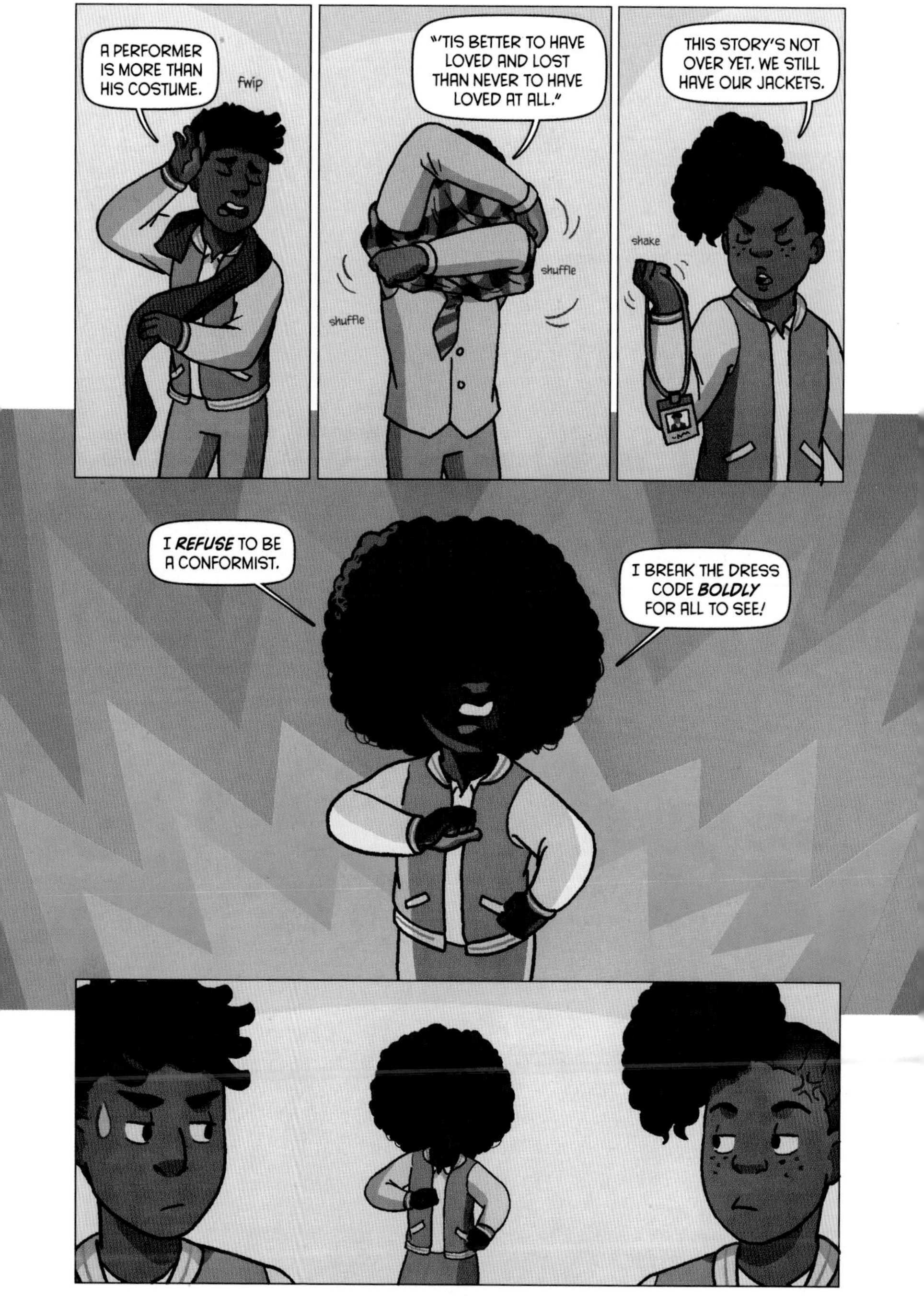

A PERFORMER IS MORE THAN HIS COSTUME.
fwip
"'TIS BETTER TO HAVE LOVED AND LOST THAN NEVER TO HAVE LOVED AT ALL."
shuffle
shuffle
THIS STORY'S NOT OVER YET. WE STILL HAVE OUR JACKETS.
shake
I **REFUSE** TO BE A CONFORMIST.
I BREAK THE DRESS CODE **BOLDLY** FOR ALL TO SEE!

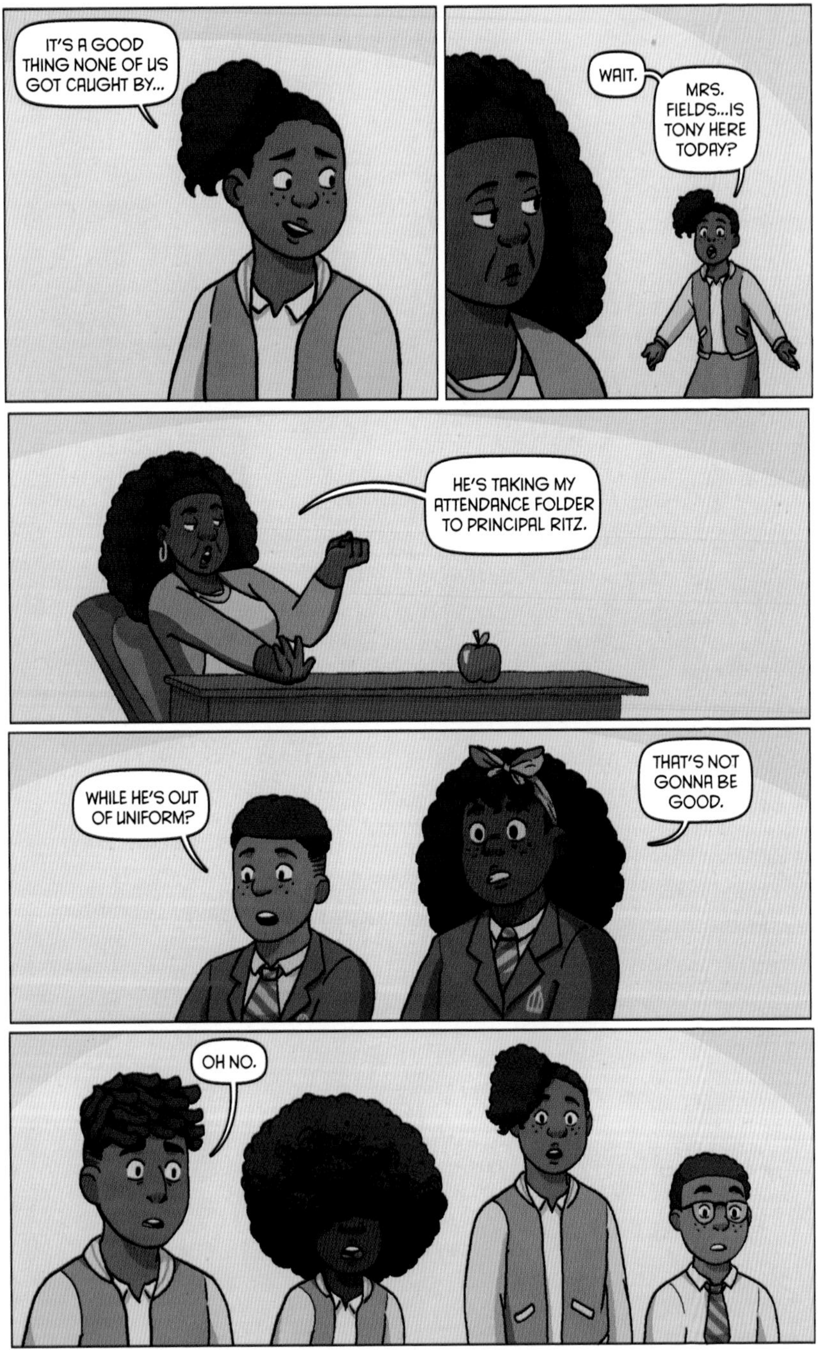
IT'S A GOOD THING NONE OF US GOT CAUGHT BY...
WAIT.
MRS. FIELDS...IS TONY HERE TODAY?
HE'S TAKING MY ATTENDANCE FOLDER TO PRINCIPAL RITZ.
WHILE HE'S OUT OF UNIFORM?
THAT'S NOT GONNA BE GOOD.
OH NO.

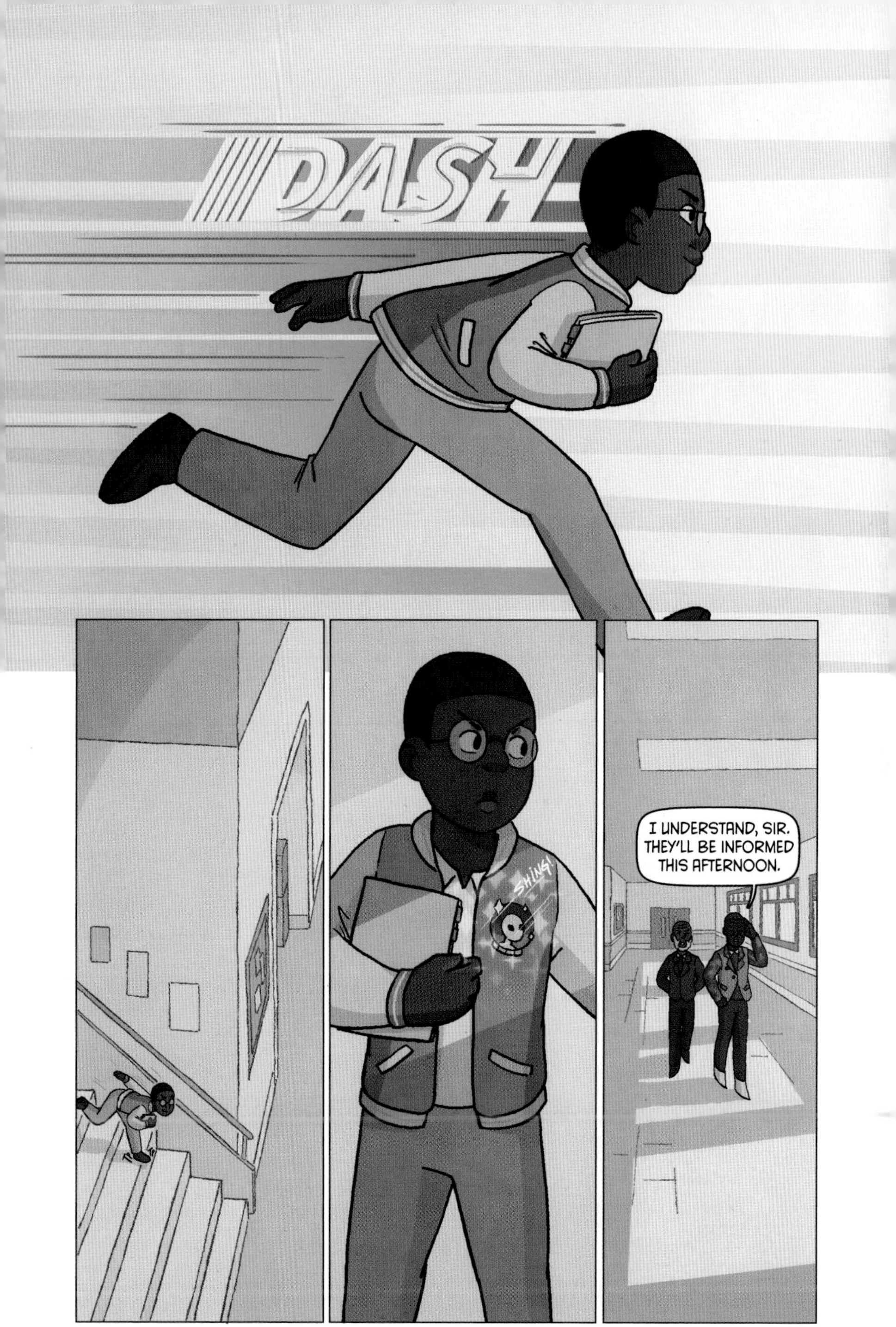
DASH
SHING!
I UNDERSTAND, SIR. THEY'LL BE INFORMED THIS AFTERNOON.

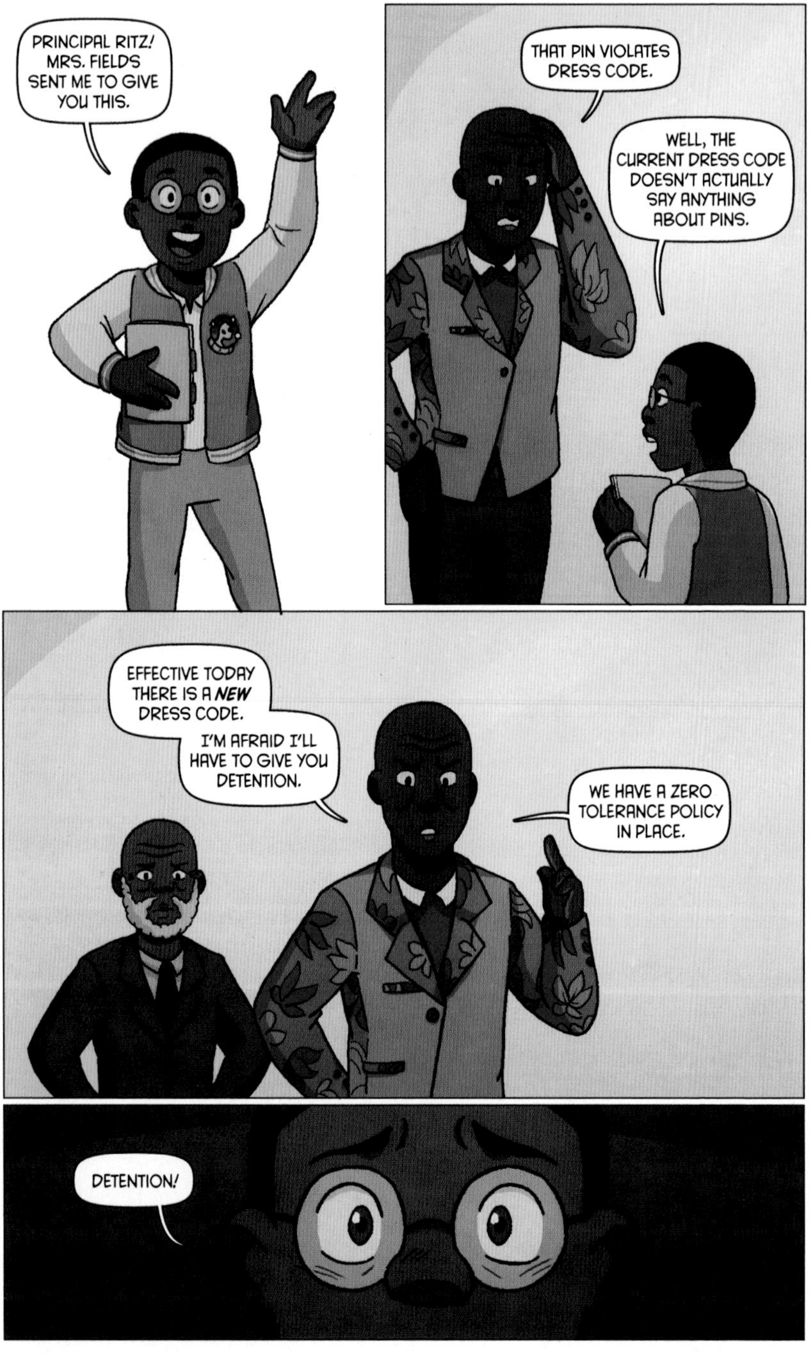
PRINCIPAL RITZ! MRS. FIELDS SENT ME TO GIVE YOU THIS.
THAT PIN VIOLATES DRESS CODE.
WELL, THE CURRENT DRESS CODE DOESN'T ACTUALLY SAY ANYTHING ABOUT PINS.
EFFECTIVE TODAY THERE IS A *NEW* DRESS CODE.
I'M AFRAID I'LL HAVE TO GIVE YOU DETENTION.
WE HAVE A ZERO TOLERANCE POLICY IN PLACE.
DETENTION!

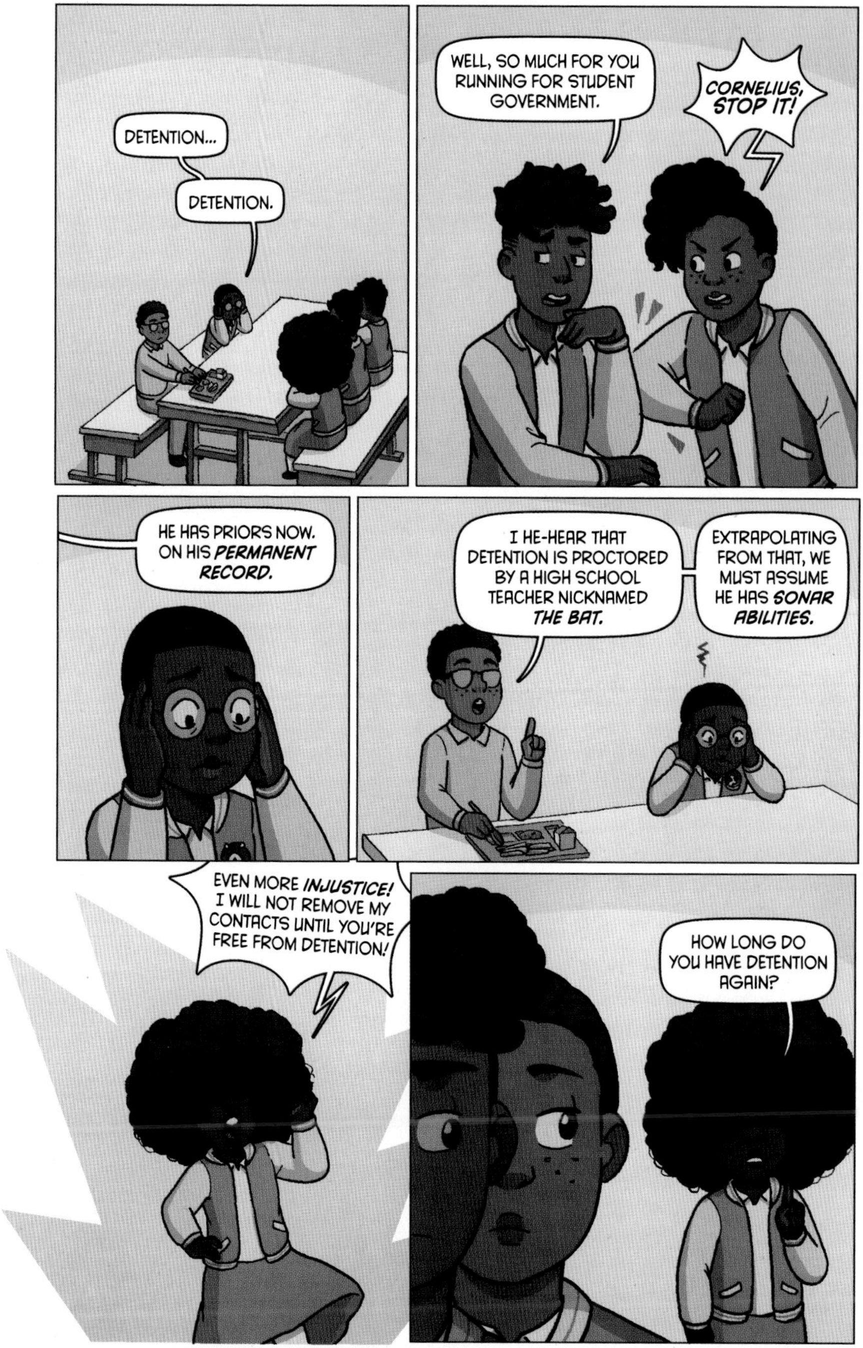
DETENTION...
DETENTION.
WELL, SO MUCH FOR YOU RUNNING FOR STUDENT GOVERNMENT.
CORNELIUS, STOP IT!
HE HAS PRIORS NOW. ON HIS PERMANENT RECORD.
I HE-HEAR THAT DETENTION IS PROCTORED BY A HIGH SCHOOL TEACHER NICKNAMED THE BAT.
EXTRAPOLATING FROM THAT, WE MUST ASSUME HE HAS SONAR ABILITIES.
EVEN MORE INJUSTICE! I WILL NOT REMOVE MY CONTACTS UNTIL YOU'RE FREE FROM DETENTION!
HOW LONG DO YOU HAVE DETENTION AGAIN?

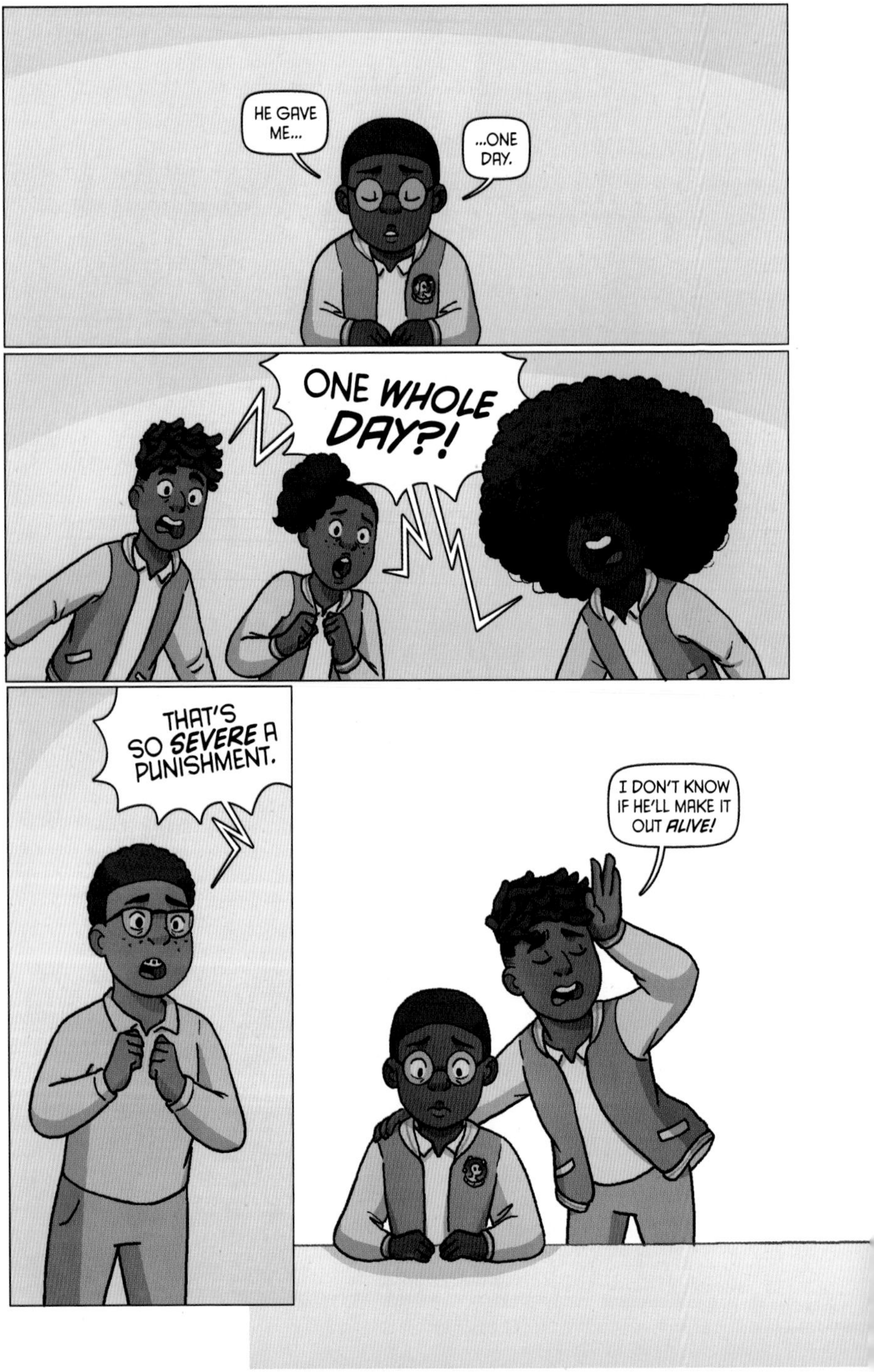
HE GAVE ME...
...ONE DAY.
ONE WHOLE DAY?!
THAT'S SO SEVERE A PUNISHMENT.
I DON'T KNOW IF HE'LL MAKE IT OUT ALIVE!

DING DONG DING

WHERE DID WE GO WRONG?!

FREE TONY!!!

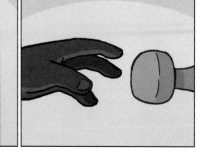

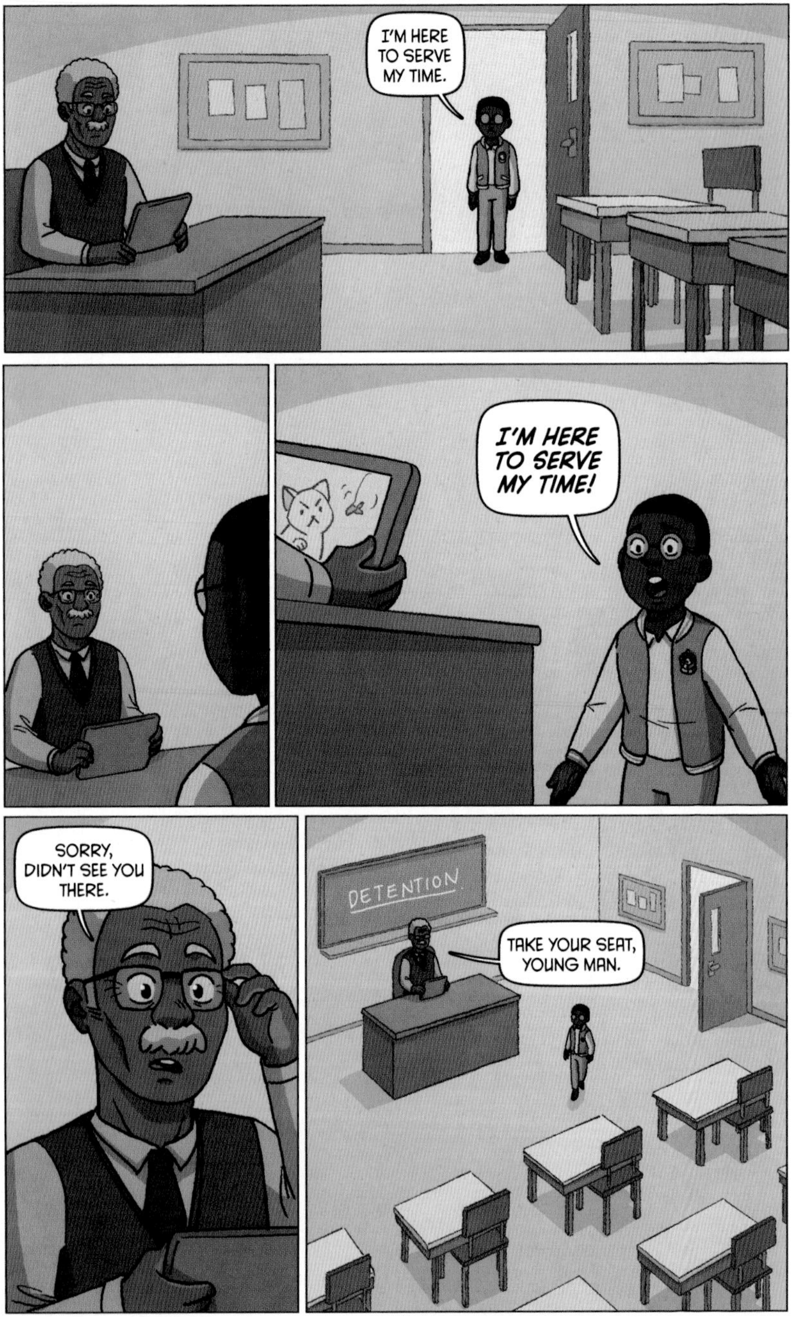
I'M HERE TO SERVE MY TIME.
I'M HERE TO SERVE MY TIME!
SORRY, DIDN'T SEE YOU THERE.
DETENTION
TAKE YOUR SEAT, YOUNG MAN.

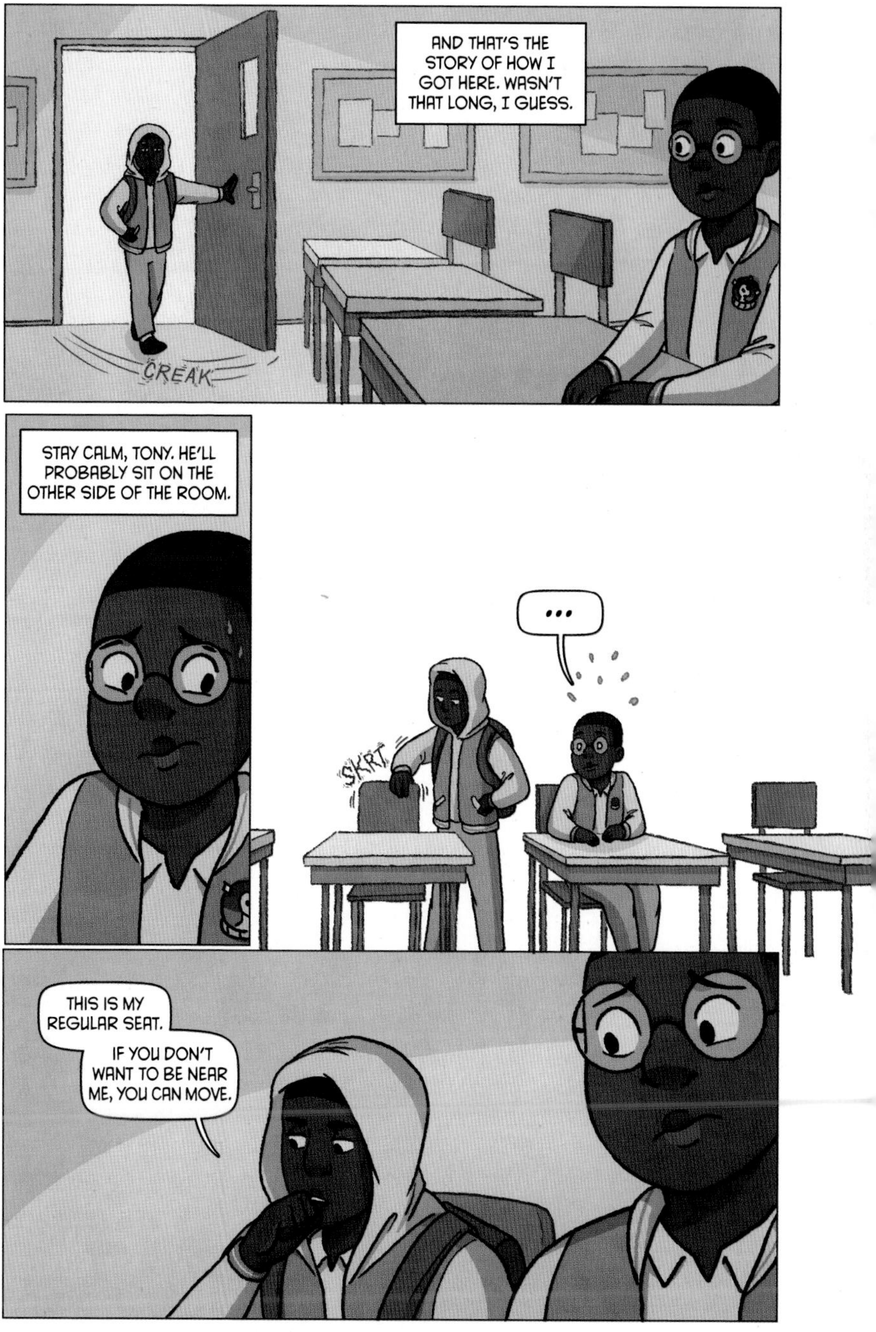
AND THAT'S THE STORY OF HOW I GOT HERE. WASN'T THAT LONG, I GUESS.
CREAK
STAY CALM, TONY. HE'LL PROBABLY SIT ON THE OTHER SIDE OF THE ROOM.
SKRT
...
THIS IS MY REGULAR SEAT.
IF YOU DON'T WANT TO BE NEAR ME, YOU CAN MOVE.

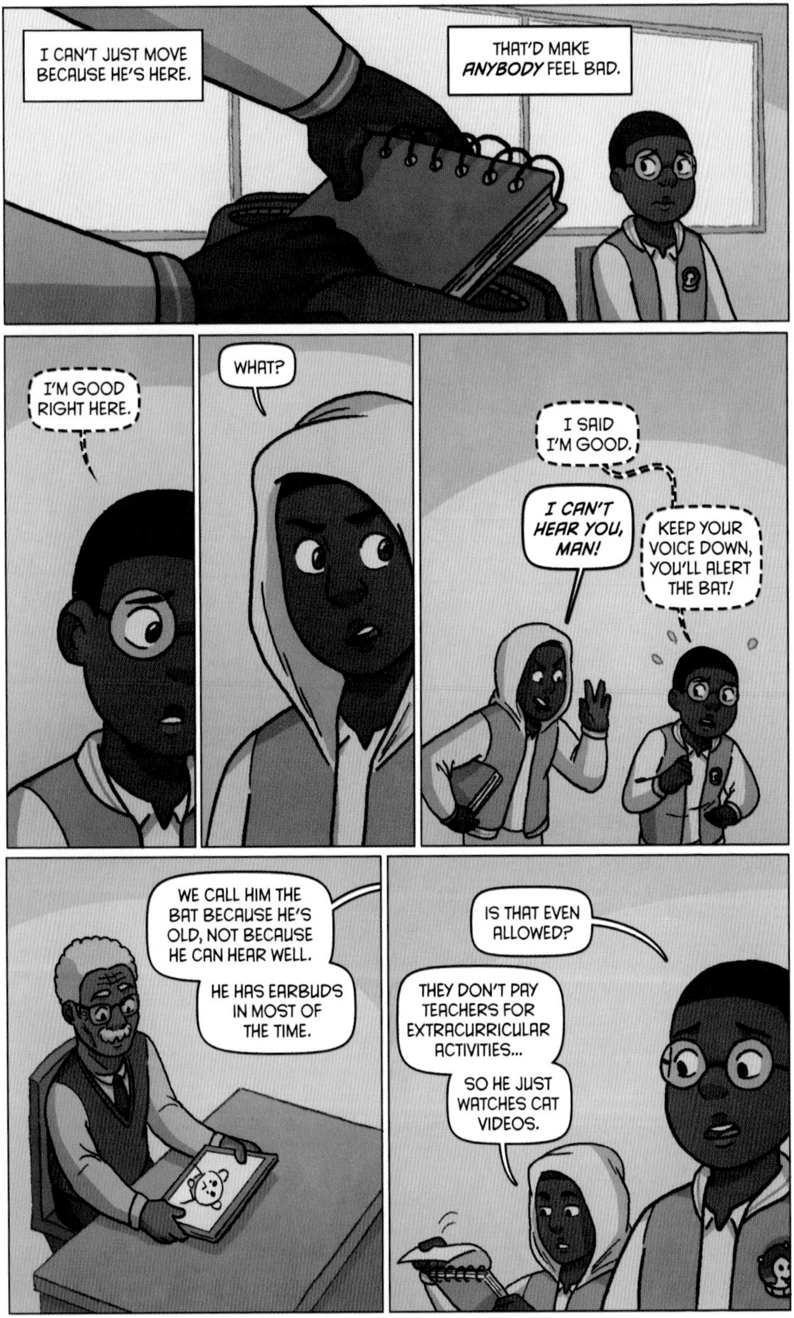
I CAN'T JUST MOVE BECAUSE HE'S HERE.
THAT'D MAKE *ANYBODY* FEEL BAD.
I'M GOOD RIGHT HERE.
WHAT?
I SAID I'M GOOD.
I CAN'T HEAR YOU, MAN!
KEEP YOUR VOICE DOWN, YOU'LL ALERT THE BAT!
WE CALL HIM THE BAT BECAUSE HE'S OLD, NOT BECAUSE HE CAN HEAR WELL.
HE HAS EARBUDS IN MOST OF THE TIME.
IS THAT EVEN ALLOWED?
THEY DON'T PAY TEACHERS FOR EXTRACURRICULAR ACTIVITIES...
SO HE JUST WATCHES CAT VIDEOS.

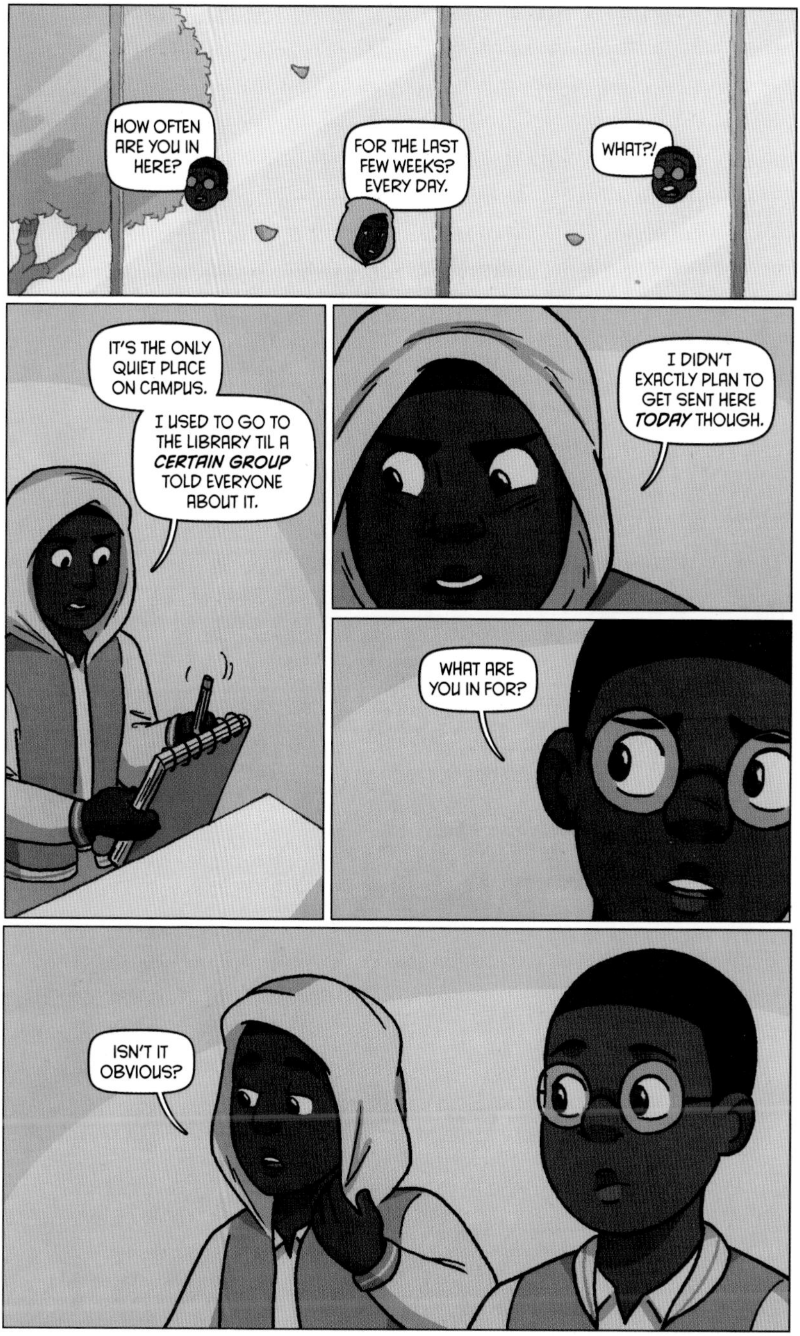
HOW OFTEN ARE YOU IN HERE?
FOR THE LAST FEW WEEKS? EVERY DAY.
WHAT?!
IT'S THE ONLY QUIET PLACE ON CAMPUS.
I USED TO GO TO THE LIBRARY TIL A ***CERTAIN GROUP*** TOLD EVERYONE ABOUT IT.
I DIDN'T EXACTLY PLAN TO GET SENT HERE ***TODAY*** THOUGH.
WHAT ARE YOU IN FOR?
ISN'T IT OBVIOUS?

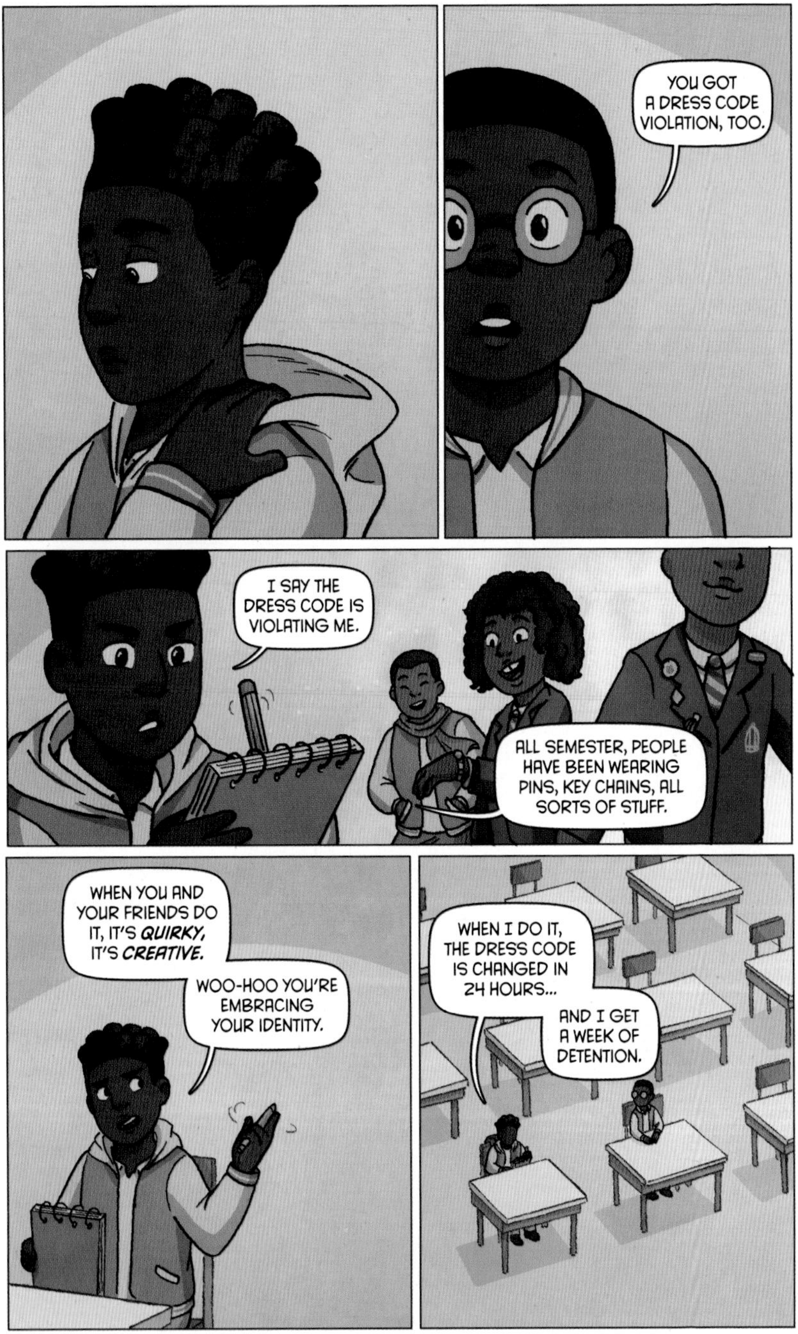
YOU GOT A DRESS CODE VIOLATION, TOO.
I SAY THE DRESS CODE IS VIOLATING ME.
ALL SEMESTER, PEOPLE HAVE BEEN WEARING PINS, KEY CHAINS, ALL SORTS OF STUFF.
WHEN YOU AND YOUR FRIENDS DO IT, IT'S *QUIRKY,* IT'S *CREATIVE.*
WOO-HOO YOU'RE EMBRACING YOUR IDENTITY.
WHEN I DO IT, THE DRESS CODE IS CHANGED IN 24 HOURS...
AND I GET A WEEK OF DETENTION.

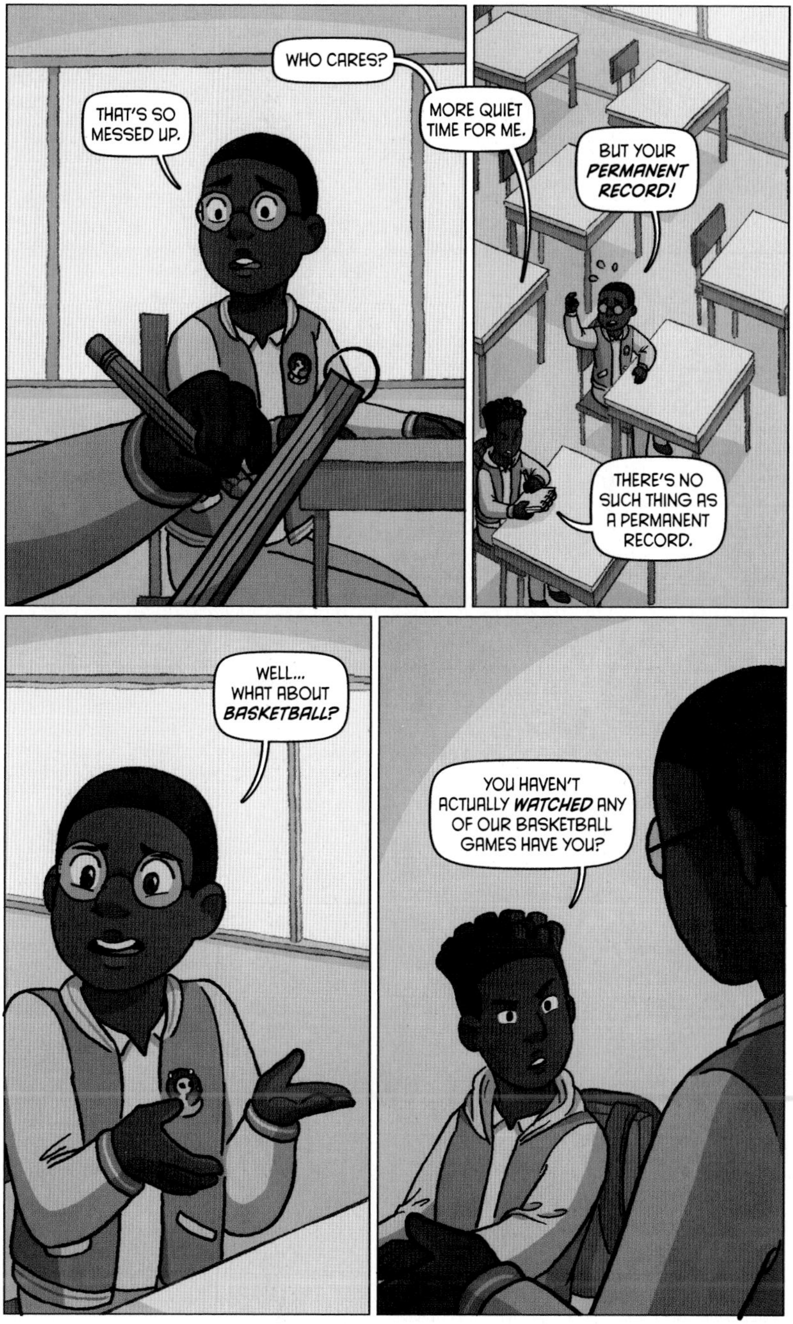
THAT'S SO MESSED UP.
WHO CARES?
MORE QUIET TIME FOR ME.
BUT YOUR *PERMANENT RECORD!*
THERE'S NO SUCH THING AS A PERMANENT RECORD.
WELL... WHAT ABOUT *BASKETBALL?*
YOU HAVEN'T ACTUALLY *WATCHED* ANY OF OUR BASKETBALL GAMES HAVE YOU?

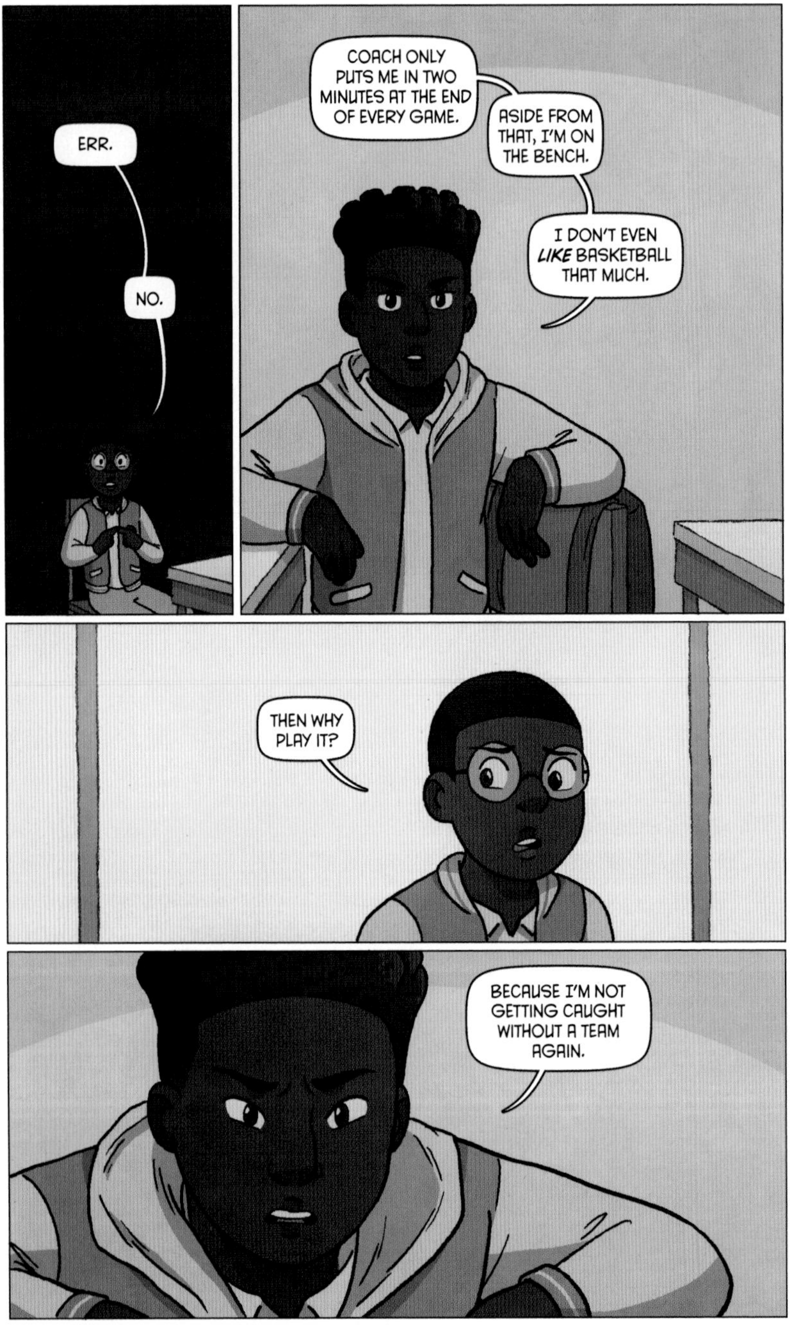
ERR.
NO.
COACH ONLY PUTS ME IN TWO MINUTES AT THE END OF EVERY GAME.
ASIDE FROM THAT, I'M ON THE BENCH.
I DON'T EVEN *LIKE* BASKETBALL THAT MUCH.
THEN WHY PLAY IT?
BECAUSE I'M NOT GETTING CAUGHT WITHOUT A TEAM AGAIN.

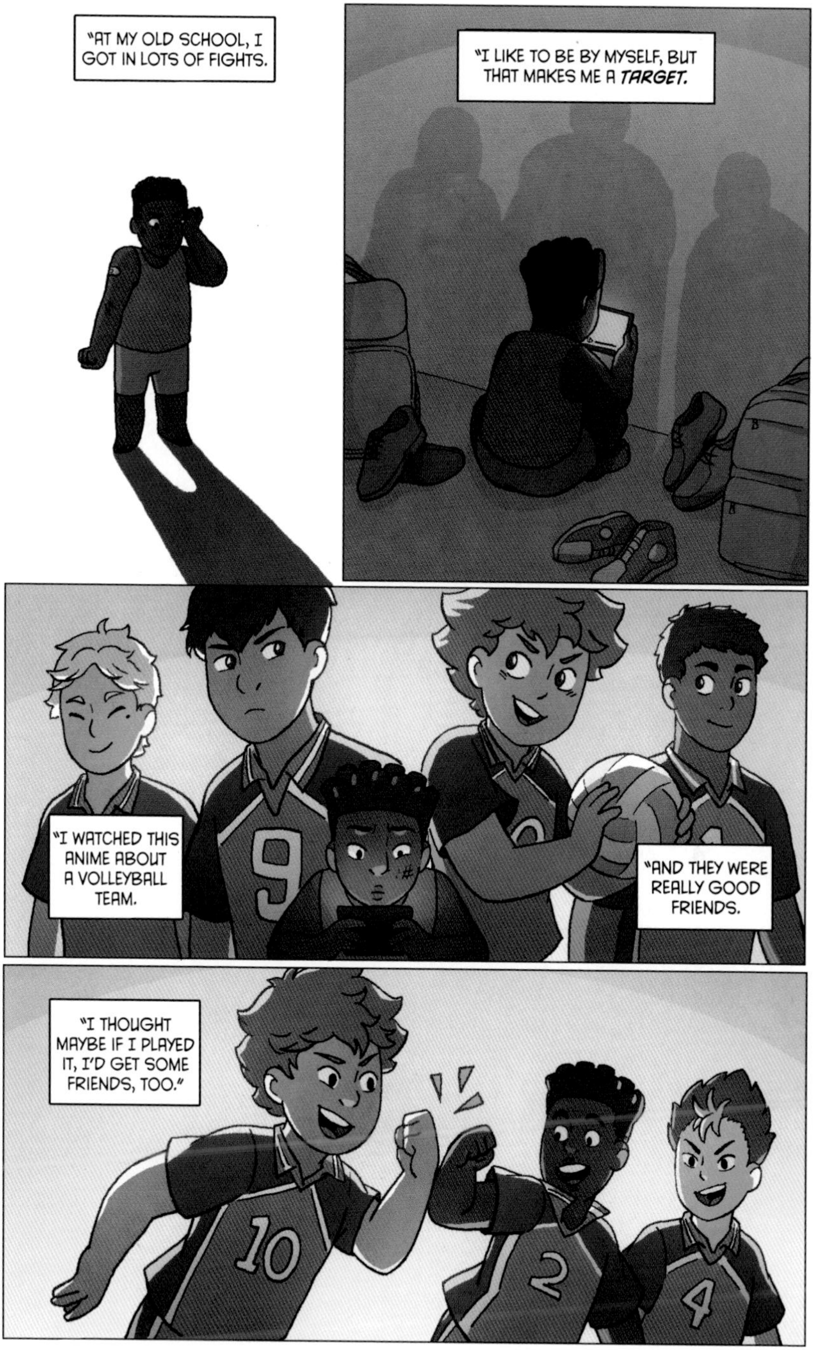
"AT MY OLD SCHOOL, I GOT IN LOTS OF FIGHTS.
"I LIKE TO BE BY MYSELF, BUT THAT MAKES ME A *TARGET.*
"I WATCHED THIS ANIME ABOUT A VOLLEYBALL TEAM.
"AND THEY WERE REALLY GOOD FRIENDS.
"I THOUGHT MAYBE IF I PLAYED IT, I'D GET SOME FRIENDS, TOO."

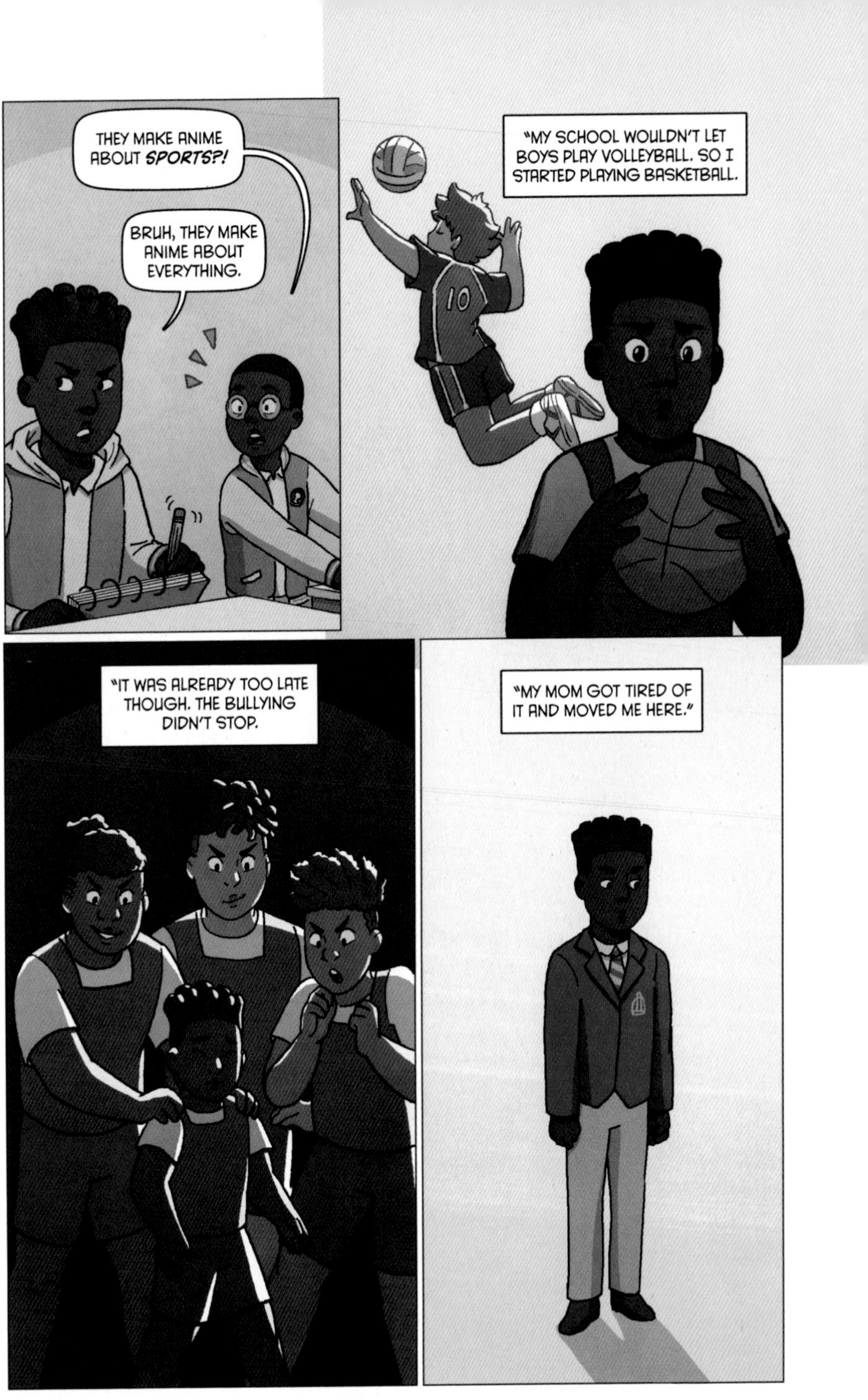
THEY MAKE ANIME ABOUT *SPORTS?!*
BRUH, THEY MAKE ANIME ABOUT EVERYTHING.
"MY SCHOOL WOULDN'T LET BOYS PLAY VOLLEYBALL. SO I STARTED PLAYING BASKETBALL.
10
"IT WAS ALREADY TOO LATE THOUGH. THE BULLYING DIDN'T STOP.
"MY MOM GOT TIRED OF IT AND MOVED ME HERE."

YOU'RE A *NEW KID*, TOO?!

YOU THOUGHT YOU WERE THE *ONLY ONE?*

I HEAR YOU'RE A BASKETBALL PLAYER.

"APPARENTLY MY MOM TOLD RITZ ABOUT ME BEFOREHAND.

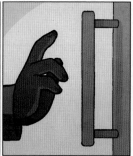

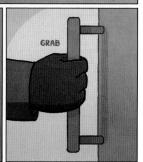

GRAB

"I WAS INTRODUCED TO THE TEAM.

"THEY'VE BEEN SHOWING ME THE ROPES EVER SINCE."

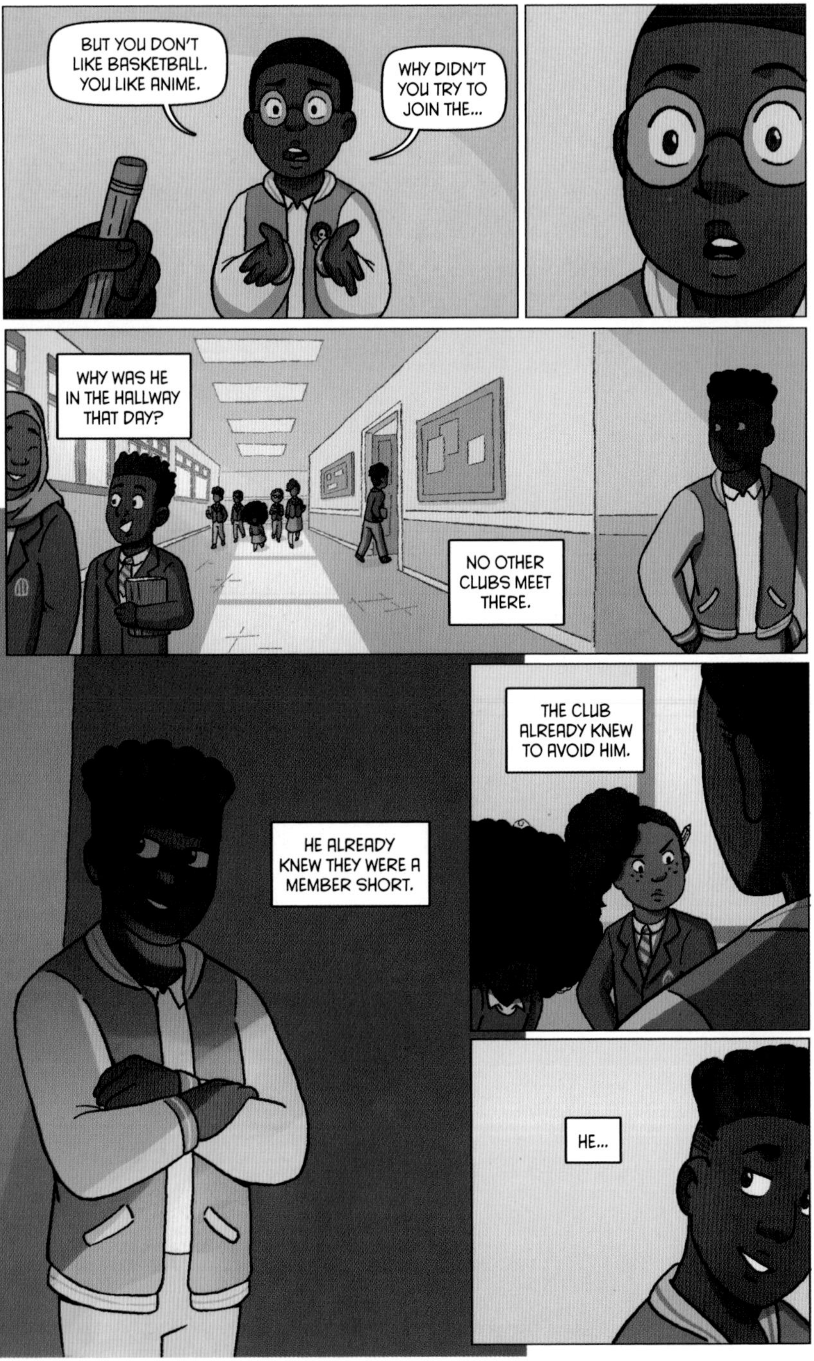
BUT YOU DON'T LIKE BASKETBALL. YOU LIKE ANIME.
WHY DIDN'T YOU TRY TO JOIN THE...
WHY WAS HE IN THE HALLWAY THAT DAY?
NO OTHER CLUBS MEET THERE.
HE ALREADY KNEW THEY WERE A MEMBER SHORT.
THE CLUB ALREADY KNEW TO AVOID HIM.
HE...

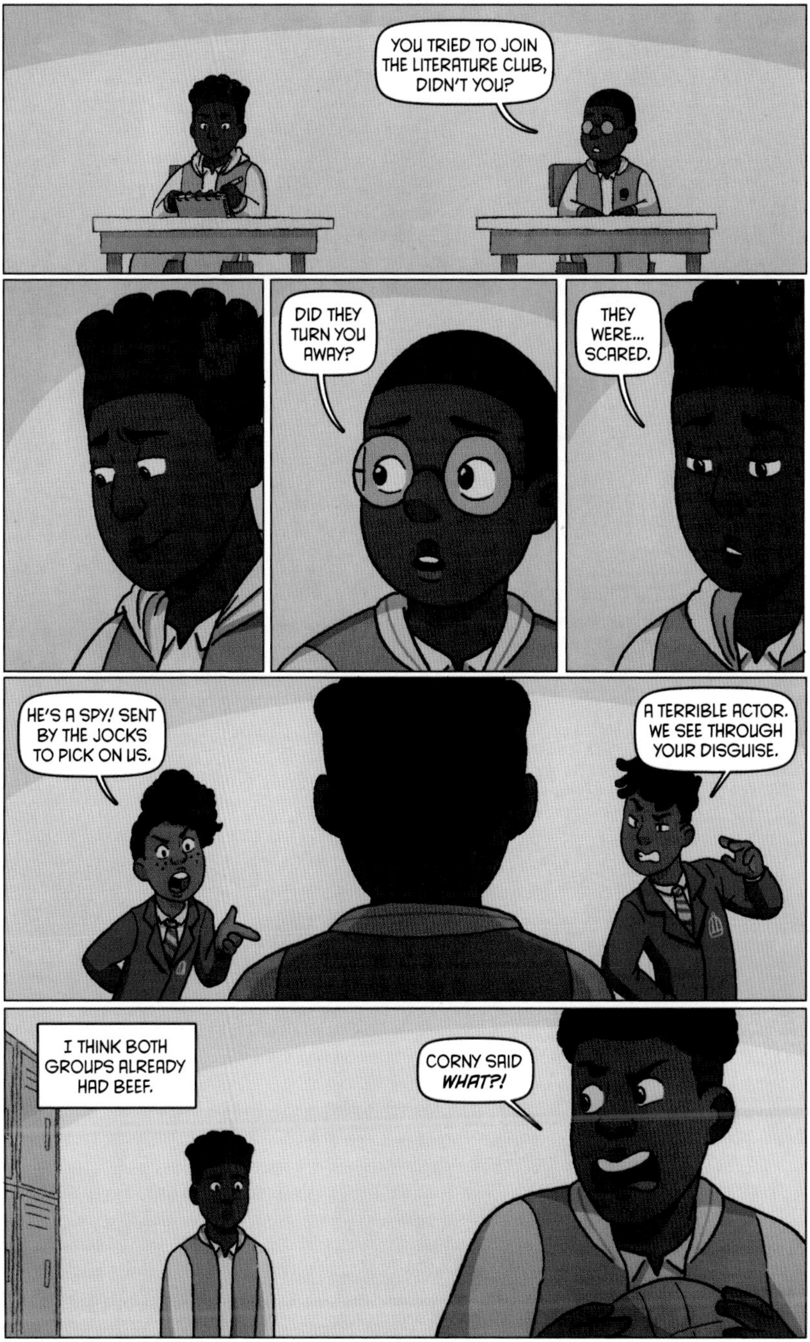
YOU TRIED TO JOIN THE LITERATURE CLUB, DIDN'T YOU?
DID THEY TURN YOU AWAY?
THEY WERE... SCARED.
HE'S A SPY! SENT BY THE JOCKS TO PICK ON US.
A TERRIBLE ACTOR. WE SEE THROUGH YOUR DISGUISE.
I THINK BOTH GROUPS ALREADY HAD BEEF.
CORNY SAID *WHAT?!*

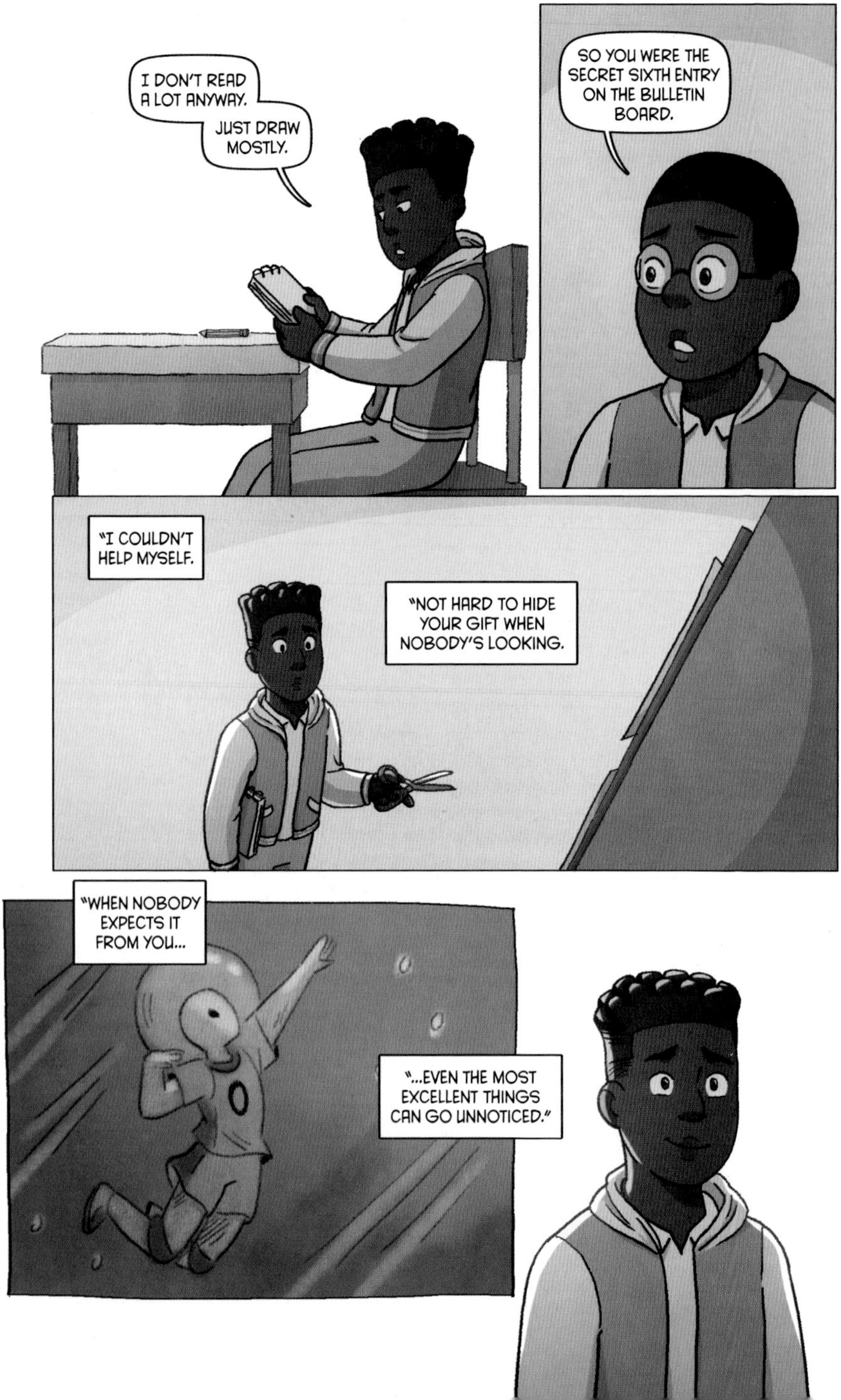
I DON'T READ A LOT ANYWAY.
JUST DRAW MOSTLY.
SO YOU WERE THE SECRET SIXTH ENTRY ON THE BULLETIN BOARD.
"I COULDN'T HELP MYSELF.
"NOT HARD TO HIDE YOUR GIFT WHEN NOBODY'S LOOKING.
"WHEN NOBODY EXPECTS IT FROM YOU...
"...EVEN THE MOST EXCELLENT THINGS CAN GO UNNOTICED."

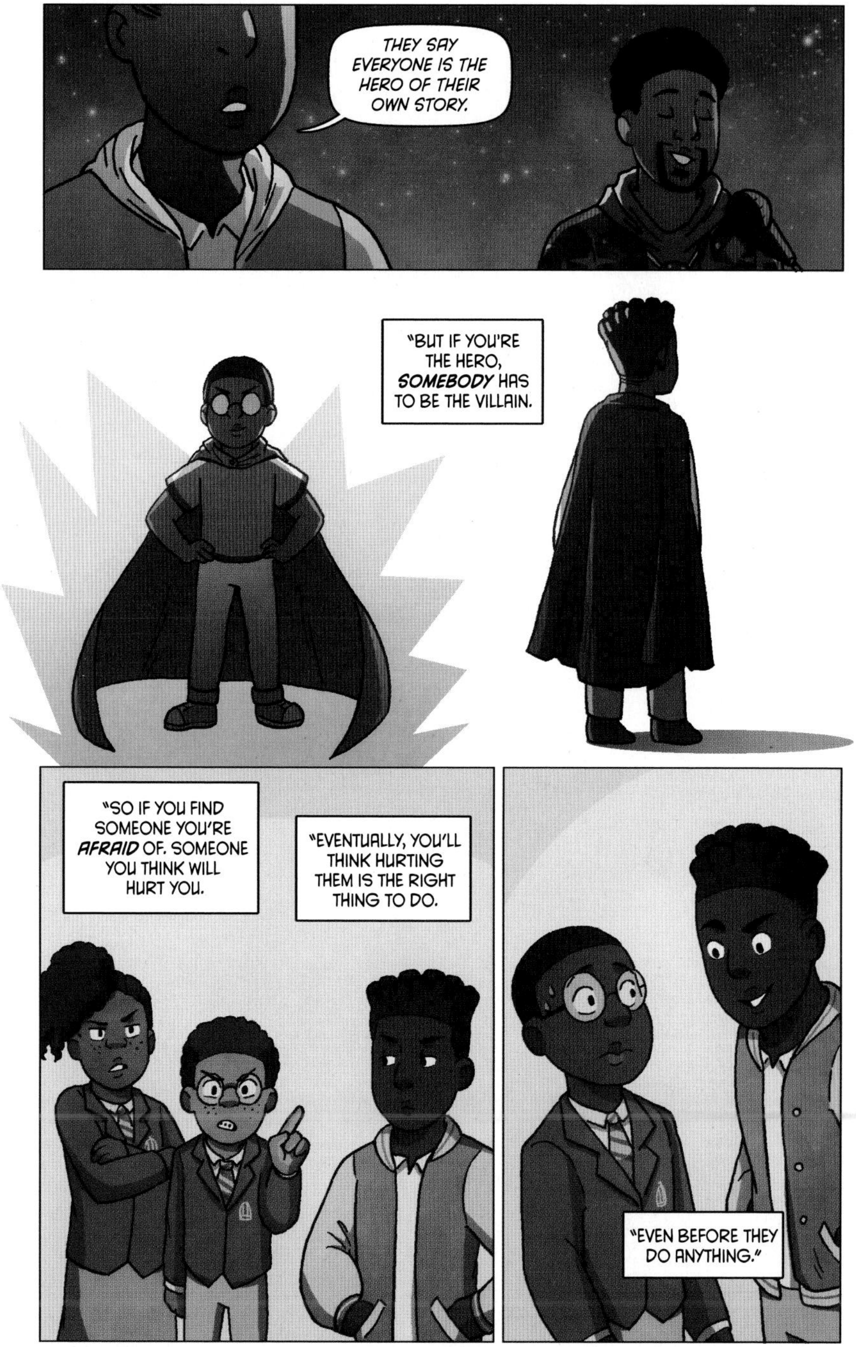
THEY SAY EVERYONE IS THE HERO OF THEIR OWN STORY.
"BUT IF YOU'RE THE HERO, SOMEBODY HAS TO BE THE VILLAIN.
"SO IF YOU FIND SOMEONE YOU'RE AFRAID OF. SOMEONE YOU THINK WILL HURT YOU.
"EVENTUALLY, YOU'LL THINK HURTING THEM IS THE RIGHT THING TO DO.
"EVEN BEFORE THEY DO ANYTHING."

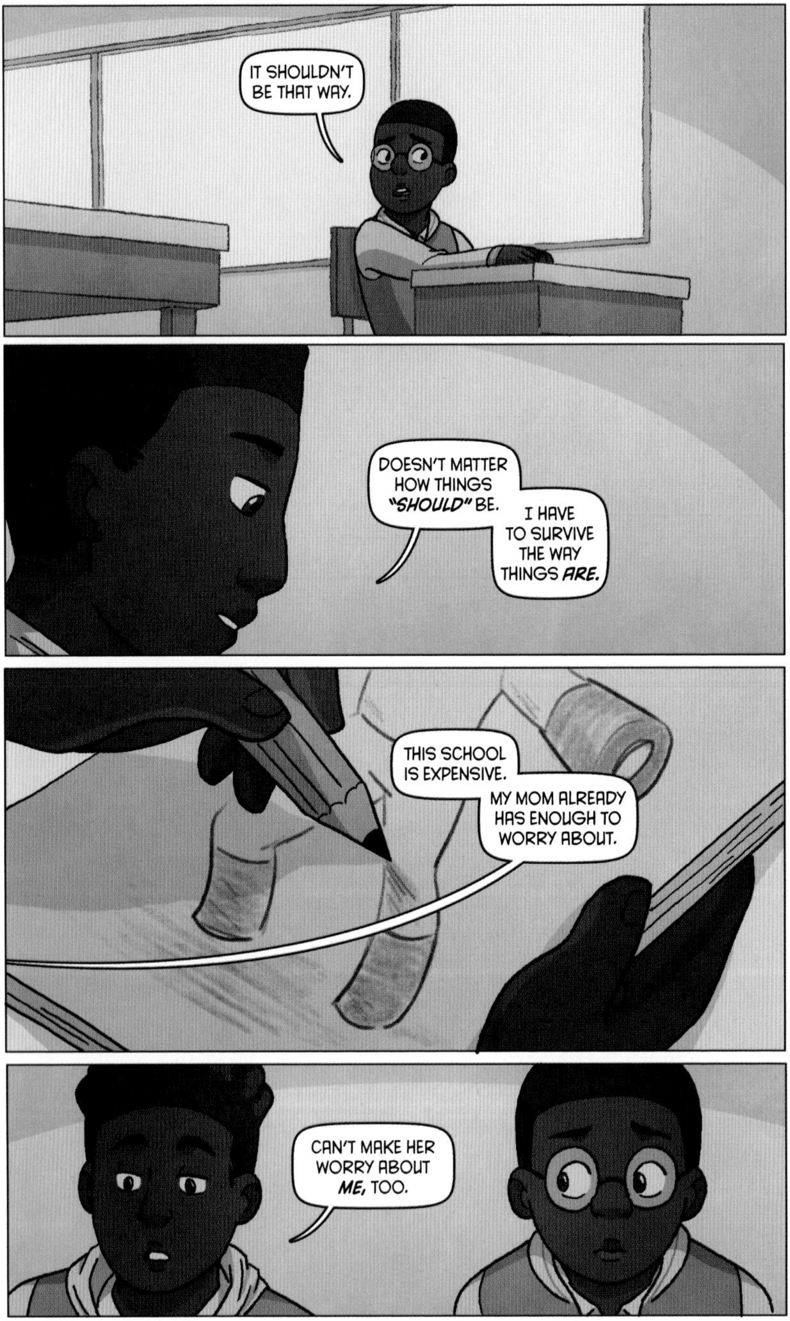
IT SHOULDN'T BE THAT WAY.
DOESN'T MATTER HOW THINGS *"SHOULD"* BE.
I HAVE TO SURVIVE THE WAY THINGS ***ARE.***
THIS SCHOOL IS EXPENSIVE.
MY MOM ALREADY HAS ENOUGH TO WORRY ABOUT.
CAN'T MAKE HER WORRY ABOUT ***ME,*** TOO.

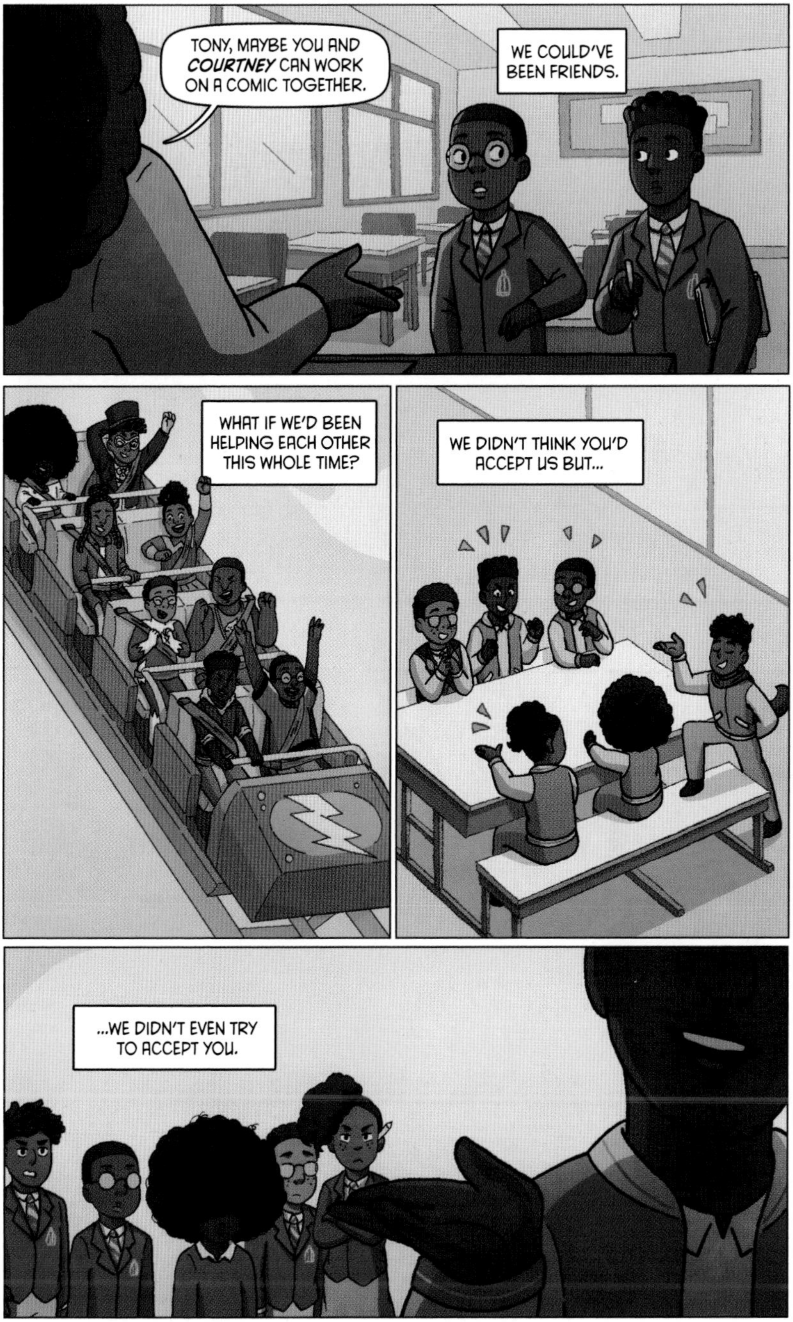
TONY, MAYBE YOU AND *COURTNEY* CAN WORK ON A COMIC TOGETHER.
WE COULD'VE BEEN FRIENDS.
WHAT IF WE'D BEEN HELPING EACH OTHER THIS WHOLE TIME?
WE DIDN'T THINK YOU'D ACCEPT US BUT...
...WE DIDN'T EVEN TRY TO ACCEPT YOU.

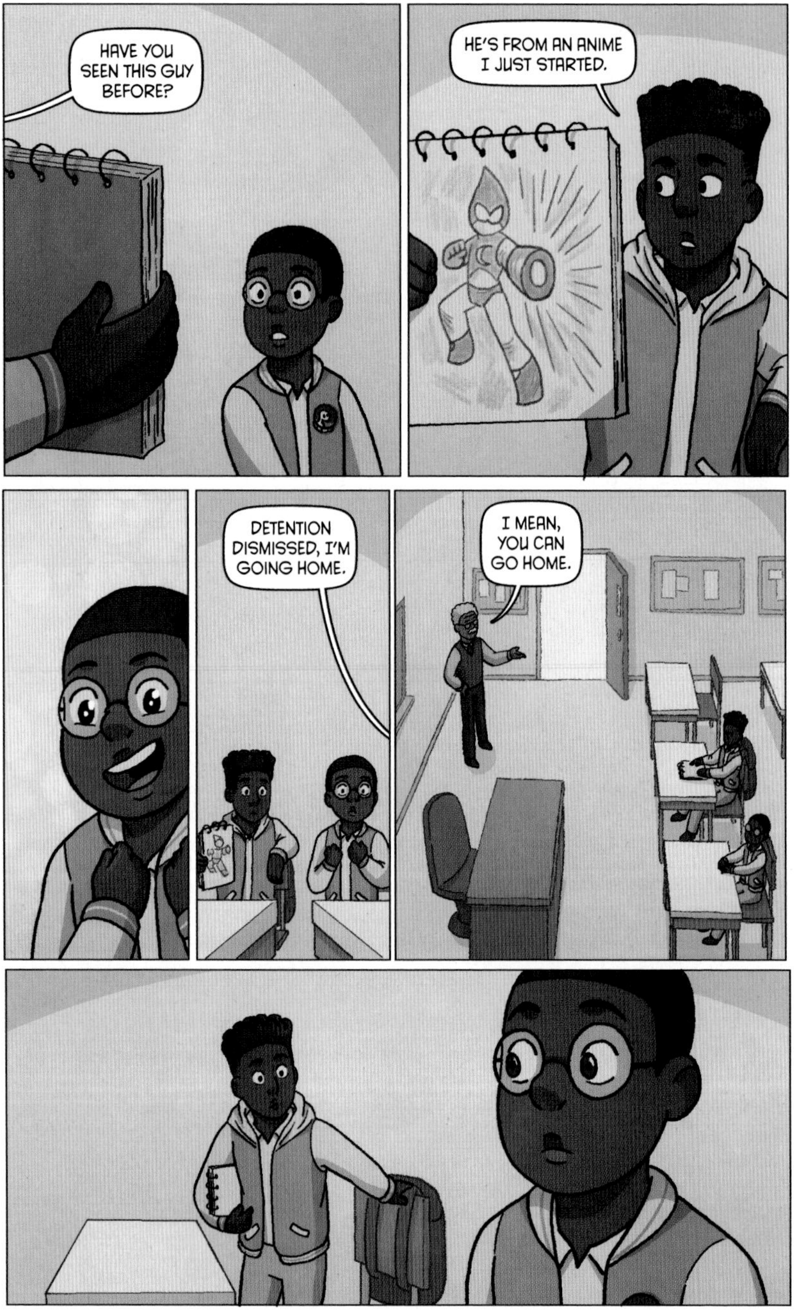
HAVE YOU SEEN THIS GUY BEFORE?
HE'S FROM AN ANIME I JUST STARTED.
DETENTION DISMISSED, I'M GOING HOME.
I MEAN, YOU CAN GO HOME.

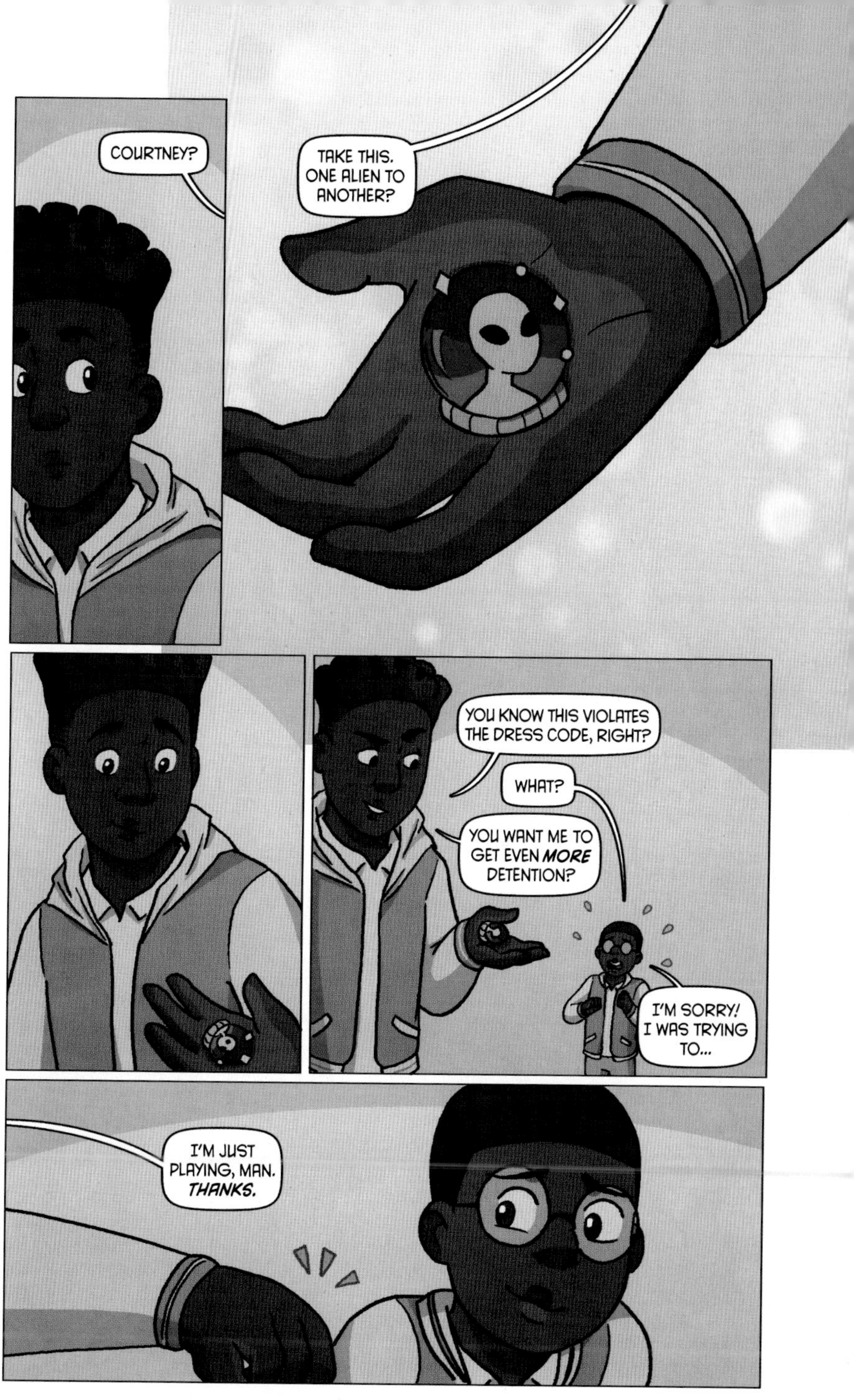
COURTNEY?
TAKE THIS. ONE ALIEN TO ANOTHER?
YOU KNOW THIS VIOLATES THE DRESS CODE, RIGHT?
WHAT?
YOU WANT ME TO GET EVEN *MORE* DETENTION?
I'M SORRY! I WAS TRYING TO...
I'M JUST PLAYING, MAN. *THANKS.*

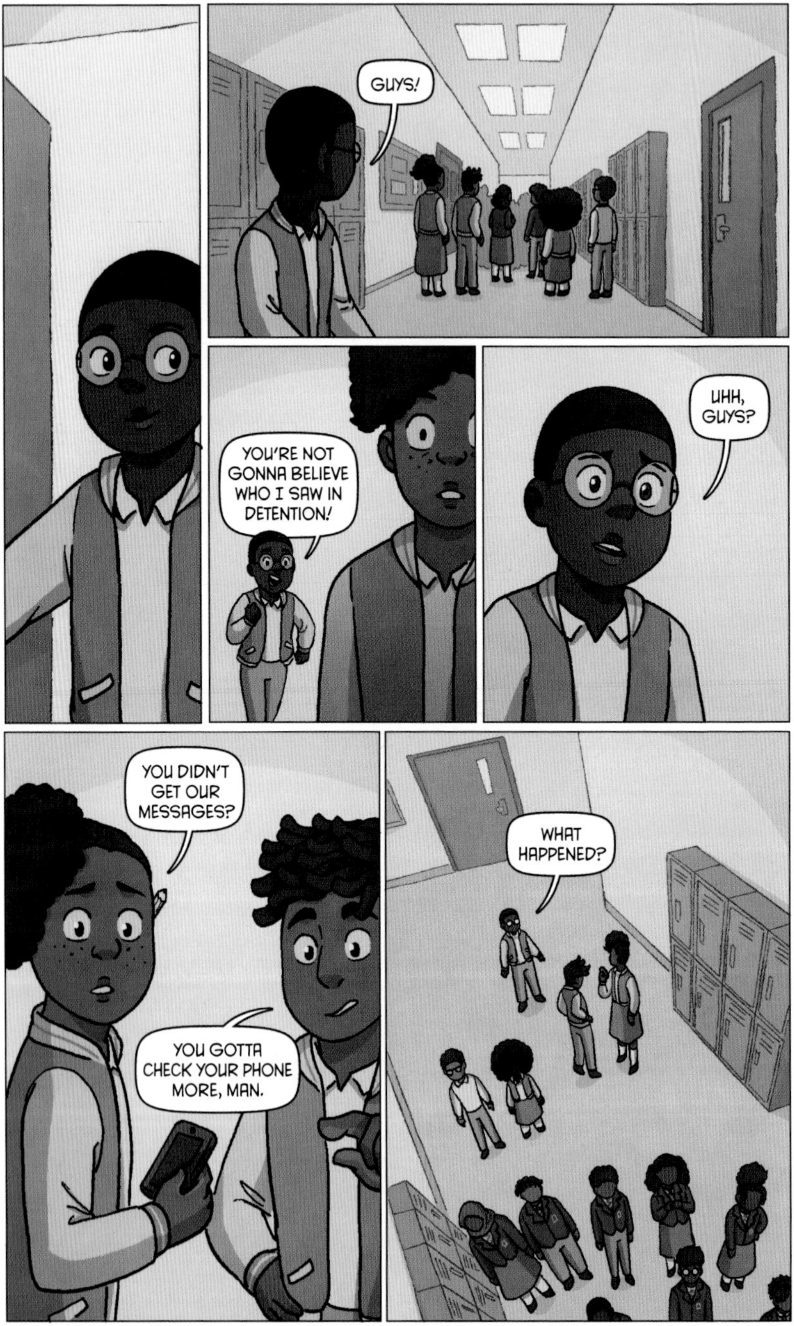
GUYS!
YOU'RE NOT GONNA BELIEVE WHO I SAW IN DETENTION!
UHH, GUYS?
YOU DIDN'T GET OUR MESSAGES?
YOU GOTTA CHECK YOUR PHONE MORE, MAN.
WHAT HAPPENED?

CHAPTER 10

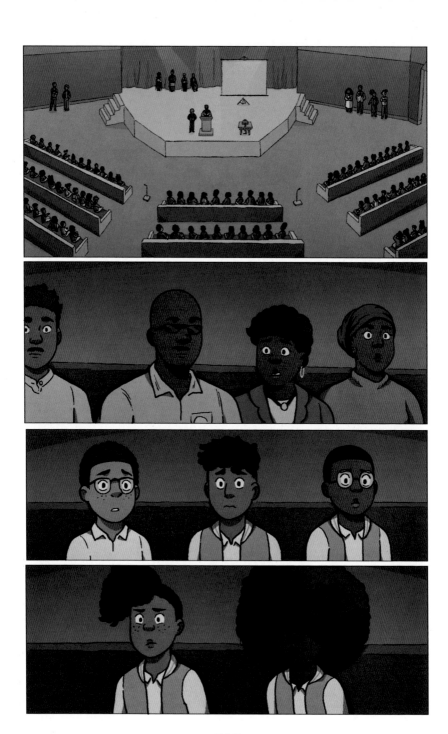

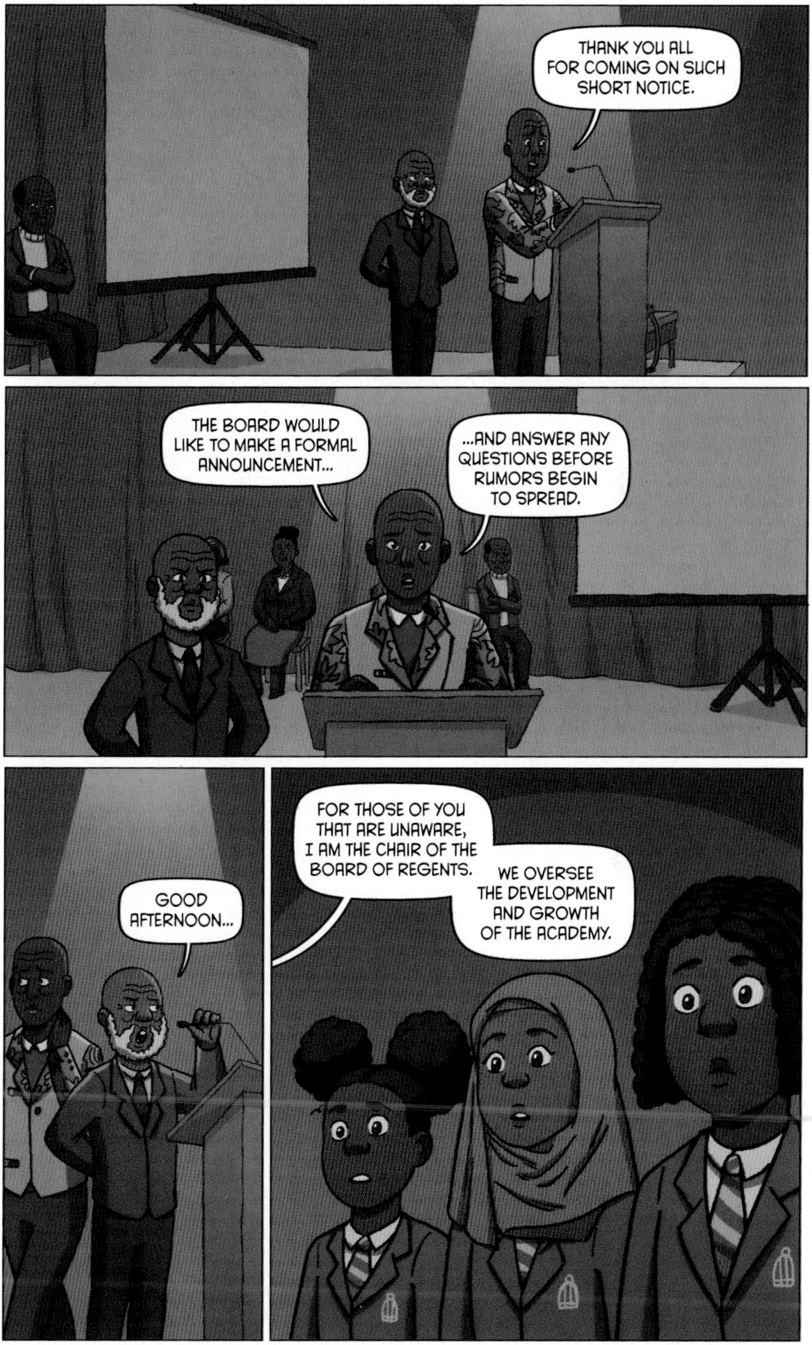
THANK YOU ALL FOR COMING ON SUCH SHORT NOTICE.
THE BOARD WOULD LIKE TO MAKE A FORMAL ANNOUNCEMENT...
...AND ANSWER ANY QUESTIONS BEFORE RUMORS BEGIN TO SPREAD.
GOOD AFTERNOON...
FOR THOSE OF YOU THAT ARE UNAWARE, I AM THE CHAIR OF THE BOARD OF REGENTS.
WE OVERSEE THE DEVELOPMENT AND GROWTH OF THE ACADEMY.

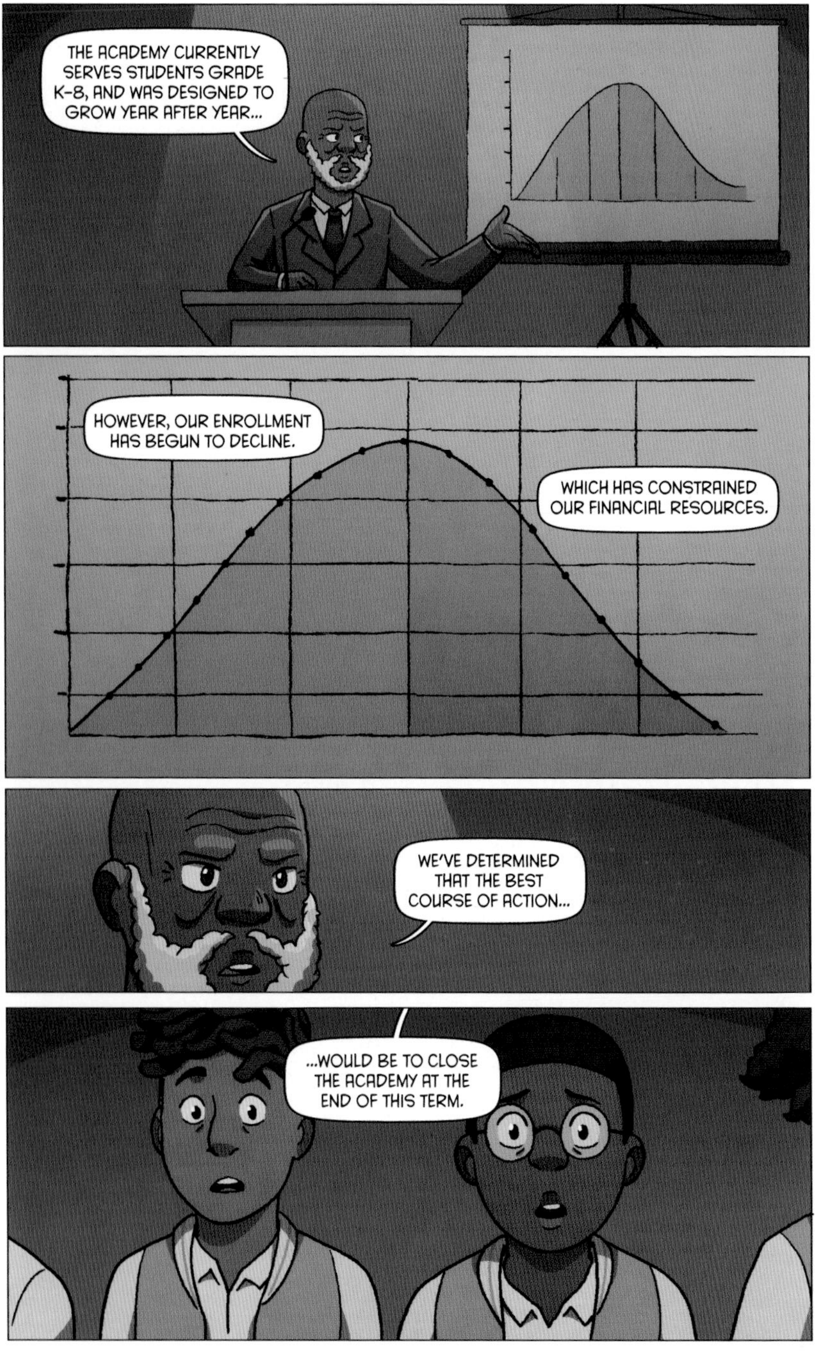
THE ACADEMY CURRENTLY SERVES STUDENTS GRADE K-8, AND WAS DESIGNED TO GROW YEAR AFTER YEAR...
HOWEVER, OUR ENROLLMENT HAS BEGUN TO DECLINE.
WHICH HAS CONSTRAINED OUR FINANCIAL RESOURCES.
WE'VE DETERMINED THAT THE BEST COURSE OF ACTION...
...WOULD BE TO CLOSE THE ACADEMY AT THE END OF THIS TERM.

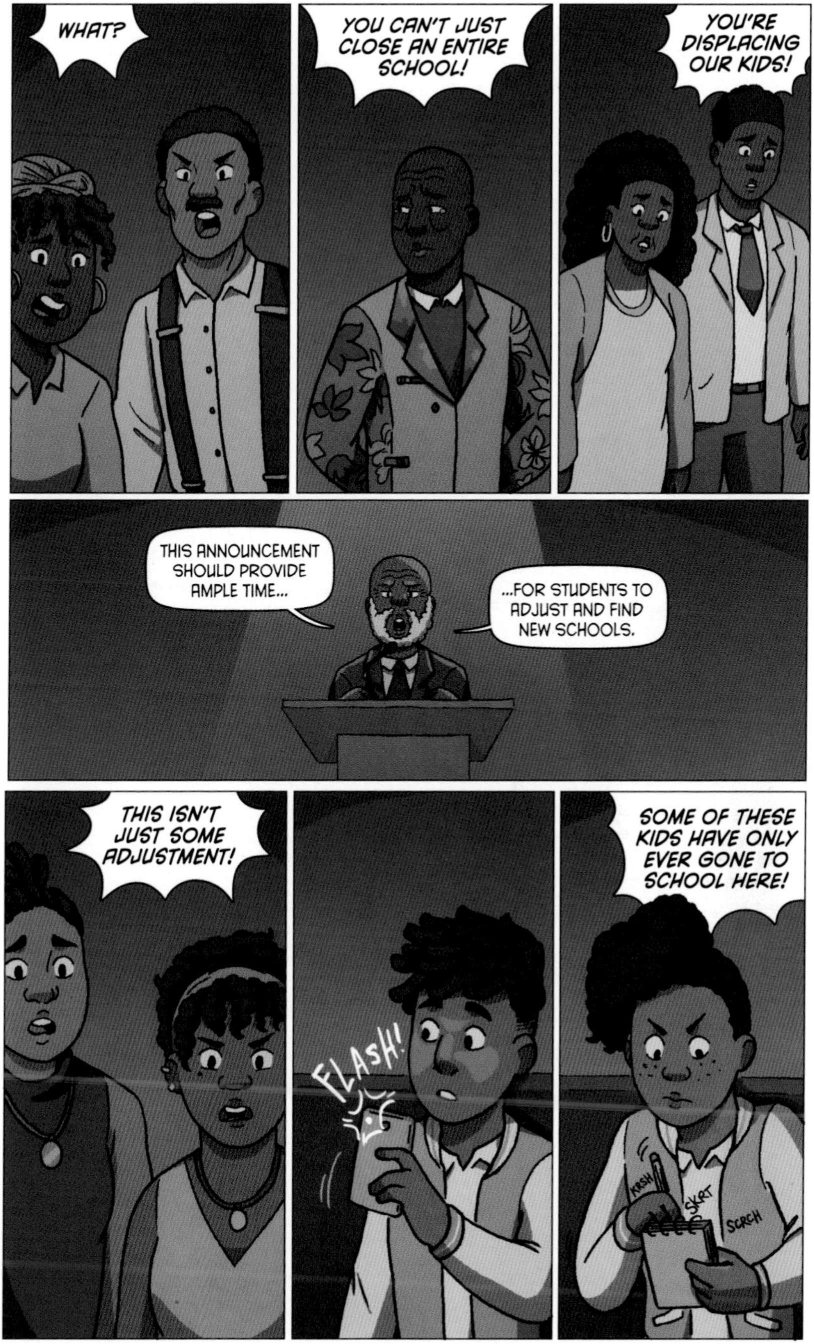
WHAT?
YOU CAN'T JUST CLOSE AN ENTIRE SCHOOL!
YOU'RE DISPLACING OUR KIDS!
THIS ANNOUNCEMENT SHOULD PROVIDE AMPLE TIME...
...FOR STUDENTS TO ADJUST AND FIND NEW SCHOOLS.
THIS ISN'T JUST SOME ADJUSTMENT!
FLASH!
SOME OF THESE KIDS HAVE ONLY EVER GONE TO SCHOOL HERE!
KRSH
SKRT
SCRCH

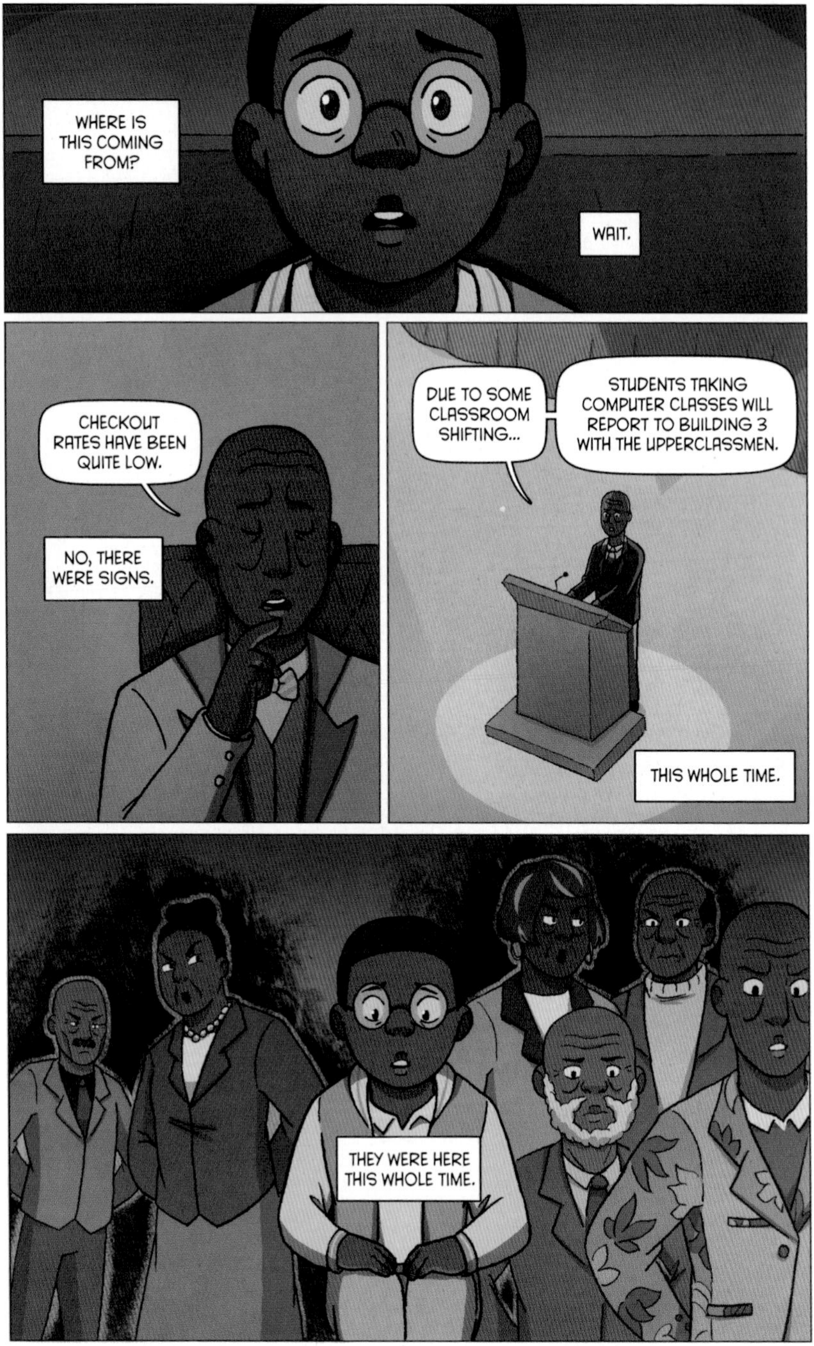
WHERE IS THIS COMING FROM?
WAIT.
CHECKOUT RATES HAVE BEEN QUITE LOW.
NO, THERE WERE SIGNS.
DUE TO SOME CLASSROOM SHIFTING...
STUDENTS TAKING COMPUTER CLASSES WILL REPORT TO BUILDING 3 WITH THE UPPERCLASSMEN.
THIS WHOLE TIME.
THEY WERE HERE THIS WHOLE TIME.

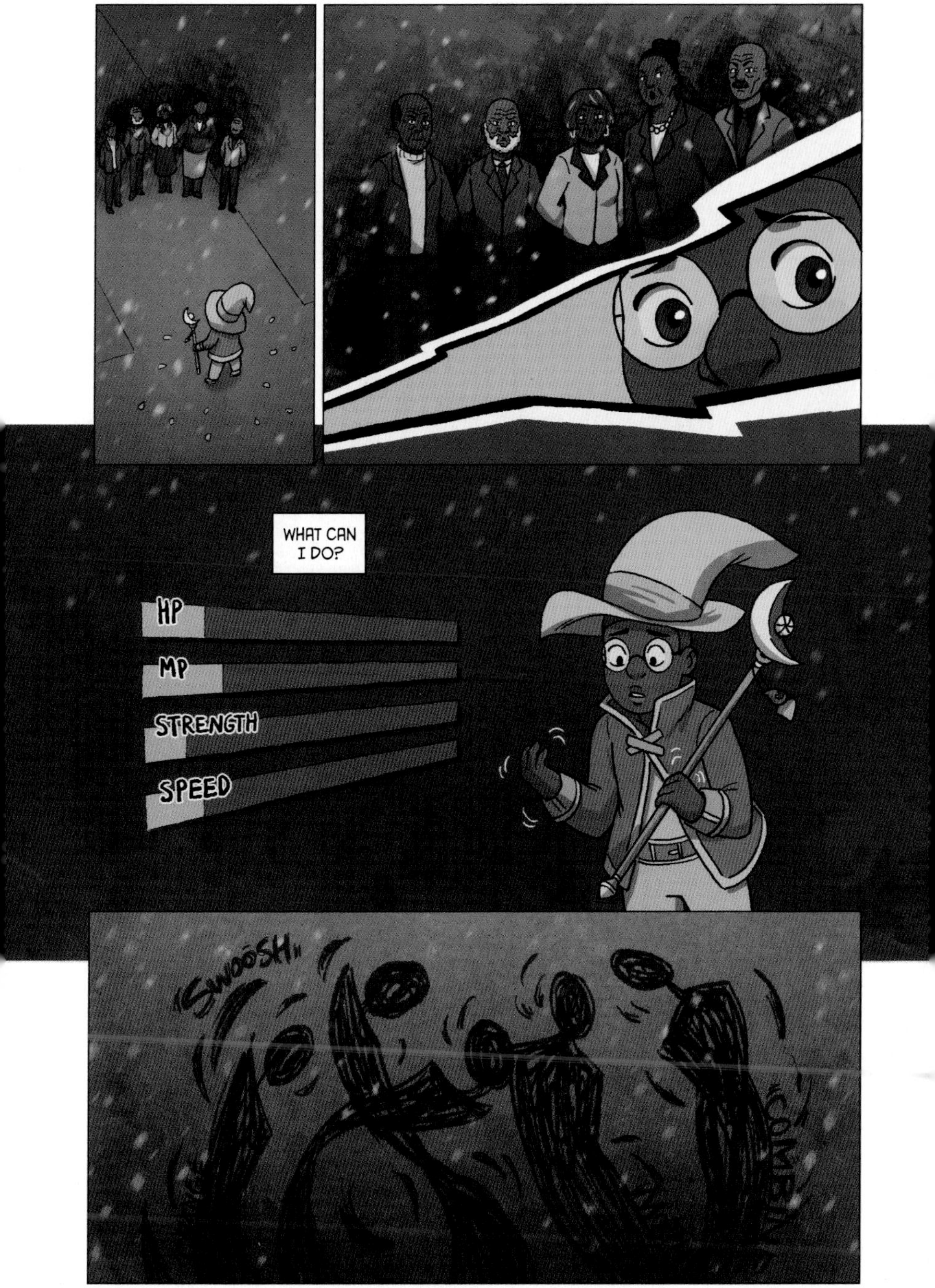
WHAT CAN I DO?
HP
MP
STRENGTH
SPEED
SWOOSH
COMBIN

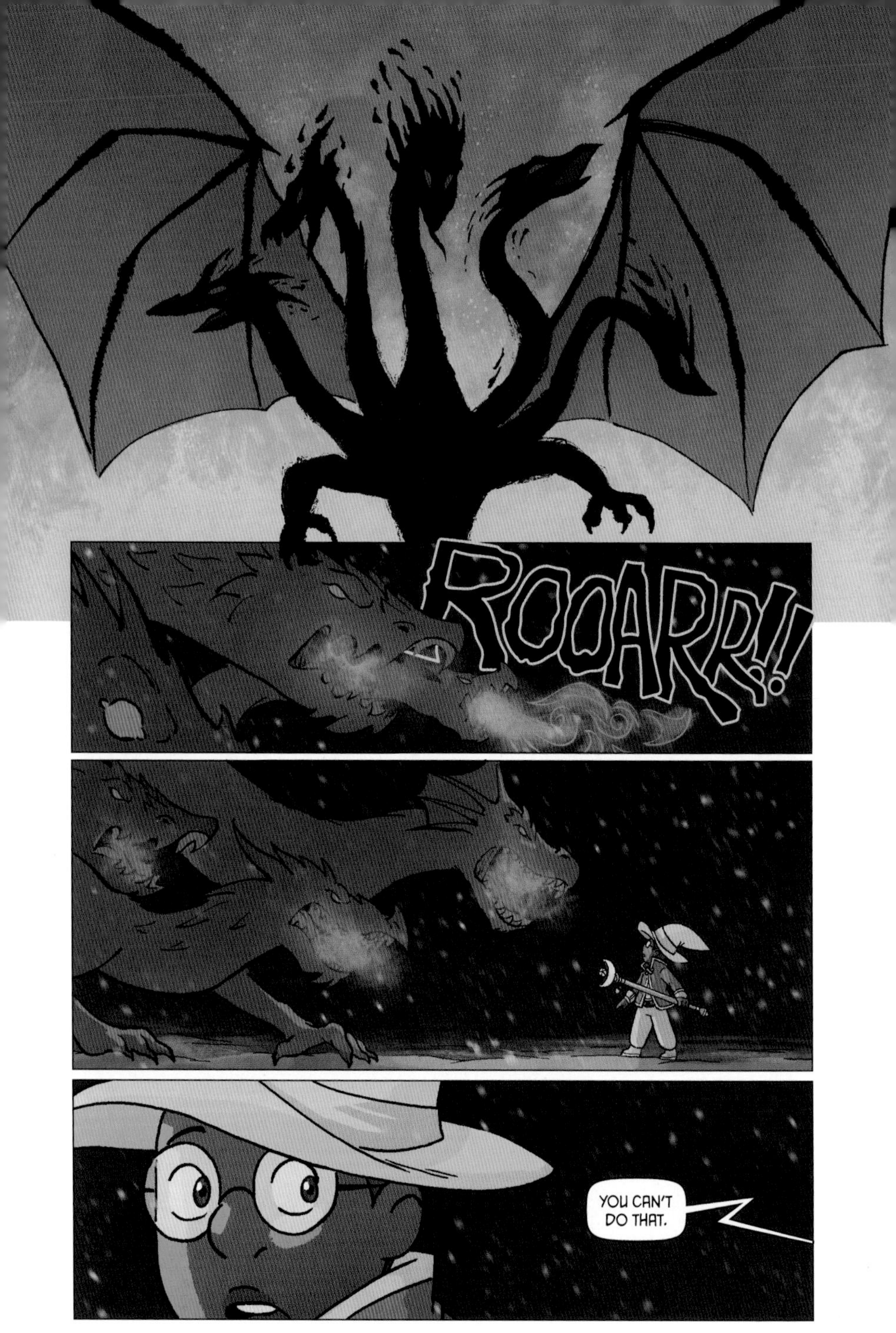
ROOARR!!
YOU CAN'T DO THAT.

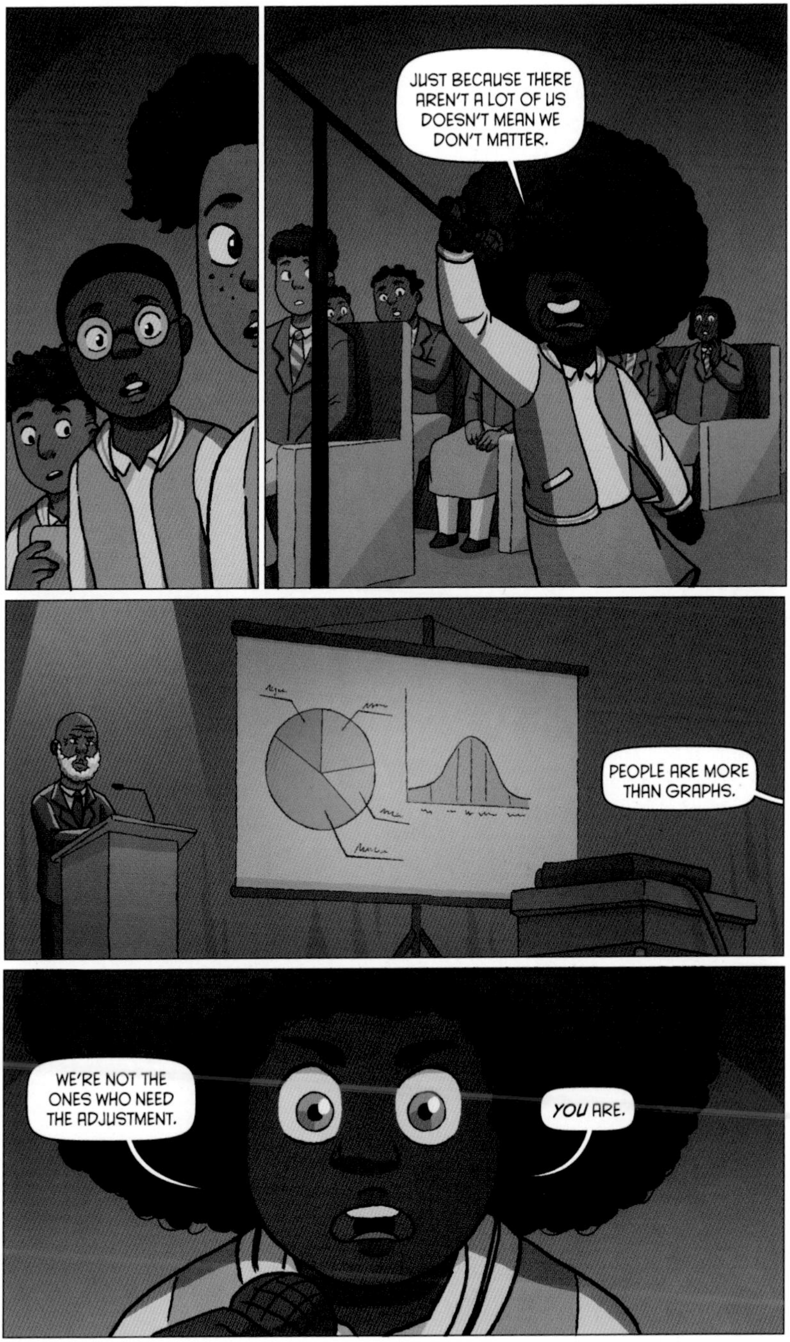
JUST BECAUSE THERE AREN'T A LOT OF US DOESN'T MEAN WE DON'T MATTER.
PEOPLE ARE MORE THAN GRAPHS.
WE'RE NOT THE ONES WHO NEED THE ADJUSTMENT.
YOU ARE.

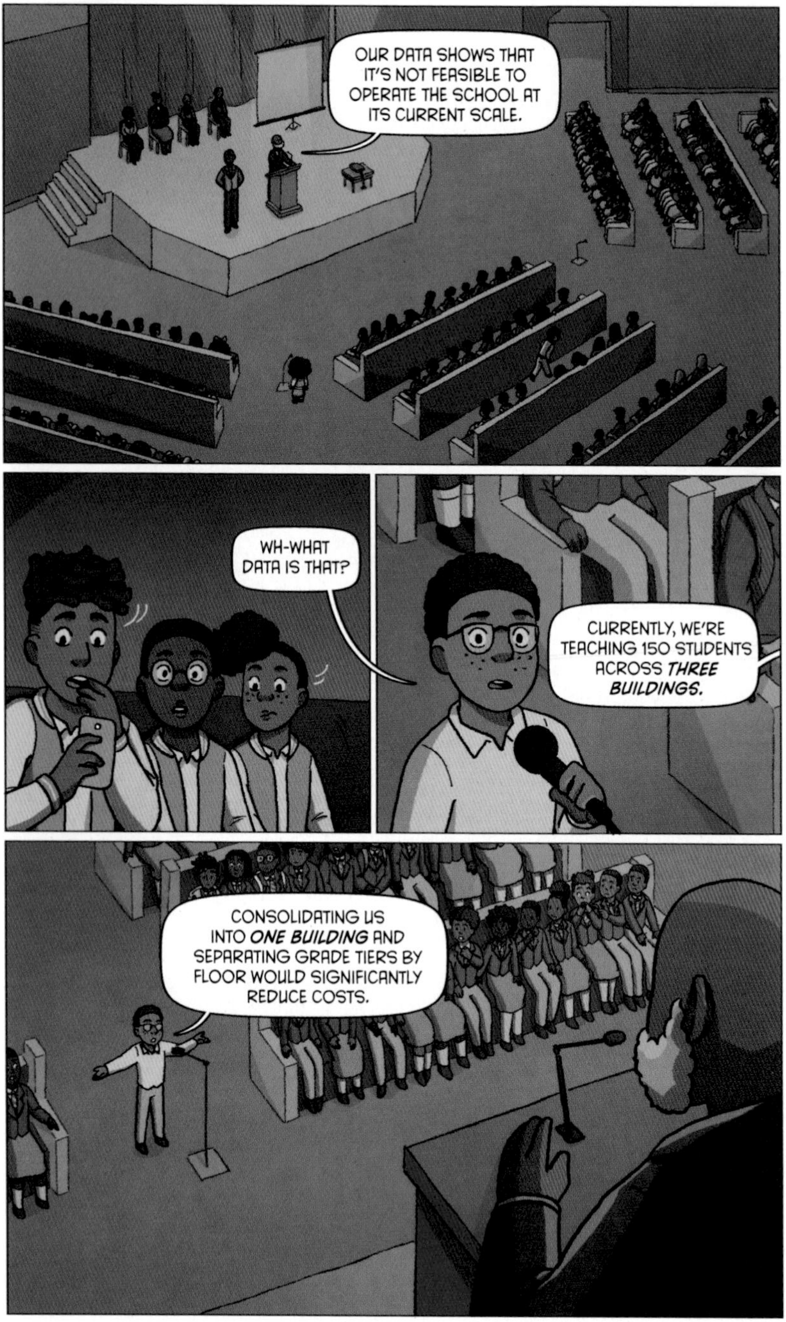
OUR DATA SHOWS THAT IT'S NOT FEASIBLE TO OPERATE THE SCHOOL AT ITS CURRENT SCALE.
WH-WHAT DATA IS THAT?
CURRENTLY, WE'RE TEACHING 150 STUDENTS ACROSS *THREE BUILDINGS.*
CONSOLIDATING US INTO *ONE BUILDING* AND SEPARATING GRADE TIERS BY FLOOR WOULD SIGNIFICANTLY REDUCE COSTS.

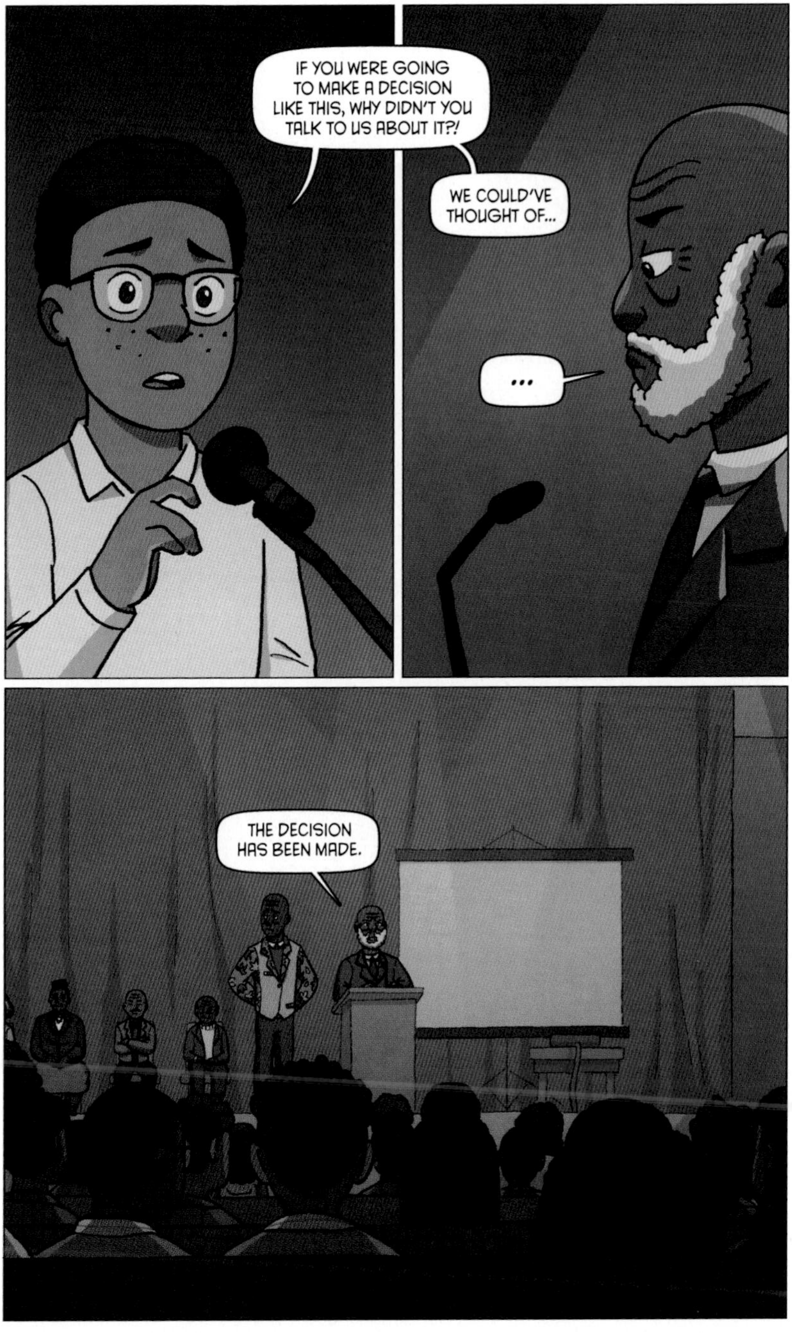
IF YOU WERE GOING TO MAKE A DECISION LIKE THIS, WHY DIDN'T YOU TALK TO US ABOUT IT?!
WE COULD'VE THOUGHT OF...
...
THE DECISION HAS BEEN MADE.

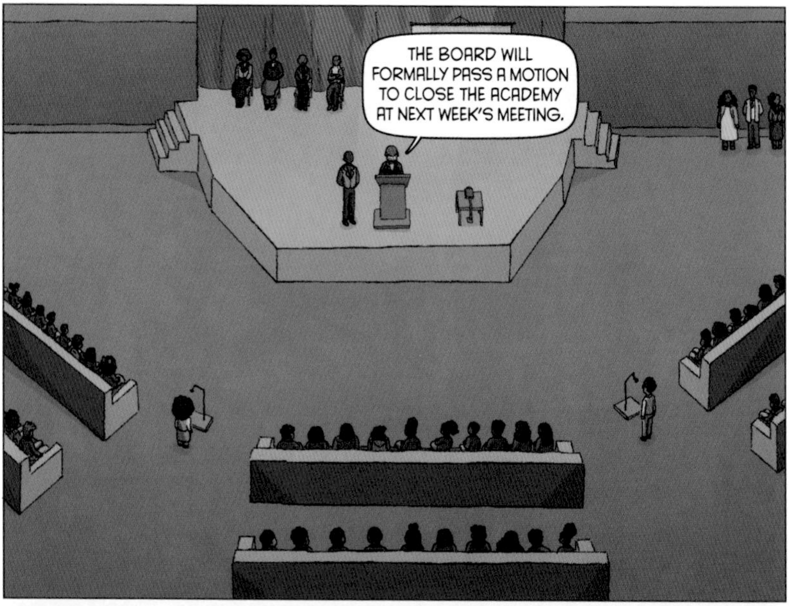
THE BOARD WILL FORMALLY PASS A MOTION TO CLOSE THE ACADEMY AT NEXT WEEK'S MEETING.

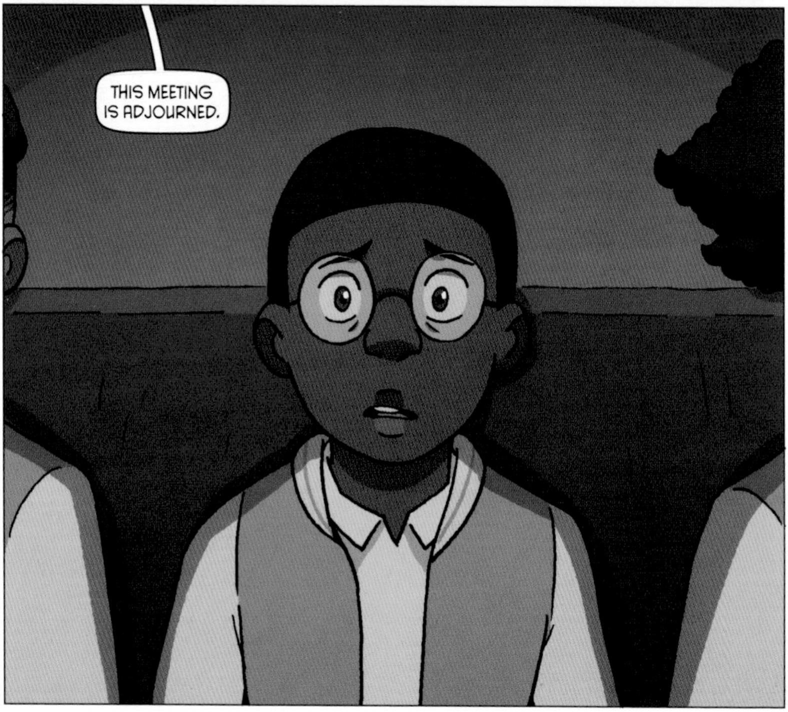
THIS MEETING IS ADJOURNED.

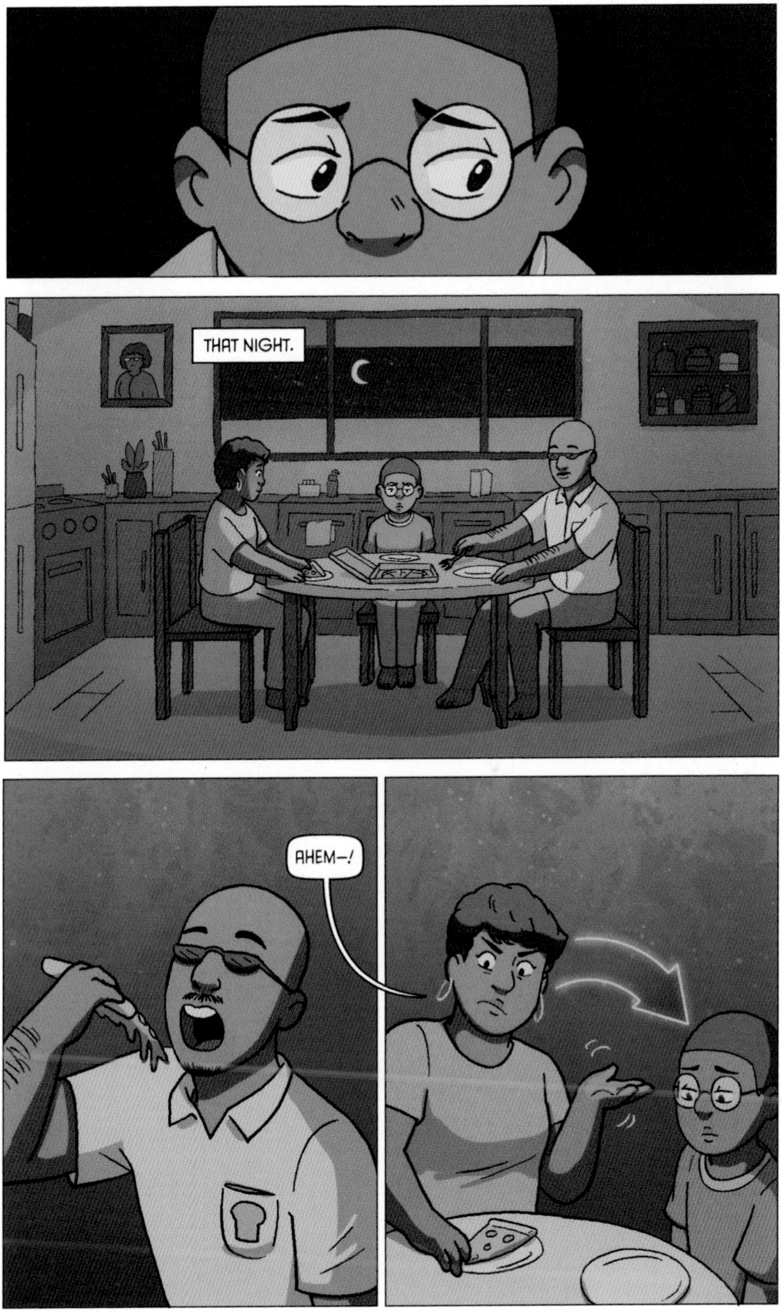
THAT NIGHT.
AHEM–!

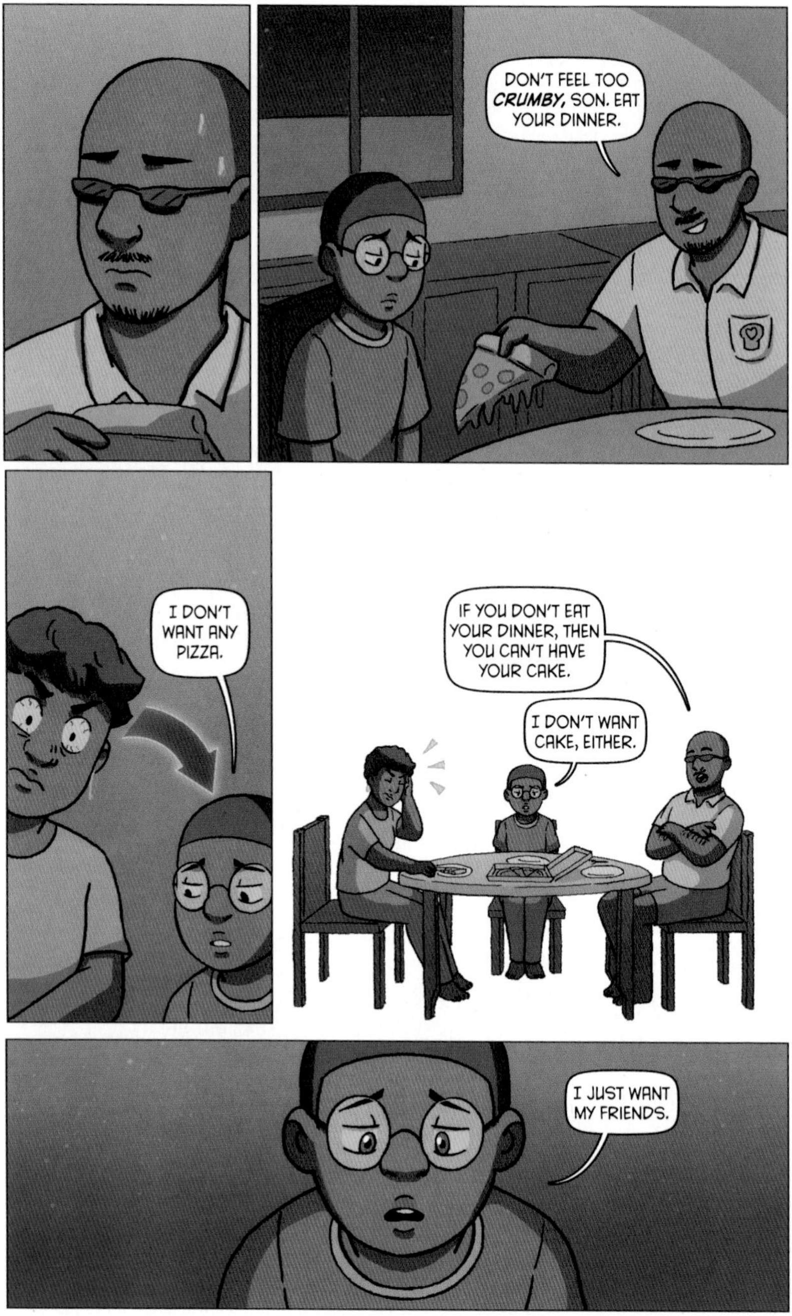
DON'T FEEL TOO *CRUMBY,* SON. EAT YOUR DINNER.
I DON'T WANT ANY PIZZA.
IF YOU DON'T EAT YOUR DINNER, THEN YOU CAN'T HAVE YOUR CAKE.
I DON'T WANT CAKE, EITHER.
I JUST WANT MY FRIENDS.

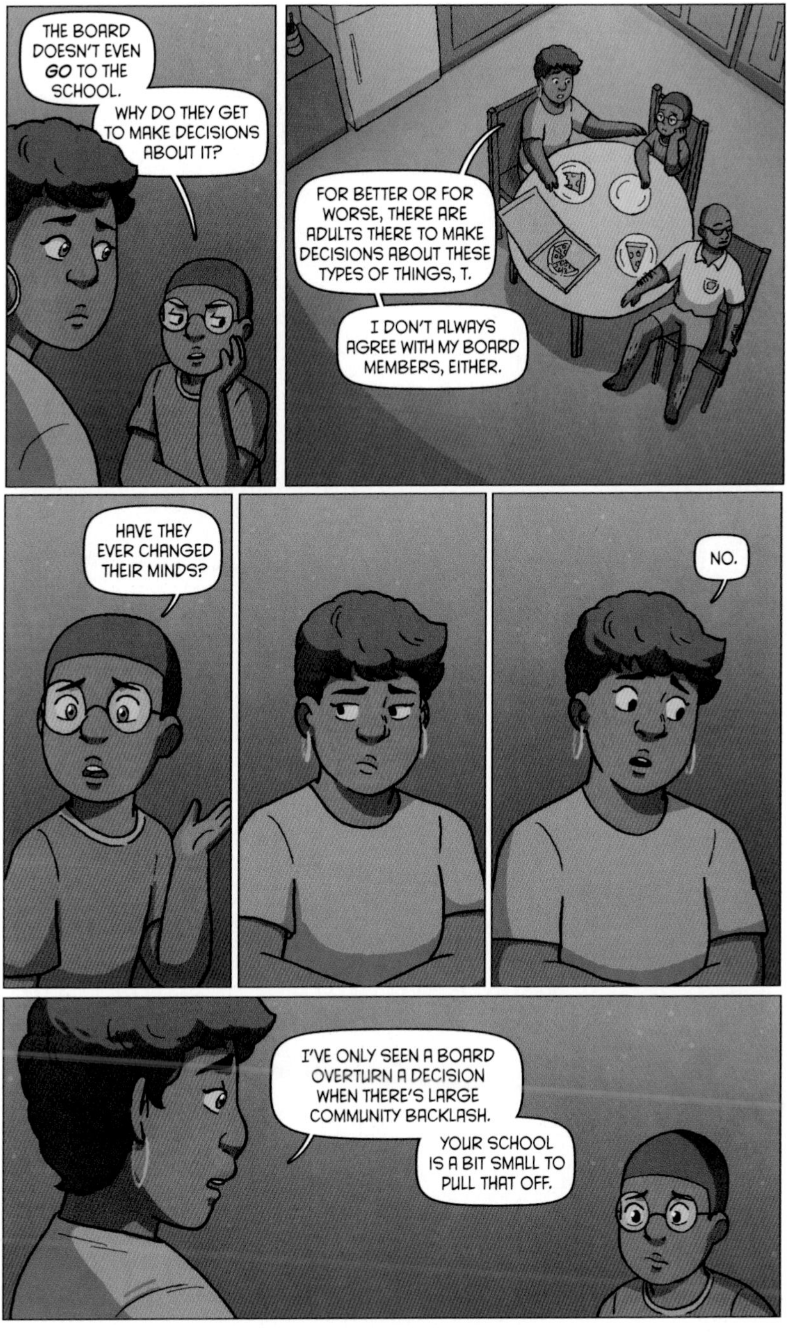
THE BOARD DOESN'T EVEN *GO* TO THE SCHOOL.
WHY DO THEY GET TO MAKE DECISIONS ABOUT IT?
FOR BETTER OR FOR WORSE, THERE ARE ADULTS THERE TO MAKE DECISIONS ABOUT THESE TYPES OF THINGS, T.
I DON'T ALWAYS AGREE WITH MY BOARD MEMBERS, EITHER.
HAVE THEY EVER CHANGED THEIR MINDS?
NO.
I'VE ONLY SEEN A BOARD OVERTURN A DECISION WHEN THERE'S LARGE COMMUNITY BACKLASH.
YOUR SCHOOL IS A BIT SMALL TO PULL THAT OFF.

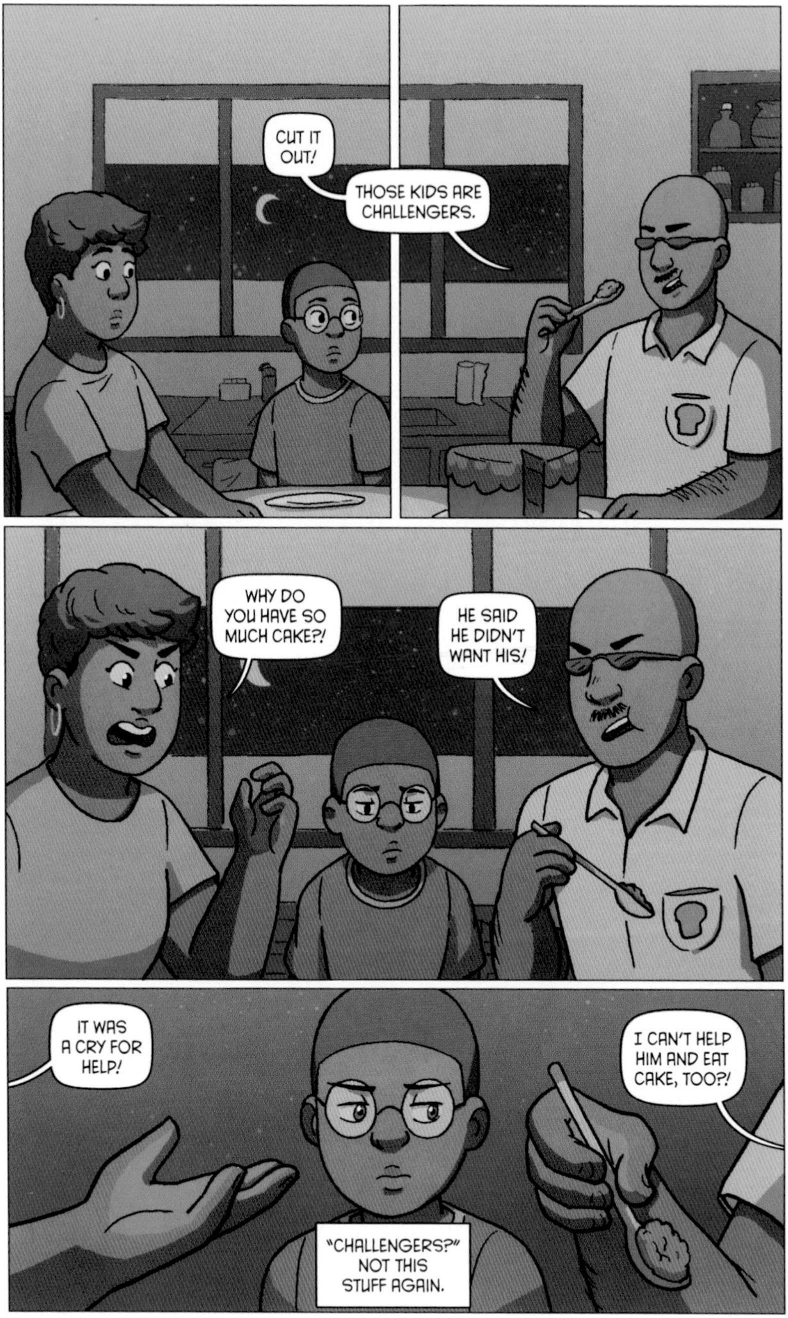
CUT IT OUT!
THOSE KIDS ARE CHALLENGERS.
WHY DO YOU HAVE SO MUCH CAKE?!
HE SAID HE DIDN'T WANT HIS!
IT WAS A CRY FOR HELP!
I CAN'T HELP HIM AND EAT CAKE, TOO?!
"CHALLENGERS?" NOT THIS STUFF AGAIN.

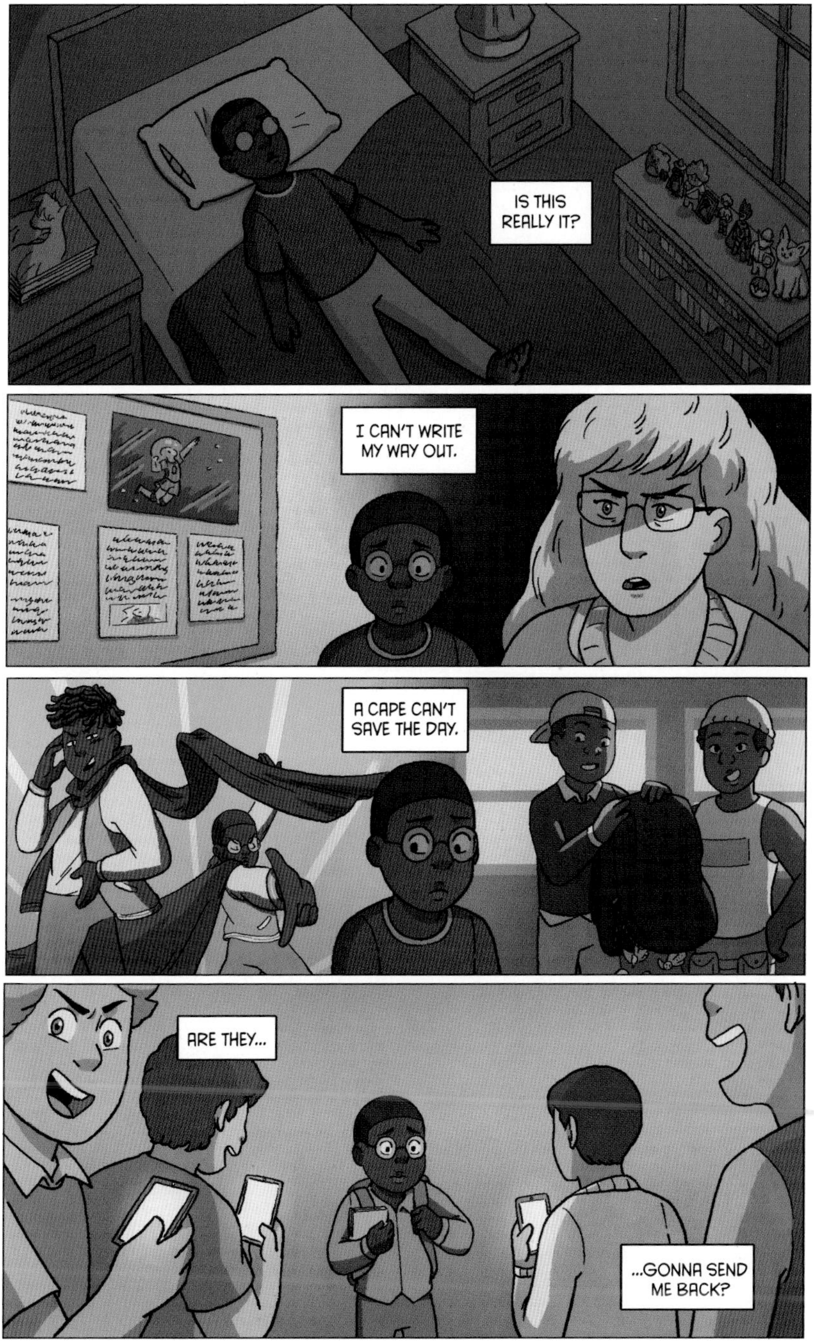
IS THIS REALLY IT?
I CAN'T WRITE MY WAY OUT.
A CAPE CAN'T SAVE THE DAY.
ARE THEY...
...GONNA SEND ME BACK?

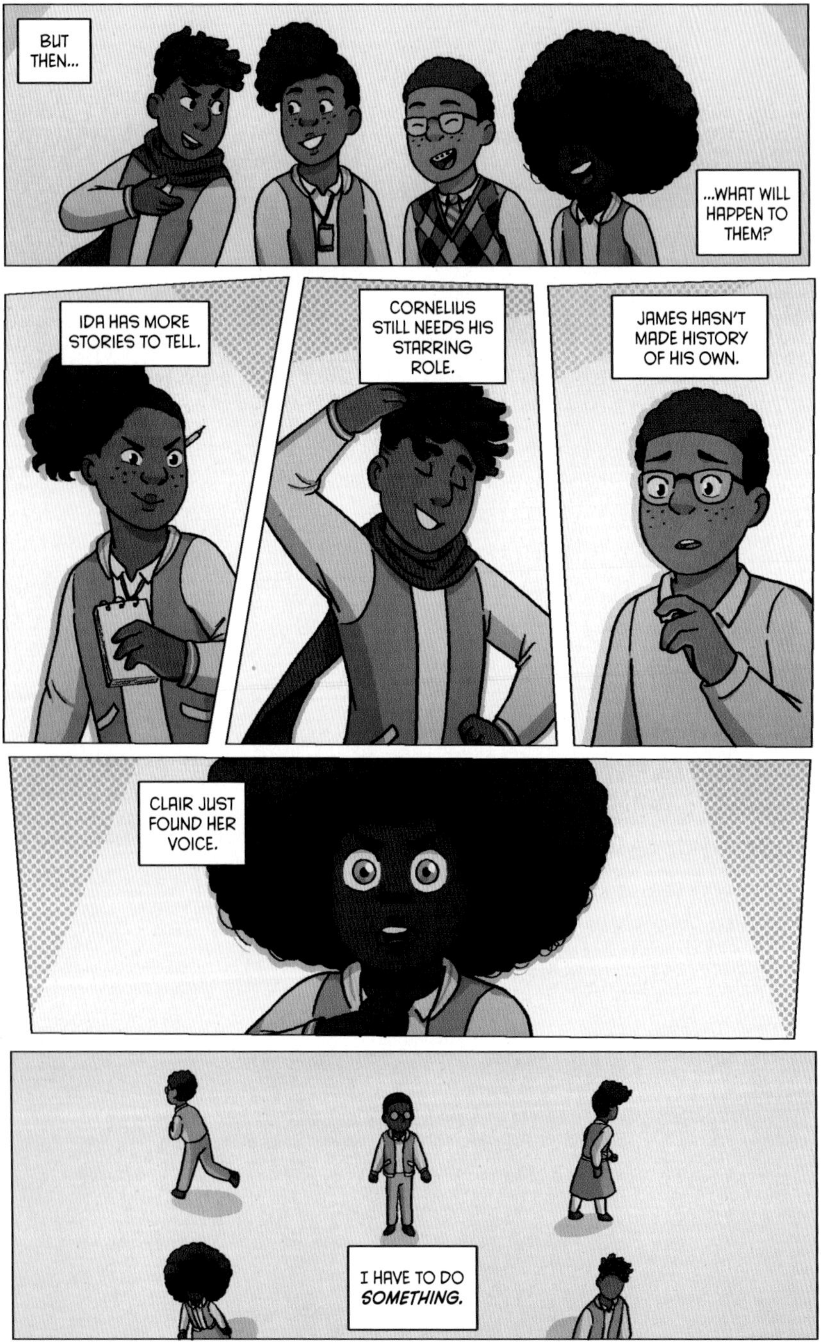
BUT THEN...
...WHAT WILL HAPPEN TO THEM?
IDA HAS MORE STORIES TO TELL.
CORNELIUS STILL NEEDS HIS STARRING ROLE.
JAMES HASN'T MADE HISTORY OF HIS OWN.
CLAIR JUST FOUND HER VOICE.
I HAVE TO DO *SOMETHING.*

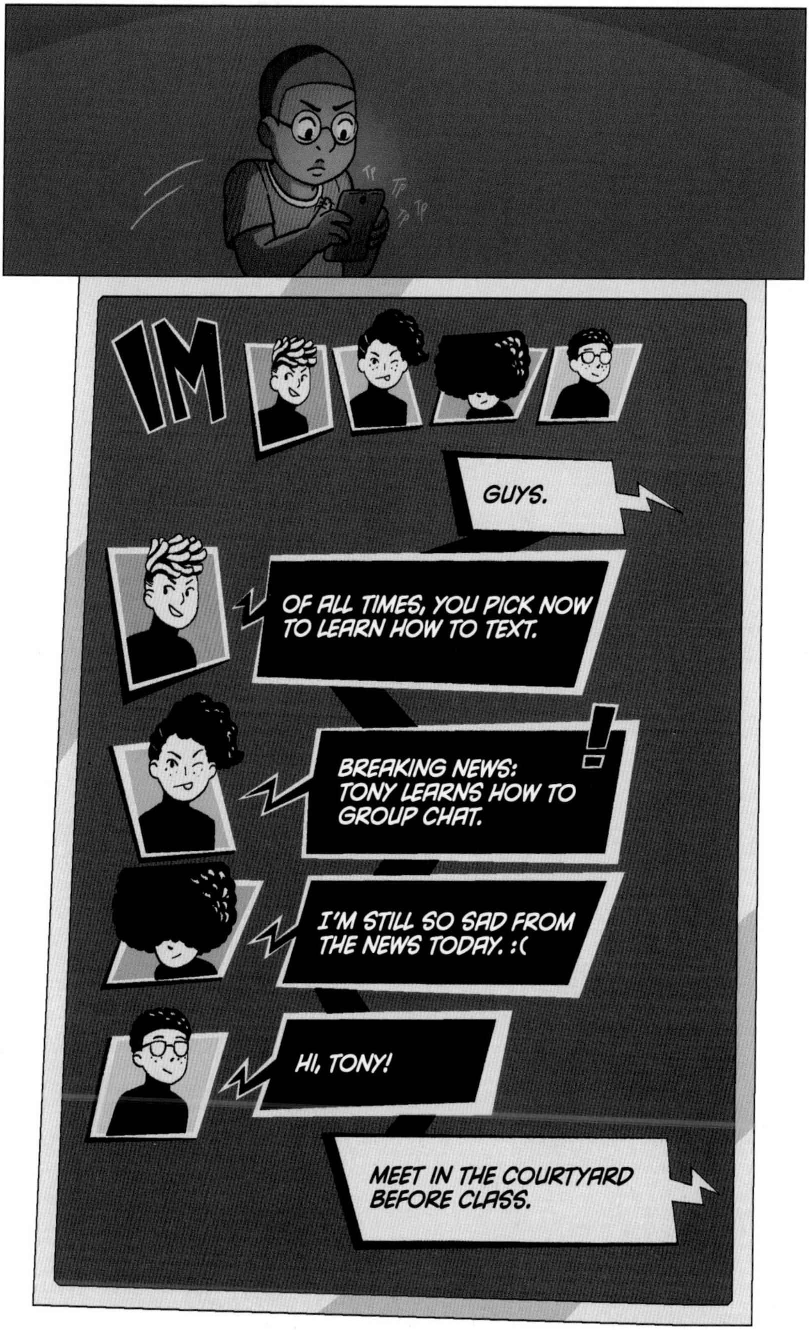
TP TP TP TP
IM
GUYS.
OF ALL TIMES, YOU PICK NOW TO LEARN HOW TO TEXT.
BREAKING NEWS: TONY LEARNS HOW TO GROUP CHAT.
I'M STILL SO SAD FROM THE NEWS TODAY. :(
HI, TONY!
MEET IN THE COURTYARD BEFORE CLASS.

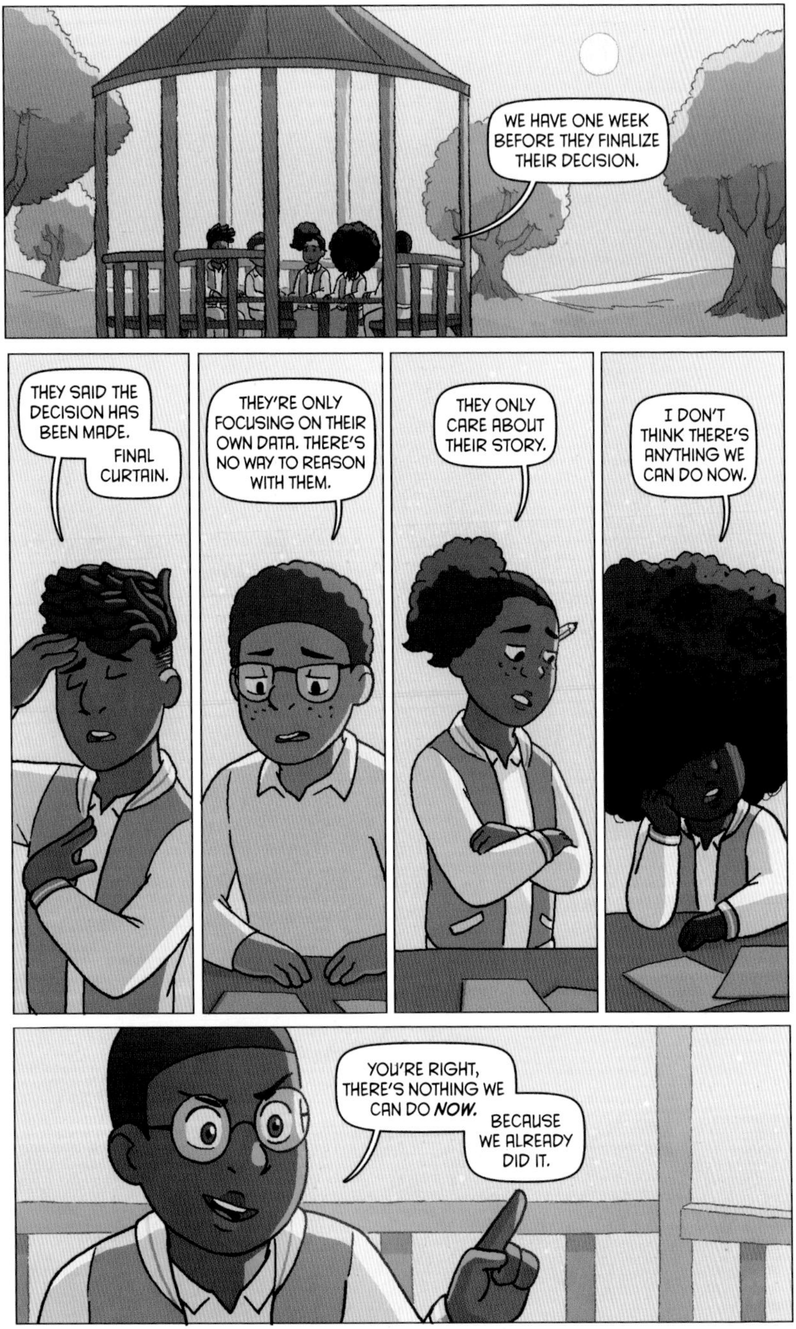
WE HAVE ONE WEEK BEFORE THEY FINALIZE THEIR DECISION.
THEY SAID THE DECISION HAS BEEN MADE.
FINAL CURTAIN.
THEY'RE ONLY FOCUSING ON THEIR OWN DATA. THERE'S NO WAY TO REASON WITH THEM.
THEY ONLY CARE ABOUT THEIR STORY.
I DON'T THINK THERE'S ANYTHING WE CAN DO NOW.
YOU'RE RIGHT, THERE'S NOTHING WE CAN DO ***NOW.***
BECAUSE WE ALREADY DID IT.

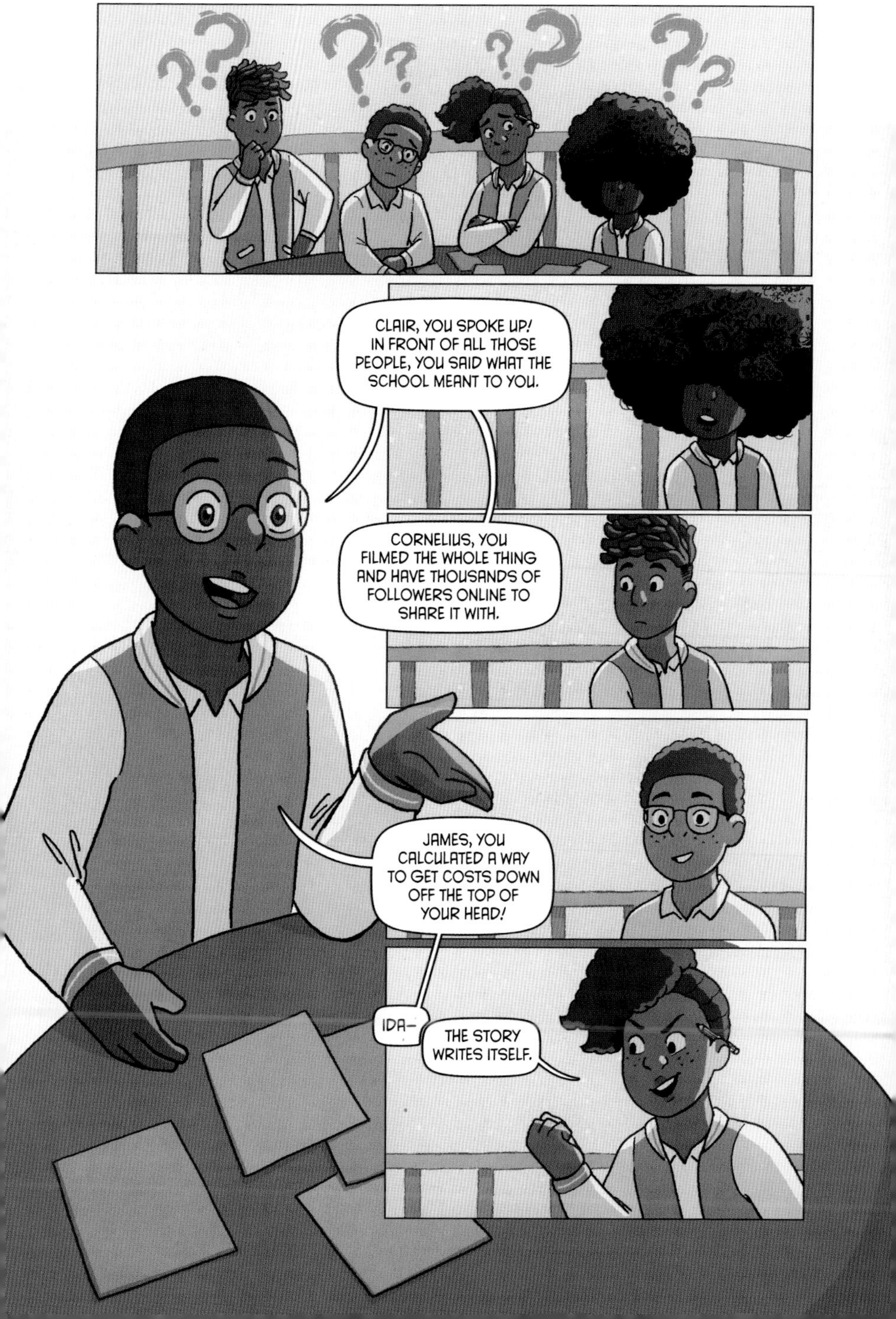
CLAIR, YOU SPOKE UP! IN FRONT OF ALL THOSE PEOPLE, YOU SAID WHAT THE SCHOOL MEANT TO YOU.
CORNELIUS, YOU FILMED THE WHOLE THING AND HAVE THOUSANDS OF FOLLOWERS ONLINE TO SHARE IT WITH.
JAMES, YOU CALCULATED A WAY TO GET COSTS DOWN OFF THE TOP OF YOUR HEAD!
IDA—
THE STORY WRITES ITSELF.

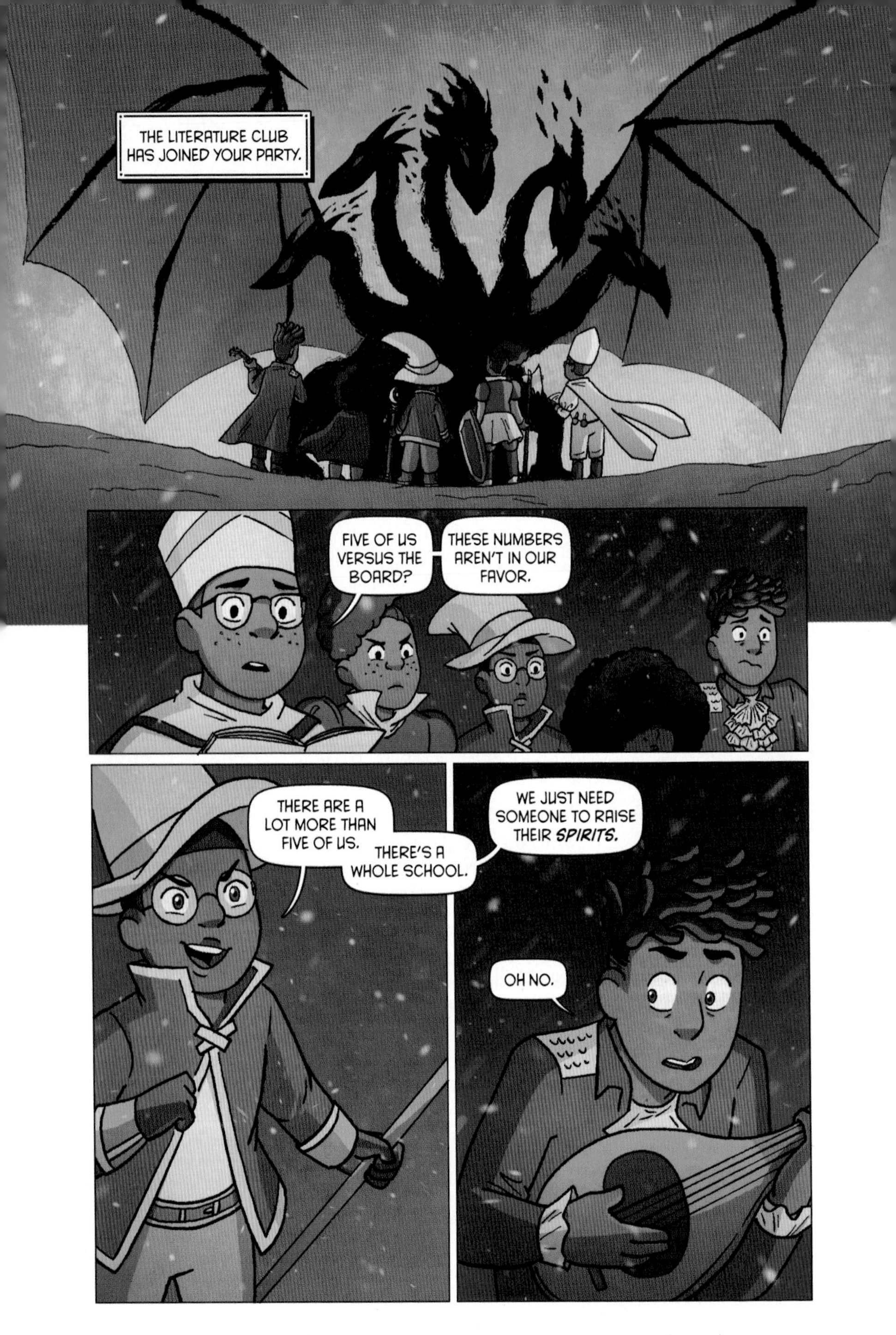
THE LITERATURE CLUB HAS JOINED YOUR PARTY.
FIVE OF US VERSUS THE BOARD?
THESE NUMBERS AREN'T IN OUR FAVOR.
THERE ARE A LOT MORE THAN FIVE OF US.
THERE'S A WHOLE SCHOOL.
WE JUST NEED SOMEONE TO RAISE THEIR *SPIRITS.*
OH NO.

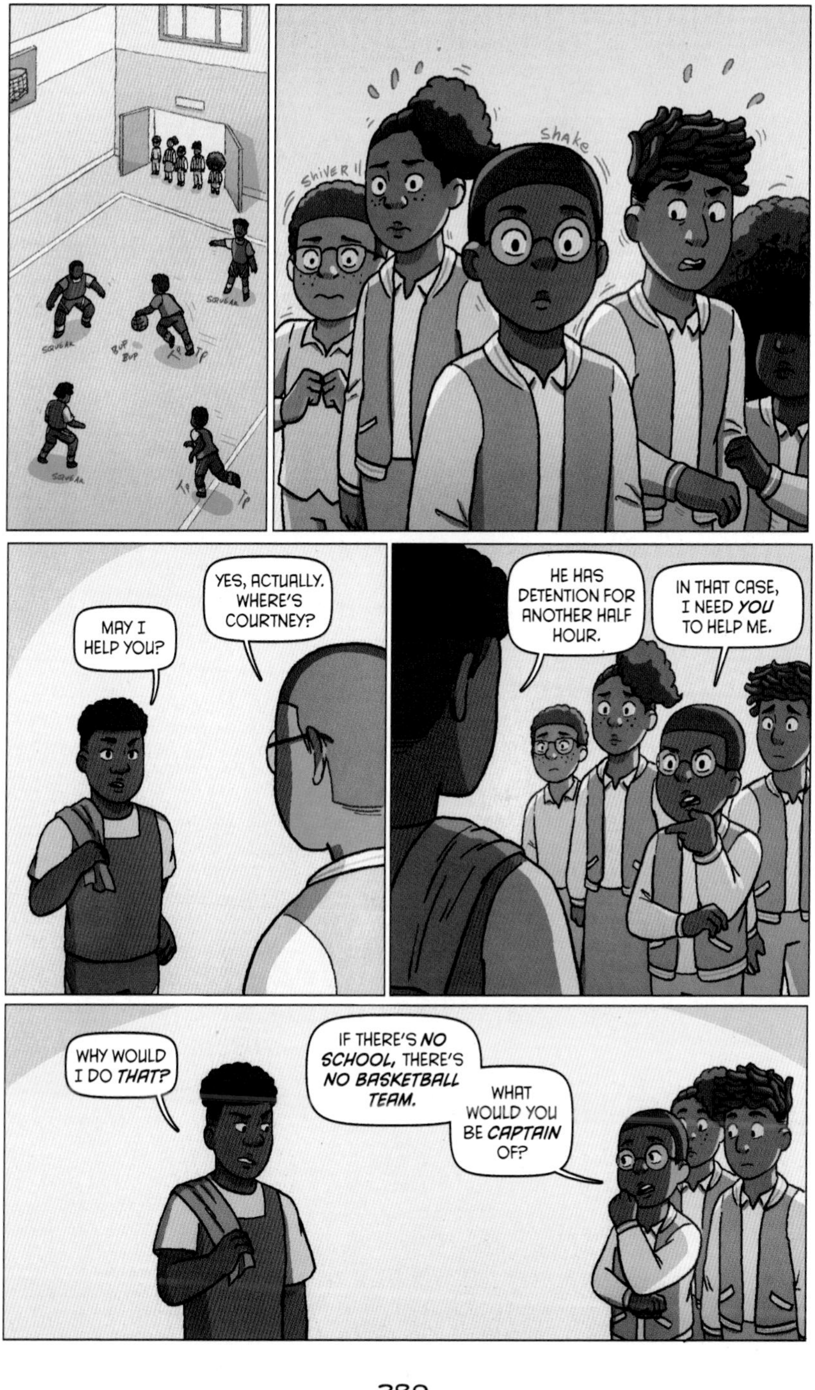

BUP BUP
SQUEAK
SHIVER
SHAKE
MAY I HELP YOU?
YES, ACTUALLY. WHERE'S COURTNEY?
HE HAS DETENTION FOR ANOTHER HALF HOUR.
IN THAT CASE, I NEED *YOU* TO HELP ME.
WHY WOULD I DO *THAT?*
IF THERE'S ***NO SCHOOL,*** THERE'S ***NO BASKETBALL TEAM.***
WHAT WOULD YOU BE ***CAPTAIN*** OF?

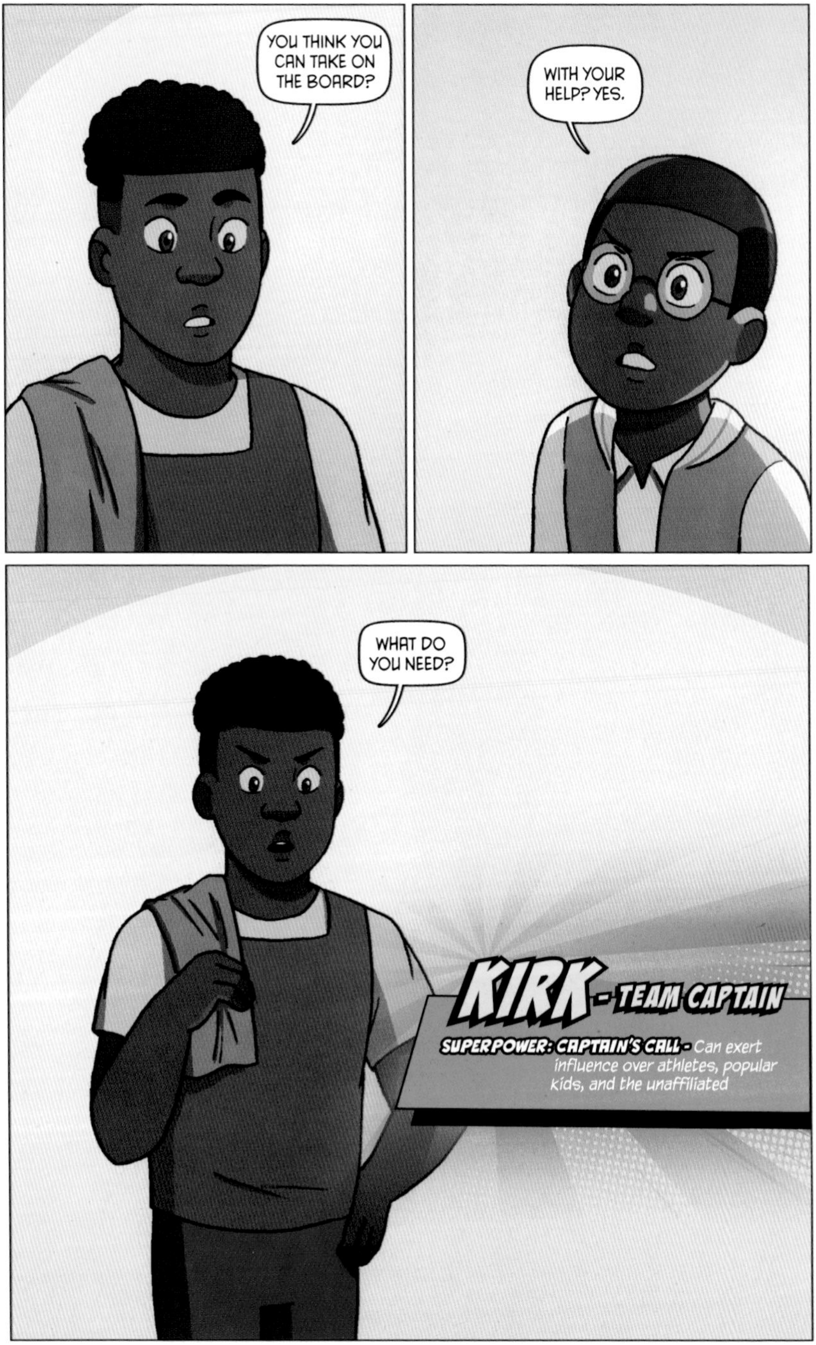
YOU THINK YOU CAN TAKE ON THE BOARD?
WITH YOUR HELP? YES.
WHAT DO YOU NEED?
KIRK - TEAM CAPTAIN
SUPERPOWER: CAPTAIN'S CALL - Can exert influence over athletes, popular kids, and the unaffiliated

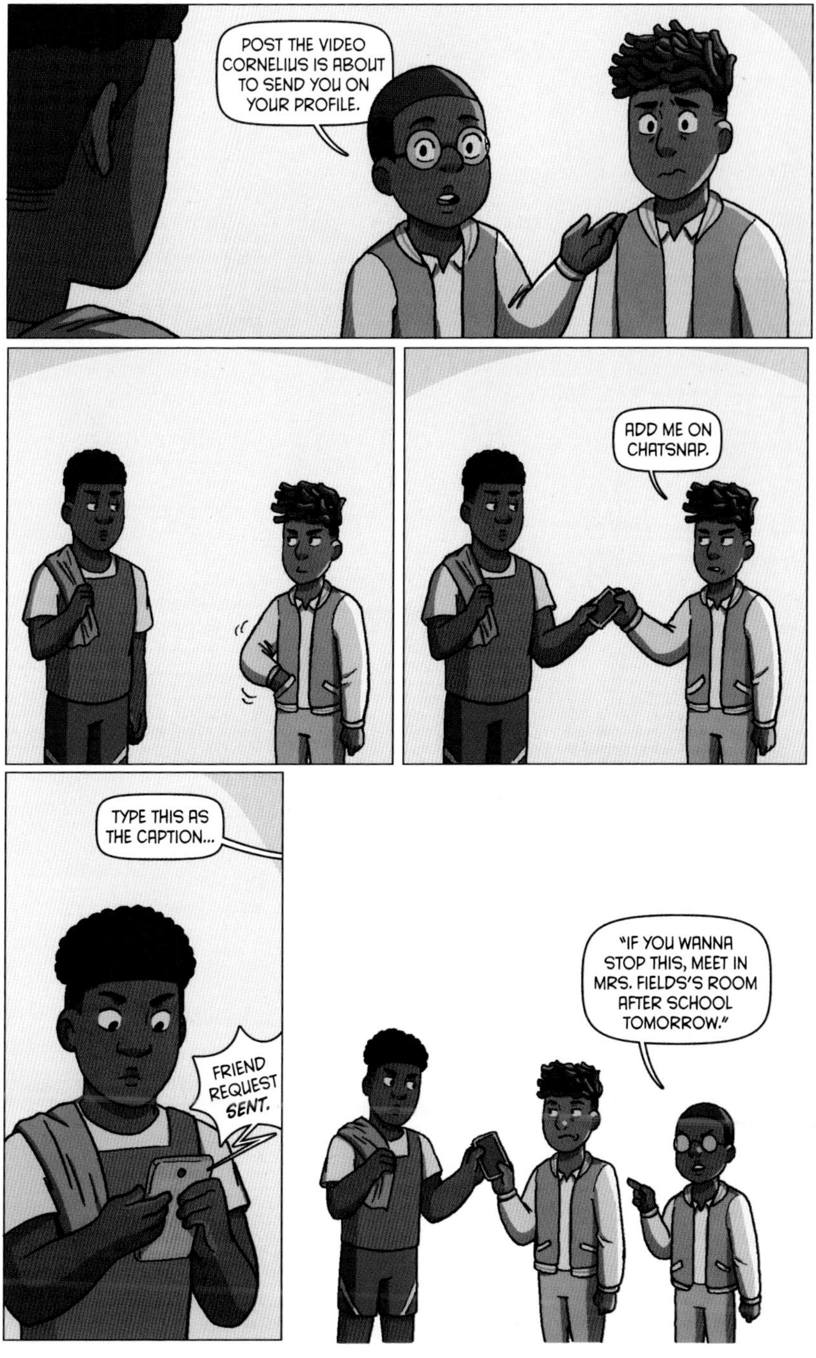
POST THE VIDEO CORNELIUS IS ABOUT TO SEND YOU ON YOUR PROFILE.
ADD ME ON CHATSNAP.
TYPE THIS AS THE CAPTION...
FRIEND REQUEST SENT.
"IF YOU WANNA STOP THIS, MEET IN MRS. FIELDS'S ROOM AFTER SCHOOL TOMORROW."

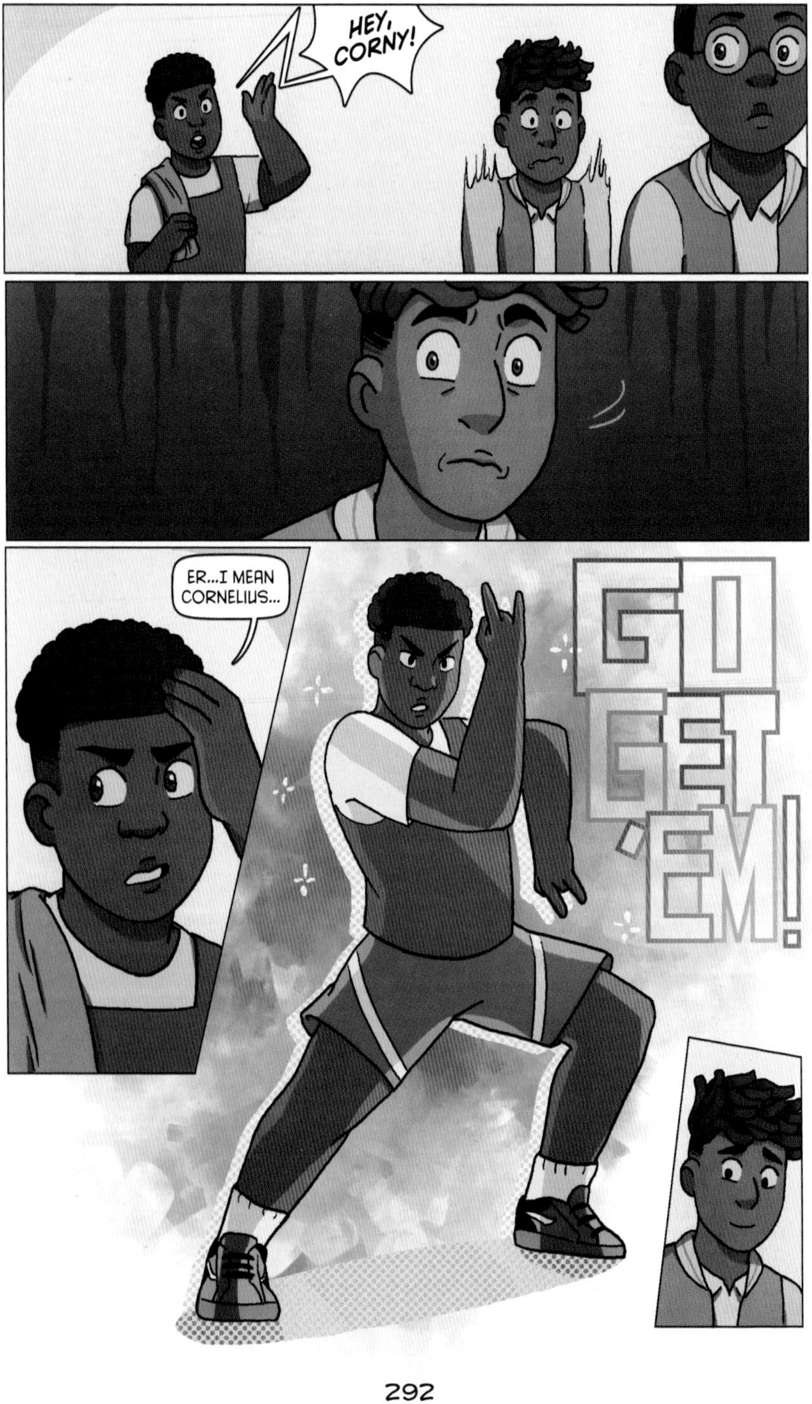
HEY, CORNY!
ER...I MEAN CORNELIUS...
GO GET 'EM!

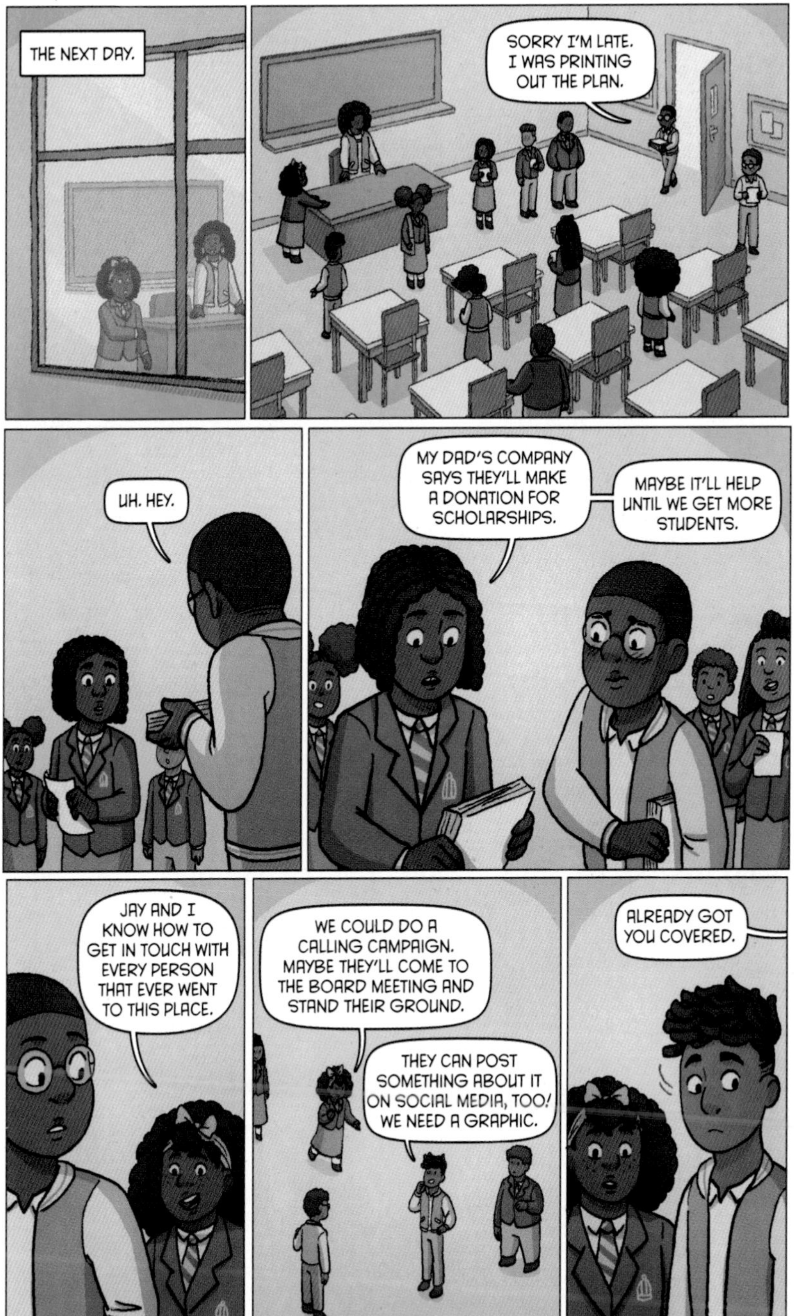
THE NEXT DAY.
SORRY I'M LATE. I WAS PRINTING OUT THE PLAN.
UH. HEY.
MY DAD'S COMPANY SAYS THEY'LL MAKE A DONATION FOR SCHOLARSHIPS.
MAYBE IT'LL HELP UNTIL WE GET MORE STUDENTS.
JAY AND I KNOW HOW TO GET IN TOUCH WITH EVERY PERSON THAT EVER WENT TO THIS PLACE.
WE COULD DO A CALLING CAMPAIGN. MAYBE THEY'LL COME TO THE BOARD MEETING AND STAND THEIR GROUND.
THEY CAN POST SOMETHING ABOUT IT ON SOCIAL MEDIA, TOO! WE NEED A GRAPHIC.
ALREADY GOT YOU COVERED.

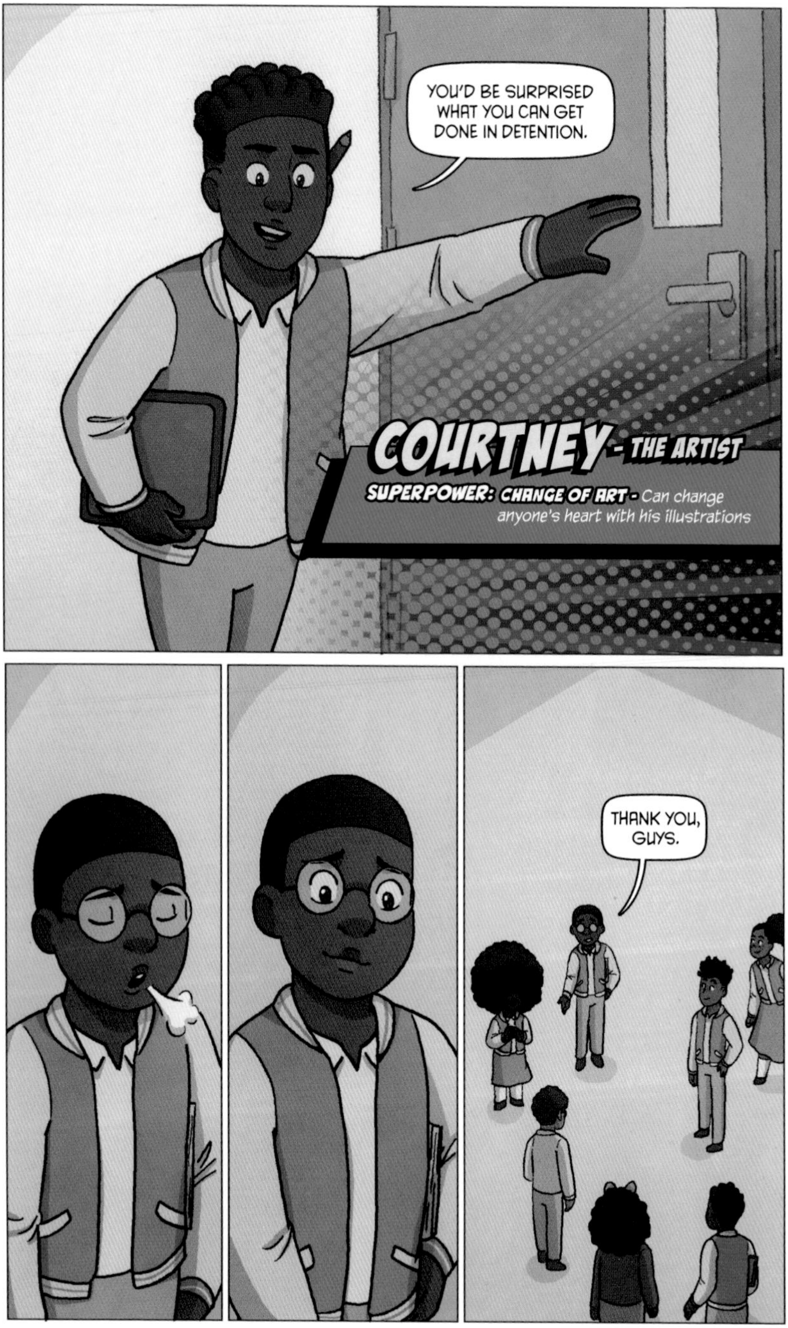
YOU'D BE SURPRISED WHAT YOU CAN GET DONE IN DETENTION.
COURTNEY - THE ARTIST
SUPERPOWER: CHANGE OF ART - Can change anyone's heart with his illustrations
THANK YOU, GUYS.

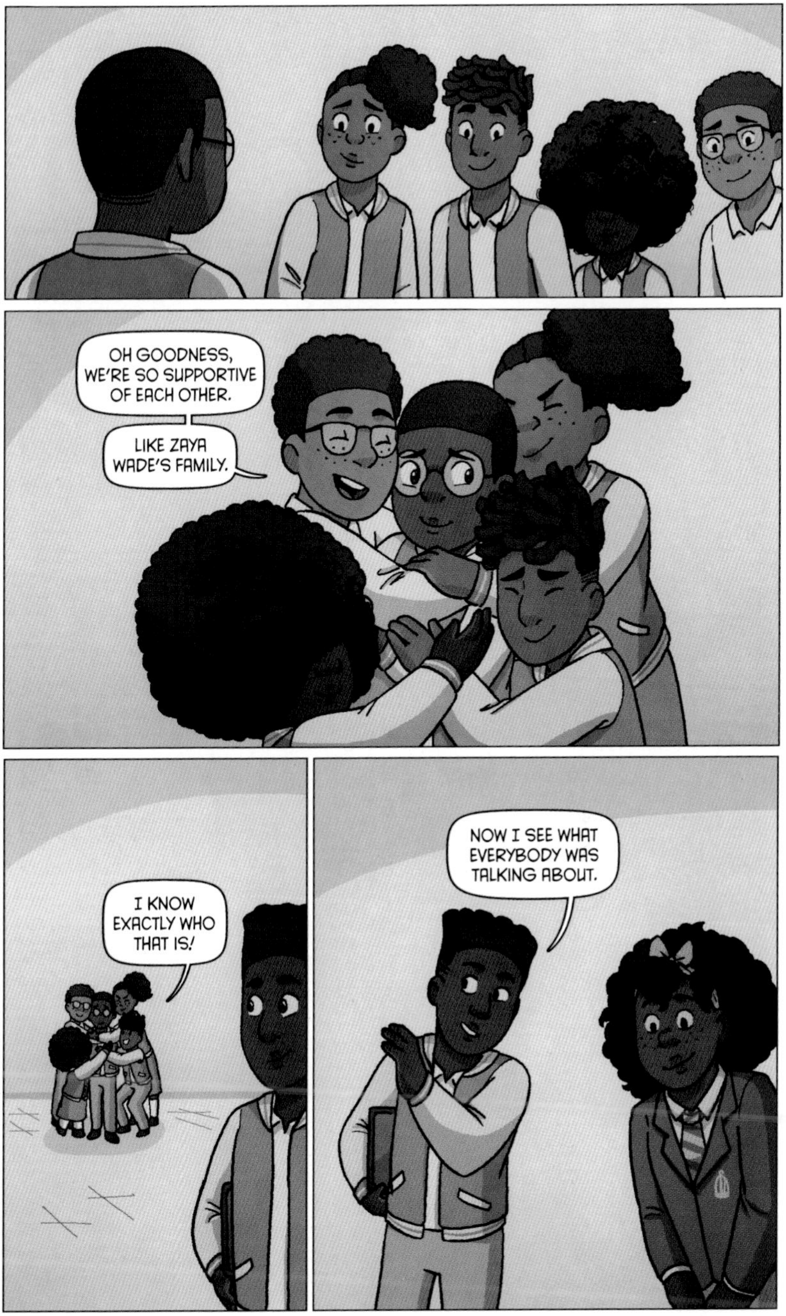
OH GOODNESS, WE'RE SO SUPPORTIVE OF EACH OTHER.
LIKE ZAYA WADE'S FAMILY.
I KNOW EXACTLY WHO THAT IS!
NOW I SEE WHAT EVERYBODY WAS TALKING ABOUT.

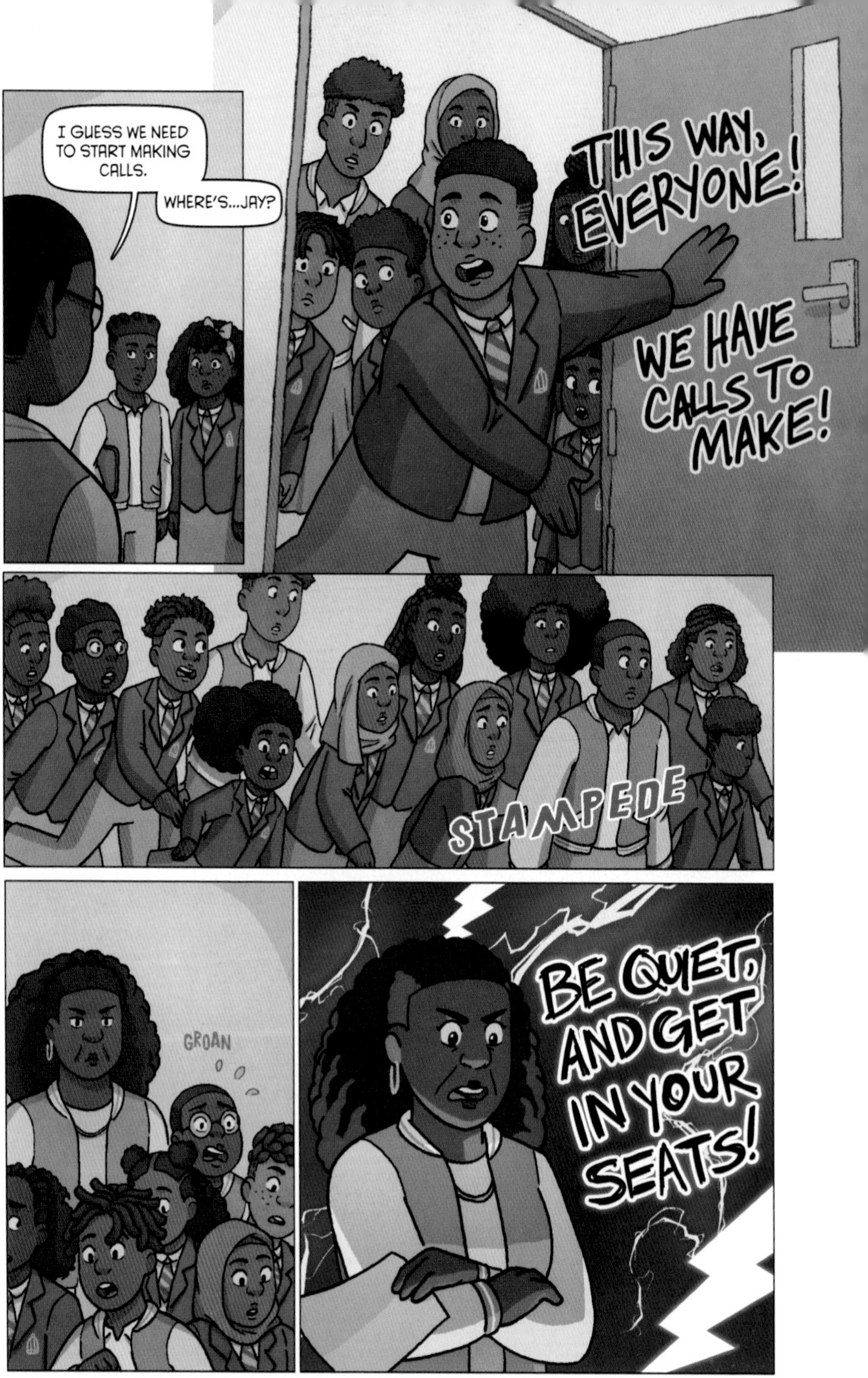
I GUESS WE NEED TO START MAKING CALLS.
WHERE'S...JAY?
THIS WAY, EVERYONE!
WE HAVE CALLS TO MAKE!
STAMPEDE
GROAN
BE QUIET, AND GET IN YOUR SEATS!

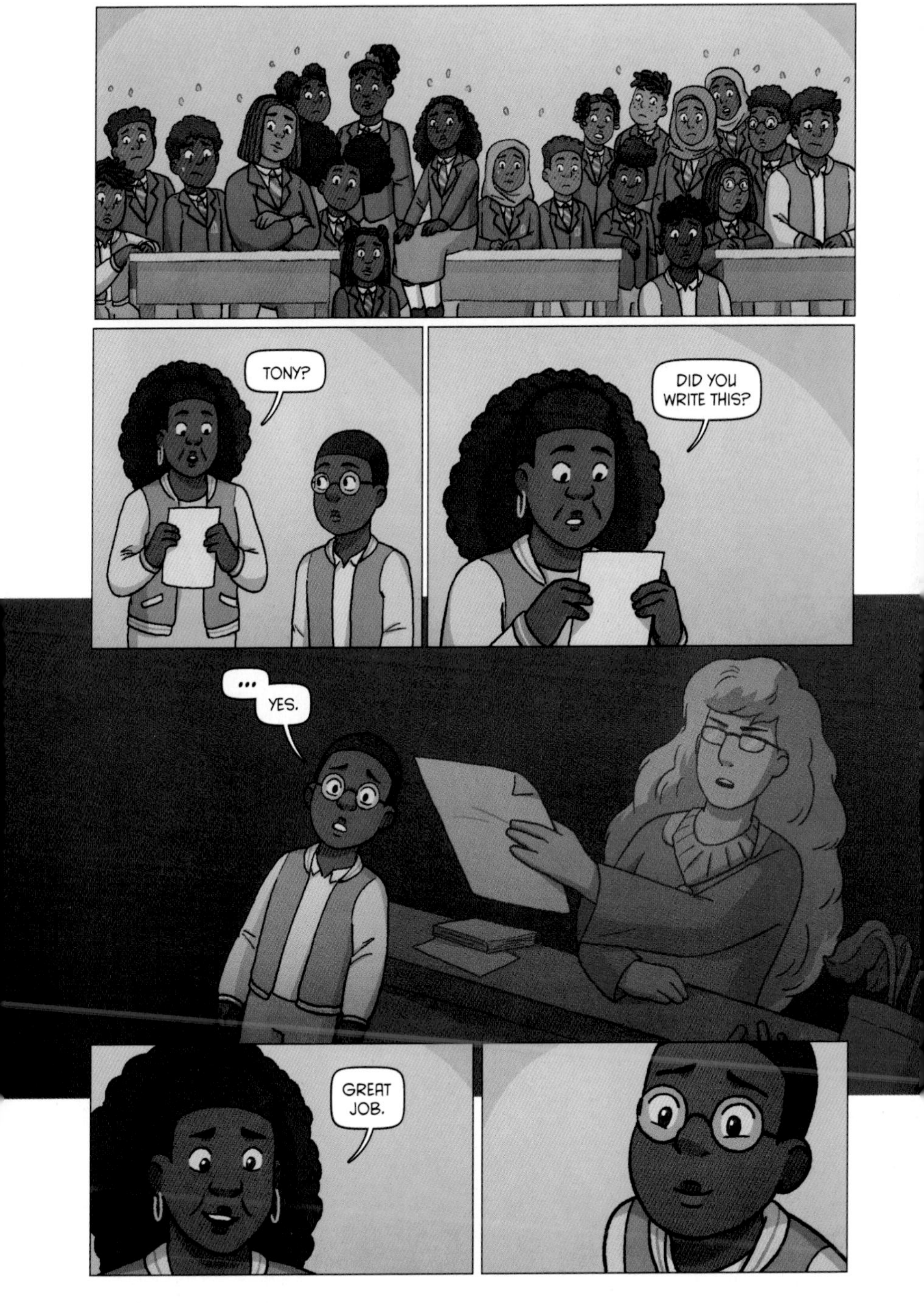

TONY?
DID YOU WRITE THIS?
...
YES.
GREAT JOB.

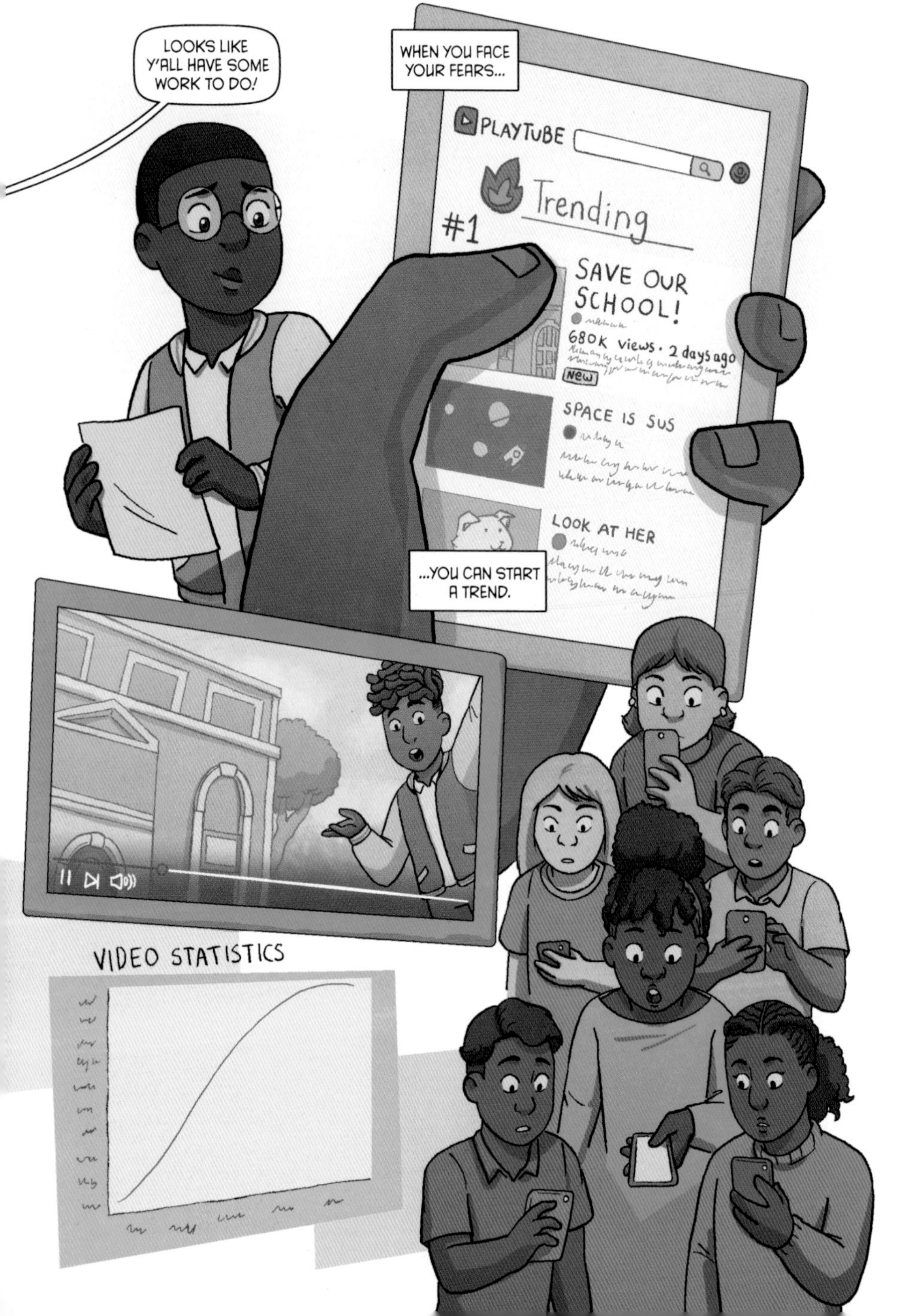
LOOKS LIKE Y'ALL HAVE SOME WORK TO DO!
WHEN YOU FACE YOUR FEARS...
PLAYTUBE
Trending
#1
SAVE OUR SCHOOL!
680K views · 2 days ago
NEW
SPACE IS SUS
LOOK AT HER
...YOU CAN START A TREND.
VIDEO STATISTICS

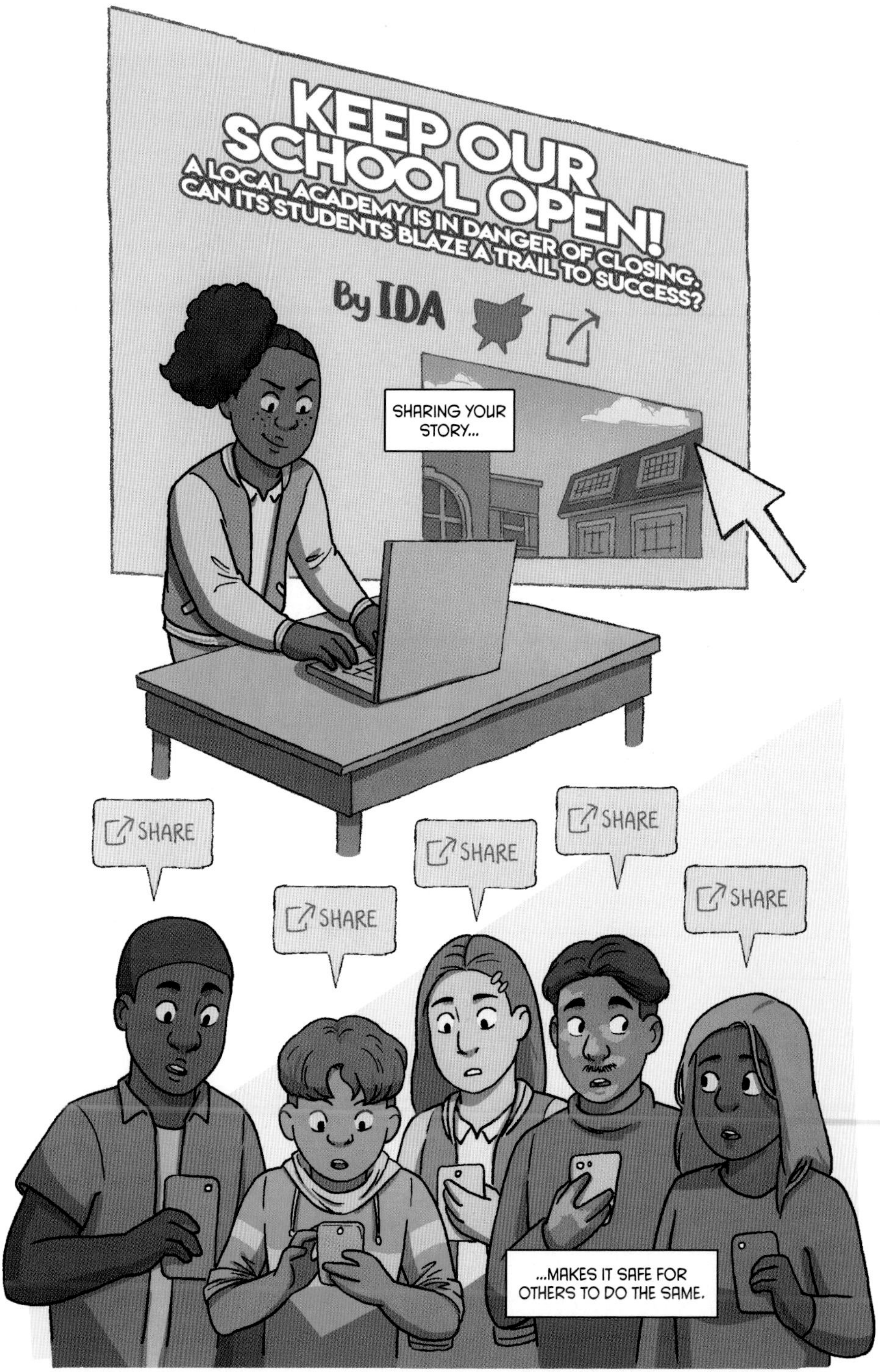
KEEP OUR SCHOOL OPEN!
A LOCAL ACADEMY IS IN DANGER OF CLOSING.
CAN ITS STUDENTS BLAZE A TRAIL TO SUCCESS?
By IDA
SHARING YOUR STORY...
SHARE
SHARE
SHARE
SHARE
SHARE
...MAKES IT SAFE FOR OTHERS TO DO THE SAME.

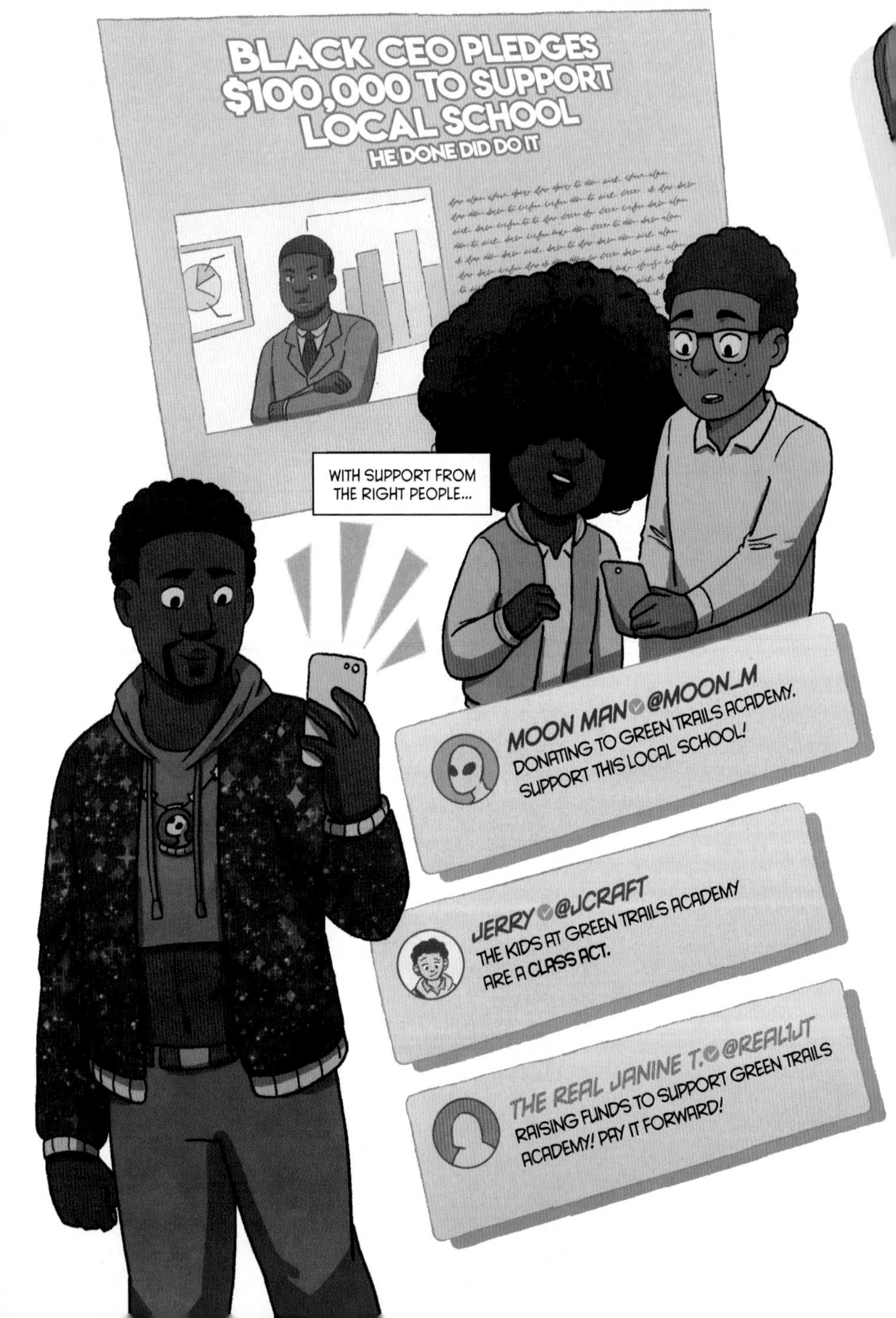
BLACK CEO PLEDGES $100,000 TO SUPPORT LOCAL SCHOOL
HE DONE DID DO IT
WITH SUPPORT FROM THE RIGHT PEOPLE...
MOON MAN @MOON_M
DONATING TO GREEN TRAILS ACADEMY. SUPPORT THIS LOCAL SCHOOL!
JERRY @JCRAFT
THE KIDS AT GREEN TRAILS ACADEMY ARE A CLASS ACT.
THE REAL JANINE T. @REAL1JT
RAISING FUNDS TO SUPPORT GREEN TRAILS ACADEMY! PAY IT FORWARD!

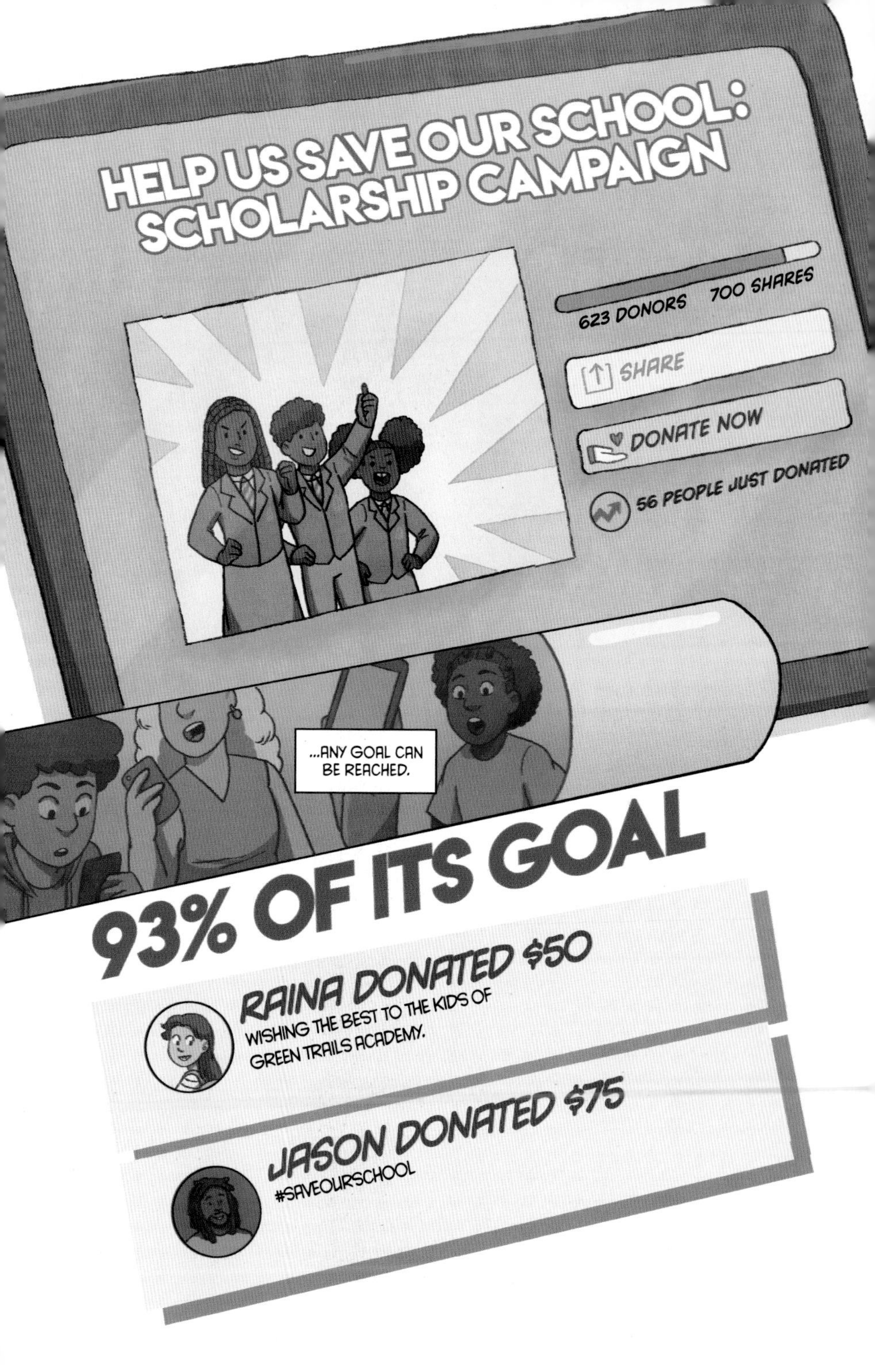
HELP US SAVE OUR SCHOOL: SCHOLARSHIP CAMPAIGN
623 DONORS
700 SHARES
SHARE
DONATE NOW
56 PEOPLE JUST DONATED
...ANY GOAL CAN BE REACHED.
93% OF ITS GOAL
RAINA DONATED $50
WISHING THE BEST TO THE KIDS OF GREEN TRAILS ACADEMY.
JASON DONATED $75
#SAVEOURSCHOOL

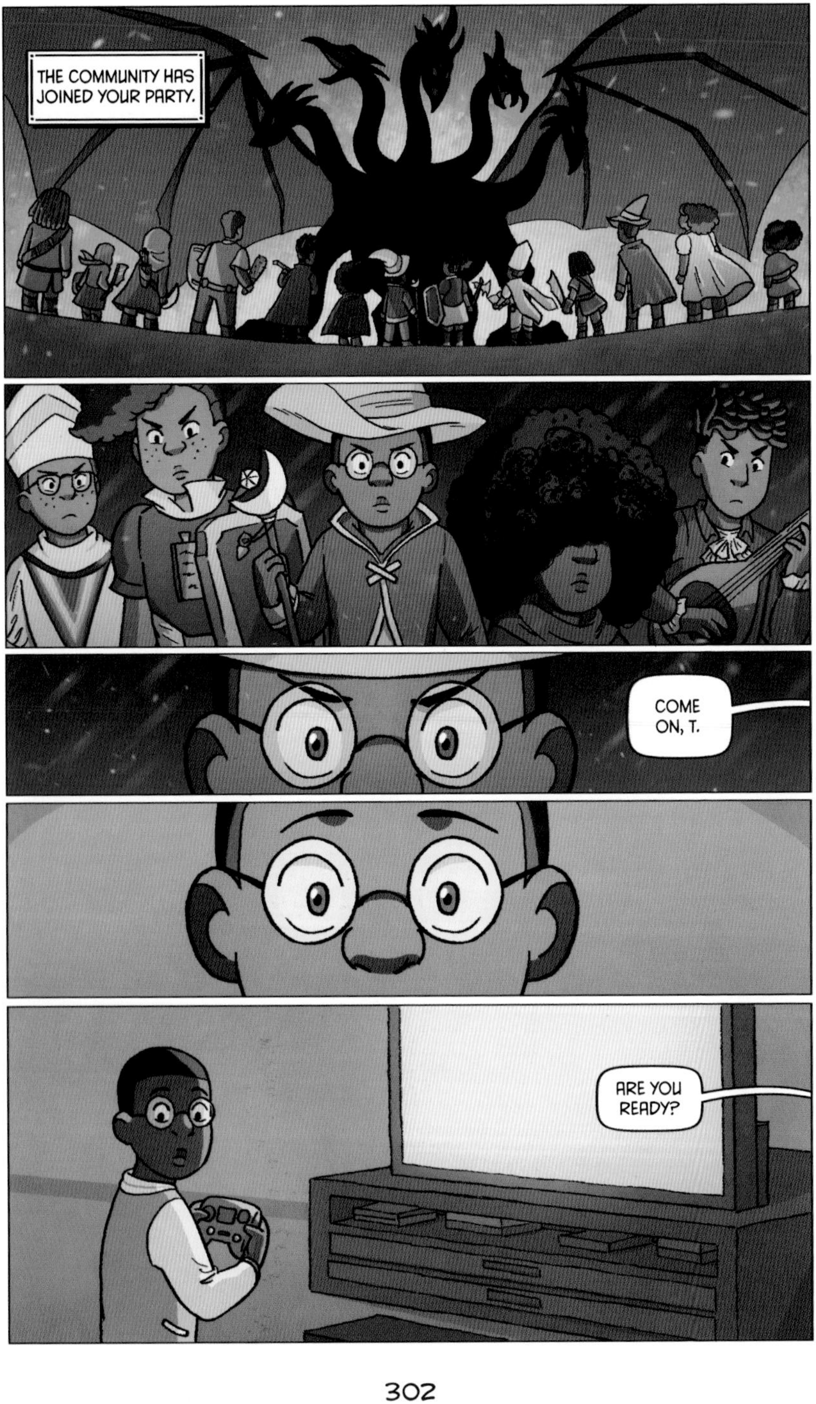
THE COMMUNITY HAS JOINED YOUR PARTY.
COME ON, T.
ARE YOU READY?

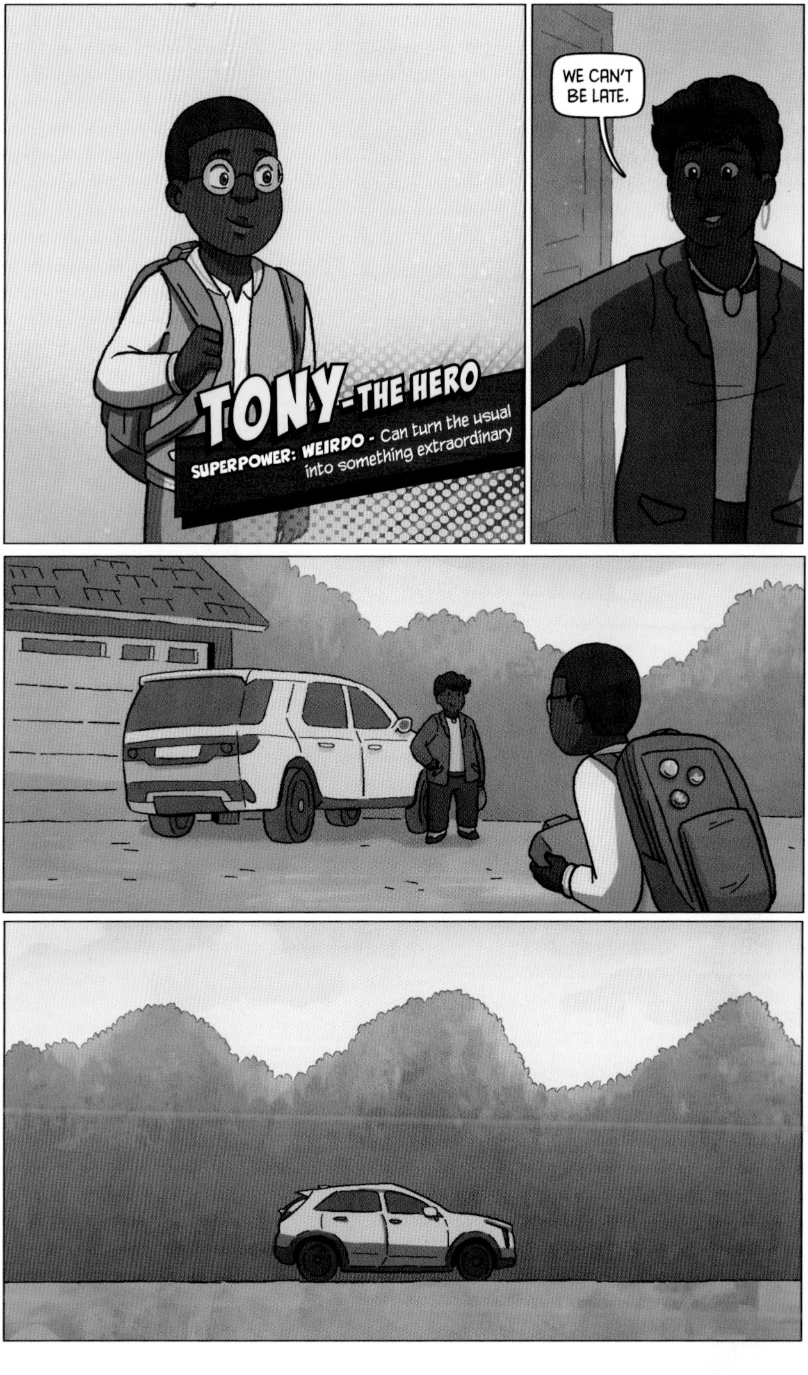
TONY - THE HERO
SUPERPOWER: WEIRDO - Can turn the usual into something extraordinary
WE CAN'T BE LATE.

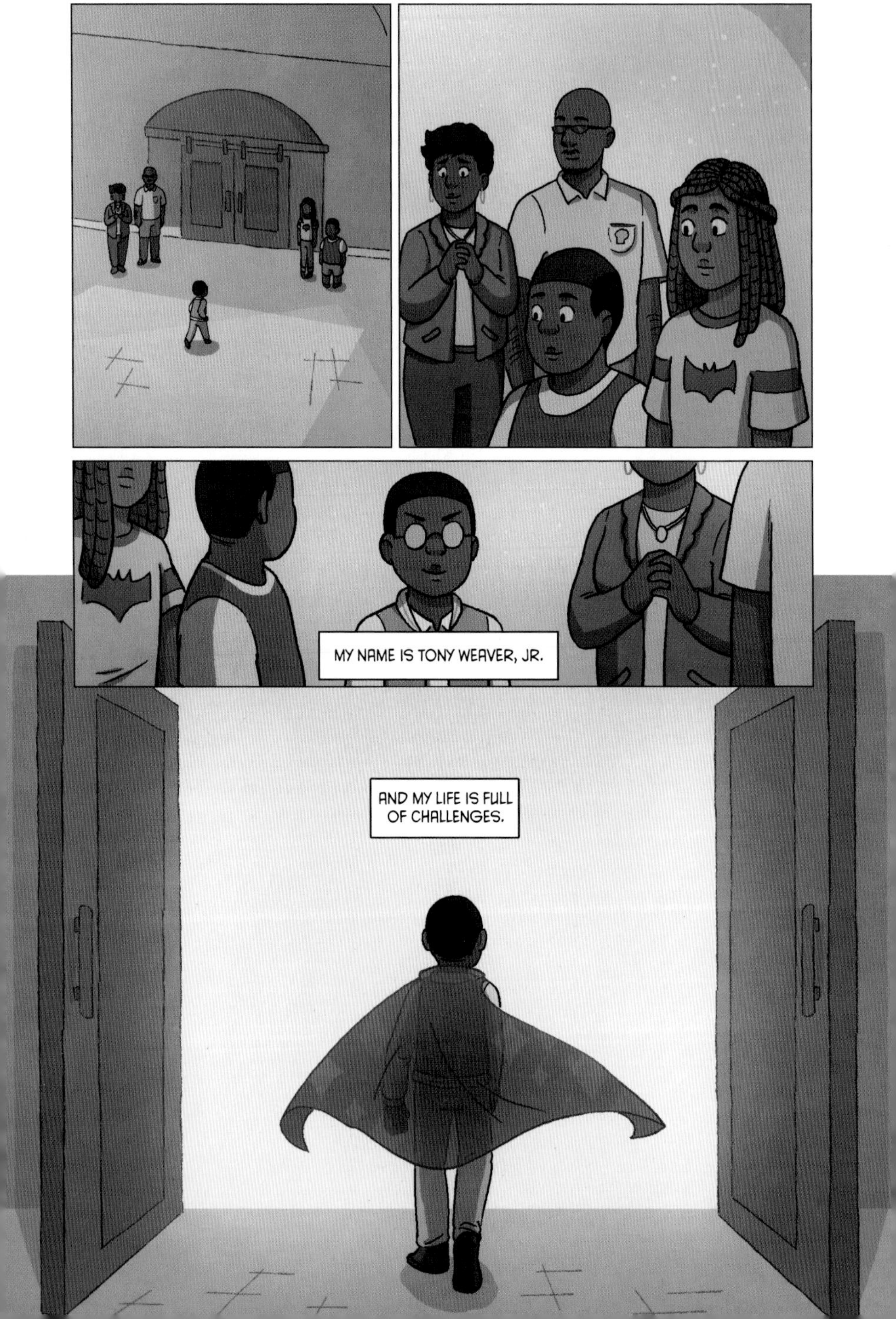
MY NAME IS TONY WEAVER, JR.
AND MY LIFE IS FULL OF CHALLENGES.

EPILOGUE

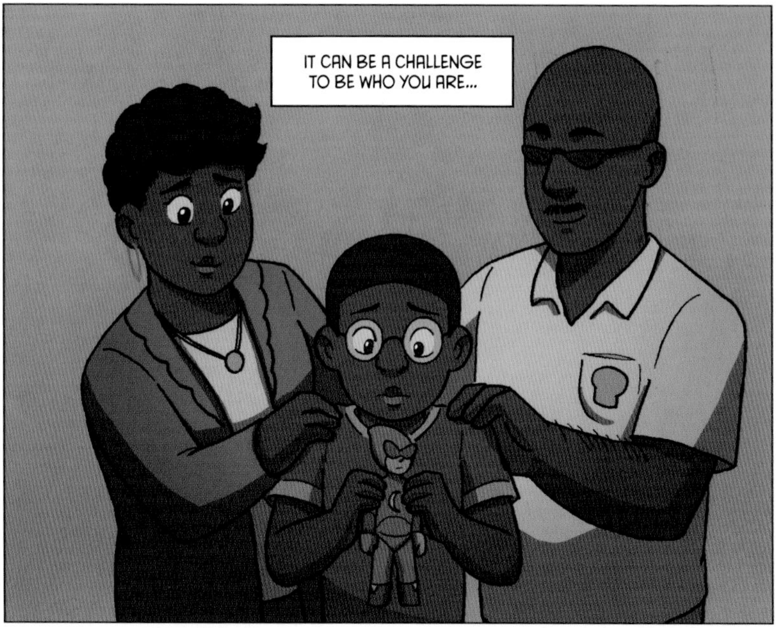
IT CAN BE A CHALLENGE
TO BE WHO YOU ARE...

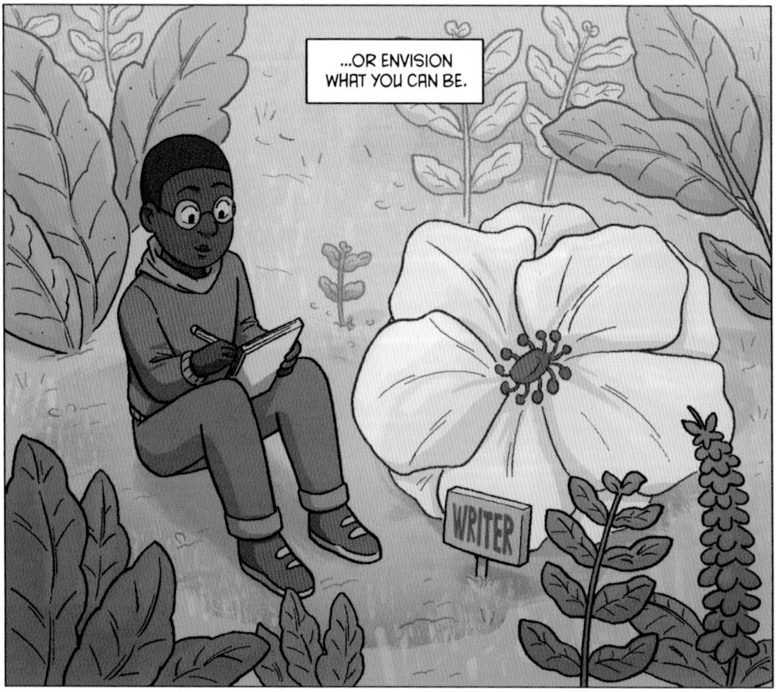
...OR ENVISION
WHAT YOU CAN BE.
WRITER

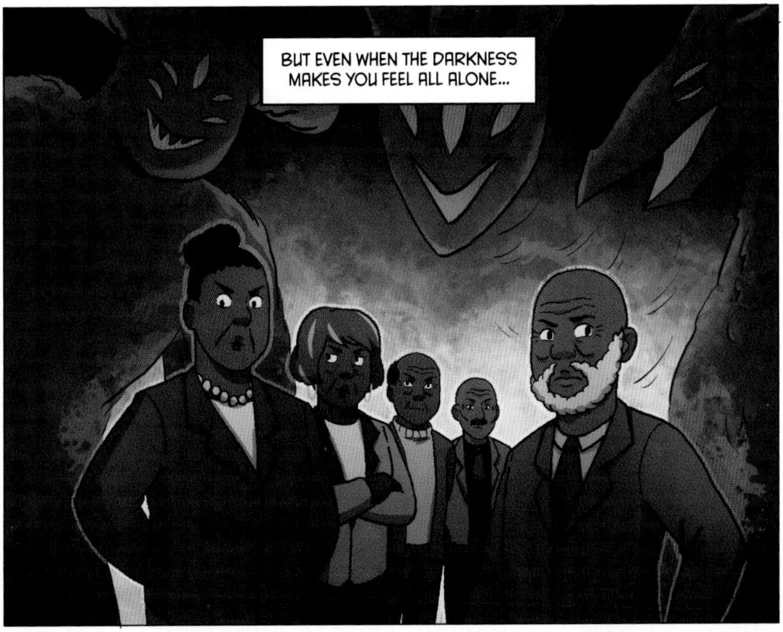
BUT EVEN WHEN THE DARKNESS MAKES YOU FEEL ALL ALONE...

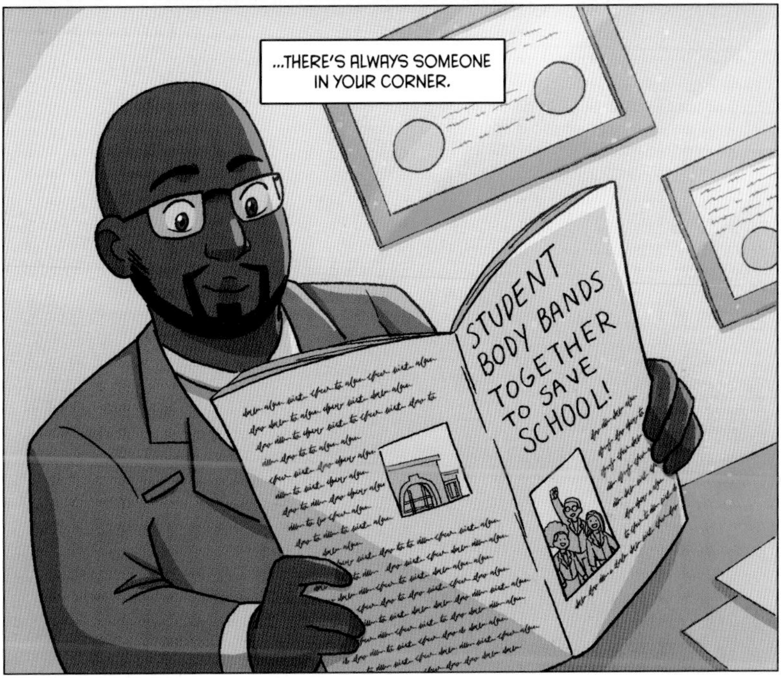
...THERE'S ALWAYS SOMEONE IN YOUR CORNER.
STUDENT BODY BANDS TOGETHER TO SAVE SCHOOL!

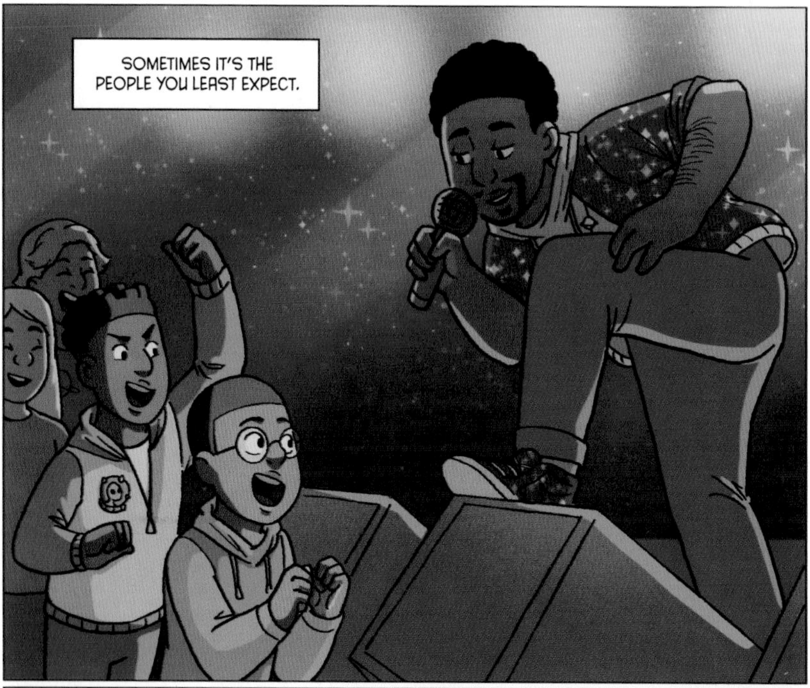
SOMETIMES IT'S THE PEOPLE YOU LEAST EXPECT.

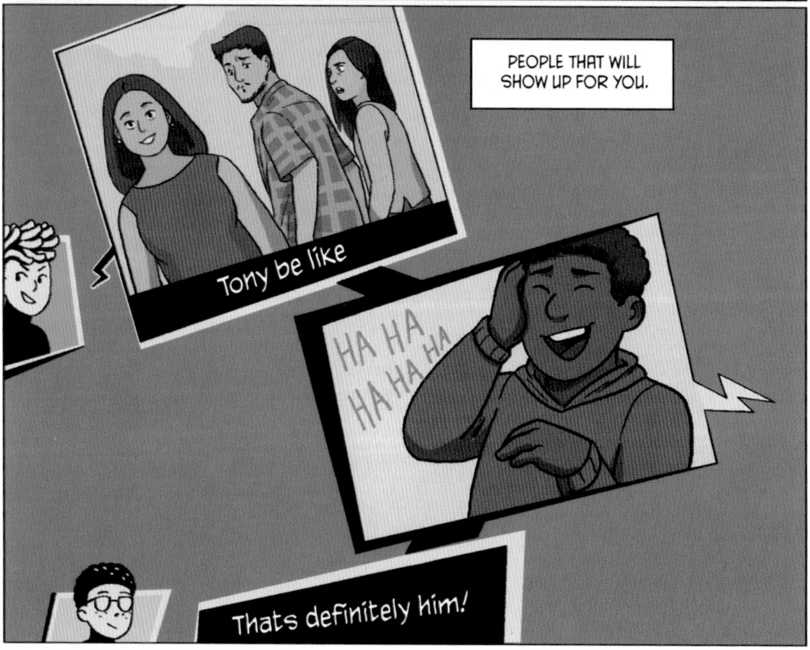
PEOPLE THAT WILL SHOW UP FOR YOU.
Tony be like
HA HA HA HA HA
Thats definitely him!

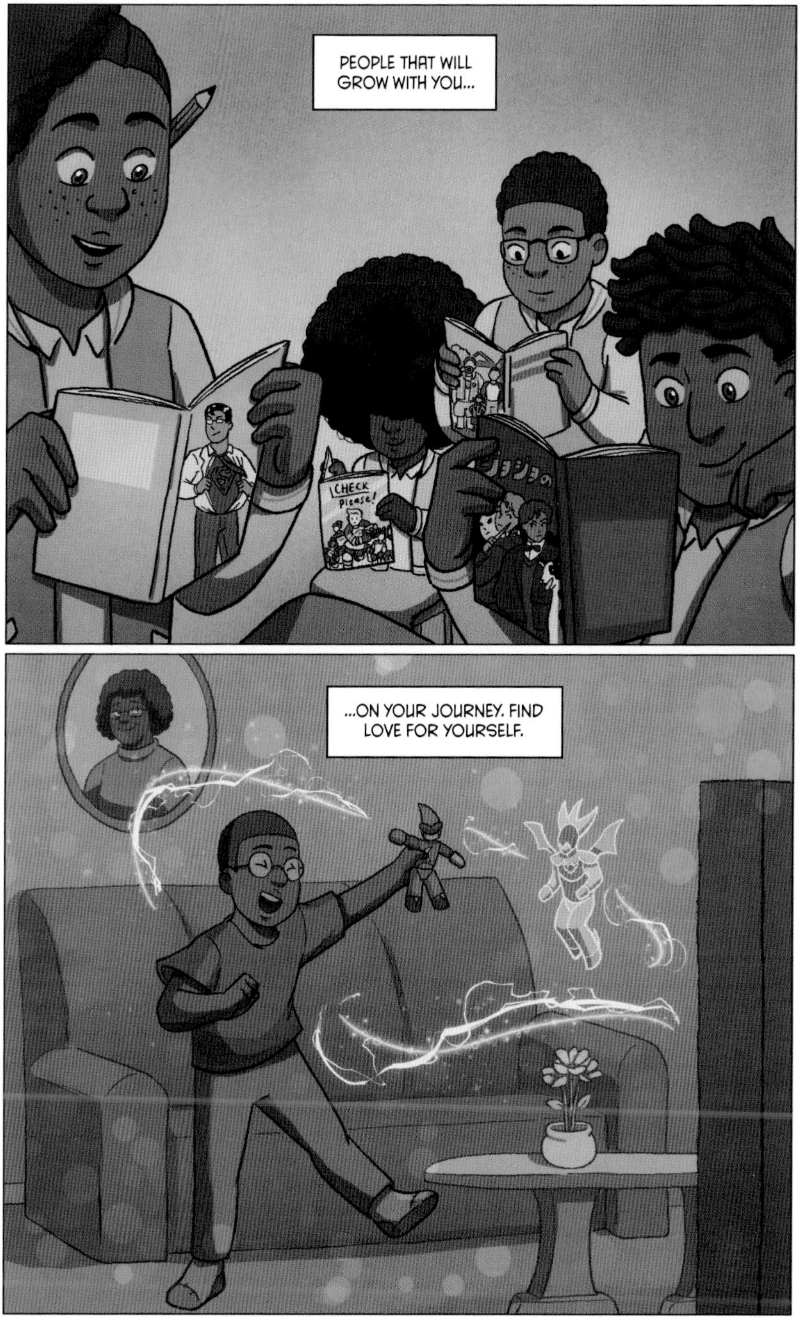
PEOPLE THAT WILL GROW WITH YOU...
CHECK Please!
...ON YOUR JOURNEY. FIND LOVE FOR YOURSELF.

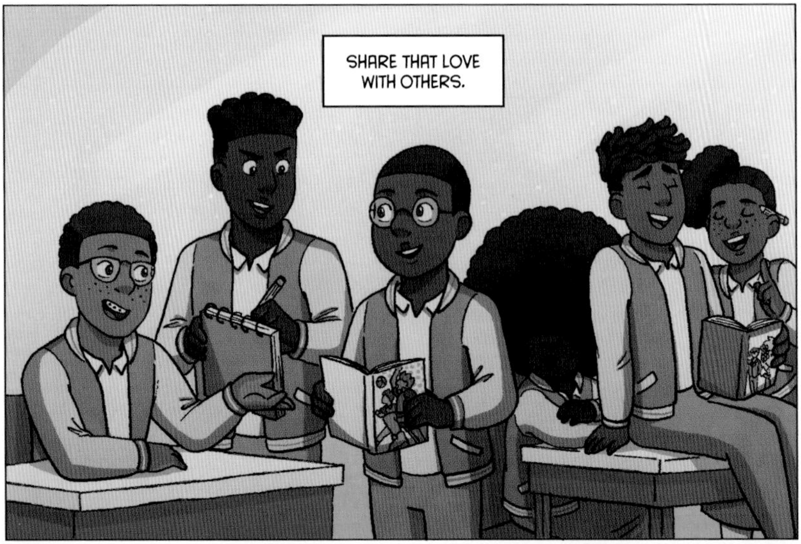
SHARE THAT LOVE WITH OTHERS.

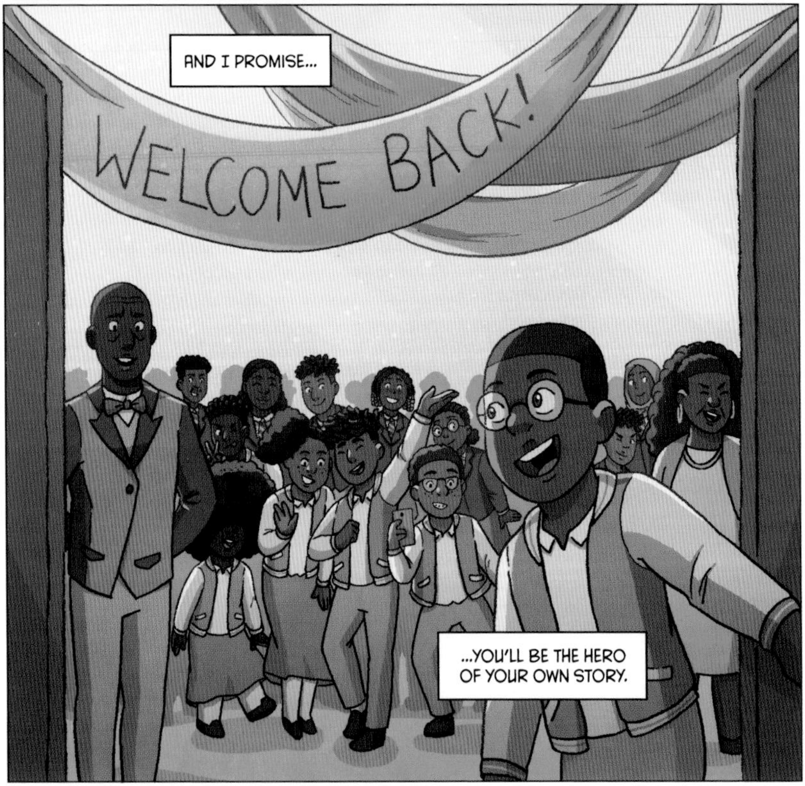
AND I PROMISE...
WELCOME BACK!
...YOU'LL BE THE HERO OF YOUR OWN STORY.

...SEE YOU NEXT TIME!

AUTHOR'S LETTER

WOAH, YOU READ THE WHOLE BOOK? GOOD JOB!

If I was there, I'd give you a high five! But I'm not . . . so the best I can manage is this letter. There's a cool surprise at the end.

What you just read is a highlight reel of my mental health journey's defining moments. Some of the details were edited to create a compelling book, and I changed names for people's privacy, but the core events are true. My mom was really a principal and my dad really does make corny bread puns. (That might not be too hard to believe.)

All the events you saw in chapters two and three actually happened, which is a little sad, but all the stuff after happened, too! I moved to a new school with a principal that was way too stylish for someone with that job title, my parents put me in therapy, my English teacher helped rekindle my love for writing, and I made a nerdy squad of friends just as weird as me! Oh, and my school did legitimately get

YOUR OWN STORY
MOON MAN

shut down by the Board of Regents until a MASSIVE campaign led by the students and parents made them reverse their decision.

Each event made me who I was meant to be. And I hope that from this book, and all the adventures your life will contain, you'll grow into the person you're meant to become. A person who's happy, kind, and who can unapologetically love what they see when they look in the mirror.

I pray you never have to experience the darkness I did. But if you do . . . remember that you're not alone. No matter how much the dark tries to tell you you are.

Oh, I promised you a surprise, didn't I?

You know how at the end of the book my superpower is called "Weirdo"? You have that superpower, too! EVERYBODY IS WEIRD. Every day you have the chance to turn the usual into something extraordinary. Use your weird wisely. The world is depending on it.

Good luck.

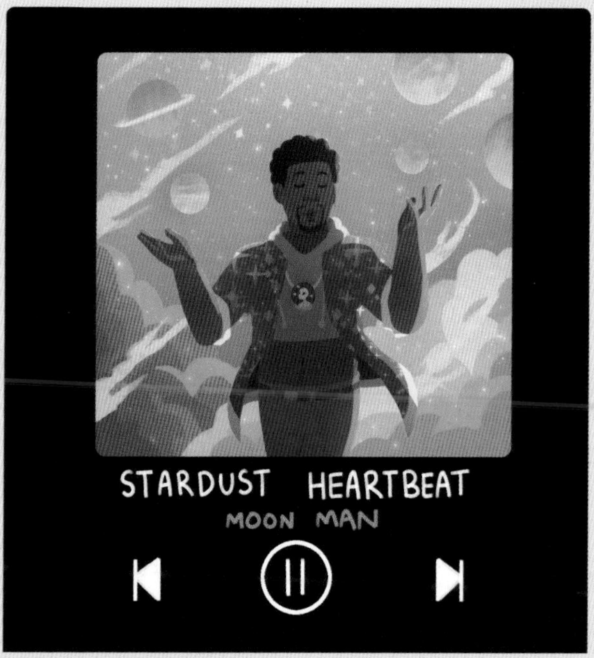
STARDUST HEARTBEAT
MOON MAN

ACKNOWLEDGMENTS

MANY THANKS TO:

Jennifer Gates and Erica Bauman, for seeing the value in this project every step of the way. Kiara, Mark, Kirk, and the entire First Second team, for helping me craft such a meaningful debut. JesnCin, for pouring thought and meaning into every detail. Jerry Craft, Jason Reynolds, Raina Telgemeier, Dan Santat, and Jarrett Krosoczka, for guiding me with your kindness and advice. LENAR, Shrimp, and Sola, for diving in with me on every draft. Kyle and the Hill family, for accepting me into their home. Leia, Maya, and Nasir. I can't wait to see what you grow into. The faculty and staff of Green Forest Christian Academy. Isaiah 40:31.

—TONY

Making a graphic novel is truly a team effort, and so we want to thank our metaphorical volleyball team for helping make this book a reality! Thank you to our family, but especially Bro, Mom, and Dad, for cheering us on as our coaches. Thank you, Jenni and Kevin, for being our wing spikers. Thank you, Britt, for being our libero, the best defense we could have in a team as our agent. Thank you, Kiara, for being our starring setter, facilitating communication through this project. Thank you, multi-hour video essays and music fixations (MLP Equestria Girls, you really came through), for being our pinch server.

Thank you to our sequential art professors, but especially Mia Goodwin and Damian Fox, for being our team captains—teaching us everything we know; we wouldn't be the artists we are now without you! Thank you to the Comic Support Discord, for being our middle blockers; we cherish talking comics with you all! A special thanks to Lune and Audris from the SEA crew for lending your ears to us when we needed it. And thank you to Tony, our vice captain, for trusting us with this story.

—JESNCIN

First Second

Published by First Second
First Second is an imprint of Roaring Brook Press,
a division of Holtzbrinck Publishing Holdings Limited Partnership
120 Broadway, New York, NY 10271
firstsecondbooks.com
mackids.com

Library of Congress Control Number: 2023948821

Our books may be purchased in bulk for promotional, educational, or business use.
Please contact your local bookseller or the Macmillan Corporate and Premium Sales Department
at (800) 221-7945 ext. 5442 or by email at MacmillanSpecialMarkets@macmillan.com.

FIRST
EDITION

First edition, 2024
Edited by Mark Siegel and Kiara Valdez
Cover design by Kirk Benshoff
Interior book design by Sunny Lee and Yan L. Moy
Production editing by Dawn Ryan
Lettering by Andy Jewett

Drawn in Photoshop and Fire Alpaca, inked and colored in Photoshop with occasional touch-ups in Clip Studio

Printed in China by Hung Hing Off-set Printing Co. Ltd., Heshan City, Guangdong Province

ISBN 978-1-250-77287-9 (paperback)
1 3 5 7 9 10 8 6 4 2

ISBN 978-1-250-77286-2 (hardcover)
1 3 5 7 9 10 8 6 4 2

Don't miss your next favorite book from First Second!
For the latest updates go to firstsecondnewsletter.com and sign up for our enewsletter.